# THE NEW
## REVISED AND UPDATED
# McCALL'S
# COOKBOOK

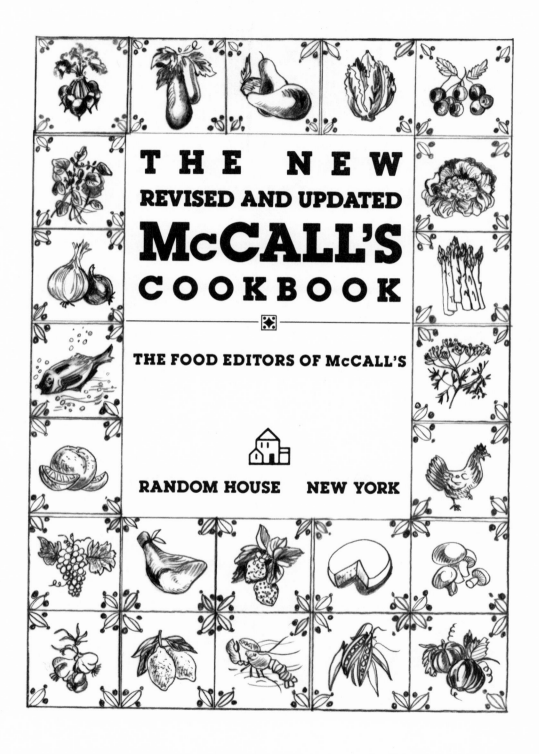

# THE NEW
## REVISED AND UPDATED
# McCALL'S
## COOKBOOK

### THE FOOD EDITORS OF McCALL'S

**RANDOM HOUSE**   **NEW YORK**

THIS BOOK WOULD NOT HAVE BEEN POSSIBLE
WITHOUT THE TALENT AND DEVOTION OF
MARY ECKLEY, MARY J. NORTON AND
DIANE MOGELEVER

Library of Congress Cataloging in Publication
Data
Main entry under title:
The New revised and updated McCall's cookbook.
Rev. ed. of: The new McCall's cookbook / Mary
Eckley. 1st ed. 1973.
Includes index.
1. Cookery. I. Eckley, Mary. The new McCall's
cookbook. II. McCall's.
TX715.N5257   1984      641.5        83-43176
ISBN 0-394-53720-3

Manufactured in the United States of America
98765432
First Edition

BOOK DESIGN AND ILLUSTRATIONS BY
LILLY LANGOTSKY

# CONTENTS

# INTRODUCTION to COOKING

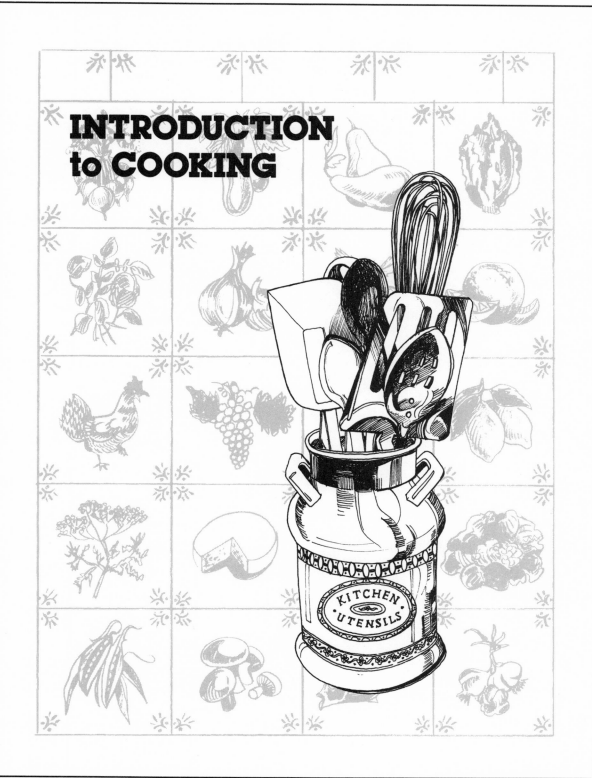

KITCHEN UTENSILS

We decided to revise *The New McCall's Cookbook* because so much has happened in the world of food since 1973, when it was published. Americans have come to appreciate good cooking more than ever before in our history. They are more concerned about nutrition, about international cuisine, about weight watching, about the value of fresh ingredients, and they are more sophisticated. Today we are incorporating in our recipes more whole grains, yogurt, and fresh fish plus a varied selection of vegetables and fruits as well as more imaginative uses of convenience foods. Since the last edition of this book, many appliances have come—and gone—but a few have made their mark and will, we suspect, be with us for many years. The food processor and the microwave oven are examples of such widely used and well-established equipment.

In the present volume, we have added a lot of new material that our readers have indicated they need and want. We have also retained some of the old favorites of *McCall's* fans, which have been tested, retested, and improved over the years. With this combination, you will feel, we hope, that the editors of *McCall's* are there beside you in the kitchen helping you make of cooking a valuable contribution to the lives of those you love, as well as a wonderful adventure for yourself.

## THE RECIPES

The recipes in this book include all the favorites our readers have requested over the years, recipes from all over the country, and the specialties of cooking experts from around the world.

They all work—*if* you follow them carefully. Before you begin to cook, read the recipe thoroughly. Make sure you understand it. Make sure you have the equipment that's called for, and prepare a shopping list if you don't have all the ingredients on hand. When you're ready to begin, assemble everything you need, then do the preliminary preparations, like preheating the oven or soaking the beans or greasing the pan. Now, the first time you try a recipe, *follow the instructions exactly.* You can be imaginative and add your own variations after you've gotten it down pat and seen how it works and how you like it.

## MEASURING

All the recipes in this book have been tested with standard measuring cups and spoons.

To measure dry ingredients or fats, use the plastic or metal cups that you can buy in sets and that hold ¼, ⅓, ½, and 1 cup.

Measuring spoons also come in sets, and generally indicate 1 tablespoon, 1 teaspoon, ½ teaspoon, ¼ teaspoon, and ⅛ teaspoon.

It's important to measure dry ingredients level. In each instance, heap the cup or spoon to overflowing and then level it off with a straight-edged knife or spatula.

Brown sugar and confectioners' sugar may get lumpy on standing, which makes them difficult to measure accurately. To keep brown sugar soft, store it in a tightly covered jar with a piece of bread or a chunk of apple. If confectioners' sugar is lumpy, rub it through a sieve before measuring.

Fats should be brought to room temperature if you keep them in the refrigerator and then firmly pressed into the spoon or cup before you level them off. However, many wrappers of butter or margarine show the measure right on the bar. One bar or stick of butter or margarine measures ½ cup or 8 tablespoons.

We use a standard glass measuring cup, with lip, for liquids. It has quarters and thirds marked off and is heat-resistant. The cup should be held at eye level so that you can accurately see how much you've got, and it should, of course, be held flat.

# COMMON FOOD WEIGHTS AND MEASURES

Dash: less than ⅛ teaspoon
1 tablespoon: 3 teaspoons
4 tablespoons: ¼ cup
5⅓ tablespoons: ⅓ cup
8 tablespoons: ½ cup
10⅔ tablespoons: ⅔ cup
12 tablespoons: ¾ cup
16 tablespoons: 1 cup

1 fluid ounce: 2 tablespoons
1 cup: ½ pint (liquid)
2 cups: 1 pint
2 pints (4 cups): 1 quart
4 quarts: 1 gallon
8 quarts: 1 peck (dry)
4 pecks: 1 bushel
16 ounces: 1 pound

# COOKING TERMINOLOGY

*Bake*: To cook by dry heat, usually in the oven. When applied to meats and vegetables, this is called roasting.

*Barbecue*: To roast meats very slowly on a spit or rack over heat, basting with a seasoned sauce.

*Baste*: To moisten foods (usually roasting meats) while cooking, with meat drippings, melted fat, or sauces, to prevent drying and to add flavor.

*Beat*: To work a mixture smooth with a regular, hard, rhythmic movement.

*Blanch*: To remove the skins from fruits, vegetables, or nuts by letting them stand in boiling water until the skins peel off easily. Occasionally, it is necessary to drain off the first water and to add more boiling water.

*Blend*: To mix thoroughly two or more ingredients using a wooden spoon, a portable or stand electric mixer, a food processor, or a food blender.

*Braise*: To brown meat or vegetables in a small amount of hot fat and then to cook slowly, tightly covered. In some recipes, other liquids are added after the initial browning.

*Bring to boiling, bring to the boiling point, or bring to a boil*: The step before cooking. You'll know that water or any liquid is reaching that point when bubbles appear at the bottom, rise to the top, and break. When all the liquid is in motion, it has come to boiling.

*Boil*: To cook at the boiling point. When this point is reached, adjust the heat to maintain it.

*Boil rapidly*: The point at which a liquid goes into rapid motion; the surface breaks into small, lumpy waves. A rapid boil won't cook food faster, but for some uses, it is better. For example, to start cereals it helps to keep the particles separated and to evaporate soup, jam, or other liquids quickly.

*Full, rolling boil*: The point at which the liquid rises in the pan, then tumbles into waves that can't be stirred down. It usually occurs in heavy sugar mixtures, like candy or frosting.

*Broil*: To cook directly under a flame or heating unit, or over an open fire or grill.

*Brush*: To spread food with butter, margarine, or egg, using a small brush.

*Candy*: To cook fruit in a heavy sugar syrup until transparent, then to drain and dry (orange peel, for example). Also, to cook vegetables with sugar or syrup to give a coating or glaze when cooked.

*Caramelize*: To melt sugar slowly over very low heat until the sugar is liquid, brown, and caramel flavored.

*Chop*: To cut food into smaller pieces, usually

with a large knife on a cutting board. One hand holds the knife tip and board; the other moves the blade up and down, cutting through the food.

*Coat*: To roll foods in flour, nuts, sugar, crumbs, etc., until all the sides are evenly covered, or to dip first into slightly beaten egg or milk, then to cover with whatever coating is called for in the recipe.

*Coat a spoon*: A method of testing the thickness of a custard sauce. A metal spoon dipped in the sauce will be thoroughly coated with a thin film.

*Coddle*: To cook slowly and gently in water just below the boiling point. Eggs are frequently coddled.

*Combine*: To mix together all the ingredients.

*Cook*: To prepare food by applying heat in any form.

*Cream*: To beat shortening until smooth, creamy, and light, with wooden spoon or beater. Usually applied to shortening when combined with sugar, for example, in making cakes.

*Crisp*: To make firm and brittle in very cold water or in the refrigerator (lettuce and other greens, for example).

*Cube*: To cut a solid into little cubes of about ½ to 1 inch. Use a cutting board and a very sharp knife.

*Cut*: To break up food into pieces, with a knife or scissors.

*Cut in*: To combine shortening with dry ingredients by working together two knives in scissor fashion or by using a pastry blender. Usually applied to pastry making.

*Dash*: A scant ⅛ teaspoon of dry or liquid ingredient, for example, a dash of salt.

*Devil*: To coat with a hot seasoning, such as mustard or a hot sauce. Eggs are "deviled" when the yolk is mixed with hot seasonings.

*Dice*: To cube but to make the cubes smaller —less than ½ inch. Use a cutting board and a very sharp knife, or a special cubing gadget.

*Dissolve*: To make a liquid and a dry substance go into solution.

*Dot*: To scatter small amounts of butter, nuts, chocolate, etc., over the surface of a food.

*Dredge*: To coat food with some dry ingredient, such as seasoned flour or sugar.

*Dust*: To sprinkle a food or coat lightly with flour or sugar.

*Flake*: To break or pull apart a food that di-

vides naturally, like chicken or fish. All you do is follow these divisions, pulling at them gently with one or two forks. Or flake with your fingers.

*Flambé*: To cover a food with liquor, such as brandy or cognac, then to light it and serve flaming, for example, plum pudding.

*Fold*: To combine two ingredients—more often than not beaten egg whites and batter— very gently with a wire whisk or rubber spatula, using an under-and-over motion, until thoroughly mixed.

*Fry*: (1) To cook in a small amount of fat on top of the stove; also sauté, pan-fry, and stir-fry. (2) To cook a food in a deep layer of hot fat; also deep-fry. The aim is to produce foods with a crisp golden-brown crust and a thoroughly cooked interior without letting them absorb too much fat. The type of fat and the quantity and temperature are important in accomplishing this result.

*Garnish*: To decorate any food. Nuts, olives, parsley, etc., are called garnishes when used to give a finish to a dish.

*Glacé*: To coat with a thin sugar syrup cooked to the hard crack stage—300 to 310F on a candy thermometer, or when syrup dropped into water separates into threads, which are hard and brittle.

*Glaze*: To cover with aspic, to coat with a thin sugar syrup, or to cover with melted fruit jelly. For example, cold meats, fish, and fruit are often glazed.

*Grate*: To tear off coarse-to-fine particles of food with a hand grater or mechanical device.

*Grill*: See "Broil."

*Grind*: To put food through a chopper. Choppers have two or three blades. Use the blade with the smaller holes to grind foods fine and the one with the larger holes for coarse chopping or grinding.

*Julienne*: To cut potatoes or vegetables into matchlike sticks.

*Knead*: To work and press dough hard with the heels of your hands so the dough becomes stretched and elastic.

*Marinate*: To let food stand in an acidic liquid, such as lemon juice, tomato juice, or wine, or in an oil-acid mixture, like French dressing. Acts as a tenderizer and steps up flavor.

*Melt*: To heat solid food, like sugar, butter, or fat, until it becomes liquid.

*Mince*: To cut food into pieces that are finer than chopped. Mincing follows the same steps: Use cutting board and sharp knife, chopping knife and wooden bowl, or scissors —just do it longer.

*Mix*: To stir, usually with a spoon, until the ingredients are thoroughly combined.

*Pan-broil*: To cook, uncovered, on a hot surface, usually a skillet. The fat is poured off as it accumulates.

*Pan-fry*: To cook or fry on top of a range in a hot, uncovered skillet with little or no fat. Steaks, chops, and potatoes are frequently cooked this way.

*Parboil*: To cook food in a boiling liquid until partially done. This is usually a preliminary step to further cooking. Beans and ham, for instance, are first parboiled, then baked.

*Pare*: To cut away the coverings of vegetables and fruits.

*Peel*: To strip or slip off the outer coverings of some vegetables or fruit. May also mean the same as pare.

*Plank*: To bake or broil meat, fish, or vegetables on a wooden or metal plank.

*Poach*: To cook eggs, fish, or vegetables in liquid at simmering, or to cook eggs over water in a special pan.

*Pot-roast*: To brown meat in a small amount of fat, then finish cooking in a small amount of liquid.

*Preheat*: To heat the oven to the stated temperature before using.

*Process*: The action performed by a food processor. Depending upon the blades used, it can mean to slice, chop, grate, blend, mix, or grind. See the chapter "Food Processor Recipes," page 201.

*Purée*: To press fruits or vegetables through a sieve or food mill or to blend in an electric blender or food processor until the food is pulpy. Sauces, soups, baby foods, and vegetables are often puréed.

*Reduce*: To boil a liquid until a small, concentrated amount remains.

*Roast*: To cook meat or vegetables in an oven by dry heat. See "Bake."

*Sauté*: To fry foods until golden and tender in a small amount of fat on top of the range. See "Fry."

*Scald*: To heat liquids like milk almost to boiling; tiny bubbles will appear at the edge. Or when freezing or canning vegetables, to heat by steam or in boiling water.

*Scallop*: To arrange foods in layers in a casserole, with a sauce or liquid, and then bake. Usually has a topping of bread crumbs.

*Score*: To cut narrow gashes, partway through the fat, in meats before cooking; for example, in steaks to prevent curling. Also, to cut diamond-shaped gashes partway through fat in ham just before glazing.

*Scramble*: To stir or mix foods gently while cooking, as eggs.

*Sear*: To brown the surface of meat over high heat on top of the range or in the oven.

*Shirr*: To break eggs into a dish with cream or bread crumbs, then bake.

*Shred*: To cut or tear into long, narrow pieces. The fineness varies—recipes often say that foods should be finely" or "coarsely" shredded. Use a hand or mechanical shredder, or cut crisp vegetables, like cabbage, to shreds with a sharp knife.

*Sift*: To put dry ingredients through a fine sieve.

*Sifted flour*: When a recipe calls for a quantity of sifted flour it means you should sift the flour before measuring it.

*Simmer*: To cook just below the boiling point; adjust the heat to maintain this stage. In simmering, the food cooks so slowly that the surface moves just slightly; no bubbles show.

*Skewer*: To thread foods, such as meat, fish, poultry, and vegetables, on a wooden or metal skewer so they hold their shape during cooking.

*Sliver*: To cut or split into long, thin strips, with a knife on a cutting board.

*Steam*: To cook by steam in a closed container. Dumplings, puddings, and vegetables are examples. You can cook by steam under pressure, in a pressure cooker, in less time than usual.

*Steep*: To let a food stand in hot liquid, below boiling, to extract flavor, color, or both.

*Sterilize*: To heat in boiling water or steam for at least 20 minutes, until all living organisms are destroyed.

*Stew*: To cook foods, in enough liquid to cover, very slowly—always below the boiling point.

*Stir*: To mix, usually with a spoon or fork, until the ingredients are worked together.

*Stir-fry*: To cook thinly sliced or slivered vegetables for a few minutes in a small amount of oil in an open skillet or wok, tossing constantly as they cook.

*Toast*: To brown and dry the surface of foods

with heat, such as bread and nuts.
*Toss*: To tumble ingredients lightly with a lifting motion.

*Whip*: To rapidly beat eggs, heavy cream, etc., in order to incorporate air and expand the volume.

# THE BASICS OF KITCHEN EQUIPMENT

Some of the best food in the world came out of the simple kitchens of our great-grandmothers, who ground their spices with a mortar and pestle, and drained their pasta with a skillfully angled pot cover. Nevertheless, cooking can be a lot easier—and recipes a lot more predictable—if you stock your kitchen with a modest and carefully purchased set of basic equipment. Buy good-quality utensils—so you won't have to replace them—of standard size and capacity.

## FOR TOP-OF-RANGE USE:

*Coffee maker, sized to suit family
Double boiler, 1½ quarts
Dutch oven, 4 to 6 quarts
Small frying pan, 7 to 8 inches top diameter
*Large frying pan, 9 to 10 inches top diameter

*Griddle
3 saucepans with covers, 1 quart, 2 quarts, and 3 quarts
*Teakettle, 2½ quarts

*These utensils may be electric for top-of-counter use.

## FOR OVEN USE:

Shallow baking dish, 1½ quarts
2 round layer-cake pans, 8 or 9 inches by 1½ inches
Square cake pan, 8 by 8 by 2 inches or 9 by 9 by 2 inches
2 casseroles, 1½ quarts and 3 quarts
Cookie sheets, 15½ by 12 inches
6 custard cups, 5- or 6-ounce

Jelly-roll pan, 15½ by 10½ by 1 inch
2 loaf pans, 9 by 5 by 3 inches
Muffin pan with 6 to 12 individual cups
Oblong pan, 13 by 9 by 2 inches
Pie plate, 9-inch diameter
Shallow roasting pan with rack
Tube pan, 10 by 4 inches

## PREPARATION AND MEASURING TOOLS:

Biscuit cutter
Bottle opener and corkscrew
Bread or cutting board
Can opener
Colander
Flour sifter, single strainer only
French cook's knife
Fruit juicer
Set of assorted graters
Jar opener
Pair of kitchen shears
Ladle

Long-handled slotted metal spoon
Long-handled 2-tined kitchen fork
Minute timer
Nest of mixing bowls, 4 sizes
Narrow spatula, ¾ inch wide
Pair of tongs
Pancake turner
Paring knife
Pastry blender
Pastry brush
Potato masher
Rolling pin

Rotary beater
2 rubber spatulas, one narrow and one wide
Slicing knife, 8- or 9-inch blade
Set of standard dry measuring cups
3 standard liquid measuring cups, 1 cup, 2
    cups, and 4 cups
Set of standard measuring spoons

Medium-large strainer
Small strainer
Vegetable brush
Vegetable peeler
Wire rack
Wooden spoon

## NICE TO HAVE:

Apple corer
Baster
Blender
Bread knife with serrated or scalloped edge
Assorted cutters for cookies, doughnuts, and
    biscuits
Flexible steamer basket
Food grinder or chopper
Food processor
French wire whisk
Funnel
Grapefruit knife
Ice-cream spade or scoop
Knife sharpener
Melon-ball cutter

Molds, large and individual for puddings and
    salads
Mortar and pestle for crushing garlic, herbs,
    and seeds
Nutmeg grater
Pasta maker
Pastry cloth and rolling pin cover
Pepper mill
Poultry pins
Salad spinner
Slicer for eggs
Soufflé dish
Thermometers, roast-meat, deep-fry, and
    candy
Wok

## FOR STORAGE:

Bins for fruits and vegetables
Canister set
Cookie jar
Juice jug

Refrigerator dishes with covers
Waxed paper, aluminum foil, plastic sand-
    wich wrap, and plastic bags

# APPETIZERS, HORS D'OEUVRES, and CANAPÉS

Serve the appetizer course in the living room, instead of a first course, and you save clearing the table one time as well as whet everybody's appetite for what's to come. If you're having a heavy dinner—meat, starch, vegetables, and dessert—keep the hors d'oeuvres light: Guacamole Dip with Crisp Vegetables or Pickled Mushrooms would be good. If the meal to follow is light and you can use some "filler," try Mexican Meatballs with Chili Sauce or Indonesian Satays. Don't undertake too many separate starters, and try not to have the flavor or the ingredients duplicate what's to come in the meal.

Take care to select bowls and plates or trays that will make your appetizers look appealing. They are the first impression the guests will have of your meal. Or, if you are serving only assorted hors d'oeuvres at a party, their presentation becomes even more challenging and important.

## ◈ GUACAMOLE DIP WITH CRISP VEGETABLES

*1 medium tomato, peeled*
*2 ripe avocados (about 1½ lb in all)*
*¼ cup finely chopped onion*
*2 tablespoons finely chopped canned chili peppers*
*1½ tablespoons white vinegar*
*1 teaspoon salt*
*Chilled cauliflowerets*
*Crisp celery sticks*
*Green onions*
*Radishes*
*Cucumber sticks*

1. In medium bowl, crush tomato with potato masher.
2. Halve avocados lengthwise; remove pits and peel. Slice avocados into crushed tomato; then mash until well blended.
3. Add onion, chili pepper, vinegar, and salt; mix well.
4. Place guacamole in bowl. Surround with vegetables.
Makes about 2 cups.

## ◈ FRESH HERB CREAM-CHEESE SPREAD

*2 pkg (8-oz size) cream cheese, softened*
*1 tablespoon sour cream*
*2 tablespoons chopped chives*
*2 tablespoons snipped fresh dill*
*2 tablespoons chopped parsley*
*1 tablespoon cracked black pepper*

1. In food processor or large bowl, combine cream cheese, sour cream, chives, dill, and parsley. Mix until smooth.
2. Turn out into serving bowl; refrigerate, covered, 3 hours or overnight.
3. To serve: Sprinkle top with cracked pepper.
4. Place on serving dish. Nice with crackers or party rye-bread slices.
Makes 20 servings.

# HOT CHEESE BALLS

½ lb grated Parmesan cheese
½ lb cream cheese, softened
2 eggs
Dash ground red pepper
1 cup Japanese-style bread crumbs
 (see Note)
Peanut or salad oil for deep-frying

1. In medium bowl, combine cheeses, eggs, and red pepper. Beat with wooden spoon until smooth. Form into 1¼-inch balls.
2. Roll each lightly in bread crumbs on waxed paper. Refrigerate.
3. In deep skillet or deep-fat fryer, slowly heat oil (about 2 inches) to 350F on deep-frying thermometer. Fry cheese balls, turning once, 1 minute, or until golden-brown. Drain on paper towels. Serve hot. Makes 24.

*Note*: Japanese-style bread crumbs may be purchased in Japanese food shops, or they can be made by removing crusts from loaf of firm white bread, grating bread, and spreading crumbs on cookie sheets, uncovered, to dry at room temperature for several days. Or dry out in 150F oven several hours.

# HOT FETA CHEESE PASTRIES

**FILLING:**

2 pkg (8-oz size) cream cheese, softened
½ lb Greek cheese (feta), crumbled
1 egg
3 tablespoons butter or margarine, melted

1 pkg (1 lb) prepared phyllo-pastry or strudel-pastry leaves
1 cup butter or margarine, melted

1. Make Filling: In small bowl of electric mixer, combine cream cheese, Greek cheese, egg, and 3 tablespoons butter; beat at medium speed until well blended and smooth.
2. Preheat oven to 350F.
3. Place 2 leaves of phyllo pastry on board; brush with melted butter. Cut lengthwise into strips about 2 inches wide.
4. Place 1 teaspoon filling at end of a strip. Fold over one corner to opposite side, to make triangle. Continue folding, keeping triangle shape, to other end of strip. Arrange filled triangle on ungreased cookie sheet. Repeat with remaining strips.
5. Repeat with other pastry leaves.
6. Bake 20 minutes, or until deep golden-brown. Serve hot.
Makes about 7 dozen.

*Note*: If desired, make and bake ahead. Cool; then refrigerate, covered, overnight. To serve: Arrange on cookie sheet; bake in 350F oven about 10 minutes, or until heated.

# ✜ THE BEST QUICHE LORRAINE

**PIE SHELL:**

*1 pkg (10-oz size) piecrust mix*
*1 egg white, slightly beaten*

**FILLING:**

*½ lb sliced bacon*
*¾ lb natural Swiss cheese, grated (3 cups)*
*6 whole eggs*
*1 egg yolk*
*1¼ teaspoons salt*
*⅛ teaspoon ground nutmeg*
*⅛ teaspoon black pepper*
*Dash ground red pepper*
*3 cups light cream*

*3 slices bacon, crisp-cooked*

1. Make piecrust as label directs. Shape three fourths of pastry into ball; flatten to make 6-inch round. Freeze remaining dough for another use.
2. On lightly floured pastry cloth or surface, with light strokes, roll pastry from center to edge, alternating directions, to form 14-inch circle. Trim edge to make 13-inch circle. Fold pastry in half; place, with fold in center, in bottom of 9-inch springform pan.
3. Unfold pastry; fit carefully into pan. Pastry will measure 2 inches high on side of pan. Pat pastry to fit snugly and evenly in pan. Brush bottom and side of pastry lightly with egg white. Refrigerate to chill slightly, until ready to use. Preheat oven to 375F.
4. Make Filling: Fry ½ pound bacon until crisp; drain and crumble. Sprinkle over bottom of pie shell. Sprinkle cheese over bacon. In bowl, with wire whisk or rotary beater, beat eggs, egg yolk, salt, nutmeg, black pepper, and red pepper slightly. Gradually beat in cream.
5. Beat mixture just until well combined, not frothy. Slowly pour over bacon and cheese in pie shell. Bake 50 to 55 minutes, or until top is golden-brown and puffy and the center seems firm when pressed with fingertip. Remove to wire rack.
6. Let cool 15 minutes on wire rack. With sharp knife, loosen edge of pastry from side of pan; gently remove side of springform pan. Place, still on bottom of springform pan, on plate. Garnish with bacon slices. Serve warm.
Makes 12 servings.

# ✜ PISSALADIÈRE

*2 pkg (10-oz size) piecrust mix*
*10 large ripe tomatoes (about 5 lb)*
*2 tablespoons olive or salad oil*
*¼ cup butter or margarine*
*3 Spanish onions (2 lb), thinly sliced*
*½ cup grated Parmesan cheese*
*1 teaspoon dried rosemary leaves*
*2 cans (2-oz size) anchovy fillets*
*15 pitted ripe olives, halved*
*Olive oil*

1. Prepare piecrust, both packages at same time, as label directs.
2. On lightly floured pastry cloth, or waxed paper, roll out pastry, ¼ inch thick to form rectangle, about 17 by 12 inches. Fit into 15½-by-10½-by-1-inch jelly-roll pan; trim edges. Refrigerate.
3. To remove skin from tomatoes: Hold tomato on fork over flame just until skin "pops," or dip in boiling water until skin loosens. Seed and cut tomatoes in very small pieces. In hot olive oil, in large skillet, cook tomatoes over high heat, until water evaporates and tomatoes form a paste—about 15 minutes.

4. Preheat oven to 375F.
5. In hot butter, in skillet, sauté onions until soft and slightly golden.
6. Sprinkle bottom of pastry with grated cheese. Layer onions evenly over cheese; sprinkle with rosemary. Then make layer of tomato mixture over all.
7. Arrange anchovies in rows on top, 5 lengthwise and 4 crosswise, to make lattice effect. In center of each square, place olive half. Brush each olive with a little olive oil.
8. Bake 35 minutes, or until crust is golden and baked through.
9. Let cool slightly. Then brush with a little olive oil. Cut into 30 squares with an olive in center of each. Makes 30 servings.

# ❖ CAPONATA

1 large eggplant
½ cup plus 2 tablespoons olive or
  salad oil
2½ cups sliced onion
1 cup diced celery
2 cans (8-oz size) tomato sauce
¼ cup red-wine vinegar
2 tablespoons sugar
2 tablespoons drained capers
½ teaspoon salt
Dash pepper
12 pitted black olives, cut in slivers
Toast rounds

1. Wash eggplant; do not peel. Cut into ½-inch cubes.
2. In ½ cup hot oil in large skillet, sauté eggplant until tender and golden-brown. Remove eggplant, and set aside.
3. In 2 tablespoons hot oil in same skillet, sauté onion and celery until tender—about 5 minutes.
4. Return eggplant to skillet. Stir in tomato sauce; bring to boiling. Lower heat, and simmer, covered, 15 minutes.
5. Add vinegar, sugar, capers, salt, pepper, and olives. Simmer, covered and stirring occasionally, 20 minutes longer.
6. Refrigerate, covered, overnight.
7. To serve: Turn out into serving bowl. Surround with toast rounds.
Makes 12 servings.

# ❖ PICKLED MUSHROOMS

1 tablespoon salt
6 cups cold water
1 lb fresh button mushrooms
½ cup chopped onion
1 clove garlic, finely chopped
¼ cup chopped parsley
2 bay leaves
⅛ teaspoon black pepper
½ teaspoon dried thyme leaves
2 cups white wine
2 cups white vinegar
½ cup olive or salad oil
2 tablespoons lemon juice

1. Add salt to cold water. Wash mushrooms in this; drain.
2. Combine remaining ingredients in large saucepan. Add mushrooms; bring to boiling point.
3. Then reduce heat, and simmer, covered, 8 to 10 minutes, or until mushrooms are tender. Cool.
4. Refrigerate, covered, at least 1 hour, or until ready to use.
Makes 6 servings.

# ❖ ROASTED RED PEPPERS

8 medium-size sweet red peppers
  (2½ lb)
1 cup olive or salad oil
¼ cup lemon juice
2 teaspoons salt
3 small cloves garlic
3 anchovy fillets

1. Preheat oven to 450F.
2. Wash red peppers; drain well.
3. Place peppers on cookie sheet; bake about 20 minutes, or until skin of peppers becomes blistered and charred. With tongs, turn peppers every 5 minutes.
4. Place hot peppers in large kettle. Cover kettle and let stand 15 minutes.
5. Peel off charred skin with sharp knife. Cut each pepper into fourths. Remove ribs and seeds, and cut out any dark spots.
6. In large bowl, combine oil, lemon juice, salt, and garlic. Add peppers, and toss lightly to coat with oil mixture.
7. Pack pepper mixture and anchovy fillets into 1-quart jar; cap. Refrigerate several hours or overnight. Serve as appetizer or in tossed salad.
Makes 12 servings.

# ❖ LIVER PÂTÉ EN GELÉE

1½ teaspoons unflavored gelatine
1 cup canned condensed beef broth
4 canned whole mushrooms
1 can (4¾ oz) liver pâté
1 tablespoon butter or regular margarine
1 teaspoon brandy
Thin slices toast

1. In small saucepan, sprinkle gelatine over ¼ cup undiluted broth; let stand 5 minutes, to soften. Heat over low heat, stirring constantly, until gelatine dissolves. Remove from heat. Add remaining broth.
2. Place 1½-cup decorative mold in pan of ice and water. Spoon about 2 tablespoons gelatine mixture into mold. Let stand a few minutes, until almost set.
3. Cut mushrooms in half. Arrange, in a pattern, on set gelatine in mold. Add enough additional gelatine mixture to cover mushrooms.
4. In small bowl, combine liver pâté, butter, and brandy. With electric mixer or fork, beat until combined.
5. Turn out mixture into empty liver-pâté can, making top even; invert onto waxed paper. With can opener, remove end of can. Lift can, and carefully push pâté, through can, onto center of set gelatine in mold, being careful to keep its shape.
6. Spoon remaining chilled gelatine mixture around and over pâté. Refrigerate, covered, 3 hours, or until firm.
7. To unmold: Run sharp knife around edge of mold. Invert over serving plate. Place hot damp dishcloth over mold; shake gently to release. Lift off mold.
8. Remove crusts from toast; cut toast diagonally in quarters. Arrange triangles around mold. Or serve mold with crackers, if you wish.
Makes 8 servings.

# ⊡ PARTY PÂTÉ

2½ lb chicken livers
1 cup (2 sticks) sweet butter
2 large onions, sliced
3 hard-cooked eggs, quartered
¼ cup cognac or brandy
1 teaspoon salt
Dash pepper

## GLAZE:

1 env unflavored gelatine
¼ cup water
1 cup dry white wine
½ teaspoon dried tarragon leaves
½ teaspoon chopped fresh parsley

1 pimiento
Pitted black olives
White-toast triangles or rye-bread
 rounds

1. Day before: Wash livers, and drain on paper towels. Line inside of 1½-quart mold with plastic wrap.
2. In ¼ cup hot butter in medium skillet, sauté onions until tender—about 10 minutes. Remove from skillet.
3. Heat half of remaining butter in same skillet. Add half of chicken livers. Sauté over high heat, stirring constantly, 3 to 5 minutes; remove. Repeat with remaining butter and chicken livers.
4. Purée onions, chicken livers, eggs, and cognac, half at a time, in food processor (in thirds if using blender). Stir in salt and pepper.
5. Turn out into prepared mold. Refrigerate, covered, overnight.
6. Next day, unmold: Loosen edge with spatula; turn out on wire rack on tray. Smooth surface with spatula. Refrigerate.
7. Prepare Glaze: Sprinkle gelatine over ¼ cup water in small saucepan; let stand 5 minutes to soften. Add wine, tarragon, and parsley. Stir over low heat until gelatine is dissolved; strain. Set pan in ice water; stir until slightly thickened (starts to jell)—about 15 minutes.
8. Spoon half of glaze over pâté, to cover completely.
9. Meanwhile, cut pimiento into ½-inch triangles. Place around edge of pâté. Cut olives into slices; arrange in center to simulate flower. Place a bit of pimiento in center. Refrigerate to set glaze—about 30 minutes.
10. Reheat remaining glaze and any glaze drippings on tray; rechill. Spoon over design; repeat with any remaining glaze. Chill. Serve on white-toast triangles or rye-bread rounds.
Makes 35 servings.

# ❖ CLAMS OREGANO

2 dozen clams in shells, well scrubbed
¾ cup butter or margarine, melted
1 cup packaged dry bread crumbs
2 cloves garlic, crushed
2 tablespoons chopped parsley
2 tablespoons grated Parmesan
  cheese
4 teaspoons lemon juice
1 teaspoon dried oregano leaves
⅛ teaspoon liquid hot-pepper seasoning
Rock salt
Lemon wedges
Parsley sprigs

1. In large kettle, bring ½ inch water to boiling. Add clams; simmer, covered, until clams open—6 to 10 minutes.
2. Meanwhile, combine butter with bread crumbs, garlic, chopped parsley, Parmesan, lemon juice, oregano, and hot-pepper seasoning.
3. Remove clams from kettle; discard top shells. Remove clams from bottom shells; chop coarsely; add to crumb mixture. Spoon into bottom shells.
4. Place layer of rock salt, ½ inch deep, in large roasting pan or 2 shallow casseroles; sprinkle with water to dampen.
5. Arrange filled clam shells on salt. Run under broiler just until golden-brown—about 5 minutes. Garnish with lemon wedges and parsley sprigs. Serve at once.
Makes 8 servings.

# ❖ HERRING IN DILL SAUCE

1 cup prepared mustard
1 cup olive oil
¼ cup vinegar
3 tablespoons lemon juice
½ cup chopped fresh dill
1 teaspoon pepper
1½ teaspoons salt
1½ teaspoons whole allspice
2 tablespoons sugar
8 salt-herring fillets
Fresh dill sprigs

1. Combine mustard and oil in small bowl; beat, with rotary beater, until as thick as mayonnaise.
2. Gradually beat in vinegar and lemon juice, then dill, pepper, salt, allspice, and sugar.
3. Rinse herring; drain well on paper towels. Place in large glass bowl; cover with sauce.
4. Refrigerate, covered, at least 3 days.
5. To serve: Cut into 1-inch pieces; serve with wooden picks. Garnish with dill sprigs.
Makes 10 to 12 servings.

# ❖ SWEDISH COLD SALMON WITH MUSTARD SAUCE
### (GRAVLAX)

5 to 6 lb fresh salmon
¼ cup sugar
¼ cup salt
1 tablespoon white pepper
½ cup snipped fresh dill
Fresh dill and lemon slices (optional)
Mustard Sauce, below
Party rye or pumpernickel bread

1. Two days before: With sharp knife, carefully remove skin from salmon. Cut salmon in half along bone; remove bone.
2. Combine sugar, salt, and pepper; mix well. Use about one third of sugar mixture to sprinkle both sides of salmon, lightly rubbing into surface.
3. On tray, covered with waxed paper, place one salmon half. Cover with half of snipped dill. Place

other half of salmon, cut side sprinkled with rest of dill, on top.

4. Place bread board on top of fish; weight down with very heavy skillet or iron. Refrigerate two days.

5. During refrigeration, sprinkle two more times with sugar mixture, turning fish and basting with juices in tray.

6. When ready to serve, lightly dry salmon with paper towels. If desired, garnish with fresh dill and thin lemon slices. Slice thin. Serve with Mustard Sauce and dark bread.

Makes 20 servings.

## MUSTARD SAUCE

½ cup prepared brown mustard
½ cup sugar
½ cup salad oil
½ cup chopped fresh dill
¼ cup white-wine vinegar

In small bowl, combine mustard, sugar, and salad oil; mix well with wooden spoon. Add dill and wine vinegar; beat well. Refrigerate, covered, until well chilled—several hours.
Makes 1½ cups.

*Note*: If stronger mustard flavor is desired, add dry mustard to taste.

# ⬛ SALMON MOUSSE

2 cans (1-lb size) red salmon
½ cup white wine
½ cup sour cream
2 tablespoons prepared horseradish
2 env unflavored gelatine
¼ cup water
¼ cup lemon juice
2 tablespoons chopped fresh chives
2 tablespoons snipped fresh dill
1 teaspoon salt
1 tablespoon prepared mustard
1 cup heavy cream, whipped
Fresh dill sprigs
White toast rounds or unsalted
   crackers

1. Drain salmon; remove any bones and skin.

2. Place salmon and wine in food processor; process until smooth, to make purée. (Or place salmon and wine in large bowl. With fork, break salmon into small pieces; beat at high speed with electric mixer until it is as smooth as possible.) Turn out into large bowl; fold in sour cream and horseradish.

3. In measuring cup, sprinkle gelatine over water and lemon juice; let stand 5 minutes. Set in pan of simmering water; stir to dissolve gelatine. Gradually stir into salmon mixture, along with chives, dill, salt, and mustard.

4. Fold in whipped cream. Turn out into 1½-quart decorative mold. Refrigerate, covered, until firm—at least 4 hours.

5. To serve: Run small spatula carefully around edge of mold; invert onto platter. Place hot damp cloth over mold; shake to release. Garnish with dill sprigs. Serve on white toast rounds or unsalted crackers.
Makes 40 servings.

# ❖ INDONESIAN SATAYS

**(HYATT REGENCY WAIKIKI, HONOLULU)**

½ lb beef tenderloin
½ lb pork tenderloin
½ lb chicken cutlet
½ cup soy sauce
1 tablespoon grated fresh ginger root
1 tablespoon pressed garlic
Dash pepper
¼ cup water
1 teaspoon sugar
1 bunch green onions

1. Cut the beef, pork, and chicken into silver-dollar-size medallions, about ¼ inch thick. Pound lightly to flatten. Insert bamboo skewer into each medallion, keeping medallion as flat as possible.

2. In small glass bowl, combine soy sauce, ginger, garlic, pepper, water, and sugar. Arrange satays in marinade, with skewers resting on edge of bowl. Cover tightly with plastic wrap, and refrigerate 3 hours.

3. Wash and trim green onions. Make several lengthwise cuts through green ends. Place, green end down, in small bowl of ice water. Cover and refrigerate.

4. Preheat broiler or charcoal grill. Arrange satays on broiler pan, with skewers all on one side. Cover skewers with foil. Broil, 3 inches from heat, 3 minutes; turn, and broil until desired doneness—about 2 minutes longer. Chicken and beef satays may be removed and pan returned to broiler to continue cooking pork satays to well done. Arrange on board or platter; garnish with green onions.

Makes 12 servings (4 per serving).

# ❖MINIATURE EGG ROLLS

## BATTER:

2½ cups water
2 cups all-purpose flour
1 egg
½ teaspoon salt

## FILLING:

¼ cup salad oil
½ cup finely chopped celery
¼ cup finely chopped green onion
1 clove garlic, pressed
¾ cup finely chopped cooked shrimp
¾ cup finely chopped cooked pork
¾ cup finely chopped water chestnuts
¾ cup bean sprouts
¼ cup soy sauce
½ teaspoon ground ginger
1 teaspoon sugar

Salad oil for deep-frying
Hot mustard (see Note)

1. Make Batter: Gradually add water to flour in medium bowl, beating at medium speed with portable electric mixer to make smooth batter. Beat in egg and salt; beat until smooth, not frothy. Refrigerate until ready to use.
2. Make Filling: Heat 2 tablespoons oil in large heavy skillet; add celery, green onion, and garlic. Cook, stirring, until tender—about 3 minutes.
3. Add 2 tablespoons oil, the shrimp, pork, water chestnuts, bean sprouts, soy sauce, ginger, and sugar; cook, stirring, 5 minutes. Set aside.
4. Lightly grease 5-inch skillet (nonstick finish if possible); heat slowly. Beat batter; pour 2 tablespoons batter into skillet, turning pan to spread batter all over. Cook until bubbles appear on surface. Turn and cook on other side. Do not brown. Cool on wire rack; stack pancakes with squares of waxed paper between them. Continue making rest of pancakes. Lightly grease skillet in between.
5. Place 1 tablespoon filling in center of each pancake; fold four sides over filling.
6. Slowly heat oil (1 inch deep) in large skillet to 375F. Fry several egg rolls at a time just until crisp and golden-brown. Lift out with slotted spoon; drain on paper towels.
7. To freeze: Place egg rolls in single layer on tray; freeze until firm. Then freezer-wrap; store in freezer.
8. To serve: Preheat oven to 375F. Place as many frozen egg rolls as needed on cookie sheet. Bake 12 minutes, or until crisp and hot. Serve at once with hot mustard.
Makes 26 egg rolls.

Note: For hot mustard, use 2 tablespoons dry mustard mixed with ¼ cup water to form smooth mixture.

# ❖ FROZEN CANAPÉ TRAY

Canapé Butters (recipes follow)
Sliced white bread (use firm type of bread)
Sliced rye bread (use firm type of bread)
Thin-sliced ham, bologna, salami, olive loaf, turkey, Cheddar cheese, Swiss cheese
Sieved egg yolks
Red salmon caviar, drained
Chives
Canned pimiento, drained
Ripe olives
Stuffed green olives
Small gherkins
Cherry tomatoes, sliced
Cucumber slices

## SALAMI-AND-CREAM-CHEESE CORNUCOPIAS:

Salami
Cream cheese, softened

Lemon Glaze (recipe follows)
Watercress sprigs

1. Make Canapé Butters.
2. Using pastry cutters, cut bread into various shapes (about 2-inch size): hearts, ovals, rounds, diamonds.
3. Spread with various canapé butters. (For example, Curry Butter for turkey, Mustard Butter for bologna, etc.)
4. Cut meats and cheeses with fancy cutters to fit bread bases. Arrange on matching bread bases. Cover half of some bread bases with egg yolk and the other half with red caviar. Garnish, using cutouts of chives, pimiento, olives, and small gherkins, leaving tomato and cucumber garnish until serving time.
5. Make Salami-and-Cream-Cheese Cornucopias: Trim rind from slices of salami. Spread with cream cheese. Roll up salami at one end; fasten with wooden pick, leaving other end open. Freeze along with sandwiches.
6. Arrange on cardboard trays. Cover with plastic wrap, then foil. Freeze until ready to serve.
7. To serve: Remove sandwiches from freezer; let stand at room temperature, still wrapped, about ½ hour. While thawing, make Lemon Glaze.
8. Remove sandwiches to serving tray. Finish garnishing with cucumber rounds and cherry tomatoes. Brush sandwiches with lemon glaze. Garnish tray with watercress. Place a sprig of watercress in open ends of cornucopias.

# ❖ CANAPÉ BUTTERS

## CAPER BUTTER:

⅓ cup butter or margarine, softened
1½ tablespoons finely chopped capers

In small bowl, combine butter and capers, mixing well.
Makes about ⅓ cup.

## CHIVE BUTTER:

⅓ cup butter or margarine, softened
2 tablespoons finely snipped chives
1½ teaspoons lemon juice

In small bowl, combine butter, chives, and lemon juice, mixing well.
Makes about ⅓ cup.

### CURRY BUTTER:

⅓ cup butter or margarine, softened
½ teaspoon curry powder

In small bowl, combine butter and curry powder, mixing well.
Makes about ⅓ cup.

### MUSTARD BUTTER:

⅓ cup butter or margarine, softened
½ teaspoon dry mustard

In small bowl, combine butter and mustard, mixing well.
Makes about ⅓ cup.

## ✤ LEMON GLAZE

1 env unflavored gelatine
1¼ cups water
¼ cup lemon juice

1. Sprinkle gelatine over water in saucepan; let stand 5 minutes to soften.
2. Over very low heat, melt gelatine; stir in lemon juice.
3. Pour into bowl, and place in larger bowl of ice cubes; stir until mixture begins to set slightly. Spoon a little over each canapé, just enough to moisten surface.
Makes about 1½ cups.

## ✤ HOT MUSHROOM CANAPÉS

1 lb mushrooms
¼ cup butter or margarine
1 cup finely chopped onion
⅓ cup flour
⅓ cup milk
½ teaspoon salt
⅛ teaspoon pepper
1 loaf sliced white bread
Grated Parmesan cheese
Sliced stuffed olives

1. Wash mushrooms; dry on paper towels. Chop fine.
2. In 2 tablespoons of butter in large skillet, sauté onion, stirring, until golden—about 5 minutes. Add rest of butter and the mushrooms; sauté, stirring, 5 minutes longer, or until tender and liquid has almost evaporated. Remove skillet from heat.
3. Add flour gradually, sprinkling over surface and stirring to mix well. Gradually stir in milk; add salt and pepper. Cook, stirring, until mixture is quite thick. Set aside to cool.
4. Using 2-inch round cutter, cut bread into rounds. Spread with mushroom mixture, using about 1 tablespoon for each round. Sprinkle with a little Parmesan cheese.
5. Preheat broiler. Arrange canapés on cookie sheets. Run under broiler about 2 minutes, to brown top and heat through. Garnish each with olive slice.
Makes 30 canapés.

# BREADS

# QUICK BREADS

✦ **B**aking-powder biscuits come to mind when you think of quick breads, but there's a whole repertoire of breads, muffins, biscuits, and pancakes that take their rising power from baking soda and baking powder instead of yeast. Since they can be mixed very easily and baked as soon as mixed, they are great for providing warm homemade breads quickly and stylishly. And they can make a simple meal a special one. A fruit salad served with slices of cheese-spread Nut Bread; a bowl of chili, with Corn Muffins; scrambled eggs, with hot Popovers—the home-baked bread will make an ordinary main dish taste better.

## ✦ SAVORY CHEESE BREAD

2 cups sifted all-purpose flour
2 teaspoons baking powder
1 tablespoon sugar
½ teaspoon salt
¼ cup butter or margarine, cut into 4 parts
1 cup grated sharp natural Cheddar cheese
1 tablespoon grated onion
1½ teaspoons dried dillweed
¾ cup milk
1 egg, slightly beaten

1. Preheat oven to 350F. Lightly grease 9-by-5-by-3-inch loaf pan.
2. Sift flour with baking powder, sugar, and salt into large bowl.
3. With 2 knives or pastry blender, cut in butter until mixture resembles coarse crumbs. Stir in cheese, onion, and dill; mix well.
4. Combine milk and beaten egg; pour into flour mixture all at once. Stir quickly with fork just to moisten flour mixture.
5. Turn out into prepared pan. Bake 40 to 45 minutes, or until cake tester inserted in center comes out clean.
6. Let cool in pan 10 minutes. Turn out on wire rack to cool completely, or serve slightly warm.
Makes 1 loaf.

## ✦ IRISH SODA BREAD

2 cups all-purpose flour
2 tablespoons sugar
1 teaspoon baking powder
1 teaspoon baking soda
½ teaspoon salt
3 tablespoons butter or margarine, softened
½ cup seedless raisins
1 cup buttermilk
1 tablespoon butter or margarine, melted

1. Preheat oven to 375F. Lightly grease small cookie sheet.
2. In large bowl, sift flour, sugar, baking powder, baking soda, and salt.
3. Cut in butter with pastry blender or fork until mixture looks like fine crumbs. Add raisins.
4. Add buttermilk; mix with fork only until dry ingredients are moistened.
5. Turn out onto lightly floured pastry cloth or board. Knead gently until smooth—about 1 minute. Shape into ball. Place on prepared cookie sheet: flatten into

7-inch circle. (Dough will be about 1½ inches thick.) Press large floured knife into center of loaf halfway through to bottom. Repeat, at right angle, to divide loaf into quarters.

6. Bake 30 to 40 minutes, or until top is golden and loaf sounds hollow when tapped.

7. Remove to wire rack to cool. Brush top with melted butter. Later, dust top with flour, if desired.

Makes 1 loaf.

# ❖ WHOLE-WHEAT IRISH SODA BREAD

*1 cup all-purpose flour*
*1 teaspoon baking powder*
*1 teaspoon baking soda*
*1 teaspoon salt*
*2 tablespoons sugar*
*2 cups whole-wheat flour*
*1½ cups buttermilk*
*1 tablespoon butter or margarine,*
   *melted*

1. Preheat oven to 375F. Grease well small cookie sheet.

2. Into large mixing bowl, sift together all-purpose flour, baking powder, baking soda, salt, and sugar. Add whole-wheat flour; mix well with fork.

3. Add buttermilk; mix just until dry ingredients are moistened.

4. Turn out onto lightly floured pastry cloth or board. Knead gently until smooth—about 1 minute.

5. Shape dough into ball. Place on prepared cookie sheet; flatten into 7-inch circle. (Dough will be about 1½ inches thick.) Press large floured knife into center of loaf halfway through to bottom. Repeat, at right angle, to divide loaf into quarters.

6. Bake 40 minutes, or until top is golden and loaf sounds hollow when tapped.

7. Remove to wire rack to cool. Brush top with melted butter. Cool completely.

Makes 1 loaf.

# SWEET QUICK BREADS

## ✠ McCALL'S BEST NUT BREAD

2½ cups sifted all-purpose flour
3 teaspoons baking powder
½ teaspoon salt
1 egg, beaten
1 teaspoon vanilla extract
¾ cup sugar
¼ cup butter or margarine, melted, or
　salad oil
1¼ cups milk
1 cup finely chopped walnuts or pe-
　cans

1. Preheat oven to 350F. Grease 9-by-5-by-3-inch loaf pan.
2. Sift flour with baking powder and salt.
3. In large bowl, combine egg, vanilla, sugar, and butter. Using wooden spoon or portable electric mixer, beat until well blended. Add milk, blending well.
4. Add flour mixture, beating until smooth. Stir in nuts.
5. Pour batter into prepared pan; bake 60 to 65 minutes, or until cake tester inserted in center comes out clean.
6. Let cool in pan 10 minutes. Remove from pan; cool completely on wire rack.
Makes 1 loaf.

## ✠ DATE-NUT BREAD

1 pkg (8 oz) pitted dates, coarsely
　chopped
1½ cups boiling water
2¾ cups sifted all-purpose flour
1 teaspoon baking powder
1½ teaspoons baking soda
1 teaspoon salt
1 egg, beaten
1 cup sugar
2 tablespoons butter or margarine,
　melted
1 teaspoon vanilla extract
1 cup coarsely chopped walnuts
Dates and walnut halves (optional)

1. In small bowl, combine dates with boiling water; let cool to room temperature.
2. Meanwhile, preheat oven to 350F. Grease 2 loaf pans, 7-by-3½-by-2-inches.
3. Sift flour with baking powder, baking soda, and salt; set aside.
4. In medium bowl, with wooden spoon or with portable electric mixer at low speed, beat egg, sugar, butter, and vanilla until smooth.
5. Add cooled date mixture, mixing well. Then add flour mixture, beating with wooden spoon until well combined. Stir in nuts.
6. Turn out batter into prepared pans. Place on cookie sheet. Bake 45 to 50 minutes, or until cake tester inserted in center comes out clean.
7. Let cool in pans 10 minutes. Remove from pans; cool completely on wire rack.
8. To store: Wrap each loaf in foil, plastic wrap, or moisture- and vapor-proof freezer paper; seal and label. Freeze.
9. Remove number of loaves desired from freezer. Let thaw, still in wrapping, at room temperature several hours, or until room temperature. If desired, decorate with dates and walnut halves.
Makes 2 loaves.

# ❖ HOLIDAY BANANA BREAD

1¾ cups sifted all-purpose flour
⅔ cup sugar
3 teaspoons baking powder
½ teaspoon salt
¼ teaspoon baking soda
⅓ cup margarine
1 cup mashed very ripe banana (2 or 3)
2 eggs
½ cup chopped walnuts
¼ cup chopped candied citron
¼ cup chopped candied orange peel
¼ cup chopped candied cherries
¼ cup chopped candied pineapple
¼ cup dark raisins

1. Preheat oven to 350F. Grease well 9-by-5-by-3-inch loaf pan.
2. Into large bowl, sift flour with sugar, baking powder, salt, and baking soda. With pastry blender or with 2 knives, cut in margarine until mixture resembles coarse crumbs.
3. Add banana and eggs; with electric mixer at low speed, beat 2 minutes.
4. Add nuts, candied fruit, and raisins; beat until well blended. Turn out into prepared pan.
5. Bake 1 hour and 10 minutes, or until cake tester inserted in center comes out clean.
6. Let cool in pan on wire rack 10 minutes. Remove from pan; let cool completely on rack. Wrap in plastic wrap, then in foil, and store overnight before serving.
Makes 1 loaf.

# ❖ CRANBERRY-NUT BREAD

1 cup fresh cranberries
2 cups sifted all-purpose flour
¾ cup sugar
3 teaspoons baking powder
¼ teaspoon salt
½ cup walnuts, chopped
2 eggs
1 cup milk
¼ cup butter or margarine, melted
1 teaspoon vanilla extract

1. Preheat oven to 350F. Grease 2 loaf pans, 7 by 3½ by 2 inches. Wash cranberries, removing stems; chop coarsely.
2. Sift flour with sugar, baking powder, and salt into large bowl. Stir in cranberries and walnuts.
3. In small bowl, with wire whisk or portable electric mixer, beat eggs with milk, butter, and vanilla.
4. Make well in center of cranberry mixture. Pour in egg mixture; with fork, stir just until dry ingredients are moistened.
5. Turn out into prepared pans. Place on cookie sheet. Bake 40 to 45 minutes, or until golden-brown on top and cake tester inserted in center comes out clean.
6. Cool in pan 10 minutes. Remove from pan; cool on wire rack.
Makes 2 loaves.

# ✠ WHOLE-WHEAT NUT BREAD

1½ cups sifted all-purpose flour
1 tablespoon baking powder
½ teaspoon salt
1 cup unsifted whole-wheat flour
1 egg, beaten
1 teaspoon vanilla extract
¾ cup sugar
¼ cup butter or margarine, melted, or
    salad oil
1¼ cups milk
1 cup finely chopped walnuts

1. Preheat oven to 350F. Grease 9-by-5-by-3-inch loaf pan.
2. Sift all-purpose flour with baking powder and salt. Stir in whole-wheat flour.
3. In large bowl, combine egg, vanilla, sugar, and butter. Using wooden spoon or portable electric mixer at low speed, beat until well blended. Add milk, blending well.
4. Add flour mixture, beating with wooden spoon just until combined. Do not overbeat. Stir in nuts.
5. Pour batter into prepared pan. Bake 60 to 65 minutes, or until cake tester inserted in center comes out clean.
6. Let cool in pan 10 minutes. Remove from pan; cool completely on wire rack.
Makes 1 loaf.

# ✠ LEMON TEA BREAD

2 cups all-purpose flour
1½ teaspoons baking powder
¼ teaspoon salt
½ cup butter or margarine
1 cup sugar
2 eggs
⅓ cup milk
½ cup chopped walnuts
2 teaspoons grated lemon peel

## SYRUP:

¼ cup lemon juice
⅓ cup sugar

1. Preheat oven to 350F. Lightly grease 9-by-5-by-3-inch loaf pan.
2. Sift flour with baking powder and salt; set aside.
3. In large bowl of electric mixer, at medium speed, beat butter with 1 cup sugar until light and fluffy. Add eggs, one at a time, beating well after each addition; beat until very light and fluffy.
4. At low speed, beat in flour mixture alternately with milk, beginning and ending with flour mixture; beat just until combined.
5. Stir in nuts and lemon peel. Turn out batter into prepared pan. Bake 55 to 60 minutes, or until cake tester inserted in center comes out clean.
6. Make Syrup: In small saucepan, combine lemon juice and sugar; cook, stirring, 1 minute, or until syrupy. Pour evenly over bread as soon as it is removed from oven.
7. Let cool in pan 10 minutes. Remove to wire rack; let cool completely.
Makes 1 loaf.

# ✜ PINEAPPLE-APRICOT-NUT LOAF

2¾ cups sifted all-purpose flour
1 tablespoon baking powder
¼ teaspoon baking soda
¼ teaspoon salt
¾ cup sugar
⅓ cup butter or margarine, melted
1 egg
⅓ cup milk
1 cup canned crushed pineapple, undrained
⅓ cup chopped dried apricots
¼ cup light raisins
1 tablespoon chopped candied cherries or citron
1 cup chopped walnuts

1. Preheat oven to 350F. Grease and flour 9-by-5-by-3-inch loaf pan. Sift flour with baking powder, baking soda, and salt; set aside.
2. In large bowl, combine sugar, melted butter, and egg; using wooden spoon, beat until ingredients are well blended.
3. Add milk, pineapple, apricots, raisins, and cherries; blend well.
4. Add flour mixture; beat just until combined. Stir in nuts. Turn out into prepared pan.
5. Bake 1¼ hours, or until cake tester inserted in center comes out clean.
6. Let cool in pan 10 minutes. Remove from pan; let cool completely on wire rack.
Makes 1 loaf.

# ✜ CINNAMON-ZUCCHINI-WALNUT BREAD

2½ cups all-purpose flour
1½ teaspoons ground cinnamon
½ teaspoon ground cloves
2 teaspoons baking soda
1 teaspoon baking powder
1 teaspoon salt
1½ cups sugar
¾ cup salad oil
3 eggs
2 cups grated unpeeled zucchini (1 lb)
1 cup finely chopped walnuts
1 teaspoon vanilla extract
½ teaspoon ground cinnamon (optional)
¼ cup sugar (optional)
10 walnut pieces (optional)

1. Preheat oven to 350F. Grease well 9-by-5-by-3-inch loaf pan.
2. Sift flour with cinnamon, cloves, baking soda, baking powder, and salt.
3. In large mixing bowl, with wooden spoon or portable electric mixer, combine 1½ cups sugar, the oil, and eggs; beat until smooth.
4. Add sifted dry ingredients, mixing until smooth.
5. Add zucchini, chopped nuts, and vanilla; stir until well combined.
6. Pour batter into prepared pan. Bake 1 hour and 15 minutes, or until cake tester inserted in center comes out clean.
7. Let cool in pan 10 minutes. Remove from pan; cool bread completely on wire rack.
8. If desired, before serving combine cinnamon and sugar. Turn bread upside down. Decorate edge with cinnamon-sugar, and center with nuts.
Makes 1 loaf.

# MUFFINS

## ✦ BUTTERMILK BRAN MUFFINS

*1 cup sifted all-purpose flour*
*2 teaspoons baking powder*
*½ teaspoon baking soda*
*¾ teaspoon salt*
*3 cups whole-bran cereal*
*½ cup seedless raisins*
*⅓ cup shortening*
*½ cup sugar*
*1 egg*
*1 cup buttermilk*

1. Preheat oven to 400F. Grease bottoms of 12 (3-inch) muffin-pan cups, or line each with paper liner.
2. Sift flour with baking powder, baking soda, and salt into medium bowl. Add bran and raisins; mix well.
3. In large bowl, using wooden spoon, cream shortening with sugar until light and fluffy. Beat in egg.
4. Using fork, add flour mixture alternately with buttermilk, stirring only until dry ingredients are moistened. Do not beat. Batter will be lumpy.
5. Quickly scoop batter into muffin-pan cups, filling not quite two thirds full. Bake 20 to 25 minutes, or until golden.
6. Loosen edge of each muffin with spatula; turn out. Serve hot.
Makes 12.

## ✦ BLUEBERRY CAKE MUFFINS

*2 cups sifted all-purpose flour*
*1½ teaspoons baking powder*
*¼ teaspoon salt*
*½ cup butter or margarine, softened*
*1 cup granulated sugar*
*2 eggs, unbeaten*
*1 teaspoon vanilla extract*
*½ cup milk*
*1 cup fresh or thawed frozen and*
  *drained blueberries*
*Confectioners' sugar*

1. Preheat oven to 375F. With paper liners, line 18 muffin-pan cups (2½ by 1¼ inches), or grease them well.
2. Sift flour with baking powder and salt. Set aside.
3. In large bowl, with electric mixer at high speed, beat butter with granulated sugar, eggs, and vanilla until light and fluffy—about 4 minutes—occasionally scraping side of bowl and beaters with rubber scraper.
4. At low speed, beat in flour mixture (in fourths), alternately with milk, beginning and ending with flour mixture. Beat just until smooth.
5. With rubber spatula, gently fold in blueberries just until combined.
6. Scoop about ¼ cup batter into each prepared muffin cup, to fill each about two thirds full.
7. Bake 20 to 25 minutes, or until golden-brown and cake tester inserted in center comes out clean.
8. Remove muffins to wire rack; let cool slightly.
9. Serve warm or cold, sprinkled with confectioners' sugar.
Makes 18.

# ❖ CINNAMON-SUGAR MUFFINS

## TOPPING:

¼ cup granulated sugar
¼ cup sifted all-purpose flour
2 tablespoons butter or margarine
1 teaspoon ground cinnamon

## BATTER:

1⅓ cups sifted all-purpose flour
1 teaspoon baking powder
¼ teaspoon salt
¼ cup butter or margarine, softened
¼ cup light-brown sugar, packed
1 egg
½ cup milk

1. Preheat oven to 375F. Lightly grease bottoms of 8 (3-inch) muffin-pan cups.
2. Make Topping: In small bowl, combine topping ingredients; mix until crumbly.
3. Make Batter: Sift flour with baking powder and salt.
4. In large bowl of electric mixer, at medium speed, beat butter until fluffy. Beat in brown sugar, then egg, until very light and fluffy. At low speed, blend in milk, then flour mixture, just until combined. Pour into muffin cups, dividing evenly.
5. Sprinkle 1 tablespoon topping over each muffin. Bake 20 minutes, or until cake tester comes out clean.
6. Cool slightly in cups on wire rack. Gently remove from cups. Serve warm.
Makes 8.

# ❖ CHEESE MUFFINS

2 cups sifted all-purpose flour
¼ cup sugar
3 teaspoons baking powder
½ teaspoon salt
⅛ teaspoon ground red pepper
½ cup grated sharp Cheddar cheese
1 cup milk
¼ cup salad oil or melted shortening
1 egg, slightly beaten

1. Preheat oven to 425F. Grease bottoms of 14 (2½-inch) muffin-pan cups.
2. Sift flour with sugar, baking powder, salt, and red pepper into large bowl. Stir in cheese.
3. Measure milk in 2-cup measure. Add oil and egg; beat with fork to mix well.
4. Make well in center of flour mixture. Pour in milk mixture all at once; stir quickly, with fork, just until dry ingredients are moistened. Do not beat. Batter will be lumpy.
5. Using ¼-cup measuring cup (not quite full), quickly scoop batter into muffin cups, filling each slightly more than half full.
6. Bake 15 to 20 minutes, or until golden and cake tester inserted in center comes out clean.
7. Loosen edge of each muffin with spatula; turn out. Serve hot.
Makes 14.

# ❖ OATMEAL-RAISIN MUFFINS

*1 cup buttermilk*
*1 cup rolled oats*
*1 cup sifted all-purpose flour*
*1 teaspoon baking powder*
*½ teaspoon baking soda*
*½ teaspoon salt*
*2 tablespoons wheat germ*
*½ cup seedless raisins*
*⅓ cup butter or margarine, softened*
*¼ cup light-brown sugar, packed*
*1 egg*
*1 tablespoon honey*

1. Pour buttermilk over oats in medium bowl; let stand until buttermilk is absorbed—about ½ hour. Grease bottoms of 10 (3-inch) muffin-pan cups, or line each with paper liners.
2. Preheat oven to 400F. Sift flour with baking powder, baking soda, and salt into medium bowl. Add wheat germ and raisins; mix well.
3. In large bowl, using wooden spoon, cream butter with sugar until light and fluffy. Beat in egg and honey.
4. Using fork, add flour mixture alternately with oat mixture, stirring only until dry ingredients are moistened. Do not beat. Batter will be lumpy.
5. Quickly scoop batter into muffin-pan cups, filling about two thirds full. Bake 25 to 30 minutes, or until golden.
6. Loosen edge of each muffin with spatula; turn out. Serve hot.
Makes 10.

# BISCUITS

# ❖ BAKING-POWDER BISCUITS

*2 cups sifted all-purpose flour*
*3 teaspoons baking powder*
*½ teaspoon salt*
*⅓ cup shortening*
*About ¾ cup milk*

1. Preheat oven to 450F. Sift flour with baking powder and salt into medium bowl.
2. Cut shortening into flour mixture, with pastry blender or 2 knives, until mixture resembles coarse cornmeal.
3. Make well in center. Pour in ⅔ cup milk all at once. Stir quickly around bowl with fork. If mixture seems dry, add a little more milk, to form dough just moist enough (but not wet) to leave side of bowl and form ball.
4. Turn out dough onto lightly floured surface to knead. Gently pick up dough from side away from you; fold over toward you, and press out lightly with palm of hand. Give dough quarter turn. Repeat 10 times.
5. Gently roll out dough, from center, to ¾-inch thickness.
6. With floured 2½-inch biscuit cutter, cut straight down into dough, being careful not to twist cutter.
7. Place on ungreased cookie sheet; bake 12 to 15 minutes.
Makes 8.

*Note*: To prepare ahead: Make biscuits through first part of Step 7; refrigerate up to 3 hours. Let warm 15 minutes to room temperature, while preheating oven; bake as directed. Serve at once.

*Drop Biscuits*: Make Baking-Powder Biscuits, increasing milk to 1 cup. Do not knead or roll out. Drop dough, by tablespoonfuls, onto lightly greased cookie sheet; bake at 450F for 10 minutes, or until golden-brown. Makes 20.

*Cheese Biscuits*: Adding ¾ cup grated sharp Cheddar cheese to sifted dry ingredients, make Baking-Powder Biscuits.

*Buttermilk Biscuits*: Substitute ¾ cup buttermilk for regular milk in Baking-Powder Biscuits.

# ❖ HOT SCONES

3 cups packaged biscuit mix
¼ cup sugar
2 whole eggs
1 cup mashed potato
2 tablespoons butter or margarine, melted
1 egg white, slightly beaten

1. Preheat oven to 400F. Lightly grease baking sheet.
2. In large mixing bowl, combine biscuit mix, sugar, whole eggs, and mashed potato; using fork, mix until smooth—dough will be soft.
3. Turn out dough onto lightly floured pastry cloth. Knead five times.
4. Roll dough to ¼-inch thickness. Cut into 2½-inch squares. Brush with melted butter; fold over to make triangle, pressing edges lightly to seal.
5. Place, 2 inches apart, on prepared baking sheet. Brush with egg white.
6. Bake 8 to 10 minutes, or until golden-brown. Serve warm with butter.
Makes 18.

# ❖ THE PALACE HOTEL "GOLD ROOM" SCONES

3⅔ cups all-purpose flour
½ cup sugar
1½ tablespoons baking powder
1 teaspoon salt
½ cup butter
2 eggs
¾ cup milk
¾ cup raisins
⅓ cup honey

1. Preheat oven to 425F. Combine flour, sugar, baking powder, and salt in large bowl; mix well.
2. Cut butter into flour mixture with pastry blender or 2 knives until mixture resembles coarse cornmeal.
3. Add eggs, milk, and raisins to flour mixture. Stir quickly with fork until dough leaves side of bowl and forms ball.
4. Spoon onto ungreased cookie sheets to make 20 scones in all. Be careful to leave 1-inch space between scones. Bake 12 to 15 minutes, or until golden.
5. Remove to wire rack; brush immediately with honey. Serve at once with butter, jam, and whipped cream.
Makes 20.

# COFFEECAKES

## ✦ STREUSEL-LAYERED COFFEECAKE

### STREUSEL MIXTURE:

½ cup light-brown sugar, firmly
   packed
2 tablespoons butter or margarine,
   softened
2 tablespoons all-purpose flour
1 teaspoon ground cinnamon
½ cup coarsely chopped walnuts (optional)

### BATTER:

1½ cups sifted all-purpose flour
2½ teaspoons baking powder
½ teaspoon salt
1 egg
¾ cup granulated sugar
⅓ cup butter or margarine, melted
½ cup milk
1 teaspoon vanilla extract

1. Preheat oven to 375F. Grease 8-by-8-by-2-inch baking pan or 9-by-1½-inch round layer-cake pan.
2. Make Streusel Mixture: In small bowl, combine
brown sugar, 2 tablespoons soft butter, 2 tablespoons
flour, the cinnamon, and nuts; mix with fork until
crumbly. Set aside.
3. Make Batter: Sift flour with baking powder and
salt. Set aside.
4. In medium bowl, with rotary beater, beat egg until
frothy. Beat in sugar and butter until well combined.
Add milk and vanilla. With wooden spoon, stir in
flour mixture until well combined.
5. Turn out half of batter into prepared pan. Sprinkle
evenly with half of streusel mixture. Repeat with
remaining batter and streusel mixture.
6. Bake 25 to 30 minutes, or until cake tester inserted
in center comes out clean. Cool slightly in pan on
wire rack. Serve warm.
Makes 9 servings.

## ✦ BLUEBERRY COFFEECAKE

2 cups sifted all-purpose flour
2 teaspoons baking powder
½ teaspoon salt
½ cup butter or margarine
1½ cups plus 2 tablespoons sugar
2 eggs
½ cup milk
2 cups blueberries

1. Preheat oven to 350F. Grease well 9-inch round
layer-cake pan.
2. Sift flour with baking powder and salt; set aside.
3. In large bowl, with portable electric mixer at medium speed or wooden spoon, cream butter with
1½ cups sugar until light and fluffy. Add eggs, one at
a time, beating after each addition until well
blended.
4. Add flour mixture, alternately with milk, beating
by hand just until combined.
5. Turn out into prepared pan. Gently sprinkle berries over top; then sprinkle with remaining sugar.
Bake 55 minutes, or until top springs back when
gently pressed with fingertip. Let cool in pan 5 to 10
minutes before serving in wedges. Serve warm.
Makes 10 servings.

# ❖ SOUR-CREAM PLUM CAKE

2 cups all-purpose flour
1 teaspoon baking powder
½ teaspoon baking soda
¼ teaspoon salt
½ cup butter or margarine, softened
1 cup sugar
3 eggs
1 teaspoon vanilla extract
¾ cup sour cream

## CRUMB TOPPING:

¼ cup sugar
2 tablespoons all-purpose flour
1 tablespoon butter or margarine, softened
½ teaspoon ground cinnamon

9 fresh Italian plums or 9 canned purple plums, drained
2 tablespoons plum jam or currant jelly, melted

1. Preheat oven to 350F. Grease well and flour 9-inch springform pan.
2. Sift flour with baking powder, baking soda, and salt; set aside.
3. In large bowl of electric mixer, at high speed, beat butter, 1 cup sugar, the eggs, and vanilla until light and fluffy—about 5 minutes—occasionally scraping bowl with rubber spatula.
4. At low speed, beat in flour mixture (in fourths), alternately with sour cream, beginning and ending with flour mixture. Beat just until smooth—about 1 minute.
5. Turn out batter into prepared pan.
6. Bake 50 minutes, or until cake tester inserted in center comes out clean.
7. Make Crumb Topping: In small bowl, combine sugar, flour, butter, and cinnamon; toss lightly with fork until crumbly.
8. Wash plums; dry well. Cut in half, and remove pits. (If using canned plums, drain and remove pits.)
9. Remove cake from oven; sprinkle crumb topping evenly over top. Arrange plums on top; return to oven 10 minutes.
10. Let cool in pan on wire rack 10 minutes. Remove from pan. Brush plums with melted jam. Serve warm.
Makes 10 servings.

# CORNBREADS AND POPOVERS

# ❖ CORNBREAD

1 cup sifted all-purpose flour
2 tablespoons sugar
3 teaspoons baking powder
½ teaspoon salt
1 cup yellow cornmeal
1 egg, beaten
¼ cup salad oil or melted shortening
1 cup milk

1. Preheat oven to 425F. Grease 8-by-8-by-2-inch baking pan.
2. Sift flour with sugar, baking powder, and salt. Add cornmeal, mixing well; set aside.
3. In medium bowl, combine egg, salad oil, and milk, mixing well. Add flour mixture, stirring only until flour mixture is moistened.
4. Spoon batter into prepared pan; bake 20 to 25 minutes, or until golden-brown. To serve: Cut into squares. Serve hot with butter.
Makes 9 servings.

# ✠ CORN MUFFINS

*1 recipe Cornbread*

1. Preheat oven to 425F. Grease bottoms of 12 (2½-inch) muffin-pan cups, or line each with paper liner.
2. Prepare batter for Cornbread, above: Sift flour with sugar, baking powder, and salt into large bowl. Add cornmeal; mix well.
3. In medium bowl, combine egg, salad oil, and milk; beat with fork to mix well.
4. Make well in center of flour mixture. Pour in milk mixture all at once; stir quickly, with fork, just until dry ingredients are moistened. Do not beat. Batter will be lumpy.
5. Quickly scoop batter into muffin-pan cups, filling not quite two thirds full. Bake 15 to 20 minutes, or until golden.
6. Loosen edge of each muffin with spatula; turn out. Serve hot.
Makes 12.

# ✠ DOUBLE-CORN MUFFINS

*1 cup sifted all-purpose flour*
*1 cup yellow cornmeal*
*4 teaspoons baking powder*
*1 teaspoon salt*
*¼ cup sugar*
*2 eggs, slightly beaten*
*1 cup milk*
*3 tablespoons butter or margarine, melted*
*1 cup canned cream-style corn*

1. Preheat oven to 425F. Lightly grease bottoms of 12 (3-inch) muffin-pan cups, or line each with paper liner.
2. Sift flour with cornmeal, baking powder, salt, and sugar; set aside.
3. In medium bowl, using wooden spoon, combine eggs, milk, butter, and corn. Add flour mixture, stirring only until flour mixture is moistened.
4. Spoon batter into prepared muffin-pan cups; bake 20 to 25 minutes, or until cake tester inserted in center comes out clean and tops are golden-brown. Serve hot.
Makes 12.

# ❖ CHEESE-AND-CHILI CORNBREAD

3 eggs
1 can (8 oz) whole-kernel corn,
   drained
1 can (4 oz) green chilis, drained and
   coarsely chopped
1 cup yellow cornmeal
1 teaspoon salt
1½ tablespoons baking powder
1 cup sour cream
¾ cup butter or margarine, melted
¼ lb Monterey Jack cheese, coarsely
   grated

1. Preheat oven to 350F. Lightly grease 9-by-9-by-1½-inch baking pan.
2. In large bowl, beat eggs slightly. Add corn and chilis; mix well. Stir in rest of ingredients. Turn out into baking pan.
3. Bake 40 minutes, or until golden on top and cake tester inserted in center comes out clean.
4. Cut into squares. Serve hot with butter.
Makes 16 servings.

# ❖ POPOVERS

Butter or margarine
4 eggs
1¼ cups milk
¼ butter or margarine, melted
1¼ cups sifted all-purpose flour
½ teaspoon salt

1. Preheat oven to 400F. Grease well, with butter, 8 custard cups.
2. Beat eggs well with rotary beater; then beat in milk and melted butter.
3. Sift flour with salt; beat into egg mixture until smooth.
4. Pour into prepared custard cups, placed, not too close together, on large cookie sheet. Bake 50 minutes. Serve hot.
Makes 8.

# PANCAKES AND WAFFLES

## ❖ BUTTERMILK PANCAKES

3 eggs
1 cup sifted all-purpose flour
3 teaspoons baking powder
½ teaspoon salt
2 teaspoons granulated sugar
1 teaspoon light-brown sugar
½ cup buttermilk
2 tablespoons butter or margarine,
   melted

1. In large bowl of electric mixer, at high speed, beat eggs until light and fluffy—about 2 minutes.
2. Into eggs, sift flour with baking powder, salt, and granulated sugar. Add brown sugar; beat until smooth.
3. Stir in buttermilk and butter just until combined; do not overbeat.
4. Meanwhile, slowly heat griddle or heavy skillet. To test temperature, drop a little cold water onto hot griddle; water should roll off in drops.
5. Use ¼ cup batter for each pancake; cook until bubbles form on surface and edges become dry. Turn; cook 2 minutes longer, or until nicely browned on underside.

6. Serve hot with butter and maple syrup.
Makes 8 (4-inch) pancakes.

*Blueberry Buttermilk Pancakes*: To Buttermilk Pancakes Batter, gently add 1 pkg (12 oz) thawed frozen blueberries, drained; or 1¼ cups fresh blueberries. Stir just until combined. Be careful not to break berries as you stir. Cook and serve pancakes as directed above. Makes 12 (4-inch) pancakes.

## ✦ GRIDDLECAKES

*1 cup sifted all-purpose flour*
*2 teaspoons baking powder*
*½ teaspoon salt*
*2 tablespoons sugar*
*1 egg*
*1 cup milk*
*3 tablespoons butter or margarine,*
*melted*

1. Sift flour with baking powder, salt, and sugar into medium bowl.
2. With rotary beater, beat egg. Add milk and butter; beat until well mixed.
3. Pour into dry ingredients; beat only until combined—batter will be lumpy.
4. Meanwhile, slowly heat griddle or heavy skillet. To test temperature, drop a little cold water onto hot griddle; water should roll off in drops.
5. Use about ¼ cup batter for each griddlecake; cook until bubbles form on surface and edges become dry. Turn; cook 2 minutes longer, or until nicely browned on underside. Serve with whipped butter.
Makes 8 (4-inch) griddlecakes.

## ✦ H.R.M.'S FAVORITE WAFFLES

*4 eggs*
*2 cups sifted all-purpose flour*
*1 teaspoon salt*
*1 teaspoon baking soda*
*1 teaspoon baking powder*
*2 cups buttermilk; or 1 cup sour*
*cream mixed with 1 cup milk*
*1 cup butter, melted*

1. Preheat waffle iron.
2. Beat eggs until light.
3. Sift together flour, salt, baking soda, and baking powder.
4. Add flour mixture and buttermilk alternately to beaten eggs, beginning and ending with flour mixture. Add melted butter; blend thoroughly.
5. For each waffle, pour batter into center of lower half of waffle iron until it spreads to 1 inch from edge—about ½ cup.
6. Lower cover on batter; cook as manufacturer directs, or until waffle iron stops steaming. Do not raise cover during baking.
7. Carefully loosen edge of waffle with fork; remove. Serve hot with butter and Strawberry Syrup, below. Makes 8 waffles.

## STRAWBERRY SYRUP

1 pkg (12 oz) thawed frozen sliced
  strawberries
2 teaspoons cornstarch
1 teaspoon lemon juice

1. Drain strawberries, reserving liquid. In medium saucepan, combine 1 tablespoon strawberry liquid and the cornstarch; stir until smooth.
2. Add remaining liquid, the berries, and lemon juice; bring to boiling, stirring. Sauce will be slightly thickened and translucent. Serve warm.
Makes about 1½ cups.

## ❖ FRENCH TOAST

4 slices white bread (see Note), ¾ inch
  thick
3 eggs
¾ cup milk
1 tablespoon granulated sugar
¼ teaspoon salt
2 tablespoons butter or margarine
Confectioners' sugar or cinnamon-
  sugar

1. Arrange bread in single layer in 9-inch square baking dish.
2. In small bowl, with rotary beater, beat eggs, milk, granulated sugar, and salt until blended. Pour over bread; turn slices to coat evenly.
3. Refrigerate, covered, overnight, or at least 4 hours.
4. In hot butter in skillet, sauté bread until golden— about 4 minutes on each side. Sprinkle with confectioners' sugar or cinnamon-sugar, and serve with bacon and syrup.
Makes 4 servings.

Note: Brioche or French bread can be used instead of white bread.

# YEAST BREADS

❖ The excitement of feeling a kneaded yeast dough come alive under your hands is matched only by the pleasure everyone will take in savoring the fragrance and tasting the goodness of *home-baked* bread.

## BREAD-BAKING TIPS

*Yeast.* Yeast is the magic ingredient that makes bread rise. Active dry yeast is the most common form, and it can be found in supermarket refrigerated cases in a dated foil package. Make sure that the "pull date" is far sults in fine, evenly textured bread, without pockets or dense spots and with a smooth, rounded surface. If you have a food processor or an electric mixer with a dough hook, follow the manufacturer's instructions for kneading enough in the future so that the yeast will be fresh when you use it. Yeast is also available in moist compressed form. Compressed yeast is more perishable and is not carried by all stores. All the recipes that follow have been tested with active dry yeast.

To be activated, yeast must be mixed with warm water, 105 to 115F. The more accurate you can be about the temperature of the water, the better. We suggest using a thermometer. Water must not be too hot or it will kill the yeast. Cold water will slow down the yeast's action.

*Flour.* Most all-purpose flours are presifted and it is unnecessary to sift before measuring unless an exact measurement is critical to the recipe. If so, the recipe will specify a measure of sifted flour. All-purpose flours are available bleached or unbleached. There is also bread flour with a high gluten content, which is formulated to use only for bread making. All of our recipes were tested using bleached all-purpose flour unless otherwise specified.

*Kneading.* Kneading develops the gluten in flour that forms a framework of tiny pockets that trap the leavening gas produced by the yeast. Good, thorough, prolonged kneading re-

dough. Generally speaking, you will make one loaf at a time in most of these machines.

To knead by hand, turn out the dough onto a lightly floured surface. Pick up the dough and fold it toward you. Then push it down and away from you with the heel of your hand. Repeat this process, giving the dough a quarter turn each time, in a nice rhythm. Continue kneading and turning 10 minutes for white flour and 20 minutes for whole-wheat flour, until the dough is smooth and elastic and the surface looks blistered.

*Rising.* It is important to keep rising dough away from drafts and at an even temperature of 85F. Again, this is important enough so that you should test it with a thermometer. Put the dough in a lightly oiled bowl and cover it well with a towel or plastic wrap. Keep it out of drafts. On chilly days an unlighted oven with a large pan of hot water placed in the bottom of the oven will make a good rising spot.

*Crust.* The texture of the crust can be as you like it. For a soft crust, brush the loaf with shortening after you take it from the oven and cover it with a clean towel. If you want a crisp, crunchy crust, omit the shortening and let the bread cool uncovered.

## � McCALL'S BASIC WHITE BREAD

2 cups milk
3 tablespoons sugar
2 teaspoons salt
¼ cup butter or margarine
½ cup warm water (105 to 115F)
2 pkg active dry yeast
7 to 7½ cups all-purpose flour
2 tablespoons melted butter or margarine

1. In small saucepan, heat milk just until bubbles form around edge of pan. Remove from heat. Add sugar, salt, and ¼ cup butter, stirring until butter is melted. Let cool to lukewarm (a drop sprinkled on wrist will not feel warm).
2. If possible, check temperature of warm water with thermometer. Sprinkle yeast over water in large bowl, stirring until dissolved. Stir in milk mixture.
3. Add half the flour; beat, with wooden spoon, until smooth—about 2 minutes. Gradually add remaining flour, mixing it in with hand until dough is stiff enough to leave side of bowl.
4. Turn out dough onto lightly floured board. Cover with bowl; let rest 10 minutes. Knead by folding dough toward you, then pushing down and away from you, with heel of hand. Give dough a quarter turn; repeat kneading, developing a rocking rhythm. Continue kneading and turning 10 minutes, or until dough is smooth and elastic and blisters appear on surface.

5. Place in lightly greased large bowl; turn dough to bring up greased side. Cover with towel; let rise in warm place (85F), free from drafts, about 1 hour, or until double in bulk. When two fingers poked into dough leave indentations, rising is sufficient. Punch down dough with fist; turn out onto lightly floured pastry cloth. Divide in half; shape each half into smooth ball. Cover with towel; let rest 10 minutes. Roll out one half into 16-by-8-inch rectangle; roll up, lengthwise. Press ends even; pinch to seal, and tuck under loaf. Place, seam side down, in greased 9-by-5-by-3-inch loaf pan. Repeat with second part of dough.

6. Brush top of each loaf with 1 tablespoon melted butter. Cover with towel; let rise in warm place (85F), free from drafts, until double in bulk, or until sides of dough reach tops of pans—about 1 hour.

7. Meanwhile, preheat oven to 400F.

8. Bake loaves 40 to 50 minutes—tops should be well browned and sound hollow when tapped with knuckle. Remove from pans immediately; cool well on wire rack, away from drafts.

*Note*: If a lighter-color crust is desired, cover top of loaves with aluminum foil after bread has baked 25 minutes.

Makes 2 loaves.

# ◈ SPIRAL HERB BREAD

*1½ cups milk*
*¼ cup sugar*
*2 teaspoons salt*
*½ cup butter or margarine*
*½ cup warm water (105 to 115F)*
*2 pkg active dry yeast*
*3 eggs*
*7½ cups all-purpose flour*

**FILLING:**

*2 cups finely chopped parsley*
*1 cup finely chopped green onions or*
  *chives*
*2 tablespoons butter or margarine*
*¾ teaspoon salt*
*⅛ teaspoon black pepper*
*Dash Tabasco*
*1 egg, slightly beaten*
*¼ cup butter or margarine, melted*

1. In small saucepan, heat milk until bubbles form around edge of pan; remove from heat. Add sugar, 2 teaspoons salt, and ½ cup butter. Stir until butter melts; cool to lukewarm.

2. If possible, check temperature of water with thermometer. Sprinkle yeast over water in large bowl, stirring until dissolved. Stir in milk mixture.

3. Add eggs and 4 cups flour; beat vigorously with wooden spoon until smooth—about 2 minutes.

4. Gradually add remaining flour; mix in last of it with hand until dough is stiff enough to leave side of bowl.

5. Turn out dough onto lightly floured pastry cloth or board. Knead until smooth and elastic—10 minutes.

6. Place in lightly greased large bowl; turn dough over to bring up greased side. Cover with towel; let rise in warm place (85F), free from drafts, until double in bulk—about 1½ hours.

7. Make Filling: In small saucepan, combine parsley, green onions, and butter. Sauté over medium heat, stirring constantly, until mixture is soft but not browned—about 2 minutes. Remove from heat; cool

5 minutes. Add salt, pepper, and Tabasco. Reserve about 2 tablespoons egg; add remaining egg to parsley mixture.

8. Turn out dough onto lightly floured pastry cloth or board. Divide in half. Roll out one half into 16-by-8-inch rectangle. Brush with 1 tablespoon reserved egg; spread with ⅔ cup herb mixture.

9. Starting at narrow end, roll up jelly-roll fashion. Pinch edges and ends together to seal. Tuck ends under to give smooth shape.

10. Place, seam side down, in greased 9-by-5-by-3-inch loaf pan. Brush surface lightly with 1 tablespoon melted butter. Cover with towel. Repeat with other half of dough.

11. Let rise in warm place, free from drafts, until sides come to top of pan and tops are rounded—about 1 hour.

12. Place oven rack in middle of oven. Preheat oven to 375F.

13. Brush loaves with remaining melted butter. Bake 35 to 40 minutes—tops should be well browned. (If crust seems too brown after 25 minutes of baking, cover loosely with foil.) Baked loaf should sound hollow when tapped with knuckle.

14. Remove from pan immediately; cool completely on wire rack, away from drafts.

Makes 2 loaves.

# ❖ CARAWAY RYE BREAD

2 cups warm water (105 to 115F)
2 pkg active dry yeast
1 tablespoon salt
¼ cup dark molasses
2 tablespoons butter or margarine, softened
1 to 2 tablespoons caraway seed, to taste
3 cups unsifted rye flour
3 cups all-purpose flour
Cornmeal
1 egg white, slightly beaten
Caraway seed or coarse salt

1. If possible, check temperature of warm water with thermometer. Sprinkle yeast over water in large bowl, stirring until dissolved.

2. Add salt, molasses, butter, caraway seed, rye flour, and 1½ cups all-purpose flour; beat with wooden spoon until smooth—2 minutes.

3. Gradually add rest of flour; mix in with hand until dough leaves side of bowl.

4. Turn out dough onto lightly floured pastry cloth or board. Dough will be stiff. Knead until smooth—about 10 minutes.

5. Place in lightly greased large bowl; turn dough over to bring up greased side. Cover with towel; let rise in warm place (85F), free from drafts, until double in bulk—about 1 hour.

6. Grease 2 large cookie sheets; sprinkle with cornmeal.

7. Punch down dough. Turn out onto lightly floured pastry cloth. Divide in half.

8. Make round loaves: Shape each half into ball. Roll

each into 10-inch loaf; tuck edges underneath. Place each loaf on cookie sheet. With sharp knife, cut 3 slashes in each loaf to make triangle.

9. Cover with towel; let rise in warm place (85F), free from drafts, until double in bulk—about 60 minutes.

10. Meanwhile, preheat oven to 375F.

11. Bake bread 40 to 50 minutes, or until loaf sounds hollow when tapped with knuckle. Remove to wire rack. Brush tops of loaves with egg white. Sprinkle with caraway seed; cool.

Makes 2 loaves.

# ✠ OLD-FASHIONED POTATO BREAD

Packaged instant mashed potato
2 cups warm water (105 to 115F)
2 pkg active dry yeast
¼ cup sugar
1 tablespoon salt
½ cup butter or margarine, softened
7½ to 7¾ cups all-purpose flour
2 tablespoons butter or margarine, melted

1. Make instant mashed potato for 2 servings as package label directs, using liquid but omitting butter and seasonings. Measure 1 cup.

2. If possible, check temperature of warm water with thermometer. Sprinkle yeast over water in large bowl, stirring until dissolved. Stir in sugar and salt until dissolved.

3. Add 1 cup mashed potato, ½ cup softened butter, and 3½ cups flour. With electric mixer at medium speed, beat until smooth—about 2 minutes.

4. Gradually add 4 cups more flour, mixing with hands until dough is smooth and stiff enough to leave side of bowl; mix in remaining ¼ cup flour if needed.

5. Turn out dough onto lightly floured board or pastry cloth. Knead until dough is smooth and elastic and small blisters appear on surface—about 10 minutes.

6. Place in lightly greased large bowl; turn dough over to bring up greased side. Cover with towel; let rise in warm place (85F), free from drafts, until double in bulk—about 1 hour.

7. Turn out dough onto lightly floured pastry cloth or board. Divide in half. Roll out one half into 16-by-8-inch rectangle; roll up, starting at one end. Press ends even; pinch to seal, and tuck under loaf.

8. Place, seam side down, in greased 9-by-5-by-3-inch loaf pan. Brush surface lightly with some of the melted butter. Repeat with other half of dough.

9. Let loaves rise in warm place (85F), free from drafts, until sides come to top of pan and tops are rounded. Set oven rack at lowest level. Preheat oven to 400F.

10. Bake 30 to 40 minutes, or until crust is deep golden-brown and loaves sound hollow when tapped. If crust becomes too brown, cover with a piece of aluminum foil.

11. Turn out of pans onto wire racks; brush tops with remaining melted butter. Let cool completely.

Makes 2 loaves.

# ✤ WHOLE-WHEAT BREAD

2 cups milk
½ cup light-brown sugar, packed
2 teaspoons salt
¼ cup butter or margarine
1 cup warm water (105 to 115F)
2 pkg active dry yeast
7 cups whole-wheat flour
1¼ cups all-purpose flour
3 tablespoons butter or margarine,
    melted

1. In small saucepan, heat milk until bubbles form around edge of pan; remove from heat. Add sugar, salt, and ¼ cup butter. Stir until butter melts; cool to lukewarm.

2. If possible, check temperature of water with thermometer. Sprinkle yeast over water in large bowl, stirring until dissolved. Stir in milk mixture.

3. Add 4 cups whole-wheat flour; beat vigorously with wooden spoon until smooth. Gradually add remaining whole-wheat flour and the all-purpose flour, mixing in last of it with hand until dough is stiff enough to leave side of bowl.

4. Turn out dough onto lightly floured pastry cloth or board. Knead until dough is smooth and elastic— about 10 minutes.

5. Place in lightly greased large bowl; turn dough to bring up greased side. Cover with towel; let rise in warm place (85F), free from drafts, until double in bulk—about 1 hour.

6. Turn out dough onto lightly floured pastry cloth or board. Divide in half. Let rest, covered, 10 minutes. Roll out one half into 16-by-8-inch rectangle; roll up, starting at one end. Press ends even; pinch to seal, and tuck under loaf.

7. Place, seam side down, in greased 9-by-5-by-3-inch loaf pan. Brush surface lightly with some of the melted butter. Repeat with other half of dough.

8. Let loaves rise in warm place, free from drafts, until sides come to top of pans and tops are rounded —about 1 hour.

9. Place oven rack in middle of oven. Preheat oven to 400F.

10. Bake 35 to 40 minutes, or until crust is deep golden-brown and loaves sound hollow when tapped. (If crust seems too brown after 35 minutes of baking, cover loosely with aluminum foil.)

11. Turn out of pans onto wire racks; brush tops with remaining melted butter. Serve slightly warm, or let cool completely.

Makes 2 loaves.

# RUSSIAN BLACK BREAD

*4 cups rye flour*
*3 cups white flour*
*1 teaspoon sugar*
*2 teaspoons salt*
*2 cups whole-bran cereal*
*2 tablespoons caraway seed, crushed*
*2 teaspoons instant coffee*
*2 teaspoons onion powder*
*½ teaspoon fennel seed, crushed*
*2 pkg active dry yeast*
*3 cups cold water*
*¼ cup vinegar*
*¼ cup dark molasses*
*1 square (1 oz) unsweetened chocolate*
*¼ cup butter or margarine*
*1 teaspoon cornstarch*

1. Combine rye and white flours.
2. In large bowl, thoroughly mix 2⅓ cups flour mixture, the sugar, salt, bran cereal, caraway, instant coffee, onion powder, fennel seed, and undissolved yeast.
3. Combine 2½ cups water, vinegar, molasses, chocolate, and butter in saucepan. Heat over low heat until liquids are warm (120 to 125F)—butter and chocolate do not need to melt. Gradually add to dry ingredients. With electric mixer at medium speed, beat 2 minutes, scraping bowl occasionally. Add ½ cup flour mixture. Beat at high speed 2 minutes, scraping bowl occasionally. Stir in remaining flour mixture. Mix in last of it with hand until dough leaves side of bowl. This is a stiff dough.
4. Turn out onto lightly floured board. Knead until smooth and elastic—about 5 minutes. Place in greased bowl, turning dough to bring up greased side. Cover; let rise in warm place, free from drafts, until double in bulk—about 1½ hours.
5. Punch down dough. Turn out onto lightly floured board. Divide in half. Shape each half into ball about 5 inches in diameter. Place each ball in center of greased 8-inch round layer-cake pan. Cover; let rise in warm place, free from drafts, until double in bulk—about 1½ hours.
6. Preheat oven to 350F. Bake 40 to 45 minutes, or until loaf sounds hollow when tapped with knuckle.
7. Meanwhile, combine cornstarch and ½ cup cold water. Cook over medium heat, stirring constantly, until mixture boils; continue to cook, stirring constantly, 1 minute.
8. As soon as bread is baked, brush cornstarch mixture over tops of loaves. Return bread to oven and bake 2 to 3 minutes, or until glaze is set. Remove from pans and cool on wire racks.

Makes 2 loaves.

# SWEDISH LIMPA BREAD

*2½ cups warm water (105 to 115F)*
*2 pkg active dry yeast*
*1 tablespoon salt*
*¼ cup light or dark molasses*
*½ cup light-brown sugar, packed*
*¼ cup butter or margarine, softened*
*2 tablespoons grated orange peel*
*1 teaspoon anise seed*
*4 cups rye flour*
*4½ cups all-purpose flour*
*Cornmeal*
*2 tablespoons butter or margarine, melted*

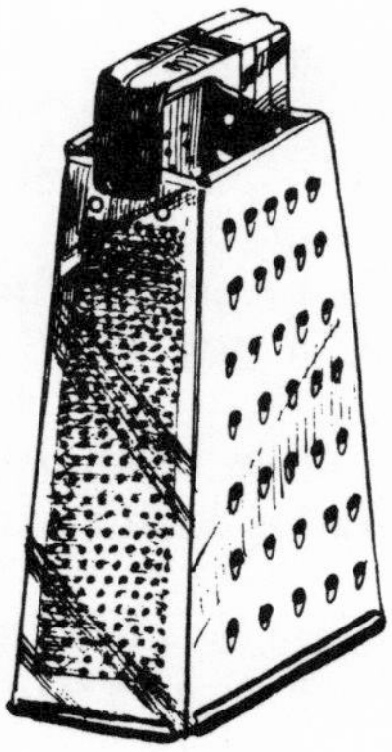

1. If possible, check temperature of water with thermometer. Sprinkle yeast over water in large bowl, stirring until dissolved.
2. Add salt, molasses, brown sugar, ¼ cup butter, the orange peel, anise seed, and rye flour. With wooden spoon, beat vigorously until smooth.
3. Gradually add all-purpose flour; mix in with hand until dough leaves side of bowl. Dough will be stiff.
4. Turn out dough onto lightly floured pastry cloth or board. (Use all-purpose flour for pastry cloth or board.) Knead until smooth and elastic—about 10 minutes.
5. Place in lightly greased large bowl; turn dough to bring up greased side. Cover with towel; let rise in warm place (85F), free from drafts, until double in bulk—about 1½ hours.
6. Grease large cookie sheet; sprinkle sheet lightly with cornmeal.
7. Punch down dough. Turn out onto lightly floured pastry cloth or board. Divide in half.
8. Shape each half into smooth ball 6 inches in diameter; tuck edges under. Place on opposite ends of cookie sheet. (To make oval loaf, shape into loaf 8 inches long, tapering ends.) With sharp knife, cut 3 diagonal slashes on top of loaf—about ¼ inch deep.
9. Cover with towel; let rise in warm place, free from drafts, until double in bulk—1 to 1½ hours.
10. Preheat oven to 375F. Bake on middle shelf of oven 30 to 35 minutes; cover with aluminum foil the last 10 minutes. Remove to rack; brush with melted butter. Serve slightly warm, or let cool completely. Makes 2 loaves.

# 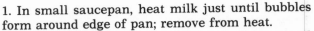 BLACK-PEPPER BREAD

1½ cups milk
3 tablespoons sugar
½ teaspoon crushed dried basil leaves
1 tablespoon salt
¼ cup butter or margarine
¾ cup warm water (105 to 115F)
2 pkg active dry yeast
7 cups all-purpose flour
1 egg
1¾ teaspoons cracked black peppercorns
4 bacon strips, cut up
1 egg yolk
2 teaspoons water

1. In small saucepan, heat milk just until bubbles form around edge of pan; remove from heat.
2. Add sugar, basil, salt, and butter, stirring until butter is melted; cool to lukewarm.
3. If possible, check temperature of warm water with thermometer. Sprinkle yeast over water in large bowl, stirring until dissolved.
4. Stir in milk mixture. Add 3 cups flour and the egg; beat with wooden spoon until smooth—2 minutes.
5. Gradually add remaining flour and 1½ teaspoons black peppercorns; mix in last of flour with hand until dough leaves side of bowl.
6. Turn out dough onto lightly floured board or pastry cloth. Knead until smooth and elastic—10 minutes.
7. Place in lightly greased large bowl; turn dough over to bring up greased side. Cover with towel; let rise in warm place (85F), free from drafts, until double in bulk—1 hour.
8. Meanwhile, in skillet over medium heat, fry bacon, stirring occasionally, until crisp and brown. Drain fat; place crumbled bacon on absorbent paper.
9. Grease large cookie sheet or two 9-by-5-by-3-inch loaf pans.
10. Punch down dough; knead in crisp bacon. Turn out dough onto lightly floured board or pastry cloth. Divide in half.
11. For crescent shape: Cut each half into three parts. With palms of hands, roll each part on floured board or pastry cloth to make 20-inch strip, tapering ends. Twist strips together; pinch ends to seal. Place on prepared cookie sheet; shape into crescent. With sharp knife, cut slashes, 2 inches apart, on top of loaf.
12. For loaf: Divide dough in half; cut each half into 3 parts. With palms of hands, on floured board or pastry cloth roll each part to make 12-inch strip. Braid 3 strips; pinch ends to seal. Place in prepared loaf pans.
13. Cover with towel; let rise in warm place (85F), free from drafts, until double in bulk—1 hour.
14. Preheat oven to 375F. Brush surface of bread lightly with egg yolk mixed with 2 teaspoons water. Sprinkle each half with ⅛ teaspoon peppercorns. Bake 30 to 35 minutes, or until nicely browned. Remove from pan to wire rack; cool.
Makes 2 loaves.

# BATTER BREADS

The easiest yeast breads to make are batter breads. In these the batters are beaten vigorously instead of being kneaded. For this reason, they have a more open, lacy texture. In color, aroma, flavor, and all-around goodness, they are comparable to kneaded breads. Batter breads do not keep as well, but they make marvelous toast.

## ❖ HONEY WHOLE-WHEAT CASSEROLE BREAD

*1 cup milk*
*¾ cup shortening*
*½ cup honey*
*2 teaspoons salt*
*¾ cup warm water (105 to 115F)*
*2 pkg active dry yeast*
*3 eggs, slightly beaten*
*4½ cups all-purpose flour*
*1½ cups whole-wheat flour*
*½ cup unprocessed bran*
*1 teaspoon soft butter or margarine*

1. In small saucepan, heat milk until bubbles form around edge of pan; remove from heat. Stir in shortening, honey, and salt until shortening is melted. Cool to lukewarm.
2. If possible, check temperature of water with thermometer. Sprinkle yeast over warm water in large bowl; stir until yeast is dissolved. Stir in milk mixture and eggs.
3. Combine all-purpose and whole-wheat flours and bran. Add two thirds of flour mixture to yeast mixture; with electric mixer at low speed, beat until blended. Then beat at medium speed until smooth—about 2 minutes. With wooden spoon, gradually beat in remaining flour mixture. Then beat 20 to 30 times.
4. Cover with waxed paper and towel. Let rise in warm place (85F), free from drafts, until double in bulk—about 1 hour.
5. Lightly grease 2½- or 3-quart casserole or ovenproof bowl. Punch down dough, and beat with spoon until smooth—about 30 seconds. Turn out into casserole. Cover, and let rise until double in bulk—20 to 30 minutes.
6. Preheat oven to 375F.
7. With sharp knife, cut 4-inch cross about ½ inch deep in top of dough.
8. Bake 45 to 50 minutes, or until bread is nicely browned and sounds hollow when tapped with knuckle.
9. Remove from casserole to wire rack. Rub butter over top of bread. Serve slightly warm, cut into wedges.
Makes 1 round loaf.

# ❖ VIRGINIA SALLY LUNN

1 cup milk
2 tablespoons sugar
1 teaspoon salt
⅓ cup butter or margarine
½ cup warm water (105 to 115F)
1 pkg active dry yeast
3 eggs
4 cups sifted all-purpose flour

1. In small saucepan, heat milk until bubbles form around edge of pan; remove from heat.
2. Add sugar, salt, and butter, stirring until butter is melted; let cool to lukewarm.
3. If possible, check temperature of warm water with thermometer. Sprinkle yeast over water in large bowl of electric mixer; stir to dissolve.
4. Add milk mixture, eggs, and all of flour; at medium speed, beat till smooth—2 minutes.
5. Cover with waxed paper and towel; let rise in warm place (85F), free from drafts, until double in bulk and bubbly—about 1 hour.
6. Grease 2 (9-by-5-by-3-inch) loaf pans.
7. With wooden spoon, beat batter vigorously ½ minute. Pour batter evenly into prepared pans. Cover with towel; let rise in warm place (85F), free from drafts, to within 1 inch of tops of pans—about 45 minutes.
8. Meanwhile, preheat oven to 350F.
9. Bake loaves 35 to 40 minutes, or until golden-brown. Remove from pans to wire rack. Serve hot, slicing with serrated knife.
Makes 2 loaves.

# ❖ ANADAMA BATTER BREAD

¾ cup boiling water
½ cup yellow cornmeal
3 tablespoons shortening
¼ cup light molasses
2 teaspoons salt
¼ cup warm water (105 to 115F)
1 pkg active dry yeast
1 egg
2¾ cups sifted all-purpose flour
¼ teaspoon salt
1 teaspoon yellow cornmeal
1 teaspoon soft butter or margarine

1. Lightly grease 9-by-5-by-3-inch loaf pan.
2. In large bowl, pour boiling water over cornmeal. Stir in shortening, molasses, and salt; let cool to lukewarm.
3. If possible, check temperature of warm water with thermometer. Sprinkle yeast over warm water in large bowl of electric mixer, stirring until dissolved. Stir into cornmeal mixture.
4. Add egg and half of flour; beat 2 minutes at medium speed, frequently scraping down side of bowl and beaters with rubber spatula. Add rest of flour; beat 1 minute longer.
5. Spread batter evenly in prepared pan, using buttered spatula to smooth top. Cover with towel; let rise in warm place (85F), free from drafts, until double in bulk—about 1½ hours. Then sprinkle top with salt and cornmeal.
6. Meanwhile, preheat oven to 375F.
7. Bake loaf 50 to 55 minutes, or until it sounds hollow when tapped with knuckle. Remove from pan to wire rack. Brush top with butter; cool completely.
Makes 1 loaf.

# ✦ BRIOCHE

½ cup warm water (105 to 115F)
1 pkg active dry yeast
¼ cup sugar
1 teaspoon salt
1 teaspoon grated lemon peel
1 cup butter or margarine, softened
6 eggs
4½ cups all-purpose flour
1 egg yolk
1 tablespoon water

1. If possible, check temperature of warm water with thermometer. Sprinkle yeast over water in large bowl of electric mixer; stir until dissolved.
2. Add sugar, salt, lemon peel, butter, 6 eggs, and 3 cups flour; at medium speed, beat 4 minutes. Add remaining flour; at low speed, beat until smooth— about 2 minutes.
3. Cover bowl with waxed paper and damp towel; let rise in warm place (85F), free from drafts, until double in bulk—about 1 hour. Refrigerate, covered, overnight.
4. Next day, grease 24 (3-inch) muffin-pan cups.
5. Stir down dough with wooden spoon. Dough will be soft. Turn out onto lightly floured board; divide in half. Return half to bowl; refrigerate until ready to use.
6. Working quickly, shape three fourths of dough on board into 12-inch roll. With floured knife, cut into 12 pieces. Shape each into ball; place in prepared muffin cup.
7. Divide other fourth of dough into 12 parts; shape into balls. With finger, press indentation in center of each large ball; fill with small ball.
8. Cover with towel; let rise in warm place (85F), free from drafts, until double in bulk—about 1 hour.
9. Meanwhile, shape refrigerated half of dough, and let rise, as directed.
10. Preheat oven to 400F.
11. Combine egg yolk with 1 tablespoon water; brush on brioche. Bake 15 to 20 minutes, or until golden-brown. Serve hot or cold.
Makes 24.

# FESTIVE BREADS

## ✖ BABKA

1 cup milk
¼ cup warm water (105 to 115F)
2 pkg active dry yeast
½ cup sugar
1 teaspoon salt
½ cup butter or margarine, softened
4 eggs
1 egg yolk
4½ cups all-purpose flour
½ cup seedless raisins

### TOPPING:

1 egg white
1 tablespoon water
2 tablespoons flour
2 tablespoons sugar
¼ teaspoon cinnamon
2 tablespoons butter or margarine

1. In small saucepan, heat milk until bubbles form around edge. Remove from heat; cool to lukewarm.
2. If possible, check temperature of warm water with thermometer. In large bowl, sprinkle yeast over water, stirring until dissolved. Add lukewarm milk, ½ cup sugar, the salt, ½ cup butter, the eggs, egg yolk, and 3 cups flour. With electric mixer at medium speed, beat until smooth and blended. With wooden spoon, stir in 1½ cups flour; beat vigorously 2 minutes, or until dough leaves side of bowl. Mix in raisins.
3. Cover with towel; let rise in warm place (85F), free from drafts, until double in bulk—about 1 hour.
4. Grease and flour 9-inch springform pan. Turn out dough into prepared pan. Cover with towel; let rise in warm place (85F), free from drafts, until dough is ½ inch from top of pan—about 1 hour.
5. Meanwhile, preheat oven to 350F.
6. Make Topping: Beat egg white with 1 tablespoon water; use to brush top of babka. Mix flour, sugar, cinnamon, and butter; sprinkle on babka.
7. Bake 60 minutes, or until cake tester inserted in center comes out clean. Cool in pan on wire rack 15 minutes.
8. To serve: Remove side and bottom of springform pan. Cut into wedges. Serve warm, if desired.
Makes 1 babka.

## ✖ ITALIAN PANETTONE

1 cup warm water (105 to 115F)
2 pkg active dry yeast
½ cup plus 2 tablespoons sugar
2 teaspoons salt
½ cup butter or margarine, softened
3 eggs, beaten
1 egg, separated
5½ cups all-purpose flour
1 cup raisins
1 cup (8 oz) mixed candied peel
½ cup (4 oz) candied cherries, halved
1 tablespoon butter or margarine, melted
2 tablespoons water

1. If possible, check temperature of warm water with thermometer. Sprinkle yeast over water in large bowl, stirring until dissolved.
2. Add ½ cup sugar, the salt, ½ cup butter, 3 eggs, the egg yolk, and 3 cups flour; beat with wooden spoon or electric mixer until smooth—about 2 minutes.
3. Gradually add remaining flour; mix in last part with hand until dough leaves side of bowl.
4. Turn out onto lightly floured board or pastry cloth. Knead until smooth—5 minutes. (Dough is soft.)
5. Place in lightly greased large bowl; turn dough to bring up greased side. Cover with towel; let rise in warm place (85F), free from drafts, until double in bulk—about 1 hour.

6. Grease well and line inside of 8-inch springform pan with 4-inch-wide strip of buttered brown paper.
7. Punch down dough; turn out onto lightly floured pastry cloth or board. Knead in raisins and candied fruits until well distributed—about 5 minutes.
8. Place dough in prepared pan. Brush top with 1 tablespoon melted butter. Cover with towel; let rise in warm place (85F), free from drafts, until more than double in bulk—about 2 hours.
9. Preheat oven to 350F.
10. With sharp knife, cut deep cross on top of bread. Brush with egg white combined with 2 tablespoons water. Bake 30 minutes.
11. Remove bread from oven. Brush again with egg white, and sprinkle with sugar. Continue baking 30 minutes, or until golden-brown.
12. Remove from pan; cool on rack.
Makes 1 loaf.

# ❖ STOLLEN

1 cup milk
½ cup granulated sugar
1 cup butter or margarine
½ teaspoon salt
2 pkg active dry yeast
½ cup warm water (105 to 115F)
6 cups all-purpose flour
½ teaspoon ground nutmeg or mace
1 tablespoon grated lemon peel
2 eggs
1 cup dark raisins
1 jar (4 oz) candied cherries, coarsely chopped
1 jar (8 oz) diced mixed candied peel
½ cup finely chopped blanched almonds
¼ cup butter or margarine, melted
Confectioners' sugar

1. In small saucepan, heat milk just until bubbles form around edge of pan; remove from heat. Add ½ cup sugar, 1 cup butter, and the salt, stirring until dissolved. Let cool to lukewarm.
2. In large bowl rinsed with hot water, sprinkle yeast over warm water (if possible, check temperature of warm water with thermometer); stir until dissolved.
3. Stir in milk mixture, 3 cups flour, the nutmeg, lemon peel, and eggs; beat with wooden spoon or with electric mixer, at medium speed, until smooth —at least 2 minutes.
4. Gradually add remaining flour; mix in last of it with hand until dough is stiff enough to leave side of bowl.
5. Turn out onto lightly floured pastry cloth or board. Knead until smooth and elastic—about 5 minutes.
6. Place in lightly greased large bowl; turn dough over to bring up greased side. Cover with towel; let rise in warm place (85F), free from drafts, until double in bulk—about 1 hour. Grease 2 cookie sheets.
7. Punch down dough. Turn out onto lightly floured pastry cloth or board. Knead in raisins, candied fruit, and almonds until well distributed—about 5 minutes.
8. Divide dough in half; shape each half into oval 10 inches long and 6 inches across at widest part. Brush each with 1 tablespoon melted butter.
9. Fold dough in half lengthwise. Place on prepared cookie sheet. Press folded edge lightly, to crease; then curve into crescent shape. Repeat with other half of dough.

10. Cover stollen with towels; let rise in warm place (85F), free from drafts, until double in bulk—1½ to 2 hours.

11. Preheat oven to 375F.

12. Bake 25 to 30 minutes, or until nicely browned (if crust seems to brown after 20 minutes of baking, cover with foil).

13. Remove to wire rack. Brush each with 1 tablespoon butter; cool.

14. To store: Wrap in plastic wrap, then in foil. Store in refrigerator or freezer several weeks.

15. To serve: Let warm to room temperature. Just before serving, sprinkle with confectioners' sugar. Makes 2 stollen.

# SWEET ROLLS

## ❖ SWEET-ROLL DOUGH

¾ cup milk
½ cup sugar
2 teaspoons salt
½ cup butter or margarine
½ cup warm water (105 to 115F)
2 pkg active dry yeast
2 eggs, beaten
4¼ cups all-purpose flour
Soft butter or margarine

1. Heat milk just until bubbles form around edge of pan. Add sugar, salt, and ½ cup butter; stir to dissolve. Cool to lukewarm.

2. If possible, check temperature of warm water with thermometer. Pour into warm large bowl. Sprinkle yeast over water, and stir to dissolve.

3. With wooden spoon, stir in milk mixture, eggs, and 2 cups flour; beat until smooth—about 2 minutes.

4. Gradually add rest of flour, beating until dough is stiff, smooth, and cleans side of bowl. Turn out into greased large bowl. Brush with butter.

5. Cover bowl with foil; refrigerate 2 hours. Dough will rise to top. (May be refrigerated up to 3 days.)

6. To use: Cut off amount needed; refrigerate remainder. Shape and bake as directed below.

Makes 2 dozen rolls.

# ✠ CRESCENTS

⅓ cup light-brown sugar, firmly
   packed
⅓ cup finely chopped walnuts
¾ teaspoon ground cinnamon
⅓ Sweet-Roll Dough, (page 54)
2 tablespoons butter or margarine,
   melted
1 egg yolk
1 tablespoon water
Cinnamon
Granulated sugar

1. Lightly grease large cookie sheet.
2. In small bowl, toss brown sugar, chopped walnuts,
and ¾ teaspoon cinnamon, mixing well.
3. On lightly floured surface, pat dough into a round;
let rest 5 minutes.
4. Roll out dough to 12-inch circle; brush with butter.
Sprinkle with brown-sugar mixture to within ½ inch
of edge. Cut into 8 equal pie-shaped wedges.
5. Starting from wide end, roll up each wedge toward
point. Place, with center point down, 2 inches apart, on
prepared cookie sheet. Curve ends to form crescents.
6. Cover loosely with waxed paper. Set in warm place
(85F), free from drafts, until double in bulk—about
45 minutes. Meanwhile, preheat oven to 350F.
7. With fork, beat egg yolk with water. Use to brush
tops of rolls. Sprinkle lightly with cinnamon and
sugar.
8. Bake 15 minutes, or until golden-brown.
9. Let cool slightly on wire rack.
Makes 8.

# ✠ BOW TIES

## STREUSEL TOPPING:

2 tablespoons butter or margarine,
   softened
2 tablespoons light-brown sugar
½ teaspoon cinnamon
⅓ cup unsifted all-purpose flour

⅓ Sweet-Roll Dough, page 54
¼ cup butter or margarine, melted
Cinnamon
Sugar

1. Make Streusel Topping: Combine butter with
sugar, cinnamon, and flour; mix well. Set aside until
ready to use.
2. Lightly grease large cookie sheet.
3. On lightly floured pastry cloth, roll dough to 20-by-
10-inch rectangle. Spread surface with half of
melted butter; then sprinkle generously with cinnamon and sugar.
4. Fold over dough in half, from long side, to form
20-by-5-inch rectangle.
5. Cut crosswise into 2½-inch strips, making 8 (5-by-
2½-inch) strips.
6. Place strips on prepared cookie sheet, making
twist in center of each, to give bow effect.
7. Brush tops with rest of melted butter. Sprinkle
with Streusel Topping; cover loosely with waxed
paper.
8. Let rise in warm place (85F), free from drafts,
until double in bulk—about 45 minutes. Meanwhile,
preheat oven to 350F.
9. Bake 15 minutes, or until golden-brown. Remove
to wire rack; let cool slightly. Serve while still warm.
Makes 8.

# ✦ PHILADELPHIA STICKY BUNS

### FILLING:

¼ cup butter or margarine, softened
¼ cup light-brown sugar
½ cup pecans, halved

½ Sweet-Roll Dough, page 54
½ cup butter, softened
½ cup brown sugar
½ cup chopped raisins
½ teaspoon ground cinnamon

1. Make Filling: In small bowl, with wooden spoon, cream ¼ cup butter with ¼ cup light-brown sugar. Spread on bottom and sides of 9-by-9-by-2-inch baking pan. Sprinkle with pecans.
2. On lightly floured pastry cloth or surface, roll out dough into 12-by-16-inch rectangle.
3. Spread with softened butter. Sprinkle with ½ cup brown sugar, raisins, and cinnamon.
4. Roll up from long side, jelly-roll fashion; pinch edges to seal.
5. Cut crosswise into 12 pieces; place, cut side down, in baking pan. Let rise, covered, in warm place (85F), free from drafts, until double in bulk—1 to 1½ hours (dough should rise to top of pan).
6. Meanwhile, preheat oven to 375F.
7. Bake 25 to 30 minutes, or until golden-brown.
8. Invert baking pan onto large cookie sheet or serving platter; let stand 1 minute, then remove pan. Serve warm.
Makes 12.

# ✦ HOT CROSS BUNS

1 cup milk
½ cup granulated sugar
½ teaspoon salt
½ cup butter or margarine
¼ cup warm water (105 to 115F)
1 pkg active dry yeast
2 eggs
5¼ cups all-purpose flour
1 cup currants or raisins
½ cup chopped mixed candied fruit
2 tablespoons melted butter or margarine

### ICING:

1½ cups sifted confectioners' sugar
1½ tablespoons milk

1. In small saucepan, heat milk just until bubbles form around edge of pan; remove from heat. Add granulated sugar, salt, and ½ cup butter, stirring until butter is melted. Let cool to lukewarm.
2. If possible, check temperature of warm water with thermometer. Sprinkle yeast over water in large bowl, stirring until dissolved. Stir in milk mixture.
3. Add eggs and 2 cups flour; beat with electric beater, at medium speed, until dough is smooth.
4. Stir in remaining flour, currants, and candied fruit with wooden spoon; then mix with hand until dough leaves side of bowl.
5. Place in lightly greased large bowl; turn dough over to bring up greased side. Cover with towel; let rise in warm place (85F), free from drafts, until double in bulk—about 1½ hours.
6. To shape: On lightly floured board or pastry cloth, using palms of hands, shape dough into roll 15 inches long. Cut roll crosswise into 15 pieces. With fingertips, shape each piece into ball; tuck edges underneath to make smooth top.
7. Arrange, ½ inch apart, on greased 13-by-9-by-2-inch baking pan. Cover with towel; let rise in warm place (85F), free from drafts, until double in bulk—about 1½ hours.

8. Preheat oven to 375F. Carefully cut cross ¼ inch deep on top of each bun. Brush well with melted butter. Bake 25 to 30 minutes, or until golden-brown.
9. Remove to rack; cool 10 minutes.
10. Make Icing: Combine confectioners' sugar and milk. With tip of spoon or pastry tube with number-10 tip, drizzle cross on each bun.
Makes 15.

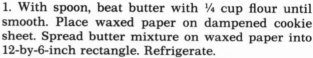

## CROISSANTS

*1½ cups butter or margarine, softened*
*3¼ cups all-purpose flour*
*¾ cup milk*
*2 tablespoons sugar*
*1 teaspoon salt*
*½ cup warm water (105 to 115F)*
*2 pkg active dry yeast*
*1 egg yolk*
*1 tablespoon milk*

1. With spoon, beat butter with ¼ cup flour until smooth. Place waxed paper on dampened cookie sheet. Spread butter mixture on waxed paper into 12-by-6-inch rectangle. Refrigerate.
2. In small saucepan, heat milk until small bubbles form around edge. Add sugar and salt, stirring until dissolved. Cool to lukewarm.
3. If possible, check temperature of water with thermometer. In large bowl, sprinkle yeast over water, and stir until dissolved.
4. With wooden spoon, beat in milk mixture and 3 cups flour, beating until smooth. Turn out onto lightly floured board or pastry cloth; knead until smooth. Let rise, covered, in warm place (85F), free from drafts, until double in bulk—1 hour. Refrigerate ½ hour.
5. On lightly floured board or pastry cloth, with stockinette-covered rolling pin, roll out into 14-by-14-inch square. Place butter mixture on half of dough; remove paper. Fold other half of dough over butter; pinch edges to seal. With fold at your right, rolling dough from center, make 20-by-8-inch rectangle.
6. From short side, fold dough into thirds, making 3 layers; pinch edges to seal. Wrap in foil and chill 1 hour. With fold at your left, roll dough into 20-by-8-inch rectangle; fold into thirds. Chill ½ hour. Repeat. Chill overnight.
7. Next day, roll and fold dough 2 more times, chilling ½ hour between rollings. Then chill 1 hour longer.
8. To shape: Cut dough into 4 parts. On lightly floured pastry cloth, roll each part into 12-inch circle. Cut each circle into 6 wedges. Roll up, beginning at wide end. Form into crescent. Place, point side down, 2 inches apart, on brown paper on cookie sheet.
9. Cover. Let rise in warm place (85F), free from drafts, until double in bulk—1 hour.

10. Preheat oven to 425F. Brush each croissant with egg yolk beaten with 1 tablespoon milk. Bake 5 minutes. Reduce oven to 375F. Bake 10 minutes, or until croissants are puffed and golden-brown. Cool on rack 10 minutes.
Makes 24.

# JELLY DOUGHNUTS

½ cup milk
⅓ cup sugar
1 teaspoon salt
⅓ cup butter or margarine
½ cup warm water (105 to 115F)
2 pkg active dry yeast
3 egg yolks
3¾ cups sifted all-purpose flour
Raspberry or strawberry jam or jelly
Egg white
Salad oil for deep-frying
Sugar

1. Heat milk in small saucepan until bubbles form around edge of pan; remove from heat. Add sugar, salt, and butter; stir until butter is melted. Let cool to lukewarm.
2. If possible, check temperature of water with thermometer. In large bowl, sprinkle yeast over warm water. Stir until dissolved.
3. Add milk mixture, egg yolks, and 2 cups flour. With electric mixer at medium speed, beat until smooth—about 2 minutes.
4. With wooden spoon, beat in remaining flour; beat until smooth.
5. Cover with foil; let rise in warm place (85F), free from drafts, until double in bulk—about 1 hour.
6. Punch down dough. Turn out onto lightly floured surface; turn over to coat with flour. Knead 10 times, or until dough is smooth. Divide in half.
7. Roll out half of dough to ¼-inch thickness. Cut into 12 (3-inch) rounds. Place 1 teaspoon jam in center of half of rounds; brush edges with egg white. Top with remaining rounds, and press together firmly to seal. Arrange on floured cookie sheet. Repeat with rest of dough.
8. Cover with towel; let rise until double in bulk—about 45 minutes.
9. Meanwhile, in deep-fat fryer or heavy skillet, slowly heat salad oil (2 inches deep) to 350F on deep-frying thermometer.
10. Gently drop doughnuts, 3 or 4 at a time, into hot oil. Fry, turning as they rise to surface, turning once again, until golden-brown—about 4 minutes in all. (Break one open to test for doneness; fry others longer if necessary.)
11. Remove with slotted utensil. Drain on paper towels. While still warm, dust with sugar.
Makes 12.

INDONESIAN SATAYS (p. 19)

IRISH SODA BREAD (p. 25), WHOLE WHEAT SODA BREAD (p. 26)

*OPPOSITE:* A BASKET OF BREADS

LADY BALTIMORE CAKE (p. 72)

OPPOSITE: McCALL'S BEST DAFFODIL CAKE (p. 67)

PEACH CHARLOTTE (p. 134), CHOCOLATE TRUFFLE CAKE (p. 75), YOGURT AND PRUNES IN GRAHAM CRACKER CRUST (p. 356)

*OPPOSITE:* SPRITZ COOKIES (p. 112)

BAKED CRANBERRY-APPLE DUMPLING (p. 129)

# CAKES, FROSTINGS, and FILLINGS

✦ **P**eople may eat less cake than they used to, but when they do, they want it to be delicious—and there is nothing more ambrosial than a piece of perfect homemade cake. Whether it's a Chocolate-Mousse Dessert Cake made for a party, McCall's Best Devil's-Food Cake prepared for a birthday, or Pineapple Upside-Down Cake baked in a skillet for a family supper, accurate measurements and careful following of the recipe are the key to perfection. Also, the "Cake Hints" below will help you do it the way we did it in the *McCall's* test kitchens.

## CAKE HINTS

1. Use the ingredients called for in the recipe; no changes, please. All ingredients should be at room temperature unless otherwise stated. All our cake recipes were tested using:
• Either sifted or unsifted all-purpose or cake flour. If the flour is to be sifted before measuring, the recipe will call for sifted flour. After sifting, spoon flour into a measuring cup and level off with a straight-edged frosting spreader or the dull edge of a knife blade.
• Regular or stick margarine or butter. Don't use the diet or whipped varieties. When a recipe calls for butter or margarine, don't substitute shortening. When a recipe calls for butter, use lightly salted butter.
• Soft, emulsified shortening when shortening is called for.
• Double-acting baking powder.
• Large eggs.
2. Try, if possible, to use the pan sizes called for in the recipe. Bright shiny metal pans were used for most of the cakes. If you choose to use oven-proof glass pans (unless the recipe calls for them), decrease the oven temperature 25 degrees.
3. Be sure to turn on your oven and set it to the correct temperature 10 minutes before putting the cake in the oven. For one or two cakes, use the rack in the center of the oven, being careful that the pans don't touch each other or the sides of the oven. If you need to use two oven racks, make sure that one pan is not directly over another. Resist the impulse to open the oven door to see how the cake is doing until the minimum baking time is up.
4. The cake will be finished when it has shrunk slightly from the side of the pan and the surface springs back when you gently press it with your fingertip. Insert a wooden pick or a wire cake tester near the center. If it comes out clean, the cake is done. Remove from oven and cool on wire rack as the recipe directs.
5. Unless otherwise stated, carefully run a knife or spatula around the edge of the cake to loosen it from the pan. Holding wire rack over the pan with both hands, invert the cake onto the rack; remove the pan. Now place another wire rack over the cake; invert again so cake cools right side up.
6. To get a tube cake out of its pan, use your knife or spatula in an up and down motion carefully all around the edge of the cake pan and its tube. If it doesn't have a lift-out bottom, hit the pan sharply on the table, then invert it and turn out the cake.
7. Most cakes can be cut best with a thin sharp-edged knife. If the cake is frosted, rinse the knife in hot water between cuts. Angel food, chiffon, and sponge cakes are best cut with a serrated-edged knife or in the old-fashioned way, by pulling the cake apart with two forks.
8. All unfrosted cakes, as well as cakes with butter or fudge frostings, can be frozen. Don't freeze cakes with whipped cream or fluffy frostings made with egg whites. Freeze the cakes unwrapped until the frosting is firm, and then wrap, label, and freeze. Make sure that the cakes you freeze are *thoroughly* cool before you wrap them. If you're wrapping unfrosted layer cakes, wrap and freeze each layer separately. Unfrosted cakes may be stored in the freezer for 2 to 3 months, and frosted cakes, for 1 to 2 months.

When thawing unfrosted cake layers, let them stand, still wrapped, at room temperature for about an hour before frosting. Frosted cakes should be allowed to stand, wrapped, for 2 hours in order to thaw thoroughly.

9. To store cakes unfrozen, cover them loosely with a moisture-proof wrap—after they have cooled. You can store them in covered cake stands or under a large inverted bowl. Cakes with cream frostings or fillings must be stored in the refrigerator.

# BASIC CAKE LAYERS

Basic cake layers can be turned into any kind of cake you fancy. Vary the frosting or the filling; ice one layer and use the other as the base of another dessert with a custard or fruits. In the "Special Cakes" section in this chapter, we show you some of our favorite ways to serve them.

## ✠ FAVORITE ONE-EGG CAKE

2 cups sifted cake flour
1 cup sugar
2½ teaspoons baking powder
1 teaspoon salt
⅓ cup shortening
1 cup milk
1 egg
1 teaspoon vanilla extract

1. Preheat oven to 350F. Grease well and flour 2 (8-by-1½-inch round) layer-cake pans or a 9-by-9-by-2-inch baking pan.
2. Into large bowl of electric mixer, sift flour with sugar, baking powder, and salt.
3. Add shortening and milk. At medium speed, beat 2 minutes, occasionally scraping side of bowl and guiding mixture into beaters with rubber spatula.
4. Add egg and vanilla; beat 2 minutes longer.
5. Pour batter into prepared pans. Bake round layers 25 to 30 minutes, and square, 30 to 35 minutes, or until surface springs back when gently pressed with fingertip.
6. Cool in pans 10 minutes. Remove from pans; cool thoroughly on wire racks. Fill and frost as desired. Makes 2 (8-inch) layers or 1 (9-inch) square cake.

## ✠ McCALL'S BEST WHITE CAKE

1 cup egg whites (7 or 8)
3½ cups sifted cake flour
4 teaspoons baking powder
1 teaspoon salt
1 cup butter or margarine, softened
2 teaspoons vanilla extract
2 cups sugar
1 cup milk

1. In large bowl, let egg whites warm to room temperature—1 hour. Preheat oven to 375F. Grease well and flour 3 (9-by-1½-inch) round layer-cake pans.
2. Sift flour with baking powder and salt.
3. In large bowl of electric mixer, at high speed, beat butter until light and fluffy. Add vanilla. Gradually add 1½ cups sugar, beating until very light and fluffy —about 2 minutes.

4. With rubber spatula, gently fold in flour mixture alternately with milk, in 3 additions, beginning and ending with flour.

5. With mixer at high speed, beat egg whites just until soft peaks form when beater is slowly raised.

6. Gradually beat in remaining ½ cup sugar, 1 tablespoon at a time, beating well after each addition; continue beating until stiff peaks form when beater is slowly raised.

7. With wire whisk or rubber spatula, using under-and-over motion, gently fold egg whites into batter just until combined. Do not overmix.

8. Pour batter into prepared pans.

9. Bake 20 to 25 minutes, or until surface springs back when gently pressed with fingertip.

10. Let cool in pans on wire rack 10 minutes. Turn out of pans; let cool completely on wire rack. Fill and frost as desired. (For Lady Baltimore Cake, see page 72.)

Makes 3 (9-inch) layers.

# ✠ McCALL'S BEST YELLOW CAKE

*3 cups sifted cake flour*
*2½ teaspoons baking powder*
*½ teaspoon salt*
*1 cup butter or margarine, softened*
*2 cups sugar*
*4 eggs*
*1 teaspoon vanilla extract*
*1 cup milk*

1. Preheat oven to 350F. Grease well and flour 3 (9-by-1½-inch) round layer-cake pans.

2. Sift flour with baking powder and salt. In large bowl of electric mixer, at high speed, beat butter and sugar until light. Add eggs, one at a time, beating well after each addition. Add vanilla. Continue beating, occasionally scraping side of bowl with rubber spatula, until light and fluffy—about 2 minutes.

3. At low speed, beat in flour mixture (in fourths), alternately with milk, beginning and ending with flour mixture. Beat just until smooth—about 1 minute.

4. Pour batter into prepared pans; bake 20 to 25 minutes, or until surface springs back when gently pressed with fingertip. Cool in pans on wire racks 10 minutes. Remove from pans; cool thoroughly on wire racks. Fill and frost as desired.

Makes 3 (9-inch) layers.

# ❖ SOUR-CREAM FUDGE CAKE

*2 squares unsweetened chocolate*
*2 cups sifted cake flour*
*1½ cups sugar*
*1 teaspoon baking soda*
*1 teaspoon salt*
*½ cup butter, softened*
*1 cup sour cream*
*2 eggs*
*1 teaspoon vanilla extract*
*¼ cup hot water*

1. Preheat oven to 350F. Grease well and flour 2 (8-by-1½-inch) round layer-cake pans or a 13-by-9-by-2-inch baking pan.
2. Melt chocolate over hot, not boiling, water; let cool.
3. Into large bowl of electric mixer, sift flour with sugar, baking soda, and salt.
4. Add butter and sour cream. At medium speed, beat 2 minutes, occasionally scraping side of bowl and guiding mixture into beaters with rubber spatula.
5. Add eggs, vanilla, chocolate, and ¼ cup hot water; beat 2 minutes longer.
6. Pour batter into prepared pans. Bake layers 30 to 35 minutes, and oblong cake, 35 to 40 minutes, or until surface springs back when gently pressed with fingertip.
7. Cool in pans 10 minutes. Remove from pans; cool thoroughly on wire racks. Fill and frost as desired. Makes 2 (8-inch) layers or 1 (13-by-9-by-2-inch) sheet cake.

# ❖ CHOCOLATE CAKE LAYERS

*1 cup unsifted unsweetened cocoa*
*2 cups boiling water*
*2¾ cups sifted all-purpose flour*
*2 teaspoons baking soda*
*½ teaspoon salt*
*½ teaspoon baking powder*
*1 cup butter or margarine, softened*
*2½ cups sugar*
*4 eggs*
*1½ teaspoons vanilla extract*

1. In medium bowl, combine cocoa with boiling water, mixing with wire whisk until smooth. Cool completely.
2. Sift flour with baking soda, salt, and baking powder. Preheat oven to 350F. Grease well and lightly flour 3 (9-by-1½-inch) round layer-cake pans.
3. In large bowl of electric mixer, at high speed, beat butter, sugar, eggs, and vanilla, scraping bowl occasionally, until light—about 5 minutes.
4. At low speed, beat in flour mixture (in fourths), alternately with cocoa mixture, beginning and ending with flour mixture. Do not overbeat.
5. Pour batter into pans, dividing evenly; smooth top. Bake 25 to 30 minutes, or until surface springs back when gently pressed with fingertip.
6. Cool in pans 10 minutes. Carefully loosen sides with spatula. Remove from pans; cool on wire racks. Frost and fill as for Perfect Chocolate Cake, page 129. Makes 3 (9-inch) layers.

# ❖ McCALL'S BEST DEVIL'S-FOOD CAKE

*3 squares unsweetened chocolate*
*2¼ cups sifted cake flour*
*2 teaspoons baking soda*
*½ teaspoon salt*
*½ cup butter or margarine, softened*
*2½ cups light-brown sugar, firmly packed*
*3 eggs*
*2 teaspoons vanilla extract*
*½ cup sour milk (see Note) or butter-milk*
*1 cup boiling water*
*Quick Fudge Frosting, page 260*

1. Melt chocolate over hot, not boiling, water. Let cool.
2. Preheat oven to 350F. Grease well and flour 2 (9-by-1½-inch) round layer-cake pans or 3 (8-by-1½-inch) layer-cake pans.
3. Sift flour with baking soda and salt; set aside.
4. In large bowl of electric mixer, at high speed, beat butter, sugar, eggs, and vanilla until light and fluffy —about 5 minutes—occasionally scraping side of bowl with rubber spatula.
5. At low speed, beat in chocolate.
6. Beat in flour mixture (in fourths), alternately with milk, beginning and ending with flour mixture. Beat just until smooth—about 1 minute.
7. Beat in water just until mixture is smooth. Batter will be thin.
8. Pour batter into prepared pans; bake 30 to 35 minutes, or until surface springs back when gently pressed with fingertip.
9. Cool in pans 10 minutes. Remove from pans; cool thoroughly on wire racks. Fill and frost with Quick Fudge Frosting, or as desired.
Makes 2 (9-inch) or 3 (8-inch) layers.

*Note*: To sour milk: Place 1½ teaspoons lemon juice or vinegar in measuring cup. Add milk to measure ½ cup; stir. Let stand a few minutes before using.

# ❖ BUTTERMILK CLOVE CAKE

*3 cups all-purpose flour*
*1½ teaspoons baking soda*
*2 teaspoons ground cloves*
*1 teaspoon ground cinnamon*
*½ teaspoon ground nutmeg*
*¼ teaspoon ground allspice*
*1 cup butter or margarine, softened*
*1½ cups light-brown sugar, packed*
*2 eggs*
*1 egg yolk*
*1½ cups buttermilk*
*Seafoam Frosting, page 92*

1. Preheat oven to 350F. Grease and flour 2 (9-by-1½-inch) round layer-cake pans.
2. Sift flour with baking soda, cloves, cinnamon, nutmeg, and allspice; set aside.
3. In large bowl of electric mixer, at high speed, beat butter, brown sugar, eggs, and egg yolk, occasionally scraping side of bowl with rubber spatula, until light and fluffy—about 5 minutes.
4. At low speed, beat in flour mixture (in fourths), alternately with buttermilk, beginning and ending with flour mixture. Beat just until smooth—about 1 minute.
5. Pour batter into prepared pans; bake 25 to 30 minutes, or until surface springs back when gently pressed with fingertip.
6. Cool in pans 10 minutes. Remove from pans; cool completely on wire rack before filling and frosting. Frost with Seafoam Frosting.
Makes 2 (9-inch) layers.

# SPONGE AND ANGEL-FOOD CAKES

No fat, no baking powder—what makes these cakes so light and airy? Egg whites, stiffly beaten; flour, sifted several times; and no fat or oil, not even on the pan. The secret of a good sponge cake lies primarily in the proper beating of the egg whites. Careful handling of the batter prevents the escape of incorporated air. Chiffon cakes are close cousins. They use fewer eggs and they do require oil.

## ✜ McCALL'S BEST ANGEL-FOOD CAKE

*1¾ cups egg whites (12 to 14)*
*1¼ cups sifted cake flour*
*1¾ cups sugar*
*½ teaspoon salt*
*1½ teaspoons cream of tartar*
*1 teaspoon vanilla extract*
*½ teaspoon almond extract*

1. In large bowl, let egg whites warm to room temperature—about 1 hour.
2. Meanwhile, preheat oven to 375F.
3. Sift flour with ¾ cup sugar; resift 3 times. Set aside.
4. With portable electric mixer, at high speed, beat egg whites with salt and cream of tartar until soft peaks form when beater is slowly raised.
5. Gradually beat in remaining sugar, ¼ cup at a time, beating well after each addition. Continue beating until stiff peaks form when beater is slowly raised.
6. With rubber spatula, or wire whisk, gently fold extracts into egg whites until combined.
7. Sift flour mixture, one fourth at a time, over egg whites. With wire whisk or rubber spatula, using an under-and-over motion, gently fold in each addition with 15 strokes, rotating bowl a quarter of a turn after each addition.
8. Then fold an additional 10 strokes; flour mixture should be blended into egg whites.
9. With rubber spatula, gently push batter into ungreased 10-inch tube pan. With spatula or knife, cut through batter twice.
10. With rubber spatula, gently spread batter in pan until it is smooth on top and touches side of pan.
11. Bake, on lower oven rack, 35 to 40 minutes, or until cake springs back when gently pressed with fingertip.
12. Invert and fit tube-pan opening over neck of bottle; let cake cool completely—about 2 hours.
13. With spatula, carefully loosen cake from pan; remove. Serve plain, or frost as desired.
Makes 16 servings.

# ✧ McCALL'S BEST DAFFODIL CAKE

## WHITE BATTER:

*1¾ cups egg whites (12 to 14)*
*1¼ cups sifted cake flour*
*1¾ cups sugar*
*½ teaspoon salt*
*1½ teaspoons cream of tartar*
*1½ teaspoons vanilla extract*

## YELLOW BATTER:

*5 egg yolks*
*2 tablespoons cake flour*
*2 tablespoons sugar*
*1 tablespoon grated orange peel*

1. In large bowl, let egg whites warm to room temperature—about 1 hour.
2. Meanwhile, preheat oven to 375F.
3. Make White Batter: Sift flour with ¾ cup sugar; resift 3 times. Set aside.
4. With portable electric mixer at high speed, beat egg whites with salt and cream of tartar until soft peaks form when beater is slowly raised.
5. Gradually beat in remaining sugar, ¼ cup at a time, beating well after each addition. Continue beating until stiff peaks form when beater is slowly raised.
6. With rubber spatula or wire whisk, gently fold vanilla into egg whites until well combined.
7. Sift flour mixture, one fourth at a time, over egg whites. With wire whisk or rubber spatula, using an under-and-over motion, gently fold in each addition with 15 strokes, rotating bowl a quarter of a turn after each addition.
8. Then fold an additional 10 strokes; flour mixture should be completely blended into egg whites. Put one third batter into medium bowl.
9. Make Yellow Batter: In small bowl, combine egg yolks with cake flour and sugar. With portable electric mixer at high speed, beat until thick and lemon-colored. Stir in orange peel.
10. With rubber spatula or wire whisk, using an under-and-over motion, gently fold egg-yolk mixture into one third batter, with 15 strokes.
11. For marbled effect, spoon batters alternately into ungreased 10-inch tube pan, ending with white batter on top. With spatula or knife, cut through batter twice.
12. With rubber spatula, gently spread batter in pan until it is smooth on top and touches side of pan.
13. Bake, on lower oven rack, 35 to 40 minutes, or until cake springs back when gently pressed with fingertip.
14. Invert and fit tube-pan opening over neck of bottle; let cake cool completely—about 2 hours.
15. With spatula, carefully loosen cake from pan; remove. Serve plain, or frost as desired.
Makes 16 servings.

## MOCHA CHIFFON CAKE

*1 cup egg whites (7 or 8)*
*2 teaspoons instant coffee*
*½ cup sifted unsweetened cocoa*
*¾ cup boiling water*
*1¾ cups sifted cake flour*
*1¾ cups sugar*
*1½ teaspoons baking soda*
*1 teaspoon salt*
*½ cup salad oil*
*7 egg yolks*
*2 teaspoons vanilla extract*
*½ teaspoon cream of tartar*

1. In large bowl of electric mixer, let egg whites warm to room temperature—about 1 hour. Meanwhile, preheat oven to 325F.
2. Combine coffee and cocoa in small bowl. Add boiling water, stirring until smooth. Let cool.
3. Sift flour with sugar, baking soda, and salt into large bowl. Make well in center.
4. Pour in oil, egg yolks, vanilla, and cooled coffee mixture. With spoon or with portable electric mixer at medium speed, beat just until smooth.
5. Sprinkle cream of tartar over egg whites; with mixer at high speed, beat until very stiff peaks form when beater is slowly raised. Do not underbeat.
6. Pour batter over egg whites; with rubber spatula or wire whisk, using an under-and-over motion, gently fold into egg whites just until blended.
7. Turn out into ungreased 10-inch tube pan; bake 60 minutes, or until cake springs back when gently pressed with fingertip.
8. Invert and fit tube-pan opening over neck of bottle; let cake cool completely—about 1½ hours.
9. With spatula, carefully loosen cake from pan; remove. Serve plain, or frost as desired.

Makes 10 to 12 servings.

## ORANGE CHIFFON CAKE LAYERS

*1 cup egg whites (7 or 8)*
*2¼ cups sifted cake flour*
*1½ cups sugar*
*1 tablespoon baking powder*
*1 teaspoon salt*
*½ cup salad oil*
*4 egg yolks*
*¾ cup orange juice*
*3 tablespoons grated orange peel*
*½ teaspoon cream of tartar*

1. In large bowl of electric mixer, let egg whites warm to room temperature—about 1 hour. Meanwhile, preheat oven to 350F.
2. Sift flour with sugar, baking powder, and salt into another bowl; make well in center. Add oil, egg yolks, orange juice, and orange peel; beat with spoon until smooth.
3. With electric mixer at high speed, in separate bowl, beat egg whites with cream of tartar until very stiff peaks form.
4. With wire whisk or rubber spatula, using an under-and-over motion, gradually fold batter gently into egg whites just until blended. Do not stir.
5. Pour into 2 ungreased 9-by-1½-inch round layer-cake pans; bake 30 to 35 minutes, or until cake tester inserted in center comes out clean.
6. Invert pans, setting rims on 2 other pans; let cool completely—about 1 hour.
7. With spatula, carefully loosen cake from pan. Hit pan sharply on table; remove cake. Frost and fill as for Super-Bowl-Sunday Cake (page 76).

Makes 2 (9-inch) layers.

# ❖ HOT-MILK SPONGE CAKE

½ cup milk
1 cup sifted all-purpose flour
1 teaspoon baking powder
¼ teaspoon salt
3 eggs (⅔ cup)
1 cup sugar
1 teaspoon vanilla extract

1. In small saucepan, heat milk until bubbles form around edge of pan. Remove from heat; set aside.
2. Preheat oven to 350F.
3. Sift flour with baking powder and salt; set aside.
4. In small bowl of electric mixer, at high speed, beat eggs until thick and lemon-colored. Gradually add sugar, beating until mixture is smooth and well blended—about 5 minutes.
5. At low speed, blend in flour mixture just until smooth.
6. Add warm milk and vanilla, beating just until combined.
7. Pour batter immediately into ungreased 9-by-9-by-2-inch baking pan or 2 (8-by-1½-inch) round layer-cake pans; bake 25 to 30 minutes, or until cake springs back when gently pressed with fingertip.
8. Invert square cake by setting rims on 2 other pans; let cool completely. Remove from pan. Let layer cakes cool in pans 10 minutes. Remove from pans; cool thoroughly on wire racks. Serve plain, or frost as desired.
Makes 1 (9-by-9-by-2-inch) square cake or 2 (8-inch) layers.

*Note*: If larger cake is desired, double amounts of ingredients above. Use large bowl of electric mixer. Bake in ungreased 10-inch tube pan 35 to 40 minutes. Invert and fit tube-pan opening over neck of bottle; let cake cool completely.

# ❖ JELLY-ROLL CAKE

4 eggs
¾ cup sifted cake flour
1 teaspoon baking powder
½ teaspoon salt
¾ cup granulated sugar
Confectioners' sugar
1 cup raspberry preserves
Sweetened whipped cream (optional)

1. In small bowl of electric mixer, let eggs warm to room temperature—about 1 hour.
2. Preheat oven to 400F. Lightly grease bottom of 15½-by-10½-by-1-inch jelly-roll pan; line bottom of pan with waxed paper.
3. Sift flour with baking powder and salt; set aside.
4. At high speed, beat eggs until very thick and lemon-colored. Beat in granulated sugar, 2 table-spoons at a time; continue beating 5 minutes longer, or until very thick.
5. With rubber spatula, gently fold in flour mixture just until combined.
6. Turn out into prepared pan, spreading evenly. Bake 9 minutes, or just until surface springs back when gently pressed with fingertip.

7. Meanwhile, on clean tea towel, sift confectioners' sugar, forming a 15-by-10-inch rectangle.

8. Invert cake on sugar; gently peel off waxed paper.

9. Starting with narrow end, roll up cake (towel and all); place, seam side down, on wire rack to cool—20 minutes.

10. Gently unroll cake; remove towel. Spread with raspberry preserves; roll up again.

11. Place, seam side down, on serving plate; let stand, covered, at least 1 hour before serving.

12. To serve, sift confectioners' sugar over top; slice on diagonal. Serve with bowl of chilled sweetened whipped cream, if desired.

Makes 8 to 10 servings.

# ❖ CHOCOLATE-ROLL CAKE

*6 eggs*
*¾ cup granulated sugar*
*⅓ cup unsweetened cocoa*
*1 teaspoon vanilla extract*
*½ teaspoon almond extract*
*Confectioners' sugar*
*Chocolate Whipped-Cream*
*Filling and Frosting, page 89*

1. Separate egg yolks into small bowl and egg whites into large bowl of electric mixer. Let egg whites warm to room temperature—about 1 hour.

2. Preheat oven to 375F. Lightly grease bottom of 15½-by-10½-by-1-inch jelly-roll pan; line with waxed paper.

3. At high speed, beat egg whites just until soft peaks form when beater is slowly raised. Gradually beat in ¼ cup sugar, beating until stiff peaks form. Meringue will be shiny and moist.

4. With same beater, at high speed, beat egg yolks with rest of sugar until thick and lemon-colored—about 5 minutes. At low speed, beat in cocoa and extracts just until combined.

5. With wire whisk or rubber spatula, using an under-and-over motion, gently fold yolk mixture into egg whites just until combined.

6. Turn out into prepared pan, spreading evenly. Bake 12 to 14 minutes, or just until surface springs back when gently pressed with fingertip.

7. Meanwhile, onto clean towel, sift confectioners' sugar in 15-by-10-inch rectangle.

8. Turn out cake onto sugar; gently peel off waxed paper. With very sharp knife, trim edges.

9. Starting with long edge, roll up cake in towel, jelly-roll fashion. (Cake tends to crack slightly when rolled.) Place, seam side down, on wire rack 30 minutes, or until cool.

10. Meanwhile, make Chocolate Whipped-Cream Filling and Frosting.

11. Gently unroll cake; remove towel. Spread cake with half of filling; reroll, then frost with remaining filling.

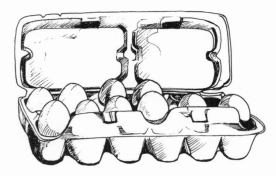

12. Place, seam side down, on serving plate; cover loosely with foil. Refrigerate 1 hour, or until serving time.

13. To serve: Slice on diagonal with serrated knife. Makes 8 to 10 servings.

*Chocolate Ice-Cream Roll*: Fill roll with 1 pint slightly soft vanilla ice cream. Roll up as directed. Freezer-wrap, and freeze about 1 hour, or until serving time.

# POUNDCAKES

## ✠ AUSTRIAN BUTTER CAKE

*1 cup egg whites (7 or 8)*
*¼ cup dry unflavored bread crumbs*
*3 cups sifted all-purpose flour*
*1 teaspoon baking powder*
*¾ teaspoon salt*
*2 cups granulated sugar*
*2 cups butter or margarine, softened*
*2 tablespoons grated lemon peel*
*1 teaspoon vanilla extract*
*8 egg yolks*
*2 tablespoons lemon juice*
*1 tablespoon water*
*Confectioners' sugar*

1. In large bowl of electric mixer, let egg whites warm to room temperature—about 1 hour.

2. Meanwhile, preheat oven to 350F. Grease well and sprinkle with bread crumbs 10-inch tube pan or bundt pan.

3. Sift flour with baking powder and ½ teaspoon salt.

4. With electric mixer at high speed, beat egg whites with ¼ teaspoon salt until foamy. Gradually beat in 1 cup granulated sugar, ¼ cup at a time, beating after each addition. Continue beating until soft peaks form when beater is slowly raised. Gently transfer egg whites to medium bowl.

5. In the bowl of electric mixer, at high speed, beat butter, remaining granulated sugar, the lemon peel, and vanilla until light and fluffy—about 5 minutes. Beat in egg yolks until light and fluffy. Add lemon juice and 1 tablespoon water; beat until smooth.

6. At low speed, beat in flour mixture, one third at a time, just until smooth and well combined.

7. At low speed, gradually beat in egg whites just until blended, scraping side of bowl and guiding batter into beater with rubber spatula.

8. Turn out batter into prepared pan; bake 60 minutes, or until cake tester inserted in center comes out clean.

9. Cool in pan on wire rack 15 minutes. Remove from pan; cool thoroughly on wire rack.

10. Serve plain or sprinkled with confectioners' sugar.

Makes 12 to 16 servings.

# SPECIAL CAKES

Here are some of our own all-time favorites, as well as some cakes that make wonderful displays. In fact, this section is a catch-all of goodies, many of them created from our basic cake layers (pages 62–65).

## ❖ LADY BALTIMORE CAKE

3 (9-inch) layers McCall's Best White Cake, page 62
Lady Baltimore Filling, below
Dates, candied cherries, and pecan halves (optional)

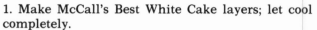

1. Make McCall's Best White Cake layers; let cool completely.
2. On cake plate, put layers together with Lady Baltimore Filling, using half of filling mixture between each two layers.
3. Frost top and sides with Lady Baltimore Frosting. Decorate with dates, candied cherries, and pecan halves, if desired. Refrigerate if keeping overnight. Makes 12 servings.

### LADY BALTIMORE FILLING AND FROSTING

**Filling:**

¾ cup chopped dates
½ cup chopped candied cherries
1 cup chopped pecans
½ cup chopped raisins
¼ cup brandy or bourbon

**Frosting:**

¾ cup egg whites (about 6 eggs)
2¼ cups sugar
¾ teaspoon cream of tartar
½ cup water
¾ teaspoon vanilla extract

1. Make Filling: In medium bowl, combine dates, cherries, pecans, raisins, and brandy; mix well. Let mixture stand at room temperature 1 hour.
2. Make Frosting: In large bowl of electric mixer, let egg whites warm to room temperature—about 1 hour.
3. In medium saucepan, combine sugar and cream of tartar with water. Cook, stirring, over medium heat, until sugar is dissolved and syrup is clear. Continue cooking over medium heat, without stirring, to 240F on candy thermometer, or until a little of the mixture spins thin thread 6 to 8 inches long when dropped from tip of spoon.
4. Meanwhile, with mixer at medium speed, beat egg whites until soft peaks form when beater is slowly raised. With mixer at high speed, slowly pour hot syrup in thin stream over egg whites, beating constantly.
5. Add vanilla; continue beating until stiff peaks form when beater is slowly raised and frosting is thick enough to spread.
6. Measure 2 cups frosting, and add to filling; mix lightly. Use between cake layers. Use remaining frosting on top and sides of cake.

# ◈ PERFECT CHOCOLATE CAKE

*3 (9-inch) Chocolate Cake Layers,*
*page 64*

**FILLING:**

*1 cup heavy cream, chilled*
*¼ cup unsifted confectioners' sugar*
*1 teaspoon vanilla extract*

**FROSTING:**

*1 pkg (6 oz) semisweet chocolate*
*pieces*
*½ cup light cream*
*1 cup butter or margarine*
*2½ cups unsifted confectioners' sugar*

1. Make Chocolate Cake Layers.
2. Make Filling: Whip heavy cream with ¼ cup confectioners' sugar and vanilla. Refrigerate until ready to use.
3. Make Frosting: In medium saucepan, combine chocolate pieces, light cream, and butter. Cook over medium heat, stirring, until smooth; remove from heat.
4. With wire whisk, blend in 2½ cups confectioners' sugar. Set saucepan in bowl filled with ice and beat until frosting holds shape and is of spreading consistency.
5. Put cake layers together with filling, using half the filling mixture between each 2 layers.
6. Frost top and sides with frosting, swirling decoratively.
Makes 12 servings.

# ◈ LEMON COCONUT CAKE

*3 (9-inch) layers McCall's Best Yellow*
*Cake, page 63*

**FILLING:**

*1 cup sugar*
*3 tablespoons cornstarch*
*¼ teaspoon salt*
*¾ cup orange juice*
*¼ cup lemon juice*
*½ cup water*
*3 egg yolks*
*1 tablespoon grated lemon peel*
*1 can (3½ oz) flaked coconut*

**FROSTING:**

*½ cup egg whites*
*1½ cups sugar*
*½ teaspoon cream of tartar*
*½ cup water*
*½ teaspoon vanilla extract*

1. Make McCall's Best Yellow Cake layers.
2. Make Filling: In small saucepan, combine 1 cup sugar, the cornstarch, and salt, mixing well. Gradually stir in orange and lemon juices and ½ cup water.
3. Bring to boiling over medium heat, stirring. Remove from heat. Add egg yolks, one at a time, beating well after each addition.
4. Bring to boiling, stirring; boil 1 minute. Remove from heat. Stir in lemon peel and coconut. Cool completely before spreading between cake layers.
5. Make Frosting: In small bowl of electric mixer, let egg whites warm to room temperature.
6. In medium saucepan, combine 1½ cups sugar, the cream of tartar, and ½ cup water. Cook, stirring, over medium heat until sugar is dissolved and syrup is clear. Continue cooking over medium heat, without stirring, to 240F on candy thermometer, or until a little spins thin thread 6 or 8 inches long when dropped from tip of spoon.
7. Meanwhile, with mixer at medium speed, beat egg whites until soft peaks form when beater is slowly raised.
8. With mixer at high speed, slowly pour hot syrup in thin stream over egg whites, beating constantly.

9. Add vanilla; continue beating until stiff peaks form when beater is slowly raised and frosting is thick enough to spread.

10. On cake plate, put layers together with filling, using half of mixture between each 2 layers.

11. Spread frosting on top and sides, swirling decoratively.

Makes 12 servings.

# ✠ ORANGE-CRÈME CHIFFON CAKE

## ORANGE CHIFFON CAKE:

1 cup egg whites (7 or 8)
2 cups sifted all-purpose flour
1½ cups granulated sugar
1 tablespoon baking powder
1 teaspoon salt
½ cup salad oil
5 egg yolks
¾ cup water
3 tablespoons grated orange peel
1 teaspoon vanilla extract
½ teaspoon cream of tartar

## ORANGE CRÈME:

1 cup heavy cream
½ cup confectioners' sugar
2 tablespoons grated orange peel

1 tablespoon shredded orange peel

1. Make Orange Chiffon Cake: Let egg whites warm to room temperature in large bowl of electric mixer —1 hour.

2. Preheat oven to 325F. Sift flour with 1½ cups granulated sugar, baking powder, and salt into another large bowl. Make well in center.

3. Add oil, egg yolks, water, 3 tablespoons grated orange peel, and the vanilla; beat with spoon until smooth.

4. In large bowl of electric mixer, at high speed, beat egg whites with cream of tartar until stiff peaks form when beater is slowly raised.

5. Pour egg-yolk mixture gradually over egg whites; with rubber spatula or wire whisk, using an under-and-over motion, gently fold into egg whites just until blended.

6. Turn out into ungreased 10-inch tube pan; bake 60 minutes, or until cake tester inserted in center comes out clean.

7. Invert and fit tube-pan opening over neck of bottle; let cake cool completely—1½ hours.

8. Carefully loosen cake from pan. Invert onto wire rack; then turn out, top side up, onto serving plate.

9. Make Orange Crème: In medium bowl, mix cream, confectioners' sugar, and grated orange peel. Refrigerate until very cold—30 minutes. With electric beater, beat just until stiff.

10. Frost top and sides of cake with orange crème. Sprinkle edge with shredded orange peel.

Makes 12 servings.

# ❖ CARROT WHIPPED-CREAM CAKE

*3 cups sifted all-purpose flour*
*2 teaspoons baking powder*
*1 teaspoon baking soda*
*2 teaspoons ground cinnamon*
*1 teaspoon salt*
*2 cups granulated sugar*
*1½ cups salad oil*
*4 eggs*
*3 cups grated carrot (1 lb)*

**WHIPPED-CREAM FROSTING:**

*2 cups heavy cream, chilled*
*½ cup confectioners' sugar*
*1 teaspoon vanilla extract*

*Pecan or walnut halves*

1. Preheat oven to 350F. Sift flour with baking powder, baking soda, cinnamon, and salt. Grease well and flour 3 (9-by-1½-inch) round layer-cake pans.
2. In large mixing bowl of electric mixer, at medium speed, beat granulated sugar, oil, and eggs until well blended—about 2 minutes. Add carrot; mix well.
3. At low speed, gradually add flour mixture, beating just until well combined. Batter will be thin. Pour batter into prepared pans, dividing evenly. Bake 30 to 35 minutes, or until surface springs back when gently pressed with fingertip.
4. Cool in pans 10 minutes. Carefully loosen sides with spatula; remove from pan. Cool completely on racks.
5. Make Whipped-Cream Frosting: In medium bowl, whip cream with confectioners' sugar and vanilla until stiff. Refrigerate if not using at once.
6. To frost: Put layers together with frosting, using ¾ cup for each layer. Frost sides and top. Arrange pecan halves on top. Refrigerate 1 hour before serving.
Makes 10 to 12 servings.

# ❖ CHOCOLATE TRUFFLE CAKE

*3 (9-inch) Chocolate Cake Layers,*
*  page 64*
*¾ cup raspberry jam*
*Chocolate Buttercream, below*
*12 Chocolate Truffles, below*
*Chocolate sprinkles*

1. Make Chocolate Cake Layers. Let cool completely.
2. Place one cake layer on cake plate, and spread with raspberry jam.
3. Place second layer on top, and spread with 1 cup chocolate buttercream.
4. Top with third layer.
5. Set aside ¾ cup buttercream for decoration. With remaining buttercream, frost sides and top of cake.
6. Swirl decorating comb around sides and top of cake to create grooved effect, if desired.
7. Place reserved buttercream in pastry bag fitted with number-30 star tip.
8. Decorate cake top with Chocolate Truffles, and a buttercream ruching. Press chocolate sprinkles onto lower two thirds of side of cake.
Makes 12 servings.

## CHOCOLATE BUTTERCREAM

*¾ lb soft butter*
*2 cups sifted confectioners' sugar*
*3 egg yolks, unbeaten*
*1 pkg (6 oz) semisweet-chocolate*
  *pieces*

1. With electric mixer at medium speed, beat butter until fluffy.
2. Gradually beat in sugar; then add egg yolks, one at a time, beating until very fluffy.
3. In top of double boiler, melt chocolate pieces over hot, not boiling, water; remove from heat to cool completely.
4. Then beat chocolate into butter mixture, beating until spreading consistency.

## CHOCOLATE TRUFFLES

*½ cup walnuts*
*3 squares (1-oz size) semisweet choco-*
  *late*
*2 tablespoons heavy cream*
*⅔ cup confectioners' sugar*
*1 tablespoon Grand Marnier,*
  *Cointreau, or rum*
*⅓ cup chocolate sprinkles*

1. Grind nuts in blender or food processor. Line bottom of 9-by-5-by-3-inch loaf pan with waxed paper.
2. In small heavy saucepan, combine chocolate and cream. Heat over low heat just until chocolate is melted. Remove from heat.
3. In medium bowl, stir nuts and sugar with wooden spoon until combined. Add chocolate mixture and liqueur, stirring to combine well.
4. Turn out into prepared pan. Refrigerate until firm. Shape into 30 round balls. Roll in chocolate sprinkles. Store, covered, in refrigerator until ready to use. Makes about 30 pieces.

# ▣ SUPER-BOWL-SUNDAY CAKE

*2 (9-inch) Orange Chiffon Cake Lay-*
  *ers, page 68*

## CREAM FILLING:

*½ cup granulated sugar*
*3 tablespoons cornstarch*
*2¾ cups milk*
*2 tablespoons butter or margarine*
*6 egg yolks, slightly beaten*
*½ teaspoon vanilla extract*
*1 cup (8 oz) chopped mixed candied*
  *fruit*
*½ cup miniature semisweet chocolate*
  *pieces*
*3 tablespoons light rum*

1. Make Orange Chiffon Cake Layers. Cool completely.
2. Make Cream Filling: In medium saucepan, combine granulated sugar and cornstarch; mix well. Gradually add 2¾ cups milk, stirring until smooth. Add butter.
3. Bring to boiling, stirring constantly; boil 1 minute. Stir a little of hot mixture into beaten egg yolks; return to saucepan, stirring. Bring to boiling; then remove from heat. Stir in vanilla.
4. Turn out into medium bowl. Place in larger bowl filled with ice cubes to cool completely—about 40 minutes. Stir occasionally.
5. Stir in candied fruit, chocolate, and rum. Refrigerate until needed. Makes about 3 cups.
6. To assemble cake: Slice layers in half horizontally to make 4 layers.

## APRICOT COATING:

⅔ cup apricot preserves
2 teaspoons lemon juice

## GLAZE:

1¼ cups sifted confectioners' sugar
3 tablespoons milk

5 pieces of citron 3 to 4 inches long
1 candied cherry

7. Place a layer, cut side up, on cake plate. Spread with one third of cream filling. Repeat with remaining layers and filling, ending with top layer, cut side down.
8. Make Apricot Coating: Melt preserves in small saucepan; strain. Add lemon juice. Brush over entire surface of cake. Refrigerate.
9. Make Glaze: In small bowl, combine confectioners' sugar with milk, beating until smooth.
10. Brush glaze over top of cake. Decorate with citron and candied cherry. Refrigerate.
Makes 16 servings.

# ✦ PINEAPPLE UPSIDE-DOWN CAKE

1 can (1 lb, 4 oz) sliced pineapple
¼ cup butter or margarine
⅔ cup light-brown sugar, firmly
   packed
½ cup pecan halves or broken walnuts
1½ cups sifted all-purpose flour
1 cup granulated sugar
2 teaspoons baking powder
½ teaspoon salt
⅓ cup shortening
¾ cup milk
1 egg
Whipped cream
Ice cream (optional)

1. Preheat oven to 350F. Drain pineapple, reserving 2 tablespoons of syrup.
2. Melt butter in 10-inch heavy skillet, over low heat (see Note). Add brown sugar, stirring until sugar is melted. Remove from heat.
3. Arrange drained pineapple on sugar mixture in skillet. Fill centers of pineapple slices and spaces between slices with pecans. Set skillet aside.
4. Into medium bowl, sift flour with granulated sugar, baking powder, and salt. Add shortening and milk. With electric mixer at medium speed, beat 2 minutes.
5. Add egg and reserved pineapple syrup; beat 2 minutes longer. Pour cake batter over pineapple in skillet, spreading evenly.
6. Bake 40 to 45 minutes, or until cake springs back when gently pressed with fingertip.
7. Let stand on wire rack just 5 minutes. With small spatula, loosen cake from edge of skillet. Cover with serving plate. Invert, and shake gently; lift off pan.
8. Serve cake warm. Top individual servings with whipped cream. Or top with small spoonfuls of vanilla ice cream, if desired.
Makes 8 servings.

Note: If skillet does not have an iron or oven-safe handle, wrap handle in aluminum foil.

# ❖ MARZIPAN TORTE

6 eggs
½ cup all-purpose flour
1 teaspoon baking powder
¼ teaspoon salt
½ cup sugar
1 can (8 oz) almond paste
1 teaspoon vanilla extract
½ teaspoon almond extract
Custard Filling, below
1 jar (12 oz) cherry preserves, melted
½ cup chopped toasted blanched al-
    monds
10 whole blanched almonds, toasted

1. Separate eggs, placing whites in large bowl of elec-tric mixer and yolks in small bowl. Let whites stand at room temperature 1 hour.
2. Preheat oven to 350F. Butter and flour 9-inch Turk's head or tube pan. Sift together flour and bak-ing powder.
3. In large bowl of electric mixer, beat egg whites with salt until soft peaks form when beater is slowly raised. Add sugar, 2 tablespoons at a time, beating well after each addition until moist stiff peaks form when beater is slowly raised.
4. Using same beater, beat egg yolks until thick and lemon-colored. Add almond paste, vanilla extract, and almond extract; beat until smooth
5. At low speed, blend in flour mixture, guiding mix-ture into beater with rubber spatula.
6. With rubber spatula or wire whisk, using an under-and-over motion, gently fold egg-yolk mixture into egg whites just until blended.
7. Pour batter into prepared pan; bake 30 to 35 min-utes, or until cake tester inserted in center comes out clean. Cool completely on wire rack. Cake will fall slightly.
8. Meanwhile, make Custard Filling.
9. To assemble: Cut cake crosswise into 3 parts. Place bottom layer, cut side up, on plate; spread with half of filling. Repeat with second layer. Top with last layer, cut side down.
10. Brush entire cake with melted cherry preserves. Sprinkle sides with chopped almonds. Arrange whole almonds on top.
Makes 10 servings.

## CUSTARD FILLING

⅓ cup sugar
2 tablespoons cornstarch
2 cups hot milk
2 egg yolks
½ teaspoon almond extract

1. In small saucepan, combine sugar and cornstarch; mix well. Slowly add hot milk, stirring constantly.
2. With wooden spoon stir over medium heat, until mixture starts to boil; remove from heat.
3. Beat egg yolks in bowl. Add ½ cup hot mixture and mix well. Return to saucepan. Continue cooking, stirring, until filling is thick. Remove from heat; add almond extract.
4. Place pan in bowl of ice water to cool completely —about 30 minutes.

# ⊞ CHOCOLATE RASPBERRY TORTE

2 cups sifted all-purpose flour
2 teaspoons baking soda
½ teaspoon salt
½ teaspoon baking powder
3 squares (1-oz size) unsweetened
  chocolate
½ cup butter or margarine
2 cups light-brown sugar, firmly
  packed
3 eggs
1½ teaspoons vanilla extract
¾ cup sour cream
½ cup strong coffee
⅓ cup coffee-flavored liqueur
¾ cup heavy cream
2 tablespoons confectioners' sugar
1 jar (12 oz) raspberry or strawberry
  preserves
Chocolate Sour-Cream Frosting,
  below
Fresh raspberries or strawberries

1. Sift flour with baking soda, salt, and baking powder. Preheat oven to 350F. Grease well and lightly flour 2 (9-by-1½-inch) round layer-cake pans.
2. Melt chocolate in custard cup placed in hot, not boiling, water; let cool.
3. In large bowl of electric mixer, at high speed, beat butter, brown sugar, eggs, and vanilla, scraping bowl occasionally, until light—about 5 minutes. Beat in chocolate.
4. At low speed, beat in flour mixture (in fourths), alternating with sour cream, beginning and ending with flour mixture. Add coffee and liqueur, blending until smooth.
5. Divide batter evenly between pans; smooth tops. Bake 30 to 35 minutes, or until surface springs back when gently pressed with fingertip.
6. Cool in pans 10 minutes. Carefully loosen sides with spatula. Remove from pans; cool on racks.
7. Beat cream with confectioners' sugar until stiff; refrigerate.
8. To assemble: Slice layers in half horizontally to make 4 layers. Place a layer, cut side up, on cake plate. Spread with ⅓ cup raspberry preserves and ½ cup whipped cream. Repeat with remaining layers, ending with top layer, cut side down.
9. Frost top and sides with Chocolate Sour-Cream Frosting, swirling it as you spread. Arrange whole berries around edge.
Makes 12 servings.

## CHOCOLATE SOUR-CREAM FROSTING

1½ pkg (6-oz size) semisweet chocolate pieces
¾ cup sour cream
Dash salt

1. Melt chocolate pieces in top of double boiler over hot water. Remove top of double boiler from hot water.
2. Add sour cream and salt. With portable mixer, at medium speed, or with rotary beater, beat frosting until creamy and of spreading consistency.

# CAKES FROM MIXES

Even when you don't have time to start from scratch, you can present cakes that are pretty close to homemade by starting with the pre-pared mixes and elaborating on them—which is what we've done in this section.

---

# ❖ CHOCOLATE-MOUSSE DESSERT CAKE

1 pkg angel-food-cake mix
1 square unsweetened chocolate,
  grated

**COCOA-CREAM FILLING AND FROSTING:**

3 cups heavy cream
1½ cups sifted confectioners' sugar
¾ cup unsweetened cocoa
1 teaspoon unflavored gelatine
2 tablespoons cold water
2 teaspoons vanilla extract
¼ teaspoon salt

Whipped cream and grated chocolate
  (optional)

1. Preheat oven and prepare cake mix as package label directs, adding grated chocolate to flour mix-ture.
2. Turn out batter into ungreased 10-inch tube pan; bake 30 to 40 minutes, or until surface springs back when gently pressed with fingertip.
3. Invert and fit tube-pan opening over neck of bottle. Let cake hang to cool completely.
4. Meanwhile, make Cocoa-Cream Filling and Frost-ing: Refrigerate heavy cream, confectioners' sugar, and cocoa (in large bowl) until very cold.
5. Sprinkle gelatine over cold water; let stand 5 min-utes to soften. Heat, stirring, over hot water until dissolved. Let cool.
6. Add vanilla and salt to chilled cocoa cream. Beat with portable electric mixer until stiff enough to hold its shape.
7. Remove 3 cups cocoa cream; into this, stir in cooled gelatine. Use for filling cake.
8. To prepare cake for filling: Remove cake from pan; place upside down on cake plate. Cut 1-inch slice crosswise from top of cake; set aside. With knife, outline cavity in cake, leaving 1-inch-thick walls.
9. With spoon, carefully remove cake from this area, leaving 1-inch-thick base. Reserve 1¼ cups crum-bled cake.
10. Fill cavity in cake with gelatine mixture. Replace top of cake.
11. Mix ½ cup cocoa cream with reserved cake pieces. Use to fill center hole of cake.
12. Frost top and sides of cake with remaining cocoa cream. Refrigerate until well chilled—several hours or overnight. Just before serving, decorate top with rosettes of whipped cream and grated chocolate, if desired.
Makes 10 to 12 servings.

# ❖ HOLIDAY LOAF CAKE

1 pkg (1 lb, 1 oz) poundcake mix
½ cup milk
1 cup grated tart apple (1 large)
2 eggs
½ cup mixed candied peel
½ cup chopped walnuts or pecans
¼ cup raisins
2 tablespoons light corn syrup
Walnut halves
Candied cherries, halved

1. Preheat oven to 325F. Lightly grease 9-by-5-by-3-inch loaf pan.
2. Turn out package of cake mix into large bowl. Add milk. Blend just until dry ingredients are moistened. With electric beater, at medium speed, beat 1 minute. Add apple and eggs; beat 2 minutes, scraping side of bowl frequently.
3. Add candied peel, walnuts, and raisins; mix well with wooden spoon just until blended.
4. Turn out into prepared pan. Bake 1 hour and 15 minutes, or until cake tester inserted in center comes out clean. Cool in pan on wire rack 10 minutes. Turn out of pan.
5. Brush warm loaf with corn syrup; decorate with walnuts and candied cherries. Cool completely before serving.
Makes 1 loaf.

# ❖ PETITS FOURS

2 pkg (1-lb, 1-oz size) poundcake mix
4 eggs
Petits Fours Glaze, below
Fondant Frosting, below
Pink and green cake-decorating frosting tubes

1. Preheat oven to 350F. Lightly grease and flour 15½-by-10½-by-1-inch jelly-roll pan.
2. Prepare both packages of poundcake mix as package label directs, using 4 eggs and liquid called for.
3. Turn out into prepared pan. Bake 30 to 35 minutes, or until top springs back when pressed with fingertip.
4. Cool 10 minutes in pan. Turn out on wire rack; let cool completely.
5. Meanwhile, make Petits Fours Glaze and Fondant Frosting.
6. Using 2-inch cookie cutter, cut out diamonds, hearts, rounds, and squares from cooled cake. (You'll have 32 or 33.)
7. To glaze cakes: Place on fork, one at a time. Hold over bowl of glaze, and spoon glaze over cake, completely covering top and sides.
8. Place cakes, uncoated side down and 2 inches apart, on wire racks placed on cookie sheets. Let stand until glaze is set—at least 1 hour.
9. To frost: Place glazed cakes on fork, one at a time. Spoon frosting over cake, to run over top and down side evenly. Frost half of cakes white and half pink or make all white.
10. Let cakes dry completely on wire racks—about 1 hour. Repeat frosting, if necessary. Let dry.

11. To decorate: Make little posies and leaves with decorating tubes, or drizzle any remaining frosting over tops. Refrigerate several hours. Let stand at room temperature 1 hour.
Makes 32 or 33.

## PETITS FOURS GLAZE

*1½ cups apricot preserves*
*½ cup sugar*
*½ cup water*

1. In medium saucepan, combine preserves, sugar, and water; bring to boiling over medium heat. Boil, stirring, 5 minutes.
2. Remove from heat. Press through sieve into bowl. Makes 1½ cups.

## FONDANT FROSTING

*2¾ cups granulated sugar*
*Dash salt*
*¼ teaspoon cream of tartar*
*1½ cups water*
*About 2¼ cups sifted confectioners'*
  *sugar*
*½ teaspoon almond extract*
*Food color (optional)*

1. In medium saucepan, combine granulated sugar, salt, cream of tartar, and water. Over low heat, cook, stirring, until sugar is dissolved.
2. Over medium heat, cook, without stirring, to 226F on candy thermometer.
3. Transfer to top of double boiler; let cool to lukewarm (110F on candy thermometer).
4. With wooden spoon, gradually beat in just enough confectioners' sugar to make frosting thick enough to coat spoon but thin enough to pour. Add almond extract. Remove half of frosting (about 1½ cups) to small bowl. Add a few drops food color to tint a delicate color, if you like.
5. Keep half of frosting over hot, not boiling, water, to keep thin enough to pour. If frosting is too thin, add a little more confectioners' sugar; if too thick, thin with a little warm water. After using frosting, heat remaining frosting, and use in same way.
Makes 3 cups.

# FRUITCAKES

These cakes are, of course, standard for Christmas and New Year's, but they store so well and are so rich and delicious that it's a great surprise for the family to serve them at other times of the year. They also make great gifts for Christmas, as well as for birthdays and weddings and even the Fourth of July.

# ❖ ENGLISH FRUITCAKE

*1 box (15 oz) raisins*
*1 box (10 oz) currants*
*2 jars (4-oz size) citron, chopped*
*2 jars (3½-oz size) candied cherries,*
  *halved*
*1 can (8 oz) walnuts, chopped*
*1 cup brandy or rum*
*2 cups all-purpose flour*
*½ teaspoon ground nutmeg*
*½ teaspoon ground cinnamon*
*1 cup butter, softened*
*1 cup sugar*
*5 eggs*
*Creamy Frosting, below*
*Citron or angelica*
*Candied cherries*

1. Lightly grease 10-inch tube pan. Line bottom and side with heavy brown wrapping paper (see Note); grease paper.
2. In very large bowl, toss raisins, currants, citron, cherries, and walnuts with ½ cup brandy until well mixed.
3. Preheat oven to 275F. Sift together flour, nutmeg, and cinnamon; set aside.
4. In large bowl of electric mixer, at medium speed, beat butter with sugar until mixture is fluffy.
5. Add eggs, one at a time, beating after each addition; beat until very light and fluffy.
6. At low speed, beat in flour mixture (in fourths), alternately with remaining brandy, beginning and ending with flour mixture.
7. Pour batter over fruit mixture; mix until well combined. Turn out into prepared pan.
8. On low rack in oven, bake 2½ to 3 hours, or until cake tester inserted in center comes out clean. (If top of cake is browning too much, halfway through baking, place sheet of foil loosely over top.) Cool cake completely in pan on wire rack. Remove from pan, and peel off paper. In a bowl of brandy, soak a piece of cheesecloth large enough to cover cake. Wrap cake in cloth, then in foil, and store for several weeks. (Resoak cheesecloth several times, as necessary.)
9. To decorate cake for serving: Make Creamy Frosting. With spatula, spread even layer on top. Decorate with leaves cut from citron or angelica and the cherries.
Makes one 5-pound fruitcake.

*For individual cakes*: Prepare pans; line five 5¾-by-3-by-2-inch greased loaf pans with strips of greased brown paper. Turn batter out into prepared pans, dividing evenly. Bake 2 to 2½ hours at 275F, or until cake tester inserted in center of cake comes out clean.
Makes 5 (1-pound) cakes.

*Note*: To line 10-inch tube pan: On heavy brown paper, draw 18-inch circle and cut out. Set pan in center of circle; draw around base of pan and tube. With pencil lines outside, fold paper into eighths; snip off tip. Unfold circle; cut along folds to second circle. Grease well both tube pan and unpenciled side of paper. Fit paper, greased side up, into pan. If necessary, trim paper to top of pan.

## CREAMY FROSTING

1½ cups confectioners' sugar
1 to 2 tablespoons light cream
¼ teaspoon almond extract

In small bowl of electric mixer, combine all ingredients; beat until smooth and creamy. Use to decorate top of cake only.

# ✚ DEARBORN INN FRUITCAKE

1½ cups light raisins
1½ cups dark raisins
1½ cups currants
1 cup coarsely chopped pitted dates
1 jar (8 oz) diced mixed candied peel
¾ cup coarsely chopped blanched almonds
¾ cup coarsely chopped walnuts
½ cup candied red cherries, quartered
½ cup candied green cherries, quartered
¾ cup finely chopped cored pared tart apple
½ cup finely chopped whole orange
3 cups sifted all-purpose flour
½ teaspoon salt
1 teaspoon baking powder
1 teaspoon ground cinnamon
1 teaspoon ground ginger
1 teaspoon ground mace
¾ teaspoon ground cloves
1 cup butter or margarine
1 cup light-brown sugar, packed
6 eggs, beaten
2 tablespoons light or dark molasses
3 tablespoons dark rum
Dark rum or brandy (optional)

1. Lightly grease 10-inch tube pan. Line bottom and side with heavy brown paper; lightly grease paper.
2. In very large bowl, combine raisins, currants, dates, candied peel, nuts, candied cherries, apple, and orange. Sift ¼ cup flour over mixture; toss to mix well.
3. Sift rest of flour with salt, baking powder, cinnamon, ginger, mace, and cloves; set aside. Preheat oven to 275F.
4. In large bowl of electric mixer, at medium speed, beat butter with sugar until light and fluffy. Beat in eggs until well combined; then beat in molasses and 3 tablespoons rum.
5. With wooden spoon, stir fruit-nut mixture into egg mixture until well combined. Then add flour mixture, combining well.
6. Turn out into prepared pan. Press batter with spatula to spread evenly.
7. Bake about 2½ hours, or until cake tester inserted in center comes out clean. Let cool completely in pan on wire rack. Then remove from pan, and peel off paper.
8. To age cake: Place ⅓ cup of rum in bowl and soak in it a piece of cheesecloth large enough to cover cake. Wrap cake in cloth, then in foil. Store in airtight tin container or in refrigerator at least 2 weeks. Resoak cheesecloth from time to time as it dries out. Makes 1 (6-pound) cake.

To make 3 (8½-by-4½-by-2⅝-inch) loaves: Line greased pans with strips of brown paper; lightly grease paper. Turn out batter into prepared pans, dividing evenly. Bake 1¾ to 2 hours at 275F, or until cake tester inserted in center comes out clean.

# ✠ EASY CHRISTMAS CHERRY CAKE

*1 pkg (15 oz) light raisins*
*1 jar (8 oz) candied cherries*
*1 jar (8 oz) chopped candied citron*
*¼ cup brandy or rum*
*1 cup butter, softened*
*2 cups sugar*
*1 teaspoon almond extract*
*8 eggs*
*4 cups all-purpose flour*

1. In medium bowl, combine raisins, cherries, citron, and brandy; with spoon, mix until well combined.
2. Preheat oven to 300F. Grease 10-inch tube pan. Line bottom and side with brown paper (see Note, page 83).
3. In large bowl of electric mixer, at medium speed, beat butter with sugar and almond extract until light and fluffy.
4. Add eggs, one at a time, beating well after each addition.
5. At low speed, gradually beat in flour.
6. Add prepared raisin mixture. Turn out into prepared pan.
7. Bake about 2 hours and 25 minutes, or until cake tester inserted in center comes out clean.
8. Let cool in pan on wire rack 30 minutes. Turn out of pan; let cool completely on rack.
Makes 1 (5-pound) cake.

# SHORTCAKES, COBBLERS, AND KUCHEN

These cakes have as their base biscuit dough, sponge cake, or other rather plain batters, but they become sinful delights by the addition of fruit, butter, and whipped cream. They are among the favorite desserts of our readers.

# ✠ OLD-FASHIONED STRAWBERRY SHORTCAKE

**TOPPING:**

*2 boxes (1-pint size) fresh strawberries*
*½ cup granulated sugar*
*1 cup heavy cream*
*2 tablespoons confectioners' sugar*

1. Preheat oven to 425F. Wash berries in cold water; drain. Set aside several nice ones for garnish. Remove stems from rest of berries. Slice half of berries into bowl; toss with ¼ cup granulated sugar. With fork, crush other half of berries with ¼ cup granulated sugar.
2. With portable electric mixer at high speed, beat

## SHORTCAKE:

2 cups sifted all-purpose flour
¼ cup granulated sugar
3 teaspoons baking powder
½ teaspoon salt
½ cup butter or margarine, cut into
  chunks
1 egg
Milk

2 tablespoons butter or margarine,
  melted

cream with confectioners' sugar just until stiff; refrigerate. Lightly grease 8-by-1½-inch round layer-cake pan.

3. Make Shortcake: With sifter placed in medium bowl, sift flour with granulated sugar, baking powder, and salt. With pastry blender or 2 knives used scissor fashion, cut butter into flour mixture until it is in very small particles, each coated with flour (resembles small peas). Break egg into 1-cup measuring cup. Add milk to measure ¾ cup. Mix with fork.

4. Make well in center of flour mixture. Pour in milk-egg mixture all at once; mix vigorously with fork until moistened. Turn out into prepared pan, scraping bowl with rubber spatula. With spatula, smooth top of dough so that it is even.

5. Bake 25 to 30 minutes, or until golden and cake tester inserted in center comes out clean. Loosen edge with sharp knife; turn out on wire rack. Using long serrated knife, cut cake in half crosswise. Place bottom of cake, cut side up, on serving plate.

6. Brush surface with melted butter. Spoon on half of crushed and sliced berries; set top in place, cut side down. Spoon on rest of berries. Mound whipped cream lightly in center. Garnish top with whole berries. Serve warm.

Makes 9 servings.

# ◈ APRICOT KUCHEN

⅔ cup butter
1 cup confectioners' sugar
1 egg
2 cups unsifted cake flour
1½ teaspoons baking powder
3 cups poundcake crumbs
½ teaspoon almond extract
17 fresh apricots or Italian plums,
  washed, split, and pitted
2 tablespoons granulated sugar
¼ teaspoon ground cinnamon
¼ cup apricot preserves
Confectioners' sugar

1. Combine butter, 1 cup confectioners' sugar, the egg, flour, and baking powder in food processor with cutting blade or in bowl of electric mixer. Process or beat until combined.

2. Grease and flour 9-inch cake pan with removable bottom or fluted quiche pan with removable bottom. Preheat oven to 350F.

3. Press kuchen dough into bottom and side of pan. Toss together poundcake crumbs and almond extract. Turn out into kuchen shell.

4. Arrange apricots on crumbs in circular pattern. Stir together granulated sugar and cinnamon; sprinkle over apricots. Bake 30 to 35 minutes, or until crust is golden and feels firm.

5. Warm apricot preserves; brush over apricots. Loosen edges with small spatula; remove side of pan. Sift confectioners' sugar around edges. Serve warm or at room temperature.

Makes 8 servings.

# ❖ FRESH BERRY COBBLER

4 cups blueberries, strawberries,
  blackberries, or raspberries,
  washed and, if necessary, hulled
⅔ cup sugar
½ teaspoon lemon juice
2 tablespoons butter or margarine
1½ cups packaged buttermilk-biscuit
  mix
3 tablespoons butter or margarine,
  melted
1 egg, slightly beaten
½ cup milk
Whipped cream or ice cream

1. Preheat oven to 400F. Grease well 10-by-6½-by-2-inch baking dish.
2. Toss berries lightly with sugar and lemon juice. Place in baking dish. Dot with 2 tablespoons butter.
3. In medium bowl, combine biscuit mix, melted butter, egg, and milk. Lightly mix with fork just until combined. With spoon, drop dough over fruit.
4. Bake 30 to 35 minutes, or until top is golden-brown. Serve warm with whipped cream or ice cream.
Makes 6 servings.

# ❖ ENGLISH TRIFLE

## CUSTARD:

1 cup sugar
1 tablespoon cornstarch
½ teaspoon salt
4 cups milk
8 egg yolks
2 teaspoons vanilla extract
1 tablespoon cream sherry

2 (8-inch) bakers' sponge-cake layers
¾ cup cream sherry
6 tablespoons raspberry preserves
6 tablespoons toasted slivered almonds
½ cup heavy cream, whipped
Candied cherries

1. Make Custard: In medium-size heavy saucepan, combine sugar, cornstarch, and salt. Gradually add milk; stir until smooth.
2. Cook over medium heat, stirring constantly, until mixture is thickened and comes to boil. Boil 1 minute. Remove from heat.
3. In medium bowl, slightly beat egg yolks. Gradually add a little hot mixture, beating well.
4. Stir into rest of hot mixture; cook over medium heat, stirring constantly, just until mixture boils. Remove from heat; stir in vanilla and 1 tablespoon sherry.
5. Strain custard immediately into bowl. Refrigerate until well chilled—several hours or overnight.
6. Split sponge-cake layers in half crosswise, to make 4 layers in all. Sprinkle each layer with sherry.
7. Spread each of 3 layers with 2 tablespoons preserves, and sprinkle each with 2 tablespoons almonds. In attractive deep serving bowl, stack prepared layers, jam side up, spreading each with about 1 cup custard. Top with plain layer, then remaining custard.
8. Decorate with whipped cream and candied cherries. Refrigerate until serving time.
Makes 8 to 10 servings.

# FROSTINGS AND FILLINGS

## FROSTING THE CAKE

1. Prepare a cake plate or tray that is 2 or 3 inches larger than the cake itself and fairly flat. You can use the traditional cake stand or improvise with what you have at hand. Make sure that the surface of the dish you choose is not so fragile that it will be harmed by a knife cutting down onto it. Cut strips of foil or waxed paper to protect the edge of the plate from dripping frosting.

2. Thoroughly cool both the cake and the frosting before you begin.

3. Use a pastry brush to brush off any loose crumbs, and scissors to trim off any ragged edges. (But remember, the nice thing about frostings is that they cover mistakes.)

4. Invert the cake layer onto the plate. If you're making a layer cake, and the layers are of different thickness, use the thicker one for the bottom layer.

5. Using a flexible metal spatula, spread the top of the layer smoothly with frosting or filling, not quite to the outer edge.

6. Place the next layer, right side up, on top, and if there are to be other layers, frost and repeat. Use wooden picks to anchor the layers if they seem to be sliding and then remove them before frosting the sides and top of the cake.

7. Frost the sides of the cake with a thin coating and then spread the frosting from the top edge down over the sides to completely cover. Swirl the frosting if it's creamy or fluffy.

8. Pile the remaining frosting on the top of the cake and spread it lightly to the edge, swirling as you go.

9. Decorate the top, if you like, with grated chocolate, nuts, or coconut while the frosting is still moist.

10. When the frosting is set, remove the foil or waxed paper from the edge of the plate.

## ❖ COFFEE BUTTER FROSTING

⅓ cup butter or margarine, softened
3½ cups sifted confectioners' sugar
1 tablespoon instant coffee
3 tablespoons hot milk
1 teaspoon vanilla or rum extract, or brandy flavoring

1. In medium bowl, combine butter, sugar, coffee, 2 tablespoons hot milk, and the vanilla.

2. With portable electric mixer at medium speed or with wooden spoon, beat mixture until smooth and fluffy.

3. If frosting seems too thick to spread, gradually beat in a little more hot milk.

Makes enough to fill and frost an 8-inch or 9-inch 2-layer cake.

## ❖ BROILED COCONUT TOPPING

¼ cup butter or margarine, softened
¼ cup light cream
½ cup light-brown sugar, firmly packed
1 cup flaked or shredded coconut

1. In small bowl, combine all ingredients; mix well.

2. Spread evenly over top of hot 8-inch or 9-inch square cake.

3. Run under broiler, 4 inches from heat, 2 to 3 minutes, or until topping is bubbly and golden. Cool cake in pan on wire rack; serve slightly warm.

# ✥ CARAMEL FROSTING

¾ *cup butter or margarine*
1½ *cups light-brown sugar, packed*
½ *cup light cream or evaporated*
  *milk, undiluted*
3 *cups confectioners' sugar*
1½ *teaspoons vanilla extract*

1. Melt butter in small saucepan over low heat. Remove from heat.
2. Add brown sugar, stirring until smooth. Over low heat, bring to boiling, stirring; boil, stirring, 1 minute. Remove from heat.
3. Add cream. Over low heat, return just to boiling. Remove from heat; let cool to 110F on candy thermometer, or until bottom of pan feels lukewarm.
4. With portable electric mixer at medium speed or with wooden spoon, beat in confectioners' sugar until frosting is thick, adding a little more confectioners' sugar if necessary. Add vanilla.
5. Set in bowl of ice water; beat until frosting is thick enough to spread.
Makes enough to fill and frost top and side of an 8-inch or 9-inch 2-layer cake.

# ✥ CHOCOLATE WHIPPED-CREAM FILLING AND FROSTING

2 *cups heavy cream*
1 *cup sifted confectioners' sugar*
½ *cup sifted unsweetened cocoa*
⅛ *teaspoon salt*

1. Combine all ingredients in medium bowl. Refrigerate, covered, 30 minutes.
2. With portable electric mixer at high speed or with rotary beater, beat mixture until stiff. Refrigerate until ready to use.
Makes enough to fill and frost an angel-food or chiffon cake split crosswise into 3 layers; or to spoon over individual slices of angel-food or chiffon cake.

*Mocha Whipped-Cream Filling and Frosting*: Combine 2 tablespoons instant coffee with rest of ingredients.

# ✥ CHOCOLATE SOUR-CREAM FROSTING

1 *pkg (6 oz) semisweet-chocolate*
  *pieces*
½ *cup sour cream*
*Dash salt*

1. Melt chocolate pieces in top of double boiler, over hot water. Remove top of double boiler from hot water.
2. Add sour cream and salt. With portable electric mixer at medium speed or with rotary beater, beat frosting until creamy and of spreading consistency.
Makes enough to frost top and side of an 8-inch or 9-inch 2-layer cake; or top of a 13-by-9-by-2-inch cake; or top and side of a 10-inch tube cake.

*Note*: To make enough frosting to fill and frost an 8-inch or 9-inch 2-layer cake, use 1½ pkg (6-oz size) semisweet-chocolate pieces and ¾ cup sour cream.

# ❖ QUICK FUDGE FROSTING

2 squares unsweetened chocolate
¼ cup butter or margarine, softened
3 cups sifted confectioners' sugar
⅛ teaspoon salt
¼ to ⅓ cup hot light cream
1 teaspoon vanilla extract or ½ teaspoon rum extract

1. Melt chocolate over hot, not boiling, water. Remove from heat; let cool.
2. In medium bowl, combine butter, sugar, salt, and ¼ cup hot cream. With wooden spoon or with portable electric mixer at medium speed, beat until mixture is smooth.
3. Add chocolate; continue beating until frosting is thick enough to spread. Add vanilla.
4. If frosting seems too thick, gradually beat in a little more hot cream.
Makes enough to fill and frost an 8-inch or 9-inch 2-layer cake.

# ❖ CREAM-CHEESE FROSTING

1 pkg (8 oz) cream cheese, softened
1 tablespoon butter or margarine
1 teaspoon vanilla extract
2½ to 3 cups confectioners' sugar

1. In medium bowl, with electric mixer at medium speed, beat cheese with butter and vanilla until creamy.
2. Add confectioners' sugar; beat until light and fluffy. Spread thickly over top of cake; make swirls with knife.
Makes enough to fill and frost an 8-inch 2-layer cake.

# ❖ CHOCOLATE BUTTERCREAM FROSTING

½ cup cold water
4 squares (1-oz size) unsweetened
  chocolate
½ cup butter or margarine
1 egg
2⅔ cups confectioners' sugar
⅓ cup water
1 teaspoon vanilla extract
⅛ teaspoon salt

1. Fill large bowl half full of ice cubes; add ½ cup cold water.
2. In top of double boiler, combine chocolate and butter. Place over hot, not boiling, water, stirring occasionally, until chocolate is melted. Remove from hot water.
3. Quickly stir in egg. Add sugar, ⅓ cup water, the vanilla, and salt; stir until well blended.
4. Place pan in prepared ice water. With portable electric mixer at high speed, beat until of spreading consistency—about 5 minutes.
Makes enough to fill and frost a 9-inch layer cake.

# ✥ BROWNED-BUTTER FROSTING

¼ cup butter
3½ cups sifted confectioners' sugar
4 to 5 tablespoons light cream
1 teaspoon vanilla extract

1. Lightly brown butter in small skillet over low heat. Remove from heat.
2. In medium bowl, combine butter with sugar, 4 tablespoons light cream, and vanilla.
3. With portable electric mixer at medium speed or with wooden spoon, beat until mixture is smooth and fluffy.
4. If frosting seems too thick to spread, beat in a little more cream.
Makes enough to fill and frost an 8-inch or 9-inch 2-layer cake.

# ✥ ORANGE FROSTING

2 tablespoons butter or margarine, softened
2 egg yolks
1 tablespoon grated orange peel
4 cups sifted confectioners' sugar
2 to 3 tablespoons orange juice

1. In small bowl of electric mixer, combine butter, egg yolks, orange peel, sugar, and 2 tablespoons orange juice.
2. With mixer at medium speed, beat until frosting is smooth and easy to spread. If frosting seems too thick to spread, gradually beat in a little more orange juice.
Makes enough to frost top and side of a 10-inch tube cake.

*Orange Glaze*: Prepare half recipe, adding enough orange juice so glaze can be poured over top of cake and run unevenly down sides.

# ✥ SEVEN-MINUTE FROSTING

2 egg whites (¼ cup)
1½ cups granulated sugar
1 tablespoon light corn syrup or ¼ teaspoon cream of tartar
⅓ cup water
1 teaspoon vanilla extract

1. In top of double boiler, combine egg whites, sugar, corn syrup, and water.
2. With portable electric mixer at low speed, or with rotary beater, beat about 1 minute to combine ingredients.
3. Cook over rapidly boiling water (water in bottom should not touch top of double boiler), beating constantly, about 7 minutes, or until stiff peaks form when beater is slowly raised.
4. Remove from boiling water. Add vanilla; continue beating until frosting is thick enough to spread—about 2 minutes.

Makes enough to fill and frost an 8-inch or 9-inch 2-layer cake; or to frost a 13-by-9-by-2-inch sheet cake.

*Seafoam Frosting*: Substitute 1½ cups light-brown sugar, firmly packed, for 1½ cups granulated sugar.

# ❖ LEMON FILLING

*4 egg yolks*
*½ cup sugar*
*¼ cup lemon juice*
*2 teaspoons grated lemon peel*
*1 tablespoon heavy cream*

1. In top of double boiler, with rotary beater, beat egg yolks with sugar until smooth.
2. Stir in lemon juice and peel; cook over boiling water, stirring, 5 to 8 minutes, or until mixture thickens.
3. Remove from heat. Stir in cream; cool.
Makes enough to fill an 8-inch two-layer cake.

# ❖ FRESH-ORANGE FILLING

*¾ cup sugar*
*2½ tablespoons cornstarch*
*⅛ teaspoon salt*
*½ cup orange juice*
*½ cup water*
*2 tablespoons grated orange peel*
*2 tablespoons lemon juice*
*2 tablespoons butter or margarine*

1. In small saucepan, combine sugar with cornstarch and salt.
2. Gradually stir in orange juice and water; over medium heat, bring to boiling, stirring. Boil 1 minute. Remove from heat.
3. Stir in remaining ingredients. Cool well.
Makes enough to fill a 9-inch 3-layer cake.

# ❖ VANILLA-CREAM FILLING

*½ cup sugar*
*¼ cup cornstarch*
*¼ teaspoon salt*
*2 cups milk*
*4 egg yolks, slightly beaten*
*1 teaspoon vanilla extract*

1. In medium saucepan, combine sugar with cornstarch and salt.
2. Gradually add milk; over medium heat, bring to boiling, stirring. Remove from heat.
3. Add half of hot mixture to egg yolks; mix well. Gradually return to saucepan, stirring.
4. Over medium heat, bring to boiling, stirring. Remove from heat. Add vanilla. Cool completely before using to fill cake.
Makes enough to fill a 9-inch 3-layer cake.

*Coconut-Cream Filling*: Add ½ cup flaked coconut and ½ teaspoon almond extract along with vanilla.

*Chocolate-Cream Filling*: Increase sugar to ¾ cup. Combine ¼ cup sifted unsweetened cocoa with sugar, cornstarch, and salt.

# CONFECTIONS

Perhaps you haven't thought of making fudge in a long time, and, indeed, homemade candies are not everyday fare. But they are a lovely treat—and no doubt a surprise to guests —to serve with after-dinner coffee or at an afternoon tea. These are some of our great favorites.

## ❖ HAZELNUT TRUFFLES

¾ cup hazelnuts
6 squares (1-oz size) semisweet chocolate
⅓ cup heavy cream
1⅓ cups confectioners' sugar
1 egg white
1 tablespoon Grand Marnier, Cointreau, or rum

1. Grind hazelnuts in blender or in Mouli grater. Line bottom of 9-by-5-by-3-inch loaf pan with waxed paper.
2. In small heavy saucepan, combine chocolate and cream. Heat over low heat just until chocolate is melted. Remove from heat.
3. In medium bowl, combine nuts, sugar, and egg white. With wooden spoon, stir until combined. Stir in chocolate mixture and liqueur, to combine well.
4. Turn out into prepared pan, or use to fill fluted paper bonbon cups. Refrigerate until firm. Cut into ¾-inch squares. Store, covered, in refrigerator. Makes about 60 pieces.

## ❖ HOLIDAY CHOCOLATE CLUSTERS

1 pkg (6 oz) semisweet-chocolate pieces or 1 cup semisweet-chocolate-flavor pieces
¼ cup light corn syrup
1 tablespoon water
2 cups raisins or salted peanuts (or use half and half)
Cinnamon candies
Angelica

1. In top of double boiler, combine chocolate pieces, corn syrup, and water. Over hot, not boiling, water, melt chocolate.
2. Remove from heat. Add raisins; mix well.
3. Drop by teaspoonfuls onto cookie sheet covered with waxed paper. Top each with 3 candies and 3 angelica slivers to make a flower.
4. Refrigerate to harden chocolate slightly—1 hour. Makes about 30 pieces.

## ❖ ROCKY ROADS

18 large marshmallows
½ cup coarsely chopped walnuts
8 squares (1-oz size) semisweet chocolate

1. Line 9-by-5-by-3-inch loaf pan with waxed paper. Lightly butter waxed paper.
2. Arrange marshmallows over bottom of prepared pan. Sprinkle walnuts on and around marshmallows.
3. In top of double boiler, over hot, not boiling, water, melt chocolate, stirring occasionally.
4. Remove from heat. Pour melted chocolate over marshmallows and nuts, smoothing with spatula. Let cool.

5. When firm, cut into rough squares with sharp knife.

6. To store: Wrap each piece individually in waxed paper or plastic wrap. Will keep several weeks at room temperature.

Makes about 18 (1½-inch) squares.

# ❖ PECAN PRALINES

1 cup granulated sugar
1 cup light-brown sugar, packed
½ cup light cream
1½ cups pecan halves
2 tablespoons butter or margarine

1. In heavy 2-quart saucepan, combine sugars and cream. Over medium heat, bring to boiling, stirring occasionally with wooden spoon. Continue cooking, stirring occasionally, to 228F on candy thermometer, or until syrup spins 2-inch thread when dropped from spoon.

2. Add pecans and butter. Cook over medium heat, stirring frequently, to 236F on candy thermometer, or until a little in cold water forms a soft ball.

3. Remove pan to wire rack. Let cool 10 minutes—to 200F. Stir about 1 minute, or until slightly thick but still glossy.

4. Drop by rounded tablespoonfuls, 3 inches apart, onto sheet of foil or double thickness of waxed paper. Pralines will spread into large patties. If mixture becomes too stiff, stir in a drop or two of cold water.

5. To store: Arrange in layers in plastic refrigerator container or in tin with tight-fitting lid, with waxed paper between layers. Store in cool, dry place. Will keep several weeks.

Makes 12 pieces.

# ❖ PENUCHE

2 cups light-brown sugar, packed
⅔ cup milk
1 tablespoon butter or margarine
1 teaspoon vanilla extract
⅔ cup chopped walnuts

1. Lightly butter 9-by-5-by-3-inch loaf pan. Line with heavy-duty foil; lightly grease foil with butter or margarine.

2. In heavy 3-quart saucepan, mix brown sugar and milk. Cook over low heat, stirring constantly with wooden spoon, until sugar dissolves and mixture comes to boiling.

3. Cook, stirring occasionally, until candy thermometer registers 236F, or a little in cold water forms a soft ball.

4. Remove from heat; add butter. Set aside, without stirring, to cool to lukewarm (110F).

5. With wooden spoon, beat until thick and creamy. Stir in vanilla and nuts.

6. Quickly turn out into prepared loaf pan. Cool completely; refrigerate.

7. Turn out of pan in one block. Discard foil. Cut into pieces.

Makes 24 pieces.

# ✦ DIVINITY FUDGE

*3 egg whites (⅓ cup)*
*3 cups sugar*
*⅔ cup light corn syrup*
*¾ cup water*
*¼ teaspoon salt*
*1 teaspoon vanilla extract*
*1 cup coarsely chopped pecans or*
*walnuts*
*6 candied cherries, quartered*
*12 pecan or walnut halves*
*6 candied cherries, halved*

1. Place egg whites in large bowl of electric mixer; let warm to room temperature—about 1 hour. Line 11-by-7-by-1½-inch pan with waxed paper.
2. In heavy 3-quart saucepan, combine sugar and corn syrup with ¾ cup water. Cook, stirring, over low heat, to dissolve sugar. Cover; cook 1 minute longer to dissolve sugar crystals on side of pan.
3. Uncover; bring to boiling, without stirring. Cook to 260F on candy thermometer, or until a little in cold water forms a ball hard enough to hold its shape. Let cool slightly.
4. When candy thermometer goes down to 250F, with portable electric mixer at high speed, beat egg whites with salt until stiff peaks form when beater is slowly raised.
5. Gradually pour hot syrup over egg whites in thin stream, beating constantly at high speed until stiff peaks form when beater is raised—5 minutes.
6. Using wooden spoon, beat in vanilla, pecans, and quartered cherries. Continue beating until mixture is stiff enough to hold its shape and looks dull.
7. Turn out into prepared pan. Do not scrape saucepan. Let mixture stand until firm. With sharp knife, cut into squares. Top each with cherry half or pecan. Makes 24 pieces.

*Note*: Divinity may be kept for at least a week if wrapped in waxed paper and stored in closed container.

# ✦ PEANUT-BUTTER CARAMELS

*1 cup light corn syrup*
*1 cup sugar*
*½ cup heavy cream*
*½ cup chunky peanut butter*

1. Line 9-by-5-by-3-inch loaf pan with foil. Lightly butter foil. In heavy 2-quart saucepan, combine corn syrup and sugar.
2. Bring to boiling, stirring constantly. Over medium heat, cook, uncovered and stirring frequently, to 245F on candy thermometer, or until syrup dropped into very cold water forms a ball that flattens on removal from water.
3. Gradually stir in cream and peanut butter; mixture should not stop boiling.
4. Over medium heat, cook, stirring constantly, until mixture returns to 245F.
5. Remove from heat. Turn out into prepared pan; let cool.
6. Turn out of pan; remove foil. With sharp knife, cut into pieces. Wrap each individually in waxed paper. Keep refrigerated.
Makes 24 pieces.

## ❖ SUGAR-PLUMS

*1 can (8 oz) almond paste, crumbled*
*1 cup flaked coconut*
*¼ cup light corn syrup*
*¼ cup chopped candied cherries*
*1 pkg (12 oz) pitted dried prunes*
*Sugar*

1. In small bowl, combine almond paste, coconut, corn syrup, and cherries; mix well.
2. With sharp knife, make lengthwise slit in each prune. Force open and fill each with about 2 teaspoons almond-paste mixture. Close prunes partially, leaving about ½ inch of filling showing.
3. Roll each prune in sugar. Pack in tightly covered container, and refrigerate. Prunes will keep several weeks. Reroll in sugar before serving.
Makes about 40 pieces.

## ❖ CHOCOLATE FUDGE DELUXE

*3 cups sugar*
*1 env unflavored gelatine*
*1 cup milk*
*½ cup light corn syrup*
*3 squares (1-oz size) unsweetened chocolate*
*1¼ cups butter or margarine*
*2 teaspoons vanilla extract*
*1 cup coarsely chopped walnuts*

1. Butter 8-by-8-by-2-inch pan.
2. In 3½-quart saucepan, mix sugar with dry gelatine. Add milk, corn syrup, chocolate, and butter.
3. Cook over medium heat, stirring frequently, to 238F on candy thermometer, or until a little in cold water forms a soft ball that flattens when removed from water.
4. Remove from heat; pour into large mixing bowl. Stir in vanilla. Cool 25 minutes.
5. Beat with wooden spoon until candy thickens. Stir in walnuts. Spread in prepared pan. Let cool; then cut into squares.
Makes about 36 pieces.

## ❖ SUGARED NUTS

*2 cups light-brown sugar, packed*
*1 cup granulated sugar*
*1 cup sour cream*
*2 teaspoons vanilla extract*
*2 cups walnut halves*
*1 cup pecans*
*1 cup unblanched almonds*

1. Combine both kinds of sugar and the sour cream in large saucepan. Cook over medium heat, stirring, until sugar is dissolved.
2. Continue cooking, without stirring, to 238F on candy thermometer, or until a little in cold water forms a soft ball. Remove from heat.
3. Add vanilla and nuts. Stir gently until all nuts are coated.
4. Turn out onto waxed paper; with fork, separate nuts. Let dry.
Makes about 2 pounds.

# COOKIES

✦ Cookie stores have sprung up all over the country, attesting to the American passion for these little sweets. Chocolate cookies, oatmeal cookies, butter cookies, are all loved not only by children but by adults as well.

In this chapter there are drop cookies to be spooned onto a baking sheet that will produce soft cookies or crisp cookies, depending on the recipe. There are refrigerator cookies that are ready to slice and bake whenever you need them, cut-out cookies to make into a myriad of shapes, molded cookies to use in a cookie press, and elegant bar cookies that are akin to rich cakes. The cookies that follow include the all-time favorites, cookies from other nations, and special holiday treats.

## COOKIE HINTS

1. Occasionally a delicate cookie will call for sifted all-purpose flour; this means flour should be sifted before measuring.
2. Bright, shiny baking sheets, or the back of any large baking pan, will produce the best cookies. Be sure the pans are at least an inch shorter and narrower than your oven.
3. To bake one sheet of cookies at a time, have the oven rack centered in the oven; for two sheets, place the racks to divide the oven into thirds. If the cookies on the bottom rack aren't browning enough on top, move them to the upper rack for the last few minutes of baking.
4. Check cookies when the minimum baking time is up. Remove from the pan with a spatula; cool on wire racks.
5. Store soft cookies in a container with a tight-fitting lid. Slip a slice of apple, placed on waxed paper, in the container to keep the cookies moist. Store crisp cookies in a container with a loose-fitting lid. If they show signs of limpness, recrisp them in a 300F oven for 5 minutes. Bar cookies keep best in their own baking pan, covered and refrigerated.
6. A batch of ready-to-bake cookie dough is nice to have in the freezer. Drop- or rolled-cookie dough is best packed in a freezer container. Thaw dough in the refrigerator until it's easy to handle. Refrigerator cookie dough can be frozen in the roll, wrapped in foil or plastic wrap. To use, cut frozen dough into slices. All baked cookies can be frozen. Wrap or store in freezer containers. Let thaw 15 minutes at room temperature before eating.

## ✦ APPLE-WALNUT DROP COOKIES

*3 cups sifted all-purpose flour*
*1½ teaspoons baking soda*
*¾ cup soft shortening*
*2 cups light-brown sugar, packed*
*¾ teaspoon salt*
*1½ teaspoons ground cinnamon*
*1½ teaspoons ground cloves*
*¾ teaspoon ground nutmeg*
*2 eggs, unbeaten*
*1½ cups chopped walnuts*
*1½ cups finely chopped unpared*
  *apple*
*1½ cups dark raisins, chopped*
*⅓ cup apple juice or milk*

1. Preheat oven to 400F. Lightly grease cookie sheets.
2. Sift flour with baking soda. With portable electric beater at medium speed or with wooden spoon, mix shortening, sugar, salt, cinnamon, cloves, nutmeg, and eggs until well blended.
3. Stir in half of flour mixture, then nuts, apple, and raisins. Blend in apple juice, then the remaining flour mixture.
4. Drop by rounded tablespoonfuls, 2 inches apart, onto cookie sheets.
5. Bake 11 to 14 minutes, or until done.
6. Make Glaze: In small bowl combine all ingredients. Mix well.
7. While cookies are still hot, spread thinly with glaze. Decorate with bits of apple, if desired.
Makes 3½ to 4 dozen.

**GLAZE:**

2 cups sifted confectioners' sugar
1½ tablespoons butter or margarine,
  softened
½ teaspoon vanilla extract
¼ teaspoon salt
¼ cup milk

# ❖ CHOCOLATE-CHIP COOKIES

1¼ cups sifted all-purpose flour
½ teaspoon baking soda
½ teaspoon salt
½ cup granulated sugar
¼ cup light-brown sugar, firmly
  packed
1 egg
1 teaspoon vanilla extract
½ cup butter or margarine, softened
½ cup coarsely chopped walnuts
1 pkg (6 oz) semisweet-chocolate
  pieces

1. Preheat oven to 375F.
2. Into large bowl, sift flour with baking soda and salt.
3. Add sugars, egg, vanilla, and butter. With wooden spoon or with portable electric mixer at medium speed, beat until smooth and well combined—about 1 minute.
4. Stir in walnuts and chocolate pieces.
5. Drop by teaspoonfuls, 2 inches apart, onto ungreased cookie sheets.
6. Bake 10 to 12 minutes, or until golden. Remove to wire rack; cool.
Makes about 4 dozen.

# ❖ CHOCOLATE HEART COOKIES

2 cups unsifted all-purpose flour
⅔ cup unsweetened cocoa
½ teaspoon salt
½ teaspoon baking soda
1 cup butter or margarine, softened
1½ cups sugar
2 eggs
1 teaspoon vanilla extract

1. Sift flour with cocoa, salt, and baking soda; set aside.
2. In large bowl of electric mixer, combine butter, sugar, eggs, and vanilla extract. Beat at medium speed until smooth and well blended.
3. Add flour mixture, a small amount at a time, beating at low speed after each addition. Refrigerate, covered, 1 hour.
4. Preheat oven to 350F. Lightly grease cookie sheet.
5. Remove dough from refrigerator. Divide dough in half. On lightly floured board or pastry cloth, roll dough, half at a time, ⅛ inch thick.
6. With 3¼-inch heart-shaped cookie cutter, cut out cookies.
7. Place, 2 inches apart, on prepared cookie sheet. Bake 8 to 10 minutes, or until cookies are just set. Remove to rack; cool completely.
Makes about 3½ dozen.

# ❖ OLD-FASHIONED MOLASSES DROP CAKES

2½ cups unsifted all-purpose flour
1 teaspoon baking soda
¼ teaspoon salt
¼ teaspoon ground cloves
1 teaspoon ground cinnamon
1 teaspoon ground ginger
½ cup shortening
½ cup sugar
1 egg
¾ cup molasses
½ cup sour milk (see Note)
½ cup dark raisins
Confectioners' sugar

1. Preheat oven to 350F. Lightly grease cookie sheets.
2. Sift flour, baking soda, salt, cloves, cinnamon, and ginger.
3. In large bowl, with electric mixer at medium speed or with wooden spoon, beat shortening, sugar, egg, and molasses until light and fluffy.
4. Add flour mixture and sour milk; beat with wooden spoon until well blended. Stir in raisins. Drop dough, about 3 inches apart, onto prepared cookie sheets, 1 tablespoon at a time.
5. Bake 10 minutes, or until tops feel firm when gently touched. Let cookies stand about 1 minute. Then remove to wire rack; let cool completely. Sift confectioners' sugar over tops.
Makes 3 dozen.

Note: Measure 1½ teaspoons white vinegar into glass measuring cup. Add milk to measure ½ cup. Stir. Let stand a few minutes before using.

# ❖ MACAROONS

2 egg whites
1½ cups blanched almonds, ground
1 cup sifted confectioners' sugar
¼ teaspoon salt
1 teaspoon almond extract
½ teaspoon vanilla extract
Blanched almonds

1. In large bowl of electric mixer, let egg whites warm to room temperature—about 1 hour.
2. Preheat oven to 300F. Lightly grease cookie sheets.
3. In medium bowl, combine ground almonds and sugar, mixing well.
4. Beat egg whites, at high speed, with salt until stiff peaks form when beaters are slowly raised. Using wooden spoon, stir almond mixture into beaten egg whites, along with almond and vanilla extracts, just until well combined.
5. Drop by slightly rounded teaspoonfuls, 2 inches apart, onto prepared cookie sheets. Top each with blanched almond.
6. Bake 20 minutes, or until a light-brown color. With spatula, remove to wire rack to cool completely.
7. Store, covered, overnight.
Makes 2½ to 3 dozen.

# ❖ CINNAMON STARS

⅓ cup egg whites (about 2 egg whites)
1¼ cups granulated sugar
1½ cups unblanched almonds,
   ground
1½ tablespoons cinnamon
1 cup sifted confectioners' sugar
2 tablespoons water

1. In small bowl of electric mixer, let egg whites warm to room temperature—about 1 hour.
2. With electric mixer at medium speed, beat egg whites until soft peaks form when beater is raised.
3. Add 1¼ cups granulated sugar to egg whites, 2 tablespoons at a time, beating after each addition. Continue to beat until mixture is thick and glossy—about 10 minutes.
4. In medium bowl, combine almonds with cinnamon. Stir in egg-white mixture; mix to combine well.
5. Refrigerate dough, covered, overnight.
6. Lightly sprinkle wooden board or pastry cloth with flour and granulated sugar. Roll out dough, one half at a time, ¼ inch thick.
7. Using 3-inch star cookie cutter, cut out cookies. Place, 1 inch apart, on lightly greased cookie sheets.
8. Let stand, uncovered, at room temperature 2 hours.
9. Preheat oven to 300F. In small bowl, combine confectioners' sugar and water; mix until smooth.
10. Bake cookies 20 minutes. Brush tops with glaze; bake 5 minutes longer.
11. Remove cookie sheets to wire racks; let cookies cool several minutes. With spatula, carefully remove cookies to wire racks to cool completely.
Makes about 2½ dozen.

# ❖ LEBKUCHEN HEARTS

3 cups sifted all-purpose flour
½ teaspoon baking soda
½ teaspoon salt
1 teaspoon ground allspice
1 teaspoon ground nutmeg
1 teaspoon ground cinnamon
1 teaspoon ground cloves
1 jar (4 oz) citron (see Note), finely
   chopped
1 can (4 oz) walnuts, finely chopped
1 cup honey
¾ cup light-brown sugar, packed
1 egg
1 tablespoon lemon juice
2 teaspoons grated lemon peel

1. Sift flour with baking soda, salt, and spices. Toss citron with walnuts.
2. Warm honey in small saucepan; remove from heat.
3. In large bowl, with portable electric mixer at medium speed, beat sugar and egg until smooth and fluffy.
4. Add lemon juice and honey; beat well. Beat in lemon peel and 1 cup flour mixture; beat until smooth.
5. Using wooden spoon, stir in rest of flour mixture until well combined. Stir in citron-nut mixture.
6. Refrigerate dough, covered, overnight.
7. Next day, preheat oven to 375F. Lightly grease 2 cookie sheets.
8. On lightly floured surface, roll out dough, one half at a time, ¼ inch thick. (Refrigerate remaining half until ready to roll out.)

## GLAZE:

*2 cups sifted confectioners' sugar*
*3 tablespoons water*

*Candied cherry and angelica bits (optional)*
*Unblanched almonds (optional)*

9. Using floured 2-inch heart or round cookie cutter, cut out cookies. Place, 2 inches apart, on prepared cookie sheet; bake 12 minutes. Remove to wire rack; cool slightly.
10. Make Glaze: Combine confectioners' sugar and water; stir until smooth.
11. Brush glaze on warm cookies. Decorate with candied-cherry and angelica bits and unblanched almonds, if desired. Let cookies cool completely.
12. Store, tightly covered, in cool, dry place two to three weeks before using. To keep cookies moist, keep slice of bread in container, changing bread occasionally, to prevent molding.
Makes 3 dozen.

*Note*: Or use ½ cup finely chopped mixed candied fruit.

# ❖ OLD-FASHIONED FILLED COOKIES

## COOKIE DOUGH:

*3 cups sifted all-purpose flour*
*1 teaspoon baking powder*
*½ teaspoon salt*
*¾ cup butter or margarine, softened*
*1½ cups sugar*
*2 eggs*
*1 teaspoon vanilla extract or 1 tablespoon grated lemon peel*

## FILLING:

*1 pkg (8 oz) pitted dates, cut up*
*½ cup sugar*
*½ cup water*
*1 teaspoon grated lemon peel*
*¼ cup lemon juice*
*½ cup coarsely chopped walnuts*

1. Sift flour with baking powder and salt; set aside.
2. In large bowl, with wooden spoon or with portable electric mixer at medium speed, beat butter, sugar, eggs, and vanilla until light and fluffy.
3. Gradually stir in flour mixture until smooth and well combined.
4. Using rubber spatula, form dough into ball. Wrap in waxed paper or foil; refrigerate several hours or overnight.
5. Divide dough into 4 parts; refrigerate until ready to use.
6. Meanwhile, make Filling: In small saucepan, combine dates, sugar, and water. Cook over medium heat, stirring, until mixture has thickened—about 5 minutes. Remove from heat. Stir in lemon peel, lemon juice, and walnuts. Cool completely.
7. Preheat oven to 375F. Lightly grease cookie sheets.
8. On lightly floured surface, roll dough, one part at a time, ⅛ inch thick. With floured 2½-inch plain or scalloped round cookie cutter, cut out cookies. Reroll trimmings, and cut.
9. Using spatula, place half the cookies, 2 inches apart, on cookie sheets. Spread 1 teaspoon filling over each cookie; cover with another cookie. With floured fork, seal edges firmly; also prick center of top.
10. Bake 10 to 12 minutes, or until lightly browned. Remove to wire rack; cool.
Makes 3 dozen.

# ✖ OLD-FASHIONED SUGAR COOKIES

4 cups sifted all-purpose flour
1 teaspoon baking powder
½ teaspoon baking soda
½ teaspoon salt
½ teaspoon nutmeg
1 cup butter or margarine, softened
1½ cups sugar
1 egg
½ cup sour cream
1 teaspoon vanilla extract

## TOPPING:

¼ cup sugar
Raisins or blanched almonds (optional)

1. Sift flour with baking powder, baking soda, salt, and nutmeg; set aside.
2. In large bowl of electric mixer, at medium speed, beat butter, sugar, and egg until light and fluffy.
3. At low speed, beat in sour cream and vanilla until smooth.
4. Gradually add flour mixture, beating until well combined.
5. With rubber spatula, form dough into ball. Wrap in waxed paper or foil; refrigerate several hours, or overnight.
6. Divide dough into four parts. Refrigerate until ready to roll out.
7. Meanwhile, preheat oven to 375F. Lightly grease cookie sheets.
8. On well-floured surface, roll dough, one part at a time, ¼ inch thick.
9. With floured 2½-inch plain or scalloped round cookie cutter, cut out cookies. Using spatula, place, 2 inches apart, on cookie sheets.
10. Sprinkle tops of cookies with sugar. Place raisin or almond in center of each, if desired. Reroll trimmings, and cut.
11. Bake 10 to 12 minutes, or until golden. Remove to wire rack; cool. Store in tightly covered tin.
Makes 4 dozen.

# ✖ CHOCOLATE-KISS PEANUT-BUTTER COOKIES

2⅔ cups sifted all-purpose flour
2 teaspoons baking soda
1 teaspoon salt
1 cup butter or margarine, softened
⅔ cup creamy peanut butter, at room temperature
Granulated sugar
1 cup brown sugar, firmly packed
2 eggs
2 teaspoons vanilla extract
5 dozen foil-wrapped chocolate kisses

1. Preheat oven to 375F. Sift flour with baking soda and salt. Set aside.
2. In large bowl, with electric mixer at medium speed, beat butter and peanut butter until well blended. Add 1 cup granulated sugar and the brown sugar; beat until light and fluffy.
3. Add eggs and vanilla; beat until smooth. Stir in flour mixture until well combined.
4. Using level tablespoonful for each, shape into 5 dozen balls. Roll each in granulated sugar. Place, 2 inches apart, on ungreased cookie sheets.
5. Bake 8 minutes. Remove from oven. Press an unwrapped chocolate kiss into top of each; bake 2 minutes longer. Remove cookies to wire rack; let cool completely.
Makes 5 dozen.

# ✠ BUTTERSCOTCH ICEBOX COOKIES

3½ cups sifted all-purpose flour
1 teaspoon baking soda
½ teaspoon salt
1 cup butter or margarine, softened
2 cups light-brown sugar, firmly packed
2 eggs
1 teaspoon vanilla extract
1 cup finely chopped walnuts or pecans

1. Sift flour with baking soda and salt; set aside.
2. In large bowl of electric mixer, at medium speed, beat butter until light. Gradually beat in sugar. Add eggs and vanilla; continue beating until very light and fluffy.
3. At low speed, beat in half of flour mixture until smooth. Mix in rest with hands to form stiff dough. Add nuts, mixing to combine well.
4. Turn out dough onto lightly floured surface. Divide in thirds. With hands, shape each third into roll 8 inches long.
5. Wrap each in plastic wrap or foil. Refrigerate until firm—about 8 hours or overnight—before slicing and baking. (Rolls may be stored in refrigerator a week or 10 days. Bake fresh as desired.)
6. Preheat oven to 375F. With sharp knife, cut as many ⅛-inch slices as desired for baking at one time. Rewrap rest of roll; refrigerate.
7. Place slices, 2 inches apart, on ungreased cookie sheets. Bake 7 to 10 minutes, or until lightly browned. Remove to wire rack; cool. Cookies should be crisp.
Makes about 16 dozen in all.

# ✠ CHOCOLATE-DIPPED BUTTER COOKIES

2⅓ cups sifted all-purpose flour
¼ teaspoon salt
1 cup butter or margarine, softened
⅔ cup sugar
1 egg yolk
1 teaspoon vanilla extract
1 cup finely chopped unblanched almonds

## CHOCOLATE DIP:

1 pkg (6 oz) semisweet-chocolate pieces
3 tablespoons butter or margarine
1 tablespoon hot water

Chopped almonds, chocolate shot, or multicolor nonpareils

1. Sift flour with salt; set aside.
2. In large bowl, with wooden spoon or electric mixer at medium speed, beat butter, sugar, egg yolk, and vanilla until light and fluffy.
3. Gradually stir in flour mixture and 1 cup almonds, mixing until well blended.
4. With hands, shape dough into two rolls 1½ inches in diameter. Wrap in foil or plastic wrap. Refrigerate until firm—about 2 hours.
5. Preheat oven to 350F. Lightly grease cookie sheets. With sharp knife, cut into slices ¼ inch thick. Place cookies, 1 inch apart, on prepared cookie sheets.
6. Bake 8 to 10 minutes, or until lightly browned. Remove to rack; cool.
7. Make Chocolate Dip: In small saucepan, over low heat, melt chocolate and butter; add hot water.
8. Dip half of each cooled cookie into chocolate mixture. Sprinkle with chopped almonds, chocolate shot, or multicolor nonpareils.
Makes 6 dozen.

# ❖ APRICOT PINWHEELS

## FILLING:

1 pkg (8 oz) dried apricots, finely
   chopped
½ cup sugar
½ cup water
¼ cup chopped walnuts or pecans

## COOKIE DOUGH:

2 cups unsifted all-purpose flour
½ teaspoon salt
½ teaspoon baking soda
½ cup butter or margarine, softened
1 cup sugar
1 egg
½ teaspoon vanilla extract

1. Make Filling: In small saucepan, combine apricots, ½ cup sugar, and the water. Cook, stirring constantly, 5 minutes, or until thickened. Remove from heat; stir in nuts. Cool completely.
2. Make Cookie Dough: Sift flour with salt and baking soda.
3. In small bowl of electric mixer, at medium speed, beat butter, sugar, egg, and vanilla until light and fluffy.
4. At low speed, beat in flour mixture just until combined. Divide dough into 4 parts.
5. Roll out dough, one fourth at a time, between 2 sheets of waxed paper to form 8-by-6-inch rectangle. Spread each with one fourth of filling.
6. From wide end, roll up rectangles tightly. Wrap each in waxed paper; refrigerate 2 hours or overnight, until firm.
7. Preheat oven to 375F. Slice cookies about ¼ inch thick. Arrange, 1 inch apart, on lightly greased cookie sheets. Bake 6 minutes, or until golden.
Makes 8 dozen.

# ❖ ALMOND LACE WAFERS

½ cup ground blanched almonds
½ cup butter or margarine
½ cup sugar
1 tablespoon flour
2 tablespoons milk

1. Preheat oven to 375F. Grease generously and flour well 2 cookie sheets.
2. Combine all ingredients in small saucepan. Cook, stirring and over low heat, until butter melts.
3. Drop by teaspoonfuls, 4 inches apart, onto cookie sheets. (Bake only 4 or 5 at a time.)
4. Bake 6 minutes, or until cookies are light brown and centers are bubbling. Let stand 1 minute.
5. Working quickly, roll each wafer around handle of wooden spoon.
6. Gently slide cookie off handle. Place, seam side down, on wire rack; cool. If cookies become too crisp to roll, return to oven for a minute or two.
7. Regrease and reflour cookie sheets before baking each batch.
Makes about 2 dozen.

# ALMOND TILE COOKIES

*⅓ cup egg whites (2 to 3 eggs)*
*½ cup sugar*
*¼ teaspoon vanilla extract*
*3 tablespoons butter or margarine, melted*
*3 tablespoons flour*
*½ cup sliced blanched almonds*

1. Preheat oven to 375F. Grease large cookie sheet with salad oil, and dust with flour (omit if using pan with nonstick coating).
2. In medium bowl, combine egg whites, sugar, and vanilla; with wire whisk or with portable electric mixer at high speed, beat about 2 minutes, or until sugar is dissolved and mixture is syrupy.
3. Add butter and flour; beat until smooth. Stir in almonds.
4. Drop by ½ teaspoonfuls, about 4 inches apart, onto prepared cookie sheet. With small spatula, spread each to 1½-inch round. Make no more than 8 at a time.
5. Bake 5 minutes, or until cookies are golden-brown around edge and very lightly browned in center.
6. With small spatula, carefully remove cookies at once, and place over rolling pin to curve them. (If cookies get too cool, return to oven just until hot and soft again.)
7. Repeat with remaining batter, oiling and flouring cookie sheet each time.

Makes about 5 dozen.

# GINGER CRINKLES

*2 cups sifted all-purpose flour*
*1 tablespoon baking soda*
*¼ teaspoon salt*
*1 teaspoon ground cloves*
*1 teaspoon ground cinnamon*
*1 teaspoon ground ginger*
*1⅓ cups sugar*
*¾ cup shortening*
*¼ cup light molasses*
*1 egg, slightly beaten*

1. Preheat oven to 350F.
2. Sift flour with baking soda, salt, cloves, cinnamon, and ginger; set aside.
3. In large bowl of electric mixer, at medium speed, gradually add 1 cup sugar to shortening, creaming until very light and fluffy—about 5 minutes. Blend in molasses and egg.
4. At low speed, beat in flour mixture just until well combined, scraping down side of bowl with rubber spatula. Refrigerate 1 hour.
5. Shape dough into 1-inch balls; roll in remaining ⅓ cup sugar.
6. Place, 2 inches apart, on ungreased cookie sheets. Bake 8 to 10 minutes (no longer), or until golden brown. Let stand 1 minute before removing to wire rack to cool.

Makes about 4 dozen.

# ❖ JEWEL COOKIES

½ cup butter or margarine, softened
¼ cup light-brown sugar, firmly
    packed
1 egg yolk
1 teaspoon vanilla extract
1 cup sifted all-purpose flour
1 egg white, slightly beaten
1 cup finely chopped walnuts or pe-
    cans
2 tablespoons currant jelly

1. In medium bowl, with wooden spoon or with portable electric mixer at medium speed, beat butter, sugar, egg yolk, and vanilla until smooth.
2. Stir in flour just until combined. Refrigerate 30 minutes.
3. Meanwhile, preheat oven to 375F. Using hands, roll dough into balls 1 inch in diameter. Dip in egg white; then roll in walnuts.
4. Place, 1 inch apart, on ungreased cookie sheets. With floured thimble or thumb, press center of each cookie.
5. Bake 10 to 12 minutes, or until delicate golden-brown. Remove to wire rack; cool.
6. Place ¼ teaspoon jelly in center of each cookie. (Diced candied fruit may be used, instead of jelly, if desired.)
Makes 2 dozen.

# ❖ OATMEAL-RAISIN COOKIES

1½ cups sifted all-purpose flour
1 teaspoon baking soda
1 teaspoon salt
1 cup shortening
1 cup granulated sugar
1 cup light-brown sugar, firmly
    packed
2 eggs
1 teaspoon vanilla extract
3 cups raw quick-cooking oats (not
    instant)
1 cup seedless raisins

1. Preheat oven to 375F. Lightly grease cookie sheets.
2. Sift flour, baking soda, and salt.
3. In large bowl, with wooden spoon or with electric mixer at medium speed, beat shortening, sugars, eggs, and vanilla until light and fluffy.
4. Add flour mixture and oats; beat with wooden spoon until well blended. Stir in raisins.
5. With hands, roll into balls, using slightly rounded tablespoonful for each. Place, 2 inches apart, on prepared cookie sheets.
6. Bake 12 to 14 minutes, or until golden-brown. Let stand 1 minute; then remove to wire rack to cool.
Makes about 2½ dozen.

# ❖ NORWEGIAN CHRISTMAS COOKIES

*2 egg yolks*
*½ cup butter or margarine, softened*
*¼ cup granulated sugar*
*1½ cups sifted all-purpose flour*
*¼ cup heavy cream*
*1 egg white, slightly beaten*
*10 sugar cubes, crushed*

1. Gently drop egg yolks into boiling water. Simmer, uncovered, 20 minutes; drain.
2. Preheat oven to 350F. Lightly grease cookie sheets.
3. In medium bowl, with wooden spoon or electric mixer at low speed, beat butter and granulated sugar until smooth and fluffy.
4. Add hot hard-cooked egg yolks; beat until well combined.
5. Stir in flour, alternately with cream; mix until smooth.
6. On lightly floured pastry cloth or surface, with palms of hands, roll dough into 1-inch balls, then into strips 4 inches long. Cross the ends.
7. Place, 1 inch apart, on prepared cookie sheets. Brush with egg white; sprinkle with crushed sugar.
8. Bake 20 to 25 minutes, or until golden-brown. Remove to wire rack to cool.
Makes 2 dozen.

# ❖ PECAN CRESCENTS

*2 cups unsifted all-purpose flour*
*1 cup butter or margarine, softened*
*1 cup ground pecans or hazelnuts*
*½ cup unsifted confectioners' sugar*
*⅛ teaspoon salt*
*1 teaspoon vanilla extract*
*¼ teaspoon almond extract*

## VANILLA SUGAR:

*3-inch strip vanilla bean, cut up*
*2 cups sifted confectioners' sugar*

1. In large bowl, combine flour, butter, nuts, ½ cup sugar, the salt, and extracts. Mix, with hands, until thoroughly combined. Refrigerate, covered, 1 hour.
2. Make Vanilla Sugar: In electric blender, combine vanilla bean and ¼ cup confectioners' sugar. Cover and blend at high speed about 8 seconds. Combine with remaining confectioners' sugar on large sheet of foil.
3. Preheat oven to 375F.
4. Shape cookies: Form dough into balls, using 1 tablespoon dough for each. Then, with palms of hands, form each ball into roll 3 inches long.
5. Place, 2 inches apart, on ungreased cookie sheets. Curve each to make crescent. Bake 12 to 15 minutes, or until set but not brown.
6. Let stand 1 minute before removing. With spatula, place hot cookies in vanilla sugar; turn gently to coat both sides. Cool completely.
7. Store in tightly covered crock or cookie tin in cool, dry place.
8. Just before serving, coat with additional vanilla sugar, if desired.
Makes about 3½ dozen.

# ✛ SPRITZ COOKIES

2 cups sifted all-purpose flour
¼ teaspoon salt
¾ cup butter or margarine, softened
½ cup sugar
1 egg yolk
1 teaspoon vanilla extract or ½ teaspoon almond extract
Cinnamon candies, angelica, or miniature multicolor nonpareils (optional)

1. Refrigerate ungreased cookie sheets until ready to use.
2. Preheat oven to 375F. Sift flour with salt. Set aside.
3. In large bowl of electric mixer, at medium speed, beat butter, sugar, egg yolk, and vanilla until smooth and fluffy.
4. At low speed, beat in flour mixture until smooth and well combined. Fill cookie press with dough.
5. Force through cookie press onto chilled cookie sheet. Cookies should be 1½ inches apart. Decorate with cinnamon candies, angelica, or miniature multicolor nonpareils, if desired.
6. Bake cookies 8 to 10 minutes, or until light golden. Remove to rack; cool. Store in airtight container. Makes 3 dozen.

# ✛ CHOCOLATE FUDGE BROWNIES

½ cup sifted all-purpose flour
⅛ teaspoon baking powder
⅛ teaspoon salt
½ cup butter, softened
1 cup sugar
2 eggs
2 squares unsweetened chocolate, melted
½ teaspoon vanilla extract
1 cup chopped walnuts

1. Preheat oven to 325F. Lightly grease 8-by-8-by-2-inch baking pan.
2. Sift flour with baking powder and salt.
3. In small bowl of electric mixer, at high speed, beat butter with sugar until light and fluffy; beat in eggs, one at a time, until very light—about 10 minutes. Beat in melted chocolate and vanilla.
4. At low speed, blend in flour mixture just until combined. Stir in nuts.
5. Turn out into prepared pan, spreading evenly. Bake 30 minutes.
6. Cool 10 minutes. With sharp knife, cut into 2-inch squares. Let cool completely in pan.
Makes 16.

Tea Brownies: Preheat oven to 325F. Lightly grease 2 (8-by-8-by-2-inch) baking pans. Prepare brownies as in Steps 2–4 above. Divide into prepared pans, spreading evenly. Bake 20 minutes. Cool 10 minutes. With sharp knife, cut into 2-inch squares. Let cool completely in pans.
Makes about 2½ dozen.

Note: By using two pans, the brownies are thinner and more suitable to serve with tea.

## ❖ DATE-WALNUT BARS

¾ cup unsifted all-purpose flour
1 teaspoon baking powder
½ teaspoon salt
2 eggs
1 cup light-brown sugar, packed
1 cup sliced dates
1 cup coarsely chopped walnuts
1 teaspoon vanilla extract
Confectioners' sugar

1. Preheat oven to 350F. Lightly grease and line bottom of 9-by-9-by-2-inch baking pan with waxed paper.
2. Sift flour with baking powder and salt; set aside.
3. In medium bowl, with electric mixer at medium speed or with wire whisk, beat eggs until light.
4. Gradually add brown sugar, beating until smooth and fluffy.
5. Add dates, nuts, and vanilla; mix thoroughly. Stir in dry ingredients; mix well. Spread in prepared pan.
6. Bake 25 to 30 minutes, or until surface springs back when lightly pressed with fingertip.
7. Cool slightly. Remove from pan to wire rack; peel off waxed paper.
8. With sharp knife, cut into 24 bars while still warm. To serve, roll in confectioners' sugar.
Makes 2 dozen.

## ❖ TOFFEE BARS

### COOKIE CRUST:

½ cup butter or margarine, softened
½ cup light-brown sugar, firmly packed
1 egg yolk
1 teaspoon vanilla extract
½ cup sifted all-purpose flour
½ cup raw quick-cooking oats (not instant)

### TOPPING:

3 squares semisweet chocolate
1 tablespoon butter or margarine
½ cup coarsely chopped walnuts or pecans

1. Preheat oven to 375F. Lightly grease 13-by-9-by-2-inch pan.
2. Make Cookie Crust: In large bowl, with wooden spoon or with portable electric mixer at medium speed, beat butter, sugar, egg yolk, and vanilla until smooth.
3. Add flour and oats; stir to combine well.
4. Press mixture evenly into bottom of prepared pan.
5. Bake 15 minutes, or until golden. Cool slightly.
6. Make Topping: In small saucepan, melt chocolate and butter over hot, not boiling, water.
7. Spread over warm cookie crust; sprinkle with nuts.
8. With sharp knife, cut into bars while still warm. Let cool completely in pan.
Makes 2 dozen.

## ❖ WALNUT BARS

### COOKIE CRUST:

¼ cup butter or margarine, softened
¼ cup light-brown sugar, packed
½ cup unsifted all-purpose flour

1. Preheat oven to 350F. Make Cookie Crust: In small bowl, with wooden spoon or with portable electric mixer at medium speed, cream butter with ¼ cup brown sugar until fluffy. Stir in ½ cup flour until mixture is smooth.

**WALNUT FILLING:**

*1 egg*
*½ cup light-brown sugar, packed*
*½ teaspoon vanilla extract*
*½ tablespoon flour*
*Dash salt*
*⅛ teaspoon baking powder*
*¾ cup chopped walnuts*

2. Press evenly into bottom of 8-by-8-by-2-inch baking pan; bake 10 minutes, or just until golden. Let cool.
3. Make Walnut Filling: In small bowl of electric mixer, at medium speed, beat egg until light. Gradually beat in sugar. Add vanilla, flour, salt, and baking powder, beating just until combined.
4. Stir in walnuts. Spread mixture evenly over cooled crust; bake 10 minutes, or just until golden-brown.
5. Remove to rack; cool 10 minutes. Cut lengthwise into 4 strips; cut each strip into 8 bars.
Makes about 2½ dozen.

# ❖ APPLE-OATMEAL-WHEAT BARS

*¼ cup unsifted all-purpose flour*
*¾ teaspoon baking powder*
*½ teaspoon baking soda*
*½ teaspoon salt*
*1 teaspoon ground cinnamon*
*½ teaspoon ground nutmeg*
*½ cup unsifted whole-wheat flour*
*⅓ cup soft shortening*
*¾ cup light-brown sugar, packed*
*2 eggs*
*¼ cup milk*
*1 cup old-fashioned rolled oats*
*¼ cup wheat germ*
*3 cups diced pared apple*
*½ cup coarsely chopped walnuts*
*Confectioners' sugar (optional)*

1. Preheat oven to 375F. Lightly grease 13-by-9-by-2-inch pan.
2. Sift all-purpose flour with baking powder, baking soda, salt, cinnamon, and nutmeg. Stir in whole-wheat flour; set aside.
3. In large bowl of electric mixer, at medium speed, beat shortening with brown sugar until light and fluffy. Beat in eggs, one at a time, beating until very light and fluffy.
4. At low speed, beat in milk, then flour mixture, just until combined. Then, with spoon, stir in oats, wheat germ, apple, and walnuts. Turn out into prepared pan.
5. Bake 30 to 40 minutes, or until cake tester inserted in center comes out clean. Let cool completely on wire rack.
6. Sprinkle with confectioners' sugar, if desired. Cut into bars.
Makes 3 dozen.

*Note*: If desired, mix ¼ cup confectioners' sugar with 2 teaspoons water. Drizzle over top.

# ❖ OATMEAL LACE WAFERS

*½ cup butter or margarine, softened*
*¾ cup light-brown sugar, packed*
*2 tablespoons flour*
*¼ teaspoon salt*
*2 tablespoons milk*
*1 teaspoon vanilla extract*
*1¼ cups raw quick-cooking oats (not instant)*

1. Preheat oven to 350F.
2. In medium bowl, with portable electric mixer at medium speed, beat butter with sugar until light and creamy.
3. Stir in flour, salt, milk, vanilla, and oats, mixing well.
4. Drop by teaspoonfuls, about 2 inches apart, onto ungreased cookie sheets.

5. Bake 8 to 10 minutes, or until light golden color. Cool 1 minute. Remove with spatula; roll each around handle of wooden spoon. Gently remove from spoon. Cool wafers on wire rack.
Makes about 3 dozen.

# ❖ SPICY APPLE-OATMEAL BARS

¾ cup sifted all-purpose flour
¾ teaspoon baking powder
½ teaspoon baking soda
½ teaspoon salt
1 tablespoon cocoa
1 teaspoon ground cinnamon
½ teaspoon ground nutmeg
¼ teaspoon ground cloves
⅓ cup soft shortening
¾ cup granulated sugar
2 eggs
1 cup raw rolled oats
1½ cups diced pared apple
½ cup coarsely chopped walnuts
Confectioners' sugar

1. Preheat oven to 375F. Lightly grease 9-by-9-by-2-inch baking pan.
2. Sift flour with baking powder, baking soda, salt, cocoa, cinnamon, nutmeg, and cloves; set aside.
3. In large bowl of electric mixer, at low speed, beat shortening with granulated sugar until light and fluffy. Beat in eggs, one at a time, beating until very light and fluffy.
4. At low speed, beat in flour mixture just until combined. Then, with spoon, stir in oats, apple, and walnuts. Turn out into prepared pan.
5. Bake 25 minutes, or until cake tester inserted in center comes out clean. Let cool completely on wire rack.
6. Sprinkle with confectioners' sugar. Cut into bars. Makes 3 dozen.

# ❖ ORANGE-CARROT COOKIES

2 cups sifted all-purpose flour
2 teaspoons baking powder
½ teaspoon salt
½ cup shortening
½ cup butter or margarine, softened
¾ cup granulated sugar
1 egg
1 teaspoon vanilla extract
2 cups grated raw carrot
½ cup Grape Nuts

## FROSTING:

1 tablespoon butter or margarine, softened
2 cups sifted confectioners' sugar
⅓ cup orange juice
1 tablespoon grated orange peel

1. Preheat oven to 350F. Lightly grease cookie sheets.
2. Sift flour with baking powder and salt; set aside.
3. In large bowl of electric mixer, at medium speed, cream shortening, butter, and granulated sugar until light and fluffy. Add egg and vanilla; mix well. At low speed, beat in flour mixture; then beat in carrot and Grape Nuts, beating just until combined.
4. Drop by tablespoonfuls, 2 inches apart, on prepared cookie sheets. Bake 20 to 25 minutes, or until golden-brown. Remove cookies to wire rack. Frost while still warm.
5. Make Frosting: In small bowl, cream butter and confectioners' sugar. Add orange juice and orange peel; mix well. Then spread over cookies.
Makes 3 dozen.

# ❖ PEANUT-BUTTER HEALTH COOKIES

½ cup butter or margarine, softened
½ cup peanut butter
1 cup dark-brown sugar, packed
1 egg
1¼ cups sifted all-purpose flour
¾ teaspoon baking soda
½ teaspoon ground nutmeg
2 tablespoons sesame seed (optional)
½ teaspoon vanilla extract
1 egg white, slightly beaten
1 cup wheat germ

1. Preheat oven to 375F. Lightly grease cookie sheets.
2. In medium bowl, with electric mixer at medium speed, cream butter with peanut butter, sugar, and egg until mixture is light and fluffy.
3. Sift flour with baking soda and nutmeg right into butter mixture. Add sesame seed and vanilla. Beat at low speed just until combined.
4. With hands, shape mixture into 1-inch balls. Dip each into egg white; then roll in wheat germ. Place, 2 inches apart, on prepared cookie sheets.
5. Bake 10 to 12 minutes. Let cool on wire rack.
Makes 3 dozen.

# ❖ TRAIL-MIX COOKIES

¾ cup butter or margarine, melted
½ cup granulated sugar
½ cup light-brown sugar, packed
2 eggs
1¾ cups whole-wheat flour
½ teaspoon salt
1 teaspoon baking powder
½ teaspoon baking soda
1 teaspoon ground cinnamon
2 cups raw quick-cooking oatmeal (not instant)
½ cup raisins
¼ cup sunflower kernels

1. Preheat oven to 350F. Lightly grease cookie sheets.
2. In large bowl, combine butter and both kinds of sugar. With wooden spoon, beat in eggs, one at a time.
3. Add flour, salt, baking powder, baking soda, and cinnamon. Stir until well blended.
4. Stir in oatmeal, raisins, and sunflower kernels. Drop by teaspoonfuls, 1 inch apart, onto prepared pans. Bake 8 to 10 minutes, or until golden. Cool completely on wire rack, and store in airtight container.
Makes 5 dozen.

# ❖ WHOLE-WHEAT MOLASSES COOKIES

¾ cup sifted all-purpose flour
1½ teaspoons baking powder
¾ teaspoon salt
¼ teaspoon baking soda
1 teaspoon ground cinnamon
½ teaspoon ground cloves
¾ cup unsifted whole-wheat flour
½ cup shortening
½ cup sugar
1 egg
½ cup light or dark molasses
⅓ cup water
½ cup raisins

1. Sift all-purpose flour with baking powder, salt, baking soda, cinnamon, and cloves. Stir in whole-wheat flour, and mix well. Set aside.
2. In medium bowl, with portable electric mixer at medium speed, beat shortening. Beat in sugar until light and fluffy; beat in egg, molasses, and water.
3. At low speed, beat in flour mixture just until combined. Stir in raisins. Refrigerate 1 hour.
4. Preheat oven to 350F. Lightly grease cookie sheets.
5. Drop cookies by rounded tablespoonfuls, 2 inches apart, onto prepared cookie sheets. Sprinkle each with 2 or 3 raisins. Bake 12 to 15 minutes, or just until surface springs back when gently pressed with fingertip.
6. Remove to wire rack to cool.
Makes 2½ dozen.

# DESSERTS and
# DESSERT SAUCES

**S**ometimes it may seem that everyone is dieting and therefore doesn't want dessert, but, in fact, our dessert recipes remain among the most popular with the readers of *McCall's*. There is nothing so satisfying and nostalgic as a good baked custard or bread pudding, and those are included here, as well as much more elaborate and sophisticated desserts that would grace the table of the most elegant dinner party.

# CREAM PUFFS, CRULLERS, AND CRÊPES

## ✦ CREAM PUFFS

### CREAM-PUFF DOUGH:

*½ cup water*
*¼ cup butter or margarine*
*⅛ teaspoon salt*
*½ cup all-purpose flour*
*2 large eggs*

*Custard Filling, recipe follows*
*Chocolate Glaze, recipe follows*
*Confectioners' sugar*

1. Preheat oven to 400F.
2. In small saucepan, combine water, butter, and salt. Over medium heat, bring to boiling. Remove from heat.
3. Immediately, with wooden spoon, beat in all the flour.
4. Over low heat, beat until mixture leaves side of pan and forms ball—1 to 2 minutes. Remove from heat.
5. Add 1 egg; with portable electric mixer at low speed, or with wooden spoon, beat until well blended. Then add other egg, and beat until dough is shiny and satiny—about 1 minute.
6. Drop dough by rounded tablespoonfuls, 2 inches apart, onto ungreased cookie sheet.
7. Bake 35 to 40 minutes, or until puffed and golden-brown. Puffs should sound hollow when lightly tapped with fingertip.
8. Meanwhile make Custard Filling.
9. Carefully remove puffs to wire rack. Let cool completely, away from drafts.
10. Shortly before serving: Cut off tops of cream puffs with sharp knife. With fork, gently remove any soft dough from inside.
11. Fill puffs with custard; replace tops. Frost tops with Chocolate Glaze, or sprinkle with confectioners' sugar. Serve soon after filling. (Filled puffs become soggy on standing.)
Makes 6 large puffs.

*Miniature Cream Puffs*: Drop batter by level teaspoonfuls, 2 inches apart, on ungreased cookie sheet. Bake 20 to 25 minutes at 400F. Proceed as directed above. Fill and frost for dessert, or fill with savory filling for hors d'oeuvres.
Makes 36 miniature puffs.

*Note*: To make double recipe of Cream-Puff Dough: Make as above in medium saucepan, using 1 cup water, ½ cup butter or margarine, ¼ teaspoon salt, 1 cup flour, and 4 eggs.

## CUSTARD FILLING

¼ cup sugar
2½ tablespoons cornstarch
1½ cups milk
1 tablespoon butter or margarine
3 egg yolks, beaten
½ teaspoon vanilla extract
⅓ cup heavy cream, whipped until
  stiff

1. In medium saucepan, combine sugar and corn-starch; mix well. Gradually add milk, stirring until smooth. Add butter.
2. Bring to boiling, stirring constantly; boil 1 minute. Stir a little of hot mixture into egg yolks; return to saucepan, stirring. Bring to boiling. Remove from heat and stir in vanilla.
3. Turn out into medium bowl. Place in larger bowl filled with ice cubes to cool completely—about 40 minutes. Stir occasionally.
4. Fold in heavy cream. Use to fill cream puffs.
Makes 2 cups; enough to fill 6 large cream puffs or 36 miniature puffs.

## CHOCOLATE GLAZE

½ cup semisweet-chocolate pieces
1 tablespoon shortening
1 tablespoon light corn syrup
1½ tablespoons milk

1. In top of double boiler, combine chocolate pieces, shortening, corn syrup, and milk.
2. Place over hot, not boiling, water, stirring occa-sionally, until mixture is smooth and well blended. Let cool slightly before using to frost puffs.
Makes ½ cup.

## ✦ COFFEE ÉCLAIRS

Cream-Puff Dough, page 119

Filling:

½ cup heavy cream
2 tablespoons confectioners' sugar
½ teaspoon powdered instant coffee
¼ teaspoon vanilla extract

Coffee Frosting, below

1. Preheat oven to 400F. Make Cream-Puff Dough.
2. For éclairs, put dough into small pastry bag with round decorating tip, ½ inch in diameter. On un-greased cookie sheet, press mixture in 2-inch strips 2 inches apart.
3. Bake 20 to 25 minutes, or until golden-brown.
4. Let cool completely on wire rack, away from drafts.
5. Make Filling: Beat cream with sugar, coffee, and vanilla just until stiff. Refrigerate, covered, until ready to use.
6. With sharp knife, cut slice from top of each éclair. Fill each with scant teaspoon of filling; replace tops.
7. Frost tops with Coffee Frosting. Refrigerate until serving.
Makes 32 eclairs.

## COFFEE FROSTING

2½ cups sifted confectioners' sugar
2 tablespoons light corn syrup
1 teaspoon vanilla extract
1 teaspoon powdered instant coffee
2 tablespoons water

1. In top of double boiler, combine all ingredients.
2. Stir over hot, not boiling, water just until frosting becomes smooth and shiny and coats wooden spoon. Remove from hot water.
3. If frosting thickens on standing, thin with a little water.
Makes about 1 cup.

# ❖ CRÊPES SUZETTE

## CRÊPES:

1 cup all-purpose flour
¼ cup butter or margarine, melted
    and cooled, or ¼ cup salad oil
2 eggs
2 egg yolks
1½ cups milk

## ORANGE BUTTER:

¾ cup sweet butter
½ cup sugar
⅓ cup Grand Marnier
¼ cup grated orange peel

## ORANGE SAUCE:

½ cup sweet butter
¾ cup sugar
2 tablespoons shredded orange peel
⅔ cup orange juice
2 oranges, peeled and sectioned
½ cup Grand Marnier

Butter or margarine
3 tablespoons Grand Marnier

1. Make Crêpes: In medium bowl, combine flour, melted butter, eggs, egg yolks, and ½ cup milk: beat with rotary beater until smooth. Beat in remaining milk until mixture is well blended.
2. Refrigerate, covered, at least 30 minutes.
3. Meanwhile, make Orange Butter: In small bowl, with electric mixer at low speed, cream ¾ cup sweet butter with ½ cup sugar until light and fluffy. Add ⅓ cup Grand Marnier and ¼ cup orange peel; beat until well blended. Set aside.
4. Make Orange Sauce: In large skillet, melt sweet butter. Stir in sugar, orange peel, and orange juice; cook over low heat, stirring occasionally, until peel is translucent—about 20 minutes. Add orange sections and ½ cup Grand Marnier. Keep warm.
5. To cook crêpes: Slowly heat 8-inch skillet until a drop of water sizzles and rolls off. For each crêpe, brush skillet lightly with butter. Pour in about 2 tablespoons batter, rotating pan quickly, to spread batter completely over bottom of skillet.
6. Cook until lightly browned—about 30 seconds; turn, and brown other side. Turn out onto wire rack.
7. Spread each crêpe with Orange Butter, dividing evenly. Fold each in half, then in half again. When all are folded, place in Orange Sauce in chafing dish or skillet; cook over low heat until heated through.
8. To serve: Gently heat 3 tablespoons Grand Marnier in small saucepan just until vapor rises. Ignite with match, and pour over crêpes. Serve flaming.
Makes 6 to 8 servings.

# ❖ FRESH BERRY DESSERT CRÊPES

## CRÊPES:

*3 eggs*
*1 cup all-purpose flour*
*⅛ teaspoon salt*
*1 cup milk*
*¼ cup water*
*2 tablespoons butter or margarine, melted*

*2 pints fresh blueberries or raspberries, washed and tossed with ½ cup light-brown sugar, packed*
*2 cups sour cream or whipped cream*
*Confectioners' sugar*
*½ cup blueberries or raspberries*

1. Make Crêpes: In medium bowl, beat eggs well with fork until frothy.
2. Add flour and salt, beating until smooth. Gradually beat in milk and water; continue beating until smooth. Refrigerate, covered, until ready to use—at least 30 minutes.
3. To cook crêpes: Slowly heat 8-inch skillet with sloping sides or crêpe pan until a drop of water sizzles and rolls off.
4. For each crêpe, brush pan lightly with butter. Pour in about ⅓ cup batter, rotating pan quickly to spread batter completely over bottom of skillet.
5. Cook until lightly browned on bottom—about 30 seconds; turn and brown lightly on other side. Turn out onto serving plate (or keep warm in oven while making rest of crêpes).
6. Fill each crêpe with about ½ cup berries. Top with 3 tablespoons sour cream. Fold crêpe over. Sprinkle with confectioners' sugar. Garnish with more cream and berries. Serve at once.
Makes 8 servings.

*Note*: Crêpes may be made ahead, stacked between rounds of waxed paper, and reheated slightly in skillet before filling.

# CUSTARDS AND PUDDINGS

# ❖ BAKED CUSTARD

*2 eggs*
*2 cups milk*
*¼ cup sugar*
*Dash salt*
*½ teaspoon vanilla extract*
*½ teaspoon lemon extract*
*Nutmeg*

1. Preheat oven to 350F.
2. Beat eggs and milk together. Add sugar, salt, and extracts (see Note). Mix well.
3. Ladle into 5 ungreased 6-oz custard cups. Sprinkle with nutmeg.
4. Place in shallow pan. Pour hot water to ½-inch depth around custard cups.
5. Bake 35 minutes, or until knife blade inserted ½ inch in center of custard comes out clean. Be careful not to overbake.
Makes 5 servings.

*Note*: Other flavorings can be used: ½ teaspoon almond extract, 1 teaspoon vanilla extract, etc.

# ❖ BAKED RICE CUSTARD

⅓ cup raw regular white rice
5 cups milk
1 teaspoon salt
3 eggs
¾ cup sugar
1½ teaspoons vanilla extract

1. In top of double boiler, combine rice, 4 cups milk, and the salt. Cook over boiling water, stirring occasionally, 1 hour, or until rice is tender.
2. Preheat oven to 350F. Grease 2-quart casserole; place in baking pan.
3. In large bowl, combine eggs, sugar, vanilla, and remaining milk; beat just until blended. Gradually stir in hot rice mixture.
4. Pour into prepared casserole. Pour hot water to 1-inch depth around casserole.
5. Bake, uncovered, 50 to 60 minutes, or until knife blade inserted in custard 1 inch from edge of casserole comes out clean.
6. Remove from hot water to wire rack, and let cool. Then refrigerate until well chilled—at least 3 hours, or overnight.
Makes 8 servings.

# ❖ CARAMEL-CUSTARD MOLD

**CARAMELIZED SUGAR:**

1 cup sugar

**CUSTARD:**

1 quart milk
6 eggs
½ cup sugar
⅛ teaspoon salt
1 teaspoon vanilla extract

1. Preheat oven to 325F.
2. Make Caramelized Sugar: Place 1 cup sugar in heavy skillet; cook over low to medium heat, without stirring, until sugar has melted and begins to form light-brown syrup. Stir to blend. Use at once to coat 1½-quart casserole: Hold with pot holder, and slowly pour in hot syrup. Turn and rotate until bottom and side are thoroughly coated.
3. Make Custard: In medium saucepan, over medium heat, heat milk just until bubbles form around edge of pan.
4. In large bowl, with rotary beater, beat eggs slightly. Stir in ½ cup sugar, the salt, and vanilla. Gradually add hot milk, stirring constantly. Pour into prepared dish.
5. Place in shallow pan; pour hot water to ½-inch depth around dish.
6. Bake 1 hour and 15 minutes, or until knife blade inserted deep into center of custard comes out clean. Cool; refrigerate overnight.
7. To serve: Run small spatula around edge of dish to loosen. Invert onto shallow serving dish; shake gently to release. The caramel will serve as a sauce.
Makes 8 servings.

# ❖ CRÈME BRÛLÉE

*3 cups heavy cream*
*6 egg yolks*
*⅓ cup granulated sugar*
*1 teaspoon vanilla extract*
*⅓ cup light-brown sugar, packed*

1. Heat cream in heavy saucepan just until bubbles form around edge of pan.
2. In double-boiler top, with electric mixer, beat yolks with granulated sugar until thick and light yellow. Gradually stir in cream.
3. Place over hot, not boiling, water; cook, stirring constantly, until mixture coats metal spoon—about 15 minutes. Add vanilla.
4. Strain custard into shallow 1-quart baking dish. Refrigerate 8 hours or overnight.
5. Just before serving, carefully sift brown sugar evenly over surface. Set dish in baking pan; surround with ice. Run under broiler just until sugar melts slightly and caramelizes—it will form a crust. Makes 8 servings.

# ❖ FLOATING ISLAND

## CUSTARD:

*2 cups milk*
*4 egg yolks*
*⅓ cup sugar*
*Dash salt*
*1 teaspoon vanilla extract*

## MERINGUE:

*4 egg whites*
*¼ teaspoon cream of tartar*
*Dash salt*
*½ cup sugar*
*½ teaspoon vanilla extract*
*⅓ cup chopped toasted almonds (optional)*
*Whole strawberries (optional)*

1. Several hours before serving, make Custard: In top of double boiler, over direct heat, heat milk until bubbles form around edge.
2. In medium bowl, beat egg yolks with sugar and salt until well blended.
3. Gradually pour hot milk into egg mixture, beating constantly. A wire whisk is handy.
4. Return mixture to top of double boiler; place over hot, not boiling, water. (Water in lower part of double boiler should not touch upper section.)
5. Cook, stirring constantly, until custard coats metal spoon—about 10 minutes.
6. Pour custard into bowl; press waxed paper right on surface to prevent formation of skin. When cool, stir in vanilla.
7. Refrigerate, covered, until well chilled—at least 2 hours.
8. Three hours before serving, make Meringue: In large bowl of electric mixer, let egg whites warm to room temperature—about 1 hour. Meanwhile, preheat oven to 350F. Butter generously and coat with sugar 6 (5-oz) custard cups.
9. At high speed, beat egg whites until foamy. Add cream of tartar and salt.
10. Beat, adding sugar gradually, until stiff peaks form when beater is raised.
11. Add vanilla; fold in almonds (optional).
12. Spoon meringue into prepared custard cups,

pressing gently to fill air pockets. Place custard cups in shallow pan containing 1 inch hot water.

13. Bake 15 minutes, or until meringue rises and becomes lightly browned.

14. Place on wire rack. Unmold at once into individual serving dishes. Cool; then refrigerate.

15. To serve, spoon custard around meringue. If desired, garnish with additional almonds or whole strawberries.

Makes 6 servings.

# 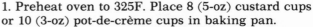 POT DE CRÈME

*3 cups heavy cream*
*½ cup sugar*
*1 tablespoon vanilla extract*
*5 egg yolks*

## CHOCOLATE CURLS:

*1 square (1 oz) semisweet or unsweet-*
*ened chocolate*

*Sweetened whipped cream (optional)*

1. Preheat oven to 325F. Place 8 (5-oz) custard cups or 10 (3-oz) pot-de-crème cups in baking pan.

2. In medium saucepan, combine cream and sugar; cook over medium heat, stirring occasionally, until sugar is dissolved and mixture is hot. Remove from heat; stir in vanilla.

3. In medium bowl, with wire whisk or rotary beater, beat egg yolks until blended—not frothy. Gradually add cream mixture, stirring constantly.

4. Strain, using fine strainer, into 4-cup measure. (If desired, first line strainer with cheesecloth.) Pour into cups.

5. Set baking pan on oven rack. Pour hot water to ½-inch depth around cups.

6. Bake 25 to 30 minutes, or until mixture just begins to set around edges.

7. Immediately remove cups from water, and place on wire rack. Let cool 30 minutes; then refrigerate, each covered with plastic wrap, foil, or lid, until chilled—at least 4 hours.

8. Make Chocolate Curls: Let chocolate stand in paper wrapper in warm place about 15 minutes, just to soften slightly. For large curls, unwrap chocolate, and carefully draw vegetable parer across broad, flat surface of square. For smaller curls, draw parer across side of square. Lift curls with a wooden pick, to avoid breaking.

9. To serve: Top with sweetened whipped cream, if desired. Then garnish with chocolate curls.

Makes 8 to 10 servings.

*Chocolate Pot de Crème:*

Make Pot de Crème, adding 1½ squares unsweetened chocolate, broken, to cream and sugar in Step 2. Cook, stirring, until chocolate is melted and mixture is hot. Proceed as directed, reducing egg yolks to 4.

# ❖ CHOCOLATE MOUSSE

4 eggs
1 pkg (6 oz) semisweet-chocolate
   pieces
5 tablespoons sweet butter
2 tablespoons cognac or brandy
Whipped cream
Candied violets

1. One or two days before serving: Separate eggs, placing whites into medium bowl. Let whites warm to room temperature.
2. In top of double boiler, over hot, not boiling, water, melt chocolate and butter; stir to blend. Remove from hot water.
3. Using wooden spoon, beat in egg yolks, one at a time, beating well after each addition. Set aside to cool. Stir in cognac.
4. When chocolate mixture has cooled, beat egg whites with rotary beater just until stiff peaks form when beater is slowly raised.
5. With rubber spatula or wire whisk, gently fold chocolate mixture into egg whites, using an under-and-over motion. Fold only enough to combine—there should be no white streaks.
6. Turn out into attractive 1-pint serving dish. Refrigerate overnight.
7. To serve: Decorate with whipped cream and candied violets.
Makes 8 servings.

# ❖ VANILLA BLANC MANGE

2¼ cups milk
3 tablespoons cornstarch
⅓ cup sugar
¼ teaspoon salt
1 teaspoon vanilla extract

1. In medium saucepan, slowly heat 2 cups milk just until bubbles form around edge of pan.
2. In small bowl, combine cornstarch, sugar, salt, and remaining milk; stir to mix well.
3. Gradually stir cornstarch mixture into hot milk; bring to boiling, stirring. Boil 1 minute, stirring constantly.
4. Remove from heat. Add vanilla.
5. Turn out into 6 individual dessert dishes; place piece of waxed paper directly on surface of each. Refrigerate 1 hour before serving. Serve with whipped cream or Raspberry Sauce, page 150, or Quick Chocolate Sauce, page 148.
Makes 6 servings.

Coconut Blanc Mange: Make Vanilla Blanc Mange, adding ½ cup flaked coconut to hot milk. Also, use ¼ teaspoon almond extract, and reduce vanilla extract to ½ teaspoon.

Mocha Blanc Mange: Make Vanilla Blanc Mange, adding 1 square unsweetened chocolate, halved, to milk along with 1 teaspoon instant coffee. Heat, stirring, until chocolate is melted. Proceed as directed, increasing sugar to ½ cup.

*Chocolate Blanc Mange*: Make Vanilla Blanc Mange, adding 2 squares unsweetened chocolate, halved, to milk. Heat, stirring, until chocolate is melted. Proceed as directed, increasing sugar to ½ cup.

# ❖ STEAMED FIG PUDDING

*2 cups sifted all-purpose flour*
*3 teaspoons baking powder*
*1¼ cups sugar*
*1¼ teaspoons ground nutmeg*
*1¼ teaspoons ground cinnamon*
*¾ teaspoon salt*
*1¼ lb dried figs*
*2¼ cups milk*
*5 eggs*
*1¾ cups ground suet*
*1¾ cups fresh white-bread crumbs*
*⅓ cup grated orange peel*
*Vanilla Hard Sauce, below*
*3 tablespoons brandy, for flaming (optional)*

1. Grease well 2- to 2½-quart pudding mold with tight-fitting cover. Sift flour with baking powder, sugar, nutmeg, cinnamon, and salt; set aside.
2. Remove stems from figs. In food processor or with scissors, cut figs into small pieces. Over medium heat, cook figs in milk, covered, 25 minutes; cool slightly.
3. In large bowl, with portable electric mixer at medium speed or with wire whisk, beat eggs until light and fluffy. With wooden spoon, beat in fig mixture, flour mixture, suet, bread crumbs, and orange peel. Beat until well combined.
4. Turn out into prepared mold; cover tightly. Place on trivet in large kettle. Add boiling water to come three quarters up side of mold. Steam, covered, 2½ hours. Add more boiling water from time to time.
5. While pudding steams, make Vanilla Hard Sauce.
6. Gently remove from mold, inverting onto serving platter. Serve hot with hard sauce. Flame, if desired. (To flame: Gently heat 3 tablespoons brandy in small saucepan just until vapor rises. Ignite with match, and pour over pudding.)
Makes 12 servings.

*Note*: If desired, make pudding a day or two before; store wrapped in refrigerator. To serve: Place in mold; resteam as directed, about 45 minutes to 1 hour, or until heated through.

## VANILLA HARD SAUCE

*⅓ cup soft butter or margarine*
*1 teaspoon vanilla extract*
*1 cup confectioners' sugar*

1. In small bowl of electric mixer, at high speed, cream butter until light.
2. Add vanilla and sugar; beat until fluffy and smooth.
Makes about ¾ cup.

## ✦ STEAMED CARROT PUDDING

*1½ cups sifted all-purpose flour*
*1½ teaspoons baking soda*
*1½ cups sugar*
*¾ teaspoon salt*
*½ teaspoon ground cloves*
*1½ teaspoons ground cinnamon*
*1½ teaspoons ground nutmeg*
*3 tablespoons butter or margarine, melted*
*3 eggs, well beaten*
*1½ cups grated raw carrot*
*1½ cups grated raw potato*
*1½ cups coarsely chopped walnuts*
*1½ cups seeded raisins*
*Pudding Sauce, below*

1. Thoroughly grease 1½-quart heat-proof glass bowl or pudding bowl.
2. Sift flour with baking soda, sugar, salt, and spices.
3. In large bowl, gradually stir butter into eggs. Stir in flour mixture and remaining ingredients; mix well.
4. Turn out into prepared bowl. Cover securely with tight-fitting cover, or wrap bowl completely in cheesecloth; tie around top with string. Place on trivet in deep kettle.
5. Add enough boiling water to come halfway up side of bowl.
6. Simmer, with cover on kettle, 1½ to 2 hours. Remove bowl from kettle. Cool pudding slightly; remove from bowl if serving at once.
7. To store: Cool pudding completely. Store in bowl wrapped in cheesecloth, and keep refrigerated until serving.
8. To serve: Steam, as above, 30 minutes, or until heated through. Serve with Pudding Sauce.

Makes 8 servings.

### PUDDING SAUCE

*1 pkg (3 oz) cream cheese, softened*
*1 egg*
*1 cup confectioners' sugar*
*2 tablespoons butter or margarine, softened*
*1 teaspoon lemon juice*
*Pinch salt*
*1 cup heavy cream, whipped*
*About 2 tablespoons golden rum or ½ to 1 tablespoon rum extract*

1. Day before: In medium bowl, with spoon, beat cheese until light. Add egg, sugar, butter, lemon juice, and salt; beat well.
2. Fold in whipped cream and rum just until combined.
3. Refrigerate, covered, overnight.

Makes 3 cups.

# FRUIT DESSERTS

## ✦ PEACHES IN MARSALA

*4 large fresh peach halves, peeled*
*½ cup cream Marsala*
*1-inch cinnamon stick*

1. In medium bowl, combine all ingredients.
2. Refrigerate, covered, until peaches are well chilled—at least 2 hours.
3. To serve: Remove cinnamon stick and turn out peaches and liquid into serving bowl.

Makes 4 servings.

# ❖ BAKED APPLE CHARLOTTE

1 loaf (1 lb) sliced white bread, crusts
   removed
1 cup sugar
4 teaspoons ground cinnamon
6 green apples (2 lb)
¼ cup butter or margarine
4 cups fresh white-bread crumbs
   (about 12 slices, crusts removed)

## SAUCE:

1 cup apple jelly
2 tablespoons golden rum

1. Lightly butter inside of 2-quart charlotte mold or straight-sided heat-proof glass bowl. Cut 6 slices bread in half; use to line sides of mold, overlapping. Using heart-shaped cookie cutter, cut 6 hearts from bread, to fit in bottom of mold.
2. Combine sugar and cinnamon.
3. Pare, core, and thinly slice apples—should measure 5½ cups.
4. Preheat oven to 350F.
5. In bottom of mold, layer 1⅓ cups apple slices. Sprinkle with ¼ cup sugar-cinnamon mixture, and dot with 1 tablespoon butter. Top with 1 cup bread crumbs. Make 3 more layers.
6. Bake 1 hour and 15 or 20 minutes, or until apples are tender when tested with wooden pick.
7. Let pudding cool on wire rack 10 minutes. (If desired, brush with a little melted apple jelly.)
8. Make Sauce: In small saucepan, over low heat, melt jelly. Remove from heat; stir in rum.
9. To serve: Carefully loosen around edge of mold with spatula. Turn out onto platter. Serve warm with sauce (see Note).
Makes 8 servings.

*Note*: Or use 1 pint softened vanilla ice cream as sauce.

# ❖ BAKED CRANBERRY-APPLE DUMPLINGS

Pastry for 2-Crust Pie, page 354
4 medium baking apples (about 2 lb)
2 tablespoons sugar
¼ teaspoon ground cinnamon
2 tablespoons butter or margarine,
   melted
1 egg yolk
1 tablespoon water
Cranberry-Apple Sauce, below
Whipped cream or vanilla ice cream
   (optional)

1. Form pastry into ball. Wrap in waxed paper, and place in refrigerator.
2. Pare and core apples. On sheet of waxed paper, combine sugar and cinnamon.
3. Preheat oven to 450F. Lightly butter 12-by-8-by-2-inch baking dish.
4. On lightly floured pastry cloth or surface, roll out pastry into rectangle, 30 inches long and 4½ inches wide. Using pastry wheel, cut lengthwise into 4 strips.
5. Roll apples in cinnamon-sugar mixture; reserve remaining mixture.

6. Starting at top, spiral a pastry strip around each apple, letting each row overlap slightly. Moisten overlapping edges with cold water; press edges to seal. Press sides and bottom of pastry against apple. Spoon melted butter into center of each apple. Brush pastry with egg yolk mixed with 1 tablespoon water. Sprinkle with reserved cinnamon-sugar mixture.

7. Bake 15 minutes. Reduce heat to 350F; continue baking dumplings 15 minutes.

8. Remove dumplings from oven. Spoon 1 tablespoon Cranberry-Apple Sauce into center of each apple and the remaining sauce around apples.

9. Bake 15 minutes longer, or until apples are tender. Serve warm. Nice with whipped cream or vanilla ice cream.

Makes 4 servings.

## CRANBERRY-APPLE SAUCE

1 cup cranberries, washed
¾ cup sugar
2 tablespoons maple or
    maple-flavored syrup
¼ cup water
2 medium apples, pared, cored, and
    chopped
2 tablespoons butter or margarine

1. In medium saucepan, combine cranberries and sugar; mash cranberries slightly with fork.

2. Add maple syrup and water; mix well. Bring to boiling, stirring constantly. Boil about 3 minutes, or until cranberries pop.

3. Add apples and butter; simmer, covered, 5 minutes.

# ❖ AVOCADO CREAM PARFAITS

1 teaspoon unflavored gelatine
¼ cup milk
2 tablespoons water
1 large ripe avocado (about 1 lb)
¼ cup superfine granulated sugar
Dash salt
Dash ground nutmeg
3 teaspoons lemon juice
2 tablespoons light rum
1½ cups heavy cream

1. Sprinkle unflavored gelatine over milk and water in small saucepan, and let stand 5 minutes to soften. Then heat gently over low heat, stirring to dissolve gelatine; cool.

2. Peel avocado; remove pit, and slice avocado. In blender, combine avocado pieces, sugar, salt, nutmeg, lemon juice, and rum; blend until smooth. Turn out into large bowl.

3. Beat ½ cup heavy cream, slowly adding cooled gelatine during beating; beat until stiff. Add to puréed avocado; fold in with rubber spatula just to combine.

4. Beat remaining heavy cream until stiff.

5. In 6 parfait glasses, layer avocado cream with whipped cream, beginning and ending with avocado.

Makes 6 servings.

# ❖ PEARS SABAYON

1 cup granulated sugar
3 cups water
4 fresh pears, peeled, halved, and
   cored

## SAUCE:

4 egg yolks
1 cup confectioners' sugar
¼ cup sherry
¾ cup heavy cream

1. In 4-quart saucepan, combine granulated sugar and water; heat until sugar dissolves.
2. Add pears. Cover, and simmer gently until tender —about 30 minutes. Remove from heat.
3. Carefully place pears, with about 1 cup syrup, in bowl; refrigerate several hours.
4. Make Sauce: In top of double boiler, with rotary beater or wire whisk, beat egg yolks, confectioners' sugar, and sherry until light.
5. Place over hot, not boiling, water; water should not touch bottom of double-boiler top. Cook, stirring constantly, 8 to 10 minutes.
6. Refrigerate, covered, several hours. Mixture thickens on standing.
7. In medium bowl, beat cream until soft peaks form when beater is raised. Carefully fold in chilled sauce.
8. Drain pears. Serve topped with sauce.
Makes 8 servings.

# ❖ BAKED SPICED RHUBARB

4 cups rhubarb, cut into 1-inch pieces
   (about 2 lb), or 2 pkg (1-lb size)
   frozen rhubarb in syrup
1 cup sugar
1-inch cinnamon stick
4 whole cloves

1. Preheat oven to 400F.
2. Place rhubarb in 2-quart casserole. Sprinkle with sugar; add cinnamon and cloves. If using frozen rhubarb, place frozen fruit in 10-by-8-by-2-inch baking dish. Sprinkle with only ¼ cup sugar; add spices.
3. Bake, covered, 10 minutes. Stir gently to dissolve sugar, and baste fruit with syrup. Bake 15 minutes longer, or until rhubarb is tender but not mushy.
4. Let stand, covered, on wire rack until cool.
Makes 4 to 6 servings.

# ❖ STRAWBERRIES ROMANOFF

2 pints fresh strawberries
1 cup confectioners' sugar
1 cup heavy cream
1 teaspoon almond extract
2 tablespoons Cointreau or orange
   juice

1. Gently wash strawberries in cold water. Drain and hull.
2. In medium bowl, sprinkle sugar over berries; toss gently.
3. Refrigerate 1 hour, stirring occasionally.
4. In chilled bowl, with rotary beater, whip cream until stiff. Add almond extract and Cointreau.
5. Fold into strawberries. Serve at once.
Makes 8 servings.

# ✦ ORANGE, BANANA, AND PINEAPPLE AMBROSIA

4 large navel oranges
1 can (1 lb, 4 oz) pineapple chunks, in
   pineapple juice
2 tablespoons orange juice
4 medium bananas
2 tablespoons confectioners' sugar
1 can (3½ oz) flaked coconut

1. Peel oranges; remove white membrane. Cut oranges crosswise into ⅛-inch-thick slices.
2. Drain pineapple, saving juice. Combine pineapple juice and orange juice; set aside.
3. Peel bananas. Cut on diagonal into ⅛-inch-thick slices.
4. In attractive serving bowl, layer half of orange slices; sprinkle with 1 tablespoon confectioners' sugar. Layer half of banana slices and half of pineapple; sprinkle with half of coconut.
5. Repeat layering. Pour juice mixture over top.
6. Refrigerate several hours, or until well chilled. Makes 10 servings.

# ✦ FRUIT MERINGUE TORTE

6 egg whites (⅔ cup)
¼ teaspoon salt
½ teaspoon cream of tartar
1½ cups sugar
1 teaspoon vanilla extract
¼ cup light rum
1 cup heavy cream, whipped
Whole strawberries, fresh or frozen
Canned pineapple slices, drained

1. Day before serving or early in morning: In large bowl of electric mixer, let egg whites warm to room temperature—about 1 hour. Lightly butter bottom, not side, of 9-inch tube pan.
2. Preheat oven to 450F.
3. To egg whites, add salt and cream of tartar; beat until frothy. At high speed, beat in sugar, 2 tablespoons at a time, beating well after each addition. Add vanilla; beat until stiff peaks form when beaters are slowly raised. Turn out into tube pan, spreading evenly.
4. Place on middle rack of oven. Immediately, turn off heat. Let stand in oven several hours or overnight.
5. Loosen edge with spatula. Turn out torte on serving plate. Sprinkle surface with rum. Refrigerate until well chilled—at least 4 hours.
6. To serve: Frost top and sides with whipped cream. Decorate top with strawberries; garnish with pineapple.
Makes 10 servings.

# GELATINE DESSERTS

## ❖ CHARLOTTE RUSSE

1 env unflavored gelatine
6 tablespoons sugar
2 eggs, separated
¾ cup milk
About ½ cup dry sherry
About 12 ladyfingers, split
1½ cups heavy cream
Toasted whole almonds (see Note)
½ cup heavy cream, whipped

1. In top of double boiler, combine gelatine and sugar; mix well.
2. Beat egg yolks slightly; beat in milk. Stir into gelatine mixture. Cook over simmering water, stirring constantly, until mixture coats metal spoon. Remove from heat; stir in ⅓ cup sherry.
3. Pour into bowl; set bowl in larger bowl filled with ice.
4. Stir occasionally until custard begins to mound slightly—20 to 30 minutes.
5. Meanwhile, sprinkle cut sides of ladyfingers lightly with sherry—about 4 tablespoons in all.
6. Rinse 7- or 8-cup charlotte or straight-sided mold with cold water; drain well. Line side of mold with 18 split ladyfingers, split side inside.
7. Beat egg whites until stiff but not dry. Beat 1½ cups cream until stiff. With rubber spatula, fold egg whites, then whipped cream, into chilled gelatine mixture, and combine thoroughly.
8. Pour half into prepared mold. Layer with remaining split ladyfingers. Cover with rest of gelatine mixture, filling mold.
9. Refrigerate until firm—about 4 hours.
10. To unmold: With small spatula, loosen around edge of mold. Invert mold over serving plate. Hold hot damp dishcloth over mold; shake to release.
11. Garnish with toasted almonds and mounds of whipped cream.
Makes 10 servings.

*Note*: To toast almonds, preheat oven to 350F. Spread almonds in single layer on cookie sheet, and bake until golden—about 7 minutes.

# ❖ PEACH CHARLOTTE

*3 cups fresh peach purée (about 8 me-*
  *dium peaches)*
*2 tablespoons lemon juice*
*¾ cup granulated sugar*
*¼ teaspoon almond extract*
*2 env unflavored gelatine*
*½ cup water*
*1 pkg (3 oz) ladyfingers*
*2 tablespoons dry sherry*
*2 cups heavy cream*
*2 tablespoons confectioners' sugar*
*6 peach slices*

1. In medium bowl, combine peach purée, lemon juice, granulated sugar, and almond extract; stir to dissolve sugar.
2. In small saucepan, sprinkle gelatine over water; let stand 5 minutes to soften. Stir over low heat until completely dissolved. Blend gelatine into peach-purée mixture.
3. Set bowl in larger bowl filled with ice, stirring occasionally, until consistency of unbeaten egg white—15 to 20 minutes.
4. Meanwhile, brush cut sides of ladyfingers lightly with sherry. Line bottom of 7-cup charlotte or straight-sided mold with waxed paper. Line inside of mold with half of split ladyfingers, cut side inside.
5. In large bowl, with electric beater at high speed, beat 1½ cups cream until stiff. With wire whisk or rubber spatula, carefully fold gelatine mixture into cream.
6. Turn out into prepared pan. Cover top with remaining ladyfingers, cut side down. Refrigerate until firm—8 hours or overnight.
7. To serve: Run spatula around edge of mold to loosen. Invert onto serving plate. If necessary, place hot damp dishcloth over bottom of mold; shake to release. Remove waxed paper.
8. In medium bowl, combine ½ cup heavy cream and confectioners' sugar. With electric beater, beat until stiff.
9. Turn out into pastry bag with number-5 tip. Use to decorate top with rosettes. Garnish with peach slices. Refrigerate until ready to be served.
Makes 8 servings.

# ❖ MOLDED PINEAPPLE BAVARIAN CREAM

*4 egg yolks*
*½ cup sugar*
*1 cup milk*
*1 can (8¼ oz) crushed pineapple*
*1 env unflavored gelatine*
*1 teaspoon vanilla extract*
*1 cup heavy cream*
*¼ cup apricot preserves*
*Sweetened whipped cream (optional)*

1. In small bowl of electric mixer, at high speed, beat egg yolks with sugar until very thick. Meanwhile, heat milk just until bubbles form around edge of pan. Gradually stir milk into yolk mixture.
2. Turn out custard into heavy saucepan; cook, stirring, over medium heat until custard thickens and coats metal spoon.
3. Meanwhile, drain pineapple, reserving liquid. Sprinkle gelatine over ¼ cup reserved pineapple juice; let stand 5 minutes to soften.

4. Remove custard from heat. Add softened gelatine and vanilla; stir to dissolve gelatine. Pour into large bowl and let cool—about 20 minutes.

5. Set in larger bowl of ice water; stir occasionally until gelatine begins to thicken and is consistency of unbeaten egg white.

6. Beat heavy cream until stiff; fold into gelatine mixture, along with drained pineapple, until combined.

7. Pour into 5-cup fancy mold. Refrigerate until firm enough to unmold—several hours or overnight.

8. To unmold: Run sharp knife around edge of mold to loosen. Invert onto serving platter. Place hot damp dishcloth over mold; shake to release. Repeat if necessary. Brush mold with preserves. Refrigerate until serving, to chill well. Serve with whipped cream, if desired.

Makes 8 servings.

# ICE-CREAM DESSERTS

## ❖ CHERRIES JUBILEE

*1 can (1 lb, 14 oz) pitted Bing cherries*
*1 tablespoon cornstarch*
*⅓ cup cherry brandy*
*⅓ cup brandy or curaçao*
*3 pints vanilla ice cream*

1. Drain cherries, reserving syrup.

2. In 10-inch skillet, combine syrup and cornstarch; stir until smooth. Add cherry brandy. Bring to boiling, stirring; boil 2 minutes.

3. Stir in cherries; heat through.

4. In small saucepan, heat brandy until bubbles form around edge of pan. Ignite with match. Pour into cherry mixture.

5. Serve over ice cream.

Makes 8 to 10 servings.

# ❖ PONTCHARTRAIN ICE-CREAM PIE

1 pkg (11 oz) piecrust mix
1 quart strawberry or favorite flavor
    ice cream
1 quart chocolate or favorite flavor
    ice cream
5 egg whites
½ teaspoon vanilla extract
½ cup sugar
Chocolate Sauce, below

1. Prepare and bake 10-inch pie shell according to package directions; cool thoroughly. Wrap and freeze remaining pastry for another use.
2. Let ice cream soften slightly. Spoon in alternate layers into baked pie shell. Wrap and freeze until very firm—several hours or overnight.
3. To serve: In large bowl of electric mixer, let egg whites warm to room temperature—about 1 hour. At high speed, beat egg whites and vanilla just until soft peaks form when beater is slowly raised.
4. Add sugar, 2 tablespoons at a time, beating well after each addition. Continue beating until meringue is shiny and stiff peaks form.
5. Spread meringue over pie, covering ice cream and edge of crust completely. Make swirls on top.
6. Broil, 5 to 6 inches from heat, until meringue is lightly browned—about 3 minutes.
7. Serve at once. Pass Chocolate Sauce.
Makes 8 servings.

Note: If ice-cream pie is frozen very hard, remove from freezer about 20 to 30 minutes before putting on meringue and broiling.

## CHOCOLATE SAUCE

½ cup sugar
¼ cup unsweetened cocoa
½ cup light cream
⅓ cup light corn syrup
¼ cup butter or margarine
2 squares unsweetened chocolate
Dash salt
1½ teaspoons vanilla extract

1. In small saucepan, combine sugar and cocoa; mix well. Add cream, corn syrup, butter, chocolate, and salt.
2. Cook over medium heat, stirring constantly, until sauce is smooth and comes to boiling. Remove from heat; stir in vanilla.
Makes 1½ cups.

# ❖ ICE-CREAM PROFITEROLES

Cream-Puff Dough, page 119
2 pints vanilla ice cream
Deluxe Chocolate Sauce, page 148
½ cup heavy cream, whipped
Chopped pistachios

1. Preheat oven to 400F. Make Cream-Puff Dough.
2. Drop dough by rounded half teaspoonfuls, 1 inch apart, onto ungreased cookie sheet, to make 40 puffs.
3. Bake 20 to 25 minutes, or until puffed and golden-brown. Remove to wire rack; let cool completely.
4. Meanwhile, with large end of melon-ball cutter or with 1-teaspoon measuring spoon, scoop ice cream into 40 balls. Place immediately in chilled pan, and store in freezer.
5. Make Deluxe Chocolate Sauce.
6. To assemble profiteroles: With sharp knife, cut slice from top of each puff. Fill each with ice-cream

ball; replace top. (Place in freezer if not serving at once.)

7. To serve: Mound puffs in serving dish. Spoon chocolate sauce over top. Garnish with whipped cream and pistachios. For individual servings: In each dessert dish, mound 5 puffs. Spoon sauce over top. Garnish with whipped cream and pistachios.
Makes 8 servings.

# ❖ STRAWBERRY-COOKIE-SHELL SUNDAES

1 pint fresh strawberries
½ cup granulated sugar

**COOKIE SHELLS:**

1 egg
⅓ cup sifted confectioners' sugar
2 tablespoons brown sugar
¼ teaspoon vanilla extract
¼ cup sifted all-purpose flour
Dash salt
2 tablespoons melted butter or margarine
2 tablespoons chopped pecans

1 quart vanilla ice cream
½ cup chopped pecans

1. Wash and hull strawberries; slice. Add granulated sugar (see Note). Refrigerate.
2. Preheat oven to 300F. Grease and flour 2 cookie sheets.
3. Make Cookie Shells: In medium bowl, with electric mixer at high speed, beat egg until soft peaks form when beater is raised. Gradually stir in sugars, folding until dissolved. Add vanilla.
4. Stir in flour and salt, mixing well. Gradually blend in butter and 2 tablespoons pecans.
5. Spoon about 2 tablespoons batter onto prepared cookie sheet. Spread thin, to make 5-inch round. Make 2 more rounds on cookie sheet and 3 rounds on other cookie sheet.
6. Bake, one sheet at a time, 12 minutes. Remove hot cookies from sheet with broad spatula. Mold each cookie, bottom down, over outside of 6-oz custard cup to form shell. Cool.
7. To serve: Fill shells with ice cream. Spoon strawberries over ice cream. Top with chopped nuts.
Makes 6 servings.

*Note*: Frozen strawberries can be substituted for fresh berries. Use 1 pkg (10 oz) frozen sliced strawberries, thawed, but omit the sugar.

# ❖ SPUMONI

3 pints chocolate ice cream, slightly soft
1 pint pistachio ice cream, slightly soft
2 pints vanilla ice cream, slightly soft
½ cup candied mixed fruits
2 teaspoons rum flavoring
1½ cups heavy cream, whipped

1. Place 2½-quart fancy mold or melon mold in freezer.
2. In large bowl, with portable electric mixer, beat chocolate ice cream until smooth but not melted. With spoon, quickly press ice cream evenly inside chilled mold, making 1-inch-thick layer. Freeze until firm.
3. In medium bowl, beat pistachio ice cream until

smooth. Then press evenly over chocolate-ice-cream layer. Freeze until firm.

4. In large bowl, combine vanilla ice cream, candied fruits, and rum flavoring; beat until well blended but not melted. Press into center of mold. Freeze until firm.

5. To unmold and decorate spumoni: Let spumoni stand at room temperature 5 minutes. Invert over serving plate. Hold hot damp dishcloth over mold, and shake to release. Return to freezer until surface is firm.

6. Spread three fourths of whipped cream over the unmolded spumoni. Place remaining whipped cream in pastry bag with decorating tip, and decorate spumoni. Return to freezer until a few minutes before serving.
Makes 16 to 20 servings.

# HOMEMADE ICE CREAM

Unless you've tried it, you won't believe how good homemade ice cream tastes. Whether you choose to make it in a crank-type freezer (either manual or electric) or in one of the newer ice-cream makers, there's a magic about pouring ingredients into a container and having it come out tasting smoothly cold and delicious in a short time. The best part of making ice cream at home is that you can make it just as you like it—with heavy cream, or with yogurt, with whatever flavor you desire. Our recipes, from Basic Vanilla Ice Cream to "Special Flavor" Ice Cream, are to inspire you to begin and experiment as your tastes and the fruits of the season dictate.

# ✦ BASIC VANILLA ICE CREAM

1½ cups half-and-half
¾ cup sugar
¼ teaspoon salt
4 egg yolks
1½ to 2 tablespoons vanilla extract
2 cups heavy cream

1. In top of double boiler, heat half-and-half until film forms on surface. Do not boil. Stir in sugar and salt.

2. In medium bowl, beat egg yolks slightly. Gradually beat in small amounts of hot half-and-half mixture until most of it is used up.

3. Return to top of double boiler; cook, over boiling water, stirring, until as smooth and thick as mayonnaise—about 15 to 20 minutes.

4. Cool custard thoroughly. Stir in vanilla to taste and the heavy cream. Cover and chill thoroughly.

5. Freeze in ice-cream maker according to manufacturer's instructions.
Makes 1 quart; 6 servings.

*Peppermint Ice Cream*: Crush coarsely about ½ lb peppermint-stripe candy (you'll need 1¼ cups crushed candy). Prepare Basic Vanilla Ice Cream. When ice cream is frozen to semihardness, stir in candy.

# ❖ CHOCOLATE-CINNAMON ICE CREAM

½ vanilla bean
2 cups light cream
2 egg yolks
½ cup sugar
1½ teaspoons cornstarch
⅛ teaspoon salt
3 squares (1-oz size) semisweet chocolate
1 tablespoon ground cinnamon
¾ cup heavy cream

1. Split vanilla bean; with tip of knife, scrape seeds into light cream in medium saucepan. Heat until bubbles appear around edge of pan.
2. In medium bowl, beat egg yolks with sugar, cornstarch, and salt until well combined. Gradually stir in hot cream. Return to saucepan; cook over medium heat, stirring constantly, until mixture is thickened and just comes to boiling.
3. Add chocolate and cinnamon. Remove from heat; stir until chocolate is melted. Set aside until cool.
4. Stir in heavy cream.
5. Freeze in ice-cream maker according to manufacturer's instructions.
6. Serve immediately, or spoon into freezer containers and place in freezer. Serve with prepared semisweet-chocolate sauce.
Makes about 1 quart; 6 servings.

# ❖ FRESH PEACH ICE CREAM

2 lb fresh ripe peaches
3 tablespoons lemon juice
1½ cups granulated sugar
2 eggs, separated
2 tablespoons confectioners' sugar
1 cup heavy cream

1. Set refrigerator control at coldest temperature.
2. Reserve 2 peaches for garnish. Peel remaining peaches. Halve, and remove pits. Place peach halves in large bowl with lemon juice. Crush with potato masher, or purée in blender. Stir in granulated sugar.
3. In medium bowl, with rotary beater, beat egg whites with confectioners' sugar until soft peaks form.
4. In small bowl, beat egg yolks well. Fold yolks gently into whites, using wire whisk or rubber spatula.
5. Whip cream until it holds soft peaks; fold gently into egg mixture.
6. Fold in crushed peaches. Pour into 8-inch square pan. Freeze until firm around edges.
7. Transfer to bowl; beat with rotary or portable elec-

tric beater until smooth and creamy. Return to tray.
Freeze until firm.
8. To serve: Peel and slice reserved peaches. Use to garnish servings.
Makes 1 quart; 6 servings.

# ✪ "SPECIAL FLAVOR" ICE CREAM

2 cups half-and-half
1 cup heavy cream
¾ cup sugar
½ teaspoon vanilla extract
Dash salt
1 cup "Special Flavoring" (see Note)

1. In large bowl, combine half-and-half, cream, sugar, vanilla, and salt. With wooden spoon or rubber spatula, stir until sugar is dissolved.
2. Process in ice-cream maker according to manufacturer's instructions. With rubber spatula, fold "Special Flavoring" into ice cream, and turn out into 1-quart freezer container. Place in freezer to ripen flavors for at least 1 hour before serving.
Makes 1 quart; 6 servings.

Note: Select one of the following for your "Special Flavoring": chopped fresh berries or fruit, miniature semisweet-chocolate pieces, crushed chocolate sandwich cookies, chopped unsalted nuts, or any combination of these.

# SHERBETS

# ✪ HONEYDEW-MELON ICE

2 cups sugar
1½ cups water
1 large ripe honeydew melon (4½ lb)
¼ cup orange juice
⅓ cup lemon juice
Mint leaves (optional)

1. Day before: In medium saucepan, combine sugar and water. Stir over low heat to dissolve sugar.
2. Bring to boiling. Boil gently, uncovered and without stirring, to 230F on candy thermometer, or until mixture spins 2-inch thread from tip of spoon—about 45 minutes.
3. Meanwhile, cut melon in half zigzag fashion. Discard seeds. Scoop out pulp but save a half shell. Blend pulp in blender or press through food mill. (There should be 4½ to 5 cups purée.)
4. In large bowl, combine puréed melon with sugar syrup; mix well. Cool 15 minutes.
5. Stir in orange and lemon juices. Turn out into a 13-by-9-by-2-inch pan; place in freezer until frozen around edge—3 hours.
6. Turn out into chilled large bowl; with electric mixer at high speed, beat just until mushy, not melted.
7. Return to pan; refreeze—several hours or overnight.
8. To serve: Mound reserved half honeydew-melon

shell with small scoops of Honeydew-Melon Ice (these may be prepared ahead and stored in freezer until ready to use). Garnish with mint leaves, if desired. Let stand about 5 minutes at room temperature before serving.
Makes 8 servings.

# ❋ ORANGE SHERBET IN ORANGE SHELLS

2 tablespoons grated orange peel
7 large oranges
½ cup honey or light corn syrup
⅔ cup sweet orange marmalade
2 cups light cream
¼ cup Cointreau
Fresh mint sprigs

1. Grate peel from one orange. Cut tops from 6 oranges, cutting about one third of the way down. Squeeze juice from tops and bottoms of 7 oranges. Scrape any pulp from tops and bottoms of 6 oranges; reserve for serving. Juice should measure 2 cups.
2. In blender, combine grated orange peel and juice, honey, marmalade, cream, and Cointreau. Blend ½ minute at high speed. Pour into 13-by-9-by-2-inch pan; freeze until firm 1 inch from edge—about 3 hours.
3. Blend again in blender ½ minute—until soft but not melted. Return to pan. Freeze until firm—several hours or overnight. (Flavor improves overnight.)
4. Remove sherbet from freezer and allow to thaw slightly. Serve in orange shells, filling bottoms and putting tops in place. Decorate each with mint sprig.
Makes 6 servings.

# ❋ LIME SHERBET

1 env unflavored gelatine
2 cups milk
1⅓ cups sugar
½ teaspoon salt
2 cups light cream
½ cup lime juice
¼ cup lemon juice
2 tablespoons grated lemon peel

1. In small heavy saucepan, sprinkle gelatine over ½ cup milk to soften.
2. In medium bowl, combine remaining milk, the sugar, salt, and cream. Stir until sugar is dissolved. Stir in lime juice, lemon juice, and lemon peel.
3. Heat gelatine mixture over low heat, stirring constantly until gelatine is dissolved. Remove from heat; slowly stir into mixture in bowl.
4. Turn out into 13-by-9-by-2-inch pan; freeze until firm 1 inch from edge.
5. Turn out into chilled bowl; with electric mixer at low speed, or rotary beater, beat mixture until smooth but not melted. Return to pan.
6. Freeze several hours, or until firm.
7. To serve: Allow to thaw slightly. Spoon into sherbet glasses.
Makes 6 servings.

# ❖ RASPBERRY SHERBET MOLD

*3 pkg (10-oz size) quick-thaw frozen raspberries*
*¾ cup currant jelly*
*½ cup crème de cassis or any fruit-flavored liqueur*
*1 cup fresh pineapple wedges*
*½ lb seedless green grapes, washed*

1. Thaw frozen raspberries as label directs.
2. Combine raspberries with their juice, the jelly, and crème de cassis in electric blender. Blend at medium speed ½ minute to make purée.
3. Place in 13-by-9-by-2-inch pan; freeze until firm ½ inch from edge—about 3 hours.
4. Blend again in blender until soft and mushy but not melted. Turn out into 5-cup ring mold (plain or decorative). Freeze until firm, preferably overnight.
5. To unmold: Invert mold onto serving platter. Cover with dishcloth dipped in hot water. Shake mold to release sherbet. Fill center of mold with pineapple and grapes.
Makes 8 servings.

# SOUFFLÉS

## ❖ APRICOT SOUFFLÉ

*8 egg whites, unbeaten*
*3½ cups water*
*2½ cups dried apricots*
*¼ teaspoon plus ⅛ teaspoon almond extract*
*Butter*
*Granulated sugar*
*¼ teaspoon cream of tartar*
*⅛ teaspoon salt*
*½ cup granulated sugar*
*1 cup cold heavy cream*
*2 tablespoons confectioners' sugar*

1. In large bowl of electric mixer, let egg whites warm to room temperature—about 1 hour. Meanwhile, in water, simmer apricots, covered, about ½ hour, or until very tender. Then press apricots, with cooking liquid, through sieve or food mill, or mix in blender, to make purée.
2. To 2 cups apricot purée, add ¼ teaspoon almond extract; refrigerate.
3. About 1 hour before dessert time, preheat oven to 325F.
4. Butter 2-quart casserole; then sprinkle with little granulated sugar.
5. Beat egg whites until foamy throughout. Add cream of tartar and salt; continue beating to form soft peaks. Gradually add ½ cup granulated sugar, 2 tablespoons at a time, beating after each addition until whites form stiff peaks.
6. Gently fold apricot purée into whites until thoroughly combined. Turn out into prepared casserole; set in pan of hot water. Bake 45 minutes.
7. At dessert time, whip cream until stiff; add confectioners' sugar and ⅛ teaspoon almond extract.
8. Serve soufflé at once with whipped cream.
Makes 8 servings.

# ❖ ORANGE SOUFFLÉ SURPRISE

8 egg whites
Butter or margarine
Sugar
4 ladyfingers, split
1¼ cups orange juice
6 egg yolks
¾ cup sugar
½ teaspoon vanilla extract
¾ cup sifted all-purpose flour
1 cup milk
2 tablespoons grated orange peel
Sweetened whipped cream

1. In large bowl of electric mixer, let egg whites warm to room temperature—about 1 hour.
2. Lightly butter bottom and side of 1½-quart straight-side soufflé dish (7½-inch diameter). Sprinkle evenly with 2 tablespoons sugar.
3. Fold 26-inch-long piece of waxed paper lengthwise into thirds. Lightly butter one side; then sprinkle evenly with sugar.
4. With string, tie collar (sugar side inside) around soufflé dish, to form 2-inch rim above top.
5. Place half of ladyfingers in single layer in shallow dish. Sprinkle with ¼ cup orange juice; set aside.
6. In medium bowl, beat yolks at high speed until thick. Add ¼ cup sugar; beat until very thick and lemon-colored—about 3 minutes.
7. Beat in remaining orange juice and the vanilla to combine well. Add flour, blending thoroughly.
8. In large saucepan, heat milk with ¼ cup sugar, stirring to dissolve sugar, until bubbles form around edge of pan.
9. Stir hot milk mixture into egg-yolk mixture; pour back into saucepan. Cook, over medium heat, stirring constantly, till it thickens and begins to boil—about 10 minutes.
10. Turn out mixture into large bowl. Add orange peel; let cool.
11. Meanwhile, at high speed, beat egg whites until foamy. Gradually beat in ¼ cup sugar. Continue beating until stiff peaks form when beater is slowly raised.
12. Gently fold egg whites into yolk mixture just until well combined.
13. Turn out half of mixture into prepared dish. Arrange remaining ladyfingers on top. Pour on the rest of the mixture. Refrigerate until baking time—no longer than 4 hours (see Note).
14. About 1 hour before serving, preheat oven to 375F. Bake soufflé, set in pan of hot water, 45 to 50 minutes, or until golden-brown. It should shake slightly in center.
15. Serve soufflé at once. The surprise is soft part in center. Serve as sauce, with sweetened whipped cream.
Makes 8 servings.

Note: If desired, soufflé may be baked at once, without refrigerating, 45 to 50 minutes, as directed above, in preheated 375F oven.

# ❖ COLD CARAMEL SOUFFLÉ

*¾ cup egg whites (about 6 eggs)*
*3¼ cups superfine granulated sugar*
*English Custard Sauce, page 149*

1. In large bowl of electric mixer, let egg whites warm to room temperature—about 1 hour.
2. Meanwhile, place 1½ cups sugar in medium-size heavy skillet. To caramelize, cook over medium heat, stirring, until sugar is completely melted and begins to boil—syrup should be a medium brown.
3. Hold 1½-quart oven-proof glass casserole with pot holder, and pour in hot syrup all at once. Tilt and rotate casserole until bottom and side are thoroughly coated. Set on wire rack, and let cool.
4. Beat egg whites, at high speed, until very stiff—about 5 minutes.
5. While continuing to beat, gradually pour in 1¼ cups sugar, in continuous stream—takes about 3 minutes. Scrape side of bowl with rubber spatula. Beat 10 minutes.
6. Meanwhile, about 5 minutes before beating time is up, place ½ cup sugar in heavy medium skillet, and caramelize as in Step 2. Remove from heat, and immediately place skillet in pan of cold water for a few seconds, or until syrup is thick; stir constantly.
7. With beater at medium speed, gradually pour syrup into beaten egg-white mixture. Scrape side of bowl with rubber spatula. Return to high speed, and continue beating 3 minutes longer.
8. Preheat oven to 250F.
9. Turn out egg-white mixture into prepared casserole, spreading evenly. Set in large baking pan; pour boiling water to 1-inch depth around casserole.
10. Bake 1 hour, or until meringue seems firm when gently shaken and rises about ½ inch above casserole.
11. Meanwhile, make English Custard Sauce.
12. Remove casserole from water; place on wire rack to cool. Refrigerate until well chilled—6 hours or overnight.
13. To unmold: Run small spatula around edge of meringue to loosen. Hold casserole in pan of very hot water at least 1 minute. Invert onto serving dish.
14. Pour some of the sauce over meringue, and pass the rest.
Makes 8 servings.

# CHESECAKES

## ❖ LINDY'S FAMOUS CHEESECAKE

### CRUST:

*1 cup sifted all-purpose flour*
*¼ cup sugar*
*1 teaspoon grated lemon peel*
*½ teaspoon vanilla extract*
*1 egg yolk*
*¼ cup soft butter or margarine*

### FILLING:

*5 pkg (8-oz size) soft cream cheese*
*1¾ cups sugar*
*3 tablespoons flour*
*1½ teaspoons grated lemon peel*
*1½ teaspoons grated orange peel*
*¼ teaspoon vanilla extract*
*5 eggs*
*2 egg yolks*
*¼ cup heavy cream*

*Cherry Glaze, page 147, or twice recipe for Strawberry Glaze, page 146, and Pineapple Glaze, page 147*

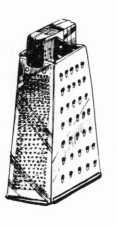

1. Make Crust: In medium bowl, combine flour, sugar, lemon peel, and vanilla. Make well in center; add egg yolk and butter. Mix, with fingertips, until dough cleans side of bowl.
2. Form into ball, and wrap in waxed paper. Refrigerate about 1 hour.
3. Preheat oven to 400F. Grease bottom and side of 9-inch springform pan. Remove side from pan.
4. Roll one third of dough on bottom of springform pan; trim edge of dough.
5. Bake 8 to 10 minutes, or until golden.
6. Meanwhile, divide rest of dough into 3 parts. Roll each part into strip 2½ inches wide and about 10 inches long.
7. Put together springform pan, with baked crust on bottom.
8. Fit dough strips to side of pan, joining ends to line inside completely. Trim dough so it comes only three fourths way up side of pan. Refrigerate until ready to fill.
9. Preheat oven to 500F.
10. Make Filling: In large bowl of electric mixer, combine cheese, sugar, flour, lemon and orange peels, and vanilla. Beat, at high speed, just to blend.
11. Beat in eggs and egg yolks, one at a time. Add cream, beating just until well combined. Pour mixture into springform pan.
12. Bake 10 minutes. Reduce oven temperature to 250F, and bake 1 hour longer.
13. Let cheesecake cool in pan on wire rack. Glaze top with Cherry Glaze. Refrigerate 3 hours or overnight.
14. To serve: Loosen pastry from side of pan with spatula. Remove side of springform pan. Cut cheesecake into wedges.
Makes 16 to 20 servings.

# ✪ GLAZED LEMON-CREAM-CHEESE CAKE

## CRUST:

2½ cups packaged graham-cracker
    crumbs
¼ cup sugar
½ cup butter or margarine, softened

## FILLING:

3 pkg (8-oz size) soft cream cheese
3 tablespoons grated lemon peel
1½ cups sugar
3 tablespoons flour
4 eggs
½ cup lemon juice

Strawberry, Blueberry, and Pineap-
    ple Glazes, below
Sour cream

1. Make Crust: In medium bowl, with hands or back of metal spoon, mix graham-cracker crumbs with sugar and butter until well combined.
2. With back of spoon, press crumb mixture into bottom and sides of greased 12-by-8-by-2-inch baking dish.
3. Preheat the oven to 350F.
4. Make Filling: In large bowl of electric mixer, at medium speed, beat cream cheese, lemon peel, sugar, and flour until smooth and well combined.
5. Beat in eggs, one at a time. Then beat in lemon juice.
6. Pour filling into crust-lined dish. Bake 35 to 40 minutes, or until center of filling seems firm when dish is shaken.
7. Cool completely on wire rack. Refrigerate 4 hours or overnight—until it is very well chilled.
8. Meanwhile, make Glazes.
9. Lightly mark filling in half crosswise. Then mark each half diagonally, forming 8 sections in all. Spoon glaze evenly over each section. Refrigerate 1 hour before cutting into squares to serve. Pass sour cream. Wonderful for large buffet or dessert party.
Makes 12 to 16 servings.

# ✪ STRAWBERRY GLAZE

1 pkg (10 oz) frozen strawberry
    halves, thawed
1 tablespoon sugar
2 teaspoons cornstarch

1. Drain strawberries, reserving ½ cup liquid.
2. In a small saucepan, combine sugar and cornstarch. Stir in reserved liquid.
3. Over medium heat, bring to boiling, stirring; boil 1 minute.
4. Remove from heat; cool slightly. Stir in strawberries; cool completely.
Makes 1 cup.

# ✪ BLUEBERRY GLAZE

1 pkg (10 oz) frozen blueberries,
    thawed
1 tablespoon sugar
2 teaspoons cornstarch

1. Drain blueberries, reserving liquid. Measure liquid; add water, if necessary, to make ½ cup.
2. In small saucepan, combine sugar and cornstarch. Stir in reserved liquid.
3. Over medium heat, bring to boiling, stirring; boil 1 minute.
4. Remove from heat; cool slightly. Stir in blueberries. Cool completely.
Makes 2 cups.

# ✣ PINEAPPLE GLAZE

*1 tablespoon sugar*
*2 teaspoons cornstarch*
*1 can (8¼ oz) crushed pineapple, un-*
  *drained*

1. In small saucepan, combine sugar and cornstarch. Stir in pineapple.
2. Over medium heat, bring to boiling, stirring; boil 1 minute. Cool completely.
Makes 1 cup.

# ✣ CHERRY GLAZE

*1 can (1 lb) sour red cherries, packed*
  *in water*
*¼ cup sugar*
*1 tablespoon cornstarch*
*1 tablespoon lemon juice*

1. Drain cherries, reserving ½ cup liquid. Set cherries aside until ready to use.
2. In small saucepan, combine sugar and cornstarch. Add reserved cherry liquid, stirring until mixture is smooth.
3. Bring to boiling, stirring, over medium heat; boil 2 or 3 minutes. The mixture will be thickened and translucent.
4. Remove from heat; let cool slightly. Add lemon juice and cherries. Cool thoroughly before spooning over top of cooled cheesecake.
Makes 2 cups glaze.

# ✣ CHOCOLATE MARBLE CHEESECAKE

*½ cup chocolate-wafer crumbs*
*1 tablespoon butter or margarine,*
  *softened*
*3 pkg (8-oz size) cream cheese, soft-*
  *ened*
*1 cup sugar*
*1½ teaspoons vanilla extract*
*5 eggs*
*2 squares semisweet chocolate,*
  *melted*
*Chocolate Sour-Cream Frosting,*
  *below*

1. In a small bowl, combine crumbs and butter. Lightly grease bottom of 9-inch springform pan. Press mixture into bottom.
2. Preheat oven to 300F. In large bowl of electric mixer, combine cream cheese, sugar, and vanilla. Beat until smooth. Add eggs, one at a time, beating well after each addition.
3. Set aside 1 cup of mixture. Pour remaining mixture into prepared pan. Fold melted chocolate into the 1 cup cheese mixture. Spoon onto mixture in pan, and cut through batter in spiral motion, for marbled effect.
4. Bake 50 to 55 minutes, or until mixture is just set. Remove to wire rack; cool completely. Refrigerate 2 hours.
5. Frost top and side of cake with Chocolate Sour-Cream Frosting. Refrigerate to chill very well before serving—about 4 hours. Place on serving plate; wrap with plastic wrap.
Makes 12 servings.

## CHOCOLATE SOUR-CREAM FROSTING

*1 pkg (6 oz) semisweet-chocolate*
  *pieces*
*½ cup sour cream*
*Dash salt*

1. Melt chocolate pieces in top of double boiler over hot, not boiling, water.
2. Add sour cream and salt. With wooden spoon, beat frosting until creamy and of spreading consistency.

# DESSERT SAUCES

## ❖ BRANDY SAUCE

*4 egg yolks*
*½ cup sugar*
*⅓ cup brandy*
*½ cup heavy cream*

1. In top of double boiler, beat egg yolks with sugar until very thick and light. Stir in brandy; cook, stirring, over hot, not boiling, water until thickened.
2. Refrigerate until well chilled.
3. Just before serving, pour cream into small bowl; beat until stiff. Fold into brandy mixture until well combined.
Makes 1½ cups.

## ❖ BUTTERSCOTCH SAUCE

*⅓ cup butter or margarine*
*1 cup light-brown sugar, firmly*
  *packed*
*2 tablespoons light corn syrup*
*⅓ cup heavy cream*

1. Melt butter in saucepan over low heat. Stir in brown sugar, corn syrup, and cream. Bring to boiling point. Then remove from heat, and cool slightly.
2. Serve warm or cold.
Makes 1¼ cups.

## ❖ QUICK CHOCOLATE SAUCE

*1 pkg (6 oz) semisweet-chocolate*
  *pieces*
*⅔ cup light cream*

1. Combine chocolate pieces and cream in medium saucepan. Stir constantly, over low heat, just until chocolate is melted.
2. Serve warm, over ice cream or cakes.
Makes about 1 cup.

## ❖ DELUXE CHOCOLATE SAUCE

*¼ cup sugar*
*⅓ cup light cream*
*1 pkg (4 oz) sweet cooking chocolate*
*1 square (1 oz) unsweetened chocolate*

1. In top of double boiler, combine sugar and 2 tablespoons cream; cook, over boiling water, until sugar is dissolved.
2. Cut up both kinds of chocolate. Remove double

boiler from heat, but leave top over bottom. Add chocolate to cream mixture, stirring until melted.
3. With spoon, beat in remaining cream. Serve warm.
Makes 1 cup.

# ✣ FUDGE SAUCE

*3 squares unsweetened chocolate*
*½ cup water*
*¾ cup sugar*
*¼ teaspoon salt*
*4½ tablespoons butter or margarine*
*¾ teaspoon vanilla extract*

1. In small saucepan, combine chocolate and water. Cook, over low heat and stirring occasionally, until chocolate is melted.
2. Add sugar and salt; cook, stirring, until sugar is dissolved and mixture thickens—about 5 minutes.
3. Remove from heat; stir in butter and vanilla. Let cool.
Makes about 1½ cups.

# ✣ ENGLISH CUSTARD SAUCE

*⅓ cup sugar*
*1 tablespoon cornstarch*
*2 cups milk*
*2 tablespoons butter or margarine*
*6 egg yolks*
*1½ teaspoons vanilla extract*
*½ cup heavy cream*

1. In medium saucepan, combine sugar and cornstarch. Gradually add milk; stir until smooth. Then add butter.
2. Cook over medium heat, stirring constantly, until mixture is thickened and comes to boil. Boil 1 minute. Remove from heat.
3. In medium bowl, slightly beat egg yolks. Gradually add a little hot mixture, beating well.
4. Stir into rest of hot mixture; cook over medium heat, stirring constantly, just until mixture boils. Remove from heat; stir in vanilla.
5. Strain custard immediately into bowl. Refrigerate, covered, until cool. Stir in heavy cream. Return to refrigerator until well chilled.
Makes about 2½ cups.

# ✣ HARD SAUCE

*¼ cup butter or margarine, softened*
*1½ cups sifted confectioners' sugar*
*2 tablespoons light rum*

1. In medium bowl, with portable electric mixer at high speed, beat butter until light.
2. Add sugar gradually, beating until sauce is smooth and fluffy. Beat in rum.
3. Refrigerate, covered, until ready to use.
4. Let stand at room temperature, to soften slightly, before serving.
Makes about 1 cup.

## RASPBERRY SAUCE

*2 pkg (10-oz size) frozen raspberries, thawed*
*Water*
*2 tablespoons cornstarch*
*½ cup currant jelly*

1. Drain raspberries, reserving liquid. Add enough water to liquid to make 2 cups.
2. In small saucepan, blend liquid with cornstarch. Bring to boiling over medium heat, stirring constantly; boil 5 minutes. Stir in jelly until melted. Remove from heat; add raspberries. Refrigerate, covered, until cold.

Makes 2 cups.

## ORANGE-YOGURT SAUCE

*1 pkg (3 oz) cream cheese, at room temperature*
*¼ cup plain yogurt*
*¼ cup orange marmalade*
*2 teaspoons Cointreau or curaçao*

1. In small bowl, with wooden spoon or with portable electric mixer at medium speed, beat cream cheese until smooth. Beat in yogurt.
2. Stir in marmalade and Cointreau until well blended. Cover and chill until serving time. Serve over crêpes or pancakes.

Makes ¾ cup.

## BERRY-YOGURT SAUCE

*1 pkg (10 oz) frozen strawberries or raspberries, thawed*
*2 cups plain yogurt*
*⅛ teaspoon almond extract*

1. Purée berries in blender or food processor until smooth. Combine with yogurt in medium bowl; add almond extract.
2. Chill, covered, until serving. Serve over fruit.

Makes 3 cups.

## YOGURT CHANTILLY

*½ cup heavy cream*
*3 tablespoons confectioners' sugar*
*1 teaspoon vanilla extract*
*½ cup plain yogurt*

1. Combine cream and confectioners' sugar in medium bowl, and refrigerate 1 hour to chill.
2. With portable electric mixer at high speed, beat cream mixture until it begins to stiffen. Add vanilla and beat until stiff.
3. Using rubber spatula or wire whisk, gently fold yogurt into whipped cream. Chill, covered, until serving. Serve over fruit.

Makes 1½ cups.

*Note*: One tablespoon of apricot brandy, Grand Marnier, or rum may be substituted for the vanilla.

# EGGS and CHEESE

# ✦ ALL ABOUT EGGS

Eggs, the most versatile of foods, are rich in protein, iron, riboflavin, vitamins A and D, and fat. They are delicate objects, both in the shell and out of it. That characteristic influences the handling and cooking of eggs.

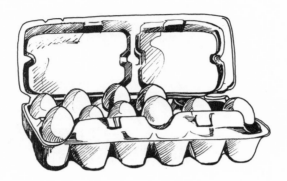

## BUYING EGGS

In the market, eggs will be priced according to their size, their grade, and, depending upon demand, their color. Eggs are available in five sizes, from jumbo to small. If the price difference between sizes is 7 cents a dozen or less, the larger size will be the better buy.

Eggs come in four grades, from AA down to C. Grade AA is the most expensive and is excellent for table use; the white covers a small area and the yolk stands high. Grade A is very good for table use; the white spreads a bit more but the yolk still stands high. Grade B is good for cooking and baking, and grade C is all right for the same uses. Most families, unless they do a lot of baking, settle on Grade A large eggs for all purposes; this is the size and grade used in tested recipes.

The contents of all eggs, whether brown- or white-shelled, are exactly the same. Where brown eggs are in demand, they will be more expensive; where they're not favored, they'll be cheaper.

## STORING EGGS

Ideally, eggs should be refrigerated from the time they're gathered until they are used. You can do your part by refrigerating them as soon as you get them home from the market. Eggs have a natural protective coating that keeps them fresh; don't wash it off until ready to use them.

Eggs separate best when they are cold; use them directly from the refrigerator. However, egg whites whip best at room temperature. Separate eggs and let the whites stand about 30 minutes before whipping. If you aren't planning to use the yolks immediately, put them in a small jar with a tight-fitting lid. Cover them with cold water, put the lid on the jar, and refrigerate. Drain and use in 2 or 3 days. Whites will keep cold and covered for about 10 days.

# ❖ FRIED EGGS SUNNY SIDE UP AND VARIATIONS

*1 to 2 tablespoons butter or margarine*
*2 eggs*

1. In small skillet, melt enough butter to just cover surface of skillet, and heat until it sizzles a drop of water.
2. Break eggs and slip them into hot pan. Immediately lower heat, and cook gently 3 to 4 minutes. To cook film over yolk, baste with hot fat, if desired.
3. With broad spatula, lift eggs out of pan onto warm, not hot, serving plate.
Makes 1 to 2 servings.

*Fried Eggs–Over*: Follow Steps 1 and 2 above but cook eggs just 3 minutes. Turn with broad spatula, and cook 1 more minute.

*Steam-Fried Eggs*: Follow Step 1 above using just enough butter to grease skillet. Break eggs and slip them into hot skillet. As soon as edges turn white, add ½ teaspoon water per egg, and cover pan tightly. Cook 3 to 4 minutes.

*Note*: When using skillet with a nonstick surface, you may omit butter.

# ❖ SOFT-COOKED AND HARD-COOKED EGGS

*2 or more eggs*
*Water to cover eggs*

*Soft-Cooked Eggs, Cold-Water Method*:
1. Put eggs in saucepan large enough to hold them without crowding.
2. Add enough cold water to cover by at least 1 inch; bring water rapidly to boiling.
3. Remove pan from heat immediately. Cover, and let stand 2 to 4 minutes, depending on hardness desired.
4. Cool briefly under cold running water to prevent further cooking. Serve in small sauce dishes or on toast.

*Soft-Cooked Eggs, Boiling-Water Method*:
1. Eggs must be at room temperature. Take them out of refrigerator 45 minutes before cooking, and bring them to room temperature in pan of warm, not hot, water.
2. In saucepan large enough to hold eggs without crowding, heat to boiling enough water to cover eggs by at least 1 inch.
3. Lower eggs gently into boiling water. Remove pan from heat. Cover, and let stand 6 to 8 minutes.
4. Cool briefly under cold running water to prevent further cooking, and serve as above.

*Hard-Cooked Eggs*:
1. Follow cold-water or boiling-water methods above.
2. For cold-water method, let eggs stand 15 minutes after removing them from heat. For boiling-water method, after placing eggs in pan, lower heat immediately to keep water below simmering, and hold at that heat 20 minutes.
3. By either method, cool eggs promptly in cold water to prevent dark surface on the yolks and to make shells easier to remove.

# ✦ SKILLET SCRAMBLED EGGS

*1½ tablespoons butter or margarine*
*4 eggs*
*¼ teaspoon salt*
*Dash pepper*
*2 tablespoons light cream*

1. Heat butter in small skillet over low heat.
2. Break eggs into skillet; stir with fork.
3. Add salt, pepper, and cream; mix well.
4. Cook slowly. As eggs start to set at bottom, gently lift cooked portion, with spatula, letting uncooked portion flow to bottom of pan.
5. When eggs are cooked but still shiny and moist, remove from skillet.
Makes 2 servings.

*Bacon Scrambled Eggs*: Sauté 4 bacon slices until crisp; drain well. Crumble bacon; stir into eggs as they cook.

*Cheese Scrambled Eggs*: Stir 1 teaspoon finely chopped onion and ¼ cup grated mild Cheddar cheese into eggs as they cook.

# ✦ SCRAMBLED EGGS À LA SUISSE

*8 eggs*
*½ cup light cream*
*½ teaspoon salt*
*Dash ground red pepper*
*1 cup grated natural Swiss cheese*
  *(¼ lb)*
*2 tablespoons butter or margarine*
*Snipped chives or parsley*

1. With rotary beater, beat eggs, cream, salt, and pepper in top of double boiler until well combined.
2. Stir in ¾ cup Swiss cheese and the butter.
3. Cook, over gently boiling water, stirring occasionally, 12 to 15 minutes, or until eggs are set but still creamy.
4. Serve eggs sprinkled with rest of cheese and the chives.
Makes 4 servings.

# ⚙ BASIC OMELET

3 eggs
¼ teaspoon salt
1 tablespoon cold water
1 tablespoon butter or margarine

1. In medium bowl, with wire whisk or rotary beater, beat eggs with salt and water just until well mixed. (Mixture should not be too frothy.) Meanwhile, slowly heat 9-inch heavy skillet or omelet pan. To test temperature, sprinkle small amount of cold water on skillet; water should sizzle and roll off in drops. Add butter; heat until it sizzles briskly—it should not brown.

2. Quickly turn out egg mixture, all at once, into skillet. Cook over medium heat.

3. As omelet sets, run spatula around edge, to loosen. Tilt pan, to let uncooked portion run underneath. Continue loosening and tilting until omelet is almost dry on top and golden-brown underneath.

4. To turn out, loosen edge with spatula. Fold, in thirds, to edge of pan; tilt out onto plate.

Makes 1 serving.

# ⚙ CHEESE OMELET

### FILLING:

1 tablespoon flour
¼ teaspoon dry mustard
⅛ teaspoon salt
⅛ teaspoon pepper
½ cup milk
2 cups grated sharp Cheddar cheese
1 teaspoon grated onion

4 Basic Omelets, above
½ cup grated sharp Cheddar cheese

1. Make Filling: In top of double boiler, over hot water, combine flour, mustard, salt, pepper, and milk, stirring until smooth.

2. Add 2 cups cheese and the onion; cook, stirring occasionally, 15 to 20 minutes, or until mixture thickens and cheese is melted.

3. Remove from heat; let stand over hot water.

4. Make 4 Basic Omelets, one by one, in omelet pan or skillet with oven-safe handle. Before pouring into pan, add 1 tablespoon cheese to each.

5. Just before folding each omelet, place ¼ cup filling in center. Fold over in thirds; sprinkle each with 1 tablespoon cheese.

6. Run under broiler, 6 inches from heat, until cheese is bubbly and golden—about 1 minute.

7. With spatula, lift out onto serving plate; keep warm until serving.

Makes 4 servings.

# BASIC PUFFY OMELET

6 egg whites
⅛ teaspoon cream of tartar
6 egg yolks
¾ teaspoon salt
Dash pepper
6 tablespoons milk
2 tablespoons butter or margarine
2 teaspoons salad oil

1. In large bowl of electric mixer, let egg whites warm to room temperature—about 1 hour.
2. Preheat oven to 350F.
3. With mixer at high speed, beat egg whites with cream of tartar just until stiff peaks form when beater is slowly raised.
4. In small bowl of electric mixer, using same beaters, beat egg yolks until thick and lemon-colored.
5. Add salt, pepper, and milk gradually; beat until well combined.
6. With wire whisk or rubber scraper, using an under-and-over motion, gently fold egg-yolk mixture into egg whites just until combined.
7. Slowly heat a 9- or 10-inch heavy skillet with heat-resistant handle, or an omelet pan. To test temperature: Sprinkle a little cold water on skillet. Water should sizzle and roll off in drops.
8. Add butter and oil; heat until it sizzles briskly—it should not brown. Tilt pan to coat side with butter mixture.
9. Spread egg mixture evenly in pan; cook, over low heat, without stirring, until lightly browned on underside—about 10 minutes.
10. Transfer skillet to oven; bake 10 to 12 minutes, or until top seems firm when gently pressed with fingertip.
11. To serve: Fold omelet in half. Turn out onto heated serving platter. Garnish with parsley sprigs, if desired.
Makes 4 servings.

# CHICKEN-LIVER OMELET

## CHICKEN-LIVER FILLING:

1 lb chicken livers
3 tablespoons butter or margarine
½ cup sliced onion
1 teaspoon flour
1 can (8 oz) tomatoes
½ cup dry white wine
2 teaspoons chopped parsley
½ teaspoon salt
½ teaspoon Worcestershire sauce

Basic Puffy Omelet, above

1. Make Chicken-Liver Filling: Wash chicken livers; drain on paper towels. Cut each in half. In hot butter in large skillet, quickly brown chicken livers—about 5 minutes. Remove from skillet.
2. Add onion to skillet; sauté until golden. Remove from heat. Stir in flour, tomatoes, wine, parsley, salt, and Worcestershire. Simmer, stirring frequently, about 5 minutes. Add chicken livers; simmer 5 minutes longer.
3. Make Basic Puffy Omelet through Step 10.
4. Cut omelet into wedges; spoon chicken livers over each serving.
Makes 6 servings.

# ❖ PUFFY SPANISH OMELET

*Basic Puffy Omelet, page 157*

## SAUCE:

2 tablespoons butter or margarine
1 clove garlic, crushed
¼ cup chopped onion
⅓ cup thinly sliced celery
½ cup chopped green pepper
½ teaspoon salt
⅛ teaspoon pepper
¼ teaspoon paprika
¼ teaspoon dried oregano
1 can (8 oz) tomato sauce
1 can (3 oz) sliced mushrooms,
  drained
9 pitted jumbo ripe olives, thickly
  sliced
1⅓ cups coarsely chopped fresh
  tomatoes

*Parsley sprigs*

1. Make Basic Puffy Omelet through Step 10.
2. Meanwhile, make Sauce: In hot butter in medium skillet, sauté garlic, onion, celery, and green pepper until tender—about 5 minutes.
3. Add salt, pepper, paprika, oregano, and tomato sauce; bring to boiling. Reduce heat; simmer, uncovered, 10 minutes.
4. Add mushrooms, olives, and tomatoes; cook, stirring, until heated through.
5. To serve: Fold half of omelet over other half. Remove to heated serving platter. Pour some of sauce over omelet; pass rest. Garnish with parsley sprigs.
Makes 4 servings.

# ❖ EGGS FLORENTINE

2 tablespoons butter or margarine
1 tablespoon finely chopped onion
1½ tablespoons flour
¼ teaspoon salt
Dash pepper
Dash ground nutmeg
1 cup milk
¼ cup grated Swiss or Parmesan
  cheese
1 pkg (10 oz) frozen chopped spinach,
  thawed and well-drained
4 eggs
1 tablespoon grated Parmesan cheese

1. In hot butter in medium-size heavy saucepan, sauté onion, stirring, until golden—about 5 minutes. Remove from heat.
2. Add flour, salt, pepper, and nutmeg; stir until smooth. Add milk, a small amount at a time, stirring after each addition. Return to heat.
3. Over medium heat, bring to boiling, stirring constantly; reduce heat, and simmer 3 minutes, stirring. Add ¼ cup grated cheese to sauce in saucepan, stirring constantly. Cook, stirring, over low heat until cheese is melted; do not boil. To keep sauce hot, cover and place over hot water.
4. Meanwhile, cook spinach as package directs; drain well.
5. Poach eggs (see poaching instructions on page 159).
6. Combine cheese sauce with spinach; mix well. Turn out into shallow 1-quart baking dish. Arrange poached eggs on top. Sprinkle top with 1 tablespoon grated cheese. Run under broiler a few minutes to melt cheese.
Makes 2 servings.

# ✦ POACHED EGGS AND TOMATOES

*4 slices bacon, diced*
*½ cup finely chopped onion*
*1 can (1 lb) Italian tomatoes, drained*
*1¼ teaspoons salt*
*¼ teaspoon pepper*
*2 tablespoons butter or margarine*
*2 tablespoons flour*
*1 cup milk*
*1 cup grated Cheddar cheese*
*Dash pepper and paprika*
*8 eggs*
*2 tablespoons fresh bread crumbs tossed with 1 tablespoon melted butter or margarine*

1. Sauté bacon in skillet until crisp. Lift out bacon with slotted spoon; drain on paper towels.
2. In 2 tablespoons bacon fat in same skillet, sauté onion until tender—about 5 minutes. Stir in tomatoes, 1 teaspoon salt, and the pepper; cook, stirring, about 10 minutes.
3. Meanwhile, melt 1 tablespoon butter. Stir in flour; then add milk. Bring to boiling, stirring; add ⅓ cup cheese, ¼ teaspoon salt, and dash pepper and paprika. Cook, stirring, until cheese is melted. Remove from heat.
4. Meanwhile, poach eggs: In shallow pan or skillet, bring water (about 1½ inches deep) to boiling point. Reduce heat to simmer. Break each egg into saucer; quickly slip egg into water. Cook, covered, 3 to 5 minutes. Lift out of water with slotted spoon.
5. Pour tomato sauce into shallow 1½-quart baking dish. Carefully arrange poached eggs evenly on top of sauce. Spoon cheese sauce over and around eggs. Sprinkle with crumbs, rest of cheese, and the bacon. Run under broiler a few minutes to brown slightly. Makes 6 servings.

# ✦ EGGS BENEDICT

*Hollandaise Sauce, page 461*
*4 English muffins*
*8 teaspoons butter or margarine*
*1 teaspoon salt*
*8 eggs*
*4 slices fully cooked ham (½ lb)*
*8 parsley or watercress sprigs*

1. Prepare Hollandaise Sauce. Keep warm over hot water.
2. Separate muffins into halves crosswise. Place on cookie sheet. Spread each side with 1 teaspoon butter. Toast until golden-brown. Cover; keep warm.
3. In large skillet, bring 1 inch water to simmering; add salt.
4. Break one egg at a time into custard cup. Slip eggs into water carefully, one by one; poach, covered, 3 to 5 minutes. If possible, use rings to keep shape circular.
5. Meanwhile, in large skillet, sauté ham about 3 minutes on each side. Cut slices in half.
6. Arrange ham slices on muffins.
7. Remove eggs with slotted utensil; trim if necessary, being careful not to break yolk.
8. Place eggs on ham; top with Hollandaise Sauce. Run under broiler until sauce is golden.
9. With broad spatula, remove to serving plates. Garnish with parsley.
Makes 4 servings.

# ❖ SHIRRED EGGS AND HAM

6 boiled-ham slices
1 cup plus 2 tablespoons light cream
12 eggs
Salt
Pepper
6 tablespoons grated Cheddar cheese

1. Preheat oven to 325F.
2. Line each of 6 ramekins or 9½-ounce casseroles with boiled-ham slice.
3. Then, into each, pour 3 tablespoons cream. Carefully slip 2 eggs on top of cream; sprinkle with salt, pepper, and 1 tablespoon cheese.
4. Cover each ramekin with foil. Bake 20 to 25 minutes, or until eggs are of desired doneness.
Makes 6 servings.

# ❖ DEVILED EGGS

12 eggs
¾ cup mayonnaise or cooked salad dressing
1 tablespoon white vinegar
1 teaspoon dry mustard
1½ teaspoons Worcestershire sauce
½ teaspoon salt
⅛ teaspoon pepper
⅛ teaspoon paprika
Parsley sprigs

1. Hard-cook eggs, as directed on page 155. Remove shells. Cool eggs completely.
2. Halve eggs lengthwise. Take out yolks, being careful not to break whites.
3. Press yolks through sieve into medium bowl. Add remaining ingredients, except parsley; mix with fork until smooth and fluffy.
4. Lightly mound yolk mixture in egg whites. Garnish each with parsley sprig. Refrigerate, covered, until serving.
Makes 12 servings.

# CHEESE

There are an enormous number of cheeses, both imported and domestic, on the market—one large New York cheese store lists more than 1,000 varieties in its mail-order catalog. Americans have become sophisticated in their use of cheese; they've gone far beyond the cheese sandwich, fondue, quiche, and the appetizer tray. Soft cheeses are served with salad and crusty bread; all cheeses except the very hard ones, like Parmesan, are delicious with fresh fruit for dessert; a dollop of soft or blue-veined cheese complements poached pears or peaches; and the grating cheeses are no longer reserved for pasta—they taste marvelous sprinkled over a fresh vegetable soup or a green salad. As a general rule, cheeses will taste best served at room temperature; only the soft, unripened cheeses should be served slightly chilled.

To describe all of the cheeses on the market is impossible in a book of this size; in these pages we give you some of our most-requested cheese recipes and a guide describing the flavor and texture of some of the most popular cheeses with suggestions for serving them. Beyond that we suggest the advice, "The only way to know cheese is to eat it." Most cheese stores are willing to let you have a nibble to taste before buying.

## GUIDE TO USING CHEESES

| TYPE OF CHEESE | TEXTURE AND FLAVOR | SUGGESTED USES |
|---|---|---|
| **Soft, unripened cheeses (serve slightly chilled, within a few days of purchasing)** | | |
| American cream cheese | Delicate, very mild flavor | In tea-bread sandwiches, softened for appetizer dips |
| Boursin | Creamy; mild flavor (also with garlic and herbs) | With plain unsalted crackers as an appetizer |
| Crème Danica | Creamy; fresh buttery flavor | With fresh fruit or berries as dessert |
| Neufchâtel | Delicate, very mild flavor | Dessert cheese, although may be used in same ways as cream cheese |
| Ricotta | Similar to cottage cheese but finer in texture | With pastas as layers or fillings |
| Ricotta salata | Firmer cheese, quite like feta | On cheese trays with crackers |
| Swedish Hablé | Soft; delicate flavor | Dessert cheese, nice with nectarines or peaches |
| **Soft, ripened cheeses (serve at room temperature and optimum ripeness; they should be very soft and creamy inside)** | | |
| Brie | Mild to pungent, with edible white crust | Excellent with fresh apples or pears for dessert |
| Camembert | Soft, buttery; mild to strong flavor | On cheese tray and for dessert; good with green salad |
| Coulommiers | Creamy, smooth; mild flavor | Good with dried or fresh fruits |
| Liederkranz | Pungent flavor | A favorite with beer and pretzels |
| Limburger | Creamy; robust flavor, highly aromatic | For sandwiches with black bread and red onion slices |
| **Semisoft cheeses (serve at room temperature, or use in cooking)** | | |
| Bel Paese | Creamy; mild to robust flavor | On cheese trays or as dessert |
| Bonbel | Smooth, soft; mild flavor; yellow | Good for snacks or appetizers |
| Caerphilly | Smooth; slight yogurtlike flavor | With fresh berries or grapes for dessert |
| Feta | White, moist, flaky | In green salads or as appetizer with black olives |
| Gruyère | Slightly nutlike flavor; small holes | To flavor sauces; in wedges with good crackers for dessert |

| TYPE OF CHEESE | TEXTURE AND FLAVOR | SUGGESTED USES |
| --- | --- | --- |
| Havarti | Smooth, small-holed cheese; rich and buttery | On cheese trays and with grapes as dessert |
| Mozzarella | Smooth; mild flavor | Commonly known as the "pizza" cheese and used in pasta casseroles; it melts smoothly |
| Muenster | Creamy white; mild, mellow flavor | Particularly good (in small wheels) with wine; sliced for sandwiches |
| Oka | Mild flavor, aromatic | On cheese tray or as dessert with apples or melon |
| Pont-l'Évêque | Pungent cheese | With tart apples for dessert |
| Port-Salut | Creamy-yellow interior; flavor mellow to robust | As appetizer or dessert |
| Trappist | Mild flavor; aromatic | For dessert with fresh or poached pears |

Semihard to hard cheeses
(serve at room temperature,
or use in cooking)

| | | |
| --- | --- | --- |
| Brick | Pale, firm, mild American cheese | Slices easily for sandwiches, snacks |
| Caciocavallo | Sharp, smoky flavor; similar to provolone | On cheese trays; grated when aged |
| Cantal | Mild with distinctive wine flavor; deep gold color | Good with red wine before or after meal |
| Cheddar | Smooth to crumbly; varies from mild to sharp | All-purpose cheese for sandwiches, sauces, crackers, snacks |
| Colby | Mild, light yellow | For sandwiches; in cooking |
| Double Gloucester | Rich, mellow, robust flavor | With fruit salad or fresh fruit for dessert |
| Edam or Gouda | Mild, nutlike flavor but pungent when aged; usually ball-shaped with red rind | On crackers, as snacks, on cheese trays, with fruit for dessert |
| Fontina | Mild to pungent flavor, depending on age | Good melted on polenta or pizza; aged, use with fruit for salad or dessert |
| Jarlsberg | Smooth; nutlike flavor | On cheese trays |
| Monterey Jack (or Jack) | Mild, buttery type of cheddar | Excellent for melting; also in cheese sauces and on sandwiches |
| Provolone | Smoky-flavored firm cheese | For hero sandwiches with salami; to flavor sauces |
| Swiss (Emmentaler) | Firm, with holes or eyes; sweetish, nutlike flavor | Melt for cheese fondue; slice for sandwiches; julienne for salads |
| Tilsit | Pungent, with small irregular holes | For cheese trays or snacks |

| TYPE OF CHEESE | TEXTURE AND FLAVOR | SUGGESTED USES |
|---|---|---|
| Blue-veined cheeses (serve at room temperature) | | |
| Blue or bleu | Semisoft; piquant spicy flavor | In dips, salads, and salad dressings; with fruit and crackers for dessert |
| Gorgonzola | Rich and creamy; delicate flavor when young, very sharp when aged | An accompaniment to green salad; with poached pears or peaches for dessert |
| Roquefort | Semisoft; sharp flavor | On cheese trays and in salads; try melting over hamburgers |
| Stilton | Semisoft; sharp flavor | For dessert with port wine |
| Very hard cheeses (serve at room temperature or use in cooking) | | |
| Parmesan | Firm; pungent flavor | May be eaten as is when young; aged, grated for sprinkling over pasta or salads |
| Romano | Firm; pungent flavor | As seasoning when grated |
| Sapsago | Sweetish, flavored with clover; pleasant aroma | As seasoning when grated |

# ❖ FABULOUS CHEESE SOUFFLÉ

6 eggs
Butter or margarine
Grated Parmesan cheese
6 tablespoons all-purpose flour
1½ teaspoons salt
Dash ground red pepper
1¼ cups milk
½ cup coarsely grated natural Swiss cheese
¼ teaspoon cream of tartar

1. Separate eggs, placing whites in large bowl, yolks in another large bowl. Set aside until whites warm to room temperature—about 1 hour.
2. Meanwhile, butter 1½-quart straight-side soufflé dish (7½ inches in diameter). Dust lightly with Parmesan—about 1 tablespoon.
3. Tear off sheet of waxed paper 26 inches long. Fold lengthwise into thirds. Lightly butter one side.
4. Wrap waxed paper around soufflé dish, with buttered side against dish and 2-inch rim extending above top edge. Tie with string.
5. Preheat oven to 350F.
6. Melt 5 tablespoons butter in medium saucepan; remove from heat. Stir in flour, 1 teaspoon salt, and the pepper until smooth. Gradually stir in milk.
7. Bring to boiling, stirring. Reduce heat, and simmer, stirring constantly, until mixture becomes very thick and begins to leave bottom and side of pan.
8. With wire whisk or wooden spoon, beat egg yolks. Gradually beat in cooked mixture. Add ½ cup Par-

mesan cheese and the Swiss cheese; beat until well combined.

9. Add remaining ½ teaspoon salt and the cream of tartar to egg whites. With portable electric mixer at high speed, beat until stiff peaks form when beater is raised.

10. With wire whisk or rubber spatula, fold one third of beaten egg whites into warm cheese mixture until well combined. Carefully fold in remaining egg whites just until combined. Turn out into prepared dish.

11. Bake 40 minutes, or until soufflé is puffed and golden-brown. Remove collar. Serve soufflé at once. Makes 4 servings.

# ❖ WELSH RABBIT EN CROÛTE

### VOL AU VENT:

1½ pkg (17¼-oz size) frozen puff pastry
1 egg yolk
1 teaspoon water

### WELSH RABBIT:

2 tablespoons butter or margarine
1 lb sharp Cheddar cheese, grated
½ cup beer
1 egg
½ teaspoon salt
½ teaspoon dry mustard
Dash ground red pepper
1 teaspoon Worcestershire sauce

1. Make Vol au Vent: Remove frozen pastry from package. Let thaw at room temperature 20 minutes. Line baking sheet with foil.

2. Unfold 1 sheet of pastry (2 in a package). Place on lightly floured surface or pastry cloth. Put 8-inch round plate in center. With sharp knife, cut around plate. Remove center round to prepared baking sheet. Prick all over with fork; brush edge with water. Refrigerate. Reserve trimmings.

3. Repeat with second sheet of pastry. In the center of 8-inch round, place 6-inch plate. Cut around plate. Remove outside ring; set on outer edge of bottom round. Place 6-inch round on baking sheet. This is for the lid.

4. Reroll trimmings into 9-inch round. Place 8-inch plate in center; cut around edge. Place 6-inch plate in center; cut around edge. Wet edge of ring lightly with water; carefully place second ring on top of first ring.

5. Remove 6-inch pastry round, and place on top of first 6-inch round.

6. Repeat Step 3 to make another ring for rim. Refreeze any leftover pastry, if desired.

7. Press dull edge of knife all around edge of ring at ½-inch intervals to make design.

8. With sharp knife, cut diamond shapes, 1 inch apart, on top of lid. Brush top lightly with egg yolk mixed with 1 teaspoon water. Also brush top of rim. Refrigerate 1 hour.

9. Preheat oven to 400F. Bake on middle shelf of oven 10 minutes; reduce oven to 350F. Bake 40 to 45 minutes longer, or until golden-brown and crisp. (If top gets too brown, cover with foil.) Remove to rack to cool slightly.

10. Meanwhile, make Welsh Rabbit: In medium saucepan, slowly heat butter. Add cheese and beer. Cook over low heat, stirring frequently, until cheese melts. Remove from heat.
11. In small bowl, beat egg with salt, mustard, pepper, and Worcestershire. Gradually add to cheese mixture, stirring until well combined. Stir over low heat until mixture is heated through and smooth—about 5 minutes.
12. To keep rabbit warm, turn out into top part of double boiler. Let stand over hot water until ready to serve.
13. To serve: Fill center of Vol au Vent with Welsh Rabbit.
Makes 8 servings.

## CHEESE FONDUE

*¾ lb Gruyère cheese, cut into ½-inch cubes*
*¼ lb Emmentaler (Swiss) cheese, cut into ½-inch cubes*
*3 tablespoons flour*
*1 clove garlic, crushed*
*2 cups dry white wine*
*2 loaves French bread*
*1 tablespoon lemon juice*
*3 tablespoons kirsch*

1. In large bowl, toss cheese and flour until well coated.
2. Rub heavy earthenware fondue pot (or heavy enamel-coated pot) with garlic; add white wine and place over medium heat. Cook until small air bubbles rise to surface.
3. Meanwhile, cut French bread into 1¼-inch cubes with some crust on each piece; arrange in serving dish.
4. Stir in lemon juice; add cheese, ⅓ cup at a time, stirring constantly, until cheese is melted. Stir in kirsch and keep mixture bubbling gently.
5. To serve: With a fondue fork, each person spears piece of bread and dips it into bubbling fondue.
Makes 4 servings.

*Note*: Steamed fresh vegetables, cut into 1¼-inch pieces, may be dipped in fondue along with bread cubes.

## HAM-AND-CHEESE FRENCH TOAST

*3 eggs*
*¾ cup milk*
*1 tablespoon sugar*
*¼ teaspoon salt*
*8 white-bread slices, lightly buttered*
*4 slices boiled ham*
*4 slices Swiss or American cheese*
*Butter or margarine*

1. With rotary beater, beat eggs with milk, sugar, and salt just to combine.
2. Make 4 sandwiches with bread, ham, and cheese; cut into quarters diagonally. Place in single layer in shallow baking dish. Pour egg mixture over top, covering completely. Refrigerate overnight.
3. Next day, just before serving, in hot butter, sauté sandwiches until golden on each side and cheese is slightly melted.
Makes 4 servings.

# ❖ SPRINGTIME QUICHE

1½ lb fresh asparagus or 2 pkg (10-oz
    size) frozen asparagus spears
1 quart water
1 teaspoon salt
1 pkg (10- or 11-oz) piecrust mix or
    Pastry for 2-Crust Pie, page 354
1 egg white, beaten slightly
8 bacon slices, sautéed until crisp,
    drained, and crumbled
½ lb natural Swiss cheese, grated
4 eggs
1½ cups half-and-half
⅛ teaspoon ground nutmeg
⅛ teaspoon salt
Dash pepper
6 cherry tomatoes, halved

1. Wash asparagus; break off and discard tough
white portion. Scrape ends of asparagus with vegetable parer. Set aside 16 of the best spears for decoration—they should be 5 inches long. Cut rest of asparagus into ½-inch pieces.
2. In large saucepan, bring water to boiling; add 1
teaspoon salt and the asparagus. Bring back to boiling. Reduce heat, and simmer, covered, 5 minutes.
Drain; rinse asparagus under cold water.
3. Prepare piecrust as package label directs. On
lightly floured board or pastry cloth, with stockinette-covered rolling pin, roll pastry to form 12-inch
circle. Use to line 11-inch quiche pan with removable side or 11-inch pie plate. Flute edge if using pie
plate. Brush bottom with egg white.
4. Preheat oven to 400F.
5. Sprinkle bottom of pie shell with bacon and
cheese, then the cut-up asparagus.
6. In medium bowl, with rotary beater, beat eggs
with half-and-half, nutmeg, salt, and pepper just
until combined.
7. Pour egg mixture into pie shell. Arrange reserved
asparagus spears, spoke fashion, and tomato halves
on pie.
8. Bake 35 minutes, or just until puffy and golden.
Serve warm.
Makes 8 servings.

# ❖ CORNED-BEEF QUICHE

1 can (15½ oz) corned-beef hash
¼ cup finely chopped onion
9-inch Unbaked Pie Shell, page 355
2 eggs
1 container (4 oz) whipped cream
    cheese with chives
1 cup cottage cheese
¼ teaspoon pepper

1. Preheat oven to 350F.
2. Combine corned beef and onion; use to line bottom
of pie shell.
3. In medium bowl, beat eggs until frothy. Add remaining ingredients; blend well. Pour over corned
beef.
4. Bake 50 minutes. Serve warm.
Makes 6 to 8 servings.

# ✪ SPINACH-AND-COTTAGE-CHEESE TART

9-inch Unbaked Pie Shell, page 355
1 egg white, slightly beaten
2 tablespoons butter or margarine
1 cup finely chopped onion
1 pkg (10 oz) frozen chopped spinach,
  thawed, or 1¼ cups chopped cooked
  spinach
1 teaspoon salt
⅛ teaspoon ground nutmeg
Dash pepper
6 eggs
½ cup milk
2 cups cream-style cottage cheese
½ cup grated Parmesan cheese

1. Preheat oven to 375F.
2. Brush pie shell lightly with beaten egg white.
3. In hot butter in medium skillet, sauté onion, stirring, until golden—about 5 minutes.
4. Drain spinach in colander; squeeze to remove excess liquid. Add to onion, along with salt, nutmeg, and pepper; mix well.
5. In medium bowl, beat together eggs and milk until well blended. Add cottage cheese, Parmesan cheese, and spinach mixture; mix well.
6. Turn out into prepared pie shell. Bake 35 to 40 minutes, or until knife inserted in center comes out clean. Serve warm.
Makes 8 servings.

# ✪ BROCCOLI-AND-CHEESE PIE

8 phyllo-pastry leaves
¼ cup butter
½ cup finely chopped onion
3 pkg (10-oz size) frozen chopped
  broccoli, thawed and well drained
3 eggs
½ lb feta cheese, crumbled
¼ cup chopped parsley
2 tablespoons chopped fresh dill
1 teaspoon salt
⅛ teaspoon pepper
½ cup butter, melted

1. Preheat oven to 350F. Let pastry leaves warm to room temperature according to directions on label.
2. In ¼ cup hot butter in medium skillet, sauté onion until golden—about 5 minutes.
3. Add broccoli; stir to combine with onion. Remove from heat.
4. In large bowl, beat eggs with rotary beater. With wooden spoon, stir in cheese, parsley, dill, salt, pepper, and broccoli-onion mixture; mix well.
5. Line inside of 9-inch round pan with removable bottom or 9-inch springform pan with rim in place with 4 phyllo-pastry leaves, overlapping and brushing top of each with melted butter. Keep unused pastry leaves covered with damp paper towels to prevent drying out.
6. Pour filling mixture into pastry-lined pan. Fold overlapping edges of pastry leaves over top of filling.
7. Cut 4 (9-inch) circles from remaining phyllo leaves. Brush each with butter; layer one over the other on top of pie. With scissors, cut through leaves to make 8 sections. Pour any remaining butter over top. Place on jelly-roll pan to catch drippings.
8. Bake 40 to 45 minutes, or until top crust is puffy and golden. Serve warm.
Makes 8 servings.

# ❖ CHILI-CHEESE CASSEROLE

2  cans  (4-oz  size)  green  chilies,
   drained
1 lb Monterey Jack cheese, coarsely
   grated
1 lb Cheddar cheese, coarsely grated
4 egg whites
4 egg yolks
⅔ cup canned evaporated milk, undiluted
1 tablespoon flour
½ teaspoon salt
⅛ teaspoon pepper
2 medium tomatoes, sliced

1. Preheat oven to 325F. Remove seeds from chilies, and dice.
2. In large bowl, combine grated cheeses and green chilies. Turn out into well-buttered shallow 2-quart casserole (12-by-8-by-2-inches).
3. In large bowl, with electric mixer at high speed, beat egg whites just until stiff peaks form when beater is slowly raised.
4. In small bowl of electric mixer, combine egg yolks, milk, flour, salt, and pepper; mix until well blended.
5. Using rubber spatula, gently fold beaten whites into egg-yolk mixture.
6. Pour egg mixture over cheese mixture in casserole, and using fork, "ooze" it through cheese.
7. Bake 30 minutes; remove from oven, and arrange sliced tomatoes, overlapping, around edge of casserole. Bake 30 minutes longer, or until knife blade inserted in center comes out clean. Garnish with sprinkling of chopped green chilies, if desired.
Makes 6 to 8 servings.

# ❖ VEGETABLE-AND-CHEESE CASSEROLE

1 small eggplant (1 lb)
3 zucchini (1 lb)
2 teaspoons salt
2 cups boiling water
¼ cup butter or margarine
2 tablespoons salad oil
2 cups sliced onion
2 small tomatoes, sliced (¾ lb)
¼ teaspoon pepper
½ lb grated Cheddar cheese

1. Wash eggplant. Cut in half lengthwise; slice ½ inch thick. Scrub zucchini; slice diagonally ½ inch thick.
2. Preheat oven to 350F. Grease well 10-inch shallow round or oval baking dish (about 2 inches deep).
3. In large skillet, layer zucchini and eggplant. Add salt and boiling water. Bring to boiling. Cover, reduce heat, and simmer, 5 minutes. Drain well in colander; set aside.
4. In same skillet, in hot butter and oil, sauté onion until tender—about 5 minutes.
5. In bottom of prepared casserole, layer half of onion, then half of eggplant, zucchini, and tomato. Sprinkle with ⅛ teaspoon pepper and 1 cup grated cheese. Repeat layering rest of vegetables; sprinkle with ⅛ teaspoon pepper and remaining cheese.
6. Bake, covered tightly with foil, 30 minutes. Uncover; bake 5 minutes more to evaporate liquid.
Makes 6 servings.

# ✦ BAKED CHEESE-AND-TOMATO FONDUE

⅔ cup butter or margarine, softened
1 clove garlic, minced
1 teaspoon dry mustard
1 loaf (8 oz) Italian bread
3 cups grated Swiss cheese or 1½ cups
　grated Cheddar cheese and 1½ cups
　grated Swiss cheese
3 tablespoons grated onion
1½ teaspoons salt
1 teaspoon paprika
Dash pepper
⅓ cup unsifted all-purpose flour
3 cups milk
1 can (16 oz) stewed tomatoes
3 eggs, beaten

1. Make fondue day before serving: In small bowl, cream ⅓ cup butter with the garlic and ½ teaspoon mustard until well blended.
2. Remove ends of bread; cut loaf into ½-inch-thick slices. Spread one side of each with butter mixture.
3. Line bottom and side of 13-by-9-by-2-inch baking dish with some of bread, buttered side down.
4. In large bowl, combine cheese, onion, salt, paprika, pepper, and remaining mustard; toss until well blended.
5. In medium saucepan, melt remaining butter; remove from heat. Stir in flour. Gradually stir in milk. Bring to boiling.
6. Stir in tomatoes. Add a little hot mixture to eggs, stirring. Pour back into saucepan, stirring.
7. Set aside ½ cup cheese mixture. In baking dish, alternate layers of remaining cheese mixture and remaining bread slices, buttered side up. Pour tomato sauce over all. Sprinkle with reserved cheese mixture.
8. Refrigerate, covered, overnight.
9. Preheat oven to 375F. Bake fondue 45 minutes, or until puffy and golden-brown on top.
Makes 8 servings.

# ✦ BROCCOLI-CHEESE FONDUE

1 pkg (10 oz) frozen chopped broccoli
10 slices day-old white bread
2 tablespoons butter or margarine,
　softened
3 cups grated sharp Cheddar cheese
6 eggs
3½ cups milk
½ teaspoon dried basil leaves
1 teaspoon salt
⅛ teaspoon pepper

1. Cook broccoli according to package directions; drain well. Set aside.
2. Trim crusts from bread slices. With doughnut cutter, cut holes 2¾ inches in diameter from 8 slices. Cut remaining bread slices and the holes into ¼-inch cubes. Spread butter inside 9-by-9-by-2-inch baking dish.
3. In large bowl, toss bread cubes with cheese and broccoli. Make layer in bottom of prepared dish. Arrange 2 rows of bread rings, overlapping slightly on top.
4. In medium bowl, with wire whisk, beat eggs. Add milk, basil, salt, and pepper. Mix until well combined.
5. Pour over fondue. Cover, and set aside ½ hour.
6. Preheat oven to 350F.
7. Bake on lower shelf of oven, uncovered, 60 to 65 minutes, or until puffed and lightly browned.
Makes 8 servings.

## ✳ CHEESE-STUFFED PEPPERS

*6 small green peppers (1½ lb), washed*
*½ lb sharp Cheddar cheese, cut into*
*¼-inch cubes*
*¼ lb Swiss cheese, cut into ¼-inch*
*cubes*
*¼ lb Gruyère cheese, cut into ¼-inch*
*cubes*
*1 medium tomato, cubed*
*½ teaspoon dried basil leaves*
*¼ teaspoon salt*
*Dash pepper*

1. Preheat oven to 375F.
2. In boiling water (2 inches deep) in 5-quart Dutch oven, parboil peppers until tender—10 minutes.
3. Drain peppers. Cut off tops; remove seeds. Place, standing upright, on lightly greased baking dish.
4. In medium bowl, combine cheeses; toss gently.
5. In small bowl, toss together tomato, basil, salt, and pepper.
6. Spoon tomato mixture into bottom of peppers, dividing evenly. Stuff peppers with cheese, rounding tops.
7. Bake 20 minutes, or until hot and cheese is melted. Makes 6 servings.

## ✳ CAMEMBERT EN CROÛTE

*½ cup sifted all-purpose flour*
*⅛ teaspoon salt*
*2 oz cream cheese (¼ cup)*
*¼ cup butter or margarine*
*1 Camembert cheese round (7 or 8 oz),*
*4-inch diameter*
*1 egg yolk*

1. Make pastry day before: Sift flour with salt into medium bowl.
2. With pastry blender, or 2 knives used scissor fashion, cut in cream cheese and butter until mixture resembles coarse crumbs.
3. Shape pastry into ball; flatten slightly. Wrap in plastic wrap or bag. Refrigerate overnight.
4. Start making Camembert en Croûte about 3 hours before serving. On lightly floured pastry cloth or board, roll out pastry to ⅛-inch (not less) thickness.
5. With pastry wheel or knife, cut out 7-inch circle; place on cookie sheet. Set Camembert cheese in center of circle. Bring pastry up around sides and ½ inch over top of cheese, taking care not to stretch or tear pastry and pressing pastry until smooth.
6. Roll out trimmings. With pastry wheel, cut out circle to fit top of cheese exactly.
7. In small bowl, with fork, beat egg yolk and 2 teaspoons water. Brush some of egg mixture on pastry rim around top edge of cheese. Place pastry circle on top.
8. With small cookie cutter, cut leaf and flower shapes from remaining pastry. Place decoratively, in center of pastry. Brush top and decoration lightly with rest of egg mixture.
9. Refrigerate at least 1 hour before baking.
10. Preheat oven to 425F.
11. Bake 20 minutes, or until pastry is golden-brown. Let cool on cookie sheet on wire rack at room temperature 30 minutes.
12. Remove to serving board or plate. Cut into wedges, and serve on small plates.
Makes 6 servings.

# FISH
# and SHELLFISH

# ✠ FISH

It used to be that some parts of the country never saw any fish at all and that other parts of the country saw only their local freshwater fish. Now, with new freezing techniques and rapid transportation, a variety of fresh and frozen fish is available everywhere.

## BUYING AND STORING FRESH FISH

When it's fresh, fish has a clean, fresh odor, without stale smells or what we think of as a "fishy" smell.

The flesh should be firm, and when you press it with your finger, it should spring back. The eyes should be clean and clear and full, almost bulging. The gills should be reddish pink and free of odor or discoloration. The scales should be shiny, firm, and not slimy.

You should figure to buy about ⅓ to ½ pound fish fillet per serving. If you're serving a small whole fish, a 1-pound fish per serving is about right.

Ideally, there should be as little time from the water to the frying pan—or oven or grill—as possible to enjoy the delicate flavor of fresh fish. Because most of us purchase fish from a market, it's important to deal with one that regularly replenishes its fish supply and keeps it stored in refrigerated cases. Try to buy fish no more than 1 day before you plan to cook it. When you get it home, remove the wrapping and refrigerate it in a sealed plastic bag until cooking time.

## BUYING AND STORING FROZEN FISH

The successful freezing of fish is a major reason why it is widely available across the country. Frozen fish should be solidly frozen when purchased. Avoid a package that feels soft, or one in which you can feel ice crystals. That means it's been partially thawed and refrozen.

When you get frozen fish home, store it in your freezer or put it in the refrigerator to thaw. Do not remove it from its package to defrost. Frozen fish must retain its juices to preserve its flavor.

## COOKING FISH

The first rule is don't overcook. The usual expressions to describe doneness of fish is "until it just loses its translucency" or "until it flakes easily with a fork." The second rule is serve immediately. Keeping fish warm to serve will lead to overcooking. Fish may be pan-fried or sautéed, broiled, baked, poached, or steamed. Our master recipes throughout this chapter will tell you how to do it.

# ✦BAKED FISH

1. Know exact weight of fish you choose to bake. Whole fish are usually baked with head on to prevent fish from drying out. It may be removed before serving, if desired.
2. Line baking pan large enough to hold whole fish with aluminum foil.
3. Preheat oven to 400F.
4. Dip fish quickly in cold salted water. Pat dry with paper towels and lay on foil in baking pan.
5. Bake fish, basting occasionally with white wine or a mixture of equal amounts of oil and lemon juice, until it flakes easily when tested with a fork but is still moist.
6. To serve: Remove fish to heated platter. Garnish with lemon wedges.

*Approximate baking time*:
  Small fish (head on): 1 to 3 minutes per oz.
  Large fish (head on): 9 to 15 minutes per oz.

# ✦BROILED FISH

1. Wash fish in cold water; pat dry with paper towels.
2. Lightly brush broiler rack with salad oil; arrange fish on rack. Brush fish with one of basting sauces below.
3. Broil, 4 inches from heat, as directed in timetable below, or until fish flakes easily when tested with fork but is still moist.
4. To serve: Remove fish to heated platter. Garnish with lemon wedges and parsley sprigs. Pass one of sauces for fish (see chapter "Sauces and Gravies," page 457), if desired.

*Herbed Basting Sauce*: Combine 2 tablespoons salad oil, 2 tablespoons lemon juice, ¼ teaspoon paprika, and ¼ teaspoon dried marjoram, basil, or thyme leaves. Use to brush on fish several times during broiling.

*Curried Basting Sauce*: Combine 2 tablespoons salad oil, 2 tablespoons lemon juice, and ¼ teaspoon curry powder. Use to brush on fish several times during broiling.

*Lemony Basting Sauce*: Combine 3 tablespoons lemon juice, ⅛ teaspoon dry mustard, and 1 bay leaf, crumbled. Use to brush on fish several times during broiling.

*Fish: Approximate Broiling Time*:
  Fillets: 5 to 8 minutes each side.
  Steaks: 5 to 8 minutes each side.
  Dressed Whole: 5 minutes per lb each side.
  Split: 5 to 8 minutes each side.

# ✤ PAN-FRIED OR SAUTÉED FISH

*Whole fish or fish fillets*
*Flour*
*Butter or margarine*
*Oil*
*Lemon wedges*

1. Small whole fish, such as trout and catfish, and all fillets are good for frying. Frozen fish should be partially defrosted before frying.
2. Rinse fish quickly and pat dry with paper towels. Dip in flour (see Note).
3. In skillet sized to fit fish without crowding, heat mixture of half butter or margarine and half oil. Be careful to keep frying fat from reaching smoking point—fat at too high temperature will emit 'fried fish' odor.
4. Fry fish, turning once, to brown on both sides.
5. Remove from pan with broad spatula.
6. Serve on heated platter with lemon wedges for each serving.

*Note*: For crisper crust, dip fish first in flour, then in beaten egg mixture (1 tablespoon of water to 1 egg), and then in fine bread crumbs or cornmeal.
*Approximate frying time*:
  Small whole fish: 5 to 8 minutes each side.
  Fish fillets: 4 to 6 minutes each side.

# ✤ OVEN-POACHED FISH

*2½ lb fish fillets or steaks*
*Butter*
*2 tablespoons minced shallots or green onions*
*1 cup white wine*
*1 cup water*

1. Wash fresh fish fillets quickly, and pat dry with paper towels.
2. Preheat oven to 350F. Butter 13-by-9½-by-2-inch baking dish
3. Sprinkle half of shallots over bottom of dish. Arrange fillets in single layer in dish, overlapping fillets if necessary.
4. Sprinkle fish with remaining shallots, and dot with 1½ tablespoons of butter, cut into small pieces. Pour in wine and water, adding water if needed so fish is just covered.
5. Place buttered piece of aluminum foil over fish, buttered side down. Bake fish in oven 10 to 15 minutes, or until fish flakes easily when tested with a fork. (Fish may be poached on top of stove, though oven poaching is easier.)
6. Remove from oven and drain immediately to prevent further cooking.
7. Poached fish may be served hot with desired sauce, (see chapter "Sauces and Gravies," page 457), at room temperature with a mayonnaise, or chilled for salads.

*Note*: Reserve poaching liquid (fish stock) to make hot sauce, or freeze it for later use.

## ◈ STEAMED FISH

1. In deep kettle equipped with metal rack and tight-fitting lid, add about 2 inches of water.
2. Wash small whole fish, steaks, or fillets quickly, and pat dry with paper towels.
3. Wrap fish in cheesecloth so it can be easily removed from kettle when done.
4. Heat water to boiling. Place cloth-wrapped fish on rack, and cover kettle tightly. Steam until fish flakes easily when pierced with fork.
5. Lift fish from kettle, unwrap cheesecloth, and put fish on hot platter.
6. Serve with sauce if desired (see chapter "Sauces and Gravies," page 457), or chill to serve cold.
*Approximate steaming time*:
   Fish less than 2 inches thick: 1 minute per oz.
   Fish over 2 inches thick are best split for steaming.

# BAKED FISH

## ◈ BAKED WHOLE FISH WITH TARRAGON STUFFING

*2½- to 3-lb whole striped bass, red snapper, cod, or haddock with head, cleaned and scaled*

### TARRAGON STUFFING:

*¼ cup butter or margarine*
*½ cup chopped green onion*
*2 tablespoons parsley*
*2 teaspoons dried tarragon leaves*
*Salt*
*¼ teaspoon pepper*
*2 cups soft bread crumbs*
*2 tablespoons butter or margarine, melted*
*1 tablespoon lemon juice*

*Lemon slices*
*Parsley*

1. Wash fish, inside and out, under cold running water. Drain well; pat dry with paper towels.
2. Make Tarragon Stuffing: In ¼ cup hot butter in medium skillet, sauté green onion, stirring, about 3 minutes. Add parsley, tarragon, ½ teaspoon salt, and ⅛ teaspoon pepper; mix well. Add bread crumbs; toss to mix well.
3. Preheat oven to 400F. Line 13-by-9-by-2-inch baking pan with foil; butter foil.
4. Spoon stuffing into cavity; close opening with skewers or wooden picks.
5. Place fish in prepared pan. Pour melted butter and lemon juice over fish. Sprinkle lightly with salt and ⅛ teaspoon pepper.
6. Bake 35 to 40 minutes, or until fish flakes easily when tested with fork.
7. To serve: With large spatula, carefully lift fish to heated serving platter. Remove skewers or wooden picks. Garnish platter with lemon slices and parsley. Makes 8 servings.

# ❖ BAKED STRIPED BASS

4- to 5-lb whole striped bass with
   head, cleaned and scaled
2 teaspoons salt
1 small lemon
Parsley
1 cup thinly sliced onion
½ cup thinly sliced carrot
½ cup thinly sliced celery
½ teaspoon dried thyme leaves
1 bay leaf
1 cup dry white wine
½ cup water
¼ cup butter or margarine, melted
Parsley and lemon (optional)
Lemon Butter, below

1. Preheat oven to 400F. Lightly grease shallow roasting pan.
2. Wash fish, inside and out, under cold running water; pat dry with paper towels. Sprinkle fish, inside and out, with the salt.
3. Slice lemon thin; cut slices in quarters. With small sharp-pointed knife, make deep cuts, about 2 inches apart, along both sides of fish. With fingers, press piece of lemon and small sprig of parsley into each cut.
4. Place fish in prepared pan. Add any remaining lemon slices and parsley, along with onion, carrot, celery, thyme, and bay leaf. Pour in wine and water. Pour butter over fish.
5. Bake, basting frequently with liquid in pan, 30 to 40 minutes, or until fish flakes easily when tested with fork.
6. With large spatulas, carefully lift fish to heated serving platter. With slotted spoon, lift out vegetables, and place around fish. Vegetables will be on the crisp side. Garnish platter with parsley and lemon, if desired. Serve with Lemon Butter.
Makes 6 servings.

## LEMON BUTTER:

6 tablespoons butter or margarine
2 tablespoons lemon juice

1. In small skillet or saucepan, heat butter over medium heat until it foams and becomes light brown.
2. Remove from heat. Stir in lemon juice. Serve at once.
Makes ½ cup.

# ❖ CRISPY BAKED FISH FILLETS

¼ cup butter or margarine, melted
¼ teaspoon paprika
¼ teaspoon salt
½ cup crushed saltine crackers
½ cup crushed potato chips
4 flounder, turbot, cod, or halibut
   fillets (about 1 lb)
Lemon slices

1. Preheat oven to 350F. Combine butter, paprika, and salt in bowl.
2. Place cracker and potato-chip crumbs on waxed paper. Wash fillets, dry on paper towels, and dip in butter mixture, then in crumbs, coating well. Place in single layer in shallow baking pan.
3. Bake 10 minutes. Then broil, 5 inches from heat, 6 to 8 minutes on each side, or until fish flakes easily when tested with fork. Serve with lemon slices.
Makes 4 servings.

# ❖ BAKED HADDOCK, NEW ENGLAND STYLE

3½-lb whole fresh haddock or cod,
  cleaned and scaled, head and tail
  removed
1½ teaspoons salt
Pepper
2 tablespoons lemon juice

## CRACKER TOPPING:

½ cup crushed unsalted crackers
½ cup chopped washed fresh mushrooms
¼ cup thinly sliced green onions
2 tablespoons chopped parsley
½ teaspoon salt
⅛ teaspoon pepper
¼ cup butter or margarine, melted
2 tablespoons lemon juice
6 slices bacon

Parsley and lemon wedges (optional)

1. Wash fish in cold water; pat dry with paper towels. With sharp knife, carefully remove bones, keeping fish joined down back. (Or have fish boned at market.)
2. Preheat oven to 400F. Line 13-by-9-by-2-inch baking pan with foil; butter foil.
3. Sprinkle inside of boned fish with ¾ teaspoon salt, dash pepper, and 1 tablespoon lemon juice. Fold fish lengthwise. Place in prepared pan. Sprinkle with ¾ teaspoon salt, dash pepper, and 1 tablespoon lemon juice.
4. Make Cracker Topping: In medium bowl, combine crushed crackers, mushrooms, green onions, parsley, salt, and pepper; mix. Pour on butter and lemon juice; toss until well combined.
5. Spoon over fish in 3-inch-wide layer. Arrange bacon slices diagonally over top.
6. Bake, basting every 10 minutes with pan juices, 30 to 35 minutes, or until fish flakes easily when tested with fork.
7. Carefully lift fish to heated serving platter. Garnish with parsley and lemon wedges, if desired.
Makes 6 servings.

# ❖ FILLETS OF SOLE WITH TARRAGON-CHIVE BUTTER

2 lb fillets of sole
½ cup butter or margarine, melted
2 tablespoons lemon juice
1 tablespoon coarsely chopped fresh
  tarragon leaves
1 tablespoon snipped chives
¼ teaspoon salt

1. Preheat oven to 350F. Wash fillets then dry on paper towels.
2. Brush fillets with ¼ cup butter. Sprinkle with lemon juice. Arrange in greased 13-by-9-by-2-inch baking dish.
3. Cover dish with foil; bake 20 minutes, or until fish flakes easily with fork.
4. Combine rest of butter with tarragon, chives, and salt; heat slightly.
5. To serve, put fillets on platter; pour warm herb butter, combined with cooking liquid, over them.
Makes 6 servings.

# ❖ BAKED FILLETS THERMIDOR

2 lb fillets of sole
5 tablespoons butter or margarine
2 teaspoons salt
¼ teaspoon pepper
1¼ cups milk
3 tablespoons flour
1 cup grated sharp Cheddar cheese
  (¼ lb)
3 tablespoons dry sherry
Paprika

1. Preheat oven to 350F.
2. Wash fillets, and dry on paper towels.
3. Melt 2 tablespoons butter. Use to brush dark side of fillets. Sprinkle with salt and pepper.
4. Roll up fillets, seasonings inside; fasten with wooden picks. Arrange in 9-by-9-by-1¾-inch baking dish. Pour on ½ cup milk.
5. Bake, uncovered, 30 minutes.
6. Meanwhile, in medium saucepan, melt rest of butter.
7. Remove from heat. Add flour, stirring until smooth. Gradually stir in remaining milk; bring to boiling, stirring constantly.
8. Reduce heat. Add cheese, stirring until it is melted. Then add sherry.
9. Carefully drain liquid from fish; stir into cheese sauce. Pour sauce over fish. Sprinkle with paprika.
10. Place under broiler, 4 inches from heat, until sauce is golden-brown.
Makes 4 servings.

# ❖ BAKED FISH IN FOIL

3-lb whole red snapper, bluefish, mackerel, bass, shad, or similar fish, cleaned and ready to cook
1 clove garlic, crushed
¼ cup butter or margarine, softened
1 teaspoon salt
⅛ teaspoon pepper
½ teaspoon dried thyme leaves
1 teaspoon flour
½ lb deveined, shelled large shrimp
  (leave shell on tail)
½ lb mushrooms, sliced
3 tablespoons lemon juice
½ cup dry white wine
¼ cup chopped parsley
1 teaspoon grated lemon peel

1. Preheat oven to 375F. Wash fish, inside and out, under cold running water. Dry well on paper towels.
2. In small bowl, combine garlic, butter, salt, pepper, thyme, and flour; mix well.
3. Place fish on double thickness of 24-by-18-inch heavy-duty foil.
4. In cavity of fish, place 1 tablespoon garlic mixture, 4 shrimp, and ½ cup mushrooms. Sprinkle with 1 tablespoon lemon juice and 2 tablespoons wine.
5. Dot top of fish with remaining garlic mixture. Arrange remaining shrimp and mushrooms over top; sprinkle with remaining lemon juice and white wine, the parsley, and lemon peel.
6. Bring long sides of foil together over fish, and secure with double fold. Fold both ends of foil upward several times. Place on cookie sheet.
7. Bake 40 minutes (allow 10 to 12 minutes per pound), or until fish flakes easily when tested with fork. Serve with juices in foil spooned over top.
Makes 4 to 6 servings.

# ❖ POMPANO EN PAPILLOTE

6 small fillets (1½ lb) of pompano, porgy, or turbot
1 tablespoon lemon juice
2 cups water
2 tablespoons brandy
5 tablespoons butter or margarine
1 cup sliced washed fresh mushrooms
1 medium green apple
¼ lb cooked shrimp, chopped
12 thin onion rings
6 teaspoons chopped chives
Salt
Pepper
Chopped parsley (optional)

1. Wash fillets in lemon juice and 2 cups water. Drain; pat dry with paper towels. Brush both sides of fillets with brandy.
2. In 3 tablespoons hot butter in medium skillet, sauté mushrooms 5 minutes, or until golden. Remove mushrooms and set aside. Pare and core apple; cut into thin wedges. Add and sauté 4 minutes, turning once.
3. Preheat oven to 375F. Tear off 6 (12-inch) squares of foil.
4. Place a fillet diagonally on half of each square 1½ inches from edge. Top with mushrooms, apple, shrimp, onion rings, and chives, dividing them evenly. Sprinkle with salt and pepper. Top each fillet with 1 teaspoon butter.
5. Fold foil on diagonal. Turn up edge, and fold over twice to seal.
6. Place foil packages on large cookie sheet or jelly-roll pan. Bake 20 to 25 minutes.
7. To serve: Slash cross in top of each package; fold back corners. Sprinkle fish with chopped parsley, if you wish.
Makes 6 servings.

# BROILED FISH

# ❖ BROILED SALMON OR SWORDFISH STEAKS WITH PARSLEY-LEMON BUTTER

4 salmon or swordfish steaks, ½ inch thick
4 tablespoons butter or margarine, melted

## PARSLEY-LEMON BUTTER:

¼ cup butter or margarine
2 tablespoons lemon juice
2 tablespoons chopped parsley

1. Rinse salmon steaks under cold running water; drain, and pat dry with paper towels.
2. Place salmon on rack of broiler pan. Brush with 1 tablespoon melted butter.
3. Broil, 4 inches from heat, 10 minutes. Turn salmon; brush with remaining melted butter. Broil 8 minutes longer, or until fish flakes easily when tested with fork.
4. Meanwhile, make Parsley-Lemon Butter: Melt butter in small saucepan. Stir in lemon juice and parsley. Keep warm.
5. Remove salmon to heated serving platter. Pour lemon butter over salmon.
Makes 4 servings.

# ✺ GRILLED FISH PROVENÇALE

*1 whole striped bass (4 lb), cleaned, scaled, and split*
*4 tablespoons salad or olive oil*
*4 tablespoons lemon juice*
*1½ teaspoons salt*
*¼ teaspoon pepper*
*1 small stalk celery with leaves, chopped*
*1½ teaspoons chopped fresh thyme leaves or ½ teaspoon dried thyme*
*2 tablespoons chopped fresh tarragon leaves or 2 teaspoons dried tarragon*
*1 teaspoon chopped fresh rosemary leaves or ¼ teaspoon dried rosemary*
*1 small onion, sliced*
*Chopped parsley*
*Lemon wedges*

1. Wash fish thoroughly; pat dry inside and out with paper towels.
2. With sharp knife, make 4 diagonal slashes through skin on each side.
3. In small bowl, combine oil and lemon juice. Brush some of mixture over inside of fish; sprinkle with 1 teaspoon salt and the pepper.
4. In small bowl, combine celery, thyme, tarragon, and rosemary. Sprinkle half of mixture over inside of fish. Add onion slices in a layer; sprinkle with remaining herb mixture. Close opening with skewers.
5. Add rest of salt to remaining oil mixture. Brush some of mixture over both sides of fish.
6. Place fish on well-oiled grill or in basket, and adjust 5 inches above prepared coals. Cook 15 to 20 minutes, or until fish flakes easily when tested with fork on underside. Brush with remaining oil mixture. Carefully turn fish with wide spatulas, or turn basket; cook 15 to 20 minutes, or until done.
7. Remove to serving platter. Sprinkle with parsley; garnish with lemon wedges.
Makes 6 servings.

# ✺ PUFFY BROILED FISH

*2 lb fish fillets, ¼ to ½ inch thick*
*2 tablespoons lemon juice*
*1 medium onion, thinly sliced*
*1½ cups mayonnaise*
*⅓ cup grated Parmesan cheese*

1. Rinse fillets under cold water; pat dry with paper towels.
2. Brush one side with lemon juice. Place fillets, 1 inch apart, on oven-proof baking dish. Arrange onion slices over tops of fillets, dividing evenly.
3. In small bowl, combine mayonnaise and Parmesan cheese. Spread ¼ cup mayonnaise mixture over each fillet. Cover baking dish with foil; broil, 6 inches from heat, 15 minutes. Remove foil; continue broiling just until top is golden-brown—about 5 minutes.
4. To serve: With wide spatula, remove fish from baking dish; arrange on platter.
Makes 6 servings.

# POACHED FISH

## ▣ FILLETS OF SOLE BONNE FEMME

4 tablespoons butter or margarine
2 shallots, chopped
6 large sole, haddock, or flounder
    fillets (about 2½ lb)
½ lb fresh mushrooms, sliced
1 teaspoon salt
⅛ teaspoon pepper
1 cup white wine
1 tablespoon chopped parsley
1½ tablespoons flour

1. Melt 2 tablespoons butter in large skillet. Add shallots, and sauté 2 minutes.
2. Wash fillets; dry on paper towels. Arrange fish over shallots, and top with mushrooms. Sprinkle salt and pepper over all. Add wine.
3. Bring to boiling; reduce heat, and simmer, covered, 10 minutes. Add parsley; cook 5 minutes longer, or until fish flakes easily with fork.
4. Drain fish well, reserving 1 cup liquid. Arrange fish and mushrooms in 12-by-8-by-2-inch baking dish.
5. Melt remaining butter in same skillet; remove from heat. Stir in flour until smooth. Gradually stir in reserved fish liquid.
6. Cook over medium heat, stirring, until thickened. Pour over fish. Run under broiler 3 to 5 minutes, or until top is golden-brown.
Makes 6 servings.

## ▣ FILLETS OF SOLE FLORENTINE

Hollandaise Sauce, page 461
6 large fillets of sole, flounder, or haddock (2½ lb)
¼ cup lemon juice
2 tablespoons finely chopped shallots
2 teaspoons dried tarragon leaves
1 teaspoon salt
1 cup dry white wine
2 pkg (10-oz size) frozen chopped spinach

### WINE SAUCE:

3 tablespoons butter or margarine
3 tablespoons flour
½ teaspoon salt
⅛ teaspoon pepper
1 cup fish stock
⅓ cup light cream
⅓ cup heavy cream

1. Make Hollandaise Sauce. Let cool completely.
2. Rinse fillets under cool water; pat dry with paper towels. Brush both sides with lemon juice. Fold into thirds, with dark side inside. Arrange in single layer in large skillet. Sprinkle with shallots, tarragon, and 1 teaspoon salt. Pour wine over all.
3. Bring to boiling; reduce heat, and simmer, covered, 5 to 10 minutes, or until fish flakes easily when tested with fork. Do not overcook.
4. Meanwhile, cook spinach as label directs. Turn out into sieve; drain well, pressing spinach to remove all liquid. Return to saucepan; cover, and keep hot.
5. With slotted spatula, remove fillets to heated platter; set aside, and keep warm. Strain liquid from skillet into 2-cup measure; reserve. (You should have about 1 cup. Boil down if necessary.)
6. Make Wine Sauce: Melt butter in small saucepan. Remove from heat. Stir in flour, salt, and pepper until smooth. Gradually stir in 1 cup fish stock and the light cream.
7. Bring to boiling, over medium heat, stirring constantly until mixture thickens. Remove from heat.

8. Stir ⅓ cup wine sauce into spinach; toss. Turn out into 12-by-8-by-2-inch broiler-proof dish; spread evenly.

9. Arrange fillets in single layer on spinach. Spoon remaining wine sauce over fillets.

10. Beat heavy cream until stiff. Fold into Hollandaise Sauce. Spoon mixture over wine sauce.

11. Place under broiler 2 to 3 minutes, or until top is golden-brown. Serve right from dish.

Makes 6 servings.

## ❖ COLD POACHED TROUT

**COURT BOUILLON:**

2 cups water
1½ cups Chablis or dry white wine
¾ cup chopped celery
1 large onion, sliced
3 parsley sprigs
6 lemon slices
1 large carrot, sliced diagonally
1 bay leaf
2 tablespoons salt

6 (10-oz size) boned fresh whole trout
   or frozen whole trout, thawed
Watercress sprigs
Lemon wedges
Sauce Verte, page 465

1. Day before serving, prepare Court Bouillon: In large (12-inch) skillet, combine water, Chablis, celery, onion, parsley, lemon slices, carrot, bay leaf, and salt. Bring to boiling. Reduce heat, and simmer, covered, 10 minutes.

2. Add trout to pan; cover pan tightly.

3. Bring to boiling over medium heat. Reduce heat, and simmer 5 to 10 minutes, or until fish flakes when tested with fork. Remove pan from heat. Cool. Refrigerate fish in Court Bouillon overnight.

4. Next day, arrange trout on serving platter. Brush with bouillon. Garnish with watercress and lemon wedges. Serve with Sauce Verte.

Makes 6 servings.

## ❖ FINNAN HADDIE DELMONICO

2-lb piece smoked haddock
¼ cup butter or margarine
3 tablespoons flour
½ teaspoon salt
Dash ground red pepper
1 cup milk
1 cup half-and-half
5 hard-cooked eggs
4 thin slices buttered toast

1. Rinse fish in cold water. If large, cut in half. Place in medium skillet. Add water to cover, and bring to boiling. Reduce heat, and simmer, covered, 15 minutes.

2. Drain well. With fork, separate fish into flakes. (You should have 2½ cups.) Set aside.

3. Melt butter in medium saucepan. Remove from heat. Blend in flour, salt, and pepper. Gradually stir in milk and half-and-half.

4. Bring to boiling over medium heat, stirring. Re-

duce heat, and simmer 5 minutes, stirring occasionally.

5. Peel eggs; slice 3. Chop whites of remaining 2 eggs, and put yolks through sieve. Cut toast into triangles.

6. Add fish and sliced egg to sauce; simmer 1 minute.

7. Turn out into heated shallow serving dish. Sprinkle with chopped egg white and sieved yolk. Arrange toast triangles around edge. Serve immediately. Makes 8 servings.

# SAUTÉED FISH

## ✠ TROUT AMANDINE

4 (½-lb size) rainbow trout, head and
   tail on, cleaned and scaled
⅓ cup all-purpose flour
½ teaspoon salt
Dash pepper
¼ cup milk
½ cup butter or margarine
⅓ cup sliced almonds

1. Wash fish under cold running water. Drain; pat dry with paper towels.

2. On 12-inch square of waxed paper, combine flour, salt, and pepper.

3. Pour milk into 9-inch pie plate. Dip trout in milk. Shake off excess; roll in flour mixture until well coated.

4. In large skillet, over medium heat, heat ¼ cup butter until golden. Add trout; sauté, over medium heat, 5 minutes, or until underside is browned. Turn, being careful not to break fish; sauté 5 minutes, or until fish are browned and flake easily when tested with a fork.

5. Carefully remove fish to heated serving platter.

6. Add ¼ cup butter to skillet. When melted, add almonds; sauté over low heat until almonds are pale golden. Pour almonds and butter over fish. Serve immediately. Makes 4 servings.

# FROZEN AND CANNED FISH

## ❖ HALIBUT WITH CHINESE VEGETABLES

1 pkg (1 lb) frozen halibut fillets, partially thawed
3 tablespoons salad or peanut oil
½ cup chopped onion
1 cup green onions, sliced thinly on diagonal
½ cup plus 3 tablespoons dry sherry
1 teaspoon salt
¼ teaspoon ground cardamom
1 can (1 lb) bean sprouts
1 tablespoon cornstarch
1 tablespoon soy sauce
2 tablespoons pimiento, in ½-inch squares

1. Preheat oven to 375F. Butter 8-by-8-by-2-inch baking dish.
2. Cut fish into 4 pieces; drain.
3. In hot oil in large skillet, sauté onion until golden. Stir in green onions, ½ cup sherry, the salt, cardamom, and bean sprouts. Cook, covered, 5 minutes.
4. Meanwhile, in small bowl, combine cornstarch, soy sauce, and 3 tablespoons sherry; mix until smooth. Gradually add to bean-sprout mixture, stirring constantly. Cook until mixture starts to boil and becomes transparent.
5. Turn out half of bean-sprout mixture into prepared dish. Arrange fish pieces on top. Spoon remaining mixture over top of fish.
6. Cover dish with foil. Bake 25 to 30 minutes, or until fish flakes easily.
7. Garnish with pimiento.
Makes 4 servings.

## ❖ FILLETS OF SOLE WITH BROCCOLI

### SAUCE:

¼ cup butter or margarine
¼ cup all-purpose flour
1 teaspoon salt
1 teaspoon dried tarragon leaves
⅛ teaspoon pepper
2 cups milk
½ cup dry white wine

2 pkg (10-oz size) frozen chopped broccoli
2 tablespoons lemon juice
2 pkg (1-lb size) frozen sole or flounder fillets, partially thawed
2 tablespoons lemon juice
Salt
Pepper
2 tablespoons grated Parmesan cheese

1. Make Sauce: In medium saucepan, slowly heat butter just until melted. Remove from heat.
2. Add flour, 1 teaspoon salt, the tarragon, and ⅛ teaspoon pepper; stir until smooth. Add milk, a little at a time, stirring after each addition.
3. Over medium heat, bring to boiling, stirring constantly. Reduce heat. Stir in wine. Simmer 3 minutes.
4. Cook broccoli according to package directions; drain well. Return to saucepan. Add 1 cup sauce and 2 tablespoons lemon juice; mix gently.
5. Preheat oven to 375F. Butter shallow 2-quart baking dish.
6. Brush fillets with lemon juice; sprinkle lightly with salt and pepper. Arrange down center of dish, overlapping. Spoon broccoli around edge.
7. Spoon remaining sauce over fish. Cover dish with foil. Bake 25 minutes.
8. Remove foil; sprinkle fish with cheese. Broil, 4 inches from heat, just until golden—about 3 minutes.
Makes 6 to 8 servings.

# ⊞ COUNTRY-STYLE FISH CASSEROLE

½ lb slab bacon, cut into ½-inch
  pieces
1 cup sliced onion
½ cup cut-up green pepper, in ½-inch
  squares
2 cups cut-up potato, in ½-inch cubes
1 cup sliced mushrooms (¼ lb)
1½ teaspoons salt
½ teaspoon dried thyme leaves
¼ teaspoon white pepper

## SAUCE:

1 tablespoon flour
1 cup dry white wine
½ teaspoon salt
Dash white pepper
Dash dried thyme leaves

2 pkg (12-oz size) frozen sole or
  flounder fillets, partially thawed

1. Preheat oven to 375F. Butter shallow 2-quart round baking dish.
2. In large skillet, sauté bacon until crisp; remove. Reserve ¼ cup fat.
3. Return fat to skillet; add onion, green pepper, potato, mushrooms, 1½ teaspoons salt, ½ teaspoon thyme, and ¼ teaspoon white pepper. Cook over medium heat, stirring frequently, until potato is almost tender—15 minutes.
4. In small saucepan, combine sauce ingredients, mixing until smooth. Bring to boiling over medium heat, stirring. Simmer 2 minutes.
5. Separate fillets; arrange in dish.
6. Spoon vegetable mixture over top. Pour sauce over all; arrange reserved bacon on top.
7. Bake, uncovered, 25 to 30 minutes, or until fish flakes easily.
Makes 4 servings.

# ⊞ DEEP-DISH SALMON (OR TUNA) POTATO PIE

1 pkg (11 oz) piecrust mix

## SAUCE:

¼ cup butter or margarine
⅓ cup flour
2½ teaspoons salt
¼ teaspoon pepper
⅛ teaspoon paprika
2 cups milk

Boiling water
2 lb potatoes, peeled and thinly sliced
4 carrots, pared and thinly sliced
4 tablespoons butter or margarine
3 medium onions, thinly sliced
1 can (15 oz) salmon, drained and
  boned, or 2 cans (6½-oz size) chunk
  light tuna, drained
1 egg yolk
1 tablespoon water

1. Prepare pastry as package label directs. Refrigerate until ready to use.
2. Preheat oven to 350F. Grease well 2-quart oval casserole or baking dish.
3. Make Sauce: In small saucepan, melt ¼ cup butter. Remove from heat; stir in flour, salt, pepper, and paprika until smooth. Blend in milk.
4. Cook, stirring, over medium heat to boiling point, or until thickened and smooth.
5. In small amount of boiling water, cook potatoes and carrots 10 minutes; drain.
6. In 2 tablespoons butter, sauté onions until golden —about 5 minutes.
7. In prepared casserole, layer half of potatoes and carrots, half of onions, and half of salmon or 1 can tuna. Top with half of sauce. Repeat, layering with potatoes, carrots, onions, remaining sauce, and salmon or tuna. Dot with 2 tablespoons butter.
8. On lightly floured pastry cloth, roll dough to 14-by-10-inch oval. With 2½-inch round cookie cutter, cut out 3 pastry rounds; reserve.
9. Fit oval pastry over salmon-potato mixture. Mix

egg yolk with 1 tablespoon water, and brush top of pie with some of mixture. Cut reserved pastry rounds in half; arrange decoratively on top of pastry. Brush with egg-yolk mixture. Trim and turn edges under; flute decoratively.

10. Bake 30 to 40 minutes, or until browned and juices bubble through steam vents. Serve warm. Makes 8 servings.

# ❖ SALMON MOUSSE

1 env unflavored gelatine
¼ cup white wine
½ cup boiling water
½ cup mayonnaise
1 tablespoon lemon juice
1 tablespoon grated onion
½ teaspoon Tabasco
½ teaspoon paprika
1 teaspoon salt
3 cans (7¾-oz size) salmon, drained
1 cup heavy cream
2 tablespoons snipped fresh dill
2 medium unpared cucumbers, washed
Bottled herb salad dressing
Watercress
Snipped fresh dill

1. In medium bowl, sprinkle gelatine over wine; let stand 5 minutes to soften. Add boiling water; stir until gelatine is dissolved. Let cool.

2. Add mayonnaise, lemon juice, onion, Tabasco, paprika, and salt; stir to mix well.

3. Set bowl in large bowl of ice cubes; let stand, stirring occasionally, until consistency of unbeaten egg white—about 10 minutes.

4. Lightly grease 4-cup mold. Remove any skin and bones from salmon. Place salmon and ½ cup heavy cream in blender; blend to make purée. Beat remaining ½ cup cream until stiff.

5. Using wire whisk, fold salmon purée, whipped cream, and 2 tablespoons dill into slightly thickened gelatine mixure, using an under-and-over motion to combine thoroughly. Turn out into prepared mold. Refrigerate until well chilled and firm enough to unmold—at least 2 hours.

6. Slice cucumbers thin. Place in shallow baking dish. Toss with enough salad dressing to coat well. Refrigerate cucumbers, covered.

7. To unmold: Loosen around edge of mold with sharp knife; invert onto serving platter. Place hot damp cloth over mold; shake to release. Repeat if necessary.

8. Garnish platter with sliced cucumbers and watercress. Sprinkle cucumbers lightly with snipped dill. Makes 8 servings.

# SHELLFISH

Some people don't eat shellfish for reasons of allergy or religious dietary restrictions. For the rest of us, clams, crabs, lobster, oysters, mussels, scallops, and shrimp are a great treat. They are also quite nutritious, being low in calories and very high in protein. There is nothing more luxurious than a Maine lobster, boiled or broiled, and served whole—and the rock lobsters of our southern waters aren't bad either. As to crabs, there are parts of the country where in even the most elegant homes, when crab season rolls around, the dinner table is covered with newspapers and the guests dig in, piling shells and claws as the crabs are attacked and emptied.

Clams, mussels, oysters, and scallops are increasingly popular, though shrimp remains the most popular shellfish in the country. Shrimp are plentiful the year round, fresh or frozen; most of the shrimp eaten in this country come from the Gulf of Mexico. Make sure the shellfish you buy are very fresh. Try to find a good market as your source, and though shellfish are never cheap, for the best price, buy when they are in season.

# PURCHASING SHELLFISH

*Live shellfish*: Be sure they are alive immediately before cooking. Lobsters and crabs should be moving. Oysters, clams, and mussels should have tightly closed shells, or if open, they should close when tapped.
*Shucked oysters or clams*: The flesh should be plump and creamy, the liquor clear, and the odor fresh and mild.
*Fresh shrimp and other shellfish sold prepared or partially prepared*: The flesh should be firm and bounce back when pressed with a finger.

# ✦ FRIED CLAMS

*1 quart shucked clams*
*1 egg, slightly beaten*
*1 teaspoon salt*
*⅛ teaspoon pepper*
*Dash paprika*
*1 cup packaged dry bread crumbs*
*½ cup butter or margarine*

1. Drain clams, reserving 2 tablespoons liquid.
2. Combine clam liquid with egg, salt, pepper, and paprika.
3. Dip clams in egg mixture; then roll in bread crumbs, coating completely.
4. In hot butter in medium skillet, sauté clams 3 to 4 minutes on each side, or until golden. Drain well on paper towels.
Makes 4 to 6 servings.

# ✠ NEW ENGLAND CLAMBAKE

*2 dozen clams in shell*
*4 ears corn*
*2 (2½-lb size) broiler-fryers, quartered*
*½ lb butter or margarine, melted*
*2 cups water*
*4 small baking potatoes, sweet*
   *potatoes, or yams, scrubbed*
*4 small onions*
*Rockweed or corn husks*
*2 (1-lb size) live lobsters (optional, see*
   *Note)*
*Lemon wedges*

1. Under cold water, scrub clam shells with stiff brush to remove sand.
2. Trim tops of ears of corn with scissors. Turn back husks and remove silk; pull back husks as they were. Remove outer husks from ears; reserve. Soak ears and reserved husks in lightly salted water until cooking time.
3. In large skillet, sauté chicken in 2 tablespoons butter until golden—about 10 minutes on each side—adding more butter as needed.
4. Place wire rack in bottom of very large kettle (at least 4-gallon capacity) with tight-fitting cover. Pour in 2 cups water. Arrange potatoes and onions on rack; cover with a layer of rockweed or reserved corn husks. Add corn and another layer of rockweed or corn husks. Then add chicken and/or lobster. Top with clams; cover with rockweed or any remaining husks.
5. Steam, covered, over medium heat 1 hour and 15 minutes, or until potatoes, onions, and corn are tender. (Check potatoes at this point to see if done.) Remove clams to large bowl and remainder of clambake to large platter. Pour broth from bottom of kettle into 4 (8-ounce) cups or bowls, and serve to dip seafood, meat, and vegetables in for flavor.
6. Serve with lemon wedges and melted butter.
Makes 4 servings. (To serve 8, make a second batch in separate kettle.)
*Note*: Since lobster is expensive and difficult to find in some areas, you may omit lobster and serve chicken. Or serve some lobster to each person and chicken as well.
To kill lobster before adding to kettle: Lay each lobster on wooden board. To sever spinal cord, insert point of knife through back shell where body and tail of lobster come together. Turn lobster over. With sharp knife, split body of lobster down middle, cutting through thin undershell just to back shell and leaving back shell intact. Discard dark intestinal vein running down center of lobster; also discard small sac below head. Crack large claws.

# ✤ BOILED CRABS

4 quarts water
¼ cup salt
16 live hard-shell crabs

1. In large kettle, bring water and salt to boiling.
2. Place crabs in colander; wash in cold water until they seem clean.
3. Holding crabs by tongs or back feelers, plunge head first into boiling water; return water to boiling. Reduce heat, and simmer, covered, 12 to 15 minutes.
4. Drain; let cool.
5. To remove meat: Twist off claws and legs; crack them with nutcracker or hammer, and remove meat.
6. Lay crab on top shell. Insert point of knife under forward end of flap that folds under body from rear; break it off, and discard.
7. Pick up crab in both hands; pull upper and lower shells apart. Discard top shell.
8. Hold crab under running water; remove gills and all spongy material.
9. Cut away any hard membrane along outer edge; carefully remove meat with fork.
Makes about 2 cups crabmeat.

# ✤ SCALLOPED CRAB

1 lb fresh crabmeat or 2 cans (7½-oz size) crabmeat
½ cup dry sherry
¼ cup butter or margarine
2 tablespoons finely chopped onion
¼ cup all-purpose flour
½ cup milk
1 cup light cream
1 tablespoon Worcestershire sauce
1 teaspoon salt
Dash pepper
2 egg yolks
2 tablespoons butter or margarine, melted
½ cup dry bread crumbs

1. Preheat oven to 350F. Lightly grease 6 or 8 scallop shells or a 1-quart casserole.
2. Drain crabmeat, removing any cartilage. Sprinkle crabmeat with ¼ cup sherry; toss to mix well.
3. In ¼ cup hot butter in medium saucepan, sauté onion until tender—5 minutes.
4. Remove from heat. Stir in flour. Gradually stir in milk and cream; bring to boiling, stirring; reduce heat, and simmer until quite thick—8 to 10 minutes.
5. Remove from heat; add Worcestershire, salt, pepper, and rest of sherry. Stir a little of sauce into egg yolks; return to rest of sauce in saucepan; mix well. Stir in crabmeat mixture.
6. Turn out into shells or casserole.
7. Toss 2 tablespoons butter with crumbs to mix well. Sprinkle crumbs evenly over crabmeat.
8. Place shells on cookie sheet; bake 20 minutes, or until mixture is bubbly and crumbs are lightly browned. (Bake casserole 25 minutes.)
Makes 6 to 8 servings.

# ❖ CRABMEAT CREOLE

¼ cup butter or margarine
1 cup chopped onion
1 cup chopped green pepper
¼ cup flour
½ cup catsup or chili sauce
2 teaspoons Worcestershire sauce
1 cup bottled clam juice
½ teaspoon salt
Dash black pepper
3 cups light cream
1 jar (4 oz) pimientos, drained and
  coarsely chopped
3 cans (6½-oz size) king-crab meat,
  flaked and cartilage removed
½ cup sherry
2 tablespoons chopped parsley
Buttered toast triangles

1. In hot butter in large skillet, sauté onion and green pepper, stirring, until soft—about 5 minutes.
2. Remove from heat; stir in flour, catsup, Worcestershire, clam juice, salt, pepper, and cream; stir to mix well. Bring to boiling, stirring. Reduce heat, and simmer several minutes.
3. Stir in pimiento, crabmeat, and sherry. Heat gently just until hot.
4. Sprinkle with parsley. Serve over toast triangles. Makes 8 servings.

# ❖ BOILED LIVE LOBSTERS

6 quarts water
1 lemon, sliced
1 medium onion, sliced
6 tablespoons salt
2 bay leaves
8 whole black peppercorns
2 (1-lb size) live lobsters
Melted butter or margarine
Lemon wedges

1. In deep 10-quart kettle, combine water, lemon, onion, salt, bay leaves, and whole black peppercorns. Bring to boiling; then reduce heat, and simmer, covered, 20 minutes.
2. Holding each lobster by the body with tongs, with claws away from you, plunge it into boiling water. Return to boiling; reduce heat. Cover kettle; simmer lobsters 12 to 15 minutes.
3. Remove lobsters from kettle; place on back. Split body lengthwise, cutting through thin undershell and lobster meat and back shell. Spread open. Remove and discard dark vein and small sac 2 inches below head. Leave in green liver (tomalley) and any red roe (coral).
4. Crack large claws, to let excess moisture drain off.
5. Serve lobsters at once, with plenty of melted butter and lemon wedges.
Makes 2 servings.

# ❖ ROCK-LOBSTER THERMIDOR

### BOILED ROCK-LOBSTER TAILS:

*3 quarts water*
*1 small onion, peeled and sliced*
*½ lemon, sliced*
*1 tablespoon salt*
*5 whole black peppercorns*
*1 bay leaf*
*5 (6-oz size) frozen rock-lobster tails*
*2 tablespoons dry sherry*

### SAUCE:

*⅓ cup butter or margarine*
*¼ cup all-purpose flour*
*½ teaspoon salt*
*Dash mace*
*¼ teaspoon paprika*
*1½ cups light cream*
*1 tablespoon dry sherry*
*½ cup grated sharp Cheddar cheese*

1. In 6-quart kettle, place water, onion, lemon, 1 tablespoon salt, the black peppercorns, and bay leaf; bring to boiling.
2. Unwrap frozen lobster tails. With tongs, lower into boiling mixture; return to boiling. Reduce heat, and simmer, covered, 9 minutes.
3. With tongs or slotted spoon, remove lobster tails from kettle. Set aside until cool enough to handle. Discard cooking liquid.
4. To remove meat from shells: With scissors, carefully cut away thin undershell, and discard. Then insert fingers between shell and meat, and gently pull out meat in one piece. Wash four shells; dry with paper towels, and set aside.
5. Cut lobster meat into bite-size pieces. Place in medium bowl; toss with 2 tablespoons sherry.
6. Preheat oven to 450F.
7. Make Sauce: Melt butter in 2-quart saucepan; remove from heat. Stir in flour, salt, mace, and paprika until smooth. Gradually stir in light cream.
8. Bring to boiling, stirring constantly. Reduce heat, and simmer 2 to 3 minutes. Add lobster meat and sherry; cook over low heat, stirring frequently, until lobster is heated through. Remove from heat.
9. Spoon into shells, mounding it high. Sprinkle with grated cheese and a little paprika, if desired. Place filled shells on cookie sheet. (Prop up tails with crushed aluminum foil to keep them steady.)
10. Bake 10 to 12 minutes, or until cheese is melted and lightly browned. If desired, garnish with lemon wedges and watercress. Serve with fluffy white rice. Makes 4 servings.

# ❖ ROCK-LOBSTER NEWBURG

Boil lobster tails as directed above, Steps 1 through 5. Make Newburg Sauce, page 464. Gently heat lobster in sauce. Serve over toast or in patty shells, or over rice.
Makes 4 or 5 servings.

# ✥ BROILED LIVE LOBSTERS

2 (1-lb size) live lobsters
Butter or margarine, melted
Salt
Pepper
Paprika
Lemon wedges

1. Kill lobster: Lay lobster on back on wooden board. To sever spinal cord, insert point of knife through to back shell where body and tail of lobster come together.
2. With sharp knife, split body lengthwise, cutting through thin undershell and lobster meat and back shell. Spread open.
3. Remove and discard dark vein and small sac 2 inches below head. Leave in green liver (tomalley) and any red roe (coral).
4. Crack large claws. Lay lobster, cut side up, on rack of broiler pan. Brush with melted butter. Sprinkle with salt, pepper, and paprika.
5. Broil, 4 inches from heat, 12 to 15 minutes, or until lightly browned.
6. Serve with more melted butter, in small dish, and lemon wedges.
Makes 2 servings.

# ✥ BROILED ROCK-LOBSTER TAILS

4 (5-oz size) frozen rock-lobster tails,
    thawed
¼ cup butter or margarine, softened
Salt or garlic salt

## LEMON BUTTER:

½ cup butter or margarine
2 tablespoons lemon juice
1 teaspoon salt
Dash ground red pepper

1. With kitchen shears, cut undershells away from lobster. Bend each shell backward until it cracks.
2. Place lobster tails, shell side up, on rack in broiler pan. Broil, 6 inches from heat, 5 minutes.
3. Turn lobster tails; spread with soft butter, and sprinkle with salt. Broil 5 to 7 minutes longer, or until tender.
4. Meanwhile, make Lemon Butter: Heat all ingredients in small saucepan, over low heat, stirring, until butter melts. Serve with lobster.
Makes 4 servings.

# ✥ BAKED LOBSTER TAILS

4 (6-oz size) frozen lobster tails,
    thawed
4 teaspoons butter or margarine, softened
8 round butter crackers, crushed
4 teaspoons Worcestershire sauce
4 teaspoons lemon juice
4 lemon wedges

1. Preheat oven to 400F.
2. With sharp knife, split each lobster tail down center, but not all the way through. Arrange in baking pan.
3. In split of each one, place 1 teaspoon butter, one fourth of crackers, 1 teaspoon Worcestershire, and 1 teaspoon lemon juice.
4. Bake 30 minutes, or until lobster is cooked through. Serve with lemon wedges.
Makes 4 servings.

# ❖ MOULES MARINIÈRE

*3 dozen mussels*
*½ cup olive oil*
*¼ cup chopped onion*
*¼ cup chopped celery*
*2 to 3 cloves garlic, crushed*
*1 teaspoon dried basil leaves*
*½ cup dry white wine*
*1 tablespoon lemon juice*
*⅛ teaspoon pepper*
*1 teaspoon salt*
*1 can (1 lb) Italian plum tomatoes,*
*    undrained*
*¼ cup chopped parsley*

1. Check mussels, discarding any that are not tightly closed. Scrub well under cold running water, to remove sand and seaweed. With sharp knife, trim off "beard" around edges. Place mussels in large bowl. Cover with cold water and let soak 1 to 2 hours.
2. Lift mussels from water, and place in colander. Rinse with cold water; let drain.
3. In olive oil in 6-quart kettle, sauté onion, celery, garlic, and basil, stirring, until golden and tender— about 10 minutes. Add wine, lemon juice, pepper, salt, tomatoes, and half of parsley; break up tomatoes with spoon. Bring to boiling.
4. Add mussels; cook over high heat, covered, 5 to 8 minutes, or until shells open. Shake kettle frequently, so mussels will cook uniformly.
5. With slotted utensil, remove mussels to heated serving dish. Keep warm.
6. Spoon sauce over mussels; sprinkle with remaining parsley. Serve immediately.
Makes 3 servings.

# ❖ MUSSELS WITH GREEN SAUCE

*1½ dozen mussels*

## GREEN SAUCE:

*1 cup mayonnaise*
*½ cup chopped spinach*
*⅓ cup chopped parsley*
*⅓ cup chopped watercress*
*1 tablespoon snipped fresh chives*
*1 tablespoon snipped fresh dill*
*2 teaspoons dried tarragon leaves*
*1 tablespoon lemon juice*
*Dash salt*

*½ cup white wine*
*½ clove garlic, crushed*

1. Check mussels, discarding any that are not tightly closed. Scrub well under cold running water to remove sand and seaweed. With sharp knife, trim off "beard" around edges. Let soak 1 to 2 hours in cold water.
2. Meanwhile, make Green Sauce: Combine all ingredients in blender or food processor, and beat until smooth. Turn out into small bowl; refrigerate, covered. Makes 1¼ cups.
3. Lift mussels from water, and place in colander. Rinse with cold water; let drain.
4. Place mussels in large skillet; add wine and garlic.
5. Cook, covered, over high heat 5 to 8 minutes. Shake skillet frequently, so mussels will cook uniformly.
6. With slotted utensil, remove mussels to serving dish; refrigerate, covered, 1 hour.
7. To serve: Spoon 1 tablespoon Green Sauce on top of each mussel in shell.
Makes 3 to 4 servings.

# ❖ OYSTER PIE

36 saltines
36 fresh oysters
3 tablespoons butter or margarine
Pepper
1 cup half-and-half

1. Break 12 crackers into fourths; layer in bottom of 8¼-inch round glass baking dish.
2. Drain oysters, reserving 1 cup liquid. Arrange half of oysters on top. Dot with 1 tablespoon butter; sprinkle lightly with pepper.
3. Repeat layering with 12 more crackers (broken into fourths), remaining oysters, 1 tablespoon butter, and a light sprinkling of pepper.
4. Arrange rest of crackers (broken into fourths) over oysters. Dot with remaining butter. Pour reserved liquid and half-and-half over all. Refrigerate 1 hour.
5. Preheat oven to 400F.
6. Bake 15 to 20 minutes, or until golden-brown but not dry.
Makes 6 to 8 servings.

# ❖ OYSTERS FLORENTINE

½ cup water
1 pkg (10 oz) frozen chopped spinach
    or 1¼ cups fresh spinach, cooked
    and chopped
¼ teaspoon salt
1 tablespoon butter or margarine
2 tablespoons finely chopped onion
½ teaspoon dried basil leaves
1 teaspoon flour
¼ cup fresh bread crumbs
1 pint medium oysters, well drained

**BATTER:**

2 eggs
¾ cup milk
¾ cup flour
¼ cup grated Parmesan cheese
½ teaspoon baking powder
¼ teaspoon salt

¼ cup grated Parmesan cheese

1. Bring water to boiling in small saucepan. Add spinach and ¼ teaspoon salt; cook according to package directions. Drain very well.
2. Melt butter in same small saucepan. Sauté onion until golden. Fold spinach, basil, and 1 teaspoon flour into sautéed onion. Spoon into 4 scallop shells or ramekins, dividing evenly.
3. Sprinkle 1 tablespoon bread crumbs into center of each shell. Arrange oysters on crumbs. Place shells or ramekins on cookie sheet with raised edges. If using shells, prop so they are level. Preheat oven to 425F.
4. Prepare Batter: In small bowl, with rotary beater, beat eggs, milk, flour, ¼ cup Parmesan cheese, baking powder, and salt, to make smooth batter.
5. Pour batter over and around spinach and oysters. Sprinkle with ¼ cup grated Parmesan cheese. Bake 18 to 20 minutes, or until puffed and golden. Serve immediately.
Makes 4 servings.

# ✦ FRIED SCALLOPS

Salad oil or shortening for frying
1 egg
½ teaspoon seasoned salt
⅛ teaspoon garlic powder
1 lb sea scallops, washed and well
    drained
½ cup packaged dry bread crumbs
Tartar Sauce (optional) page 466
Lemon wedges (optional)

1. In deep skillet, heat salad oil (at least 1 inch) to 375F on deep-frying thermometer.
2. In small bowl, beat egg with seasoned salt and garlic powder.
3. Dip scallops in egg mixture; roll in crumbs, coating evenly.
4. Fry, a few at a time, until golden-brown—2 to 3 minutes.
5. Drain on paper towels; keep warm while frying rest. Serve with well-chilled Tartar Sauce and lemon wedges, if desired.
Makes 3 or 4 servings.

# ✦ SAUTÉED SCALLOPS

2 lb sea scallops
6 tablespoons butter or margarine
2 tablespoons chopped shallots
3 tablespoons dry vermouth or dry
    white wine
2 tablespoons chopped parsley
Lemon wedges

1. Rinse scallops gently under cold water; drain. If large, cut in half.
2. In hot butter in large, heavy skillet, sauté shallots 2 minutes. Add scallops in single layer (do half at a time, if necessary). Sauté over medium heat, stirring occasionally, until browned and cooked through—5 to 8 minutes.
3. With slotted spoon, remove to heated platter; keep warm.
4. Add vermouth and parsley to skillet. Heat over low heat, stirring to dissolve browned bits, until bubbling —about 1 minute. Pour over scallops.
5. Garnish with lemon wedges and with additional parsley, if desired.
Makes 6 servings.

# ✦ QUICK SCALLOP PAELLA

2¼ cups cold water
1 cup raw long-grain white rice
1 teaspoon salt
¼ teaspoon dried thyme leaves
3 tablespoons butter or margarine
1 lb sea scallops, washed and drained
1 medium-size green pepper, cut into
    strips
1 medium-size red pepper, cut into
    strips
4 (3-inch) slices salami, cut into
    eighths

1. In medium-size heavy saucepan with tight-fitting cover, combine water, rice, salt, thyme, and 1 tablespoon butter.
2. Bring to boiling, uncovered.
3. Reduce heat; simmer, covered, 15 to 20 minutes, or until rice is tender and liquid is absorbed.
4. In 2 tablespoons butter in large skillet, sauté scallops 5 minutes, turning.
5. Add green and red peppers; sauté, stirring, until peppers and scallops are tender—about 5 minutes.
6. Add cooked rice and salami to scallop mixture. Simmer, covered, 5 minutes.
Makes 4 to 6 servings.

# ❖ FRIED SCALLOPS, SHRIMP, AND SOLE

1 lb fillets of sole
1 lb sea scallops
¾ lb shrimp, shelled and deveined
Salad oil or shortening for deep-frying
2 eggs
1½ teaspoons salt
¼ teaspoon pepper
¼ teaspoon paprika
1¼ cups packaged dry bread crumbs
Tartar Sauce, page 466
Lemon wedges (optional)

1. Wash seafood; dry with paper towels. Cut fillets in half crosswise.
2. In deep skillet, slowly heat salad oil (at least 1 inch deep) to 375F on deep-frying thermometer. Or heat oil in electric skillet at 375F.
3. In pie plate, using fork, beat eggs with salt, pepper, and paprika.
4. Place bread crumbs on waxed paper. Dip seafood in egg mixture, then in crumbs, coating evenly.
5. Gently place seafood, a few pieces at a time, in hot oil; fry until golden-brown—3 to 5 minutes.
6. Remove, and drain on paper towels. Place in warm oven until all seafood is cooked. Serve with Tartar Sauce and, if desired, with lemon wedges.
Makes 4 to 6 servings.

# ❖ BOILED SHRIMP

1½ to 2 lb unshelled raw shrimp
1 quart water
1 small onion, thinly sliced
½ lemon, thinly sliced
2 sprigs parsley
1 tablespoon salt
5 whole black peppercorns
1 bay leaf
¼ teaspoon dried thyme leaves

1. Rinse shrimp; remove shells, and devein (using small sharp knife, slit each shrimp down back; lift out sand vein).
2. In large skillet, combine water, onion, lemon, parsley, salt, peppercorns, bay leaf, and thyme. Bring to boiling, covered, over medium heat; simmer 10 minutes.
3. Add shrimp; return to boiling. Reduce heat, and simmer, covered, 3 to 5 minutes, or just until tender.
4. Drain; let cool. Refrigerate, covered, until ready to use. Use for shrimp cocktails, in salads, or in any recipe calling for boiled shrimp.
Makes 6 to 8 servings.

# ❖ SHRIMP IN SHELL

2½ lb unshelled shrimp
1 cup butter or margarine, melted
2 tablespoons lemon juice
3 cloves garlic, crushed
2 tablespoons white wine
½ cup olive or salad oil
1 teaspoon salt
3 tablespoons cracked black peppercorns
Chopped parsley

1. Rinse shrimp, and pat dry with paper towels. Place in shallow broiling pan.
2. In small bowl, mix butter, lemon juice, garlic, white wine, and oil. Pour over shrimp; sprinkle with some of salt and cracked black pepper.
3. Broil, 6 inches from heat, 6 minutes. Turn shrimp. Sprinkle with salt and pepper; broil 6 minutes. Serve in shells, sprinkled with chopped parsley.
Makes 4 to 6 servings.

# ❖ SHRIMP CURRY

## CURRY SAUCE:

*3 tablespoons butter or margarine*
*1 cup chopped onion*
*1 cup chopped pared apple*
*1 clove garlic, crushed*
*2 to 3 teaspoons curry powder*
*¼ cup flour*
*1 teaspoon salt*
*¼ teaspoon ground ginger*
*¼ teaspoon ground cardamom*
*¼ teaspoon pepper*
*2 cans (10¾-oz size) condensed*
*  chicken broth, undiluted*
*2 tablespoons lime juice*
*2 teaspoons grated lime peel*

*2 lb raw shrimp, shelled and deveined*
*  (18 to 20 per pound)*
*1 quart water*
*1 tablespoon salt*
*1 small onion, sliced*
*½ lemon, sliced*
*5 whole black peppercorns*
*¼ cup chopped chutney*

1. Make Curry Sauce: In hot butter in large skillet, sauté chopped onion, chopped apple, garlic, and curry powder until onion is tender—will take about 5 minutes.
2. Remove from heat; blend in flour, 1 teaspoon salt, the ginger, cardamom, and pepper.
3. Gradually stir in chicken broth, lime juice, and lime peel.
4. Bring to boiling, stirring constantly. Reduce heat, and simmer sauce, uncovered, 20 minutes, stirring occasionally.
5. Meanwhile, cook shrimp: Rinse shrimp under cold running water.
6. In large saucepan, combine 1 quart water, 1 tablespoon salt, the sliced onion, sliced lemon, and whole black peppercorns; bring to boiling. Add cleaned shrimp.
7. Return to boiling; reduce heat, and simmer, uncovered, 3 to 5 minutes, or just until shrimp are tender when tested with fork.
8. Drain shrimp, discarding cooking liquid. Add shrimp to curry sauce; stir in chopped chutney. Heat gently just to boiling.
9. Serve Shrimp Curry hot, with Curry Accompaniments, below, and Fluffy White Rice, page 423. Makes 6 servings.

*Curry Accompaniments:*

| | |
|---|---|
| Chutney | Diced tomato |
| Pickled watermelon rind | Salted nuts |
| Chopped green pepper | Peanuts |
| Chopped green onion | Sliced banana |
| Diced avocado | Raisins |
| Cucumber slices | Pineapple chunks |

# ❖ SHRIMP IN GARLIC BUTTER

*2 lb large unshelled raw shrimp*
*½ cup butter or margarine*
*½ cup salad or olive oil*
*¼ cup chopped parsley*
*6 cloves garlic, crushed*
*1 teaspoon salt*
*Dash ground red pepper*
*¼ cup lemon juice*
*Lemon slices (optional)*

1. Rinse shrimp; remove shells, leaving tails on. Devein (using small, sharp knife, slit each shrimp down back; lift out sand vein). Wash under cold running water. Drain; pat dry with paper towels.
2. Melt butter in shallow broiler pan, without rack, or in 13-by-9-by-2-inch baking pan. Add oil, 2 tablespoons parsley, the garlic, salt, red pepper, and lemon juice; mix well.
3. Add shrimp, tossing lightly in butter mixture to

coat well. Arrange in single layer in pan.

4. Broil, 4 to 5 inches from heat, 5 minutes. Turn shrimp; broil 5 to 10 minutes longer, or until lightly browned.

5. Using tongs, remove shrimp to heated serving platter. Pour garlic mixture over all, or pour it into small pitcher, to pass.

6. Sprinkle shrimp with remaining chopped parsley. Garnish platter with lemon slices, if you wish. Makes 8 servings.

*Note*: Shrimp may be baked at 400F for 8 to 10 minutes, or just until tender, instead of broiled.

# ✠ SHRIMP CREOLE WITH WHITE RICE

*1 quart water*
*½ lemon, sliced*
*4 whole black peppercorns*
*2 lb raw shrimp, shelled and deveined*
*4 slices bacon*
*2 tablespoons butter or margarine*
*1 clove garlic, finely chopped*
*1 cup chopped onion*
*1½ cups chopped green pepper*
*¼ cup finely chopped parsley*
*1½ cups thinly sliced celery*
*1 can (1 lb, 12 oz) tomatoes*
*1 can (6 oz) tomato paste*
*1 tablespoon lemon juice*
*1 tablespoon sugar*
*1 teaspoon salt*
*¼ to ½ teaspoon black pepper*
*¼ to ½ teaspoon crushed red pepper*
*1 bay leaf*
*½ teaspoon dried thyme leaves*
*½ teaspoon filé powder*
*Cooked white rice*

1. Bring water to boiling in large saucepan. Add lemon slices, black peppercorns, and shrimp. Reduce heat; simmer, uncovered, 3 minutes.

2. Drain shrimp, reserving 1 cup cooking liquid.

3. In same saucepan, sauté bacon, over low heat, until crisp. Remove bacon. Drain on paper towels; crumble.

4. To bacon fat, add butter, garlic, onion, green pepper, parsley, and celery; cook, stirring, about 5 minutes, or until vegetables are tender.

5. Add reserved shrimp liquid, bacon, tomatoes, tomato paste, lemon juice, sugar, salt, black pepper, red pepper, bay leaf, and thyme; bring to boiling. Reduce heat, and simmer, covered, 30 minutes.

6. Just before serving, stir in filé powder and shrimp; bring to boiling. Reduce heat, and simmer 5 minutes.

7. Serve over hot cooked white rice.
Makes 6 to 8 servings.

*Note*: This dish may be made in advance and frozen until ready to use.

# ❖ SEAFOOD PAELLA
### (RICE WITH CLAMS AND SHRIMP)

*1 dozen small clams, in shell*
*2 lb shrimp, shelled and deveined*
*6 cups water*
*4 tablespoons olive or salad oil*
*1 tablespoon butter or margarine*
*1 cup raw long-grain white rice*
*1 teaspoon salt*
*1 bay leaf*
*1 chicken-bouillon cube*
*2 cloves garlic, finely chopped*
*2 medium onions, finely chopped*
*2 green peppers, seeded and finely chopped*
*2 large tomatoes, peeled*
*½ cup pimiento-stuffed olives, sliced*
*2 teaspoons paprika*
*⅛ teaspoon ground red pepper*
*1½ cups grated Cheddar cheese (6 oz)*

1. Wash clams and shrimp thoroughly. Place clams in saucepan with the water; bring to boiling. Add shrimp; cook over high heat, covered, 5 minutes. Remove from heat.

2. Pour off enough shellfish liquid to make 2¼ cups. Set aside clams and shrimp in remaining broth; keep warm.

3. Heat 2 tablespoons olive oil and the butter in 3-quart saucepan. Add rice, and stir to coat well. Add reserved 2¼ cups liquid, the salt, bay leaf, and bouillon cube. Bring to boiling; lower heat, and simmer, covered and without stirring, 25 minutes.

4. Preheat oven to 375F. Meanwhile, in 2 tablespoons hot oil in 6-quart Dutch oven, sauté garlic, onion, and green pepper until green pepper is tender—about 10 minutes.

5. Chop tomatoes. Add to sautéed vegetables with olives, paprika, and red pepper; cook 5 minutes longer. Keep warm.

6. Drain shellfish, and add with rice to tomato mixture; stir gently to blend. Turn out into paella pan or shallow 4-quart casserole.

7. Sprinkle cheese over top of all. Bake 10 to 15 minutes, or until cheese is melted and bubbly.

Makes 6 to 8 servings.

# FOOD PROCESSOR RECIPES

❖ **M**any of us can remember our grand-mothers or great-grandmothers turning up their noses at electric mixers when they first heard of them and then, very quickly, becoming converted to those time-saving machines, which have become standard in American kitchens. More recently we have gone through the same sort of experience with the food processor. This machine, which can slice, chop, grind, grate, shred, purée, whip, and mix, has made many formerly difficult dishes a snap to prepare—pâtés, sauces, soups, dishes calling for several different chopped vegetables, and, not the least, pastries and breads, which mix up in' your processor like magic.

The recipes here are an assemblage of the wonders your processor can perform. You will also find that the more you use this machine, the more things you will think to do with it.

## FOOD PROCESSOR HINTS

If you've never used a food processor or are just experimenting with its wondrous ways, remember that you are using a powerful machine, one that will perform remarkably well if you get to know how to use it.
1. Treasure your instruction book that comes with the machine. Many of these contain recipes you'll want to try, but first master the techniques of using the machine.
2. Respect the processor. Some jobs, like chopping onion, take literally a second or two. It's best to stop and see what's happening. You can always chop more but never less.
3. Blades and cutting surfaces are sharp—that's why they do the job so well and so fast. Handle them with care and never toss them into a dishpan to wash later. You can get cut if you accidentally brush a finger over a cutting edge.
4. Experiment; try your various blades and discs. The better you know this machine, the more it will do for you.

## ❖ CURRIED CHEESE PÂTÉ WITH CHUTNEY

*3 pkg (8-oz size) cream cheese, at room*
  *temperature*
*2 pkg (10-oz size) sharp Cheddar*
  *cheese, cubed*
*2 teaspoons curry powder*
*½ teaspoon salt*
*¼ cup dry sherry*
*1 cup chutney, chopped*
*¼ cup chopped green onion*
*Small crackers*

1. Line 7-by-6-inch 1½-quart dish with waxed paper.
2. In food processor, with chopping blade, combine cream cheese, Cheddar cheese, curry powder, salt, and sherry. Process until smooth.
3. Turn out into prepared dish. Refrigerate, covered, until firm—4 hours or overnight.
4. To serve: With spatula, loosen sides. Turn out onto serving dish; remove waxed paper. Spread chutney on top. Sprinkle green onion around edge.
5. Let stand at room temperature 30 minutes before serving. Surround with small crackers.
Makes enough to spread on 48 crackers.

# ❖ BAKED CHICKEN LIVER PÂTÉ

3 lb chicken livers
6 tablespoons butter or margarine
⅓ cup coarsely chopped onion
1 tablespoon dried savory leaves
1 tablespoon dried tarragon leaves
6 tablespoons cognac or brandy
½ cup light cream
5 eggs
1 teaspoon salt
¼ teaspoon pepper
8 slices bacon
Toast rounds

1. Wash livers, and dry on paper towels. Cut in half.
2. In hot butter in skillet, sauté onion and dried herbs until onion is golden. Add chicken livers; sauté, stirring, about 5 minutes.
3. In bowl, combine livers, cognac, cream, eggs, salt, and pepper; mix well. In processor, with chopping blade, process mixture about one third at a time to make smooth purée.
4. Preheat oven to 400F. Line oval or round 1¾-quart casserole (7¾ inches in diameter) with bacon slices.
5. Transfer liver mixture to casserole; place in pan of very hot water (water should measure 1 inch). Bake 1 hour.
6. Remove casserole from hot water. Let cool on wire rack 1 hour. Serve, slightly warm or cooled completely, with toast rounds.
Makes 40 servings.

# ❖ VEAL AND HAM PÂTÉ

1 lb lean veal round steak, ¼ inch thick
½ cup chopped shallots
⅔ cup brandy
2 tablespoons butter or margarine
1 lb boneless veal, cut into ¾-inch pieces
¼ lb pork fat, coarsely chopped
¼ teaspoon salt
1 teaspoon dried thyme leaves
½ cup pitted black olives, chopped
1 lb fresh pork, cut into ¾-inch pieces
2 eggs
⅛ teaspoon ground allspice
⅛ teaspoon pepper
½ lb cooked ham, cut into ¼-inch strips
3 bay leaves
¾ cup chopped parsley (see Note)

1. Cut veal steak crosswise into ¼-inch strips. In small bowl, combine veal strips, 1 tablespoon shallots, and 2 tablespoons brandy; mix well. Refrigerate, covered.
2. In hot butter in small skillet, sauté remaining shallots just until tender—about 3 minutes. Add remaining brandy; cook over medium heat about 5 minutes, or until mixture is reduced to ½ cup.
3. In processor, with chopping blade, combine veal, pork fat, the ½ cup shallot-brandy mixture, the salt, and thyme. Process until finely chopped. Measure 1 cup mixture into small bowl; stir in olives. Set aside. To remaining mixture, add pork, eggs, allspice, and pepper; process until finely chopped. Set aside.
4. Grease well 9-by-5-by-2¼-inch loaf pan. Preheat oven to 350F.
5. Set aside 1 cup veal-pork mixture. Turn out remainder into pan and pat to make 1-inch thick layer on bottom and up each side (not ends).
6. Now line sides and bottom with three quarters of veal strips, then with three quarters of ham strips. Fill center with reserved veal-olive mixture. Top with remaining ham strips, then remaining veal strips. Pour any remaining brandy mixture from veal strips over all. Last, add reserved veal-and-pork mixture, patting it into even layer. Top with bay leaves.

7. Place loaf pan on baking pan to catch drippings. Bake about 2 hours, or until meat thermometer registers 180F. Remove pâté to wire rack. Cool to room temperature. Refrigerate overnight.

8. To serve: With sharp knife, loosen pâté around sides and ends, and invert onto serving platter. Pat chopped parsley onto top and sides of loaf.

Makes 12 servings.

*Note*: To chop parsley in processor, first wash and dry thoroughly on towels; then break into sprigs and place in clean, dry processor fitted with chopping blade. Process until finely chopped.

# ❖ TURKEY AND VEAL PÂTÉ

1 lb turkey cutlets, cubed
1 lb boneless veal, cubed
1 cup fresh bread crumbs
1 egg
¼ cup heavy cream
2 tablespoons dry sherry
¼ lb medium mushrooms, washed
   and trimmed
½ teaspoon tarragon
¼ teaspoon crumbled bay leaf
3 sprigs parsley
2 tablespoons chopped shallots
½ teaspoon salt
¼ cup chopped parsley (optional)

1. Preheat oven to 350F. Thoroughly grease 9-by-5-by-3-inch loaf pan. Wipe turkey and veal with damp paper towel. In food processor, with chopping blade, process until finely chopped.

2. Add bread crumbs, egg, cream, sherry, mushrooms, tarragon, bay leaf, parsley sprigs, shallots, and salt. Process until mixture is smooth purée.

3. Turn out into prepared pan. Bake 1 hour, or until center feels firm when gently pressed. Set aside to cool 10 minutes at room temperature. Loosen edges and invert onto wire rack over baking pan. Pat chopped parsley over outside of loaf, if desired; place on serving platter. Serve warm, or refrigerate several hours and serve cold.

Makes 8 servings.

# ❖ CHOPPED STEAK TARTARE

2 lb beef round or sirloin, cut into
   ½-inch cubes
1 small onion, halved
½ cup capers, drained
8 anchovy fillets
4 egg yolks
1 teaspoon salt
⅛ teaspoon pepper
¼ cup watercress
Small rounds of pumpernickel or rye
   bread

1. In processor, with chopping blade, chop beef, a little at a time, until fine but not mushy. Turn out into large bowl.

2. Place remaining ingredients in processor except bread. Chop, turning machine on and off several times.

3. Add beef; turn machine on and off just to mix well.

4. Mound on serving platter. Refrigerate, covered, until ready to serve—2 to 3 hours.

5. To serve: Surround with bread rounds.

Makes 20 servings.

*Note*: To make more decorative, place meat mixture into fancy mold. To serve: Unmold onto serving platter, and garnish with anchovy strips and capers.

# ❖ VEGETABLE DIP NIÇOISE

2 cloves garlic
12 anchovy fillets, cut in half
1 teaspoon capers
½ cup pitted whole black olives
½ teaspoon dried basil leaves
2 tablespoons chopped parsley
2 cups mayonnaise
2 tablespoons chopped pitted black
  olives
Celery sticks
Cherry tomatoes
Radishes
Cucumber sticks

1. In food processor, with chopping blade, combine garlic, anchovies, capers, whole black olives, basil, parsley, and mayonnaise; blend until smooth.
2. Turn out into bowl; refrigerate, tightly covered, overnight.
3. To serve: Turn out into serving bowl and garnish with chopped black olives. Surround with vegetables.
Makes about 2 cups.

# ❖ EASY GAZPACHO

2 large tomatoes (¾ lb), peeled
1 large cucumber, pared and halved
1 large onion, halved
1 medium-size green pepper, quartered and seeded
2 cans (18-oz size) tomato juice
½ cup red-wine vinegar
Dash pepper
Chopped parsley

1. In processor, with chopping blade, combine 1 tomato, cucumber half, onion half, half of green pepper, and 1 cup tomato juice. Process 30 seconds to purée vegetables.
2. In 2-quart container, mix puréed vegetables with remaining tomato juice, the vinegar, and pepper.
3. Refrigerate mixture, covered, until well chilled—about 2 hours. Also refrigerate serving bowls or mugs.
4. Chop separately remaining tomato, cucumber, onion, and green pepper. Place each in separate mounds on small plate. Serve as accompaniments.
5. At serving time, stir gazpacho, and pour into chilled bowls. Sprinkle with parsley. Pass accompaniments.
Makes 4 servings.

# ❖ CREAM OF BROCCOLI SOUP

2½ lb fresh broccoli
1 large onion, cut into eighths
2 stalks celery, quartered
¾ teaspoon salt
¼ teaspoon pepper
¼ teaspoon ground nutmeg
2 bay leaves
1½ cups water
3 cans (13¾-oz size) chicken broth
4½ tablespoons butter or margarine
3 tablespoons flour
3 cups half-and-half
1 cup heavy cream, whipped
Nutmeg

1. Trim broccoli; wash thoroughly. Split each stalk lengthwise into halves.
2. Place onion and celery in food processor fitted with chopping blade. Process until coarsely chopped.
3. In 6-quart Dutch oven or heavy kettle, combine broccoli, onion, celery, salt, pepper, ¼ teaspoon nutmeg, and the bay leaves.
4. Add water to chicken broth to make 6 cups; add to broccoli. Bring to boiling; simmer, covered, until broccoli is tender—about 30 minutes.
5. Drain; reserve broth. Purée vegetables in food processor with 1 cup broth half at a time.
6. In Dutch oven, melt butter. Remove from heat and add flour, stirring until smooth. Gradually add reserved broth, stirring. Cook over medium heat, stirring, until mixture boils.
7. Add puréed vegetables and half-and-half. Continue stirring until soup is hot and well blended—5 minutes. Top each serving with spoonful of whipped cream and dash of nutmeg.
Makes 12 servings.

# ❖ CREAMY COLESLAW

3 lb green cabbage
½ lb carrots
1 cup radishes

## DRESSING:

2 cups prepared mayonnaise or
   Processor Mayonnaise, page 208
¼ cup prepared horseradish
1 tablespoon sugar
1 tablespoon lemon juice
1 tablespoon grated onion
2 teaspoons salt
½ teaspoon paprika

1. Wash cabbage. Cut into small wedges; remove core. Wash and pare carrots; cut in half crosswise. Wash radishes; remove stems.
2. In food processor, shred cabbage with slicing or shredding disc, a few wedges at a time. Remove to large bowl.
3. Shred carrots with shredding disc; add to cabbage.
4. Slice radishes with slicing disc. Add to cabbage and carrots, and toss to mix well. Refrigerate.
5. Make Dressing: In large bowl, combine mayonnaise and rest of dressing ingredients; mix well. Add vegetables and toss with dressing to coat well.
6. Refrigerate, covered, until well chilled—several hours or overnight.
Makes 12 servings.

# ⊕ AIOLI SAUCE

1 slice white bread, crust removed
2 tablespoons milk
3 cloves garlic
2 egg yolks
1 cup olive or salad oil
2 tablespoons lemon juice
¼ teaspoon salt
Dash white pepper

1. Soak bread in milk 10 minutes; squeeze hard to remove all milk.
2. Place bread and garlic in processor fitted with chopping blade. Process 10 seconds, or until mixture forms paste.
3. Add egg yolks; blend until egg mixture is thick—10 seconds.
4. With processor running, add oil, 1 tablespoon at a time, processing until thick.
5. Continue until all oil has been used. Mixture should be thick.
6. Add lemon juice, salt, and pepper; blend a few seconds more to mix well. Refrigerate, tightly covered. Serve over chilled fish, chicken, or vegetables. Makes 1¼ cups.

# ⊕ PROCESSOR MAYONNAISE

¾ cup salad oil
2 egg yolks
2 tablespoons lemon juice or vinegar
¼ teaspoon sugar
½ teaspoon dry mustard
¼ teaspoon salt
Dash ground red pepper

1. In food processor, with chopping blade or plastic mixing blade, combine ¼ cup salad oil and rest of ingredients. Process 10 to 15 seconds.
2. Remove pusher from feed tube. With machine running, add remaining oil in very thin stream. Process until thick and creamy.
3. Store, tightly covered, in refrigerator.
Makes about 1 cup.

# ⊕ PROCESSOR HOLLANDAISE SAUCE

3 egg yolks
3 tablespoons lemon juice
¼ teaspoon salt
Dash ground red pepper
½ cup hot melted butter or margarine

1. In food processor, with chopping blade or plastic mixing blade, combine egg yolks, lemon juice, salt, and red pepper. Cover and process 10 seconds.
2. Remove pusher from feed tube of processor. With motor running, gradually add butter in steady stream.
3. Serve immediately, or keep warm by placing serving bowl in 2 inches hot, not boiling, water.
Makes 1 cup.

# ❖ POTATO PANCAKES

4 large potatoes (2 lb), peeled
1 small onion
2 eggs, slightly beaten
2 tablespoons flour
¾ teaspoon salt
Dash nutmeg and pepper
Salad oil or shortening for frying
Sour cream

1. In processor, with coarse shredding disc, shred potatoes and onion. Drain very well; pat dry with dish towel.
2. In large bowl, combine potatoes, onion, eggs, flour, salt, nutmeg, and pepper.
3. In large heavy skillet, slowly heat oil (⅛ inch) until very hot but not smoking.
4. For each pancake, drop 1 tablespoon potato mixture at a time into hot fat. With spatula, flatten against bottom of skillet to make pancake 2 inches in diameter. Fry 2 to 3 minutes on each side, or until golden-brown.
5. Drain well on paper towels. Serve hot with sour cream.
Makes 24.

# ❖ FRESH TOMATO SAUCE

4 large ripe tomatoes
1 large onion
1 tablespoon olive oil
1 clove garlic, crushed
1 teaspoon dried basil leaves
½ teaspoon dried oregano leaves
1 can (6 oz) tomato juice

1. Wash tomatoes. Cut into eighths and remove seeds.
2. Peel and quarter onion. In food processor, with chopping blade, process onion until finely chopped.
3. Heat oil in medium skillet. Add onion, garlic, basil, and oregano. Sauté over low heat until onions are tender.
4. Place tomatoes in food processor, and process until coarsely chopped. When onions are tender, add tomato juice; bring to boiling. Add fresh tomatoes. Cook, stirring, just until tomatoes are heated through. Do not overcook.
Makes 4 servings.

# ❖ PESTO SAUCE

¼ cup butter or margarine, softened
¼ cup freshly grated Parmesan cheese
1 cup parsley sprigs
1 clove garlic, crushed
1 teaspoon dried basil leaves or 1 tablespoon fresh basil leaves
½ teaspoon dried marjoram leaves
¼ cup olive oil
¼ cup pine nuts or walnuts

1. In food processor, with chopping blade, combine butter, Parmesan cheese, parsley, garlic, basil, and marjoram.
2. Remove pusher from feed tube. With motor running, gradually add ¼ cup oil. Process until well blended. Add nuts; process 10 seconds.
Makes about 2 cups.

# ❖ HOMEMADE SAUSAGE

2 lb boneless pork with fat (see Note)
1 tablespoon salt
½ teaspoon ground pepper
½ teaspoon ground allspice
1 teaspoon dried thyme or rubbed sage
2 tablespoons salad oil

1. Wipe meat with damp paper towels. Cut into 1-inch cubes. Place in large bowl. Add remaining ingredients, and toss until meat is evenly coated with spice mixture.
2. Place half of meat in food processor fitted with chopping blade. Process until evenly ground. Remove; repeat with remaining meat.
3. Shape sausage into patties or "links." Sauté over medium heat until well done, turning to brown on all sides—about 10 minutes; or wrap individually, and freeze for use at another time. Fresh sausage may be kept 2 days in the refrigerator or 3 to 4 months in the freezer.
Makes 2 pounds.

Note: 1 pound beef chuck may be substituted for 1 pound pork to make mixed sausage.

# ❖ MEAL IN A PIE

1 pkg (11 oz) pastry mix or 1 recipe Processor Pastry, below
2 medium potatoes (¾ lb), peeled
4 medium carrots (½ lb), scraped
1 medium onion
1 can (16 oz) stewed tomatoes
¾ cup catsup
½ cup oatmeal (not instant)
½ teaspoon salt
½ teaspoon dried basil leaves
⅛ teaspoon ground allspice
⅛ teaspoon ground black pepper
½ lb boneless beef chuck, cut into ½-inch cubes
2 eggs
1 teaspoon water

1. Prepare pastry for 2-crust pie. Divide into 2 balls. On lightly floured surface, roll out 1 ball of dough to form 11-inch round. Fit into bottom of 9-inch pie plate.
2. Cut potatoes, carrots, and onion into 1-inch chunks. Place in food processor fitted with chopping blade. Add 1 cup stewed tomatoes, ¼ cup catsup, the oatmeal, salt, basil, allspice, and pepper. Process until all vegetables are finely chopped.
3. Add beef chuck and 1 egg. Separate the second egg; add egg white to mixture in processor, and place the yolk in a custard cup or small dish. Process meat and vegetable mixture just until uniformly chopped. Turn out into pie shell. Preheat oven to 350F.
4. Roll out second ball of pastry to form 10-inch round. Cut 1-inch circle from center of round. Moisten edges of bottom pastry. Carefully place top pastry over filling. Fold edge of top crust under edge of bottom crust, and flute edges.
5. Add 1 teaspoon water to reserved egg yolk; mix well. Brush over top of pastry. Place pie in oven. Bake 50 to 60 minutes, or until center feels firm. Remove from oven; brush immediately with more egg-yolk mixture. Let cool 5 minutes before cutting.
6. In small saucepan, combine remaining stewed tomatoes and catsup. Heat, stirring; just to boiling. Serve with pie.
Makes 6 servings.

# ❖ PROCESSOR PASTRY

2 cups all-purpose flour
¼ teaspoon salt
⅔ cup cold butter or margarine, cut
    into ½-inch slices
¼ cup ice water

1. Combine flour and salt in food processor fitted with chopping blade.
2. With motor running, drop pieces of butter through feed tube. Process until mixture resembles coarse cornmeal.
3. With motor running, pour ice water through feed tube, and continue processing until pastry forms ball.
4. Refrigerate dough 15 minutes before rolling.
Makes pastry for 2-crust pie.

# ❖ HAM-AND-CHEESE QUICHE

Cheese Pastry, below

**FILLING:**

6 oz ham, cubed
½ lb Swiss cheese
1½ cups milk
½ teaspoon salt
3 eggs

1. Preheat oven to 375F. Prepare Cheese Pastry as directed. Bake pie shell 5 minutes; remove to rack.
2. Meanwhile, make Filling: In food processor, with chopping blade, chop ham.
3. Spread ham on bottom of cooled pastry shell. Chop cheese in processor; sprinkle over ham.
4. In processor, combine milk, salt, and eggs. Blend just until mixture is smooth, not frothy—3 seconds.
5. Pour egg mixture into pie shell. Bake 40 to 45 minutes, or until top is golden and center is firm when pressed with fingertip.
6. Cool on wire rack 10 minutes. Remove side of pan. Keep quiche on bottom; place on serving plate.
Makes 10 servings.

**CHEESE PASTRY:**

¼ lb Swiss cheese, cubed
1⅔ cups sifted all-purpose flour
½ teaspoon salt
⅓ cup cold butter, cut into ½-inch
    cubes
3 to 4 tablespoons ice water

1. In processor, with chopping blade, chop cheese.
2. Add flour, salt, and butter to processor. Chop until butter is in fine lumps.
3. Add ice water, and mix until well combined. Form into ball.
4. Roll pastry on lightly floured pastry cloth to form 12-inch circle. Lift into fluted 9-inch quiche pan with removable bottom in place.
5. Press evenly into bottom and side. Refrigerate.

# ◈ PROCESSOR WHITE BREAD

*1 pkg active dry yeast*
*1 cup cool water*
*3 cups all-purpose or bread flour*
*1 teaspoon salt*
*Salad oil*
*1 tablespoon honey*

1. Sprinkle yeast over water in food processor fitted with chopping blade.
2. Add 1½ cups flour, the salt, 1 tablespoon oil, and the honey. Process 3 minutes. Add remaining flour, and process until dough forms compact ball and leaves side of bowl.
3. Lightly oil large bowl. On lightly floured surface, knead dough several times; form into ball. Place in bowl; turn dough so oiled surface is on top. Cover with towel; let rise in warm place (85F), free from drafts, about 1 hour, or until double in bulk.
4. Grease and flour 8-by-4-by-2½-inch loaf pan. Punch down dough with fist; turn out onto lightly floured board or pastry cloth. Knead several times.
5. Shape dough into loaf, and place in prepared pan.
6. Brush lightly with oil. Cover with towel; let rise in warm place until double in bulk—about 1 hour.
7. Meanwhile, preheat oven to 400F. Bake until golden-brown—30 to 40 minutes. Loaf should sound hollow when tapped with knuckle.
8. Cool on wire rack 5 minutes. Remove from pan; cool completely.
Makes 1 loaf.

*Whole-Wheat Bread*: Substitute 1½ cups whole-wheat flour for 1½ cups all-purpose flour. Follow directions for white bread.
Makes 1 loaf.

*Whole-Wheat Swirl Bread*: Prepare 1 recipe white bread and 1 recipe whole-wheat bread. Follow directions above up to Step 5, keeping doughs separate. Then divide each dough in half. Roll out one half of white dough to make 8-inch square. Repeat with one half of whole-wheat dough. Place one square of dough on top of other. Whichever dough is on bottom will form outside of loaf. Roll, jelly-roll fashion, and place, seam side down, in prepared pan. Repeat with remaining dough. Proceed with Step 6 above.
Makes 2 loaves.

# ❖ PUMPERNICKEL

1 pkg active dry yeast
1 cup cool water
1¾ cups all-purpose or bread flour
1 teaspoon salt
Salad oil
¼ cup dark molasses
1 square unsweetened chocolate, melted
1½ cups rye flour
¼ cup cornmeal
1 teaspoon caraway seeds

1. Sprinkle yeast over water in food processor fitted with chopping blade.
2. Add all-purpose flour, salt, 1 tablespoon oil, the molasses, and melted chocolate. Process 3 minutes. Add rye flour and cornmeal, and process until dough forms compact ball and leaves side of bowl.
3. Lightly oil large bowl. Place dough on lightly floured board or pastry cloth. Set aside ¼ teaspoon caraway seeds. Sprinkle rest over dough. Knead dough until smooth and seeds are well distributed; form into ball. Place in bowl; turn dough so oiled surface is on top. Cover with towel; let rise in warm place (85F), free from drafts, about 1 hour, or until double in bulk.
4. Grease and flour 8-inch circle in center of cookie sheet. Punch down dough with fist; turn out onto lightly floured board. Knead several times.
5. Shape dough into 5-inch ball, and place on prepared pan. Cut 3 slashes across top.
6. Brush lightly with oil. Sprinkle with reserved caraway seeds, patting them into surface. Let rise in warm place until double in bulk—about 1 hour.
7. Meanwhile, preheat oven to 400F. Bake until golden-brown—20 to 30 minutes. Loaf should sound hollow when tapped with knuckle.
8. Cool on wire rack 5 minutes. Remove from pan; cool completely.
Makes 1 loaf.

# ❖ FAMILY RYE BREAD

1 pkg active dry yeast
1 cup cool water
1½ cups all-purpose or bread flour
1 teaspoon salt
Salad oil
2 tablespoons dark molasses
1½ cups rye flour
2 tablespoons unprocessed bran

1. Sprinkle yeast over water in food processor fitted with chopping blade.
2. Add all-purpose flour, salt, 1 tablespoon oil, and the molasses. Process 3 minutes. Add rye flour, and process until dough forms compact ball and leaves side of bowl.
3. Grease and flour 8-by-4-by-2½-inch loaf pan. On lightly floured board or pastry cloth, knead dough several times. Shape dough into loaf; roll in bran to coat surface. Place in prepared pan. Make several diagonal cuts across top.
4. Let rise in warm place (85F), free from drafts, until double in bulk—1 to 1½ hours.
5. Meanwhile, preheat oven to 400F. Bake until golden-brown—30 to 40 minutes. Loaf should sound hollow when tapped with knuckle.
6. Cool on wire rack 5 minutes. Remove from pan; cool completely.
Makes 1 loaf.

# ❖ REFRIGERATOR ROLLS

1 pkg active dry yeast
⅔ cup cool water
2 tablespoons granulated sugar
1 teaspoon salt
1 egg, unbeaten
2 tablespoons butter or margarine, softened
3 cups all-purpose flour
Salad oil

1. Sprinkle yeast over water in food processor fitted with chopping blade.
2. Add sugar, salt, egg, butter, and 1½ cups flour. Process 2 minutes. Gradually add remaining flour. Process until dough forms ball.
3. Place dough in lightly oiled medium bowl; turn dough over to oil top. Cover with double thickness of plastic wrap or with damp towel. Let rise in refrigerator at least 2 hours, or until double in bulk.
4. Punch down dough, and refrigerate. Store in refrigerator at least 1 day or up to 3 days, punching it down once a day.
5. When ready to make rolls, remove dough from refrigerator. On lightly floured surface, with palms of hands, roll into 18-inch strip. Cut into 18 pieces.
6. With fingertips, shape each piece into ball; tuck edges underneath to make smooth top. Arrange in 2 greased 8-inch round layer-cake pans.
7. Cover with towel; let rise in warm place (85F), free from drafts, until double in bulk—about 1 hour.
8. Meanwhile, preheat oven to 400F.
9. Bake rolls 15 to 20 minutes, or until golden-brown. Serve hot. Makes 18 rolls.

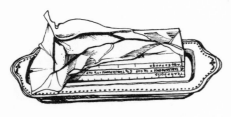

## FRUIT-FILLED STICKY BUNS

*Dough for Refrigerator Rolls, page 214*
*½ cup coarsely chopped pecans*

### SYRUP:

*⅓ cup light-brown sugar, firmly packed*
*3 tablespoons butter or margarine*
*2 tablespoons light corn syrup*

### FILLING:

*1 large cooking apple*
*¼ cup raisins*
*2 tablespoons butter or margarine, softened*
*¼ cup light-brown sugar, firmly packed*
*¼ teaspoon ground cinnamon*

1. Make Refrigerator Roll dough as directed; refrigerate.
2. When ready to bake, grease 18 (2½-inch) muffin-pan cups; divide chopped pecans among cups.
3. Make Syrup: In small saucepan, combine ⅓ cup brown sugar, 3 tablespoons butter, and corn syrup.
4. Cook over medium heat, stirring, until butter melts. Spoon evenly into prepared muffin-pan cups.
5. Make Filling: Pare apple, core, and cut into eighths. In food processor, with chopping blade, combine apple pieces, raisins, 2 tablespoons butter, ¼ cup brown sugar, and cinnamon. Process until apple is finely chopped.
6. Remove dough from refrigerator. On lightly floured surface, roll into 20-by-10-inch rectangle.
7. Spread with apple filling. Roll up from long side, jelly-roll fashion. Pinch edges to seal firmly.
8. Cut crosswise into 18 pieces. Place, with cut side down, in prepared muffin-pan cups.
9. Cover with towel; let rise in warm place (85F), free from drafts, until double in bulk—about 1 hour.
10. Meanwhile, preheat oven to 375F.
11. Bake 20 to 25 minutes, or until golden-brown.
12. Invert pan onto large cookie sheet. Let stand 1 minute; then remove pan. Serve warm.

Makes 18 buns.

## BANANA-FRUIT BREAD

*2½ cups all-purpose flour*
*2 teaspoons baking powder*
*½ teaspoon baking soda*
*¼ teaspoon salt*
*¼ cup butter or margarine, softened*
*½ cup granulated sugar*
*2 eggs*
*2 teaspoons vanilla extract*
*1¼ cups thinly sliced ripe banana*
*½ cup buttermilk*
*½ cup coarsely chopped dates*
*¼ cup dried apricot halves, quartered*
*¼ cup walnuts or pecans*
*Confectioners' sugar*

1. Preheat oven to 350F. Grease well 9-by-5-by-3-inch loaf pan. Sift flour with baking powder, baking soda, and salt.
2. In food processor, with chopping blade, beat butter, granulated sugar, eggs, and vanilla, occasionally scraping sides, until light and fluffy—about 3 minutes.
3. Add banana and buttermilk; process until smooth. Add flour mixture, dates, apricots, and nuts. Process just until uniformly combined.
4. Pour batter into prepared pan; bake 1 hour and 10 to 15 minutes, or until cake tester inserted in center comes out clean.
5. Cool in pan on wire rack 15 minutes. Then turn out on rack; cool completely. Dust top with confectioners' sugar.

Makes 1 loaf.

# ❖ FRESH APPLE CAKE

3 cups sifted all-purpose flour
1½ teaspoons baking soda
½ teaspoon salt
6 tart apples, pared and cut into
   eighths
½ cup chopped walnuts or pecans
1 teaspoon grated lemon peel
1 cup sugar
½ cup salad oil
2 eggs
Confectioners' sugar

1. Preheat oven to 350F. Grease well and flour 9-by-13-by-2-inch baking pan. Sift flour with baking soda and salt. In food processor, with chopping blade, combine apples, nuts, and lemon peel. Process until finely chopped. Turn out into large mixing bowl.
2. In processor, combine sugar, oil, and eggs; beat until light and fluffy. Add sifted dry ingredients; mix just until smooth.
3. Add to apple mixture; stir until well combined. Spread evenly into prepared pan. Bake 35 to 45 minutes, or until surface springs back when pressed lightly with fingertip.
4. Cool in pan 10 minutes. Serve warm or cool, sprinkled with sifted confectioners' sugar.
Makes 10 to 12 servings.

# ❖ PROCESSOR CHEESECAKE

12 vanilla wafers
1 teaspoon butter
1 pkg (8 oz) cream cheese, softened
½ lb creamed cottage cheese
¾ cup granulated sugar
2 eggs
1½ tablespoons cornstarch
1½ tablespoons all-purpose flour
2 teaspoons lemon juice
½ teaspoon vanilla extract
1 cup sour cream
1½ pints fresh strawberries
¼ cup currant jelly

1. Preheat oven to 325F. In food processor, with chopping blade, process vanilla wafers to make fine crumbs. Spread butter on sides and bottom of 8-inch springform pan. Sprinkle with vanilla-wafer crumbs, turning to coat sides and bottom.
2. In processor, with chopping blade, beat cream cheese and the cottage cheese until creamy and well combined. Gradually beat in granulated sugar; then beat in eggs until well combined.
3. Gradually beat in cornstarch, flour, lemon juice, and vanilla. Add sour cream; beat just until smooth.
4. Pour into prepared pan; bake 40 minutes, or until firm around edge. Turn off oven heat; let cake stand in oven 1 hour.
5. Remove cake from oven. Let cool completely in pan; then refrigerate until well chilled—several hours.
6. Wash and hull strawberries. In small saucepan, heat currant jelly over low heat until melted.
7. Remove cheesecake from pan by running spatula around edge of pan and removing sides.
8. Arrange strawberries on cake. Brush with melted currant jelly.
Makes 8 servings.

# ❖ GINGER-GINGER SHORTBREAD

1 cup butter or margarine, softened
½ cup sugar
¼ cup crystallized ginger, cut into
  pieces
2 cups all-purpose flour
¼ teaspoon ground ginger
¼ teaspoon salt
1 teaspoon vanilla

1. Place butter, sugar, and crystallized ginger in food processor fitted with chopping blade. Process until just combined.
2. Add flour, ground ginger, salt, and vanilla. Process until mixture forms ball.
3. Refrigerate dough, covered, several hours.
4. Preheat oven to 300F. Divide dough in half; refrigerate until ready to use.
5. On lightly floured surface, roll out dough, one part at a time, to ¼-inch thickness.
6. Using 1½-inch cookie cutter, cut out cookies. Place 1 inch apart, on ungreased cookie sheets.
7. Bake cookies 20 minutes, or until light golden. Remove to wire rack; cool.
Makes 4 dozen.

# ❖ CARROT CUSTARD PIE

## CRUST:

½ cup whole blanched almonds
½ cup pecans
10 gingersnaps, halved
4 graham crackers, halved
¼ cup butter or margarine, melted

## FILLING:

1 lb carrots, pared and halved
Boiling water
1 pkg (3 oz) cream cheese, softened
2 tablespoons light-brown sugar
3 eggs
1 teaspoon ground cinnamon
1 teaspoon ground nutmeg
½ teaspoon salt
1 can (8 oz) crushed pineapple, undrained
1 can (14 oz) sweetened condensed milk
1 teaspoon vanilla extract

½ cup heavy cream, whipped
Thin slices raw carrot

1. Prepare Crust: Preheat oven to 375F. In processor, with chopping blade, grind almonds and pecans; then add gingersnaps and graham crackers.
2. Continue running processor; slowly add butter; blend just until combined.
3. With fingers, press mixture evenly into bottom and side of 10-inch pie plate, not on rim.
4. Bake 8 to 10 minutes, or until golden-brown. Cool on wire rack before filling.
5. Make Filling: In medium saucepan, cook carrots, covered, in 1 inch boiling water just until tender—20 minutes. Drain; cool.
6. Purée carrots and cream cheese in processor. Turn out into large bowl.
7. Place sugar, eggs, cinnamon, nutmeg, salt, and crushed pineapple in processor; process a few seconds to combine.
8. Add condensed milk and vanilla, blending until smooth.
9. Pour into carrot and cream-cheese mixture; mix with wooden spoon until smooth.
10. Turn out into prepared crust. Bake 35 to 40 minutes. Remove to rack. Cool completely; refrigerate.
11. Before serving, decorate with rosettes of whipped cream and very thinly sliced raw carrots.
Makes 8 servings.

# ❖ PINEAPPLE SORBET

1 fresh ripe pineapple (see Note)
¼ teaspoon angostura bitters (optional)

1. Peel pineapple. Remove and discard eyes and core; cut fruit into chunks. Purée in food processor using chopping blade. Stir in angostura bitters, if desired.
2. Turn out pineapple mixture into 9-by-9-by-2-inch pan. Freeze until edges are firm and center is still a little soft—3 hours.
3. Cut sorbet into chunks and place in chilled bowl. Beat quickly with electric beater until smooth but not melted. Turn out into plastic freezer container with tight-fitting lid. Freeze several hours, until firm.
Makes 4 servings.

Note: If pineapple is not sweet enough, add 1 tablespoon confectioners' sugar to puréed pineapple.

CRISPY BAKED FISH FILLETS (p. 177)

FILLETS OF SOLE FLORENTINE (p. 182)

*OPPOSITE: BOUILLABAISSE (p. 226)*

**CARAMEL FRIED APPLES** (p. 225)

*OPPOSITE:* LEMON CHICKEN (p. 223)

STUFFED
GRAPE
LEAVES
(p. 235)

TEMPURA (p. 250)

# FAVORITE INTERNATIONAL and ETHNIC FOODS

In recent years, both in our restaurants and in our homes, American cuisine has come to reflect the melting pot of our society. We regularly eat Chinese food, French, Italian, Middle Eastern, German, Scandinavian, Japanese, . . . Food markets across the country now stock the raw ingredients for such dishes, and there are almost countless cookbooks devoted to international cuisine.

Along with this development is the resurgence of interest in regional and ethnic recipes. Mexican cooking, for example, or "Tex-Mex," is now common throughout the country, as are fast-food restaurants devoted to this cuisine. Pennsylvania Dutch cooking remains extremely popular, and in places like New York and Los Angeles, Jewish favorites are widely consumed at home and in restaurants. Our readers continue to ask us for both international and ethnic recipes, and the samples presented here are a selection of the favorites.

# CHINESE

## ❖ SHRIMP TOAST

*12 slices white bread*
*1 lb deveined, shelled shrimp*
*¼ cup finely chopped onion*
*1 tablespoon dry sherry*
*2 teaspoons salt*
*1 teaspoon sugar*
*1 tablespoon cornstarch*
*1 egg, beaten*
*1 can (5¼ oz) water chestnuts,*
  *drained and finely chopped*
*Salad oil for frying*
*Chopped parsley*

1. Trim crusts from bread; let slices dry out slightly.
2. Chop shrimp very, very fine (put in blender or food processor, if desired, to chop fine); in medium bowl, toss with onion, sherry, salt, sugar and cornstarch; mix well. Stir in beaten egg and water chestnuts; mix well.
3. Spread mixture on bread; cut each slice into quarters (squares or triangles).
4. In large heavy skillet or saucepan, heat oil (about 1 inch deep) to 375F on deep-frying thermometer.
5. Drop bread pieces, several at a time, shrimp side down, in hot oil. Fry until edges of bread begin to brown; turn on other side, and fry until golden-brown.
6. Drain well on paper towels. Sprinkle with chopped parsley. Serve warm.
Makes 48.

*Note*: These can be made ahead and reheated in 375F oven 10 minutes at serving time.

# ⊡ EGG-DROP SOUP

4 cans (13¾-oz size) clear chicken
    broth
3 tablespoons cornstarch
¼ cup cold water
½ teaspoon sugar
1 teaspoon salt
¼ teaspoon pepper
2 eggs, beaten
1 cup chopped green onions, with
    tops

1. Heat broth to boiling point in large saucepan.
2. Meanwhile, in small bowl, make smooth paste of cornstarch and cold water.
3. Into hot broth, slowly stir cornstarch mixture, with sugar, salt, and pepper. Heat to boiling point, stirring constantly—mixture should be slightly thickened and translucent.
4. Reduce heat. Add eggs, a small amount at a time, stirring to separate them into shreds.
5. Remove from heat; add green onions. Serve at once.
Makes 8 servings.

# ⊡ SWEET-AND-SOUR PORK

2¾ lb pork shoulder, cut into ½-inch
    cubes
3 tablespoons sherry
1½ teaspoons soy sauce
½ teaspoon ground ginger
1 quart salad oil

## BATTER:

3 eggs
¾ cup sifted all-purpose flour
3 tablespoons cornstarch

## SAUCE:

1 can (1 lb 4 oz) pineapple chunks
1 cup sugar
1 cup vinegar
2 large green peppers, cut in ½-inch
    strips
½ cup thinly sliced gherkins
2 tablespoons cornstarch
¼ cup water
2 teaspoons soy sauce
2 large tomatoes, cut in eighths
½ cup slivered crystallized ginger

Cooked white rice

1. In large, shallow dish, toss pork with sherry, soy sauce, and ginger; let stand 10 minutes.
2. Meanwhile, in 3-quart saucepan or deep-fat fryer, slowly heat oil to 375F on deep-frying thermometer.
3. Make Batter: In medium bowl, with rotary beater or wire whisk, beat eggs very well. Add flour and cornstarch; beat until smooth.
4. Drain pork cubes well. Pour batter over them; mix well, to coat evenly.
5. Drop cubes (about one fourth at a time—do not crowd) into hot fat; fry about 5 minutes, turning, until golden on all sides. With slotted spoon, remove pork; drain on paper towels.
6. Keep warm in oven set at very low temperature.
7. Make Sauce: Drain pineapple chunks, reserving juice. Add water to juice to make 1 cup.
8. In large saucepan, combine juice, sugar, and vinegar; heat, stirring, until sugar is dissolved. Then bring to boiling point.
9. Add green peppers and gherkins; boil 2 minutes. Remove from heat.
10. In small bowl, combine cornstarch and water; stir until smooth. Add to pineapple-juice mixture, with soy sauce, tomatoes, ginger, and pineapple chunks.
11. Cook, stirring, over moderate heat until thickened and translucent.
12. Arrange pork cubes in serving dish. Pour on the sauce. Serve with hot rice.
Makes 6 to 8 servings.

# ❖ LEMON CHICKEN

2 chicken breasts (1½ lb), boned and
   skinned
1½ tablespoons plus ¼ cup oil
1 teaspoon salt
Dash pepper
6 medium-size dried Chinese mushrooms
1 large red pepper
2 whole lemons
6 green onions
½ teaspoon grated fresh ginger
2 teaspoons cornstarch
1½ teaspoons sugar
½ cup chicken broth
¼ cup dry sherry
2 tablespoons soy sauce
6 lemon slices

1. Slice chicken into ¼-inch-wide strips. In small bowl, combine 1½ tablespoons oil, the salt, and pepper. Add chicken; mix well. Set aside for 30 minutes.
2. In small bowl, soak mushrooms in 1½ cups warm water for 30 minutes.
3. Wash pepper; cut in half and remove ribs and seeds. Cut into thin julienne strips.
4. With sharp paring knife, remove peel from whole lemon in strips; cut into pieces ⅛ inch wide. Squeeze lemon to make 3 tablespoons juice; set aside.
5. Wash green onions; cut into ½-inch diagonal slices. Drain mushrooms; remove and discard stems. Slice caps into ⅛-inch-wide strips.
6. In large heavy skillet or wok, heat ¼ cup salad oil. Add chicken, and stir-fry 2 minutes. Remove from skillet; keep warm.
7. Add ginger, mushrooms, and red pepper. Stir-fry 1 minute. Add lemon peel and green onions. Stir-fry 1 minute longer.
8. In small bowl, combine cornstarch, sugar, chicken broth, sherry, soy sauce, and reserved lemon juice; mix until smooth. Add to vegetables, and cook, stirring, until thickened.
9. Return chicken to skillet; stir 1 minute, or until vegetables and chicken are well coated. Turn out into warm serving dish. Garnish with lemon slices. Serve with rice and more soy sauce, if desired. Makes 6 servings.

# ❖ SCALLOPS WITH SNOW PEAS

1 lb sea scallops, cut in half
2 leeks
½ lb snow peas
1 tablespoon cornstarch
2 teaspoons soy sauce
¼ teaspoon salt
⅓ cup water
2 tablespoons salad or peanut oil
1 teaspoon grated fresh ginger
Cooked white rice (optional)

1. Wash scallops; drain well. Prepare leeks: Cut off root ends and green stems. Wash thoroughly. Cut on diagonal into slices ¼ inch thick. Trim ends of snow peas, and remove strings.
2. In small cup, mix cornstarch, soy sauce, salt, and water; stir until smooth.
3. Heat salad oil in large heavy skillet or wok over high heat. Add scallops; stir-fry 1 minute. Add leeks, snow peas, and ginger; stir-fry 1 minute longer.
4. Pour cornstarch mixture over scallops and vegetables. Stir until sauce is thickened. Serve with rice and more soy sauce, if desired.
Makes 4 servings.

# ✦ CHICKEN WITH TOASTED ALMONDS

3 (2-lb size) broiler-fryers
5 tablespoons salad oil
2 tablespoons soy sauce
2 teaspoons salt
1½ teaspoons sugar
Dash pepper
¼ cup cornstarch
⅓ cup water
1 can (13¾ oz) clear chicken broth
1 can (5 oz) water chestnuts, drained
    and chopped
½ cup frozen peas, thawed, or
    canned, peas, drained
1 cup thinly sliced celery
1 can (4 oz) whole mushrooms,
    drained
½ cup toasted slivered almonds

1. Have butcher bone and skin broiler-fryers. To make them easier to slice, store in freezing compartment until partially frozen. Then slice into long, thin slivers; let thaw completely at room temperature.
2. Heat oil in large skillet. Add chicken slivers, soy sauce, salt, sugar, and pepper; cook, stirring, a few minutes, or just until chicken is no longer pink.
3. In small bowl, make smooth paste of cornstarch and water. Stir into chicken mixture, with chicken broth, water chestnuts, peas, celery, and mushrooms; cook, stirring, until slightly thickened and translucent. Sprinkle top with almonds.
Makes 6 servings.

# ✦ FRIED RICE

¼ cup salad oil
2 cups cold cooked white rice
3 eggs, beaten
2 cooked bacon slices, crumbled
2 tablespoons soy sauce
⅛ teaspoon pepper
3 green onions, with tops, sliced

1. Heat oil in heavy skillet. In hot oil, sauté rice, over medium heat, stirring with metal spoon, about 5 minutes, or until golden.
2. Stir eggs into rice; cook, stirring constantly and over medium heat, until eggs are cooked—about 3 minutes.
3. Then stir in bacon, soy sauce, and pepper; combine well. Garnish with green onions.
Makes 6 servings.

# ✦ STEAMED RICE

1 cup converted raw white rice
2⅓ cups cold water
1 teaspoon salt
2 tablespoons butter or 1 tablespoon
    peanut oil

1. In heavy 3-quart saucepan with lid, combine rice, water, and salt. Bring to boiling; reduce heat to very low.
2. Fold kitchen towel in quarters. Place over pan; cover with heavy lid. Cook 25 to 30 minutes. Rice should be tender and water absorbed. Add butter or oil; stir with fork. Turn out into heated serving dish.
Makes 4 to 6 servings.

Note: Do not double recipe; it is better to make recipe twice.

# ✦ STIR-FRIED "HOT SALAD"

2 tablespoons salad oil
1 medium onion, thinly sliced
1 tablespoon shredded fresh ginger
3 cloves garlic, crushed
1 teaspoon salt
2 stalks celery, cut on diagonal into
    ½-inch pieces
½ large green pepper, cut into ¼-inch
    strips
½ large red pepper, cut into ¼-inch
    strips
2 cups bean sprouts
1½ teaspoons sugar
2 tablespoons soy sauce
½ medium cucumber, peeled and cut
    into strips
6 lettuce leaves, coarsely chopped
1 tablespoon lemon juice
1 tablespoon sesame oil
Cooked white rice (optional)

1. In wok or large heavy skillet, heat oil over medium heat. Add onion, ginger, garlic, and salt; stir-fry ½ minute.
2. Add celery, green and red peppers, and bean sprouts. Stir-fry over high heat 2 minutes.
3. Add sugar, soy sauce, cucumber, and lettuce. Stir-fry 1½ minutes. Sprinkle with lemon juice and sesame oil; mix well. Turn out into warm serving dish. Serve with rice, if desired.
Makes 6 servings.

# ✦ CARAMEL FRIED APPLES

½ cup all-purpose flour
2 tablespoons cornstarch
¾ teaspoon baking powder
½ cup water
2 large Golden Delicious apples (1 lb)
Salad oil for frying

## CARAMEL COATING:

1 cup sugar
¼ cup warm water
1 tablespoon salad oil
2 tablespoons sesame seeds

1. In medium bowl, combine flour, cornstarch, and baking powder; mix well. Add water; stir until smooth.
2. Pare and core apples; cut each apple into 8 wedges. Add apples to batter; toss to coat evenly.
3. Meanwhile, in deep skillet or deep-fat fryer, slowly heat oil (1½ inches deep) to 375F on deep-frying thermometer.
4. Lift out apple wedges with tongs; let excess batter drip off. Place wedges in hot oil, 4 at a time. Fry until golden-brown—about 2 minutes. Remove with slotted spoon; drain on paper towels. Keep warm.
5. Lightly oil small cookie sheet. Half fill large bowl with ice cubes; cover with water.
6. Make Caramel Coating: In 10-inch skillet, combine sugar, warm water, and 1 tablespoon oil; mix well. Cook over medium heat, stirring occasionally with wooden spoon, until mixture starts to boil—about 1 minute. Continue cooking until syrup turns golden-brown—about 5 minutes. Remove from heat. Stir in sesame seeds. (Syrup will continue to cook for a few seconds after removing from heat.)

7. Drop half of prepared apple wedges into syrup, turning with fork to coat evenly. Using two forks, immediately remove apples and place, 1 inch apart, on prepared cookie sheet.

8. Dip each apple wedge in ice water to harden caramel and cool fruit.

Makes 6 servings.

# FRENCH

## ❖ BOUILLABAISSE

¼ cup olive or salad oil
1 cup chopped onion
3 cloves garlic, crushed
4 bottles (8-oz size) clam juice
2 cans (1-lb 12-oz size) whole peeled
   tomatoes, undrained
¾ cup water
1 teaspoon grated orange peel
¾ teaspoon salt
¼ teaspoon crumbled saffron
¼ teaspoon fennel seed
⅛ teaspoon dried thyme leaves
⅛ teaspoon pepper
2 bay leaves
2 pkg (8-oz size) frozen rock-lobster
   tails
1 lb cod steaks
1 lb halibut steaks
½ lb sea scallops
1 loaf French bread, thinly sliced and
   toasted or fried, or garlic bread

1. Heat oil in 8-quart kettle. Add onion and garlic; sauté until onion is tender—about 5 minutes.

2. Add clam juice, tomatoes with their liquid, the water, orange peel, salt, saffron, fennel seed, thyme, pepper, and bay leaves; bring to boiling. Reduce heat, and simmer mixture, covered, 30 minutes.

3. Remove from heat, and let mixture cool. Then refrigerate, covered, overnight.

4. Next day, cut lobster tails (shell and all) in half crosswise. Wipe cod and halibut steaks with damp paper towels. Cut into 1½-inch pieces. Rinse sea scallops in running cold water and drain.

5. About 20 minutes before serving, bring tomato mixture just to boiling. Add lobster; simmer, covered, 4 minutes. Add cod and halibut pieces; simmer, covered, 10 minutes. Then add sea scallops, and cook over low heat for 5 minutes, or just until scallops are tender.

6. Spoon seafood and broth into soup tureen. Serve bouillabaisse with thin slices of toasted French bread or garlic bread.

Makes 8 servings.

*Note*: Since this dish calls for many fish found only in the Mediterranean, substitutions have been made. These fish and shellfish may be used also: crab; perch; red or gray snapper; rock, calico, or sea bass; flounder.

# ✦ BEEF BOURGUIGNON

Butter or margarine
2½ lb boneless beef chuck, cut into
   1½-inch cubes
3 tablespoons brandy
½ lb small white onions (about 12)
½ lb small fresh mushrooms
2½ tablespoons potato flour
½ teaspoon salt
2 tablespoons tomato paste
1½ cups red Burgundy wine
¾ cup dry sherry
¾ cup ruby port
1 can (10½ oz) condensed beef broth,
   undiluted
⅛ teaspoon pepper
1 bay leaf

1. Slowly heat 4-quart Dutch oven with tight-fitting lid. Add 2 tablespoons butter; heat—do not burn.
2. In hot butter, over high heat, brown beef cubes well all over (about a fourth at a time—just enough to cover bottom of Dutch oven).
3. Lift out beef as it browns. Continue until all beef is browned, adding more butter as needed. Then return beef to Dutch oven.
4. In small saucepan, heat 2 tablespoons brandy just until vapor rises. Ignite, and pour over beef. As flame dies, remove beef cubes; set aside.
5. Add 2 tablespoons butter to Dutch oven; heat slightly. Add onions; cook over low heat, covered, until onions brown slightly. Then add mushrooms; cook, stirring, 3 minutes. Remove from heat.
6. Stir in flour, salt, and tomato paste until well blended. Stir in Burgundy, sherry, port, and beef broth.
7. Preheat oven to 350F.
8. Bring wine mixture just to boiling, stirring; remove from heat. Add beef, pepper, and bay leaf; mix well.
9. Bake, covered and stirring occasionally, 1½ hours, or until beef is tender, adding remaining brandy, little by little.
Makes 6 servings.

Note: This dish is better if made day before, refrigerated, and reheated gently for serving. (If necessary, add a little more wine, to thin sauce.)

## ❖ BEEF STEW PROVENÇALE

*3 lb lean beef chuck, cut into 1½-inch*
*cubes*
*⅓ cup all-purpose flour*
*2 teaspoons salt*
*¼ teaspoon pepper*
*¼ cup butter or margarine*
*4 tablespoons olive or salad oil*
*8 small onions (1 lb)*
*1 clove garlic, crushed*
*1 cup chopped leek or shallot*
*1½ teaspoons dried thyme leaves*
*2 bay leaves*
*1 can (1 lb 12 oz) tomatoes, undrained*
*2 beef-bouillon cubes*
*1½ cups dry red wine*
*1 strip orange peel, 1 inch wide and 3*
*inches long*
*8 small new potatoes, scrubbed*
*4 zucchini (1½ lb), cut into ½-inch-*
*thick slices*
*12 pitted green olives*
*12 ripe olives*
*¼ cup water*
*Chopped parsley*

1. Wipe meat with damp paper towels. Coat beef with flour mixed with salt and pepper; reserve remaining flour mixture for later use.
2. In hot butter and 2 tablespoons oil in 6-quart Dutch oven, sauté beef, one half at a time, until well browned on all sides. Remove as browned.
3. Sauté whole onions until golden-brown—about 5 minutes; remove.
4. Add remaining oil to drippings in pan; sauté garlic, leek, thyme, and bay leaves until leek is golden —5 minutes. Add tomatoes, bouillon cubes, wine, browned beef, and orange peel.
5. Bring to boiling; simmer, covered (place waxed paper on top, under lid), 2 hours, or until meat is tender. During last hour of cooking, add potatoes and sautéed onions; cook 30 minutes. Add zucchini and green and ripe olives; cook until meat and vegetables are tender.
6. In small bowl, combine reserved flour mixture and water; mix until smooth. Stir into stew; simmer, stirring, until mixture thickens—about 5 minutes. Sprinkle with parsley. Serve with French bread. Makes 8 servings.

## ❖ LEG OF LAMB WITH WHITE BEANS

*1 lb dried pea beans*
*6 cups water*
*2 cloves garlic*
*¼ cup butter or margarine*
*2 lb onions, thinly sliced*
*Seasoned salt*
*½ teaspoon salt*
*¼ teaspoon pepper*
*1 teaspoon dried rosemary leaves*
*2 cans (1-lb size) Italian plum*
*tomatoes, undrained*
*7-lb leg of lamb*
*Chopped parsley*

1. In 6-quart kettle, combine beans and water. Bring to boiling; simmer 2 minutes. Cover; remove from heat, and let stand 1 hour.
2. Drain beans, reserving liquid. Add water to liquid to measure 2 quarts. Return beans and liquid to kettle; bring to boiling. Reduce heat; simmer, covered, 1 hour, or until beans are tender. Drain.
3. Preheat oven to 325F. Crush 1 clove garlic.
4. In hot butter in large skillet, sauté onion and crushed garlic until golden—about 10 minutes.
5. In shallow roasting pan, combine cooked beans, onion mixture, 2 teaspoons seasoned salt, ½ teaspoon salt, pepper, ½ teaspoon rosemary, and the tomatoes; mix well.
6. Split remaining clove garlic; rub over lamb. Sprinkle lamb lightly with seasoned salt and remaining rosemary. Place lamb on beans; insert meat ther-

mometer into meaty part—it should not rest against bone.

7. Roast, uncovered, 2½ to 3 hours, or to 160F on meat thermometer, for medium.

8. To serve: Remove lamb to heated serving platter or carving board. Turn out beans into serving dish; sprinkle with parsley.

Makes 10 servings.

## ✦ SOLE NORMANDE

*6 fillets of sole (2½ lb)*
*3 tablespoons lemon juice*
*1 teaspoon salt*
*⅛ teaspoon white pepper*
*2 tablespoons butter or margarine*
*½ cup dry white wine*
*1 small onion, sliced*
*1 bay leaf*
*½ teaspoon dried tarragon leaves*
*½ pint oysters or mussels in liquid (optional)*

### SAUCE NORMANDE:

*3 tablespoons butter or margarine*
*½ lb fresh mushrooms, washed, trimmed, and sliced*
*3 tablespoons flour*
*1 cup reserved fish stock*
*½ cup dry white wine or cider*
*2 egg yolks, slightly beaten*
*½ cup heavy cream*
*Cooked shrimp, below (optional)*

### TO COOK SHRIMP

*½ lb unshelled raw shrimp*
*2 cups water*
*½ small onion, thinly sliced*
*¼ lemon, thinly sliced*
*1 sprig parsley*
*½ tablespoon salt*
*3 whole black peppercorns*
*½ bay leaf*
*⅛ teaspoon dried thyme leaves*

1. Preheat oven to 350F.

2. Rinse fillets under cold water; dry well on paper towels. Fold over in thirds. Arrange in single layer in lightly buttered 13-by-9-by-2-inch baking dish. Sprinkle with lemon juice, salt, and pepper; dot with butter.

3. Pour ½ cup wine over all. Top with onion, bay leaf, and tarragon.

4. Bake, uncovered, 20 minutes, or until fish flakes easily when tested with fork.

5. Meanwhile, in small saucepan, cook oysters in their liquid just until edges begin to curl. Drain; set aside.

6. With slotted spatula, lift fillets to large shallow serving dish; keep warm. Reserve cooking stock.

7. Meanwhile, make Sauce Normande: Melt 3 tablespoons butter in medium saucepan. Add mushrooms; sauté, stirring occasionally, about 5 minutes. Remove from heat; stir in flour until smooth. Add reserved fish stock and the wine. Cook over medium heat, stirring constantly, until mixture comes to boiling. Reduce heat; simmer 3 minutes.

8. In medium bowl, combine egg yolks and cream; mix well. Stir in a little of hot mushroom mixture. Pour back into saucepan. Cook, stirring, several minutes, or until slightly thickened.

9. Add oysters and shrimp to sauce; drain off any liquid from fillets in dish. Pour sauce over all, and serve at once.

Makes 6 servings.

1. Rinse shrimp; shell and devein.

2. In large skillet, combine the water, onion, lemon, parsley, salt, peppercorns, bay leaf, and thyme. Bring to boiling, covered, over medium heat; simmer 10 minutes.

3. Add shrimp; return to boiling. Reduce heat, and simmer, covered, 1 to 2 minutes, or just until cooked.

4. Drain. Add to Sauce Normande.

# ✦ MADELEINES

*2 eggs*
*1 cup granulated sugar*
*1 cup sifted all-purpose flour*
*¾ cup butter, melted and cooled*
*1 teaspoon grated lemon peel*
*Confectioners' sugar*

1. Preheat oven to 350F. Grease and lightly flour madeleine pans.
2. In top of double boiler, over hot, not boiling, water (water in bottom of double boiler should not touch base of pan above), with electric mixer at medium speed, beat eggs and granulated sugar while mixture heats to lukewarm—takes about 2 minutes.
3. Set top of double boiler in cold water. Beat egg mixture, at high speed, 5 minutes, or until very light and fluffy.
4. With wire whisk or rubber spatula, gently fold in flour until well combined. Stir in cooled butter and lemon peel just until blended. Pour into prepared pans, using 1 tablespoon batter for each pan.
5. Bake 12 to 15 minutes, or until golden. Cool 1 minute. Then remove from pans with small spatula; cool completely on wire racks. Sprinkle with confectioners' sugar.
Makes 3½ dozen.

# ✦ STRASBOURG APPLE PIE

*½ pkg (11-oz size) piecrust mix*
*2½ lb tart cooking apples*
*¾ cup sugar*
*1 teaspoon ground cinnamon*
*4 egg yolks*
*½ cup heavy cream*

1. Make pastry as package label directs for 9-inch pie shell. On lightly floured surface, roll out into 11-inch circle. Use to line 9-inch pie plate. Fold under edge of crust, and press into upright rim about 1 inch high. Flute decoratively. Refrigerate.
2. Preheat oven to 350F.
3. Pare apples; slice into eighths. Arrange apples in pie shell in an attractive pattern. Sprinkle with ½ cup sugar combined with cinnamon.
4. Bake 30 minutes. Meanwhile, in small bowl, beat together egg yolks, cream, and remaining ¼ cup sugar.
5. Remove pie from oven. Pour egg-yolk mixture over apples; return to oven. Bake 35 minutes, or until apples are tender and topping turns golden-brown. Serve slightly warm.
Makes 8 servings.

# ❖ BRETON CAKE

1½ cups all-purpose flour
½ cup sugar
½ cup butter or margarine, softened
1 jar (8 oz) mixed candied fruit,
  chopped
2 whole eggs
1 egg yolk, slightly beaten

1. Preheat oven to 350F. Lightly grease and flour 9-inch round layer-cake pan.
2. In medium bowl, combine flour and sugar. Add butter; mash with fork until evenly distributed.
3. Stir in fruit and whole eggs; mix well. Turn out into prepared pan.
4. Bake 30 minutes; remove from oven. With knife, make cuts in surface, not all the way through, to form 1½-inch diamonds. Brush with egg yolk. Bake 10 to 15 minutes longer, or until golden. Remove from pan. Let cool on wire rack before serving. Makes 30 small pieces.

# ❖ PEAR TARTE TATIN

2 cans (1-lb 14-oz size) pear halves
1 cup sugar
1 tablespoon butter or margarine
½ pkg (11-oz size) piecrust mix
1 cup heavy cream, whipped and
  sweetened

1. Preheat oven to 450F.
2. Drain pears well. Cut each in half lengthwise; drain on paper towels.
3. Caramelize sugar: Cook sugar in large skillet over medium heat, stirring occasionally, until sugar melts and becomes light-brown syrup.
4. Immediately pour into bottom of 8½-inch round baking dish. Arrange pears, rounded side down, spoke fashion, in caramelized sugar. Top with second layer of pears, rounded side up, fitting pieces over bottom layer to fill open spaces.
5. Dot with butter. Bake, uncovered, 25 minutes, or just until caramelized sugar is melted.
6. Let stand in baking dish on wire rack until cooled to room temperature—about 1½ hours.
7. Meanwhile, prepare pastry, following package directions. On lightly floured surface, roll out to 9-inch circle. Place on ungreased cookie sheet; prick with fork. Refrigerate 30 minutes.
8. Bake pastry at 450F for 10 minutes, or until golden-brown. Let stand on cookie sheet on wire rack until ready to use.
9. To serve: Place pastry circle over pears in baking dish. Top with serving plate; invert, and remove baking dish. Serve with whipped cream.
Makes 6 to 8 servings.

# GERMAN

## ❖ SAUERBRATEN WITH RED CABBAGE

### MARINADE:

1 cup cider vinegar
1 cup Burgundy
2 onions, sliced
1 carrot, sliced
1 stalk celery, chopped
2 whole allspice
4 whole cloves
1 tablespoon salt
1½ teaspoons pepper

4-lb rump or boned chuck pot roast
2 tablespoons all-purpose flour
⅓ cup salad oil

### RED CABBAGE:

1 medium-size red cabbage
1 tablespoon salt
2 tablespoons butter or margarine
½ cup cider vinegar
½ cup sugar
½ cup water
2 tart red cooking apples
3 tablespoons flour
⅓ cup cold water
1 tablespoon sugar
½ cup crushed gingersnaps

1. In large bowl, mix 1 cup vinegar, the wine, onions, carrot, celery, allspice, cloves, salt, and pepper.
2. Wipe meat with damp paper towels. Place in marinade; refrigerate, covered, 2 days, turning occasionally. Remove meat from marinade. Reserve marinade.
3. Dry meat on paper towels. Coat with 2 tablespoons flour. In hot oil in Dutch oven, over medium heat, brown meat all over, turning with wooden spoons—20 minutes. Add marinade; bring to boil. Reduce heat, and simmer, covered, 2½ to 3 hours, or until tender.
4. Meanwhile, prepare Red Cabbage: Discard outer leaves. Quarter cabbage, remove core, and shred cabbage. There should be 10 cups. In large skillet, combine cabbage, salt, butter, ½ cup vinegar, ½ cup sugar, and ½ cup water. Cook over medium heat, covered and stirring occasionally, 15 minutes.
5. Core apples; do not pare. Slice thin. Stir into cabbage. Set aside.
6. When meat is fork-tender, remove from Dutch oven. Press liquid and vegetables through coarse sieve; skim off fat. Measure 3½ cups liquid (add water if needed).
7. Return liquid to Dutch oven. Mix 2 tablespoons flour with ⅓ cup cold water and 1 tablespoon sugar. Stir into liquid; bring to boiling, stirring. Stir in gingersnaps.
7. Return meat to Dutch oven. Spoon gravy over it; simmer, covered, 20 minutes.
8. Cook cabbage and apples 10 minutes. Sprinkle with 1 tablespoon flour; cook, stirring, until thickened. Cabbage should be tender but crisp.
9. Remove meat to hot platter and slice thin. Add cabbage, and pour some gravy over all. Serve with additional gravy.
Makes 6 to 8 servings.

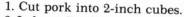

# ❖ PORK-AND-SAUERKRAUT GOULASH

2-lb boneless pork-shoulder roast, trimmed
2 cups chopped onion
1 clove garlic, finely chopped
1 teaspoon dried dillweed
1 teaspoon caraway seed
1 tablespoon salt
1 beef-bouillon cube
½ cup boiling water
1 tablespoon paprika
1 can (1 lb 11 oz) sauerkraut, drained and rinsed
2 cups sour cream

1. Cut pork into 2-inch cubes.
2. In large Dutch oven or heavy kettle, combine pork, onion, garlic, dill, caraway seed, salt, bouillon cube, and boiling water.
3. Bring to boiling. Reduce heat, and simmer, covered, 1 hour.
4. Add paprika; stir until dissolved. Add sauerkraut; mix well.
5. Simmer, covered, until meat is tender—1 hour longer.
6. Stir in sour cream; heat thoroughly, being careful not to boil.
Makes 6 servings.

# ❖ APPLE KUCHEN

1¼ cups sifted all-purpose flour
¼ cup sugar
1½ teaspoons baking powder
½ teaspoon salt
¼ cup butter or margarine
1 egg, beaten
¼ cup milk
1 teaspoon vanilla extract
5 cups thinly sliced pared tart apple

## TOPPING:

¼ cup sugar
1 teaspoon cinnamon
¼ cup butter or margarine, melted

⅓ cup apricot preserves
1 tablespoon hot water
Whipped cream (optional)

1. Preheat oven to 400F. Lightly grease 13-by-9-by-2-inch baking pan.
2. Into medium bowl, sift flour with ¼ cup sugar, the baking powder, and salt. With pastry blender, cut in ¼ cup butter until mixture resembles coarse crumbs.
3. Add beaten egg, milk, and vanilla extract, stirring with fork until mixture is smooth—will take about 1 minute.
4. Spread batter evenly in bottom of prepared pan. Arrange apple slices, slightly overlapping, in parallel rows over batter.
5. Make Topping: Combine sugar, cinnamon, and melted butter. Sprinkle sugar mixture over apple slices.
6. Bake 35 minutes, or until apple slices are tender. Remove to wire rack.
7. Mix apricot preserves with hot water. Brush over apples. Cut apple kuchen into rectangles, and serve warm, with whipped cream, if desired.
Makes 12 servings.

# ✪ APPLE STRUDEL

½ pkg (1-lb size) phyllo-pastry or strudel-pastry leaves (16 sheets, 12-by-15-inches)
½ cup unseasoned dry bread crumbs
¾ cup ground almonds
½ cup granulated sugar
¼ teaspoon ground nutmeg
¼ teaspoon ground cinnamon

## APPLE FILLING:

½ cup granulated sugar
¼ cup brown sugar, packed
2 tablespoons flour
¼ teaspoon ground nutmeg
½ teaspoon ground cinnamon
¼ teaspoon salt
1 tablespoon grated lemon peel
1 can (1 lb 4 oz) sliced apples, drained
½ cup raisins

¾ cup butter or margarine, melted
2 tablespoons butter or margarine
Confectioners' sugar
Sour-Cream Sauce, below

## SOUR-CREAM SAUCE:

1 pint sour cream
6 tablespoons confectioners' sugar
1 teaspoon ground cinnamon
½ teaspoon ground nutmeg

1. If pastry leaves are frozen, defrost as label directs. Remove pastry leaves from package. In small bowl, combine bread crumbs, almonds, ½ cup granulated sugar, ¼ teaspoon nutmeg, and ¼ teaspoon cinnamon; mix well.
2. Make Apple Filling: In medium bowl, combine ½ cup granulated sugar, the brown sugar, flour, ¼ teaspoon nutmeg, ½ teaspoon cinnamon, the salt, and lemon peel; mix well. Add apples and raisins; toss lightly to combine.
3. Preheat oven to 375F. Line 15½-by-10½-by-1-inch jelly-roll pan with brown paper.
4. Layer 2 sheets pastry at a time in pan. Brush with 2 tablespoons melted butter; then sprinkle with 2 tablespoons crumb mixture. Continue layering 2 pastry leaves and sprinkling with butter and crumbs 5 more times, using 12 pastry leaves in all.
5. Then sprinkle remaining crumb mixture over one fourth of pastry, on short side. Spoon apple filling over crumb mixture. Dot top of filling with 2 tablespoons butter. Roll up like jelly roll as tightly as possible.
6. Brush all over with remaining melted butter. Bake 1 hour, or until nicely browned.
7. Let cool 5 minutes; transfer to wooden board or serving platter. Sprinkle lightly with confectioners' sugar. Slice, and serve warm with Sour-Cream Sauce.
Makes 10 to 12 servings.

In small bowl, combine all ingredients; mix well. Turn out into serving bowl; refrigerate to chill well. Makes 2 cups.

# GREEK

## ❖ STUFFED MUSSELS

24 mussels
1 bottle (8 oz) clam juice
¼ cup olive oil
½ cup chopped onion
½ cup raw long-grain white rice
1 jar (3 oz) pine nuts (pignolis)
¼ cup dried currants
½ cup white wine
1 teaspoon salt
¼ teaspoon pepper
2 tablespoons chopped parsley
Lemon wedges (optional)

1. Scrub mussels well, or scrape with knife, until shells are clean. Rinse well in cold water.
2. In medium saucepan, bring half of clam juice to boiling; add mussels, and cook just until shells are open—3 to 5 minutes. Drain, reserving liquid; strain liquid. Arrange mussels, in shells, in a single layer in shallow baking dish. Discard any mussels that are not open.
3. In hot oil in medium saucepan, sauté onion until golden. Add rice and pine nuts; sauté, stirring, until nuts turn golden. Add remaining clam juice and reserved liquid, currants, wine, salt, and pepper; bring to boiling. Reduce heat, and simmer, covered, 20 minutes, or until all liquid is absorbed. Remove from heat.
4. Add parsley; mix well. Place 1 tablespoon of mixture in each mussel shell. (If desired, mussels may be prepared several hours ahead and refrigerated until just before serving.)
5. Preheat oven to 400F. Bake, uncovered, 10 minutes, or until hot. Garnish, if desired, with more chopped parsley. Or refrigerate; serve cold with lemon wedges.

Makes 6 entrée servings or 24 hors d'oeuvres.

## ❖ STUFFED GRAPE LEAVES

⅓ cup olive or salad oil
½ cup finely chopped onion
1 lb ground lean lamb or beef
½ cup raw white rice
1 jar (3 oz) pine nuts (pignolis)
1 tablespoon dried dillweed
½ teaspoon salt
⅛ teaspoon pepper
¾ cup water
1 jar (16 oz) grape leaves, drained (see Note)
2 tablespoons lemon juice
2 cups tomato juice

1. In hot oil in large (12-inch) skillet over medium heat, sauté onion, stirring, until golden—about 5 minutes. Add ground lamb; cook, stirring, until lamb is no longer pink—10 minutes.
2. Add rice, pine nuts, dillweed, salt, pepper, and water. Simmer, covered, 10 minutes, or until water is absorbed and rice is half cooked. Remove from heat. Turn out into bowl; let cool 30 minutes before stuffing grape leaves.
3. Separate grape leaves. Use imperfect leaves for layering in bottom of skillet. Put 1 tablespoon lamb mixture in center of each leaf; fold in edges like envelope, and roll.

4. Cover bottom of skillet with closely fitted layers of stuffed grape leaves. Repeat layering until all stuffing and leaves are used. Pour lemon juice and tomato juice over them.

5. Put heavy plate upside down on top, to prevent leaves from unrolling. Bring to boiling; reduce heat, and simmer, covered, until liquid is absorbed—about 30 minutes. Cool slightly before serving, or refrigerate and serve cold.

Makes 40 to 45.

*Note*: Separate grape leaves. Rinse very well in cold water to wash away brine. Dry well on paper towels.

# ❖ SPINACH PIE

½ pkg (1-lb size) prepared phyllo- or strudel-pastry leaves (16 sheets, 12 by 15 inches)
¼ cup butter or margarine
½ cup finely chopped onion
3 pkg (10-oz size) frozen chopped spinach, thawed and well drained
3 eggs
½ lb feta cheese, crumbled
¼ cup chopped parsley
2 tablespoons chopped fresh dill
1 teaspoon salt
⅛ teaspoon pepper
¾ cup butter or margarine, melted

1. Preheat oven to 350F. Let pastry leaves warm to room temperature, according to directions on package label.

2. In ¼ cup hot butter in medium skillet, sauté onion until golden—about 5 minutes.

3. Add spinach; stir to combine with onion. Remove from heat.

4. In large bowl, beat eggs with rotary beater. With wooden spoon, stir in cheese, parsley, dill, salt, pepper, and spinach-onion mixture; mix well.

5. Brush 13-by-9-by-2-inch baking pan lightly with some of melted butter. In bottom of baking pan, layer 8 phyllo-pastry leaves (see Note), one by one, brushing top of each with melted butter. Spread evenly with spinach mixture.

6. Cover with 8 more leaves, brushing each with butter; pour any remaining melted butter over top.

7. Using scissors, trim off any uneven edges of pastry. Cut through top pastry layer on diagonal, then cut in opposite direction, to form about 9 (3-inch) diamonds.

8. Bake 30 to 35 minutes, or until top crust is puffy and golden. Serve warm.

Makes 8 to 10 servings.

*Note*: Keep unused pastry leaves covered with damp paper towels to prevent drying out.

# ❖ SOUVLAKIA

*¼ cup butter or margarine*
*1½ lb cubed boneless lamb (for stew)*
*1 cup sliced onion*
*1 clove garlic, crushed*
*¼ cup water*
*1 teaspoon salt*
*⅛ teaspoon pepper*
*3 tablespoons tomato paste*
*½ cup red wine*
*1 teaspoon dried oregano leaves*
*¼ teaspoon dried thyme leaves*
*¼ teaspoon dried rosemary leaves*
*1 chicken-bouillon cube*
*4 pita breads*

## GARNISH:

*1 small tomato, sliced*
*4 large onion slices*
*1 cup shredded lettuce*

1. In hot butter in large saucepan, sauté lamb (just enough at a time to cover bottom of pan) until well browned all over—about 10 minutes. Remove lamb as it browns; continue browning rest.
2. Add 1 cup onion and the garlic; sauté about 5 minutes. Return lamb to saucepan, along with water and remaining ingredients, except bread and garnish.
3. Bring to boiling; reduce heat, and simmer, covered, 45 minutes, or until meat is tender.
4. Preheat oven to 350F. Heat bread 15 minutes, or until heated through. Split each loaf partway through. Fill with lamb mixture. Garnish with tomato, onion, and lettuce.
Makes 4 servings.

# ❖ GREEK MEATBALLS WITH LEMON SAUCE

## MEATBALLS:

*2 lb ground beef chuck*
*½ cup finely chopped onion*
*¼ cup raw regular white rice*
*¼ cup chopped parsley*
*2 teaspoons salt*
*¼ teaspoon pepper*
*4¼ cups cold water*
*4 beef-bouillon cubes*
*2 tablespoons butter or margarine*

## LEMON SAUCE:

*4 eggs*
*2 tablespoons cold water*
*¼ cup lemon juice*
*¼ teaspoon salt*

*Chopped parsley*

1. Make Meatballs: In medium bowl, combine beef, onion, rice, parsley, salt, pepper, and ¼ cup cold water. Using hands, mix well to combine.
2. Shape mixture into meatballs 1¼ inches in diameter.
3. In large kettle, combine bouillon cubes, butter, and 4 cups water; bring to boiling.
4. Drop meatballs, one by one, into boiling liquid. Return to boiling; reduce heat, and simmer, covered, 50 minutes.
5. Meanwhile, make Lemon Sauce: In top of double boiler, over hot, not boiling, water, using rotary beater or wire whisk, beat eggs with 2 tablespoons cold water until light and fluffy.
6. Remove ¼ cup hot bouillon from kettle; gradually add to egg mixture, beating constantly.
7. Gradually stir in lemon juice. Cook, stirring occasionally, until sauce thickens. Add salt. Remove from heat; let stand over hot water 5 minutes before serving.
8. To serve: With slotted spoon, remove meatballs to serving dish. Pour sauce over them. Sprinkle with chopped parsley. Serve the meatballs with cooked rice or mashed potatoes, if desired.
Makes 6 to 8 servings.

# ⊞ MOUSSAKA

## MEAT SAUCE:

2 tablespoons butter or margarine
1 cup finely chopped onion
1½ lb ground beef chuck or lamb
1 clove garlic, crushed
½ teaspoon dried oregano leaves
1 teaspoon dried basil leaves
½ teaspoon ground cinnamon
1 teaspoon salt
Dash pepper
2 cans (8-oz size) tomato sauce

2 eggplants (about 1½ lb each),
   washed and dried
Salt
½ cup butter or margarine, melted

## CREAM SAUCE:

2 tablespoons butter or margarine
2 tablespoons flour
½ teaspoon salt
Dash pepper
2 cups milk
2 eggs

½ cup grated Parmesan cheese
½ cup grated Cheddar cheese
2 tablespoons dry bread crumbs

1. Make Meat Sauce: In 2 tablespoons hot butter in 3½-quart Dutch oven, sauté onion, meat, and garlic, stirring, until brown—10 minutes. Add oregano, basil, cinnamon, ½ teaspoon salt, the pepper, and tomato sauce; bring to boiling, stirring. Reduce heat; simmer, uncovered, ½ hour.

2. Halve unpeeled eggplant lengthwise; cut crosswise into ½-inch-thick slices. Place in bottom of broiler pan. Sprinkle lightly with salt; brush lightly with melted butter. Broil, 4 inches from heat, 4 minutes on each side, or until golden.

3. Make Cream Sauce: In medium saucepan, melt butter. Remove from heat; stir in flour, salt, and pepper. Add milk gradually. Bring to boiling, stirring until mixture is thickened. Remove from heat.

4. In small bowl, beat eggs with wire whisk. Beat in some hot cream-sauce mixture. Return mixture to saucepan; mix well.

5. Preheat oven to 350F. To assemble casserole: In bottom of 12-by-7½-by-2-inch baking dish, layer half of eggplant, overlapping slightly; sprinkle with 2 tablespoons each grated Parmesan and Cheddar cheeses.

6. Stir bread crumbs into meat sauce. Spoon evenly over eggplant in casserole; then sprinkle with 2 tablespoons each Parmesan and Cheddar cheeses. Layer rest of eggplant slices, overlapping, as before.

7. Pour cream sauce over all. Sprinkle top with remaining cheese. Bake 35 to 40 minutes, or until golden-brown and top is set. If desired, brown top a little more under broiler—1 minute. Cool slightly to serve. Cut in squares.

Makes 12 servings.

*Note*: Moussaka can be baked day before or early in day, refrigerated, and reheated just in time for serving in 350F oven, uncovered, 35 to 40 minutes.

# ❖ EGGPLANT SALAD

2 medium eggplants (about 1 lb each)
2 cloves garlic
½ teaspoon salt
⅛ teaspoon pepper
1 tablespoon white-wine vinegar or
   white vinegar
2 tablespoons olive or salad oil
¼ cup chopped parsley
½ teaspoon dried oregano leaves
1 large tomato, sliced
Greek olives

1. Wash eggplant; peel and cut into large cubes. In boiling water 1 inch deep in 6-quart saucepan, simmer eggplant, covered, 10 minutes, or until tender. Drain very well.
2. In blender, or food processor, combine eggplant, garlic, salt, pepper, vinegar, and oil. Blend at medium speed to make purée. (Or press ingredients through a food mill.) Refrigerate overnight to blend flavors.
3. Mound eggplant mixture on platter; sprinkle with parsley and oregano. Garnish with tomato slices and olives. Refrigerate until serving. Use as spread for crackers.
Makes 4 cups.

# ❖ BAKLAVA

1 pkg (1 lb) prepared phyllo- or strudel-pastry leaves (12 by 15 inches)
1 cup finely chopped or ground walnuts
1 cup finely chopped or ground blanched almonds
½ cup sugar
¼ teaspoon ground cinnamon
⅛ teaspoon ground cloves
1½ cups sweet butter, melted

## SYRUP:

¾ cup sugar
¾ cup honey
1-inch cinnamon stick
4 lemon slices
4 orange slices
1¾ cups water

1. Preheat oven to 325F. Let pastry leaves warm to room temperature as label directs.
2. In small bowl, mix walnuts, almonds, ½ cup sugar, the ground cinnamon, and cloves.
3. Place 2 leaves of phyllo pastry in 15½-by-10½-by-1-inch jelly-roll pan; brush top leaf with melted butter. Repeat, stacking 14 leaves in all and buttering every other leaf. (Keep rest of pastry leaves covered with damp paper towels to prevent drying out.)
4. Sprinkle top with one third of nut mixture. Add 6 more leaves, brushing every other one with butter.
5. Repeat Step 4 twice. Stack any remaining pastry leaves on top, brushing every other one with remaining melted butter and buttering top leaf.
6. Bake 60 minutes. Turn off heat, and let baklava remain in oven 60 minutes longer.
7. Meanwhile, make Syrup: In small saucepan, combine sugar, honey, cinnamon stick, lemon and orange slices, and water.
8. Bring to boiling, stirring until sugar is dissolved Reduce heat; simmer, uncovered, 20 minutes. Strain.
9. As soon as baklava is removed from oven, cut into diamond-shaped pieces. (On long side, make 9 crosswise cuts, at 1½-inch intervals. Then, starting at one corner, make 11 cuts on diagonal, at 1½-inch intervals, to form diamonds.) Pour syrup over top. Cool in pan on wire rack 2 hours. Cover with foil; let stand overnight.
Makes about 40 servings.

# ✦ GREEK BUTTER COOKIES

1 cup butter or margarine, softened
¼ cup granulated sugar
2 egg yolks
1 teaspoon vanilla extract
½ teaspoon almond extract
2½ cups all-purpose flour
½ cup finely chopped walnuts
Whole cloves
Confectioners' sugar

1. Preheat oven to 350F.
2. In large bowl, with electric mixer at medium speed, beat butter, granulated sugar, egg yolks, and vanilla and almond extracts until light and fluffy.
3. Add flour and nuts; mix well with hands.
4. Turn out dough onto lightly floured surface. Divide dough in half. With your hands, shape each half into roll 16 inches long. Cut each roll into 16 (1-inch) pieces and then shape into balls. Press whole clove into each ball.
5. Place, 1 inch apart, on ungreased cookie sheets.
6. Bake 20 minutes, or until cookies are set but not brown. Remove to wire rack; sprinkle lightly with confectioners' sugar while still warm. Cool completely.
7. Just before serving, sprinkle with confectioners' sugar again.
Makes 32.

# ITALIAN

## ✦ CHICKEN CACCIATORE WITH POLENTA

2 (2-lb size) ready-to-cook broiler-fryers, cut up
3 tablespoons olive or salad oil
2 tablespoons butter or margarine
1½ cups sliced onion
1 clove garlic, crushed
1 can (1 lb 1 oz) Italian tomatoes, undrained
2 tablespoons chopped parsley
1½ teaspoons salt
½ teaspoon dried basil leaves
¼ teaspoon pepper
½ cup red wine
Polenta, page 426

1. Wash chicken; pat dry with paper towels.
2. Heat oil and butter in Dutch oven. Add chicken, a few pieces at a time, and brown well on all sides. Remove as browned, and set aside.
3. Add onion and garlic to Dutch oven, and sauté until golden-brown—about 5 minutes. Add tomatoes, parsley, salt, basil, and pepper; mix well, mashing tomatoes with fork.
4. Bring to boiling. Reduce heat, and simmer, uncovered, 20 minutes.
5. Add browned chicken and the wine; simmer, covered, 45 to 50 minutes, or until chicken is tender.
6. Meanwhile, make Polenta.
7. To serve, spoon chicken and some of sauce over polenta. Pass rest of sauce. If desired, garnish with chopped parsley.
Makes 6 to 8 servings.

# ❖ VEAL PARMIGIANA

1 lb thin veal scallopini
2 eggs, beaten
1 cup seasoned dry bread crumbs
½ cup olive or salad oil

## SAUCE:

2 tablespoons olive or salad oil
½ cup chopped onion
1 clove garlic, crushed
1 can (1 lb 1 oz) Italian tomatoes, undrained
2 teaspoons sugar
¾ teaspoon salt
½ teaspoon dried oregano leaves
¼ teaspoon dried basil leaves
¼ teaspoon pepper

1 pkg (8 oz) mozzarella cheese, sliced
¼ cup grated Parmesan cheese

1. Preheat oven to 350F.
2. Wipe veal with damp paper towels. Dip in egg, then in bread crumbs, coating lightly.
3. In large skillet, heat about ¼ cup oil. Add veal slices, a few at a time, and cook until golden-brown on each side—2 to 3 minutes for each side. Add more oil as needed.
4. Make Sauce: In hot oil in medium saucepan, sauté onion and garlic until golden-brown—about 5 minutes. Add tomatoes, sugar, salt, oregano, basil, and pepper; mix well, mashing tomatoes with fork. Bring to boiling. Reduce heat; simmer, covered, 10 minutes.
5. Place veal in 10-by-6½-by-2-inch baking dish, to cover bottom in single layer. Add half of sauce and half of mozzarella and Parmesan cheeses. Repeat layers, ending with Parmesan cheese.
6. Cover baking dish with foil. Bake 30 minutes, or until bubbly.
Makes 4 to 6 servings.

# ❖ SPINACH FRITTATA

3 tablespoons olive oil
½ cup thinly sliced onion
10 eggs
1 cup finely chopped raw spinach
  (½ lb) or 1 cup frozen spinach,
  thawed
⅓ cup grated Parmesan cheese
1 tablespoon chopped parsley
1 small clove garlic, crushed
1 teaspoon salt
¼ teaspoon pepper

1. Preheat oven to 350F. Heat oil in heavy 10-inch skillet with oven safe handle. Add onion; sauté until onion is tender and golden-brown—will take about 5 minutes.
2. In large bowl, combine remaining ingredients; with wire whisk or fork, beat until well blended. Turn out into skillet with onion.
3. Cook over low heat, lifting from bottom with spatula as eggs set—3 minutes.
4. Bake, uncovered, 10 minutes, or until top is set. With spatula, loosen from bottom and around edge, and slide onto serving platter. Cut into wedges.
Makes 4 to 6 servings.

Note: Frittata can also be made with leftover cooked vegetables, such as stringbeans, asparagus, zucchini, broccoli, tomatoes, or even sliced boiled potatoes.

# ❖ STEWED SWEET PEPPERS

6 or 7 sweet green or yellow peppers (2
  lb)
½ cup olive or salad oil
1 cup sliced onion
1 clove garlic
1 can (1 lb 12 oz) Italian tomatoes,
  undrained
1½ teaspoons salt
⅛ teaspoon pepper
2 tablespoons chopped parsley

1. Wash peppers. Cut in half lengthwise. Discard cores and seeds. Slice each half into three long strips.
2. In hot oil in large skillet, sauté pepper strips, onion, and garlic, stirring occasionally, 15 minutes.
3. Add tomatoes, salt, and pepper. Bring to boiling; reduce heat, and simmer, uncovered and over medium heat, 45 minutes, or until mixture is like thick sauce. Remove and discard garlic.
4. Serve hot or cold, garnished with parsley. Nice as accompaniment to meat.
Makes 8 to 10 servings.

# ❖ HOMEMADE RAVIOLI

Italian Tomato Sauce, below

### RAVIOLI FILLING:

1 carton (15 oz) ricotta cheese
1 pkg (8 oz) mozzarella cheese, diced
¼ cup grated Parmesan cheese
1 egg
1 tablespoon chopped parsley
¾ teaspoon salt
⅛ teaspoon pepper

### NOODLE DOUGH:

3 cups all-purpose flour
½ teaspoon salt
4 eggs
4 tablespoons water

8 quarts water
2 tablespoons salt
2 tablespoons olive or salad oil
Grated Parmesan cheese

1. Make Italian Tomato Sauce.
2. Meanwhile, make Ravioli Filling: In medium bowl, combine all filling ingredients. Beat with wooden spoon until well blended. Set aside.
3. Make Noodle Dough: Combine flour and ½ teaspoon salt in medium bowl; make well in center. Add eggs and water. Beat with wooden spoon until dough forms ball and leaves side of bowl.
4. Turn out onto floured surface. Knead until smooth and elastic—6 to 8 minutes. Divide in quarters.
5. On lightly floured surface, roll one quarter (keep remaining dough covered with plastic wrap) into 17-by-13-inch rectangle. Cover with plastic wrap.
6. Roll second quarter into 17-by-13-inch rectangle. Drop filling by teaspoonfuls in 24 evenly spaced mounds on this dough rectangle (6 lengthwise and 4 across). Lightly brush edges and spaces between mounds of filling with water. Place first dough rectangle on top; trim edges with pastry wheel. Run pastry wheel between mounds of filling, to make 24 ravioli; press edges of each with tines of fork to seal.
7. Place on flour-covered sheet of waxed paper to dry —about 15 minutes. Turn once. Repeat with remaining dough and filling.
8. In large kettle, bring 8 quarts water to boil. Add salt, oil, and ravioli. Boil gently, uncovered, 25 to 30 minutes, or until pasta is tender. Turn out half of ravioli into colander at one time; drain well.
9. Turn out ravioli into heated large serving dish. Top with some tomato sauce; pass remaining sauce. Sprinkle ravioli with Parmesan.
Makes 8 to 10 servings.

## ITALIAN TOMATO SAUCE:

1 can (2 lb 3 oz) Italian tomatoes
¼ cup olive or salad oil
1 cup finely chopped onion
1 clove garlic, crushed
1 can (6 oz) tomato paste
1½ cups water
2 sprigs parsley
1 tablespoon salt
2 teaspoons sugar
1 teaspoon dried oregano leaves
½ teaspoon dried basil leaves
¼ teaspoon pepper

1. Purée undrained tomatoes in blender.
2. In hot oil in large saucepan, sauté onion and garlic until golden-brown—about 5 minutes.
3. Add puréed tomato, tomato paste, water, parsley sprigs, salt, sugar, oregano, basil, and pepper; mix well.
4. Bring to boiling; reduce heat, and simmer, covered, 1 hour, stirring occasionally.

## ⊞ GNOCCHI VERDE

¼ cup butter or margarine
1½ cups chopped fresh spinach, washed and drained well on paper towels
1 cup ricotta cheese
2 eggs
⅓ cup all-purpose flour
¼ cup plus ⅓ cup grated Parmesan cheese
3¼ teaspoons salt
¼ teaspoon pepper
¼ teaspoon ground nutmeg
4 quarts water
Melted butter or margarine

1. In ¼ cup hot butter in large skillet, cook spinach, stirring, just enough to dry out. Add ricotta cheese; cook, stirring, several minutes, or until well blended.
2. In medium bowl, beat eggs slightly; beat in flour until smooth. Add ¼ cup Parmesan cheese, ¼ teaspoon salt, the pepper, and nutmeg; mix well. Stir in spinach-cheese mixture; mix well. Refrigerate until firm—several hours.
3. In large Dutch oven or kettle, bring water to boiling; add 3 teaspoons salt.
4. Form dumplings: With floured hands, carefully shape chilled mixture into balls, 1½ inches wide. Drop into gently boiling water, about one third at a time. Simmer 5 minutes, or until gnocchi rise to top of water. Lift out with slotted spoon; drain on paper towels.
5. Continue shaping and cooking until all are cooked. Arrange gnocchi in single layer in greased shallow heat-proof dish (about 12 by 8 inches). Sprinkle with 2 to 3 tablespoons melted butter, then with ⅓ cup grated Parmesan cheese.
6. Broil, about 4 inches from heat, until heated through and golden-brown—3 to 5 minutes.
Makes 28 gnocchi; 6 to 7 servings.

# ⊠ GNOCCHETTI

## POLENTA:

3 cups water
1 teaspoon salt
1 cup yellow cornmeal

## SAUCE:

3 tablespoons olive or salad oil
¼ cup finely chopped onion
1 stalk celery with leaves, finely
  chopped (about ½ cup)
1 large carrot, pared and finely
  chopped (about ½ cup)
1 can (10¾ oz) condensed chicken
  broth, undiluted
¼ cup tomato paste
½ cup dried mushroom pieces
¾ cup water
¼ teaspoon salt
⅛ teaspoon pepper

Flour
¼ cup grated Parmesan cheese

1. In heavy 2-quart saucepan, bring 3 cups water and 1 teaspoon salt to full, rolling boil.
2. Slowly add cornmeal, stirring constantly with wire whisk—mixture will get very thick.
3. Reduce heat to very low, and cook, covered, about 5 minutes.
4. On cookie sheet that has been moistened with cold water, spread mixture to ½-inch thickness. Refrigerate until firm—several hours.
5. Make Sauce: In hot oil in large skillet, sauté onion, celery, and carrot, stirring, until tender—10 minutes.
6. Add water to chicken broth to measure 2 cups. Combine with tomato paste, mixing until smooth. Stir into vegetables in skillet. Simmer, covered, 15 minutes, stirring occasionally.
7. Meanwhile, soak dried mushrooms in ¾ cup water about 15 minutes. When soft, drain well; chop.
8. Add to sauce with salt and pepper. Simmer, covered, 20 minutes, or until mushrooms are tender.
9. Meanwhile, cut polenta into 1-inch squares. Dust lightly with flour. Preheat oven to 400F. Place polenta dumplings in 1½-quart baking dish. Pour sauce over top. Sprinkle with grated cheese. Bake 15 minutes, or until heated and golden-brown.
Makes 4 servings.

# ⊠ ANCHOVY ANTIPASTO SALAD

2 cans (2-oz size) anchovy fillets,
  drained
¼ cup diced pickled beets
2 tablespoons finely chopped green
  pepper
1 tablespoon finely chopped onion
1 tablespoon drained capers
2 tablespoons olive or salad oil
4 teaspoons red-wine vinegar
½ teaspoon sugar
½ teaspoon dried oregano leaves
Dash pepper
Crisp chicory leaves
Hard-cooked-egg wedges
Whole pickled beets
Drained capers

1. In bowl, combine anchovies, diced beets, green pepper, onion, and 1 tablespoon capers.
2. In jar with tight-fitting lid, combine oil, vinegar, sugar, oregano, and pepper; shake vigorously. Pour over anchovy mixture, and toss.
3. Refrigerate, covered, at least 2 hours.
4. To serve: Spoon on chicory on serving plate. Garnish with egg, beets, and capers. Pass chunks of Italian bread.
Makes 4 servings.

# ◆ ZABAIONE

*6 egg yolks*
*3 tablespoons sugar*
*⅓ cup Marsala*

1. In top of double boiler, with portable electric mixer at high speed or with rotary beater, beat egg yolks with sugar until light and fluffy.
2. Gradually add Marsala, beating until well combined.
3. Over hot, not boiling, water, beat at medium speed 8 minutes, or until mixture begins to hold its shape.
4. Turn out into 4 dessert glasses. Serve at once, or while still slightly warm. (Zabaione separates on standing.)
Makes 4 servings.

# ◆ CANNOLI

## FILLING:

*3 lb ricotta cheese*
*2½ cups confectioners' sugar*
*¼ cup semisweet-chocolate pieces or*
  *chopped sweet chocolate*
*2 tablespoons chopped citron*
*10 candied cherries, finely chopped*
*½ teaspoon ground cinnamon*

*Cannoli Shells, below*
*Chopped pistachio nuts (optional)*
*Confectioners' sugar*

1. In a large bowl, with portable electric mixer, at medium speed, beat ricotta cheese 1 minute. Add 2½ cups confectioners' sugar, and beat until light and creamy—about 1 minute.
2. Add chocolate, citron, cherries, and cinnamon; beat at low speed until well blended. Refrigerate, covered, until well chilled—at least 2 hours. Meanwhile, make Cannoli Shells.
3. Just before serving, with teaspoon or small spatula, fill shells with ricotta mixture. Garnish ends with chopped pistachios; sprinkle tops with confectioners' sugar.
Makes 24.

## CANNOLI SHELLS:

3 cups sifted all-purpose flour
1 tablespoon sugar
¼ teaspoon ground cinnamon
¾ cup port
Salad oil or shortening for deep-
   frying
1 egg yolk, slightly beaten

1. Sift flour with sugar and cinnamon onto board. Make well in center, and fill with port. With fork, gradually blend flour into port. When dough is stiff enough to handle, knead about 15 minutes, or until dough is smooth and stiff (if too moist and sticky, knead in a little more sifted flour).
2. Refrigerate dough, covered, 2 hours.
3. In deep-fat fryer, electric skillet, or heavy saucepan, slowly heat salad oil (3 to 4 inches deep), to 400F on deep-frying thermometer.
4. Meanwhile, on lightly floured surface, roll one third of dough to paper thinness, making 16-inch round. Cut into 8 (5-inch) circles. Wrap circle loosely around 6-inch-long cannoli form or dowel measuring 1 inch in diameter; seal with egg yolk.
5. Gently drop dough forms, 2 at a time, into hot oil, and fry 1 minute, or until browned on all sides (turn if necessary). With tongs or slotted utensil, lift out of oil, and drain on paper towels. Carefully remove forms. Continue until all dough is used.
Makes 24.

*Note*: Cannoli Shells can be made a day or two ahead and stored, covered, at room temperature, then filled about 1 hour before serving.

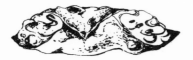

# ❖ COFFEE TORTONI

2 egg whites, at room temperature
2 tablespoons instant coffee
¼ teaspoon salt
¼ cup granulated sugar
2 cups heavy cream
½ cup confectioners' sugar
2 teaspoons vanilla extract
2 teaspoons almond extract
½ cup coarsely chopped toasted almonds

1. In medium bowl, with portable electric mixer, beat egg whites until foamy. Beat in coffee and salt; beat in granulated sugar, a little at a time. Continue beating until stiff peaks form when beaters are slowly raised.
2. Beat cream in medium bowl (use clean beaters) with confectioners' sugar just until stiff.
3. With wire whisk or rubber spatula, gently fold whipped cream into egg whites, along with vanilla and almond extracts.
4. Use to fill 10 paper tortoni cups; sprinkle top of each with chopped toasted almonds. Freeze until firm—overnight. Let stand 5 minutes at room temperature before serving. (If storing in freezer longer, freezer-wrap.)
Makes 10 servings.

# ITALIAN CHEESE PIE

## CRUST:

*1½ cups all-purpose flour*
*1¼ teaspoons baking powder*
*½ teaspoon salt*
*3 tablespoons butter or margarine, softened*
*¼ cup sugar*
*1 egg*
*½ teaspoon vanilla extract*
*½ teaspoon grated orange peel*
*1 tablespoon orange juice*

## FILLING:

*1 container (15 oz) ricotta cheese*
*¾ cup sugar*
*3 eggs*
*1½ teaspoons all-purpose flour*
*1 teaspoon almond extract*
*2 tablespoons finely chopped citron*

*1 egg, separated*
*1 tablespoon water*

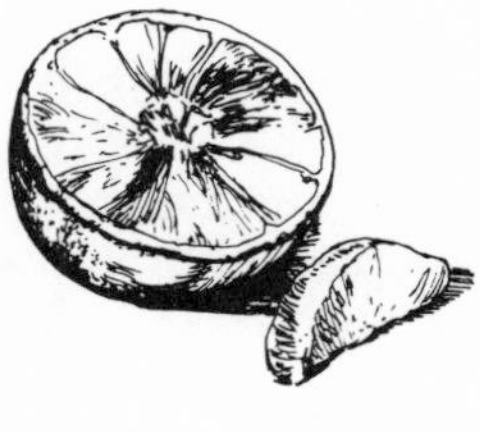

1. Make Crust: Sift flour with baking powder and salt; set aside.
2. In medium bowl, with electric mixer at high speed, beat butter with ¼ cup sugar and 1 egg until light and fluffy. Beat in vanilla, orange peel, and orange juice.
3. Add half of flour mixture; with wooden spoon, beat until well blended. Add remaining flour mixture, mixing with hand until dough leaves side of bowl and holds shape.
4. Turn out onto lightly floured board or pastry cloth; knead several times to blend well. Set aside, covered.
5. Make Filling: In medium bowl, with portable electric mixer, beat ricotta cheese until creamy. Add sugar, eggs, flour, almond extract, and citron; beat until well combined.
6. Preheat oven to 350F.
7. Divide crust in half. Roll one half, between 2 sheets of waxed paper, to 11-inch circle. Remove top paper. Fit crust into 9-inch pie plate; trim to edge of plate. Brush with egg white.
8. Roll remaining crust to ⅛-inch thickness. With pastry cutter, cut into 10 strips, each ½ inch wide.
9. Turn out filling into lined pie plate. Place 5 pastry strips across filling, pressing firmly to edge of pie plate. Place remaining strips across first ones, to make lattice.
10. Reroll trimmings and cut into ½-inch-wide strips. Place around edge of pie; with fork, press firmly to plate.
11. Beat egg yolk with 1 tablespoon water; brush over crust. To prevent overbrowning, place strip of foil, about 2 inches wide, around edge of crust.
12. Bake about 50 minutes, or until top is golden-brown and filling is set.
13. Cool on wire rack. Refrigerate until well chilled —8 hours or overnight.

Makes 8 servings.

# JAPANESE

## ❖ WHITE RADISH SALAD

½ lb fresh green beans
4 carrots (½ lb), pared and cut into
  3-inch julienne pieces
Boiling water

### DRESSING:

½ cup white vinegar
¼ cup sugar
1 tablespoon soy sauce

1½ cups white radish, cut into 3-inch
  pieces, ¼ inch wide (see Note)

1. Wash beans under cold running water; drain. Trim ends of beans, then cut each in half lengthwise. (If beans are large and wide, cut in thirds.)
2. Arrange carrots on one side of medium skillet and beans on other side; add boiling water to measure 1 inch.
3. Boil carrots and beans gently, uncovered, 5 minutes. Drain. Chill in ice water; drain well.
4. Make Dressing: In small bowl, combine vinegar, sugar, and soy sauce; mix well.
5. Arrange radish, carrots, and green beans in shallow serving dish. Garnish, if desired, with additional white radish and carrot slices.
6. Spoon dressing over vegetables. Refrigerate, covered, 1 hour before serving.
Makes 6 servings.

*Note*: Daikon (white radish) is often used instead of turnips in Japanese dishes. It is large, can weigh up to 3 lb, and is always peeled. Long white radishes may be substituted.

## ❖ SUSHI
### (HAM-AND-CUCUMBER RICE BARS)

Sushi Rice, below
2 thin slices (8 by 4 inches) boiled
  ham
1 cucumber
2 teaspoons prepared mustard

1. Make Sushi Rice.
2. Line bottom of 8-inch square pan with waxed paper. Place ham slices, one on top of the other, on one half of bottom of pan.
3. Wash cucumber, and cut into thin lengthwise strips. Trim off ends of each strip, leaving pieces 4 inches wide. Make layer of cucumber strips on remaining half of pan, overlapping if necessary.
4. Spread ham and cucumber with mustard. Spoon in all of Sushi Rice, and spread to make even layer.
5. Cut 8-inch strip of waxed paper, and place over rice. Place second 8-inch square pan in first. Press to pack rice firmly. Place weight (several cans or heavy pot) in top pan. Refrigerate until rice is completely cool—1 to 1½ hours.
6. To serve: Remove weight and top pan. Peel off waxed paper. Invert sushi onto cutting board, and peel off remaining waxed paper. Using sharp knife, cut into 24 bars.
Makes 24 sushi bars.

## SUSHI RICE:

1½ cups water
1¼ cups raw short-grain rice
¼ cup rice vinegar or white vinegar
3½ tablespoons sugar
2½ teaspoons salt
1½ tablespoons sweet sake or sherry

1. In very heavy saucepan, bring water to boiling. Add rice; cover, and simmer until rice is tender and all water has been absorbed—15 to 18 minutes.
2. Add vinegar, sugar, salt, and sake to rice. Stir until combined. Cover; set aside 15 minutes.
Makes 4 cups.

## ❖ SKEWERED NIBBLERS

½ lb boned chicken breast
½ lb boneless beef chuck
½ lb boneless pork shoulder
½ large green pepper
½ large red pepper
12 small white onions
12 fresh Brussels sprouts
6 sea scallops, cut in half
6 medium shrimp, shelled and deveined
½ cup soy or shoyu sauce
½ cup sake or dry sherry
2 green onions
1½ teaspoons grated fresh ginger
3 eggs, well beaten
½ cup all-purpose flour
1¼ cups unseasoned bread crumbs
Salad oil for frying
Freshly grated radishes
Mustard

1. With sharp knife, cut chicken into 1-inch cubes and beef into ½-inch cubes. Slice pork ¼ inch thick. Cut into 1½-by-2½-inch pieces.
2. Cut pepper into slices 2 inches long and 1 inch wide.
3. Peel onions. Cut off stem ends of Brussels sprouts. Drop onions and Brussels sprouts into 1 inch boiling salted water. Boil, uncovered, 5 minutes; drain well. Cool.
4. In bottom of shallow 12-by-8-inch dish, arrange in rows scallops, shrimp, cut-up meats, onions, and Brussels sprouts. In small bowl, combine soy sauce and sake. Pour over seafood, meat, and vegetables.
5. To assemble skewered nibblers: Remove seafood, meat, and vegetables from marinade; reserve marinade. Insert skewer into Brussels sprout and piece of chicken; repeat on another skewer with beef and onion. Cut green onions into 1-inch strips. Sprinkle pork piece with ⅛ teaspoon ginger; roll pork around green onion, and insert skewer. Repeat with rest of Brussels sprouts, chicken, beef, onions, pork, ginger, and green onions.
6. Insert skewer into each scallop, adding shrimp and green- and red-pepper slice.
7. Add 1 tablespoon marinade to eggs; mix well. Dip skewered meat and vegetables first in flour, then in egg mixture, then coat with crumbs. Continue with shrimp and scallops.
8. Meanwhile, in deep-fat fryer or heavy 1-quart saucepan, heat oil (2 inches) to 350F on deep-frying thermometer.
9. Deep-fry, holding skewers, 3 at a time, with potholder—about 1 or 2 minutes, or until lightly browned.
10. Drain well on paper towels. Bring remaining marinade to boiling. Pour into bowl; use as sauce for dipping, along with grated radish and mustard. Serve a selection of nibblers to each guest, along with a small bowl of sauce for dipping.
Makes 6 servings.

# 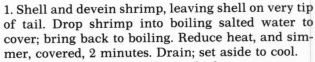 TEMPURA

½ lb large fresh shrimp
1 lb sea scallops (if large, cut in half)
6 large parsley sprigs
½ small eggplant, cut into 2-by-
   ¼-inch strips
¾ lb sweet potatoes, peeled and sliced
   ⅛ inch thick
1 large green pepper, sliced lengthwise into ¼-inch strips
½ lb small fresh mushrooms

## SAUCE:

½ cup dry sherry
½ cup beef broth
1 cup soy or shoyu sauce
Freshly grated radish
Freshly grated horseradish
Freshly grated ginger root

## BATTER:

1 egg yolk
2 cups ice-cold water
⅛ teaspoon baking soda
1⅔ cups all-purpose flour
Salad oil for frying

1. Shell and devein shrimp, leaving shell on very tip of tail. Drop shrimp into boiling salted water to cover; bring back to boiling. Reduce heat, and simmer, covered, 2 minutes. Drain; set aside to cool.
2. Drop scallops into boiling salted water to cover; bring back to boiling. Reduce heat, and simmer, covered, 3 minutes. Drain; set aside to cool.
3. On large serving platter or tray, have shrimp and scallops ready for frying, with parsley, eggplant, sweet potatoes, green pepper, and whole mushrooms. Refrigerate, covered, until ready to cook.
4. Make Sauce: In small saucepan, combine sherry, beef broth, and soy sauce; bring to boiling. Spoon equal amounts into 6 individual bowls. Place on tray with 3 small bowls filled with grated radish, horseradish, and ginger root as accompaniments.
5. Make Batter: In large mixing bowl, with wooden spoon, combine egg yolk with water and baking soda. With wire whisk, stir in flour to make smooth batter; it will be thin. Use batter soon after it is made; it should not stand.
6. In deep-fat fryer, electric skillet, or heavy skillet, heat oil (at least 3 inches deep) to 375F on deep-frying thermometer. With tongs, dip shrimp, scallops, and vegetables, one by one, into batter, to coat lightly. Deep-fry, a few at a time, until lightly browned—about 3 minutes.
7. Tempura is traditionally cooked at table, and should be served immediately. Serve with small bowl of dipping sauce for each guest.
Makes 6 servings as main course; 10 to 12 servings as hors d'oeuvre.

# ✤ SUKIYAKI
### (TO BE COOKED AT TABLE)

2 lb boneless sirloin steak, sliced
⅛ inch thick (see Note)
2 onions
2 bunches green onions
12 large fresh mushrooms
1 can (5 oz) bamboo shoots, drained
½ lb fresh spinach
½ small head cabbage
¾ cup soy or shoyu sauce
2 tablespoons sugar
2 beef-bouillon cubes, dissolved in
1-½ cups boiling water
¼ lb beef suet or shortening
Cooked white rice

1. Cut beef into 2-inch strips.
2. Prepare vegetables: Peel onions, and slice very thin. Diagonally slice green onions, including tops, into 1-inch pieces. Slice mushrooms and bamboo shoots ¼ inch thick. Cut spinach into 1-inch strips. Shred cabbage.
3. Arrange all ingredients attractively on large serving platter.
4. In small saucepan, combine soy, sugar, and bouillon; heat, stirring, until sugar is dissolved.
5. Preheat electric skillet to 350F. Fry suet in skillet to lubricate pan; remove.
6. Add onion and green onion slices, sauté, stirring occasionally, until golden. Add remaining vegetables.
7. Cover with beef strips, overlapping if necessary. Pour on sauce mixture; simmer, uncovered, 10 minutes.
8. Turn meat; simmer just until vegetables are tender—about 5 minutes.
9. Serve at once with hot rice.
Makes 6 servings.

*Note*: Have butcher slice on meat slicer.

# JEWISH

# ✤ CHOPPED CHICKEN LIVERS

¾ cup chicken fat
2½ cups thinly sliced onion
1 lb chicken livers, rinsed and dried
2 hard-cooked eggs, peeled and quartered
¾ cup white-bread cubes
1½ teaspoons salt
¼ teaspoon pepper
Crisp lettuce leaves
2 tablespoons finely chopped parsley
Crackers or white toast

1. In large skillet, heat ¼ cup chicken fat. Add onion; sauté, stirring, until golden—about 10 minutes. Remove onion with slotted spoon; set aside.
2. Add ¼ cup chicken fat to same skillet; heat. Add chicken livers; sauté just until they are cooked through and no longer pink—about 10 minutes. Reserve pan drippings.
3. Using medium blade of meat grinder, or in food processor, grind eggs, then onion and livers into medium bowl. Grind bread cubes. Toss liver mixture with pan drippings, 3 tablespoons chicken fat, salt, and pepper. Mix well; refrigerate, covered, to chill well.
4. To serve: Mound chopped chicken livers on crisp lettuce on chilled serving plate. Spoon remaining 1 tablespoon chicken fat over top; sprinkle with parsley. Serve with crackers.
Makes 2½ cups.

## ❖ TZIMMES
### (BEEF BRISKET WITH CARROTS AND SWEET POTATOES)

3-lb beef brisket
3 teaspoons salt
½ teaspoon pepper
2 medium onions, peeled and chopped
2 tablespoons flour
3 cups boiling water
8 carrots, pared and quartered
3 sweet potatoes, peeled and quartered
¼ cup honey
1 cup pitted prunes

1. Wipe beef with damp paper towels. Combine 2 teaspoons salt and the pepper; rub into surface of meat.
2. Slowly heat 6-quart Dutch oven. Over low heat, brown meat with onions, turning to brown on all sides.
3. Remove from heat; gradually add flour to meat drippings, stirring until smooth. Gradually stir in boiling water. Add 1 teaspoon salt.
4. Bring to boiling, stirring. Reduce heat, and simmer, covered, over low heat 1 hour.
5. Meanwhile, preheat oven to 375F. Add carrots, sweet potatoes, honey, and prunes to Dutch oven. Bake, covered, 1½ to 1¾ hours, or until beef is tender; remove cover during last 15 minutes of baking. (Be careful not to overcook potatoes.)
6. Serve with pan liquid spooned over meat.
Makes 8 servings.

## ❖ POTATO PUDDING
### (KUGEL)

3 lb Idaho potatoes
4 eggs
⅓ cup potato flour
1½ teaspoons salt
¾ teaspoon baking powder
⅛ teaspoon pepper
¼ cup grated onion
About ½ cup melted butter

1. Wash and peel potatoes. Grate potatoes on coarse grater into large bowl filled with ice water. Let stand 15 minutes.
2. Preheat oven to 350F. Grease inside of 1½-quart baking dish.
3. Drain potatoes; pat dry with clean dish towel or paper towels. Measure about 5½ cups.
4. In large bowl, with electric mixer at high speed, beat eggs until thick and light. Stir in potatoes, potato flour, salt, baking powder, pepper, onion, and ¼ cup melted butter; mix well.
5. Turn out into prepared baking dish. Bake, uncovered, ½ hour; brush top with some melted butter. Bake 45 minutes longer, brushing every 10 minutes with butter, until top is crusty and golden-brown.
Makes 8 servings.

# ❖ KASHA VARNISHKES

1 cup uncooked kasha (buckwheat
    groats)
1 egg
½ cup chopped onion
2 tablespoons butter
1 teaspoon salt
⅛ teaspoon pepper
2 cups boiling water
1½ cups bow-tie noodles
Chopped parsley

1. In medium bowl, combine kasha and egg; mix well until well blended.
2. In medium skillet, over medium heat, heat kasha mixture, stirring, until grains become dry and separated (about 3 minutes). Remove from heat.
3. In small skillet, sauté onion in butter until golden.
4. Add onion, salt, pepper, and boiling water to kasha mixture; mix well.
5. Cook, covered, over medium heat 15 minutes, stirring occasionally so kasha doesn't stick to bottom of pan.
6. Meanwhile, cook bow-tie noodles according to package directions; drain.
7. Add noodles to kasha; toss lightly to combine. Sprinkle with chopped parsley. Serve while hot.
Makes 8 servings.

# ❖ NOODLE PUDDING

1 pkg (8 oz) medium noodles
2 tablespoons butter or margarine,
    melted
1 large tart apple, pared and grated
1 teaspoon kosher salt
¼ teaspoon white pepper
2 eggs
½ cup white raisins
1 teaspoon ground cinnamon
½ cup sugar
4 candied cherries, quartered

1. Preheat oven to 350F. Grease well 8-by-8-by-2-inch or 1½-quart shallow oval baking dish.
2. Cook noodles according to package directions; drain well.
3. In large mixing bowl, combine noodles, butter, apple, salt, pepper, eggs, raisins, cinnamon, and sugar; mix well.
4. Turn out into prepared baking dish, spreading evenly.
5. Bake 1 hour, or until top is crisp and richly browned. Serve warm or cold with meat, or as a dessert. For dessert, decorate with candied cherries.
Makes 8 servings.

# ❖ MANDEL BREAD

6 eggs
1 cup granulated sugar
1 cup salad oil
6 cups all-purpose flour
4 teaspoons baking powder

## FILLING:

1 cup chopped pecans or walnuts
1 cup (8 oz) chopped mixed candied
  fruit
⅓ cup granulated sugar
2 teaspoons ground cinnamon
1 cup white raisins

Salad oil
2 jars (12-oz size) cherry preserves
Confectioners' sugar (optional)

1. In medium bowl, combine eggs and 1 cup each granulated sugar and salad oil; with rotary beater or wire whisk, beat just until well combined.
2. Into large bowl, sift flour with baking powder.
3. Make well in center; pour in egg mixture all at once. Using wooden spoon, stir around bowl until well blended.
4. Turn out dough onto lightly floured pastry cloth. Coat lightly with flour; knead until smooth—about 5 minutes.
5. Preheat oven to 350F. Lightly grease 2 cookie sheets.
6. Make Filling: In small bowl, mix together all filling ingredients.
7. Divide dough into 5 equal parts.
8. On lightly floured pastry cloth, roll each fifth of dough into 12-by-10-inch rectangle.
9. Brush lightly with 1 teaspoon oil. Spread ¼ cup preserves over surface; sprinkle with ½ cup filling. From long side, roll tightly as for jelly roll; pinch ends to seal.
10. Place 3 rolls, seam side down and 2 inches apart, on cookie sheet. Place 2 rolls, 2 inches apart, on other pan.
11. Bake 45 to 50 minutes, or until golden-brown.
12. Remove to wire rack; cool 10 minutes before taking bread from cookie sheets. Cool completely.
13. If desired, sprinkle with confectioners' sugar. Makes 5 loaves.

*Note*: This bread mellows with storage. Slice; then store, covered, in cool, dry place.

# ❖ HONEY CAKE

3 cups sifted cake flour
2 teaspoons baking powder
1¼ teaspoons ground cinnamon
½ teaspoon ground ginger
½ teaspoon ground nutmeg
2 tablespoons salad oil
1 cup sugar
3 eggs
1 cup cold black coffee
1 cup honey
Confectioners' sugar (optional)

1. Preheat oven to 350F.
2. Sift together flour, baking powder, cinnamon, ginger, and nutmeg; set aside. Grease and flour 10-inch bundt or tube pan.
3. In large bowl of electric mixer, combine oil, sugar, and eggs; beat, at high speed, until thick and fluffy—about 2 minutes.
4. In small bowl, combine coffee and honey; mix well.
5. At low speed, add flour mixture (in fourths) to sugar mixture, alternately with honey mixture, be-

ginning and ending with flour mixture. Beat just until combined. Turn out into prepared pan.

6. Bake 55 to 60 minutes, or until cake tester inserted in center comes out clean.

7. Cool in pan on wire rack—5 minutes. With spatula, carefully loosen cake from pan. Let stand until completely cool.

8. Serve plain, or sprinkle with confectioners' sugar before serving.

Makes 16 servings.

# ❖ CHALLAH
## (SABBATH TWIST)

*1¼ cups warm water (105 to 115F)*
*1 pkg active dry yeast*
*¼ cup sugar*
*1½ teaspoons salt*
*¼ cup salad oil*
*2 eggs, slightly beaten*
*5½ cups all-purpose flour*
*1 egg yolk*
*2 tablespoons water*
*2 tablespoons sesame seed*

1. If possible, check temperature of water with thermometer. In large bowl, sprinkle yeast and sugar over water, stirring until dissolved.

2. Add salt, oil, eggs, and 3 cups flour; beat with electric mixer at low speed, until smooth—about 2 minutes. Gradually add remaining flour, mixing in flour with wooden spoon or by hand until dough is stiff enough to leave side of bowl.

3. Turn out dough onto lightly floured pastry cloth or board. Knead until smooth and elastic—about 5 minutes.

4. Place in lightly greased large bowl; turn dough over to bring up greased side. Cover with towel; let rise in warm place (85F), free from drafts, about 1 hour, or until double in bulk.

5. Turn out dough onto lightly floured pastry cloth or board. Divide two thirds into 3 equal parts. Using palms of hands, roll each part into 20-inch-long strips. Braid 3 strips; pinch ends together. Place on greased large cookie sheet.

6. Divide remaining one third of dough into 3 equal parts. Roll each part into 18-inch-long strips. Braid 3 strips together; pinch ends together. Place on top of larger braid.

7. Cover with clean dish towel; let rise in warm place (85F), free from drafts, until double in bulk—50 to 60 minutes.

8. Preheat oven to 375F.

9. Brush surface of loaf with egg yolk mixed with 2 tablespoons water. Sprinkle with sesame seed.

10. Bake 35 to 40 minutes, or until rich golden-brown. (If crust seems too brown after 25 minutes of baking, cover with foil.) Remove to wire rack to cool. Serve warm or cold.

Makes 1 braid.

FLOUR

# PENNSYLVANIA DUTCH

## ❖ BEEF STEW WITH POTATO DUMPLING

2 lb boneless beef chuck or round, cut into 1½-inch cubes
4 medium carrots, pared and cut in half
3 celery stalks, cut into 2-inch pieces
2 medium onions, quartered
2 bay leaves
1 teaspoon salt
10 whole black peppercorns
2 cans (10½-oz size) condensed beef broth, undiluted
1 cup water


### POTATO DUMPLING:

Boiling water
1¼ lb potatoes, peeled and thinly sliced
1½ tablespoons butter or margarine
½ cup chopped onion
2 tablespoons chopped parsley
½ teaspoon salt
⅛ teaspoon pepper
1 egg, beaten
1¼ cups all-purpose flour
1 teaspoon baking powder
¼ teaspoon salt
2 tablespoons shortening
5 tablespoons ice water

Chopped parsley

1. Place beef cubes in 6-quart oval Dutch oven. Add carrots, celery, quartered onions, bay leaves, 1 teaspoon salt, the peppercorns, beef broth, and 1 cup water.
2. Bring to boiling. Reduce heat; simmer, covered, 2½ hours, or until meat is tender. Remove bay leaves.
3. Meanwhile, make Potato Dumpling: In boiling water, cook potatoes, covered, until tender—20 minutes; drain well. Turn out potatoes into large bowl.
4. In small skillet in hot butter, sauté onion until golden—5 minutes.
5. To potato, add sautéed onion, parsley, salt, pepper, and egg. Toss lightly to combine; set aside.
6. Sift flour, baking powder, and salt into medium bowl.
7. Cut in shortening with pastry blender or 2 knives until mixture resembles coarse cornmeal.
8. Gradually add ice water, stirring briskly with fork, just until mixture holds together. Shape pastry into ball.
9. On lightly floured pastry cloth or floured surface, roll out into 10-inch circle. Spread potato filling on half of circle. Loosen dough with spatula, and fold in half over filling; seal edges with tines of fork.
10. Carefully drop dumpling into boiling stew; simmer, covered, 25 minutes.
11. Lift cooked dumpling with 2 spatulas.
12. To serve, spoon hot meat stew and broth over dumpling. Sprinkle with parsley.
Makes 6 servings.

# ✠ BRAISED PORK LOIN WITH TURNIP AND POTATOES

4 lb loin of pork
2 teaspoons salt
½ teaspoon plus ¼ teaspoon pepper
¼ teaspoon ground allspice
4 cups apple cider
1 large (2½ lb) turnip (rutabaga),
    pared, quartered, and sliced ⅓ inch
    thick
5 medium potatoes (about 3 lb)
Paprika (optional)

1. Preheat oven to 350F.
2. Wipe pork with damp paper towels. Mix 1 teaspoon salt, ½ teaspoon pepper, and the allspice; rub into surface of pork. Place pork, fat side up, in large roasting pan with cover. Roast, uncovered, 1 hour.
3. Pour apple cider into bottom of pan. Add turnip slices. Roast, covered, 1 hour.
4. Meanwhile, peel and quarter potatoes.
5. Remove roasting pan from oven. Add potatoes to pan drippings around roast. Baste vegetables with drippings; then sprinkle with 1 teaspoon salt and ¼ teaspoon pepper.
6. Roast, covered, 1 hour longer, or until turnip and potatoes are tender. If desired, sprinkle potatoes with paprika.
7. Remove roast and vegetables to heated platter; keep warm.
8. Skim off excess fat from drippings. Over direct heat, bring remaining drippings to boiling; boil, uncovered, 15 minutes. Spoon over pork and vegetables. Makes 8 servings.

# ✠ SCRAPPLE

1½ cups yellow cornmeal
3 cups water
1 lb ground pork sausage
½ teaspoon dried sage leaves
½ teaspoon salt
1 tablespoon chopped parsley
1 can (10¾ oz) condensed chicken
    broth, undiluted
Butter

1. In small bowl, blend together cornmeal and 1 cup water.
2. In large saucepan, combine pork sausage, sage, salt, parsley, and chicken broth. Gradually stir in 2 cups water, being careful to separate sausage into fine pieces. Bring to boiling.
3. Slowly add cornmeal to boiling mixture, stirring constantly with wire whisk. Reduce heat; simmer, uncovered, 15 minutes.
4. Turn out into 9-by-5-by-3-inch loaf pan. Cool; refrigerate, covered.
5. To serve: Turn out of pan; cut into ¼-inch-thick slices. Sauté in hot butter in skillet until golden-brown on both sides. Serve with pancake syrup. Makes 8 servings.

# ✦ CHICKEN-AND-NOODLE POTPIE

5-lb roasting chicken, cut up
6 cups water
1 celery stalk, cut up
6 whole black peppercorns
1½ teaspoons salt
⅛ teaspoon saffron threads, crumbled
4 medium potatoes (2 lb), peeled and
    sliced ¼ inch thick
1 cup sliced onion

## NOODLES:

1 cup all-purpose flour
1 tablespoon butter or margarine
1 teaspoon salt
1 egg
2 tablespoons water

Chopped parsley

1. Wipe chicken pieces with damp paper towels. Place in 6-quart Dutch oven with 6 cups water. Add celery, peppercorns, 1½ teaspoons salt, and the saffron.
2. Bring to boiling; reduce heat, and simmer, covered, 60 minutes, or until tender. Remove chicken pieces from broth; reserve broth.
3. Remove chicken meat from bones in large pieces; discard skin and bones.
4. To broth, add potatoes and onion. Bring to boiling; reduce heat and simmer, covered, until potatoes are tender—15 minutes. Remove from broth with slotted utensil.
5. Meanwhile, make Noodles: In medium bowl, combine flour, butter, and salt; mix with fork. Make well in center. Add egg and 2 tablespoons water; beat with fork until ingredients are combined.
6. On lightly floured pastry cloth or surface, roll dough ⅛ inch thick.
7. With sharp knife or pastry wheel, cut into strips 4 inches long and 1 inch wide.
8. To boiling broth, add noodle strips; return to boiling. Boil, uncovered and stirring occasionally, until tender—about 15 minutes.
9. Add reserved chicken pieces and vegetables to broth. Simmer, uncovered, 5 minutes. Sprinkle with chopped parsley.
Makes 6 servings.

# ✦ SCALLOPED SWEET POTATOES AND APPLES

3 medium-size sweet potatoes (2½ lb)
Boiling water
½ cup butter or margarine
¾ cup light- or dark-brown sugar,
    packed
½ cup apple cider
½ teaspoon mace
¼ teaspoon salt
1 large apple, pared and thinly sliced

1. Scrub potatoes. Place in large saucepan, and cover with boiling water. Bring back to boiling. Reduce heat, and simmer, covered, 25 minutes.
2. Drain; let cool. Peel and cut into slices ¼ inch thick. Preheat oven to 400F.
3. Melt butter in small skillet. Add sugar, cider, mace, and salt; bring to boiling, stirring until sugar is dissolved. Simmer, uncovered, 10 minutes.
4. In shallow 2-quart casserole, alternate potato and apple slices around edge and in center.
5. Spoon half of syrup evenly over sweet potato and apple. Bake, covered with foil, 25 minutes, or until tender.
6. Remove foil; baste with remaining syrup. Bake, uncovered, 20 minutes, or until glazed.
Makes 6 servings.

# ❖ SAUERKRAUT

3 tablespoons butter or margarine
¾ cup chopped onion
3 cans (14-oz size) sauerkraut,
    drained and rinsed
1 cup grated raw potato
1½ teaspoons caraway seeds
2 tablespoons light-brown sugar
2½ cups boiling water

1. In hot butter in 5-quart Dutch oven, sauté onion until golden—about 3 minutes.
2. Add sauerkraut, potato, caraway seeds, sugar, and boiling water.
3. Bring to boiling; reduce heat, and simmer, uncovered, 20 minutes, stirring occasionally. Nice with pork.
Makes 8 servings.

# ❖ RED BEET EGGS

2 cans (1-lb size) small whole beets
1 cup cider vinegar
½ cup sugar
1 teaspoon salt
6 hard-cooked eggs, shelled
Salad greens

1. Drain beets, reserving liquid. Place drained beets in 1½-quart jar.
2. Measure reserved liquid. If necessary, add enough water to measure 1 cup.
3. In small saucepan, combine beet liquid, vinegar, sugar, and salt; bring to boiling, stirring. Pour over beets; then refrigerate, tightly covered, 24 hours.
4. Next day, remove beets from jar, reserving liquid, and put eggs in jar with liquid; refrigerate, covered, 24 hours. Also, refrigerate beets, covered.
5. To serve: Drain eggs; halve lengthwise. Slice beets. Arrange eggs on salad greens, along with sliced beets.
Makes 6 servings.

# ❖ BOILED-RAISIN CAKE

1 box (15 oz) raisins
1 cup sugar
1⅓ cups water
⅓ cup butter or margarine, softened
2 cups all-purpose flour
1 teaspoon baking soda
¾ teaspoon ground cinnamon
¼ teaspoon ground cloves
½ teaspoon salt
¾ cup chopped walnuts
1 teaspoon vanilla extract

1. In large saucepan, combine raisins, sugar, water, and butter; mix well. Bring to boiling. Remove from heat; let cool 30 minutes.
2. Lightly grease and flour 9-by-5-by-3-inch loaf pan. Preheat oven to 350F.
3. Sift flour with baking soda, cinnamon, cloves, and salt. Add to cooled raisin mixture, along with walnuts and vanilla. With wooden spoon, mix until well combined.
4. Turn out into prepared pan. Bake 1 hour and 25 minutes, or until cake tester inserted in center comes out clean.
5. Let cool in pan on wire rack. Remove from pan; cut into slices.
Makes 10 to 12 servings.

## ❖ FUNNEL CAKES

Salad oil or shortening for deep-
  frying
1¼ cups sifted all-purpose flour
2 tablespoons sugar
1 teaspoon baking powder
¼ teaspoon salt
⅔ cup milk
1 egg, beaten
Confectioners' sugar

1. In deep-fat fryer or heavy skillet, slowly heat salad oil (2 inches deep) to 350F on deep-frying thermometer.
2. Into medium bowl, sift together flour, sugar, baking powder, and salt.
3. Make well in center; pour in milk and egg. Mix thoroughly with wooden spoon just until batter is smooth.
4. Holding finger over spout, pour ½ cup batter into funnel with tip opening ⅝ inch in diameter.
5. Drop batter into hot oil; starting in center, move funnel in circle to make snail-like coil of 4 rings, each about 6 inches in diameter. (Make 2 at a time.)
6. Fry, turning once with slotted utensil, until golden-brown—about 2 minutes on each side.
7. With slotted utensil, lift cakes from hot oil; hold over skillet a few seconds, to drain slightly.
8. Drain well on paper towels; keep warm in oven. If batter becomes too stiff, gradually add a little more milk.
9. Sprinkle with confectioners' sugar, and serve with pork sausage on the side and maple syrup on top, if desired.
Makes 7.

# SCANDINAVIAN

## ❖ MATJES HERRING BUFFET

Ice Tray, below
3 cans (7-oz size) whole fillets Matjes
  herring, drained
1 bunch fresh dill
1 large leek, thinly sliced
1 large green pepper, coarsely
  chopped
1 medium-size red onion, chopped
1 pint sour cream
Hot boiled unpeeled new potatoes,
  drained
Snipped fresh dill

1. Day before: Make Ice Tray.
2. To serve: Arrange herring fillets, each rolled around sprig of dill, on ice tray.
3. Serve surrounded with small bowls of leek, green pepper, onion, and sour cream.
4. Serve hot boiled potatoes sprinkled with snipped dill as an accompaniment.
Makes 8 servings.

### ICE TRAY

1. Day before needed, fill 8-inch round cake-layer pan with cold water. Freeze overnight.
2. To remove: Invert onto large serving platter. Arrange food on top and serve at once.

# ❖ SWEDISH GLAZED HAM

2 bay leaves, crushed
1½ teaspoons ground cloves
1 teaspoon ground ginger
10-to-12-lb fully cooked bone-in
  whole ham
2 parsley sprigs
1 cup sliced onion
2 carrots, sliced
2 cups apple cider

## MUSTARD GLAZE:

1 egg
3 tablespoons spicy prepared mustard
3 tablespoons sugar
¼ cup unseasoned dry bread crumbs

## BUTTER FROSTING:

3 tablespoons butter or margarine,
  softened
2 cups sifted confectioners' sugar
1 teaspoon vanilla extract

Whole cloves

1. Day before: Preheat oven to 325F. Combine bay leaves, ground cloves, and ginger.
2. Carefully remove ham rind. Place ham, fat side up, in shallow roasting pan. Rub surface of ham with bay-leaf mixture. Insert meat thermometer in center of meat, away from bone.
3. Place parsley, onion, and carrot around ham; pour cider into pan. Cover pan tightly with foil.
4. Bake, basting every 20 minutes with cider mixture in pan, until thermometer registers 130F—about 3 hours. Remove ham from oven. Pour off liquid; discard vegetables. Increase oven temperature to 450F.
5. Make Mustard Glaze: In small bowl, beat together egg, mustard, and sugar.
6. Spread glaze over ham. Sprinkle with bread crumbs. Bake, uncovered, 15 minutes, or until golden-brown. Remove from roasting pan; cool completely. Refrigerate, covered, overnight.
7. Next day: Remove ham to serving platter. Make Butter Frosting: In small bowl, mix together butter, confectioners' sugar, and vanilla extract until smooth.
8. Transfer butter frosting to pastry bag with number-53 decorating tip. Make diagonal lines 1½ inches apart to form diamond pattern on ham. Insert whole clove in center of each diamond.
9. To serve: Carve a few slices and arrange around ham. Serve with additional mustard, if desired. Makes 24 servings.

# ❖ GRETA'S MEATBALLS WITH SPICED CRANBERRIES

½ cup dry bread crumbs
¾ cup bottled club soda or water
2 lb ground beef chuck
1 small potato, peeled and grated
  (¼ cup)
1 small onion, grated
2 teaspoons salt
¼ teaspoon white pepper
¾ teaspoon ground allspice
1 egg
2 tablespoons butter or margarine
Spiced Cranberries, below

1. In large bowl, combine bread crumbs and club soda. Let stand until liquid is absorbed.
2. Add ground chuck, potato, onion, salt, and spices; mix lightly. Add egg; mix gently until combined.
3. Shape into 30 medium-size meatballs.
4. In slightly browned butter in large skillet, sauté meatballs over medium heat about 8 minutes, turning on all sides to keep round. (Cook only enough at one time to make single layer in pan.) Remove; sauté rest of meatballs.
5. Serve hot, with Spiced Cranberries. Makes 8 to 10 servings.

## SPICED CRANBERRIES:

1 pkg (12 oz) fresh cranberries
5 whole cloves
5 whole allspice
2 (3-inch) cinnamon sticks
1½ cups sugar

1. Wash cranberries. Drain; remove stems, if necessary.
2. Turn out into 3½-quart saucepan. Add water and spices.
3. Cook, covered, over medium heat just until cranberries burst—about 10 minutes.
4. Remove from heat; stir in sugar. Cook, stirring, over low heat 5 minutes.
5. Cool; refrigerate, covered. Serve cold. (This is better refrigerated overnight.)
Makes 1 quart.

# ✖ YELLOW-PEA SOUP WITH PORK

1 lb quick-cooking dried split yellow
    peas (2¼ cups), washed
1 bay leaf
2 quarts water
2½-lb pork shoulder, bone in
1 cup finely chopped onion
3 teaspoons salt
1 teaspoon dried marjoram leaves
½ teaspoon ground ginger
¼ teaspoon dried thyme leaves
¼ teaspoon pepper
Lemon slices

1. In deep 8-quart kettle, combine peas, bay leaf, and water; bring to boiling. Reduce heat, and simmer, covered and stirring occasionally, 1 hour.
2. Add pork shoulder, onion, salt, marjoram, ginger, thyme, and pepper; bring to boiling. Reduce heat, and simmer, covered and stirring occasionally, 2 hours, or until pork is tender. (If soup seems too thick, stir in a little water—about ½ cup.)
3. Lift pork out of soup. Cut into slices.
4. Turn out into soup tureen, and garnish with lemon slices. Serve with pork, along with mustard and dark bread.
Makes about 2 quarts; 6 to 8 servings.

Note: Flavor is improved if soup is made day before, refrigerated, then reheated and served next day.

# ✖ STEWED RED CABBAGE

¼ cup butter or margarine
3 tablespoons sugar
3 quarts shredded red cabbage (3 lb)
½ cup chopped onion
1 tablespoon salt
1 cup dry red wine
2 tart apples, sliced
1 cup currant jelly

1. Day before: Melt butter in 5-quart Dutch oven or iron saucepan. Stir in sugar. Add cabbage and onion; sauté, stirring occasionally, over medium heat 15 minutes.
2. Add salt and wine. Bring to boiling, stirring; simmer, covered, and stirring occasionally, 1 hour, or until tender.
3. Add apple slices and currant jelly. Simmer, covered, 15 minutes. Remove from heat. Cool completely before refrigerating.
4. Next day: Return cabbage to boiling; simmer, covered, 10 minutes.
Makes 8 to 10 servings.

### SWEDISH-STYLE BROWN BEANS

*2 cups dried brown beans*
*6 cups water*
*2 teaspoons salt*
*¾ cup cider vinegar*
*¾ cup dark corn syrup*
*¼ cup light-brown sugar, firmly packed*

1. Wash beans; turn out into 3-quart saucepan with 6 cups water. Refrigerate, covered, overnight.
2. Next day, bring to boiling. Reduce heat; simmer, covered, 1 hour.
3. Add remaining ingredients. Simmer, covered, about 4 hours, or until beans are tender and mixture is thick; stir occasionally.

Makes 6 to 8 servings.

## TEX-MEX

### CHILI CON QUESO WITH RAW VEGETABLES

*¼ cup butter or margarine*
*½ cup finely chopped onion*
*1 can (1 lb) tomatoes, undrained*
*1½ to 2 cans (4-oz size) green chilies (see Note), drained and chopped*
*½ teaspoon salt*
*1 lb Monterey Jack cheese, cubed*
*½ cup heavy cream*
*Carrot sticks*
*Celery hearts*
*Cucumber sticks*
*Corn chips*

1. In hot butter, in medium skillet, sauté onion until tender. Add tomatoes, chilies, and salt, mashing tomatoes with fork. Simmer, stirring occasionally, 15 minutes.
2. Add cheese cubes, stirring until cheese is melted. Stir in cream. Cook, stirring constantly, 2 minutes.
3. Remove from heat, and let stand 15 minutes. Serve warm, in casserole over candle warmer, as dip with carrot sticks, celery hearts, cucumber sticks, and large corn chips.

Makes 10 to 12 servings.

*Note*: Use larger amount of green chilies if you like this really hot.

### TACO SALAD BOWL

*1 lb ground beef chuck*
*½ clove garlic, crushed*
*1 can (4 oz) green chilies, finely chopped*
*1 can (1 lb) tomatoes, undrained*
*1 teaspoon salt*
*⅛ teaspoon pepper*
*2 quarts bite-size pieces crisp salad greens*
*1 cup grated Cheddar cheese*
*1 pkg (6 oz) corn chips, regular size*
*1 cup chopped green onion*
*1 medium tomato, coarsely chopped*

1. In medium skillet, sauté beef (breaking up with fork) and garlic until chuck is browned—about 10 minutes. Drain excess fat.
2. Add green chilies, tomatoes, salt, and pepper; mix well. Cook over low heat, uncovered, about 30 minutes.
3. Just before serving, in large chilled salad bowl arrange salad greens, cheese, corn chips, and green onion with cooked meat mixture; toss lightly until well combined. Garnish with chopped tomato. Serve immediately. Nice as main course.

Makes 6 to 8 servings.

# ❖ BEEF TACOS WITH GREEN-CHILI SALSA

## FILLING:

1 lb ground beef chuck
1 medium onion, chopped
1 clove garlic, crushed
2 tablespoons soy sauce
1 tablespoon Worcestershire sauce
1 can (8 oz) tomato sauce

Salad oil for deep-frying
Tortillas, page 269 (or use canned or
  frozen tortillas)
1 medium tomato, coarsely chopped
  (1 cup)
1 cup shredded lettuce
1 cup grated Monterey Jack or sharp
  Cheddar cheese
Green-Chili Salsa, below

1. Make Filling: In hot skillet, sauté chuck with onion until meat loses red color. Add garlic, soy sauce, Worcestershire, and tomato sauce; simmer about 10 minutes. Keep warm.
2. In heavy saucepan, slowly heat salad oil (at least 3 inches) to 420F on deep-frying thermometer.
3. Use 12 tortillas. Gently drop 1 tortilla into hot oil; when it rises to top, grasp it with two tongs, and bend into U shape. Hold in oil until crisp—about 2 minutes. Remove, and drain on paper towels. Continue until all tortillas are used, frying one at a time.
4. Preheat oven to 400F.
5. In each tortilla, arrange, in order, a layer of filling, a little chopped tomato, a small mound of shredded lettuce, and some grated cheese. Place in shallow baking dish.
6. Bake, uncovered, 10 minutes, or just until cheese melts. Serve with Green-Chili Salsa.
Makes 6 servings.

## GREEN-CHILI SALSA:

1½ cups chopped peeled tomato
1 cup chopped Bermuda onion
2 canned green chilies, chopped
2 cloves garlic, crushed
½ teaspoon salt

1. In medium bowl, combine all ingredients; mix well.
2. Let stand about 15 minutes, to develop flavor, before serving.
Makes about 2½ cups.

# ❖ BEEF EMPANADAS

## FILLING:

2 tablespoons butter or margarine
½ cup chopped onion
1 lb ground beef
2 large ripe tomatoes (1 lb), chopped
1 can (3 oz) green chilies, drained and
  chopped
1 teaspoon salt
1 bay leaf
2 tablespoons chopped black olives

1. Make Filling: In hot butter in large skillet, sauté onion until tender. Add beef, and sauté until no longer red.
2. Add tomato, chilies, 1 teaspoon salt, and the bay leaf; simmer, stirring occasionally, 30 to 35 minutes, or until most of liquid has evaporated. Remove from heat; discard bay leaf. Stir in olives.
3. Preheat oven to 400F.
4. Meanwhile, make Pastry (see Note): In medium bowl, combine flour and salt. With pastry blender, cut in shortening until well blended. Sprinkle with

## PASTRY:

1½ cups all-purpose flour
¾ teaspoon salt
½ cup shortening
4 to 4½ tablespoons ice water

1 egg yolk
1 tablespoon water
Salsa, below

ice water; stir with fork until mixture holds together. Shape into ball.

5. Divide pastry into 12 pieces. On lightly floured surface, roll each piece into 6-inch round. Place about 3 tablespoons filling on half of each round; fold over other half.

6. Press edges together with fingers to seal; flute edges. Cut slits on top of each empanada. Brush with egg yolk beaten with 1 tablespoon water.

7. Bake 20 to 25 minutes, or until golden-brown. Serve hot with Salsa.

Makes 6 servings.

*Note*: If you wish, you can use packaged pastry mix; prepare as label directs. Continue recipe as in Step 5.

## SALSA:

1 can (1 lb 12 oz) tomatoes, drained
  and chopped
1 cup finely chopped onion
1 can (3 oz) green chilies, drained and
  finely chopped
1 tablespoon finely chopped canned
  jalapeño pepper
1 clove garlic, crushed
2 tablespoons peanut or salad oil
½ teaspoon salt
¼ teaspoon pepper
¼ teaspoon chili powder

1. Make 1 or 2 days ahead: In medium saucepan, combine all ingredients; stir to mix well. Bring to boiling, stirring. Reduce heat, and simmer 20 minutes, stirring occasionally. Refrigerate, covered, overnight or longer.

2. To serve, reheat gently, or serve cold, if desired. Makes 2½ cups.

## ✦ BEEF ENCHILADAS

## FILLING:

1 lb ground beef chuck
1 clove garlic, finely chopped
2 teaspoons salt
1 tablespoon vinegar
1 tablespoon tequila, cognac, or water
1 tablespoon chili powder
1 can (1 lb) kidney beans, undrained

1. Prepare Filling: In medium skillet, over low heat, sauté beef with 1 clove garlic, 2 teaspoons salt, 1 tablespoon vinegar, the tequila, and chili powder until chuck is browned. Stir in kidney beans.

2. Make Tomato Sauce: In hot oil in skillet, sauté garlic and onion until golden.

3. Remove from heat. Stir in flour until smooth; stir in tomato purée, vinegar, and bouillon cube dissolved in boiling water.

4. Bring mixture to boiling, stirring, over medium heat.

## TOMATO SAUCE:

3 tablespoons salad oil
1 clove garlic, very finely chopped
¼ cup chopped onion
2 tablespoons flour
2 cans (10½-oz size) tomato purée
1 tablespoon vinegar
1 beef-bouillon cube
1 cup boiling water
2 tablespoons finely chopped canned
   green chilies
Dash ground cumin
½ teaspoon salt
Dash pepper

## ENCHILADAS:

10 Tortillas, page 269 (or use canned
   or frozen tortillas)
1 cup grated sharp Cheddar cheese or
   1 cup cubed Monterey Jack cheese

5. Add chilies, cumin, salt, and pepper; simmer, uncovered and stirring occasionally, about 5 minutes.
6. Preheat oven to 350F.
7. To assemble Enchiladas: Place about ⅓ cup filling in center of each tortilla; roll up. Arrange, seam side down, in 13-by-9-by-2-inch baking dish. Pour tomato sauce over all; sprinkle with cheese.
8. Bake 25 minutes.
Makes 10 small, 5 large servings.

*Note*: Meat filling and tomato sauce may be made ahead of time and refrigerated. Reheat slightly when ready to use.

# ⊠ CHILI FOR A CROWD

2½ lb ground beef chuck
2 cups chopped onion
2 cloves garlic, crushed
2 to 3 tablespoons chili powder
1½ teaspoons dried oregano leaves
1 teaspoon dried basil leaves
¼ teaspoon crushed red pepper (optional)
1 teaspoon ground cumin
1 tablespoon sugar
2 teaspoons salt
2 cans (1-lb size) tomatoes, undrained
2 cans (8-oz size) tomato sauce
1 can (6 oz) tomato paste
3 cans (1-lb size) kidney beans, drained

4 cups fluffy cooked rice
1 cup finely chopped onion

1. In 6-quart Dutch oven, over medium heat, sauté ground beef, stirring occasionally, until red color disappears. Keep ground beef in small chunks. Pour off fat.
2. Add 2 cups onion, the garlic, chili powder, oregano, basil, crushed red pepper, and cumin to Dutch oven, and mix well. Cook, stirring, until onion is tender—about 5 minutes.
3. Stir in sugar, salt, tomatoes, tomato sauce, and tomato paste; mix well. Bring to boiling, breaking up tomatoes with fork. Simmer slowly, covered and stirring occasionally, until thickened and flavors are blended—about 40 minutes.
4. Add kidney beans; simmer, covered, 10 minutes.
5. Serve over rice; top with finely chopped onion.
Makes 16 servings.

# ✥ CHILIES RELLENOS

*2 cans (4-oz size) green chilies*
*½ lb Monterey Jack cheese*
*4 tablespoons all-purpose flour*
*3 eggs, separated*
*¼ teaspoon salt*
*Salad oil for deep-frying*
*Red Chili Sauce, below*

1. Drain chilies; discard seeds. Cut into 24 strips.
2. Cut cheese into 24 cubes; wrap chili strip around each cheese cube. Roll lightly in 1 tablespoon flour, coating lightly all over.
3. In medium bowl, beat egg whites with rotary beater or wire whisk until soft peaks form.
4. Beat egg yolks with salt until thick. Stir in 3 tablespoons flour. Using rubber spatula, fold into egg whites until combined.
5. Start heating oil in electric skillet or large skillet —about 1½ inches deep—to 425F on deep-frying thermometer.
6. Coat each chili cube with egg mixture. Drop into hot fat, a few at a time. Fry about 4 minutes; turn and fry on other side 4 minutes. Lift out with slotted utensil; drain on paper towels. Keep warm while frying rest.
7. Serve with Red-Chili Sauce.
Makes 24.

*Note*: Chilies Rellenos may be prepared ahead of time and reheated in oven, uncovered, 15 to 20 minutes at 375F.

## RED-CHILI SAUCE:

*4 medium-size ripe tomatoes, peeled*
*2 canned hot red chilies, stems removed*
*3 small cloves garlic*
*3 tablespoons salad oil*
*2 tablespoons chopped coriander leaves or 1 teaspoon crushed coriander*
*1 tablespoon salt*
*¼ teaspoon black pepper*

1. Cut tomatoes into chunks; blend in blender or food processor with chilies and garlic.
2. Turn out purée into medium saucepan; add remaining ingredients. Bring to boiling, stirring; reduce heat, and simmer 1 minute. Serve hot.
Makes 2½ cups.

## ❖ REFRIED BEANS

1 pkg (1 lb) dried pinto beans
6 cups cold water
6 slices bacon
¼ cup finely chopped onion
¼ cup finely chopped green pepper
1 clove garlic, crushed
2 teaspoons salt
1 teaspoon chili powder
Chopped green pepper, bacon bits, or
   cheese strips (optional)

1. Wash beans. Turn out into large bowl; cover with 6 cups cold water. Refrigerate, covered, overnight.
2. Next day, turn out beans and liquid into large saucepan. Bring to boiling; reduce heat, and simmer, covered, about 1½ hours, or until tender. Drain beans, reserving liquid. Add water to liquid, if necessary, to make 1 cup.
3. In large skillet, sauté bacon until crisp. Drain on paper towels, and crumble.
4. In bacon drippings in skillet, sauté onion, green pepper, and garlic until tender—about 5 minutes.
5. With wooden spoon, stir in beans, bacon, salt, and chili powder. Cook over medium heat, stirring in reserved bean liquid a little at a time and mashing beans until all are mashed and mixture is creamy.
6. Turn out into serving dish. If desired, sprinkle with chopped green pepper, crisp bacon bits, or strips of cheese.
Makes 6 to 8 servings.

## ❖ BARBECUED CHICKEN WITH MEXICAN RICE

### BARBECUE SAUCE:

½ cup cider vinegar
¼ cup brown sugar, packed
2 tablespoons prepared mustard
2 teaspoons salt
¼ teaspoon crushed red pepper
½ teaspoon black pepper
Dash Tabasco
1 cup chopped onion
1 small lemon, sliced
1 tablespoon Worcestershire sauce
¼ cup water
¼ cup chili sauce
1 cup catsup

3 (2-lb size) broiler-fryers, cut up
Mexican Rice, below

1. Make Barbecue Sauce: In large saucepan, combine vinegar, sugar, mustard, salt, red and black pepper, Tabasco, onion, lemon, Worcestershire, and water; mix well. Bring to boiling; reduce heat, and simmer, uncovered, 20 minutes.
2. Add chili sauce and catsup; bring just to boiling.
3. Preheat oven to 400F. Wash chicken; pat dry with paper towels.
4. Place chicken, skin side down, in large shallow roasting pan.
5. Spoon some barbecue sauce over chicken. Bake 30 minutes; turn chicken, skin side up. Meanwhile, make Mexican Rice.
6. Brush chicken liberally with Barbecue Sauce; bake 30 minutes longer, basting frequently. Serve barbecued chicken with more of the sauce, if desired, and with Mexican Rice.
Makes 6 servings.

## MEXICAN RICE:

⅔ cup chopped onion
3 tablespoons bacon fat
1½ cups raw converted white rice
1 cup chopped green pepper
1 teaspoon chili powder
1 cup tomato juice
½ cup catsup
2 teaspoons salt
3 cups water
Chopped fresh tomato and chopped
   green pepper (optional)

1. In heavy 5-quart Dutch oven with tight-fitting cover, sauté onion in hot bacon fat. Stir in rice, 1 cup chopped green pepper, the chili powder, tomato juice, catsup, and salt.
2. Add water. Bring to boiling. Reduce heat; simmer, covered, 20 minutes, or until liquid is absorbed and rice is cooked. Garnish with chopped tomato and green pepper, if desired.
Makes 6 servings.

#  TORTILLAS

1½ cups yellow cornmeal (see Note)
1½ cups all-purpose flour
¾ teaspoon salt
3 tablespoons shortening
¾ cup warm water

1. In large bowl, combine cornmeal, flour, and salt. With pastry blender or 2 knives, cut in shortening until well blended.
2. Add water (use more if necessary), stirring until mixture is completely moistened. Form into ball.
3. On lightly floured surface, knead or work dough with hands until it is no longer sticky—about 5 minutes. Divide into 2 equal balls. Let dough rest 20 minutes at room temperature.
4. Shape each piece into 6-inch cylinder. Cut each into 6 parts. Form each into round ball; then roll out into 5¾-inch circle.
5. With paring knife, trim edge evenly. (Reuse trimmings.)
6. On heated, ungreased griddle, bake tortillas 1 minute. Turn, and bake 1 minute longer.
Makes 14.

*Note*: Authentic tortillas are made with *masa*, which is not nationally available. Our adaptation uses regular cornmeal.

# ✦ PINEAPPLE SOPAPILLAS

## PILLOWS:

2 cups sifted all-purpose flour
3 teaspoons baking powder
1 teaspoon salt
1 tablespoon peanut oil
¾ cup water

## FILLING:

2½ tablespoons sugar
2 tablespoons cornstarch
1 can (20 oz) crushed pineapple, un-
    drained

Peanut or salad oil for frying
Confectioners' sugar

1. Make Pillows: Sift flour with baking powder and salt into medium bowl.
2. Make well in center of ingredients. Pour in 1 tablespoon oil and the water; mix well with fork to form soft, smooth dough. Divide dough into 4 parts. With hands, knead each part 4 or 5 times—until smooth; form each part into round. On lightly floured pastry cloth, roll one part at a time into 8-by-4-by-¼-inch rectangle. Cut each rectangle into 4 pieces, each 2 by 4 inches; move to edge of pastry cloth to rest.
3. Make Filling: In medium saucepan, thoroughly combine sugar and cornstarch. With wooden spoon, stir in pineapple. Cook mixture over medium heat, stirring, until boiling; boil 1 minute, stirring constantly. Cool slightly.
4. In deep skillet, slowly heat peanut oil (at least 3 inches) to 385F on deep-frying thermometer. Gently drop dough pieces, 3 or 4 at a time, and fry until puffy —like pillows—about 1 minute. Turn and brown other side. With slotted utensil, lift from oil; drain well on paper towels.
5. While pillows are still hot, with sharp knife make slit along one long side and one short side of each. Gently lift up tops and fill each with slightly rounded tablespoon of warm filling.
6. Sprinkle tops with sifted confectioners' sugar. Serve warm.
Makes 16.

# ✦ MEXICAN HOT CHOCOLATE

¼ cup unsweetened cocoa
¼ cup sugar
¾ teaspoon ground cinnamon
Dash salt
1 quart milk
¼ cup light cream
¾ teaspoon vanilla extract

1. In small bowl, combine cocoa, sugar, cinnamon, and salt; mix well.
2. In medium saucepan, heat 1 cup milk until bubbling. Stir in cocoa mixture; beat with wire whisk or rotary beater until smooth.
3. Over low heat, bring to boiling, stirring. Gradually stir in rest of milk, return to boiling.
4. Stir in cream and vanilla; heat gently.
5. Before serving, beat with rotary beater until frothy.
Makes 6 servings.

# MEATS

◆ **M**aking friends with the butcher used to be the important first step to cooking good meals. The friendly shopkeeper who would save the "first cut" for a favorite customer or slice a steak the way he knew you liked it is harder to find—but still there in smaller butcher shops, as well as in supermarkets that have special fresh-cut meat sections. Even in large supermarkets that feature only packaged meat, you'll find that when you "ring the bell for service," an obliging man or woman will answer.

## SHOPPING FOR MEAT

When you're picking meat out of the refrigerated case, it's really helpful to know what to look for. Always check the date on packaged meat; it indicates the day it was cut and wrapped. Always buy the freshest possible meat.

*Beef.* This meat should be a bright red color and well marbled with creamy-white fat. The meat itself should be firm, with a fine grain.

*Veal.* This "young" meat should be a pale pink color and have very little fat. What there is should be firm, clear, and white.

*Lamb.* Lean lamb is pinkish red and marbled with clear-white firm fat. Cuts to be roasted, like the leg, should be well covered with firm fat.

*Pork.* The fat that covers pork should be free of moisture and the meat a pale pink to rose in color, firm, and fine grained.

## PORTIONS

The rule used to be ½ pound of meat per serving with the bone in. Boneless meat was generally computed at ¼ pound per serving, and very bony meat, like spare ribs, at ¾ to 1 pound per serving. However, many main dishes we cook these days use meat that is supplemented with vegetables, pasta, and other ingredients, so that these "standard" servings have to be checked with each recipe.

## STORING MEAT

Use ground or cut-up meat within a day—no more than 2—of purchase. If you find that you're not going to use it within this time, form the ground beef into small patties with squares of waxed paper in between, wrap carefully, and freeze. Other fresh meat can be stored 2 or 3 days in the coldest part of the refrigerator. If the fresh meat is tightly wrapped in plastic, loosen the wrapping a bit to allow for air circulation.

Cooked meat can be held in a covered dish in a refrigerator for up to 4 or 5 days.

Canned meat, like ham, should be stored in a cool place until you open it. After that, cover and carefully refrigerate any leftovers.

Cured meat will keep longer than fresh meat, but it should be placed in the refrigerator and lightly covered or wrapped.

# COOKING MEAT

The purpose of cooking meat is to break down, or soften, the connective tissues that hold the flesh together and to develop flavor, usually by browning. Whether you roast, broil, grill, or fry meat, the best way to get tender meat is to use low or moderate heat.

The timetables throughout this chapter are a tested guide to the time and temperature for perfectly cooked meat. All of our recipes carefully indicate time, method, and temperature, the important criteria for cooking meats.

# ROAST BEEF

The weekly "roast" served at Sunday dinner with leftovers is, for most of us, a thing of the past. The regal standing rib roast, for example, has become a dish for very special occasions. All the more reason, then, to cook such cuts with loving care. The rib roast, the rolled rib roast, the sirloin "silver tip," and the eye of round all do beautifully roasted in the oven at a steady low temperature—though the sirloin or eye of round should be of high quality or else marinated before use. Roast these last two only to rare, and slice them on the diagonal very thin.

Use a shallow pan, with a rack, except for the standing roast, which doesn't need one. Place the meat on the rack, fat side up. Don't cover the pan, don't add liquids—you'll get a pot roast if you do. Roast in a 325F oven, unless the recipe specifies otherwise. Use a meat thermometer inserted in the thickest part of the roast to test for doneness according to the chart below. Make sure the tip of the thermometer doesn't touch bone or fat. Let the roast rest for 15 to 20 minutes before you serve it. People devoted to very rare roasts should bear in mind that the beef will continue cooking somewhat during this resting period.

# BONELESS BEEF

A boneless top round will yield a roast or two, several steaks, and cubes for braising or grinding.

The boneless beef tip yields lean roasts, steaks to braise or pan-fry, and cubes for braising—or grinding, for good, lean hamburger.

The boneless rib-eye cut (or Delmonico) provides a variety of very special meals: steaks—which may be broiled, pan-fried, or pan-broiled—or roasts.

Boneless beef tenderloin can become a series of glorious filets mignon, or a combination of filets and center-cut roast, or it can be roasted whole. The tapered end offers cubes for elegant fondue, ragouts, or kebabs.

## TIMETABLE FOR ROASTING BEEF, 325F

| CUT | WEIGHT | APPROXIMATE ROASTING TIME | INTERNAL TEMPERATURE |
|-----|--------|---------------------------|----------------------|
| Rib roast, standing (bone in)* | 4 lb | 1¾ hr | 140F (rare) |
| | | 2¼ hr | 160F (medium) |
| | | 3 hr | 170F (well done) |
| | 6 lb | 3¼ hr | 140F (rare) |
| | | 3¾ hr | 160F (medium) |
| | | 4¼ hr | 170F (well done) |
| | 8 lb | 3½ hr | 140F (rare) |
| | | 4½ hr | 160F (medium) |
| | | 5 hr | 170F (well done) |
| Rib roast, boned and rolled** | 4 lb | 2¾ hr | 140F (rare) |
| | | 3¼ hr | 160F (medium) |
| | | 3½ hr | 170F (well done) |
| | 6 lb | 3½ hr | 140F (rare) |
| | | 4¼ hr | 160F (medium) |
| | | 4¾ hr | 170F (well done) |
| Sirloin-tip roast, Prime or Choice | 3–5 lb | 1¾–2½ hr | 140F (rare) |
| | | 2¼–3 hr | 160F (medium) |
| | | 2½–3½ hr | 170F (well done) |

*Ribs that measure approximately 6 inches from chine bone to tip of ribs. If ribs are cut longer, allow less roasting time.

**Diameter of roasts: 4 lb–4½ to 5 inches; 6 lb–5½ to 6 inches, Thinner roasts of same weight require less roasting time.

NOTE: It is advisable to use meat thermometer as extra precaution since roasts vary in size and shape, in amount of meat to bone, etc. Insert thermometer in thickest part of roast. Be sure tip is not touching bone or resting in fat.

# ❖ ROAST PRIME RIBS OF BEEF

3-rib roast of beef (about 7 lb)
1 tablespoon flour
1 teaspoon dry mustard
1 teaspoon salt
½ teaspoon pepper

1. Preheat oven to 325F. Wipe roast of beef with damp paper towels.
2. Combine flour, mustard, salt, and pepper. Rub all over beef.
3. Place roast, fat side up, with ribs as rack, in roasting pan. Insert meat thermometer through fat into center of roast; point should not rest on fat or bone.
4. Roast, uncovered, 3¼ hours, or until meat thermometer registers 140F, for rare; or 4¼ hours, 160F, for medium. (See timetable.)
5. Let roast stand 20 minutes, for easier carving.
6. Serve in its own juices or with Brown Gravy for Roast Beef, page 467.
Makes 8 servings.

# ❖ SAVORY ROAST BEEF WITH YORKSHIRE PUDDING

Standing 3-rib roast beef, bone in (8 to 9 lb)
½ teaspoon salt
¼ teaspoon dried marjoram leaves
¼ teaspoon dried thyme leaves
¼ teaspoon dried basil leaves
¼ teaspoon rubbed savory
⅛ teaspoon pepper
1 teaspoon liquid gravy seasoning
½ cup red Burgundy
Yorkshire Pudding, below
Burgundy Gravy for Roast Beef, page 467

1. Preheat oven to 325F. Wipe roast with damp paper towels. Mix salt with herbs and pepper.
2. Stand roast, fat side up, in shallow roasting pan. Rub salt mixture into beef on all sides. Insert meat thermometer through outside fat into thickest part of muscle (point should not rest on fat or bone).
3. Mix gravy seasoning with wine. Spoon some of mixture over beef.
4. Roast, uncovered, basting several times with remaining wine mixture, 3½ hours, or until meat thermometer registers 140F for rare; or 4½ hours, 160F, for medium. (See timetable.)
5. Get Yorkshire Pudding ingredients ready to assemble and bake when roast is done.
6. Remove roast to heated platter. Pour drippings into 2-cup measure. Let roast stand at room temperature while pudding is baking and you're making Burgundy Gravy. The roast will be easier to carve after standing 20 to 30 minutes.
Makes 8 to 10 servings.

## YORKSHIRE PUDDING:

2 eggs
1 cup milk
1 cup all-purpose flour
½ teaspoon salt
2 tablespoons roast-beef drippings

1. As soon as roast beef has been removed from oven, increase oven temperature to 425F.
2. In medium bowl, with rotary beater, beat eggs, milk, flour, and salt to make smooth batter.
3. Pour drippings into 10-inch pie plate; tilt to coat bottom and side of pie plate. Pour in batter.
4. Bake about 25 minutes, or until pudding is deep golden-brown. Serve immediately with roast beef.
Makes 8 servings.

## ROAST BEEF PROVENÇALE

*6½-lb boneless rib eye of beef*
*2 cups fresh white-bread crumbs*
*½ cup chopped parsley*
*2 cloves garlic, minced*
*2 teaspoons salt*
*½ teaspoon pepper*
*4 tablespoons Dijon-style mustard*
*½ cup butter or margarine, melted*

**BROWN GRAVY:**

*2 tablespoons meat drippings*
*3 tablespoons flour*
*1 can (10½ oz) condensed beef broth, undiluted*
*¼ teaspoon salt*
*Dash pepper*

1. Preheat oven to 325F. Wipe roast with damp paper towels. Place in open roasting pan.
2. Combine bread crumbs, parsley, garlic, 2 teaspoons salt, and ½ teaspoon pepper.
3. Spread mustard over top of roast. Firmly pat crumb mixture into mustard. Drizzle with butter. Insert meat thermometer into center of roast.
4. Roast, uncovered, 2 to 2¼ hours, or until meat thermometer registers 140F, for rare; or 2¼ to 3 hours, 160F, for medium. (See timetable.)
5. Let roast stand 20 minutes, for easier carving.
6. Make Brown Gravy: Pour off drippings in roasting pan. Return 2 tablespoons drippings to pan.
7. Stir flour into drippings in pan, to make smooth mixture; brown over low heat, stirring to loosen any brown bits in pan.
8. Add water to beef broth to measure 2 cups; slowly stir into flour mixture. Add salt and pepper. Bring to boiling, stirring gravy until smooth and bubbly. Makes 2 cups. Nice served with cauliflower and broccoli spears.

Makes 12 servings.

## BEEF WELLINGTON

*3-lb fillet of beef*
*½ teaspoon salt*
*¼ teaspoon pepper*
*¼ cup butter or margarine*
*1 pkg (17¼ oz) frozen puff pastry*
*½ cup prepared liver pâté*
*1 egg yolk*
*1 tablespoon water*
*Béarnaise Sauce, page 460*

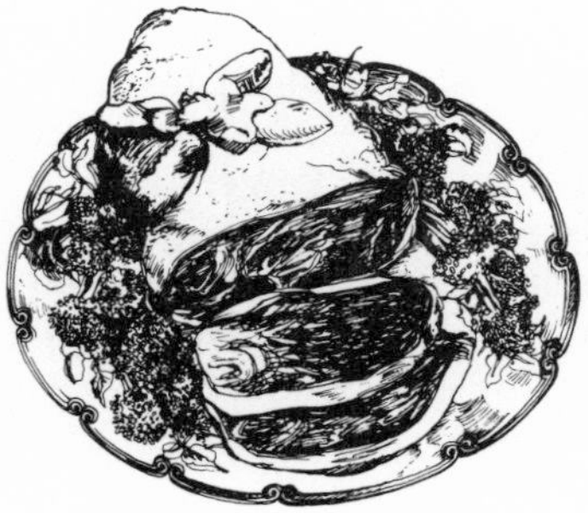

1. Preheat oven to 425F. Remove most of fat from fillet. Wipe with damp paper towels.
2. Rub salt and pepper over fillet. Place on rack in shallow roasting pan. Insert meat thermometer into thickest part. Roast 40 minutes, or to 140F, for rare; or to 160F for medium-rare. Let cool in pan.
3. Remove pastry from freezer. Let thaw at room temperature 20 minutes.
4. Preheat oven to 400F. Spread top of fillet with pâté.
5. Unfold 1 sheet of pastry (2 sheets in package). Wrap around fillet, tucking edges and sides underneath. (Cut 4-inch squares from second sheet to cover ends; press edges together to seal.) Decorate top with 4 puff-pastry leaves (cut pastry with 1½-inch leaf-shaped cookie cutter). Coil ½-inch strip of pastry to resemble rosette, and place on top.
6. In small bowl, beat together egg yolk and water. Brush leaves, rosette, and entire surface with egg-yolk mixture.
7. Bake 20 to 25 minutes, or until pastry is golden-brown.
8. To serve: Cut with sharp knife. Serve with Béarnaise Sauce.

Makes 8 servings.

# ROAST SIRLOIN OF BEEF

*3½-lb sirloin of beef*
*1 clove garlic, minced*
*1 teaspoon dry mustard*
*1 teaspoon salt*
*½ teaspoon pepper*

## GRAVY:

*¼ cup meat drippings*
*3 tablespoons flour*
*1 can (10½ oz) condensed beef broth, undiluted*
*Dash pepper*

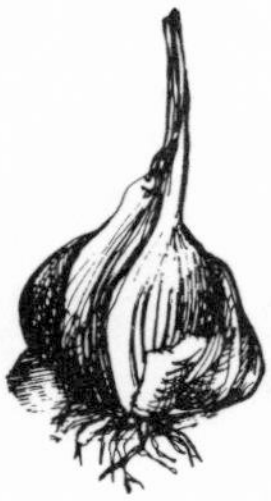

1. Preheat oven to 325F. Wipe sirloin roast with damp paper towels.
2. In small bowl, combine garlic, mustard, salt, and ½ teaspoon pepper. Rub all over beef.
3. Place roast, fat side up, in roasting pan. Insert meat thermometer through fat into center of roast.
4. Roast, uncovered, 1¼ hours, or until meat thermometer registers 140F, for rare; or 2 to 2¼ hours, 160F, for medium.
5. Let roast stand 20 minutes on heated platter for easier carving.
6. Make Gravy: Pour off fat and drippings in roasting pan; return ¼ cup to pan. Stir in flour, to make smooth mixture. Brown slightly over low heat, stirring to loosen any browned bits in pan.
7. Add water to beef broth to measure 2 cups. Gradually stir into flour mixture; add pepper.
8. Bring to boiling, stirring gravy until smooth and bubbly. Makes 2 cups.
9. To serve: Slice roast thin on diagonal. Pass gravy with roast.

Makes 8 servings.

# BROILED STEAK

Though trends in food change over the years, there is no doubt that for many Americans a good meal is by definition a good steak. Serving a luxurious steak is a way of celebrating, a way of saying to the people you're cooking for that you think that they're something special. And, of course, for the cook, serving steak is a treat because it means that in less than a half hour you can present a really festive and satisfying meal.

Whether your pocketbook allows you to buy a fillet, porterhouse, T-Bone, sirloin, or club, or whether you're using a chuck, flank, or round steak, the best way to cook steak is to broil it, either in the oven or over the charcoal grill. The trick here is precise timing combined with a precise distance from the heat. We've experimented with all sorts of methods over the years and have found that the following steps hold up best.

1. Trim excess fat from the steak; slash the remaining fat just to, not into, the meat.
2. Place the meat on a rack 2 or 3 inches from the heat for meat that is 1 inch thick or less; 3 to 5 inches from the heat for meat between 1 and 2 inches thick. Broil until the top is brown, or about half the time in the charts below. Turn the meat with tongs (do not use a fork, or the juices will escape) and brown it on the other side for the remaining time. Season the meat with salt and pepper *after* it is done. Note that barbecuing steaks calls for searing a steak over high heat for a short length of time on the first side and cooking the second side over medium heat for a longer time.
3. If your meat is especially thick, you may want to test its doneness with a meat thermometer or, better still, by cutting a slit near the bone to check the color of the meat.

## TIMETABLE FOR BROILING STEAKS

| CUT | THICKNESS | APPROXIMATE MINUTES PER SIDE | | |
|---|---|---|---|---|
| | | RARE | MEDIUM | WELL DONE |
| Fillet | 1 inch | 3 min | 5 min | 6–7 min |
| | 1½ inches | 8 min | 9 min | 11 min |
| Porterhouse | 1 inch | 6 min | 8 min | 11 min |
| | 1½ inches | 8 min | 10 min | 14 min |
| T-bone | 1 inch | 6 min | 8 min | 11 min |
| | 1½ inches | 9–10 min | 11–12 min | 14–15 min |
| Rib | 1 inch | 5–6 min | 7 min | 8–9 min |
| | 1½ inches | 9–10 min | 11–12 min | 14–15 min |
| Club | 1 inch | 5–6 min | 7 min | 8–9 min |
| | 1½ inches | 9 min | 11 min | 14–15min |
| Delmonico (rib-eye) | 1 inch | 5 min | 7 min | 8–9 min |
| | 1½ inches | 9 min | 11–12 min | 14–15 min |
| Shell or strip | 1 inch | 5 min | 7 min | 8–9 min |
| | 1½ inches | 9 min | 10–11 min | 14–15 min |
| Sirloin | 1 inch | 8–9 min | 10 min | 12 min |
| | 1½ inches | 12–14 min | 14–15 min | 17–18 min |
| Sirloin butt | 1 inch | 4 min | 6 min | |
| | 1½ inches | 12 min | 14 min | |
| Sirloin tip | 1 inch | 10 min | 11–12 min | |
| | 1½ inches | 12 min | 14 min | |
| Flank | ¾ inch | 2 min | 3 min | |
| | 1 inch | 3 min | 4 min | |
| Butterfly (eye of round) | 1 inch | 4 min | 6 min | |
| | 1½ inches | 8–9 min | 10 min | |
| Ground sirloin, round, or chuck patties | ¾ inch | 4 min | 6 min | 7 min |

NOTE: For steaks at room temperature in preheated broiler.
Broil 1-inch-thick steaks (flank steak, ¾ inch) 3 inches from heat.
Broil 1½-inch-thick steaks (flank steak, 1 inch) 4 inches from heat.

## TIMETABLE FOR BARBECUING STEAKS

| CUT | THICKNESS | APPROXIMATE MINUTES PER SIDE | |
|---|---|---|---|
| | | FIRST SIDE | SECOND SIDE |
| Club, rib, rib-eye, T-bone, porterhouse, sirloin | 1¼ inches | Sear on high, direct heat, 3–5 min | Medium to low heat Rare: 8 min Medium: 10 min Well: 12–15 min |
| Top round, chuck | 1¼ inches | Marinate to tenderize; sear on high, direct heat, 5–8 min | Medium to low heat Rare: 7–10 min Medium: 12 min Well: 15 min |

| | | APPROXIMATE MINUTES PER SIDE | |
| CUT | THICKNESS | FIRST SIDE | SECOND SIDE |
| --- | --- | --- | --- |
| Flank | ¾ inch | Score both sides; marinate; sear on high, direct heat, 3–5 min | High, direct heat<br>Rare: 3 min<br>Medium: 5 min |
| London broil | 2 inches | Marinate. Sear on high, direct heat, 8 min | Medium to low heat<br>Rare: 20 min<br>Medium: 22 min |
| Ground sirloin, round or chuck patties | 1 inch | Sear on high, direct heat, 4 min | Medium to low heat<br>Rare: 8–10 min<br>Medium: 12–16 min |

NOTE: For steaks at room temperature.
To retain juiciness, thick steaks should be seared over high heat, then cooked at medium to low heat to finish. Raise grid of grill or spread coals apart to reduce heat.

# ❖ RIB STEAKS WITH MUSTARD AND HERBS

2 (1½-lb size) rib-eye (Delmonico) steaks, 1½ inches thick
½ teaspoon dried marjoram leaves
½ teaspoon dried thyme leaves
1 teaspoon cracked black peppercorns
6 tablespoons dry mustard
3 tablespoons dry white wine
1 tablespoon chopped parsley
1 tablespoon finely chopped chives

1. Wipe steaks with damp paper towels. In small bowl, combine marjoram, thyme, and ½ teaspoon cracked peppercorns. Rub herb mixture on each side of steak.
2. In small bowl, combine mustard, ½ teaspoon cracked peppercorns, and wine to form paste.
3. Spread half of mustard paste smoothly on one side of each steak; allow to stand, uncovered, at room temperature 30 minutes.
4. Place steaks, mustard side up, on broiler rack of oven or broiler unit. Broil steaks, 4 inches from heat source, 8 minutes.
5. Remove steaks from broiler. Turn, and spread with remaining mustard paste. Return steaks to broiler, and continue to broil 6 to 8 minutes, or until steaks are cooked rare to medium and mustard paste is golden-brown and crusty.
6. To serve: Place on steak board. Sprinkle with parsley and chives.
Makes 8 servings.

# ✖ LONDON BROIL

2-lb flank steak
1 tablespoon salad oil
2 teaspoons chopped parsley
1 clove garlic, crushed
1 teaspoon salt
1 teaspoon lemon juice
⅛ teaspoon pepper
Maître d'Hôtel Butter Sauce, page 463.

1. With sharp knife, trim excess fat from steak. Wipe with damp paper towels. Lay steak on cutting board.
2. Combine salad oil, parsley, garlic, salt, lemon juice, and pepper. Brush half of mixture over steak; let stand about 45 minutes.
3. Place steak, oil side up, on lightly greased broiler pan. Broil, about 4 inches from heat, 5 minutes. Turn steak; brush with remaining oil mixture; broil 4 to 5 minutes longer. The steak will be rare, the only way London broil should be served.
4. Remove steak to board or platter. Slice very thin on diagonal, across grain. Serve with Maître d'Hôtel Sauce.
Makes 4 servings.

# ✖ FLORENTINE CHUCK STEAK

¼ cup olive or salad oil
¼ cup lemon juice
½ teaspoon salt
½ teaspoon coarsely ground pepper
4¼- to 5-lb beef round-bone chuck steak, about 2 inches thick
Lemon wedges (optional)

1. Combine olive oil, lemon juice, salt, and pepper; mix well. Place steak in mixture and refrigerate for about 1 hour, turning occasionally.
2. Wipe steak with damp paper towels. Place on rack in broiler pan; brush with about 2 tablespoons oil mixture. Broil, 5 inches from heat, 20 minutes. Turn steak, and brush with more oil mixture. Broil 20 minutes longer, for rare.
3. To serve: Slice thin. Drizzle with any remaining oil mixture. Garnish with lemon wedges, if desired.
Makes 8 to 10 servings.

# ✠ TOURNEDOS NIÇOISE

## TOMATO SAUCE:

*1 green pepper*
*4 tablespoons olive or salad oil*
*2 lb fresh tomatoes, very ripe*
*1 red onion, chopped*
*2 tablespoons chopped parsley*
*2 teaspoons salt*
*½ teaspoon sugar*
*1 teaspoon dried tarragon leaves*
*½ teaspoon dried thyme leaves*
*6 slices fillet of beef, 1 inch thick*
*2 tablespoons butter or margarine,*
  *melted*
*¼ teaspoon pepper*

*6 anchovy fillets, drained*
*6 black pitted olives*

1. Make Tomato Sauce: Slice green pepper lengthwise into ¼-inch strips, removing seeds and ribs. In 1 tablespoon hot oil in medium skillet, sauté pepper strips, stirring frequently, 5 minutes.
2. Scald tomatoes in boiling water to cover a few minutes; peel skin with paring knife. Cut tomatoes into chunks, discarding seeds.
3. In 3 tablespoons hot oil in large skillet, sauté onion, combined with parsley, until onion is transparent, not browned—about 5 minutes. Add tomato, 1 teaspoon salt, the sugar, tarragon, and thyme. Cook, uncovered and stirring occasionally, over medium heat about 30 minutes.
4. About 15 minutes before sauce is done, broil fillets: Wipe beef with damp paper towels. Arrange on greased broiler rack. Brush with 1 tablespoon melted butter; sprinkle with ½ teaspoon salt and ⅛ teaspoon pepper.
5. Broil, 4 inches from heat, 5 minutes. Turn fillets. Brush with remaining melted butter; sprinkle with ½ teaspoon salt and ⅛ teaspoon pepper. Broil 5 minutes longer, for medium-rare.
6. To serve: Arrange on heated serving platter. Place an anchovy and black olive on top of each fillet. Surround with tomato sauce.
Makes 6 servings.

# BRAISED AND SIMMERED MEATS

The recipes in this section include pot roasts and other meats that are either braised or simmered. These are methods of cooking that are good for less tender cuts, such as top and bottom round, rump, chuck, and flank. The meats are usually browned slowly on all sides in a heavy pan and then cooked with liquid in a tightly covered pan for several hours. You can make these recipes either on top of the stove or in the oven. As you will see, the meat is cooked at low temperatures to give it time for the flavor to develop and the meat to become tender. The gravy, or cooking liquid, from braised or simmered beef has a superb flavor and contains many of the nutrients from the meat and vegetables. Serve it, skimmed of fat, of course, as an integral part of the meat dish.

## PERFECT POT ROAST

*4- to 5-lb beef rump roast*
*2 tablespoons salad oil*
*2 tablespoons butter or margarine*
*1 small onion, sliced*
*1 clove garlic, crushed*
*1 teaspoon dried thyme leaves*
*1 teaspoon dried marjoram leaves*
*1 bay leaf, crumbled*
*8 whole black peppercorns*
*1 teaspoon salt*
*1 can (10½ oz) condensed beef broth, undiluted (see Note)*
*8 carrots (1 lb), pared and halved*
*12 small white onions*
*1 sprig parsley*

### GRAVY:

*2 cups meat drippings*
*3 tablespoons flour*
*¼ cup water*
*Salt (optional)*

1. Wipe pot roast with damp paper towels. Heat oil and butter in 5-quart Dutch oven or heavy kettle over medium heat. Add roast and sliced onion.
2. Turn roast occasionally with two wooden spoons, until well browned on all sides—25 minutes in all.
3. Add garlic, thyme, marjoram, bay leaf, peppercorns, and salt to pan. Cook ½ minute to restore flavor to herbs.
4. Add beef broth; bring to boiling. Reduce heat, and simmer, covered, for 2½ hours, turning meat occasionally.
5. Add carrots, onions, and parsley. Simmer, covered, 30 minutes, or until vegetables and meat are tender.
6. Remove meat and vegetables from Dutch oven to warm platter; keep in warm place, covered loosely with foil.
7. Make Gravy: Strain liquid remaining in Dutch oven into a 2-cup measure. If necessary, add water to make 2 cups liquid. Pour back into Dutch oven. In small bowl, combine flour with ¼ cup water, and mix with fork until smooth. Stir flour mixture into liquid in Dutch oven; bring to boiling, stirring. Reduce heat, and simmer 3 minutes. Taste; add salt, if desired.
8. To serve: Slice meat, and spoon a little of the gravy over it. Pass remaining gravy with meat and vegetables.

Serves 10.

*Note*: To vary flavor, you may substitute 1⅓ cups tomato juice, stewed tomatoes, beer, or red wine for beef broth.

## FRUITED POT ROAST

*5-lb chuck roast*
*2 teaspoons salt*
*¼ teaspoon pepper*
*2 tablespoons shortening*
*1 cup chopped carrot*
*1 cup chopped onion*
*1 clove garlic, crushed*
*1 can (1 lb) tomatoes, undrained*
*1 cup pitted prunes*
*½ cup dried apricots*
*½ cup raisins*

1. Wipe roast with damp paper towels. Trim excess fat.
2. Rub salt and pepper into surface of meat.
3. In hot shortening in 6-quart Dutch oven, brown meat with carrot, onion, and garlic over high heat, turning to brown on all sides—about 20 minutes.
4. Meanwhile, preheat oven to 350F.
5. Pour tomatoes over roast. Bake, covered, about 2 hours.
6. Add prunes, apricots, and raisins to Dutch oven. Bake, covered, ½ hour, or until beef is tender.
7. Remove roast and dried fruits to warm serving platter; keep warm.

**GRAVY:**

*3 tablespoons flour*
*½ cup cold water*
*Pan juices*

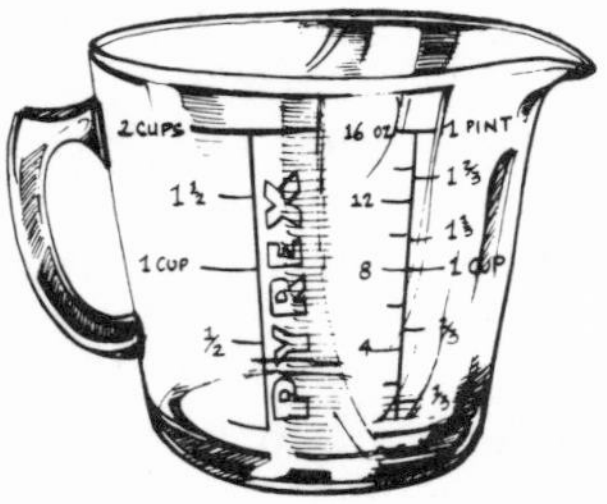

8. Pour pan drippings into 2-cup measure. Skim off and discard fat. Add water to make 2 cups. Return to Dutch oven.
9. Make Gravy: In small bowl, stir flour with ½ cup cold water until smooth. Stir into pan juices in Dutch oven; bring to boiling, stirring. Reduce heat, and simmer 3 minutes; strain. Serve with roast.
Makes 8 servings.

## ✦ SAVORY BRAISED SHORT RIBS

*4 lb beef short ribs, in serving-size pieces*
*1 cup coarsely chopped onion*
*1 clove garlic, crushed*
*4 whole black peppercorns*
*1 bay leaf*
*2 teaspoons Worcestershire sauce*
*½ teaspoon dried marjoram leaves*
*1 can (10½ oz) condensed beef broth, undiluted*
*1 cup water*

**HORSERADISH CREAM:**

*½ cup heavy cream*
*¼ cup sour cream*
*2 tablespoons prepared horseradish*
*1 teaspoon prepared mustard*
*⅛ teaspoon salt*

*3 tablespoons flour*
*½ cup water*
*Tomato wedges*
*Parsley sprigs*

1. Wipe short ribs with damp paper towels. If necessary, trim excess fat.
2. Slowly heat Dutch oven. Add short ribs, fat side down; over medium heat, brown well on all sides—about 30 minutes. Discard drippings.
3. Add onion, garlic, peppercorns, bay leaf, Worcestershire, marjoram, broth, and 1 cup water; bring to boiling. Reduce heat, and simmer, covered and turning meat once, 1½ to 2 hours, or until tender.
4. Meanwhile, make Horseradish Cream: In small bowl, beat heavy cream until stiff. Stir in sour cream, horseradish, mustard, and salt. Refrigerate, covered, until needed.
5. Remove short ribs to serving platter; keep warm. Skim fat from pan juices.
6. Mix flour with ½ cup water until smooth. Stir into pan juices; bring to boiling, stirring. Reduce heat, and simmer 3 minutes. Strain, and pour over short ribs. Garnish with tomato wedges and parsley. Pass Horseradish Cream.
Makes 8 servings.

# ✖ BEEF STROGANOFF

2-lb fillet of beef, ½ inch thick
6 tablespoons butter or margarine
1 cup chopped onion
1 clove garlic, finely chopped
½ lb fresh mushrooms, sliced ¼ inch
   thick
3 tablespoons flour
1 tablespoon catsup
½ teaspoon salt
⅛ teaspoon pepper
1 can (10½ oz) condensed beef broth,
   undiluted
¼ cup dry white wine
1 tablespoon snipped fresh dill or ¼
   teaspoon dried dillweed
1½ cups sour cream
5 cups cooked white rice
2 tablespoons snipped fresh dill or
   parsley

1. Trim fat from beef. Cut crosswise into ½-inch-thick slices. Cut each slice across grain into ½-inch-wide strips.
2. Slowly heat large heavy skillet. In it, melt 2 tablespoons butter. Add just enough beef strips to cover skillet bottom. Over high heat, sear quickly on all sides. With tongs, remove beef strips as they brown. (They should be browned outside, rare inside.) Brown rest of beef; set aside.
3. In remaining hot butter in same skillet, sauté onion, garlic, and mushrooms until onion is golden —about 5 minutes. Remove from heat. Add flour, catsup, salt, and pepper; stir until smooth. Gradually add beef broth; bring to boiling, stirring. Reduce heat; simmer 5 minutes.
4. Over low heat, add wine, 1 tablespoon snipped dill, and sour cream, stirring until well combined. Add beef; simmer just until sauce and beef are hot.
5. Serve Stroganoff with rice. Sprinkle dill or parsley over top.
Makes 6 servings.

# ✖ BRAISED SWISS STEAK, FAMILY-STYLE

2½-lb beef round steak, 1½ inches
   thick (see Note)
½ cup flour
1½ teaspoons salt
½ teaspoon pepper
⅓ cup salad oil
2 cups sliced onion
1 can (1 lb) tomatoes
½ cup water
½ teaspoon dried thyme leaves
1 bay leaf

1. Wipe steak with damp paper towels. Combine flour, salt, and pepper.
2. Spread half of flour mixture on wooden board. Place steak on flour mixture, and sprinkle with remaining flour mixture. Pound it into both sides of steak, using wooden mallet, until all of flour mixture has been pounded in.
3. In hot oil in large skillet, over medium heat, brown steak well on both sides—about 20 minutes in all. Sauté onion with steak during last 5 minutes.
4. Add tomatoes, water, thyme, and bay leaf; bring to boiling. Reduce heat, and simmer, covered, 1 hour. Turn steak, and simmer 1 hour longer, or until tender. Remove steak to heated platter.
5. Bring sauce in skillet to boiling, stirring to loosen any browned bits in pan.
6. Arrange onion on steak. Pour sauce around it.
Makes 6 servings.

*Note*: A 3½-lb blade-bone chuck steak, 1½ inches thick, may be used instead of round steak. Prepare as above, braising about 15 minutes longer. After removing steak to platter, pour pan liquid into 2-cup measure. Pour off excess fat—there should be about 1 cup liquid left. Thicken if desired.

# ✛ HUNGARIAN GOULASH

¼ cup salad oil
3-lb boneless beef chuck, cut into
    1-inch cubes
1 lb onions, sliced
1 tablespoon paprika
1½ teaspoons salt
⅛ teaspoon pepper
1 can (10½ oz) condensed beef broth,
    undiluted
3 tablespoons flour
1 cup sour cream
Poppy-Seed Noodles, page 335

1. In Dutch oven, heat oil over high heat. Add beef cubes, in single layer at a time, and cook over medium heat until cubes are well browned on all sides. As they brown, remove to bowl. This will take about 15 to 20 minutes in all.
2. Add onion to drippings; sauté until tender and golden-brown—about 10 minutes.
3. Return meat to Dutch oven. Add paprika, salt, and pepper, stirring until well blended with meat. Stir in ¾ cup beef broth.
4. Bring to boiling; then reduce heat, and simmer, covered, for 2 hours, or until beef cubes are fork-tender.
5. In small bowl, combine flour and remaining beef broth, stirring until smooth. Gradually add to beef mixture, stirring constantly. Simmer, uncovered and stirring occasionally, 15 minutes longer.
6. Just before serving, place sour cream in small bowl. Slowly add ½ cup hot gravy. Slowly add to beef mixture, stirring until well blended. Heat, but do not boil. Serve goulash with Poppy-Seed Noodles.
Makes 6 servings.

# ✛ NEW ENGLAND BOILED DINNER

4- to 5-lb corned-beef brisket
1 clove garlic, crushed
2 whole cloves
10 whole black peppercorns
2 bay leaves
8 medium carrots, pared
8 medium potatoes, peeled
8 medium yellow onions, peeled
1 medium head cabbage, cut into 8
    wedges
2 tablespoons butter or margarine
Chopped parsley
Mustard Sauce, page 463

1. Wipe corned beef with damp paper towels. Place in large kettle; cover with cold water. Add garlic, cloves, black peppercorns, and bay leaves.
2. Bring to boiling; reduce heat, and simmer 5 minutes. Skim surface; then simmer, covered, 3 to 4 hours, or until meat is fork-tender.
3. Add carrots, potatoes, and onions during last 25 minutes. Add cabbage during last 20 minutes. Cook just until vegetables are tender.
4. To serve: Slice corned beef thin across the grain. Arrange on one side of serving platter. Place cabbage wedges beside meat. Brush potatoes with butter, and place in serving dish; sprinkle with parsley. Arrange carrots and onions in another dish. Pass Mustard Sauce.
Makes 8 servings.

# ❖ OXTAIL RAGOUT

4 lb oxtails, cut crosswise into 2-inch
   pieces (if frozen, let thaw)
5 tablespoons flour
¼ cup butter or margarine
1 cup chopped celery
1 cup chopped onion
4 sprigs parsley
1 clove garlic, crushed
¼ teaspoon whole black peppercorns
2 teaspoons salt
1 teaspoon dried thyme leaves
2 bay leaves
1 can (10½ oz) condensed beef broth,
   undiluted
2¼ cups cold water
1 cup hot tomato juice
8 carrots (1½ lb), pared and cut into
   1½-inch pieces
2 lb potatoes, peeled and halved
Chopped parsley (optional)

1. Day before: Wash oxtails under cold water; dry with paper towels. Coat oxtails with 3 tablespoons flour. In some of hot butter in 6-quart Dutch oven, brown oxtails, half at a time, turning with tongs to brown well all over; add butter as needed. Lift out oxtails, as they are browned. (Slow browning gives better flavor and color—takes about 30 minutes in all.)

2. To fat in Dutch oven, add celery, onion, parsley sprigs, garlic, peppercorns, salt, and thyme and bay leaves. Sauté over medium heat, stirring, until onion is golden—about 5 minutes.

3. Add browned oxtails, beef broth, and 2 cups water. Bring to boiling. Reduce heat; simmer, covered, over low heat 3 hours, or until oxtails are tender. Remove from heat; stir in tomato juice. Cool to room temperature; refrigerate, covered, overnight.

4. Next day, about 1 hour before serving: With metal spoon, skim off hardened layer of fat from surface and discard. Heat oxtails slowly over low heat, stirring occasionally; bring just to boiling point.

5. Meanwhile, prepare carrots and potatoes. Add to oxtail mixture; bring back to boiling. Reduce heat, and simmer, covered, until vegetables are tender when pierced with fork—30 minutes.

6. To 2 tablespoons flour in small bowl, stir in ¼ cup cold water; mix with fork until smooth. Stir into bubbling liquid in Dutch oven. Simmer, stirring occasionally, until sauce has thickened—about 5 minutes. Sprinkle top of ragout with chopped parsley, if desired.

Makes 8 servings.

# GROUND BEEF

It is, it has been said, harder to make a great hamburger than a soufflé. Ground beef, just because of its relative economy and frequent use, should not be treated carelessly. You'll find several grades of ground beef. The package labeled ground beef will (legally) contain the most fat, and since fat weighs, it may not be cheaper than the next grade, ground chuck. Both are fine for meat loaves and meatballs, where the fat cooks out and may be discarded. Ground beef round or, if you're splurging, ground sirloin tip are best for hamburgers. Handle good ground meat as little as possible, shape it gently, and cook it carefully —it's just as rewarding as a roast.

# ❖ MEAT LOAF DELUXE

2 eggs
½ cup milk
1½ teaspoons salt
1 teaspoon dried thyme leaves
⅛ teaspoon nutmeg
Dash pepper
1½ cups soft white-bread crumbs
2 lb ground beef chuck
½ lb ground pork
¼ cup chopped parsley
¼ cup finely chopped onion

## MASHED-POTATO TOPPING:

8 medium potatoes (about 2½ lb)
1 tablespoon salt
½ cup milk
¼ cup butter or margarine
⅛ teaspoon white pepper
Dash ground red pepper
2 egg yolks

Parsley sprigs

1. Preheat oven to 350F. In large bowl, beat 2 eggs with ½ cup milk, 1½ teaspoons salt, the thyme, nutmeg, and pepper. Stir in bread crumbs. Let mixture stand 5 minutes.
2. Add ground meats, chopped parsley, and onion; mix lightly with fork until well combined. Grease 9-by-5-by-2¾-inch loaf pan. Pack in meat-loaf mixture. Bake 60 minutes.
3. Make Mashed-Potato Topping: Peel potatoes; cut into quarters. Cook in 1 inch boiling water with 1 tablespoon salt, covered, until tender—20 minutes. Drain well; return to saucepan.
4. Beat with portable electric mixer (or mash with potato masher) until smooth. Heat, slowly stirring, over low heat, to dry out—about 3 minutes.
5. In saucepan, heat milk and butter until butter melts—don't let milk boil.
6. Gradually beat hot milk mixture into potato until potato is smooth, light, and fluffy; beat in white pepper, red pepper, and egg yolks.
7. Remove meat loaf from oven. Swirl mashed potato evenly over entire surface.
8. Return to oven; bake until potato topping is slightly golden. Serve garnished with parsley.
Makes 10 servings.

# ❖ HAMBURGERS BASQUAISE

## SAUCE:

1 medium-size red pepper (8 oz)
2 medium zucchini (1 lb)
2 tablespoons salad or olive oil
½ cup sliced onion
1 teaspoon salt
½ teaspoon dried oregano leaves
½ teaspoon dried tarragon leaves
⅛ teaspoon crushed dried hot red pepper flakes
2 medium tomatoes, peeled and quartered

1½ lb ground beef chuck
Chopped parsley

1. Make Sauce: Wash pepper, and cut in half. Remove ribs and seeds. Cut pepper lengthwise into ¼-inch-thick slices.
2. Scrub zucchini. Cut on diagonal into ¼-inch-thick slices.
3. In hot oil in large skillet, sauté red pepper, zucchini, and onion 5 minutes, or until onion is transparent.
4. Add salt, oregano, tarragon, and pepper flakes; mix lightly to combine.
5. Cook over medium heat, covered, 10 minutes.
6. Layer tomato quarters on top; cook, covered, 5 minutes, or until vegetables are tender and water has evaporated. Keep warm.
7. Make hamburgers: Shape chuck gently into 6 thick patties. Preheat broiler. Arrange patties on cold broiler rack. Broil, 3 inches from heat, turning once, 8 to 10 minutes, or until desired doneness.
8. Serve covered with sauce and sprinkled with parsley.
Makes 6 servings.

# ✦ BEEF BALLS EN BROCHETTE

## MARINADE:

¼ cup salad oil
2 tablespoons chopped onion
1 clove garlic, crushed
1 teaspoon Worcestershire sauce
1 teaspoon dried oregano leaves
½ teaspoon dried basil leaves

## MEATBALLS:

1 egg
1½ lb ground beef chuck
½ teaspoon salt
Dash pepper
½ cup dry bread crumbs

1 medium zucchini
1 medium-size yellow squash
2 cups water
¼ teaspoon salt
8 cherry tomatoes
4 cups fluffy cooked rice

1. Make Marinade: In shallow glass baking dish, combine all marinade ingredients; mix well.
2. Make Meatballs: In large bowl, with fork, beat egg. Stir in ground beef, ½ teaspoon salt, the pepper, and bread crumbs; mix until well combined.
3. Using hands, shape into 24 meatballs, each 1 inch in diameter. Add meatballs to marinade. Refrigerate, covered, 1 hour, turning occasionally.
4. Meanwhile, scrub zucchini and yellow squash. Cut crosswise into 8 (1-inch) slices.
5. In 10-inch skillet, bring water and ¼ teaspoon salt to boiling. Add zucchini and squash. Reduce heat and simmer, covered, 5 minutes, until tender. Drain.
6. Remove meatballs from marinade; reserve marinade.
7. On 8 skewers, thread 3 meatballs alternately with zucchini, squash, and 1 tomato. Brush with marinade.
8. Place skewers on broiler rack. Broil, 6 inches from heat, 5 to 7 minutes. Turn; brush all over with marinade. Broil 5 to 7 minutes longer, or until nicely browned.
9. To serve: Place skewers on rice on heated large serving platter.
Makes 8 servings.

# ✦ BEEF BALLS STROGANOFF

## BEEF BALLS:

1 lb ground beef chuck
¾ teaspoon salt
¼ teaspoon pepper
2 teaspoons bottled steak sauce
¼ cup dry bread crumbs
1 egg
2 tablespoons butter or margarine

## SAUCE:

2 tablespoons butter or margarine
½ cup sliced onion
¼ lb mushrooms, sliced
2 tablespoons flour
1 teaspoon catsup
1 can (10½ oz) condensed beef broth, undiluted
1 cup sour cream
Cooked rice or noodles

1. Make Beef Balls: In large bowl, lightly toss ground beef with salt, pepper, steak sauce, bread crumbs, and egg until well combined.
2. Using hands, gently shape chuck mixture into 12 balls, each about 1½ inches in diameter.
3. In 2 tablespoons hot butter in large skillet, brown beef balls well all over. Remove beef balls.
4. Make Sauce: To drippings in skillet, add 2 tablespoons butter. Sauté onion 5 minutes. Add mushrooms; sauté 5 minutes longer, stirring. Remove from heat. Stir in flour and catsup.
5. Gradually stir in broth; bring to boiling, stirring. Reduce heat, and simmer, uncovered, 2 minutes.
6. Add beef balls; simmer gently, uncovered, 10 minutes, or until heated through.
7. Stir in sour cream; heat gently over low heat. Serve over rice or noodles.
Makes 6 servings.

# ⊠ NEAPOLITAN CASSEROLE

1½ lb ground beef chuck
1 cup finely chopped onion
1 cup chopped green pepper
2 cloves garlic, crushed
2 teaspoons dried basil leaves
1 teaspoon fennel seed
⅛ teaspoon crushed red pepper flakes
2 tablespoons sugar
1 tablespoon salt
1 can (2 lb, 3 oz) Italian-style
   tomatoes, undrained
1 lb fresh spinach
½ pkg (1-lb size) medium shell macaroni
1 cup grated sharp Cheddar cheese

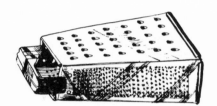

1. In 5-quart Dutch oven, over medium heat, sauté ground beef (break up into chunks with wooden spoon), onion, green pepper, garlic, basil, fennel seed, and red pepper flakes, stirring frequently, until meat is browned and vegetables are tender—about 20 minutes. Drain off fat.
2. Add sugar, salt, and tomatoes, mashing tomatoes with wooden spoon. Bring to boiling. Reduce heat, and simmer, uncovered and stirring occasionally, until thickened—20 minutes.
3. Wash spinach thoroughly, and remove stems. Place in large kettle. Cook, covered and stirring occasionally, 4 to 6 minutes, or just until leaves are wilted. Drain well; reserve.
4. Preheat oven to 350F.
5. In large kettle, cook shell macaroni according to package directions for firm macaroni; drain well. In large kettle, combine sauce, spinach, and shell macaroni; toss lightly to mix well. Turn out into 3-quart casserole.
6. Sprinkle with grated cheese. Bake, uncovered, 30 minutes, or until bubbly and lightly browned.
Makes 8 servings.

# ⊠ CORNISH PASTIES

2 pkg (11-oz size) piecrust mix

**FILLING:**

3 cups thinly sliced quartered peeled
   potato
1 cup coarsely chopped pared carrot
¼ cup chopped parsley
1½ teaspoons salt
½ teaspoon pepper
1 lb ground beef chuck

¼ cup butter or margarine
1 egg, beaten

1. Prepare pastry as package label directs. Form into ball. Wrap in waxed paper, and refrigerate until ready to use.
2. Make Filling: In large bowl, combine potato, carrot, parsley, salt, pepper, and ground beef; mix well.
3. To make pasties: Preheat oven to 425F. On lightly floured pastry cloth, divide pastry into 8 parts; roll each part into 8-inch circle. Moisten edge of each circle.
4. Spread ½ cup filling on half of each circle. Dot with butter; fold over. Fold edge of bottom crust over top; crimp edges. Make 2 gashes in center for steam to escape. Brush with beaten egg.
5. Bake, on ungreased cookie sheet, about 30 minutes, or until potato and carrot are tender.
6. Remove to wire rack. Serve hot or cold.
Makes 8 servings.

# PORK

Pork should no longer be shunned by weight-conscious people. Today's pork has a much smaller ratio of fat to lean, and it is an excellent source, not just of protein but of two important B vitamins, thiamine and niacin. The internal temperature of well-done pork—and fresh pork should always be well done—has been a source of conflict among cooking authorities. Our roasting chart reflects the result of many tests and the way we like it.

## TIMETABLE FOR ROASTING FRESH PORK, 325F

| CUT | WEIGHT | INTERNAL TEMPERATURE | APPROXIMATE ROASTING TIME |
|---|---|---|---|
| Fresh ham, bone in | 10–14 lb | 170F | 3¾–6 hr (22–26 min/lb) |
| Fresh ham, half, bone in | 5–6 lb | 170F | 2–4 hr (35–40 min/lb) |
| Center loin | 4–5 lb | 170F | 2–3¼ hr (30–35 min/lb) |
| Blade loin or sirloin | 3–4 lb | 170F | 2–3 hr (40–45 min/lb) |
| Picnic shoulder, bone in | 5–8 lb | 170F | 3–4½ hr (30–35 min/lb) |

NOTE: It is advisable to use meat thermometer as extra precaution since roasts vary in size and shape, in amount of meat to bone, etc. Insert thermometer in thickest part of roast. Be sure tip is not touching bone or resting in fat.

## ✦ ROAST PORK BOULANGER

3½-lb center pork loin
1 clove garlic, slivered
4½ teaspoons salt
½ teaspoon dried thyme leaves
¼ teaspoon plus ⅛ teaspoon pepper
3 lb medium potatoes, peeled and thinly sliced
1 cup chopped onion
1 tablespoon chopped parsley
½ cup canned condensed chicken broth, undiluted
¼ cup butter or margarine, melted
1 teaspoon paprika
Chopped parsley

1. Preheat oven to 425F. Wipe pork with damp paper towels. Trim off excess fat.
2. Rub outside of pork with cut garlic; then insert garlic slivers where possible in crevices. Combine 1½ teaspoons salt, the thyme, and ¼ teaspoon pepper; rub mixture all over surface. Place pork, fat side up, in large shallow roasting pan.
3. Roast 45 minutes. Remove pork from oven; discard fat in roasting pan.
4. Gently toss potatoes with onion, 1 tablespoon chopped parsley, and the remaining salt and pepper. Arrange around roast. Heat chicken broth to boiling; pour over potatoes. Brush potatoes with melted butter. Sprinkle with paprika.
5. Reduce oven to 400F. Roast pork 1 hour longer, or until meat thermometer registers 170F and potatoes are fork-tender and nicely browned. Sprinkle potatoes with chopped parsley. Serve pork and potatoes from roasting pan.
Makes 8 servings.

# ❖ ROAST PORK WITH SAUTÉED PEPPERS

*5-lb loin of pork*
*2 teaspoons salt*
*2 teaspoons dried rosemary leaves*
*1½ teaspoons dried oregano leaves*
*1½ teaspoons dried thyme leaves*
*1½ teaspoons dried sage*
*¼ teaspoon pepper*
*¼ teaspoon ground nutmeg*
*1 cup thinly sliced onion*
*1 cup thinly sliced carrot*
*Sautéed Sweet Peppers, below*

## HERB GRAVY:

*¼ cup pan drippings*
*¼ cup all-purpose flour*
*2¾ cups boiling water*
*½ teaspoon salt*
*¼ teaspoon dried rosemary*
*⅛ teaspoon dried oregano leaves*
*⅛ teaspoon dried thyme leaves*
*⅛ teaspoon dried sage*
*⅛ teaspoon pepper*
*Dash nutmeg*

1. Preheat oven to 325F. Wipe pork with damp paper towels.
2. In small bowl, combine 2 teaspoons each salt and rosemary; 1½ teaspoons each oregano, thyme, and sage; and ¼ teaspoon each pepper and nutmeg. With paring knife, make ½-inch-deep slits on back of roast between ribs and on fat side of meat. Press half of herb mixture into slits; rub remaining herb mixture on surface of meat.
3. Place roast, fat side up, in shallow roasting pan without rack. (Roast will rest on bones.) Scatter onion and carrot around roast.
4. Roast 2¼ hours, or until 170F on meat thermometer.
5. Meanwhile, prepare Sautéed Sweet Peppers.
6. Remove roast to heated platter. Surround roast with peppers; keep warm in low oven.
7. Make Herb Gravy; Skim off fat. Pour pan drippings with onion and carrot mixture through strainer. Reserve ¼ cup drippings; discard onion and carrot.
8. In 1-quart saucepan, combine reserved pan drippings and flour; mix until smooth. Set aside. Pour boiling water into roasting pan. Return to boiling, loosening brown particles and brown drippings from pan. Continue boiling about 2 minutes.
9. Slowly pour boiling liquid into flour mixture, stirring briskly with wire whisk. Stir in remaining gravy ingredients. Bring to boiling, stirring constantly.
10. Reduce heat, and simmer, covered, 5 minutes. Stir with wire whisk just before serving. (You should have about 2½ cups.) Serve with roast.
Makes 8 servings.

## SAUTÉED SWEET PEPPERS:

*6 or 7 green and red peppers (2 lb)*
*½ cup salad oil*
*1 cup sliced onion*
*1 clove garlic, crushed*
*1 teaspoon salt*
*⅛ teaspoon pepper*

1. Wash peppers. Slice into ¾-inch-wide strips, removing ribs and seeds.
2. In hot oil in large skillet, sauté onion and garlic, stirring occasionally, 5 minutes. Add peppers; sauté, stirring occasionally, 10 minutes. Sprinkle with salt and pepper.

# ✦ CROWN ROAST OF PORK WITH FRUIT STUFFING

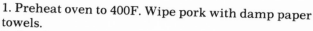

*6-lb crown roast of pork (14 ribs)*
*1 teaspoon salt*
*¼ teaspoon pepper*
*1 cup water*
*¼ cup white vinegar*

## FRUIT STUFFING:

*¼ cup butter or margarine*
*2 sweet Italian sausages (¼ lb)*
*½ cup thinly sliced celery*
*½ cup chopped onion*
*1 cup diced pared tart apple*
*½ cup chopped dried apricot*
*2 cups bread cubes (¼-inch)*
*1 teaspoon dried sage leaves*
*½ teaspoon salt*
*⅛ teaspoon pepper*

## GRAVY:

*Meat drippings*
*3 tablespoons flour*

*1 can (1 lb 13 oz) whole apricots,*
  *drained (optional)*
*Watercress (optional)*

1. Preheat oven to 400F. Wipe pork with damp paper towels.
2. Combine 1 teaspoon salt and ¼ teaspoon pepper; rub meat well with mixture. Crumple large piece of foil into ball and press down into center of crown roast to hold shape of cavity while cooking.
3. Place roast in shallow roasting pan without rack. Roast, uncovered, 15 minutes.
4. Reduce oven to 350F. Combine water and vinegar; pour into pan with roast. Cover tightly with foil. Roast 1 hour and 45 minutes.
5. Meanwhile, prepare Fruit Stuffing: In hot butter in medium skillet, sauté sausages (remove casing, and cut up sausage), celery, and onion, stirring, until onion is golden—about 5 minutes.
6. In large bowl, combine sausage mixture, apple, apricot, bread cubes, sage, ½ teaspoon salt, and ⅛ teaspoon pepper; mix well.
7. Remove roast from oven. Remove foil. Spoon stuffing into center cavity, mounding. Cover stuffing with 10-inch square of foil. Return roast to oven; roast 45 minutes. Place roast on heated platter; keep warm while making gravy.
8. Make Gravy: Strain drippings in roasting pan. Skim off fat from top, reserving 2 tablespoons. Return 2 tablespoons fat to roasting pan. Stir flour into fat until smooth. Stir in drippings (about 2 cups) and bring to boil. Reduce heat; simmer, stirring, about 3 minutes, or until thickened.
9. Before serving, garnish with apricots and watercress, if desired. Pass gravy.
Makes 10 servings.

# ❖ PORK CHOPS À L'ORANGE

6 rib pork chops, ½ inch thick (about 1¾ lb)
4 tablespoons butter or margarine
¼ cup flour
1 teaspoon dried sage
½ teaspoon salt
⅛ teaspoon pepper
1 clove garlic, crushed
1 can (10¾ oz) condensed chicken broth, undiluted
1 teaspoon grated orange peel
½ cup orange juice
1 orange, peeled and cut into segments
Parsley

1. Wipe pork chops with damp paper towels. Trim excess fat from chops; heat butter in large skillet.
2. On waxed paper, combine flour, sage, salt, and pepper; dip chops in flour mixture, coating lightly. Reserve remaining flour mixture.
3. In hot fat, brown chops, along with garlic, on both sides. Remove chops; set aside.
4. To drippings left in skillet, stir in rest of flour mixture. Add chicken broth, orange peel, and orange juice. Bring to boiling. Add chops; simmer, covered, 40 to 50 minutes, or until chops are tender. Add orange segments last 5 minutes. Taste sauce; add salt and pepper if necessary.
5. To serve: Arrange chops on heated platter. Spoon sauce over top of each chop. Garnish with orange segments and parsley.
Makes 6 servings.

# ❖ BAKED PORK CHOPS AND APPLES

6 rib pork chops, 1 inch thick (2½ lb)
1½ teaspoons sage
1½ teaspoons salt
¼ teaspoon pepper
1 lb carrots, pared
2 cups sliced onion
1 lb tart cooking apples, pared and quartered
¼ cup light-brown sugar

1. Preheat oven to 350F.
2. Wipe pork chops with damp paper towels. Trim off fat if necessary.
3. On waxed paper, combine sage, salt, and pepper. Dip both sides of chops in seasoning.
4. Slice carrots diagonally ½ inch thick. Layer in 3-quart casserole or baking dish. Top with half of onion. Then add chops, slightly overlapping; sprinkle with any remaining seasoning. Cover chops with remaining onion. Arrange apple quarters over all; sprinkle with brown sugar.
5. Bake, covered, 2 hours. Remove cover; baste with pan juices. Bake 30 minutes longer, or until tender.
6. Let stand for 5 minutes, and then skim off fat.
Makes 6 servings.

# ❖ SWISS PORK CHOPS WITH MUSTARD SAUCE

6 loin or rib pork chops, about 1 inch
  thick (2¼ lb)
2 tablespoons flour
1 teaspoon salt
¼ teaspoon pepper
2 tablespoons butter or margarine
¼ cup white wine
1 tablespoon lemon juice

## MUSTARD SAUCE:

1½ tablespoons flour
Meat drippings
1 cup light cream
2 tablespoons Dijon-style prepared
  mustard
Dash ground red pepper

1. Wipe pork chops with damp paper towels. Trim off
fat, if necessary. Mix 2 tablespoons flour, the salt,
and pepper; use to coat chops.
2. In hot butter in large skillet, brown chops well on
both sides—about 20 minutes in all.
3. Add wine and lemon juice; simmer, covered, 45 to
50 minutes, or until chops are tender. Remove chops
to warm serving platter.
4. Make Mustard Sauce: Stir flour into drippings in
skillet until smooth. Stir in cream, mustard, and red
pepper. Boil, stirring, 1 minute.
5. Serve chops with sauce.
Makes 6 servings.

# ❖ MAPLE-BARBECUED SPARERIBS

1½ cups maple syrup
2 tablespoons chili sauce
2 tablespoons cider vinegar
1½ tablespoons finely chopped onion
1 tablespoon Worcestershire sauce
1 teaspoon salt
½ teaspoon dry mustard
⅛ teaspoon pepper
3 lb spareribs, cut into serving-size
  pieces

1. Preheat oven to 350F.
2. In medium bowl, combine maple syrup with rest
of ingredients, except spareribs; mix well.
3. Wipe spareribs with damp paper towels. Brush on
both sides with maple basting sauce.
4. Place ribs, in single layer, on rack in shallow, open
roasting pan. Roast 1½ hours, or until tender, brushing frequently with sauce and turning occasionally,
to glaze evenly.
Makes 4 servings.

# ❖ BARBECUED COUNTRY-STYLE PORK RIBS

4 lb country-style pork ribs
2½ quarts boiling water
¾ cup white vinegar
1 large onion, quartered
1 teaspoon salt
⅛ teaspoon pepper
1 bay leaf

## BARBECUE SAUCE:

⅓ cup cider vinegar
¼ cup chili sauce
1 can (8 oz) tomato sauce
¼ cup chopped onion
2 tablespoons brown sugar
1 tablespoon Worcestershire sauce
1 teaspoon dry mustard

1. Wipe pork ribs with damp paper towels. Cut slits about halfway through on meaty side, between bones.
2. Pour boiling water and white vinegar into heavy 8-quart kettle. Add pork ribs, fat side up (water should cover pork ribs). Add quartered onion, salt, pepper, and bay leaf. Bring to boiling; reduce heat, and simmer, covered, very gently (liquid should barely bubble) about 1½ hours, or just until tender. Drain well. (See Note.)
3. Meanwhile, make Barbecue Sauce: In medium saucepan, combine all sauce ingredients. Bring to boiling; reduce heat and simmer, uncovered and stirring occasionally, 30 minutes. Makes 1⅓ cups.
4. Brush pork ribs with sauce, and place on grill, 6 inches from prepared coals. Cook, brushing with sauce and turning frequently, about 20 minutes. Serve any remaining sauce with ribs.
Makes 8 servings.

*To Cook Indoors*: After they have simmered for 1½ hours, arrange pork ribs, fat side up, in broiler pan without rack. Brush with sauce. Broil, 6 inches from heat, turning occasionally and basting frequently with sauce, 20 minutes.

*Note*: Ribs may be simmered day before or several hours ahead, and refrigerated until ready to cook. Let warm to room temperature before barbecuing, or cooking time may be longer.

# ❖ PORK-AND-APPLE PIE

2 tablespoons salad oil
1½ lb lean boneless pork, cut into
    1-inch cubes
1 cup chopped onion
1½ teaspoons rubbed sage
1 teaspoon salt
¼ teaspoon pepper
1 can (10¾ oz) condensed chicken
    broth, undiluted
2 tart cooking apples (1 lb), pared and
    cut into eighths
2 tablespoons flour

1. In hot oil in large skillet, sauté pork cubes until brown on all sides—20 minutes. Remove.
2. Add onion; sauté until golden—5 minutes.
3. Add sage, salt, pepper, and browned pork cubes; mix well.
4. Stir in chicken broth. Bring to boiling, stirring; simmer, covered, 30 minutes, or until pork is tender.
5. Toss apple slices with flour. Add to skillet; stir until well combined. Simmer, covered, until apples are tender and sauce is thickened. Remove from heat.
6. Meanwhile, make Mashed-Potato Topping: In 1

## MASHED-POTATO TOPPING:

*Boiling water*
*1 tablespoon salt*
*8 medium potatoes (2½ lb), peeled and quartered*
*1 cup milk*
*¼ cup plus 2 tablespoons butter or margarine*

inch boiling water, with salt, cook potatoes, covered, until tender—20 minutes. Drain well; return to saucepan.

7. With portable electric mixer at medium speed, beat until smooth. Heat slowly, stirring, over low heat, to dry out—about 3 minutes.

8. In saucepan, heat milk and ¼ cup butter just until butter melts. (Do not let milk boil.)

9. Gradually beat in hot milk mixture until potato is smooth and fluffy.

10. Turn out pork mixture into bottom of shallow 2-quart round (10-inch diameter) baking dish.

11. Swirl mashed potatoes decoratively over top of pie, spreading to edge of dish. Then brush with 2 tablespoons melted butter.

12. Place under broiler, 6 inches from heat, 5 to 7 minutes, or until nicely browned.

Makes 6 to 8 servings.

# ❖ BARBECUED PORK SATÉ

*2 cups water*
*⅓ cup white vinegar*
*1½ lb boneless pork shoulder, cut into 1¼-inch cubes (18 cubes)*

## MARINADE:

*¼ cup creamy peanut butter*
*1½ teaspoons ground coriander*
*½ teaspoon salt*
*⅛ teaspoon red-pepper flakes*
*1 teaspoon ground cumin*
*¾ cup chopped onion*
*1 clove garlic, crushed*
*1½ tablespoons lemon juice*
*1 tablespoon brown sugar*
*3 tablespoons soy sauce*

*2 medium zucchini*
*1 cup water*
*6 small onions*
*12 fresh-pineapple chunks*
*6 large mushrooms*
*Parsley sprigs*

1. Combine 2 cups water and the white vinegar in medium saucepan. Add pork cubes, and simmer, covered, 45 minutes; drain.

2. Make Marinade: In shallow baking dish, combine all marinade ingredients. Add pork, tossing until well coated.

3. Refrigerate, covered, 2 hours.

4. Meanwhile, cut zucchini into 12 (1-inch) pieces. Bring 1 cup water to boiling in medium saucepan. Add onions and simmer, covered, 5 minutes. Add zucchini, and simmer 5 minutes longer, or until fork-tender. Drain; cool.

5. On 6 skewers, thread pork cubes, alternating with zucchini, pineapple, onions, and mushrooms.

6. Adjust grill 4 to 6 inches from prepared coals. Place skewers on grill (lower hood if using one). Over low coals, grill pork, basting several times with leftover marinade (thin marinade with a little water if necessary), about 5 minutes on each side, turning once. Garnish with parsley.

Makes 6 servings.

*To Cook Indoors*: Place pork in broiler pan, without rack. Broil, 4 inches from heat, 10 minutes, turning after 5 minutes; baste several times with marinade.

# SMOKED HAM

Ham, a favorite meat for buffet tables and a tradition for Easter dinner, comes in a great variety of shapes and sizes, from bone-in whole hams to ready-to-fry slices. There are ready-to-cook hams, whole or half, fully-cooked hams, and canned hams, always fully-cooked. The fully-cooked hams may be sliced cold to serve without further cooking. If, however, you opt to serve them hot, count on the fact that it takes almost as long to heat a fully-cooked ham to serving temperature as it takes to bake a ready-to-cook ham. Our chart gives you planning time and desirable temperatures.

**TIMETABLE FOR BAKING SMOKED HAM, AT 325F**

| TYPE | WEIGHT | INTERNAL TEMPERATURE | APPROXIMATE BAKING TIME |
|---|---|---|---|
| Fully-cooked ham: | | | |
| Bone-in whole ham | 10–16 lb | 140F | 2½–4¾ hr (15–18 min/lb) |
| Bone-in half ham | 5–7 lb | 140F | 1½–2¾ hr (18–24 min/lb) |
| Arm picnic shoulder | 5–8 lb | 140F | 2–4 hr (25–30 min/lb) |
| Cook-before-eating ham: | | | |
| Bone-in whole ham | 10–16 lb | 160F | 3–5¼ hr (18–20 min/lb) |
| Bone-in half ham | 5–8 lb | 160F | 2–3¼ hr (22–25 min/lb) |
| Shank portion | 3–4 lb | 160F | 1¾–2½ hr (35–40 min/lb) |
| Rump portion | 3–4 lb | 160F | 1¾–2½ hr (35–40 min/lb) |

NOTE: It is advisable to use meat thermometer as extra precaution since roasts vary in size and shape, in amount of meat to bone, etc. Insert thermometer in thickest part of roast. Be sure tip is not touching bone or resting in fat.

# ⊞ BAKED VIRGINIA HAM

*10- to 12-lb country-style Virginia ham*
*Whole cloves*
*1 cup dark-brown sugar, firmly packed*
*1 teaspoon dry mustard*
*3 tablespoons pineapple juice*
*1 tablespoon cider vinegar*

1. Cover ham completely with cold water; let stand 24 hours.
2. Next day, scrub ham with stiff brush. Rinse well in cold water.
3. In large kettle, cover ham with cold water; bring to boiling. Reduce heat; simmer, covered, 4 to 5 hours, or until ham is almost tender.
4. Remove from heat; let cool in liquid.
5. Meanwhile, preheat oven to 325F.

6. Remove cooled ham from liquid; carefully remove skin and excess fat.

7. With tip of knife, cut fat into diamond pattern; do not cut into ham. Insert clove in each diamond.

8. Place ham on rack in shallow roasting pan.

9. Bake, uncovered, 2½ hours.

10. Combine remaining ingredients; spread over ham.

11. Bake 15 minutes longer, or until internal temperature is 160F on meat thermometer. For easy slicing, let stand 20 minutes.

Makes about 24 servings.

# ❖ BAKED HAM IN CIDER

*10- to 12-lb fully-cooked bone-in ham*
*1 cup sliced onion*
*2 bay leaves*
*¼ cup light-brown sugar, packed*
*4 sprigs parsley*
*Whole cloves*
*3 whole black peppercorns*
*2 cups cider*

## GLAZE:

*½ cup light-brown sugar, packed*
*½ cup orange marmalade*
*1 tablespoon prepared mustard*

*2 navel oranges*
*10 kumquats*
*Watercress*

1. Preheat oven to 325F. Place ham, fat side up, in shallow roasting pan. Place onion and bay leaves on ham; sprinkle with ¼ cup brown sugar, parsley, 6 cloves, and the peppers.

2. Pour cider into pan around ham. Cover pan tightly with foil. Bake, basting every 30 minutes with cider in pan (using a baster), about 3 hours, or until meat thermometer registers 140F. (To baste, remove ham from oven and take off foil.)

3. Make Glaze: In small saucepan, combine brown sugar, orange marmalade, and mustard; cook over medium heat, stirring, until sugar is dissolved. When ham is done, remove from roasting pan, and pour off all fat and drippings.

4. Increase oven temperature to 400F. With sharp knife, carefully remove any skin. To score: Make diagonal cuts in fat (be careful not to cut into meat), ¼ inch deep and 1¼ inches apart, using ruler, to form diamond pattern.

5. Stud center of each diamond shape with whole clove. To glaze ham: Brush surface with half of glaze; return ham to oven, and bake 30 minutes longer, basting every 10 minutes with more of glaze.

6. Slice oranges ⅓ inch thick. Place kumquat in center of each slice. Arrange around ham. For easy slicing, let ham stand 20 minutes.

Makes 16 to 18 servings.

# ROAST HAM WITH APRICOT-PECAN STUFFING

10- to 12-lb fully-cooked whole ham
½ cup coarsely chopped dried apricots
1½ cups finely chopped pecans or walnuts
1 can (8½ oz) crushed pineapple, undrained
1 teaspoon dried thyme leaves
1½ cups fresh white-bread crumbs
1¼ cups light-brown sugar, packed
1 tablespoon prepared Dijon-type mustard
2 egg whites
1 cup apple juice

1. Have butcher bone ham to make cavity for stuffing. Also ask to have about ½ pound lean ham removed from cavity and ground—you'll need 1 cup ground ham.
2. Preheat oven to 325F. Wipe ham with damp paper towels. Soak apricots ½ hour in warm water to cover; drain well.
3. In large bowl, combine ground ham with apricots, pecans, pineapple, thyme, ½ cup bread crumbs, ¼ cup sugar, the mustard, and egg whites; mix well. Spoon into cavity in ham; draw opening together with poultry pins, and tie with twine. Place ham on foil-lined shallow roasting pan.
4. Pour apple juice into bottom of pan; cover pan tightly with foil.
5. Bake 2 hours. Remove ham from oven; remove foil, then string. Remove rind from ham. Increase oven temperature to 375F.
6. Combine 1 cup sugar and 1 cup bread crumbs; pat mixture over surface of ham. Bake until surface is golden-brown and meat thermometer registers 140F —about 45 minutes.
7. Serve warm, if desired. Or cool 1 hour; then refrigerate, covered, several hours or overnight.
8. To serve: Slice ham, and arrange on platter with sliced filling.
Makes about 20 servings.

# BAKED HAM STEAK

¼ cup light-brown sugar, firmly packed
¼ teaspoon ground allspice
2½-lb fully-cooked ham steak, 1½ inches thick
Whole cloves
1 can (6 oz) apricot nectar

1. Preheat oven to 325F.
2. Combine sugar and allspice; spoon mixture evenly over top of ham steak. Press cloves into ham, all around side.
3. Place ham in shallow baking dish. Pour apricot nectar around ham.
4. Bake, uncovered, 1 hour, basting occasionally with pan liquid.
5. To serve: Place ham on serving platter. Spoon pan liquid over ham. Cut crosswise into slices.
Makes 6 servings.

# ✤ SMOKED PORK BUTT WITH SAUERKRAUT

3 slices bacon, halved
2-lb boneless smoked pork butt
3 cups water
6 whole cloves
3 medium onions, halved
2 lb sauerkraut, washed and drained
4 whole black peppercorns
2 bay leaves
1 cup white wine
2 tart red apples, cut into quarters and cored
3 medium potatoes, peeled and cut into thirds

1. In 6-quart Dutch oven, sauté bacon until crisp. With slotted spoon, remove bacon; crumble and set aside. With spoon, skim off excess fat.
2. In drippings in Dutch oven, place pork butt. Add water; bring to boiling. Reduce heat, and simmer, covered, 1 hour.
3. Insert clove into each onion half; add onions, sauerkraut, peppercorns, bay leaves, and white wine to Dutch oven. Cook, covered, 30 minutes. Add apples and potatoes; cook 30 minutes longer, or until pork and potatoes are tender. (As soon as apples are tender, remove and set aside.)
4. Slice meat into ½-inch-thick slices; arrange on platter with sauerkraut, potatoes, and apples. Sprinkle vegetables with reserved bacon.
Makes 8 servings.

# ✤ SMOKED HAM HOCKS WITH LIMA BEANS

6 smoked ham hocks (3 lb)
2 teaspoons celery seed
5 cups water
1 lb dried large lima beans
3 tablespoons butter or margarine
1 cup chopped onion
2 cloves garlic, finely chopped
1 cup chopped celery
1 can (1 lb 1 oz) whole tomatoes, undrained
¼ teaspoon pepper
1 teaspoon salt

1. Wipe ham hocks with damp paper towels.
2. In 6-quart Dutch oven or kettle, combine ham hocks, celery seed, and water. Bring to boiling. Reduce heat, and simmer, covered, 1 hour.
3. Wash lima beans; drain. Add to ham hocks; simmer, covered, 1 hour. Skim off excess fat.
4. Meanwhile, in hot butter in medium skillet, sauté onion and garlic until onion is soft—about 5 minutes.
5. Add celery, tomatoes, pepper, and salt; bring to boiling, stirring. Reduce heat; simmer, uncovered, 15 minutes. Remove from heat.
6. Preheat oven to 350F.
7. Add tomato mixture to ham-hock mixture. Turn out into 3-quart casserole. Bake, covered tightly, until ham hocks and beans are tender and almost all the liquid has been absorbed—30 to 40 minutes.
Makes 6 to 8 servings.

# ⊞ BAKED HAM LOAF

*1 cup milk*
*1 egg*
*2 tablespoons catsup*
*2 tablespoons prepared brown mustard*
*1 teaspoon salt*
*⅛ teaspoon pepper*
*2 cups soft fine white-bread crumbs*
*1½ lb ground cooked ham*
*½ lb ground uncooked pork*
*½ lb ground uncooked veal*
*2 tablespoons finely chopped onion*
*2 tablespoons chopped parsley*

## MUSTARD FRUIT:

*1 can (8¾ oz) mixed fruits for salad*
*2 tablespoons cider vinegar*
*¼ cup light-brown sugar*
*1 tablespoon prepared brown mustard*

1. Preheat oven to 350F. In large bowl, combine milk, egg, catsup, 2 tablespoons mustard, the salt, and pepper; mix well. Stir in bread crumbs; let stand several minutes.
2. Add ham, pork, veal, onion, and parsley; mix well. In shallow baking pan, shape meat mixture into loaf about 11 inches long and 5 inches wide. Bake, uncovered, 30 minutes.
3. Prepare Mustard Fruit: Drain mixed fruits, pouring liquid into small saucepan. Set fruit aside. Add vinegar, sugar, and mustard to saucepan. Bring to boiling, stirring occasionally. Reduce heat, and simmer, uncovered, 5 minutes, or until mixture is of glaze consistency.
4. Pour half of glaze over top of ham loaf. Bake 30 minutes. Arrange reserved fruit on top. Cover with rest of glaze; bake 20 minutes more. To serve, cut ham loaf crosswise into ½-inch slices.
Makes 8 to 10 servings.

# LAMB

Lamb, once rarely eaten in parts of this country, is now considered a great delicacy, especially if it is done rare to medium-well. Under-cooking rather than over-cooking lamb roasts or chops enhances their flavor and keeps the meat moist and tender. The portions of lamb used for stewing or braising are cooked to well done, but always in moist heat at a relatively low temperature.

**TIMETABLE FOR ROASTING LAMB, AT 325F**

| CUT | WEIGHT | INTERNAL TEMPERATURE | APPROXIMATE ROASTING TIME |
|---|---|---|---|
| Leg, whole | 6–7 lb | 145–150F (rare) | 1¼–1¾ hr (12–15 min/lb) |
| | | 160F (medium) | 1½–2½ hr (18–20 min/lb) |
| | | 175F (well done) | 3–4 hr (30–35 min/lb) |

| CUT | WEIGHT | INTERNAL TEMPERATURE | APPROXIMATE ROASTING TIME |
|---|---|---|---|
| Leg, half | 3–4 lb | 145–150F (rare) | ¾–1 hr (12–15 min/lb) |
| | | 160F (medium) | 1–1½ hr (18–20 min/lb) |
| | | 175F (well done) | 1¼–2 hr (25–30 min/lb) |
| Boned rolled shoulder | 4–6 lb | 160F (medium) | 1¾–2½ hr (25–30 min/lb) |
| | | 175F (well done) | 2–4 hr (30–40 min/lb) |
| Stuffed shoulder, bone-in | 4–5 lb | 160F (medium) | 1¾–2½ hr (25–30 min/lb) |
| | | 175F (well done) | 2–4 hr (30–40 min/lb) |

NOTE: It is advisable to use meat thermometer as extra precaution since roasts vary in size and shape, in amount of meat to bone, etc. Insert thermometer in thickest part of roast. Be sure tip is not touching bone or resting in fat.

# ✦ ROAST LEG OF LAMB

6-lb leg of lamb
1 clove garlic, slivered
½ cup salad oil
2 cups dry red wine
3 onions, sliced
¼ teaspoon ground cloves
2 teaspoons dried oregano leaves
2 teaspoons salt
1 carrot, sliced
3 sprigs parsley

1. Wipe lamb with damp paper towels. Using paring knife, make several small pockets in flesh, and insert garlic slivers.
2. Combine remaining ingredients, to make marinade. In large shallow glass baking dish, arrange lamb as flat as possible. Pour marinade over it.
3. Refrigerate, covered, at least 24 hours, turning lamb occasionally.
4. Preheat oven to 325F.
5. Place lamb, fat side up, on rack in shallow roasting pan.
6. Roast, uncovered and basting occasionally with marinade, about 2½ hours, or to 160F on meat thermometer, for medium.
7. Let roast stand 20 minutes before carving, for easier slicing. If desired, some of the marinade may be heated, to pass with roast.
Makes about 10 servings.

# ❖ ROAST LAMB KARMA

6- to 7-lb leg of lamb
2 tablespoons grated fresh ginger root
½ cup yogurt
2 tablespoons lime juice
2 cloves garlic, crushed
2½ teaspoons salt
¼ teaspoon black pepper
2½ teaspoons ground coriander
⅛ teaspoon ground red pepper
¼ teaspoon ground cinnamon
¼ teaspoon ground cloves
¼ teaspoon ground cardamom
1¼ cups water
1 tablespoon flour
7 slices navel orange
7 green olives
Fresh coriander
Fluffy cooked rice

1. Wipe lamb with damp paper towels. With sharp knife, score in diamond pattern. Place lamb in large roasting pan without rack.
2. In small bowl, combine ginger root, yogurt, lime juice, garlic, salt, and black pepper. Rub mixture into lamb well; let stand in cool place 2 hours.
3. Preheat oven to 325F. In small skillet, combine coriander, red pepper, cinnamon, cloves, and cardamom. Stir over low heat just until combined—1 minute. Cool 10 minutes.
4. Sprinkle coriander-spice mixture evenly over lamb. Rescore diamond pattern. Roast 2 to 2½ hours, or to 160F on meat thermometer, for medium.
5. Remove roast to serving platter; keep warm. Let roast stand 20 minutes for easier carving.
6. Meanwhile, skim off fat from roasting pan. Stir 1 cup water into pan; place over heat. Simmer, stirring, to dissolve browned bits. Combine flour with ¼ cup water; stir to dissolve. Stir into liquid in roasting pan. Bring to boiling, stirring, until thickened. Serve with lamb.
7. To serve: Garnish platter with orange slices, olives, and fresh coriander. Serve with rice.
Makes 10 servings.

# ❖ PARSLEY LEG OF LAMB

6- to 7-lb leg of lamb
1½ teaspoons salt
¼ teaspoon pepper
1 cup chopped onion
1 cup sliced carrot
1 cup white wine
1½ cups fresh bread crumbs
¾ cup chopped parsley
1 clove garlic, minced
¼ cup prepared brown mustard
½ cup butter or margarine, melted

**GRAVY:**

2 tablespoons flour
1 cup chicken broth
½ cup white wine

Parsley

1. Preheat oven to 350F.
2. Wipe lamb with paper towels. Rub surface with salt and pepper.
3. Place lamb in shallow roasting pan without rack. Sprinkle onion and carrot around roast.
4. Add 1 cup white wine. Roast, uncovered and basting occasionally with pan juices, 2 hours.
5. Meanwhile, in medium bowl, combine bread crumbs, chopped parsley, and garlic; toss lightly to combine.
6. Remove roast from oven; let cool about 15 minutes.
7. Spread mustard over surface of lamb. Firmly pat crumb mixture into mustard. Pour butter over bread crumbs.
8. Return roast to oven, and continue roasting, uncovered, about 30 minutes, or until meat thermometer registers 160F, for medium, or 175F, for well done.
9. Remove lamb to heated platter. Let roast stand 20 minutes for easier carving.

10. Make Gravy: Skim off fat, reserving 2 tablespoons. Return 2 tablespoons fat to roasting pan. Stir in flour to make smooth paste. Add broth and ½ cup white wine.

11. Bring to boiling, stirring. Simmer 3 minutes, or until slightly thickened. Strain; discard vegetables. Makes 1½ cups.

12. Before serving, garnish platter with parsley. Pass gravy.

Makes 10 servings.

# ✦ BRAISED POT ROAST OF LAMB

5½-lb boned shoulder of lamb (see Note)
¼ cup chopped parsley
1 clove garlic, minced
1 teaspoon salt
½ teaspoon dried basil leaves
½ teaspoon dried marjoram leaves
¼ teaspoon pepper
2 tablespoons butter or margarine
½ cup chopped onion
½ cup chopped celery
½ cup chopped carrot
1 can (10½ oz) condensed beef broth, undiluted
½ cup red wine
1 bay leaf
2 lb medium potatoes, peeled and halved
2 tablespoons flour
¼ cup cold water
¼ cup chopped fresh mint

1. Wipe lamb with damp paper towels. Trim off any excess fat; spread meat flat.

2. In small bowl, combine parsley, garlic, salt, basil, marjoram, and pepper.

3. Spread parsley mixture evenly over lamb. Starting from one end, roll up, jelly-roll fashion, as tightly as possible. Tie with twine in 3 or 4 places.

4. In hot butter in Dutch oven, brown roast well on all sides—about 20 minutes. Remove roast.

5. In same pan, sauté onion, celery, and carrot until soft and lightly golden. Drain off fat.

6. Return roast to pan. Add beef broth, wine, and bay leaf; bring to boiling. Reduce heat, and simmer, covered and turning meat once, 1½ hours.

7. Add potatoes; simmer, covered, 40 minutes longer, or until lamb and potatoes are tender.

8. Remove lamb and potatoes to heated serving platter. Remove string from lamb. Keep warm. Skim fat from pan liquid. Boil liquid, uncovered, about 8 minutes, to reduce it. (Liquid should measure 1¾ cups.)

9. Mix flour with cold water until smooth. Stir into pan liquid; bring to boiling, stirring. Add chopped mint. Reduce heat, and simmer 3 minutes. Spoon some of mint gravy over meat. Pass the rest.

Makes 8 servings.

*Note*: Weight after lamb shoulder is boned. Have butcher flatten lamb to 1½-inch thickness.

## ☒ BROILED LAMB-CHOP GRILL

6 tablespoons soft butter or margarine
3 tablespoons grated Parmesan cheese
3 firm tomatoes
1½ teaspoons dried oregano leaves
¼ cup lemon juice
½ cup salad oil
1 teaspoon dried tarragon leaves
6 loin lamb chops, 1½ inches thick
1 can (1 lb) cling-peach halves
¼ teaspoon ground cloves
Dash ground cinnamon
⅓ cup currant jelly, melted
Parsley or watercress

1. Combine butter with cheese.
2. Slice tomatoes in half. Sprinkle with oregano, and spread cut side with cheese mixture. Arrange on cold broiler rack.
3. Mix lemon juice, salad oil, and tarragon. Brush part of mixture on chops, and arrange chops on broiler rack.
4. Place broiling pan 4 inches from heat (chops will be about 2 inches from heat). For medium chops, broil 5 to 6 minutes on first side; then turn. Baste with more lemon-juice mixture, and broil 4 to 5 minutes. For well-done chops, broil 6 to 8 minutes on first side; then turn, basting as above, and broil 5 to 7 minutes.
5. Meanwhile, drain peach halves, reserving ⅓ cup syrup. Add cloves and cinnamon.
6. When chops are turned, place peach halves, cut side up, on broiler rack. Brush generously with currant jelly and peach syrup.
7. Serve chops, garnished with parsley or watercress, in center of large heated platter. Heat any remaining lemon-juice mixture, and pour over chops. Surround chops with tomatoes and peach halves.
Makes 6 servings.

## ☒ RACK OF LAMB

2-lb rack of lamb
1 teaspoon salt
¼ cup orange marmalade
¼ cup lemon juice

1. Preheat oven to 300F.
2. Cover tip of each rib bone with aluminum foil, to prevent scorching. Rub lamb with salt.
3. Place lamb, fat side up, on rack in shallow roasting pan; roast, uncovered, 30 minutes.
4. Mix marmalade with lemon juice. Brush half of glaze on lamb.
5. Roast lamb, uncovered, 30 minutes; then brush with rest of glaze. For medium lamb, roast 15 minutes more, or until meat thermometer reads 170F. For well-done lamb, roast 30 minutes more, or until thermometer reads 180F.
6. To serve: Remove foil tips. Place paper frills on bone ends, if desired.
Makes 2 or 3 servings.

# ✦ BROWN LAMB STEW

2½ lb boneless lamb, cut into 1½-inch
  cubes
⅓ cup all-purpose flour
2 teaspoons salt
¼ teaspoon pepper
¼ cup butter or margarine
12 small white onions
1 teaspoon dried thyme leaves
1 bay leaf
2¼ cups water
1 cup tomato juice
1 lb carrots
1 lb small new potatoes (about 8)
1 pkg (10 oz) frozen peas
3 tablespoons snipped fresh dill or
  parsley, or 1 teaspoon dried dillweed

1. Wipe lamb with damp paper towels. Trim excess fat. Combine flour, salt, and pepper. On waxed paper, roll lamb cubes in flour mixture, coating evenly on all sides. Reserve any remaining flour.

2. In hot butter in 5- or 6-quart Dutch oven, brown lamb well all over, turning with tongs (about one fourth at a time—just enough to cover bottom of pan).

3. Lift out lamb as it browns. Continue until all lamb is browned, adding more butter if needed (about ½ hour).

4. Add onions to drippings in Dutch oven. Cook, covered, about 5 minutes, or until lightly browned.

5. Return lamb to Dutch oven. Add thyme and bay leaf; toss with drippings to coat evenly.

6. Add 2 cups water and the tomato juice; stir to combine. Place large sheet of waxed paper just under lid. Pour off any liquid that collects on top of paper during cooking, to keep it from diluting sauce. Bring to boiling. Reduce heat, and simmer, covered, 30 minutes.

7. Meanwhile, pare carrots; cut in half crosswise. Scrub potatoes; pare 1-inch band of skin from around center of each potato. Add carrots and potatoes to lamb; stir to combine.

8. Bring back to boiling. Reduce heat, and simmer, covered, 45 minutes, or until meat and vegetables are tender when pierced with fork.

9. Remove from heat; skim fat from surface.

10. Combine reserved flour mixture with ¼ cup water; stir into lamb mixture. Add peas and dill. Remove and discard bay leaf.

11. Simmer, covered, 10 to 15 minutes longer, or until peas are tender and stew is slightly thickened. Remove from heat; let stand about 5 minutes. Turn out into large serving dish, or serve right from pot. Sprinkle top with fresh dill sprigs or parsley, if desired.

Makes 6 to 8 servings.

# ✠ LAMB-AND-FRUIT CURRY

2-lb lamb shoulder, cut into 1½-inch
   cubes
2 tablespoons salad or peanut oil
2 medium onions, thinly sliced
1 teaspoon dried thyme leaves
1 tablespoon chopped parsley
2 tablespoons curry powder
2 tablespoons flour
1½ teaspoons salt
2½ cups water
2 medium-size green apples, unpared
3 bananas (1 lb)
1 can (8 oz) pineapple chunks, undrained
Cooked rice

1. Trim any excess fat from lamb, and discard. Wipe lamb with damp paper towels.
2. In 4-quart Dutch oven, heat oil. Add onions; sauté until golden—about 5 minutes. Add thyme and parsley; cook 1 minute longer.
3. Add lamb cubes; sauté, turning, until browned on all sides—about 25 minutes.
4. Meanwhile, in small bowl, combine curry powder, flour, and salt; mix well.
5. Sprinkle curry mixture over browned meat. Cook, stirring, 2 minutes. Add water; mix well. Simmer, covered, 50 to 60 minutes, or until meat is tender.
6. Cut apples into eighths; remove cores. Add apple wedges to curry mixture, and let cook 5 minutes.
7. Peel bananas; cut into ½-inch chunks. Add, with pineapple, to curry mixture; stir gently. Cook over low heat 5 minutes. Turn out onto heated serving platter. Serve with rice.
Makes 6 to 8 servings.

# ✠ DILLED LAMB-AND-VEGETABLE PIE

3 lb boneless lamb for stew
1½ teaspoons salt
¼ teaspoon pepper
2 large carrots, pared and sliced
2 large potatoes, peeled and cut up
1 medium onion, chopped
½ cup chopped celery
2½ cups plus 1 tablespoon water
1 pkg (11 oz) piecrust mix
2 teaspoons flour
1 tablespoon vinegar
2 teaspoons sugar
2 egg yolks
½ cup heavy cream
¾ cup chopped fresh dill or 6 tablespoons dried dillweed
1 pkg (10 oz) frozen peas, thawed

1. Trim excess fat from lamb; cut meat into 1-inch cubes. Sprinkle with salt and pepper.
2. In 4-quart Dutch oven, combine lamb, carrots, potatoes, onion, celery, and 2½ cups water. Bring to boiling. Reduce heat; simmer, covered and stirring occasionally, 1 hour, or until lamb is tender. Skim off fat, if necessary.
3. Meanwhile, prepare pastry as label directs; roll out to form 12-inch circle. Preheat oven to 350F.
4. Drain lamb and vegetables, pouring liquid into medium saucepan. Liquid should measure 2 cups.
5. Combine flour and 1 tablespoon water. Stir into liquid; cook, stirring, until liquid is slightly thickened. Add vinegar and sugar.
6. In medium bowl, beat egg yolks slightly; beat in cream, then a small amount of hot sauce. Pour back into rest of sauce. Add lamb mixture, dill, and peas; mix well.
7. Turn out lamb mixture into 10-inch 3-quart casserole (about 3 inches deep). Make slits in pastry for steam vents, and adjust over top of casserole; crimp edges. Bake 45 minutes, or until top is golden.
Makes 10 servings.

# VEAL

Veal, judged by price per pound, is a luxury meat, but most of the classic veal dishes use boneless meat that has no waste. Veal has a subtle flavor and is beautifully tender when properly cooked; consider it a treat worth serving occasionally.

**TIMETABLE FOR ROASTING VEAL, AT 325F**

| CUT | WEIGHT | INTERNAL TEMPERATURE | APPROXIMATE ROASTING TIME |
|-----|--------|---------------------|---------------------------|
| Leg, center cut | 7–8 lb | 170F | 3–3½ hr |
| Loin | 4½–5 lb | 170F | 2½–3 hr |
| Boned rolled shoulder | 5–6 lb | 170F | 3½–4 hr |
| Boned rolled shoulder | 3 lb | 170F | 3 hr |

NOTE: It is advisable to use meat thermometer as extra precaution since roasts vary in size and shape, in amount of meat to bone, etc. Insert thermometer in thickest part of roast. Be sure tip is not touching bone or resting in fat.

# ❖ VEAL SCALLOPINI

3 tablespoons butter or margarine
½ lb mushrooms, sliced
1 small onion, finely chopped
1 clove garlic, crushed
1½ cups coarsely chopped peeled fresh tomatoes (about 1 lb)
⅓ cup dry white wine
Salt
¼ teaspoon dried tarragon leaves, crushed
6 thin veal scallops (1 lb)
⅛ teaspoon pepper
1 tablespoon grated Parmesan cheese

1. In 1 tablespoon hot butter in skillet, sauté mushrooms until golden-brown—about 5 minutes. Add onion and garlic; cook until onion is golden.

2. Add tomatoes, wine, ¼ teaspoon salt, and the tarragon; stir until well blended. Reduce heat; simmer, covered and stirring occasionally, 30 minutes.

3. Meanwhile, wipe veal with damp paper towels. Sprinkle with ½ teaspoon salt and the pepper.

4. Heat 2 tablespoons butter in another skillet. Add veal, a few pieces at a time, and cook until lightly browned on both sides—about 5 minutes. Remove and keep warm.

5. Return veal to skillet. Remove garlic from sauce. Pour sauce over veal; simmer, covered, 5 minutes. Sprinkle with grated Parmesan cheese.

Makes 3 or 4 servings.

# ▒ STUFFED VEAL BREAST

## APPLE-ONION STUFFING:

¼ cup butter or margarine
3 cups chopped cored pared tart
   apple
1 cup chopped onion
½ teaspoon salt
½ teaspoon dried thyme leaves
Dash pepper
¾ cup unseasoned bread crumbs
1 egg

5-lb breast of veal, with pocket for
   stuffing
1 teaspoon salt
¼ teaspoon pepper
1 clove garlic, minced
¼ cup chopped onion
¼ cup chopped celery
¼ cup chopped carrot
1 sprig parsley
1 can (10½ oz) condensed beef consommé, undiluted
¼ cup all-purpose flour
¼ cup water
Glazed Apple Rings and Onions,
   below

1. Preheat oven to 350F. Make Apple-Onion Stuffing: In hot butter in medium skillet, sauté apple and 1 cup onion until tender—about 10 minutes. Remove from heat; add ½ teaspoon salt, the thyme, dash pepper, the bread crumbs, and egg; mix well.
2. Wipe veal with damp paper towels. Lightly spoon stuffing into pocket, pushing down into cavity; do not pack. (If necessary, cut pocket larger.) Fasten with skewers; lace loosely with twine.
3. Place veal, meaty side up, in large shallow roasting pan. Rub salt, pepper, and garlic over surface of meat. Surround with onion, celery, carrot, and parsley. Pour consommé into bottom of pan.
4. Cover pan tightly with foil. Bake 2 hours; uncover, and bake, basting several times, 30 to 45 minutes longer, or until veal is fork-tender. Remove veal to platter; keep warm in low oven.
5. Make Gravy: Measure drippings. Skim fat from surface. Add water to drippings to measure 2 cups. Pour back into pan; bring to boiling, stirring to dissolve browned bits.
6. Remove from heat. Combine flour and ¼ cup water; mix well. Stir into liquid in pan. Bring to boiling, stirring until thickened. Taste for seasoning; add salt and pepper, if necessary. Pour through strainer, pressing vegetables through to purée.
7. Serve with veal roast, along with Glazed Apple Rings and Onions.
Makes 8 servings.

## GLAZED APPLE RINGS AND ONIONS:

2 lb red cooking apples
¼ cup lemon juice

### Glaze:

½ cup butter or margarine
½ cup sugar
2 tablespoons light corn syrup
½ cup water
4 small onions, halved

1. Wash apples; do not peel. Core; cut into slices about ¾ inch thick.
2. In medium bowl, toss apple slices with lemon juice.
3. Make Glaze: In large skillet, combine butter, sugar, corn syrup, and water. Cook over medium heat, stirring, until sugar melts.
4. Layer apple slices in skillet. Add any lemon juice remaining in bowl. Cook over medium heat, turning once, 5 minutes, or until glazed and tender but not mushy.
5. Remove apples. Add onion halves to skillet. Cook over medium heat, turning once, until glazed and tender.
Makes 8 servings.

# ❖ VEAL SAINT-TROPEZ

5 large veal scallops (about 2 lb)
¼ cup all-purpose flour
½ cup butter
1½ cups whole mushroom caps (½ lb)
3 shallots, peeled and chopped
1 teaspoon dried tarragon leaves
¾ cup dry white wine
¼ cup brandy
Velouté Sauce, page 466

1. Wipe veal with damp paper towels. Place each scallop between 2 pieces of waxed paper, and pound with mallet to ⅛-inch thickness. Lightly coat both sides with flour.
2. In ¼ cup hot butter in large skillet, sauté veal, a few pieces at a time. Cook until lightly browned on both sides—about 5 minutes on each side—adding more butter as needed. Remove and keep warm in oven. Add mushrooms to skillet; sauté, stirring, 5 minutes. Remove and add to veal.
3. In remaining butter, sauté shallots and tarragon, stirring, until shallots are tender—about 5 minutes. Add wine and brandy; simmer, uncovered and stirring occasionally, to reduce to ½ cup. Keep warm.
4. Meanwhile, make Velouté Sauce.
5. Add Velouté Sauce to skillet. Over high heat, bring to boiling, stirring constantly.
6. Continue cooking, stirring constantly, until sauce is smooth and blended.
7. Return veal and mushrooms to skillet; simmer, uncovered, 5 minutes.
8. Serve with Velouté Sauce poured over veal.
9. Makes 6 servings.

# ❖ PAUPIETTES DE VEAU ITALIAN-STYLE

1½ lb veal for scallopini (8 scallops)
¾ lb sliced boiled ham (8 slices)
½ lb natural Gruyère or Swiss cheese,
  cut into 8 slices
Freshly ground black pepper
2 tablespoons olive or salad oil
1 bay leaf
8 small onions
½ teaspoon salt
½ cup dry vermouth
4 small or 2 large tomatoes, or about
  2 cups canned tomatoes, drained
1 tablespoon flour dissolved in 2
  tablespoons dry vermouth

1. On each veal scallop, place slice of ham, then slice of cheese. Sprinkle each scallop lightly with pepper. Roll up, with veal outside; tie with string, or secure with wooden picks.
2. In large heavy skillet, heat oil with bay leaf. Add veal rolls in single layer; sauté, turning until golden-brown all over.
3. Add onions, salt, ¼ teaspoon pepper, and ½ cup vermouth. Simmer, covered, 30 minutes, or until tender.
4. Meanwhile, pour boiling water over tomatoes; let stand several minutes—until skin peels off easily with sharp knife. Quarter tomatoes; remove seeds. Add to skillet during last 10 minutes of cooking.
5. With slotted spoon, remove veal rolls to serving platter; remove string or wooden picks. Place vegetables around veal rolls, arranging attractively. Discard bay leaf.
6. Add flour mixture to pan liquid. Bring to boiling, stirring; boil about 3 minutes. Pour over veal rolls. Makes 8 servings.

# ❖ BRAISED VEAL CHOPS

6 veal chops, 1 inch thick
1½ teaspoons salt
¼ teaspoon pepper
⅓ cup salad oil
½ cup chopped onion
¾ cup sliced raw carrots
1 can (8 oz) tomatoes, undrained
⅓ cup dry sherry or chicken broth
1 can (6 oz) sliced mushrooms,
   drained
2 tablespoons chopped parsley

1. Wipe chops with damp paper towels. Sprinkle with salt and pepper.
2. In large skillet, over medium heat, heat oil. Brown chops on both sides, with onion.
3. Add carrots, tomatoes, and sherry. Reduce heat; simmer, covered, 45 minutes, or until meat is fork-tender.
4. Remove cover. Add mushrooms and parsley; heat 5 minutes. Serve chops with sauce.
Makes 6 servings.

# ❖ FRENCH VEAL STEW

¼ cup flour
1½ teaspoons salt
1 teaspoon dried thyme leaves
¼ teaspoon dried summer savory
Dash pepper
2 lb boned veal shoulder, cut into
   1½-inch cubes
2 tablespoons butter or margarine
2 tablespoons salad oil
1 cup sliced onion
1 clove garlic, crushed
About ¾ cup water
1 can (10¾ oz) condensed chicken
   broth, undiluted
1½ cups sliced pared carrot, in 1-inch
   pieces
1½ cups sliced celery, in 1½-inch
   pieces
1 medium (8 oz) yellow squash
2 medium (1 lb) zucchini
½ cup white wine
1 tablespoon chopped parsley

1. On waxed paper, combine flour, salt, thyme, summer savory, and pepper. Use to coat veal; reserve rest of flour mixture.
2. In hot butter and oil in 5-quart Dutch oven, brown veal, half at a time, on all sides; remove veal. In remaining fat, sauté onion and garlic until golden—about 5 minutes.
3. Return veal to Dutch oven. Add water to chicken broth to make 2 cups. Gradually add broth to veal. Bring to boiling, reduce heat, and simmer, covered, ½ hour.
4. Add carrot and celery to meat mixture; simmer, covered, ½ hour.
5. Wash yellow squash and zucchini. Cut into quarters lengthwise; slice into 2-inch pieces. Add to meat mixture; cook 15 to 20 minutes, or until meat and vegetables are tender.
6. Mix reserved flour mixture with wine until smooth. Stir into liquid in Dutch oven; bring to boiling, and boil 1 minute, or until thickened. Turn out into serving dish. Sprinkle with parsley.
Makes 8 servings.

# ✪ VEAL CREOLE

2 lb boneless veal shoulder, cut into
   1½-inch cubes
2 tablespoons butter or margarine
½ cup chopped onion
1 teaspoon salt
⅛ teaspoon pepper
¼ teaspoon dried thyme leaves
1 can (10½ oz) condensed beef broth,
   undiluted
½ small eggplant (8 oz)
1 green pepper (6 oz)
1 red pepper (4 oz)
2 large tomatoes (1 lb)
2 tablespoons flour
¼ cup water
Rice (optional)

1. Wipe veal with damp paper towels. In hot butter in 5-quart Dutch oven, over medium heat, sauté veal a few pieces at a time until well browned on all sides —about 20 minutes. Remove as browned.

2. To remaining fat in Dutch oven, add onion, salt, pepper, and thyme. Sauté, stirring, until onion is golden—about 3 minutes.

3. Return veal to Dutch oven. Add broth; mix well. Bring to boiling; reduce heat, and simmer, covered, 45 minutes.

4. Meanwhile, prepare vegetables: Wash eggplant; cut, unpeeled, into ½-inch-thick strips. Wash peppers and tomatoes; slice peppers, then cut each tomato into 8 wedges.

5. Stir flour into water, mixing until smooth. Add to veal mixture; bring to boiling, stirring, until slightly thickened and smooth.

6. Add eggplant strips. Simmer, covered, 15 minutes, or until veal is tender.

7. Add tomatoes and peppers. Simmer 10 minutes, or until peppers are just tender. Serve with rice, if desired.

Makes 8 servings.

# ✪ VEAL-PAPRIKASH-AND-NOODLE CASSEROLE

⅓ cup flour
3¼ teaspoons salt
¼ teaspoon pepper
⅓ cup salad oil
3 lb stewing veal, cut into 1½-inch
   cubes
2½ to 3 tablespoons paprika
1 lb yellow onions, sliced
12 small white onions
2 cans (10½-oz size) condensed beef
   broth, undiluted
½ teaspoon Worcestershire sauce
6 carrots, pared and halved crosswise
1 pkg (8 oz) wide noodles
2 cups sour cream
Fresh dill sprigs or chopped parsley

1. On waxed paper, combine flour, 2¼ teaspoons salt, and the pepper. Use to coat veal. Reserve remaining flour mixture.

2. In some of hot oil in Dutch oven or 4-quart casserole, brown veal, a third at a time, adding oil as needed. Remove as browned.

3. Preheat oven to 350F.

4. Stir paprika into drippings in Dutch oven. Add sliced onions and small white onions, and sauté, stirring, about 10 minutes. Remove Dutch oven from heat.

5. Stir in reserved flour mixture until well blended. Stir in beef broth, Worcestershire, carrots, browned veal, and 1 teaspoon salt. Bake, covered, 1 hour and 50 minutes.

6. Meanwhile, cook noodles as package label directs. Add cooked noodles to Dutch oven; bake 10 minutes longer.

7. Stir a little hot liquid from Dutch oven into 1 cup sour cream. Gradually stir into veal mixture until well blended. Garnish with remaining 1 cup sour cream and fresh dill sprigs.

Makes 6 to 8 servings.

# ✦ COLD ROAST VEAL LOAF

2 eggs
½ cup dry bread crumbs
2 tablespoons prepared mustard
1 teaspoon dried basil leaves
1½ teaspoons salt
½ teaspoon pepper
Dash Tabasco
½ cup finely chopped onion
½ cup finely chopped green pepper
1 cup chopped parsley
1½ lb ground veal
½ lb lean ground pork
1 lemon, thinly sliced
6 slices bacon
Prepared mustard
Salad greens
Sliced tomatoes

1. Preheat oven to 350F.
2. In large bowl, combine eggs, bread crumbs, mustard, basil, salt, pepper, Tabasco, onion, green pepper, and parsley; beat with fork until well combined. Let stand 5 minutes.
3. Add veal and pork; mix well with fork.
4. Line 13-by-9-by-1¾-inch pan with foil (use piece long enough to hang over ends of pan). Turn out meat mixture into pan; shape with hands to form loaf 8 inches long and 4 inches wide. Overlap lemon slices on top; place bacon slices lengthwise on top.
5. Bake, uncovered, 1 hour and 15 minutes.
6. Let cool in pan on wire rack 30 minutes. Lifting with foil, remove meat loaf to serving platter; refrigerate several hours, covered, to chill well.
7. Serve with mustard and garnished with salad greens and sliced tomatoes, if desired.
Makes 8 servings.

# VARIETY MEATS

The variety meats are frequently a bargain in the meat case since the price is very much influenced by demand. Liver, in particular, is a good and reasonable source of hard-to-get vitamins (thiamine and riboflavin) and an excellent source of iron. While calf's liver and lamb's liver are more delicate in flavor, look for baby-steer liver. When it's available, it's a good buy and has an excellent flavor.

# ✦ BROILED LIVER

1 lb calf's or lamb's liver, sliced ½ inch thick
Melted butter or margarine
Salt
Pepper

1. Brush liver with melted butter; sprinkle with salt and pepper.
2. Broil, 3 inches from heat, 3 minutes on each side.
Makes 4 servings.

# ✦ PAN-FRIED LIVER

2 tablespoons flour
½ teaspoon salt
⅛ teaspoon pepper
1 lb calf's or lamb's liver, sliced ½ inch thick
2 tablespoons butter or margarine

1. Combine flour, salt, and pepper on sheet of waxed paper. Dredge liver in mixture, coating well.
2. Melt butter in large skillet. Sauté liver until nicely browned—about 5 minutes on each side.
Makes 4 servings.

# ✦ VENETIAN-STYLE CALF'S LIVER

1½ lb calf's liver, sliced 1 inch thick
¼ cup flour
1½ teaspoons salt
¼ teaspoon pepper
¼ cup butter or margarine
¼ cup olive or salad oil
2 lb onions, thinly sliced
½ teaspoon dried sage leaves
¼ cup dry white wine
1 tablespoon lemon juice
2 tablespoons chopped parsley

1. With paper towels, pat liver dry. Cut into strips ⅛ inch wide (see Note).
2. On sheet of waxed paper, combine flour, salt, and pepper. Roll liver in mixture, coating well.
3. In large skillet, heat butter and 2 tablespoons oil. Sauté liver strips, turning frequently, until lightly browned on all sides—about 5 minutes. Remove, and set aside.
4. Add remaining oil to skillet. Sauté onion slices, stirring frequently, until golden—about 10 minutes. Add sage. Cook, covered, over low heat 5 minutes.
5. Combine liver with onions, tossing lightly. Cook, covered, over low heat 5 minutes. Remove liver and onions to serving dish.
6. To drippings in skillet, add white wine and lemon juice; bring to boiling, stirring. Pour over liver and onions. Sprinkle with chopped parsley.
Makes 6 to 8 servings.

*Note*: To make liver easier to slice thin, place in freezer long enough to chill thoroughly.

# ✦ VEAL KIDNEYS PROVENÇALE

2 (½-lb size) veal kidneys
¼ cup all-purpose flour
1 teaspoon salt
⅛ teaspoon pepper
½ lb fresh mushrooms
¼ cup butter or margarine
1 tablespoon olive or salad oil
1 tablespoon chopped shallot
2 tablespoons chopped parsley
1¼ cups dry white vermouth
Dash lemon juice
Chopped parsley

1. Wash kidneys. Cut in half; remove white center part. Slice thin—¼ inch thick.
2. On waxed paper, combine flour, salt, and pepper; mix well. Roll sliced kidneys in flour mixture, coating well.
3. Wipe mushrooms with damp cloth. Trim stems; slice lengthwise through cap and stem.
4. In hot butter and oil in large skillet, sauté kidneys, turning kidneys and shaking skillet, about 10 minutes, or until nicely browned on both sides. Add shallot and 2 tablespoons parsley; cook 5 minutes more.
5. Add mushrooms and ¼ cup vermouth; cook 5 minutes longer. Add rest of vermouth; cook gently, covered, 15 more minutes, or until kidneys are tender.
6. To serve: Sprinkle with lemon juice and parsley. Serve with rice or toast points, if desired.
Makes 4 servings.

# ❖ SWEETBREADS IN WHITE WINE IN PATTY SHELLS

2 lb sweetbreads
2 quarts water
2½ teaspoons salt
1 pkg (6 oz) frozen patty shells
6 tablespoons butter or margarine
½ cup thinly sliced carrot
½ cup thinly sliced onion
6 medium mushrooms, halved
1 cup dry white wine
4 tablespoons flour
¾ cup light cream
⅓ cup condensed chicken broth
Chopped parsley

1. Soak sweetbreads in cold water to cover 1 hour; drain.
2. Bring 2 quarts water to boiling in large saucepan. Add sweetbreads and 2 teaspoons salt; return to boiling. Reduce heat, and simmer, covered, 20 minutes.
3. Drain sweetbreads. Plunge into ice water, to keep white and firm; let cool completely in water. Remove outer membrane and any fat in folds of sweetbreads. Pat dry with paper towels. Cut into about 1-inch cubes. (You should have 3 cups sweetbreads.)
4. Bake patty shells as package label directs. Keep warm.
5. In 2 tablespoons butter in skillet, sauté carrots and onion until soft—about 5 minutes. Add sweetbreads; cook over medium heat, stirring occasionally, about 20 minutes, or until lightly browned.
6. Meanwhile, in 2 tablespoons butter in large saucepan, sauté mushrooms until golden—about 5 minutes. Add to sweetbread mixture with ½ cup wine; simmer, covered, 5 minutes.
7. In same saucepan, melt remaining butter. Remove from heat; blend in flour and remaining ½ teaspoon salt. Gradually stir in cream and undiluted chicken broth; bring to boiling, stirring constantly. Reduce heat, and simmer 1 minute.
8. Stir in sweetbread mixture and liquid, and remaining wine; bring mixture just to boiling.
9. Spoon about ⅔ cup sweetbreads and sauce into and over each patty shell on individual serving plates. Cover with pastry tops; sprinkle with parsley.
Makes 6 servings.

# ❖ BOILED TONGUE

3- to 4-lb smoked beef tongue
1 large onion, quartered
10 whole black peppercorns
¼ teaspoon mustard seed
2 bay leaves
4 whole cloves
About 3 quarts water
Sour-Cream Sauce, page 465

1. Wash tongue; pat dry with paper towels.
2. In 6-quart kettle, combine tongue and remaining ingredients with water to cover—about 3 quarts.
3. Bring to boiling. Reduce heat; simmer, covered, 2½ to 3 hours, or until tongue is tender.
4. Drain tongue. Plunge tongue into cold water.
5. To remove skin: With sharp knife, gently slit skin on underside from thick end to tip. Peel off skin, and remove and discard root.
6. To serve: Slice tongue thin, and serve hot or cold with Sour-Cream Sauce.
Makes 7 or 8 servings.

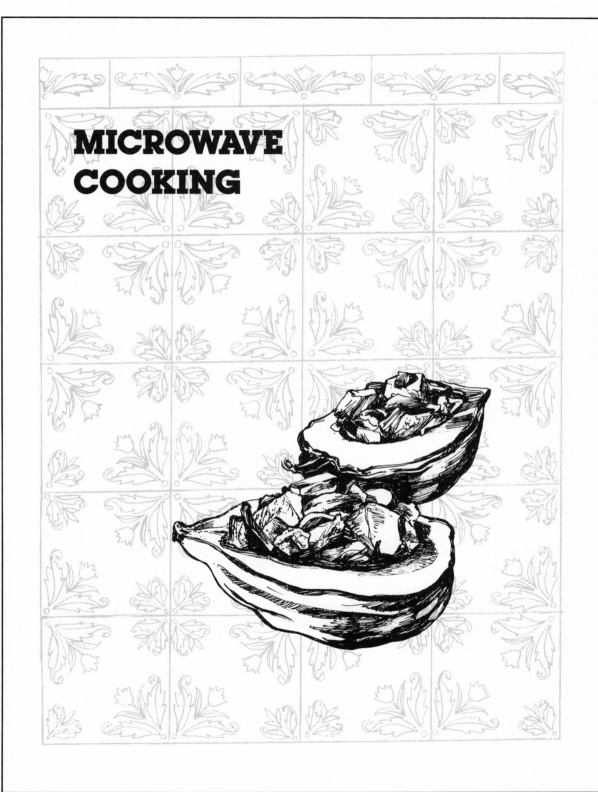

# MICROWAVE COOKING

♦ **A** microwave oven offers both convenience and speed and is the most versatile means of cooking yet developed. In it you can roast, simmer, bake, cook, defrost, and reheat foods—all in less time than it takes by conventional methods and often with better results.

It's convenient, for example, to put creamed soup into glass bowls or microwave-safe cups and have it piping hot in 3 or 4 minutes with no pan to wash. It's convenient to lay three strips of bacon on a paper towel, resting on a paper plate, and have them crisp and ready-to-serve in less than 3 minutes with no fat to discard and no pan to wash.

It's time-saving to cook a potato in less than 5 minutes, to bake acorn squash in less than 10 minutes, and to have the most perfectly baked apples in about 8 minutes.

These few simple examples are just the beginning of the advantages of microwave cooking for busy people. The use, and the results, anyone will get from a microwave oven depend entirely upon the right utensils for the food to be prepared, timing, and knowing the cooking techniques involved and when to apply them.

The way to get the best use out of your microwave oven is to start with the easy, uncomplicated uses—cooking vegetables from the frozen state, reheating leftovers, or baking a meat loaf (about 13 minutes). Learn how a microwave works, keep reading the cookbook that came with your oven, and try more complicated cooking little by little.

The general advice that follows will be useful in learning about microwaving.

## UTENSILS

Oven-proof glass dishes—casseroles, pie plates, measuring cups—are all suitable for microwave cooking. Paper plates, napkins, rigid (dishwasher-safe) plastics, china (without metallic trim), glass custard cups, and loaf pans are also safe for microwave cooking. There are utensils manufactured specifically for microwave cooking. As your use of the oven increases, you may want to add them to your store of equipment. In general, round or oval shapes are best; shallow is better than deep; and individual containers are better than large ones. The idea is to allow the microwaves to penetrate the food quickly and easily. The ring shape, not unlike the familiar tube pan, is considered ideal because it allows the microwaves to enter the food from different angles, and you can devise one by inverting a custard cup in the center of a round casserole.

Metal utensils are generally not recommended for microwave-oven use, though they can be used in some models. Check the manufacturer's use and care book.

A trivet or roasting rack is essential when roasting meats, to lift them out of their juices, and when steaming vegetables.

## TIMING

Several factors affect microwave cooking time:
*Density*: Dense, compact foods, such as potatoes, carrots, and roasts, take longer to cook or heat than light, porous foods, such as cakes, breads, and rolls.
*Size*: Small pieces cook faster than large ones. Pieces that are similar in shape and size (2 inches or less in diameter) cook more evenly. Avoid stacking foods.
*Shape*: Irregularly shaped items—chicken pieces, for example—will cook differently from meat loaf and other evenly shaped foods. Arrange irregular pieces so that thicker parts

are toward the outside edge of the utensil, and thinner parts, toward the center.

*Quantity*: Cooking time is directly related to the number of servings being cooked. Small amounts usually take less time than large amounts. As the quantity increases, microwaving time increases.

*Starting temperature*: Foods taken directly from the refrigerator take longer to microwave than those at room temperature.

*Height in oven*: For even cooking, foods that stand higher than 5 inches should be turned over or shielded during cooking. Cakes and other batters need to be elevated on another dish, such as an oven-proof glass pie plate, turned upside down or put on a roasting rack or trivet.

*Moisture*: Foods naturally high in moisture, such as fresh vegetables, fruits, fish, poultry, soups, and sauces, cook faster than foods low in moisture such as dried peas, beans, and rice. But avoid excessive moisture in such dishes as casseroles, cakes, and sauces, since it lengthens microwave-cooking time; liquids do not evaporate as they do in conventional cooking. If you are converting a conventional recipe, you may need to cut down on the liquid.

*Fat and sugar content*: Fats and sugar attract microwaves. As a result, foods high in sugar or fat cook more quickly than other foods. Meats containing large chunks of fat tend to cook more slowly because the fat attracts microwaves away from the meat; fat that is evenly distributed makes for quicker, more even cooking. Trim meats of excess exterior fat for faster, more even cooking.

# TECHNIQUES

*Arrangement*: The placement of the food within the utensil or the oven is critical. Arrange foods of more or less equal size, for example, potatoes, apples, and meat patties, in a circle, leaving the center empty. Asparagus tips and the flower ends of broccoli should be placed toward the center of the pan, and the stems, toward the edge, where the microwaves will penetrate first.

*Stirring*: Since microwaves cook from all directions, stir from outside to the center of the utensil to combine the heated portions of the food with unheated portions and shorten cooking time. Foods like puddings, sauces, and cream soups, which require constant stirring when cooked conventionally, will need only occasional stirring in a microwave.

*Rearranging*: Since corners and sides of utensils receive more energy and some spots in the oven may be warmer than others, foods that cannot be stirred, such as roasts, chops, and meat patties, need to be rearranged or turned over during the cooking process.

*Rotating*: Foods that cannot be stirred, rearranged, or turned over, such as cakes and pies, should be given a half- or quarter-turn during microwaving to permit even cooking.

*Shielding*: To slow down cooking in spots that tend to get done first, use small pieces or strips of aluminum foil as shields to cover these portions. Foil shields may be added or removed at any time during the cooking process.

*Piercing*: Foods that have thick skins or membranes—potatoes, acorn squash, egg yolks, chicken livers, frankfurters—must be pierced before microwaving to allow steam to escape and to prevent bursting.

*Covering*: The rate of evaporation is not easy to control in microwave cooking. The reason for covering some foods while they cook is to retain the steam for tenderizing, to keep the food moist, to shorten cooking time, or to help prevent spattering. When you want to keep foods really moist, use plastic wrap as a covering. In fact, when a microwave recipe specifies "heat or cook covered," it refers to the use of plastic wrap or utensil lid.

Whether or not to cover a food to be microwaved can be determined by the type of food it is and the end result you want, for example, crispness or moistness. Oven manufacturers give very specific instructions for the types of coverings to use. The chart that follows is a good general guide.

| REASON | COVER | FOOD |
|---|---|---|
| Retain moisture and steam<br>Speed cooking<br>Hold in heat<br>Promote even cooking | Plastic wrap or utensil lid | Vegetables (fresh or frozen); fish (unless bread-coated); casseroles (pasta type); meats that need steam for tenderizing |
| Prevent spattering<br>Absorb excess moisture<br>Promote even cooking | Paper towel | Bacon; sandwiches; vegetable casseroles (saucy); bread-coated meats, poultry, seafood; reheating rolls and breads |
| Retain heat<br>Allow steam to escape | Waxed paper | Fruits; meats; soups; chicken; ground-meat patties; some cakes |

NOTE: All of the following recipes were tested in a 650-watt microwave oven. For 400- to 500-watt ovens, add 30 seconds to each minute of cooking time; for 500- to 600-watt ovens, add 15 seconds to each minute of cooking time.

# ⌘ CARROT AND POTATO SOUP

2 large baking potatoes (1 lb), peeled
3 carrots (½ lb), pared
1 small onion
1 can (13¾ oz) chicken broth
1 cup milk or light cream
½ teaspoon dried dillweed or 1½ teaspoons snipped fresh dill
¼ teaspoon salt

1. Cut potatoes, carrots, and onion into small pieces or chop in food processor, using chopping blade.
2. Place chopped vegetables in microwave-safe 3-quart utensil; pour ½ of chicken broth over vegetables.
3. Cover with utensil lid or plastic wrap; microwave at HIGH (100% power) 10 minutes.
4. Transfer vegetables and liquid to food processor or blender; process to purée.
5. Return puréed vegetables to utensil; add remaining chicken broth, milk, dill, and salt. Cover; microwave at MEDIUM (50% power) for 10 minutes.
Makes 4 to 6 servings.

# ⌘ FISH FILLETS FLORENTINE

1 lb fresh or frozen fish fillets
2 pkg (10-oz size) frozen chopped spinach
½ cup diced onion
1 teaspoon dried dillweed or 1 tablespoon snipped fresh dill
Salt
Pepper
4 teaspoons lemon juice
Paprika
¾ cup grated sharp Cheddar cheese

1. To thaw frozen fish, place package in microwave oven; microwave at MEDIUM LOW (30% power) 6 minutes; halfway through, turn package over. Gently separate fillets.
2. Pierce spinach package on top several times with fork; microwave at HIGH (100% power) 5 minutes to defrost. Press spinach package to remove moisture.
3. Place spinach in bowl; add onion, dill, 1 teaspoon salt, and ¼ teaspoon pepper. Spread mixture in microwave-safe 12-by-7½-by-2-inch utensil. Top with fish fillets; place thicker edges toward outside of

dish. Sprinkle fillets with lemon juice, and season with salt, pepper, and paprika to taste.

4. Cover with waxed paper; microwave at HIGH (100% power) 6 to 8 minutes. After 4 minutes, sprinkle grated cheese over fish, and rotate dish. Remove from oven; let stand 5 minutes before serving. Makes 4 servings.

# ✦ SEAFOOD GUMBO

1 pkg (16 oz) frozen flounder
4 tablespoons butter or margarine
⅔ cup chopped green onion, with tops
1 cup chopped celery
1½ teaspoons salt
¼ teaspoon ground thyme
1 whole bay leaf
6 to 10 drops hot pepper sauce
2 cans (16-oz size) stewed tomatoes
3 tablespoons cornstarch
1 cup chicken broth
1 pkg (10 oz) frozen sliced okra
1 pkg (12 oz) frozen cleaned raw shrimp

1. Place package of flounder in microwave oven; microwave at MEDIUM LOW (30% power) 3 minutes. Remove wrapping; cut flounder into 1-inch pieces. Set aside.

2. In microwave-safe 3-quart utensil combine butter, green onion, and celery; microwave at HIGH (100% power) 5 minutes. Stir well once.

3. Add salt, thyme, bay leaf, hot pepper sauce, and tomatoes. Cover with plastic wrap, and microwave at HIGH (100% power) 10 minutes.

4. Combine cornstarch and broth; stir into tomato mixture. Add okra, shrimp, and flounder; re-cover with plastic wrap. Microwave at HIGH (100% power) 15 to 18 minutes, or until shrimp and fish are cooked. Let stand 5 minutes before serving.
Makes 8 servings.

# ✦ JIFFY CRABMEAT

1 tablespoon butter or margarine
½ cup sliced mushrooms
1 small green pepper, cut into ¼-inch strips
2 tablespoons toasted slivered almonds
½ teaspoon lemon rind
1 teaspoon lemon juice
1 can (10½ oz) condensed cream of celery soup, undiluted
2 tablespoons chopped pimiento
1 tablespoon chopped parsley
Dash Tabasco sauce
Dash pepper
1 can (6½ oz) crabmeat, drained, or 1 pkg (6 oz) frozen crabmeat, thawed and well drained
2 cups hot cooked rice

1. Place butter, mushrooms, and green pepper in microwave-safe 2-quart casserole. Cover with plastic wrap, and microwave at HIGH (100% power) 2 minutes.

2. Add all remaining ingredients except rice. Stir to mix.

3. Cover with waxed paper, and microwave at HIGH (100% power) 6 minutes, stirring after 3 minutes. Let stand, covered with waxed paper, 3 minutes. Serve crabmeat mixture over rice.
Makes 4 servings.

# ✠ FISH WITH HERB-CHEESE SAUCE

1 lb fresh or frozen fish fillets
¼ cup sliced celery
¼ cup chopped onion
3 tablespoons butter or margarine
3 tablespoons flour
¼ teaspoon salt
¼ teaspoon dried tarragon leaves,
   crushed
Dash pepper
1¼ cups milk
1 cup (4 oz) shredded Monterey Jack
   cheese
3 cups hot cooked rice (optional)

1. To thaw frozen fish, place package in microwave oven; microwave at MEDIUM LOW (30% power) 6 minutes; halfway through, turn package over. Gently separate fillets.
2. Place celery, onion, and butter in microwave-safe 2-quart utensil. Microwave at HIGH (100% power) 4 to 5 minutes, or until vegetables are tender, stirring after 2 minutes.
3. Blend in flour, salt, tarragon, and pepper. Gradually add milk, stirring constantly. Cover with plastic wrap; microwave at HIGH (100% power) 4 to 5 minutes, or until sauce boils and thickens, stirring once each minute. Add cheese; stir until melted.
4. Arrange fillets in microwave-safe 12-by-7½-by-2-inch utensil; top with cheese sauce. Cover with waxed paper; microwave at HIGH (100% power) 4½ minutes, turning utensil after 2 minutes. Let stand, covered, 2 to 3 minutes before serving, or until fish flakes easily with fork. Serve with cooked rice, if desired.
Makes 4 servings.

# ✠ CHICKEN BREASTS VERONIQUE

¼ teaspoon shredded orange peel
½ cup orange juice
1 tablespoon sliced green onion
½ teaspoon instant-chicken-bouillon
   granules
4 medium chicken-breast halves (1½
   to 2 lb), skinned
Salt
Pepper
Paprika
1 tablespoon cornstarch
1 tablespoon cold water
½ cup seedless green grapes, halved
Parsley (optional)
Orange slices (optional)
Green-grape clusters (optional)

1. In microwave-safe 12-by-7½-by-2-inch utensil, combine orange peel, orange juice, green onion, and bouillon granules. Add chicken; sprinkle with salt, pepper, and paprika to taste. Cover with waxed paper; microwave at HIGH (100% power) 10 minutes, rearranging chicken once. Remove chicken to warm platter; cover to keep warm.
2. Measure pan juices. Add water, if necessary, to measure ¾ cup liquid. Blend cornstarch with cold water; stir into pan juices. Microwave at HIGH (100% power) 2 minutes, or until thickened and bubbly, stirring after 1 minute.
3. Add halved grapes; microwave at HIGH (100% power) 30 seconds.
4. Spoon some sauce over chicken; pass remaining sauce. Garnish with parsley, orange slices, and grape clusters, if desired.
Makes 4 servings.

# ✠ FANCY BAKED CHICKEN

1 can (16 oz) whole cranberry sauce
1 tablespoon brown sugar
1 tablespoon defrosted orange juice
  concentrate
4 tablespoons butter
1 can (13¾ oz) chicken broth
1 medium onion, finely chopped
2 stalks celery, chopped (optional)
1 pkg (8 oz) herb-seasoned stuffing
  mix
1 frying chicken (2½ to 3 lb), cut into
  serving pieces

1. Combine cranberry sauce, brown sugar, and orange juice concentrate in small glass bowl. Microwave at HIGH (100% power) 45 seconds and stir. Set aside.
2. In 3-quart oblong microwave-safe baking dish, heat butter and chicken broth at HIGH (100% power). 4 minutes.
3. Add onion, celery, and stuffing mix. Toss to combine.
4. Arrange chicken pieces on top of stuffing, with meatier portions toward outside. Cover dish loosely with waxed paper, and microwave at HIGH (100% power) 10 minutes.
5. Rotate dish and brush chicken with cranberry mixture. Cover again with waxed paper. Microwave at HIGH (100% power) an additional 10 to 15 minutes, or until chicken is tender. Remove from oven and allow to stand 5 minutes.
Makes 4 to 6 servings.

# ✠ BURGUNDY BEEF STEW

1 lb boneless beef chuck, 1 inch thick
3 tablespoons flour
1 teaspoon salt
⅛ teaspoon pepper
1 tablespoon salad oil
4 medium carrots, sliced ½ inch thick
8 small onions
½ cup Burgundy
1 tablespoon catsup
1 clove garlic, minced
¼ teaspoon dried marjoram leaves
⅛ teaspoon dried thyme leaves
¼ lb fresh mushrooms, sliced
2 tablespoons water
2 tablespoons chopped parsley

1. Cut beef into 1-inch cubes. Combine 2 tablespoons flour, salt, and pepper; dredge beef. Place beef and oil in microwave-safe 2½-quart utensil. Cover with plastic wrap, venting one corner; microwave at MEDIUM LOW (30% power) 20 minutes, stirring after 10 minutes.
2. Add carrots and onions, arranging onions in circle around beef. Combine Burgundy, catsup, garlic, marjoram, and thyme; pour over beef and vegetables. Re-cover with plastic wrap, vent, and microwave at MEDIUM LOW (30% power) 45 minutes, stirring every 15 minutes.
3. Add mushrooms and continue microwaving, covered with plastic wrap, 5 minutes, or until tender.
4. Combine remaining flour and water; stir into beef and vegetables, and sprinkle with parsley. Re-cover with plastic wrap; microwave at MEDIUM LOW (30% power) 3 minutes, stirring after 1½ minutes. Remove from oven; let stand, covered, 5 minutes.
Makes 4 servings.

# ⊞ SLICED BEEF WITH VEGETABLES

1-lb top-round steak, cut 1 inch thick
1 can (16 oz) tomatoes
1 cup thinly sliced carrot
½ cup chopped onion
½ teaspoon dried basil leaves
¼ teaspoon dried oregano leaves
2 tablespoons flour
1 teaspoon salt
⅛ teaspoon ground cumin
⅛ teaspoon pepper
1 tablespoon salad oil
1 cup thinly sliced zucchini

1. Slice steak strips ⅛ inch thick or less and 2 to 2½ inches long. (See Note).
2. Drain juice from tomatoes into microwave-safe 1½-quart utensil; break up and reserve tomatoes. Add carrot, onion, basil, and oregano to tomato juice; cover with plastic wrap, and microwave at HIGH (100% power) 5 minutes, stirring after 2 minutes.
3. Combine flour, salt, cumin, and pepper; dredge steak strips. Measure oil into microwave-safe 12-by-7½-by-2-inch utensil or shallow 2½-quart casserole; spread steak strips in layer over bottom. Cover with waxed paper; microwave at MEDIUM (50% power) 6 minutes, stirring after 4 minutes.
4. Stir in carrot mixture, reserved tomatoes, and zucchini. Re-cover with plastic wrap; microwave at MEDIUM (50% power) 20 minutes, or until tender, stirring every 3 minutes. Remove from oven; let stand, covered, 3 minutes.
Makes 4 servings.

*Note*: Partially freeze steak to facilitate cutting into thin slices.

# ⊞ SPEEDY SPAGHETTI MEAT SAUCE

1 lb ground beef
½ cup chopped onion
¼ teaspoon salt
Dash pepper
1 can (14 oz) Italian tomatoes
¼ cup water
2 tablespoons Parmesan cheese
1 clove garlic, minced
½ teaspoon dried marjoram leaves
½ teaspoon crushed dried rosemary
Cooked pasta

1. Combine ground beef with onion; arrange in ring in all-plastic colander or sieve set over microwave-safe 2½-quart utensil. Cover with waxed paper; microwave at HIGH (100% power) 5 minutes, stirring and breaking up beef after 2½ minutes and again after removing from oven.
2. Place colander containing beef on absorbent paper; sprinkle with salt and pepper. Re-cover with waxed paper, and let stand 2 to 3 minutes.
3. Discard fat from 2½-quart utensil, and in it combine tomatoes, water, cheese, garlic, marjoram, and rosemary. Cover with waxed paper; microwave at HIGH (100% power) 2 minutes.
4. Stir in beef. Re-cover with waxed paper; microwave at HIGH (100% power) 8 to 10 minutes. Let stand 3 minutes. Serve over cooked pasta.
Makes 6 servings.

# ❖ PORK CHOPS À LA SUISSE

**STUFFING:**

*1 cup soft bread crumbs*
*2 tart apples, peeled and diced*
*2 tablespoons butter or margarine,*
*   melted*
*½ teaspoon liquid gravy seasoning*
*⅛ teaspoon crushed caraway seeds*
*⅛ teaspoon salt*
*Dash pepper*

*6 pork chops (2 lb), ¾ inch thick*
*1 tablespoon water*
*¼ teaspoon liquid gravy seasoning*

1. Make Stuffing: Combine all stuffing ingredients in microwave-safe medium-size utensil; mix well. Microwave at HIGH (100% power) 2 minutes, stirring several times.
2. Cut deep slit in side of each chop. Fill with stuffing. Secure with wooden picks.
3. Place prepared chops in single layer in microwave-safe 12-by-7½-by-2-inch utensil, with thickest meaty areas toward edge and end piece toward center of utensil. Combine water and ¼ teaspoon gravy seasoning; brush chops with half of mixture. Cover with waxed paper.
4. Microwave at MEDIUM (50% power) 20 minutes. Turn chops over. Brush with remaining seasoning mixture. Re-cover with waxed paper; microwave at MEDIUM (50% power) 15 minutes, or until tender. Remove from oven; let stand, covered, 5 minutes before serving.
Makes 6 servings.

# ❖ STUFFED ACORN SQUASH

*2 medium acorn squash (2½ lb)*
*2 tablespoons butter or margarine*
*3 tablespoons chopped green onion*
*1 cup diced cored apple*
*2 cups cooked, cubed chicken*
*⅓ cup chopped walnuts*
*2 tablespoons freshly squeezed lemon*
*   juice*
*½ teaspoon dried tarragon leaves*
*¼ teaspoon dried thyme leaves*
*2 tablespoons butter or margarine*
*Lemon wedges*

1. Pierce whole squash through to center in several places with long metal skewer or sharp knife. Place squash at opposite corners of microwave oven on paper towel. Microwave at HIGH (100% power) 5 minutes, rotating corners after 2½ minutes. Turn over; microwave 5 minutes more, rotating corners after 2½ minutes, or until slightly soft to the touch. Let stand 5 minutes.
2. Cut squash in half vertically; discard seeds and fibers. Scoop out approximately ⅓ cup pulp from each half. Mash pulp with fork. Set aside.
3. In microwave-safe 1-quart utensil, melt butter at HIGH (100% power). Microwave green onion and apple in melted butter at HIGH (100% power) 3 minutes, or until tender.
4. Add chicken, walnuts, lemon juice, tarragon, thyme, and reserved squash pulp; mix well. Spoon filling into squash halves, dot with butter.
5. Place squash halves in circle in microwave-safe utensil; cover with paper towels. Microwave at HIGH (100% power) 5 minutes, or until heated through. Serve with lemon wedges.
Makes 4 servings.

# ❖ EGGPLANT ITALIANO

2 medium eggplants (1 lb each)
4 green onions, sliced
½ cup chopped green pepper
1 small yellow squash (½ lb), diced
1 can (16 oz) whole tomatoes, well
  drained and chopped
3 tablespoons butter or margarine,
  melted
1½ teaspoons salt
¼ teaspoon pepper
1 teaspoon Italian seasoning
1 cup seasoned croutons
¼ cup grated Parmesan cheese

1. Pierce skin of each eggplant with fork 2 or 3 times to create vent holes. Place whole eggplant on paper towel, and arrange in opposite corners in microwave oven. Microwave at HIGH (100% power) 5 to 7 minutes. Let stand 2 to 3 minutes.

2. Split each eggplant in half lengthwise. Scoop out pulp; save shells. Mash pulp in blender or with potato masher by hand, and combine with green onions, green pepper, squash, tomatoes, butter, salt, pepper, Italian seasoning, and croutons. Fill eggplant shells with mixture.

3. Arrange filled shells on microwave-safe ribbed utensil or trivet. Cover with waxed paper; microwave at HIGH (100% power) 8 to 10 minutes. At end of cooking time, sprinkle with grated cheese. Remove from oven; let stand, covered, 3 to 5 minutes. Makes 4 servings.

# ❖ CORN-STUFFED ZUCCHINI

3 medium zucchini (1½ lb), cut in
  half lengthwise
¼ teaspoon salt
3 tablespoons butter or margarine
⅓ cup chopped onion
⅓ cup chopped green pepper
1 pkg (10 oz) frozen corn, thawed
1 teaspoon dried tarragon leaves
¼ teaspoon pepper

1. With spoon, scoop out pulp from zucchini halves, leaving ¼-inch shell intact; sprinkle with ⅛ teaspoon salt. Chop zucchini pulp.

2. Place butter in microwave-safe 1-quart utensil; microwave at HIGH (100% power) 1 minute, or until melted.

3. Stir in zucchini pulp, onion, and green pepper; microwave at HIGH (100% power) 3 minutes.

4. Combine corn, tarragon, ⅛ teaspoon salt, and the pepper with zucchini mixture; microwave at HIGH (100% power) 2 minutes. Spoon vegetable mixture into zucchini halves, mounding slightly.

5. Place filled zucchini shells in shallow microwave-safe utensil. Cover with waxed paper; microwave at HIGH (100% power) 6 to 8 minutes, or until zucchini is just tender. Remove from oven; let stand, covered, 3 to 5 minutes before serving. Makes 6 servings.

# ❖ HERBED SQUASH DELIGHT

1 lb small zucchini or yellow squash,
 sliced ¼ inch thick
⅓ cup chopped onion
1 tablespoon water
1 medium carrot, grated
½ cup sour cream
1 can (10½ oz) cream of chicken soup,
 undiluted
3 tablespoons butter or margarine,
 melted
¾ cup packaged herb stuffing mix

1. Place squash, onion, and water in microwave-safe 10-by-6-inch utensil. Cover with plastic wrap; microwave at HIGH (100% power) 5 minutes. Drain.
2. In a medium bowl, combine carrot, sour cream, and soup. Stir in squash mixture; mix well.
3. In small bowl, combine butter and stuffing mix. Spread half of stuffing mix in bottom of microwave-safe 10-by-6-inch utensil. Pour squash mixture over top. Cover with plastic wrap; microwave at HIGH (100% power) 4 minutes.
4. Sprinkle remaining stuffing mixture over top. Cover with paper towel; microwave at HIGH (100% power) 2 minutes. Remove from oven; let stand, covered, 5 minutes.
Makes 4 servings.

# ❖ POTATOES ROMANOFF

2 patties or 2 cups frozen shredded
 hash brown potatoes
1 cup cottage cheese
1 cup sour cream
2 tablespoons chopped green onion
2 tablespoons chopped parsley
1 clove garlic, minced
½ teaspoon salt
1 tablespoon butter or margarine

1. Place frozen hash brown potatoes in microwave-safe 1-quart casserole. Cover with plastic wrap; microwave at HIGH (100% power) 3 minutes. Stir; microwave at HIGH (100% power) 3 minutes longer.
2. Add cottage cheese, sour cream, green onion, parsley, garlic, and salt. Mix well; dot with butter. Cover with plastic wrap; microwave at HIGH (100% power) 4 minutes. Stir.
3. Cover with paper towel; microwave at HIGH (100% power) 2 minutes. Remove from oven; let stand 5 minutes, covered with paper towel, before serving.
Makes 4 servings.

# ❖ EGG-SPINACH BAKE

1 pkg (10 oz) frozen chopped spinach
2 eggs
1½ cups sour cream
2 tablespoons flour
3 tablespoons grated Parmesan
 cheese
½ teaspoon salt
1 tablespoon finely chopped onion
⅛ teaspoon pepper
6 hard-cooked eggs (recipe below),
 chopped

1. Pierce spinach package on top several times with fork. Microwave at HIGH (100% power) 5 minutes to defrost. Press spinach to remove moisture.
2. Beat eggs. Add sour cream, flour, Parmesan cheese, salt, onion, and pepper. Stir in spinach, and fold in hard-cooked eggs.
3. Pour into greased microwave-safe 1-quart ring mold, muffin-cup ring, or 6 custard cups. Microwave at MEDIUM LOW (30% power) 10 to 15 minutes, or until knife inserted halfway between middle and outer edge comes out clean. Remove from oven; let stand, uncovered, 10 minutes before removing from mold or cups.
Makes 6 servings.

## MICROWAVE HARD-COOKED EGGS

1. Place 1 teaspoon butter in each of 6 microwave-safe custard cups or muffin-ring cups. Break egg into each cup. Pierce yolk with toothpick.
2. Cover with plastic wrap; microwave at HIGH (100% power) 30 seconds to 1 minute per egg. Remove from oven; keep covered until ready to use.

# ❖ HOT GERMAN POTATO SALAD

3 baking potatoes (1½ lb)
2 slices bacon, diced
½ cup chopped onion
½ cup chopped celery

### DRESSING:

⅓ cup cider vinegar
¼ cup water
1 teaspoon sugar
¼ teaspoon ground celery seed
¼ teaspoon caraway seed
¼ teaspoon dried parsley
¾ teaspoon salt
Dash Tabasco sauce

4 knockwurst, cut in half lengthwise, and skin removed

1. Wash and dry potatoes; prick with fork. Arrange potatoes in ring on paper towel. Microwave at HIGH (100% power) 15 minutes, or until almost tender, turning once. Cool potatoes. Peel, and slice ¼ inch thick; set aside.
2. In microwave-safe utensil, combine bacon, onion, and celery. Cover with waxed paper; microwave at HIGH (100% power) 5 minutes. Stir.
3. In 2-cup glass measure, make Dressing: Mix vinegar, water, sugar, celery seed, caraway seed, parsley, salt, and Tabasco sauce. Microwave at HIGH (100% power) 2 minutes.
4. In microwave-safe 2½-quart casserole, arrange half of potatoes, onion, and bacon. Pour half of dressing. Repeat. Arrange knockwurst over potatoes. Cover with plastic wrap; microwave at HIGH (100% power) 3 minutes; turn dish. Uncover; microwave at HIGH (100% power) 2 minutes longer, or until heated through. Remove from oven; let stand, covered, 3 to 5 minutes before serving.
Makes 4 servings.

# ❖ NEW DELHI RICE

1 tablespoon butter or margarine
½ cup chopped onion
1 teaspoon salt
½ teaspoon curry powder
⅛ teaspoon pepper
1¼ cups chicken broth
1 cup orange juice
1 cup uncooked long-grain rice
½ cup raisins
⅓ cup slivered almonds, toasted
2 tablespoons chopped parsley

1. Place butter in microwave-safe 2-quart utensil. Microwave at HIGH (100% power) 30 seconds.
2. Add onion, salt, curry powder, and pepper to melted butter; stir. Microwave at HIGH (100% power) 2 minutes.
3. Add chicken broth, orange juice, rice, and raisins to onion mixture; stir. Cover with utensil lid or plastic wrap. Microwave at HIGH (100% power) 5 minutes, or until boiling. Reduce power to MEDIUM (50% power); cook 15 minutes, or until liquid is absorbed. Remove from oven. Let stand, covered, 5 minutes. Serve sprinkled with toasted almonds and parsley.
Makes 6 servings.

# ❖ CRANBERRY-AND-PEAR CRISP

1 pkg (12 oz) cranberries
2 unpeeled pears (1 lb), cored and
  sliced
2 tablespoons plus ½ cup flour
1 cup granulated sugar
1 teaspoon ground cinnamon
½ cup brown sugar, packed
⅓ cup butter or margarine
¾ cup regular oats
¾ cup chopped pecans or walnuts
Vanilla ice cream (optional)

1. In microwave-safe 2-quart utensil, thoroughly mix cranberries, pears, 2 tablespoons flour, the granulated sugar, and cinnamon.
2. In bowl, combine ½ cup flour and the sugar; cut in butter until mixture resembles coarse crumbs. Add oats and nuts; sprinkle evenly over fruit mixture.
3. Microwave at HIGH (100% power) 12 minutes, rotating utensil quarter-turn every 3 minutes. Remove from oven; let stand 5 minutes. Serve topped with ice cream, if desired.
Makes 6 servings.

# ❖ LEMON-ORANGE COCONUT CAKE

Solid shortening
2 tablespoons graham-cracker
  crumbs
¼ cup butter or margarine
¾ cup orange marmalade
½ cup flaked coconut
1 pkg (18¾ oz) pudding-style lemon-
  cake mix
1 cup water
⅓ cup oil
3 eggs

1. Grease microwave-safe 12-cup tube utensil with solid shortening; coat with graham-cracker crumbs.
2. In microwave-safe 2-cup glass measure, place butter; microwave at HIGH (100% power) 45 seconds, or until melted. Add marmalade and coconut; mix well. Spread evenly on bottom of prepared utensil.
3. In large bowl, blend cake mix, water, oil, and eggs until moistened. With portable electric mixer, beat 2 minutes at highest speed. Pour batter over marmalade mixture.
4. Microwave at MEDIUM LOW (30% power) 11 minutes, rotating utensil quarter-turn every 3 minutes. Microwave at HIGH (100% power) 5½ minutes longer.
5. Cool upright in utensil on flat surface 10 minutes; turn out onto serving dish. Spoon any remaining marmalade in utensil over cake. Cool completely.
Makes 16 servings.

# ❖ LIGHT 'N FLUFFY TAPIOCA

2 cups skim milk
¼ cup plus 2 tablespoons sugar
¼ cup quick-cooking tapioca
¼ teaspoon salt
2 eggs, separated
1 teaspoon vanilla

1. Place milk in 1-quart glass measure or in microwave-safe casserole. Add ¼ cup sugar, tapioca, salt, and egg yolks. Blend well. Cover with plastic wrap; microwave at MEDIUM (50% power) 8 minutes, or until mixture begins to boil. Stir well after 4 minutes.
2. Beat egg whites until frothy. Gradually add 2 tablespoons sugar, beating until mixture forms soft peaks; add vanilla. Fold into pudding mixture. Cool. Chill if desired.
Makes 6 servings.

# PASTA

◈ **A**mericans' fondness for spaghetti and meatballs or macaroni and cheese has become a full-blown love affair with pasta— pasta with fish or vegetable sauces, pasta in ravioli, stuffed shells, lasagna, pasta in soups, and, with growing frequency, pasta in intricately seasoned salads. As our nutritional knowledge of food has grown, pasta has lost the connotation of being a fattening food. It is recognized as a provider of desirable carbohydrates and protein and also as a low-fat, low-sodium product.

Pasta comes in a multitude of shapes and sizes (one estimate says 325), which can add variety to your use of pasta (see "Guide to Pasta Uses" below).

How much pasta to cook per person? It depends largely upon whether the pasta is being used as a side dish or a main dish and, of course, on your family's appetites. The general rule is 8 oz for 4 servings.

Our own treasury of pasta recipes has increased enormously over the years, and this section reflects that richness—including directions for making homemade pasta.

## GUIDE TO PASTA USES

| SHAPE | DESCRIPTION |
| --- | --- |
| Soup pastas | |
|   Alphabets and stars | Noodles cut in variety of shapes, including crowns, hearts, clubs, diamonds |
|   Bows | Tiny noodle shape; come in many sizes |
|   Ditalini | Small macaroni, cut short; comes in many sizes |
|   Egg-noodle flakes | Small squares of egg-noodle dough, about ¼ inch square |
|   Orzo | A pasta that resembles rice |
|   Tubettini | Tiny macaroni, smaller then ditalini |
| Pastas to serve with sauces | |
|   Fettuccine | Flat noodles made in long lengths; variety of widths, |
|     Trenettine | narrowest to widest, are listed at left |
|     Trenette | |
|     Fetuccelle | |
|     Fettuccine | |
|     Fetucce | |
|     Lasagnette | |
|   Linguine | Solid spaghetti rod pressed into an oval shape; variety of |
|     Bavettini | sizes, smallest to largest, are listed at left |
|     Bavette | |
|     Linguine | |
|     Linguine de passeri | |
|   Spaghetti | General name for solid rod form of pasta; comes in many |
|     Fidellini | different sizes, some of which, from smallest to largest, are |
|     Cagellini | listed at left |
|     Vermicelli | |
|     Spaghettini | |
|     Spaghetti | |
|     Spaghettoni | |
|   Fusilli | Long strands of spiraled spaghetti; easy to handle (often called "non-skid" spaghetti) |
|   Vermicelli clusters | Fine spaghetti strands twisted into cluster that separates on cooking |

| SHAPE | DESCRIPTION |
|---|---|
| Ziti | Hollow-rod macaroni; comes in long tubes or cut into short tubes |
| **Pasta to stuff with meat, vegetable, or seafood mixtures** | |
| Manicotti | Tubes about 4 inches long and 1 inch in diameter; made in both plain and green (spinach) forms |
| Rigatoni | Grooved pasta tube; smaller then manicotti |
| Shells | Made in many sizes; giant or jumbo shells best for fillings |
| Tufoli | Large tube pasta; ridged version known as tufoli rigati |
| **Pasta for casseroles** | |
| Egg noodles, wide, medium or narrow | The base of many good casseroles, but may also serve as side dish with stews |
| Elbow macaroni, large, medium, or small | Short curved pasta; blends well with cheese and chopped meat in sauced casseroles and is basis of macaroni salad |
| Lasagna | Curly-edged or flat, plain or green, this wide noodle gives a favorite dish its name |
| Shells, medium or small | Particularly good in tomato-sauced dishes; use small ones in salads |
| **Shaped pastas** | |
| Bows Spirals (rotini) Wheels | Because of shape, add variety and interest to casserole or salad |

NOTE: Ready-to-heat filled pastas, notably ravioli and tortellini, are found in freezer counters. Tortellini and cappeletti are also available in dry form.

# ❖ BASIC DIRECTIONS FOR COOKING MACARONI, SPAGHETTI, NOODLES

*1 tablespoon salt*
*3 quarts boiling water*
*1 pkg (7 or 8 oz) macaroni, spaghetti, or noodles*

1. In large kettle, bring salted water to a rapid boil. Add macaroni, breaking long pieces into short ones. You may leave long spaghetti whole; place one end in boiling water, and gradually coil in rest as it softens.
2. Bring back to boiling. Cook, uncovered, stirring occasionally with long fork to prevent sticking, just until tender—about 7 to 10 minutes. Do not overcook.
3. Drain in colander or sieve. Do not rinse.
Makes 4 to 6 servings.

*Poppy-Seed Noodles*: Cook 8-oz pkg noodles as directed above. Toss drained hot noodles with ¼ cup melted butter and 1 tablespoon poppy seed.

*Caraway Noodles*: Cook 8-oz pkg noodles as directed above. Toss drained hot noodles with ¼ cup melted butter and 1 tablespoon caraway seed.

## ❖ BAKED NOODLES ROMANOFF

1 pkg (8 oz) noodles
1 cup cottage cheese
1½ cups sour cream
1 teaspoon Worcestershire sauce
1 teaspoon salt
⅛ teaspoon pepper

1. Preheat oven to 350F.
2. Cook noodles as package label directs; drain.
3. In large bowl, blend cottage cheese, sour cream, and seasonings. Toss gently with noodles.
4. Turn out into 2-quart casserole; cover.
5. Bake 15 to 20 minutes, or until thoroughly hot.
Makes 4 to 6 servings.

## ❖ FETTUCCINE AND BROCCOLI

1 pkg (8 oz) medium noodles
¼ cup salad oil
1 clove garlic, crushed
1 pkg (10 oz) frozen chopped broccoli, thawed and drained
½ cup canned condensed chicken or beef broth, undiluted
½ teaspoon dried basil leaves
¼ cup chopped parsley
¼ cup grated Parmesan cheese
1 cup (8 oz) cottage cheese
½ teaspoon salt
Dash pepper

1. Cook noodles according to package directions; drain.
2. Meanwhile, in hot oil in medium skillet, sauté garlic and broccoli, stirring, 5 minutes.
3. Add remaining ingredients. Stir over low heat until blended—will take about 2 minutes.
4. Toss broccoli mixture with noodles. Turn out into heated serving dish.
Makes 4 servings.

## ❖ BUTTERED LINGUINE PARMESAN

1 pkg (1 lb) linguine
¾ cup butter or margarine
2 tablespoons finely chopped onion
1 small clove garlic, crushed
2 tablespoons chopped parsley
½ cup grated Parmesan cheese

1. Cook linguine as package label directs.
2. Meanwhile, melt butter in small saucepan. Add onion and garlic; simmer 5 minutes. Keep warm.
3. Drain linguine, and place on serving platter. Pour sauce over all; sprinkle with parsley; toss gently. Sprinkle with Parmesan, and serve immediately.
Makes 8 servings.

# ❖ LINGUINE CARBONARA

1 pkg (1 lb) linguine
7 bacon strips
½ cup butter or margarine
½ cup grated Parmesan cheese
4 eggs, well beaten
1 tablespoon chopped parsley

1. Cook linguine as package label directs; drain well.
2. Meanwhile, cook bacon until crisp; drain on paper towels.
3. In large skillet, combine butter and cheese; stir until margarine is melted.
4. Add linguine and eggs; toss quickly over low flame just until eggs are cooked.
5. Turn out into warm serving dish. Garnish with bacon strips; sprinkle with parsley and, if desired, additional Parmesan.
Makes 8 servings.

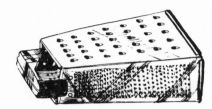

# ❖ SPAGHETTI WITH MARINARA SAUCE

⅓ cup olive or salad oil
2 or 3 cloves garlic, crushed
⅓ cup chopped parsley
1 can (1 lb 12 oz) Italian tomatoes, undrained
1 teaspoon dried oregano leaves
½ teaspoon salt
Dash pepper
1 pkg (8 oz) cooked spaghetti

1. In hot oil in large skillet, sauté garlic and parsley about 3 minutes. Add undrained tomatoes, oregano, salt, and pepper; mix well, mashing tomatoes with fork.
2. Bring mixture to boiling. Then reduce heat, and simmer, uncovered and stirring occasionally, 30 minutes, or until sauce is thickened.
3. Serve hot over spaghetti.
Makes 3 to 4 servings.

# ❖ SPAGHETTI WITH PESTO SAUCE

¼ cup butter or margarine, softened
¼ cup grated Parmesan cheese
½ cup finely chopped parsley
1 clove garlic, crushed
1 teaspoon dried basil leaves
½ teaspoon dried marjoram leaves
¼ cup olive or salad oil
¼ cup finely chopped walnuts or pine nuts
1 pkg (8 oz) cooked spaghetti or noodles

1. With wooden spoon, cream butter, Parmesan, parsley, garlic, basil, and marjoram until well blended.
2. Gradually add oil, beating constantly. Add walnuts; mix well.
3. Add to spaghetti in heated serving dish, and toss until well coated.
Makes about 4 servings.

# ❖ SPAGHETTI WITH WHITE CLAM SAUCE

2 cans (7½-oz size) minced clams
¼ cup olive or salad oil
¼ cup butter or margarine
2 or 3 cloves garlic, crushed
2 tablespoons chopped parsley
1½ teaspoons salt
1 pkg (8 oz) cooked spaghetti
Grated Parmesan cheese

1. Drain clams, reserving ¾ cup liquid. Set aside.
2. In skillet, slowly heat oil and butter. Add garlic, and sauté until golden. Remove from heat.
3. Stir in clam liquid, parsley, and salt; bring to boiling. Reduce heat; simmer, uncovered, 10 minutes.
4. Add clams; simmer 3 minutes.
5. Serve hot over spaghetti, with Parmesan cheese. Makes 4 to 6 servings.

# ❖ MORE SPAGHETTI SAUCES

## TOMATO SAUCE:

1 can (2 lb 3 oz) Italian tomatoes
¼ cup olive or salad oil
1 cup finely chopped onion
1 clove garlic, crushed
1 can (6 oz) tomato paste
1½ cups water
2 sprigs parsley
1 tablespoon salt
2 teaspoons sugar
1 teaspoon dried oregano leaves
½ teaspoon dried basil leaves
¼ teaspoon pepper

1. Purée undrained Italian tomatoes in electric blender, or press through sieve with juice.
2. In hot oil in large saucepan, sauté onion and garlic until golden-brown—about 5 minutes.
3. Add puréed tomato, tomato paste, water, parsley, salt, sugar, oregano, basil, and pepper; mix well.
4. Bring to boiling; reduce heat, and simmer, covered and stirring occasionally, 1 hour. Cook, uncovered and stirring occasionally, ½ hour longer.
Makes 4½ cups.

*Note*: Freeze any unused Tomato Sauce for another time.

## MEAT AND MUSHROOM SAUCE:

2 tablespoons olive or salad oil
2 cloves garlic, sliced
¼ lb fresh mushrooms, sliced
½ lb ground pork
½ lb ground veal
1 can (2 lb) Italian tomatoes, undrained
½ can (6-oz size) tomato paste
2 teaspoons sugar
3 teaspoons salt
¼ teaspoon pepper

1. In hot oil in large heavy skillet or saucepan, sauté garlic just until golden; lift out garlic and discard.
2. To oil, add mushrooms, pork, and veal; cook, stirring occasionally, 10 minutes.
3. Add tomatoes, tomato paste, sugar, salt, and pepper. Bring to boiling; reduce heat, and simmer, covered and stirring occasionally, 1 hour.
Makes 6 cups.

## SARDINE SAUCE:

2 tablespoons salad or olive oil
1 clove garlic, crushed
1 medium onion, finely chopped
1 can (1 lb) Italian tomatoes, un-
    drained
½ can (6-oz size) tomato paste
1 cup water
1 teaspoon sugar
¼ teaspoon salt
Dash pepper
½ teaspoon dried oregano leaves
1 tablespoon chopped parsley
1 can (3¾ oz) sardines in tomato
    sauce

1. In hot oil in large skillet, sauté garlic and onion, stirring, 5 minutes, or until tender.
2. Add tomatoes, tomato paste, water, sugar, salt, pepper, oregano, and parsley; mix well. Bring to boiling; reduce heat, and simmer, covered and stirring occasionally, 45 minutes.
3. Gently remove bones from sardines. Add sardines in tomato sauce to tomato mixture; simmer, covered, 5 minutes.
Makes 2⅔ cups.

## THREE CHEESE SAUCE:

¼ cup butter or margarine
½ cup light cream
1 cup grated Swiss cheese
1 cup grated sharp Cheddar cheese
¼ cup grated Parmesan cheese
½ teaspoon salt
Dash pepper
2 tablespoons chopped parsley

1. Heat butter and cream in medium saucepan until butter is melted.
2. Add Swiss cheese, Cheddar cheese, 2 tablespoons Parmesan cheese, the salt, and pepper. Cook over low heat, stirring constantly, until sauce is blended and fairly smooth.
3. Toss sauce with 1 lb cooked, drained pasta (spinach linguine, spaghetti, or egg noodles). Turn out into serving dish; sprinkle with chopped parsley and remaining Parmesan cheese.
Makes about 3 cups.

# ▓ SHRIMP SPAGHETTI

1 pkg (8 oz) spaghetti
½ lb unshelled raw shrimp
¼ cup salad or olive oil
½ cup chopped onion
2 cloves garlic, crushed
3 medium tomatoes (1 lb), peeled and
    coarsely chopped, or 1 can (1 lb)
    tomatoes, undrained
⅛ teaspoon pepper
1 teaspoon dried basil leaves
½ teaspoon salt
¼ cup chopped parsley
½ cup pitted black olives
Grated Parmesan cheese

1. Cook spaghetti according to package label. Drain well; return to kettle.
2. Rinse shrimp; remove shells, and devein. Using small sharp knife, split each shrimp in half down the back.
3. In hot oil in medium skillet, over medium heat, sauté onion, garlic, and shrimp, stirring, until onion is golden and shrimp turn pink—about 5 minutes. Remove shrimp; set aside.
4. Add tomatoes, pepper, basil, and salt. Bring to boiling; simmer, uncovered, 5 minutes. Return shrimp to skillet.
5. Pour shrimp mixture, with parsley, over spaghetti; toss until well coated.
6. Turn out onto platter; garnish with olives. Serve at room temperature with grated Parmesan cheese.
Makes 4 servings.

# ✦ SPAGHETTI PRIMAVERA

*1 pkg (1 lb) spaghetti*

### VEGETABLES:

*1 tablespoon butter or margarine*
*2 tablespoons salad oil*
*1 clove garlic, split*
*1 zucchini, sliced ¼ inch thick*
*½ lb broccoli, cut into 1½-inch flowerets*
*½ red pepper, cut into ¼-inch strips*
*½ lb whole fresh snow-pea pods, ends trimmed*

### SAUCE:

*½ cup butter or margarine*
*1 cup half-and-half*
*1 cup grated Parmesan cheese*
*¼ teaspoon salt*
*Dash pepper*

*2 tomatoes, peeled and chopped*

1. Start cooking spaghetti as package label directs.
2. Meanwhile, prepare Vegetables: In 1 tablespoon hot butter and the oil in large skillet, toss garlic, zucchini, broccoli, and red pepper; stir-fry 5 minutes, or until vegetables are just crisp. Add pea pods; cook 1 minute. Cook vegetables, covered, 1 to 2 minutes. Do not overcook. Discard garlic.
3. Make Sauce: In medium saucepan, heat butter and half-and-half until butter is melted. Remove from heat. Add ¾ cup cheese, the salt, and pepper; mix well.
4. Drain spaghetti. Toss with sauce; turn out onto heated serving platter. Place vegetables on top. Arrange tomatoes around edge. Sprinkle with remaining ¼ cup Parmesan cheese. Toss at table just before serving.
Makes 6 servings.

# ✦ DELUXE BAKED MACARONI AND CHEESE

*1½ cups elbow macaroni*
*¼ cup butter or margarine*
*¼ cup all-purpose flour*
*1 teaspoon salt*
*⅛ teaspoon pepper*
*1 teaspoon dry mustard*
*2½ cups milk*
*¼ cup chopped pimiento*
*¼ cup chopped green pepper*
*2 cups grated Cheddar cheese (8 oz)*
*2 tablespoons fresh bread crumbs*
*1 tablespoon butter or margarine, melted*

1. Preheat oven to 375F. Cook macaroni as label directs; drain.
2. Meanwhile, melt ¼ cup butter in medium saucepan; remove from heat. Stir in flour, salt, pepper, and mustard until smooth. Gradually stir in milk. Bring to boiling, stirring. Add pimiento and green pepper. Reduce heat; simmer, uncovered, 1 minute.
3. Stir in 1½ cups cheese and the macaroni. Pour into shallow 2-quart baking dish. Mix together bread crumbs and 1 tablespoon butter. Sprinkle bread crumbs and rest of cheese over top.
4. Bake 15 to 20 minutes, or until cheese is melted and crumbs are golden-brown.
Makes 6 servings.

# ✦OUR FAVORITE LASAGNA

*1 lb sweet or hot Italian sausage
    (5 links)*
*½ lb ground beef*
*½ cup finely chopped onion*
*2 cloves garlic, crushed*
*2 tablespoons sugar*
*1½ teaspoons dried basil leaves*
*½ teaspoon fennel seed*
*¼ teaspoon pepper*
*¼ cup chopped parsley*
*4 cups canned tomatoes, undrained,
    or 1 can (2 lb 3 oz) Italian-style
    tomatoes*
*2 cans (6-oz size) tomato paste*
*½ cup water*
*12 curly lasagna noodles (¾ of 1-lb
    pkg)*
*1 container (15 oz) ricotta or cottage
    cheese, drained*
*1 egg*
*½ teaspoon salt*
*¾ lb mozzarella cheese, thinly sliced*
*¼ cup grated Parmesan cheese*

1. Remove sausage meat from outer casings; chop meat. In 5-quart Dutch oven, over medium heat, sauté sausage, beef (break up beef with wooden spoon), onion, and garlic, stirring frequently, until well browned—20 minutes.

2. Add sugar, 1 tablespoon salt, the basil, fennel, pepper, and half the parsley; mix well. Add tomatoes, tomato paste, and ½ cup water, mashing tomatoes with wooden spoon. Bring to boiling; reduce heat, and simmer, covered and stirring occasionally, until thick—1½ hours.

3. In 8-quart kettle, bring 3 quarts water and 1 tablespoon salt to boiling. Add lasagna noodles, 2 or 3 at a time. Return to boiling; boil, uncovered and stirring occasionally, 10 minutes, or just until tender. Drain in colander; rinse under cold water. Dry noodles on paper towels.

4. Preheat oven to 375F. In medium bowl, combine ricotta, egg, remaining parsley, and salt; mix.

5. In bottom of 13-by-9-by-2-inch baking dish, spoon 1½ cups sauce. Layer with 6 lasagna noodles, lengthwise and overlapping, to cover. Spread with half of ricotta mixture; top with third of mozzarella. Spoon 1½ cups sauce over cheese; sprinkle with ¼ cup Parmesan. Repeat layering, starting with 6 lasagna noodles and ending with 1½ cups sauce sprinkled with Parmesan. Spread with remaining sauce; top with rest of mozzarella and Parmesan. Cover with foil, tucking around edge.

6. Bake 25 minutes. Remove foil; bake, uncovered, 25 minutes longer, or until bubbly. Cool 15 minutes before serving.

Makes 8 servings.

# ❖ VEGETARIAN CHEESE LASAGNA

## TOMATO SAUCE:

¼ cup olive or salad oil
1 cup finely chopped onion
1 clove garlic, crushed
1 can (2 lb 3 oz) Italian tomatoes
1 can (6 oz) tomato paste
1 can (8 oz) tomato sauce
2 tablespoons chopped parsley
1 tablespoon salt
1 tablespoon sugar
1 teaspoon dried oregano leaves
½ teaspoon dried basil leaves
¼ teaspoon pepper

1 pkg (1 lb) lasagna noodles

## CHEESE LAYER:

2 containers (15-oz size) ricotta
   cheese
1½ pkg (8-oz size) mozzarella cheese,
   grated coarsely
½ cup grated Parmesan cheese
2 eggs
1 tablespoon chopped parsley
1 teaspoon salt
¼ teaspoon pepper

3 tablespoons grated Parmesan
   cheese
½ pkg (8-oz size) mozzarella cheese,
   grated

1. Make Tomato Sauce: In hot oil in 6-quart kettle, sauté onion and garlic until golden-brown—about 10 minutes. Add undrained tomatoes, tomato paste, tomato sauce, 2 tablespoons parsley, 1 tablespoon salt, the sugar, oregano, basil, and ¼ teaspoon pepper; mix well, mashing tomatoes with fork.
2. Bring to boiling; reduce heat, and simmer, covered and stirring occasionally, 1 hour.
3. Preheat oven to 350F. Cook lasagna noodles as package label directs. Grease 14-by-10-by-2-inch baking pan.
4. Make Cheese Layer: In large bowl, combine ricotta, 1½ packages mozzarella, ½ cup Parmesan, the eggs, parsley, salt, and pepper. Beat with wooden spoon until all ingredients are blended.
5. Spoon a little tomato sauce into prepared pan. Layer noodles, cheese mixture, and tomato sauce. Repeat until all ingredients are used, ending with tomato sauce. Sprinkle with 3 tablespoons Parmesan and ½ package mozzarella.
6. Bake, uncovered, 45 to 50 minutes, or until cheese is melted, and top is browned.
Makes 10 to 12 servings.

# ❖ BAKED STUFFED TUFOLI

4 cups Tomato Sauce, page 337
2 tablespoons salt
6 quarts boiling water
½ pkg (1-lb size) tufoli (20) or manicotti

1. Make Tomato Sauce.
2. In large kettle, add salt to boiling water. Add tufoli; return to boiling. Boil 10 to 15 minutes, or until almost tender. Drain; lay flat on tray to cool.
3. Meanwhile, make Filling: In hot oil in large skillet, sauté onion and garlic until tender—about 5 min-

## FILLING:

¼ cup salad or olive oil
1 cup chopped onion
1 clove garlic, crushed
1 lb ground beef chuck
½ lb ground veal
1 pkg (10 oz) frozen chopped
    spinach, thawed, drained, and
    finely chopped
2 tablespoons chopped parsley
1 teaspoon dried oregano leaves
1 teaspoon salt
¼ teaspoon pepper
1 pkg (8 oz) mozzarella cheese, cut
    into ½-inch cubes

1 pkg (8 oz) mozzarella cheese, thinly
    sliced crosswise
½ cup grated Parmesan cheese

utes. Add beef and veal; brown lightly, stirring—about 15 minutes.
4. Remove from heat. Add spinach, parsley, oregano, salt, pepper, and cubed mozzarella. Mix well.
5. Preheat oven to 375F. With small spoon, stuff meat mixture into tufoli from each end.
6. Pour 1 cup tomato sauce in bottom of 13-by-9-by-2-inch baking dish or shallow oval baking dish.
7. Arrange tufoli in tomato sauce. Pour rest of tomato sauce over top. Cover with foil. Bake 25 minutes.
8. Remove from oven; remove foil. Place slice of mozzarella on each tufoli. Sprinkle with Parmesan cheese. Bake 10 minutes, or until cheese is melted. Makes 8 to 10 servings.

# ✖ PASTA E FAGIOLI

1½ cups dried navy or pea beans
6 cups cold water
2 teaspoons salt
½ pkg (1-lb size) shell macaroni
    (3 cups)
3 tablespoons olive oil
1 large onion, chopped
2 cups thinly sliced carrot
1 cup chopped celery
1 clove garlic, crushed
2 cups diced peeled tomato (1 lb)
1 teaspoon dried sage leaves
½ teaspoon dried oregano leaves
¼ teaspoon pepper
Chopped parsley
Grated Parmesan cheese

1. In large bowl, combine beans and cold water. Refrigerate overnight.
2. Next day, turn out beans and water into 6-quart kettle. Add 1½ teaspoons salt.
3. Bring to boiling; reduce heat, and simmer, covered, about 2 to 2½ hours, or until beans are tender. Stir several times during cooking. Drain, reserving liquid (there will be about 2½ cups).
4. Cook macaroni, following package-label directions.
5. Meanwhile, in hot oil in large skillet, sauté onion, carrot, celery, and garlic, covered, until soft—about 20 minutes. Do not brown. Add tomato, sage, oregano, ½ teaspoon salt, and the pepper. Cover; cook over medium heat 15 minutes.
6. In large saucepan or kettle, combine beans, macaroni, and vegetable mixture. Add 1½ cups reserved bean liquid. Bring to boiling. Cover, and simmer 35 to 40 minutes, stirring several times and adding more bean liquid if needed. Add salt and pepper if needed.
7. Turn out into attractive serving dish or casserole. Sprinkle with chopped parsley and grated Parmesan cheese.
Makes 8 servings.

## SAVORY PASTA AND CHEESE

*½ pkg (16-oz size) cavatelle or other pasta*

### VEGETABLE-CHEESE SAUCE:

*½ cup butter or margarine*
*1 cup thinly sliced carrot*
*1 cup thinly sliced celery*
*½ cup chopped green onion*
*¼ cup all-purpose flour*
*1 teaspoon dried oregano leaves*
*½ teaspoon salt*
*2 teaspoons prepared mustard*
*2 cups milk*
*1½ cups grated sharp Cheddar cheese*
*½ cup sour cream*

*6 cherry tomatoes*
*2 tablespoons chopped parsley*

1. Cook pasta as package label directs; drain.
2. Make Vegetable-Cheese Sauce: In hot butter in 5-quart Dutch oven, over medium heat, sauté carrot, celery, and green onion about 5 minutes, stirring constantly. Remove from heat.
3. Add flour, oregano, salt, and mustard; stir until smooth. Add milk, a small amount at a time, stirring after each addition. Return to heat.
4. Over medium heat, bring to boiling, stirring constantly. Reduce heat; simmer 3 minutes.
5. Add cheese; stir until melted. Add pasta and sour cream; stir just until heated through—about 1 minute. Turn out into serving dish. Garnish center with a row of tomatoes. Sprinkle edge with chopped parsley.

Makes 6 servings.

## HOMEMADE PASTA

Once you've tasted fresh pasta versus dried, you will probably be tempted to become a homemade-pasta maker. The recipe is simple and has few ingredients; the work of making pasta is in the stretching and rolling of the dough, a job that, like bread kneading, requires some skill developed through experience. There are, however, many pasta-making machines on the market, which take over that time-consuming job. They range from expensive to reasonable. The highest-price models require that you add ingredients only —the machine takes over the mixing, rolling, and cutting (or extruding) of the dough. Less expensive models take over the job of rolling the dough to the required thickness (the hard part) and cutting the flat dough into a variety of widths. Some brands of food processors have pasta-making attachments. No matter which you buy, be sure your machine is well anchored—that it clamps onto a tabletop or is heavy enough to stay in place when it is being used.

Fresh pasta takes less than 5 minutes to cook, depending upon the size of the strands; you can vary the flavors and the colors, and it tastes wonderful. Instructions for use, and recipes, come with pasta machines. Our recipes give instructions for hand rolling and cutting—let a machine take over if you wish.

# ✖ EGG PASTA

*3 cups all-purpose flour*
*½ teaspoon salt*
*4 eggs*
*1 tablespoon salad or olive oil*
*2 to 3 tablespoons lukewarm water*

*3 quarts water*
*1 tablespoon salt*
*1 tablespoon salad oil*

1. Sift flour with salt into medium bowl.
2. Make well in center. Add eggs and oil. Pour water in gradually, and mix with fork until well combined. Dough will be stiff. Form into ball.
3. Turn out onto lightly floured wooden board. Knead dough until smooth and elastic—about 15 minutes. Cover with bowl; let rest at least 30 minutes (this makes it easier to roll out). Makes 1½ pounds.
4. To shape: Divide dough into 4 parts. Keep covered with bowl until ready to roll out; or refrigerate in plastic bags.
5. On lightly floured pastry cloth or board, roll each part into rectangle about 16 by 14 inches and about ¹⁄₁₆ inch thick. (Or put dough through flat rollers of pasta machine several times, gradually decreasing size of opening until dough reaches desired thinness.)
6. Work quickly, because dough dries out. From long side, roll up loosely as for jelly roll.
7. With thin sharp knife, cut roll crosswise, ⅛ inch wide for fettuccine. (Or insert preferred cutting blade or disc in pasta machine and cut noodles to desired width.) For lasagna noodles, cut rolled dough into strips 2 inches wide and 6 inches long. For wide noodles, cut into strips ¾ inch wide. For narrow noodles, cut ¼ inch wide.
8. Unroll noodles, and wind loosely around fingers. For fresh pasta, cook immediately. Or freeze in plastic bags for a week.
9. To dry pasta, arrange on ungreased cookie sheets; let dry overnight. Store pasta in covered glass jar in cool place.
10. To cook: In large kettle, bring 3 quarts of water, 1 tablespoon salt and 1 tablespoon salad oil to rapid boil. Add pasta; bring back to boiling; cook, uncovered and stirring occasionally with long fork to prevent sticking, just until tender—3 to 5 minutes for fresh pasta, 7 to 10 minutes for dried. (Do not thaw frozen pasta.) Do not overcook. Drain well; do not rinse.
Makes 1½ pounds.

*Note*: For food processor, place all ingredients in processor container. Process about 1 minute, or just until mixture leaves sides of container. Continue with Step 3.

# ✖ PASTA VARIATIONS

## SPINACH OR BROCCOLI PASTA:

1 pkg (10 oz) frozen chopped spinach
  or broccoli
3 cups all-purpose flour
½ teaspoon salt
2 eggs
1 tablespoon salad or olive oil

1. Cook spinach according to package directions; drain well. Purée in food processor or blender.
2. Follow directions for making Egg Pasta, adding puréed spinach along with eggs and oil, and omitting water. (If dough seems sticky, add more flour to board during kneading.)
Makes 1½ pounds.

## TOMATO PASTA:

3 cups all-purpose flour
½ teaspoon salt
2 eggs
1 can (8 oz) tomato sauce
1 tablespoon salad or olive oil
2 teaspoons dried basil leaves

Follow directions for Egg Pasta, adding tomato sauce and basil with eggs and oil, omitting water. (If dough is sticky, add more flour to board during kneading.)
Makes 1½ pounds.

## WHOLE-WHEAT PASTA:

2 cups whole-wheat flour
1 cup all-purpose flour
½ teaspoon salt
4 eggs
1 tablespoon salad or olive oil
3 to 4 tablespoons lukewarm water

Follow directions for Egg Pasta.
Makes 1½ pounds.

## PARMESAN-CHEESE PASTA:

3 cups all-purpose flour
¼ cup grated Parmesan cheese
½ teaspoon salt
3 eggs
1 tablespoon salad or olive oil
5 to 6 tablespoons lukewarm water

Follow directions for Egg Pasta. Add Parmesan with flour and salt.
Makes 1½ pounds.

## CARROT PASTA:

2 cups sliced carrots
Boiling water
3 cups all-purpose flour
½ teaspoon salt
2 eggs
1 tablespoon salad or olive oil

1. In small saucepan, cook carrots, covered, in 2 inches boiling water until tender. Drain; purée in food processor or blender. Cool completely; use 1 cup.
2. Follow directions for making Egg Pasta, adding 1 cup carrot purée along with eggs and oil, and omitting water. (If dough seems sticky, add more flour to board during kneading.)
Makes 1½ pounds.

## ASPARAGUS PASTA:

1 pkg (10 oz) frozen asparagus
3 cups all-purpose flour
½ teaspoon salt
3 eggs
1 tablespoon salad or olive oil

1. Cook asparagus according to package directions; drain well. Purée in food processor or blender.
2. Follow directions for making Egg Pasta, adding puréed asparagus along with eggs and oil, and omitting water. (If dough seems sticky, add more flour to board during kneading.)
Makes 1⅔ pounds.

## ORANGE PASTA:

3 cups all-purpose flour
½ teaspoon salt
3 eggs
1 tablespoon salad or olive oil
2 tablespoons grated orange peel
3 to 4 tablespoons orange juice

Follow directions for making Egg Pasta, substituting orange juice for water. (If dough seems sticky, add more flour to board during kneading.)
Makes 1¼ pounds.

# ❖ PEPPERS AND BROCCOLI WITH WHOLE-WHEAT FETTUCCINE

2 large red peppers (1 lb)
3 tablespoons olive oil
2 cloves garlic
Salt
1 bunch broccoli (about 1½ lb)
Whole-Wheat Pasta, page 345 (see Note)
¼ cup butter or margarine, melted
¼ cup grated Parmesan cheese

1. Prepare peppers: Wash peppers. Cut in half, and remove seeds and ribs. Cut peppers into ½-inch-wide lengthwise strips.
2. In hot oil in large skillet, over medium heat, sauté garlic until golden—about 5 minutes. Remove and discard garlic.
3. Add peppers; cook over medium heat, stirring occasionally, just until tender but not soft. Sprinkle with 1 teaspoon salt.

4. Prepare broccoli: Remove large leaves and tough portions of broccoli. Wash thoroughly; drain. Separate, splitting larger stalks into quarters. Place in 6-quart saucepan; add boiling water to 1 inch and 1 teaspoon salt. Cook, covered, 10 minutes, or until tender. Drain in colander.

5. Prepare Whole-Wheat Pasta. For fettuccine, cut into strips ¼ inch wide. Freeze half in plastic bag for later use. Or dry it overnight, and store in a cool dry place.

6. Cook remaining half: In large kettle bring 3 quarts water, 3 teaspoons salt, and 1 tablespoon oil to rapid boil. Add pasta. Bring back to boiling. Cook, uncovered and stirring occasionally with long fork to prevent sticking, just until tender—3 to 5 minutes.

7. To serve: In large bowl, combine peppers and whole-wheat fettuccine; toss lightly. Turn out into warm serving dish. Arrange broccoli on top; pour melted butter over broccoli. Sprinkle with Parmesan cheese.

Makes 8 servings.

*Note*: Or use 1 package (8 oz) fettuccine. Cook as label directs; continue with Step 7.

## ◈ PASTA VERDE WITH ANCHOVIES

*1 recipe Broccoli Pasta, page 345, or Asparagus Pasta, page 346 (see Note)*
*Salt*
*2 tablespoons olive oil*
*2 tablespoons butter*
*2 cloves garlic, pressed*
*¼ teaspoon dried basil leaves*
*¼ cup small stuffed olives*
*1 can (2 oz) rolled anchovies, drained*
*4 tablespoons grated Parmesan cheese*
*Chopped parsley*

1. Prepare Broccoli or Asparagus Pasta. Using a fluted pastry wheel, cut pasta into 1½-by-2 inch diamonds. Moisten one corner of the long measurement. Press firmly onto opposite corner. Freeze half in plastic bag for later use. Or dry it overnight, and store in cool, dry place.

2. In large kettle, bring 3 quarts water, 1 tablespoon salt, and 1 tablespoon oil to a rapid boil. Add pasta. Bring back to boiling. Cook, uncovered and stirring occasionally, just until tender, about 3 minutes.

3. In small saucepan, warm olive oil and butter with garlic until butter is melted. Add basil, olives, and anchovies.

4. Drain pasta well. Return to saucepan. Toss with olive oil mixture and 2 tablespoons Parmesan cheese. Turn out onto serving platter. Top with 2 more tablespoons cheese and some chopped parsley. Makes 6 servings.

*Note*: Or use 1 package (8 oz) green fettuccine or egg bows. Cook as label directs. Continue with Step 3.

# ✦ SPINACH SOUP WITH TORTELLINI

1½ lb marrowbones, cracked
1 cup chopped onion
1 bay leaf
4 whole black peppercorns
¼ teaspoon salt
3 cans (10½-oz size) beef broth
1 cup chopped carrot
1 cup chopped celery
2 tablespoons chopped parsley
Tortellini, below (see Note)
½ lb fresh spinach leaves
Chopped parsley
Parmesan cheese

1. Scrape marrow (fat inside bones) into 5-quart Dutch oven. Melt marrow over medium heat, and sauté onion, stirring, until golden—about 5 minutes.
2. Add marrowbones, bay leaf, peppercorns, and salt. Add water to beef broth to make 8 cups; add to Dutch oven. Cover, and bring to boiling; lower heat, and simmer, covered, 1 hour. Drain; remove and discard marrowbones. Skim off fat.
3. Add carrot, celery, and parsley. Return soup to boiling. Reduce heat, and simmer, covered, 20 minutes. Add 24 tortellini; cook over medium heat, stirring occasionally, 10 minutes.
4. Prepare spinach: Cut off root ends. Wash spinach several times; drain.
5. During last 5 minutes of cooking, add spinach leaves. Serve sprinkled with parsley and Parmesan cheese.
Makes 8 cups; 8 servings.

Note: Or use 24 frozen packaged tortellini; do not thaw.

# ✦ TORTELLINI

### FILLING:

½ lb chicken livers
2 tablespoons butter or margarine
¼ cup chopped onion
2 tablespoons Parmesan cheese
½ teaspoon dried basil leaves
¼ teaspoon salt
Dash pepper
1 egg

Egg Pasta, page 344

1. Make Filling: Wash chicken livers; drain on paper towels. Cut each in half.
2. In hot butter in large skillet, sauté onion and chicken livers about 5 minutes.
3. Turn out chicken-liver mixture into food processor or blender; add Parmesan cheese, basil, salt, pepper, and egg; blend until smooth.
4. Prepare Egg Pasta. On lightly floured pastry cloth or board, roll one fourth of dough at a time to ¹⁄₁₆-inch thickness.
5. Cut into rounds with 2½-inch cookie cutter or small drinking glass. Wet edges; place ½ teaspoon filling on each round. Fold dough over filling; press edges together to seal. You now have semicircle. Wrap piece of dough around finger, and press ends togther.
Makes 80 tortellini.

Note: You may freeze any leftover tortellini.

# ✠ HALF-MOON RAVIOLI PRIMAVERA

*2 sweet Italian sausages*
*1 medium onion, coarsely chopped*
*1 slice whole-wheat bread*
*¼ teaspoon dried oregano leaves*
*¼ teaspoon dried basil leaves*
*1 egg*
*1 recipe Spinach Pasta, page 345 (see Note)*
*1 recipe Egg Pasta, page 344 (see Note)*
*Salt*
*½ lb fresh asparagus*
*¼ cup red-wine vinegar*
*3 tablespoons lemon juice*
*⅔ cup olive oil*
*1 teaspoon sugar*
*2 cloves garlic, pressed*
*½ lb medium mushrooms*
*½ box cherry tomatoes*

1. Remove skins from sausage meat. In medium skillet, sauté sausages and onion until sausages are cooked through—5 to 7 minutes.
2. Combine sausages, onion, bread, oregano, basil, and egg in food processor with chopping blade. Process until smooth. Or, chop sausages, onion, and bread, a little at a time, in blender, and combine with oregano, basil, and egg in medium bowl.
3. Prepare Spinach Pasta. Roll out one fourth to make 14-by-10-inch rectangle. Cut into rounds, using 2-inch plain or fluted cookie cutter. Spoon ½ teaspoon sausage filling onto each round. Moisten half of edge of each round; fold over, and press edges together with fork to make half-moon ravioli.
4. Repeat with one fourth of Egg Pasta. (Remaining dough may be rolled out, folded between pieces of floured waxed paper, tightly wrapped, and frozen for use at later time. Scraps from cutting ravioli may be finely chopped and frozen for use in soup.)
5. Cook spinach and egg ravioli together in boiling salted water as directed for Egg Pasta. Wash asparagus well; trim off ends, and peel lower part of stem with vegetable peeler. Slice diagonally to make 2-inch pieces; add to pasta for last 5 minutes. Drain well.
6. In large bowl, combine vinegar, lemon juice, olive oil, 1 teaspoon salt, the sugar, and garlic. Add pasta and asparagus; toss to coat well.
7. Wash and slice mushrooms. Wash cherry tomatoes, and cut in half. Add to pasta. Toss; refrigerate, covered, until thoroughly chilled—at least 4 hours.
Makes 8 servings.

*Note*: You may substitute 48 packaged frozen small ravioli for Spinach and Egg Pasta. Start with Step 5.

# ✠ NOODLES ALFREDO

**HOMEMADE NOODLES:**

*3 cups all-purpose flour*
*Salt*
*3 eggs*
*3 tablespoons lukewarm water*

1. Make Homemade Noodles: In medium bowl, combine flour and ½ teaspoon salt. Make well in center. Add eggs and water; beat with fork until ingredients are combined. Dough will be stiff.
2. Turn out onto lightly floured surface, and knead until smooth and elastic—about 15 minutes. Cover

## ALFREDO SAUCE:

½ cup butter or margarine
⅔ cup heavy cream
1¼ cups grated Parmesan cheese
¼ teaspoon salt
Dash pepper
Chopped parsley

with bowl; let rest 10 minutes. Then divide dough into 4 parts. Keep covered until ready to roll out.

3. Roll out each part to paper thinness, a 12-inch square. (Or put dough through flat rollers of pasta machine several times, gradually decreasing size of opening until dough reaches desired thinness.) Sprinkle lightly with flour. Then roll loosely around rolling pin, as for jelly roll. Slip out rolling pin. With sharp knife, cut into ⅛-inch-wide strips for fine noodles and ⅓-inch-wide strips for broad noodles. (Or insert preferred cutting blade or disc in pasta machine and cut noodles to desired width.) Arrange dough strips on ungreased cookie sheet.

4. In large kettle, bring 4 quarts water with 1 tablespoon salt to boiling. Add noodles; return to boiling. Boil, uncovered, stirring occasionally, 7 to 10 minutes, or until tender. Drain; keep warm.

5. Make Alfredo Sauce: Heat butter and cream in saucepan until butter is melted. Remove from heat. Add 1 cup Parmesan cheese, salt, and pepper. Stir until sauce is blended and fairly smooth.

6. Add to drained noodles, and toss until they are well coated. Sprinkle with remaining Parmesan cheese and the chopped parsley. Serve at once.

Makes 6 servings.

# ✸ PINEAPPLE-GLAZED NOODLE PUDDING

Orange Pasta, page 346 (see Note)
1 pkg (8 oz) cream cheese, at room
    temperature
½ cup butter or margarine, softened
8 eggs
2 cups sour cream
1 cup sugar
2 teaspoons vanilla extract
½ cup raisins

## PINEAPPLE GLAZE:

1 tablespoon sugar
2 teaspoons cornstarch
1 can (8 oz) crushed pineapple, un-
    drained

1. Make Orange Pasta; cut into strips ¼ inch wide.

2. Cook one fourth of noodles according to directions for Egg Pasta (page 344); drain well. (Remaining Orange Noodles can be frozen in plastic bag for a week; or dry overnight, and store in cool, dry place.)

3. Preheat oven to 350F. Lightly grease 2-quart baking dish. Line prepared dish with noodles.

4. In food processor or large bowl of electric mixer, combine cheese, butter, eggs, sour cream, 1 cup sugar, and the vanilla; blend until smooth. Stir in raisins.

5. Pour over noodles. Bake 45 to 50 minutes, or until knife blade inserted in center comes out clean. Remove to rack.

6. Make Pineapple Glaze: In small saucepan, combine sugar and cornstarch; mix well. Stir in pineapple. Over medium heat, bring to boiling, stirring; boil 1 minute. Let cool. Spread over cooled pudding. Refrigerate until serving.

Makes 10 servings.

Note: Or use 5 oz packaged wide noodles; cook as label directs. Continue with Step 3.

# PIES and
# SMALL PASTRIES

The ingredients for making a crisp, flaky, golden piecrust that literally melts in your mouth are few—flour, good fresh shortening, a little salt, and ice water. The secret of making a great piecrust—whether it's to be filled with fresh fruit, a creamy custard, or nuts swimming in a caramel syrup—is in the mixing, rolling, and shaping of the pastry. Handling pastry is an art that is rewarding and well worth learning, and it is not limited just to desserts. Once you've made—and tasted—a good pastry, you'll use your skill to make super pastry to top a casserole, tart shells to fill with creamed meat or vegetables, or cheese straws to serve as appetizers. The secrets of good pastry making are here and in the step-by-step directions in each recipe in this section.

## THE SECRETS OF GREAT PASTRY

Assemble your equipment and ingredients. Once you start to put pastry together, it should move quickly.

*The equipment:* A medium bowl; a pastry blender or two knives for mixing pastry; measuring cups and spoons; a rolling pin with stockinette cover; a pastry cloth or waxed paper; and a pie plate.

*The ingredients:* Flour (unsifted, unless otherwise noted); salt; fresh butter, lard, or vegetable shortening, no warmer than room temperature; and ice water.

*Preparation:* Mix the ingredients according to the recipe for Flaky Pastry (page 354), working quickly. Always refrigerate the pastry unless you plan to roll it out immediately.

Roll out the pastry on a *lightly* floured board or pastry cloth using a stockinette cover on the rolling pin, or roll out between two sheets of waxed paper. Use a circle of waxed paper as a guide if you wish—many pastry cloths have circles imprinted on them. Roll with light strokes, from the center out, alternating directions to make an even circle. Lift the rolling pin each time at the outer edge; never roll back and forth or from edges to center.

Pie plates of heat-resistant glass or dull-finished aluminum give a well-baked, browned bottom crust; don't use shiny metal pans.

## FREEZING PIES AND PIE SHELLS

*Unbaked pie shells* may be freezer-wrapped and frozen for future use; bake them unwrapped and unfrozen in a preheated 450F oven about 20 minutes, until golden-brown. If the pie shell is to be filled before baking, let stand in the refrigerator or at room temperature to thaw. Fill and bake as recipe directs.

*Baked pie shells* may be freezer-wrapped when cool, and frozen for future use. Reheat frozen shells in a preheated 375F oven 10 minutes before filling.

*Cracker or cookie crusts* may be frozen. Thaw before using as recipe directs.

*Fruit pies,* baked or unbaked, can be frozen successfully. Freeze unbaked fruit pies before cutting slits in upper crust. To bake, cut slits for steam vents and bake 1 hour in a preheated 425F oven. Baked fruit pies may be frozen after they have cooled completely. Reheat solidly frozen fruit pies about 40 minutes in a preheated 375F oven.

# ◈ FLAKY PASTRY

## FOR 1-CRUST PIE:

*1 cup all-purpose flour*
*½ teaspoon salt*
*⅓ cup plus 1 tablespoon shortening*
*or ⅓ cup lard*
*2½ to 3 tablespoons ice water*

1. Sift flour with salt into medium bowl.
2. With pastry blender or 2 knives, using a short cutting motion, cut in shortening until mixture resembles coarse cornmeal.
3. Quickly sprinkle ice water, 1 tablespoon at a time, over all of pastry mixture, tossing lightly with fork after each addition and pushing dampened portion to side of bowl; sprinkle only dry portion remaining. (Pastry should be just moist enough to hold together, not sticky.)
4. Shape pastry into ball; wrap in waxed paper, and refrigerate until ready to use. Flatten with palm of hand.
Makes enough pastry for 8- or 9-inch pie shell, or top of 1½-quart casserole.

## FOR 2-CRUST PIE:

*2 cups all-purpose flour*
*1 teaspoon salt*
*¾ cup shortening or ⅔ cup lard*
*5 to 6 tablespoons ice water*

1. Prepare crust following Steps 1, 2, and 3 above.
2. Shape pastry into ball; wrap in waxed paper and refrigerate until ready to use. Divide in half; flatten each half with palm of hand.
3. To make bottom crust: On lightly floured surface, roll out half of pastry to 11-inch circle, rolling with light strokes from center to edge and lifting rolling pin as you reach edge. As you roll, alternate directions, to shape even circle.
4. If rolled piecrust is too irregular in shape, carefully trim off any bulge and use as patch. Lightly moisten pastry edge to be filled in. Gently press patch in place. Smooth seam with several light strokes of rolling pin.
5. Fold rolled pastry in half; carefully transfer to pie plate, making sure fold is in center.
6. Unfold pastry, and fit carefully into pie plate. Do not stretch pastry. Trim bottom crust even with edge of pie plate.
7. Turn out prepared filling onto bottom crust.
8. To make top crust: Roll out remaining half of pastry to 11-inch circle.
9. Fold in half; make several gashes near center for steam vents.
10. Carefully place pastry on top of filling, making sure fold is in center; unfold.
11. Trim top crust ½ inch beyond edge of pie plate. Fold top crust under bottom crust; press gently together to seal. Crimp edges decoratively.

12. For shiny, glazed top, brush top crust with 1 egg yolk beaten with 1 tablespoon water, or with 1 slightly beaten egg white, or with undiluted evaporated milk.

13. To prevent edge of crust from becoming too brown, place 1½-inch strip of foil around crust; bake as recipe indicates. Remove foil last 15 minutes of baking.

Makes enough pastry for 8- or 9-inch 2-crust pie.

# ❖ UNBAKED PIE SHELL

1. On lightly floured surface, roll out Flaky Pastry for 1-Crust Pie (page 354) to 11-inch circle, rolling with light strokes from center to edge and lifting rolling pin as you reach edge. As you roll, alternate directions to shape even circle.

2. If rolled piecrust is too irregular in shape, carefully trim off any bulge and use as patch. Lightly moisten pastry edge to be filled in. Gently press patch in place. Smooth seam with several light strokes of the rolling pin.

3. Fold rolled pastry in half; carefully transfer to 9-inch pie plate, making sure fold is in center.

4. Unfold pastry, and fit carefully into pie plate, pressing gently with fingertips toward center of plate. This eliminates air bubbles under crust and helps reduce shrinkage.

5. Fold under edge of crust, and press into upright rim. Crimp decoratively.

6. Refrigerate until ready to fill and bake.

Makes 1 9-inch shell.

# ❖ BAKED PIE SHELL

1. Prepare pie shell as directed in Unbaked Pie Shell above.

2. Prick entire surface evenly with fork.

3. Refrigerate 30 minutes.

4. Meanwhile, preheat oven to 450F. Bake pie shell 8 to 10 minutes, or until golden-brown.

5. Cool completely on wire rack before filling.

Makes 1 9-inch shell.

# ❖ BAKED GRAHAM-CRACKER PIE SHELL

1¼ cups graham-cracker crumbs (about 18 crackers, crushed with rolling pin or in food processor)
⅓ cup butter or margarine, softened
¼ cup sugar
¼ teaspoon ground cinnamon

1. Preheat oven to 375F.
2. Combine all ingredients in medium bowl; blend with fingers, fork, or pastry blender.
3. Press evenly on bottom and side of 9-inch pie plate, not on rim. Set 8-inch pie plate on top of crumbs. Press firmly; remove pie plate.
4. Bake 8 minutes, or until golden-brown. Cool on wire rack before filling.
Makes 9-inch shell.

# ❖ UNBAKED GRAHAM-CRACKER PIE SHELL

Prepare pie shell as directed in Baked Graham-Cracker Pie Shell above but do *not* bake; instead, refrigerate until ready to fill.

# ❖ FRESH APPLE FLAN

Flaky Pastry for 2-Crust Pie, page 354
1 cup sugar
⅓ cup all-purpose flour
1¼ teaspoons ground cinnamon
Dash salt
3 lb tart cooking apples
2 tablespoons sugar (optional)

1. Prepare Flaky Pastry; shape into ball. On lightly floured surface, roll out pastry into 18-by-14-inch rectangle. Fold in half. Carefully lift and fit into 13-by-9-by-2-inch baking pan; fold edges over, to make shell 1½ inches high. Refrigerate.
2. Preheat oven to 425F.
3. In large bowl, combine sugar, flour, cinnamon, and salt; mix well.
4. Pare, quarter, core, and slice apples—you should have 9 cups. Add to sugar mixture. Toss lightly to coat well.
5. Place one layer of apple slices in pastry-lined pan. Arrange remaining slices in parallel rows across pan.
6. Bake 45 minutes, or until pastry is golden-brown and apple is tender. If desired, sprinkle 2 tablespoons sugar over apple slices the last 5 minutes of baking.
7. Let flan stand in pan on wire rack 20 minutes. Serve warm, cut into squares.
Makes 9 servings.

# ❖ OLD-FASHIONED APPLE PIE

*Flaky Pastry for 2-Crust Pie, page 354*
*1 cup sugar*
*1 teaspoon ground cinnamon*
*4 tablespoons all-purpose flour*
*Dash salt*
*6 cups thinly sliced cored pared tart cooking apples (2 lb)*
*2 tablespoons butter or margarine*

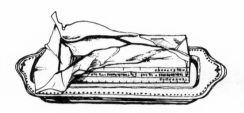

1. Prepare Flaky Pastry; shape into ball. On lightly floured surface, roll out half of pastry into 11-inch circle. Use to line 9-inch pie plate; trim. Refrigerate, with rest of pastry, until ready to use.
2. Preheat oven to 425F.
3. In small bowl, combine sugar, cinnamon, flour, and salt, mixing well.
4. Add to apples in large bowl, tossing lightly to combine.
5. Turn out into pastry-lined pie plate, mounding high in center; dot with butter.
6. Roll out remaining pastry into 11-inch circle. Make several slits near center for steam vents. Adjust over filling; trim.
7. Fold edge of top crust under bottom crust; press together with fingertips. Crimp edge decoratively.
8. Bake 45 to 50 minutes, or until apples are tender and crust is golden-brown.
9. Cool partially on wire rack. Serve warm.
Makes 6 to 8 servings.

*Note*: Test apples for doneness with wooden pick inserted in steam vent in top crust.

# ❖ SOUR-CREAM APPLE PIE

*Flaky Pastry for 2-Crust Pie, page 354*
*3 lb (about 7) tart cooking apples (see Note)*
*2 tablespoons lemon juice*
*1 cup sour cream*
*1 cup granulated sugar*
*2 tablespoons all-purpose flour*
*1 teaspoon ground cinnamon*
*⅛ teaspoon ground nutmeg*
*¼ teaspoon salt*

## TOPPING:

*3 tablespoons dark-brown sugar*
*3 tablespoons granulated sugar*
*1 teaspoon ground cinnamon*
*1 cup chopped walnuts*

*2 tablespoons butter or margarine*
*Milk*
*Granulated sugar*
*Ice cream (optional)*

1. Prepare Flaky Pastry. Shape pastry into ball; divide in half.
2. On lightly floured surface, roll out half of pastry into 12-inch circle. Use to line 9-inch pie plate. Refrigerate, along with remaining pastry, until ready to use.
3. Peel, core, and thinly slice apples into large bowl. Sprinkle with lemon juice. Toss with sour cream. In small bowl, combine 1 cup granulated sugar, the flour, 1 teaspoon cinnamon, the nutmeg, and salt; mix well. Add to apples; toss lightly to combine.
4. Make Topping: Combine brown sugar, 3 tablespoons granulated sugar, the cinnamon, and walnuts; mix well.
5. Roll out remaining half of pastry into 10-inch circle. With knife or pastry wheel, cut into 9 (1-inch-wide) strips.
6. Preheat oven to 400F. Turn out apple mixture into pastry-lined pie plate. Dot top with butter. Sprinkle topping evenly over apple mixture.
7. Moisten rim of pastry slightly with cold water. Arrange 5 pastry strips, ½ inch apart, over filling; press ends to pastry rim. Place remaining strips

across first ones at right angle, to make lattice, and press to rim. Fold overhang of bottom crust over ends of strips, and crimp decoratively. Brush lattice top, but not rim, lightly with milk, and sprinkle with granulated sugar.
8. Bake 50 minutes, or until crust is golden and juice bubbles through lattice. (After 30 minutes, place foil tent loosely over top to prevent overbrowning.)
9. Cool on wire rack. Serve warm, with ice cream, if desired.
Makes 8 servings.

Note: Use Granny Smith or Rome Beauty.

## SCOTCH APPLE TART

*Flaky Pastry for 2-Crust Pie, page 354*

### FILLING:

*3 cups diced pared tart green apple (4 apples)*
*⅓ cup butter or margarine*
*1¾ cups currants*
*⅓ cup light-brown sugar, packed*
*⅓ cup granulated sugar*
*1 teaspoon ground cinnamon*
*¼ teaspoon ground nutmeg*
*¼ teaspoon salt*
*½ cup water*
*¼ cup light or dark rum*
*2 teaspoons cornstarch*

*1 egg yolk*
*2 teaspoons water*
*Ice cream or Hard Sauce (optional)*

1. Prepare pastry; shape into ball, and divide in half.
2. Preheat oven to 400F.
3. Make Filling: In 3-quart saucepan, combine apple, butter, currants, brown sugar, granulated sugar, cinnamon, nutmeg, salt, and ½ cup water.
4. Bring to boiling; reduce heat, and cook, covered and stirring occasionally, until apple is tender but not mushy—10 to 15 minutes.
5. Mix rum with cornstarch until smooth. Add to filling; bring to boiling, stirring constantly. Remove from heat; cool completely.
6. On lightly floured pastry cloth or board, roll half of pastry to 12-inch circle. Use to line 9-inch tart pan with removable bottom. Trim edge.
7. Roll out second half of pastry to 9-inch circle. Place tart pan on pastry. Using edge of pan as guide, with pastry wheel or sharp knife, cut around pan. Remove pan.
8. With pastry wheel, cut circle into 8 triangles. From center, cut out and remove circle 2 inches in diameter; discard along with 1 triangle.
9. Turn out filling into pastry-lined pan, mounding slightly in center. On top, place 7 pastry triangles, spoke fashion. Brush pastry triangles with egg yolk mixed with 2 teaspoons water.
10. Bake 40 to 45 minutes, or until pastry is golden. Serve warm. If not serving at once, cool completely on wire rack. Refrigerate, wrapped in foil.
11. To serve: Preheat oven to 400F. Remove foil from pie; heat in oven 20 minutes. Serve warm with vanilla ice cream or Hard Sauce (page 149), if desired.
Makes 8 servings

# ✦ FRESH BERRY PIE

*Flaky Pastry for 2-Crust Pie, page 354*
*2 pint boxes fresh blackberries, rasp-*
*   berries, or blueberries*
*1 tablespoon lemon juice*
*1 cup sugar*
*¼ cup all-purpose flour*
*¼ teaspoon ground cinnamon*
*⅛ teaspoon ground nutmeg*
*Dash ground cloves*
*2 tablespoons butter or margarine*
*1 egg yolk*
*1 tablespoon water*

1. Prepare Flaky Pastry. Shape pastry into ball; divide in half. On lightly floured surface, roll out half of pastry into 11-inch circle. Use to line 9-inch pie plate. Refrigerate with rest of pastry until ready to use.
2. Preheat oven to 400F.
3. Gently wash berries; drain well. Place in large bowl; sprinkle with lemon juice.
4. Combine sugar, flour, cinnamon, nutmeg, and cloves. Add to berries, and toss lightly to combine. Turn out into pastry-lined pie plate, mounding in center. Dot with butter.
5. Roll out remaining pastry into 11-inch circle. Make several slits near center for steam vents. Adjust over filling. Fold edge of top crust under bottom crust; press together, and crimp decoratively.
6. Beat egg yolk with 1 tablespoon water. Brush lightly over top crust.
7. Bake 45 to 50 minutes, or until juices start to bubble through steam vents and crust is golden-brown.
8. Cool on wire rack at least 1 hour. Serve slightly warm.

Makes 8 servings.

# ✦ SOUR-CHERRY PIE

*Flaky Pastry for 2-Crust Pie, page 354*
*1 cup sugar*
*⅓ cup all-purpose flour*
*⅛ teaspoon salt*
*4 cups pitted fresh sour cherries*
*¼ teaspoon almond extract*
*2 tablespoons butter or margarine*

*1 egg yolk*
*1 tablespoon water*

1. Prepare Flaky Pastry; shape into ball. On lightly floured surface, roll out half of pastry into 11-inch circle. Fit into 9-inch pie plate; trim.
2. Preheat oven to 400F.
3. In large bowl, mix together sugar, flour, and salt. Add cherries and almond extract; toss lightly to combine.
4. Turn out cherry mixture into pastry-lined pie plate, mounding in center. Dot with butter.
5. Roll out remaining pastry into 11-inch circle. Make several slits near center for steam vents. Adjust over filling. Fold edge of top crust under bottom crust; press together, and crimp decoratively.
6. Beat egg yolk and water. Brush lightly over top crust.
7. Bake 40 to 45 minutes, or until juices start to bubble through steam vents and crust is golden-brown.
8. Cool on wire rack at least 1 hour. Serve slightly warm.

Makes 8 servings.

# ❋ MINCEMEAT-APPLE PIE

*Flaky Pastry for 2-Crust Pie, page 354*

## FILLING:

*1 jar (1 lb 12 oz) prepared*
  *mincemeat, plain or with brandy*
  *and rum*
*1 cup sweetened applesauce*
*1 cup diced pared tart apple*
*1 egg yolk*
*2 teaspoons water*

1. Prepare Flaky Pastry; shape into ball.
2. On lightly floured surface, roll out two thirds of pastry to ⅛-inch thickness. Fit into 9-inch pie plate; trim overhang to 1 inch.
3. Roll out remaining pastry to 10-inch circle. Cut with pastry wheel or knife into ¾-inch-wide strips.
4. Preheat oven to 400F.
5. Make Filling: In large saucepan, combine mincemeat, applesauce, and diced apple. Bring to boiling; reduce heat, and simmer, stirring, 10 minutes. Let cool. Turn out into pie shell.
6. Moisten edge of shell slightly with cold water. Arrange pastry strips across filling: press ends to rim of shell. Fold overhang of lower crust over ends of strips to make rim. Press rim with fork.
7. Beat egg yolk with 2 teaspoons water. Brush over lattice top but not on edge of pastry.
8. Bake 25 to 30 minutes, or until crust is nicely browned.
9. Let cool slightly on rack. Serve warm, with whipped cream, Hard Sauce (page 149), or vanilla ice cream, if desired.
Makes 10 servings.

# ❋ PEACH AND BLUEBERRY PIE

*2 tablespoons lemon juice*
*3 cups sliced pitted peeled peaches*
  *(2 ¼ lb)*
*1 cup blueberries*
*1 cup sugar*
*½ teaspoon ground cinnamon*
*2 tablespoons quick-cooking tapioca*
*½ teaspoon salt*
*Flaky Pastry for 2-Crust Pie, page 354*
*2 tablespoons butter or margarine*

1. Sprinkle lemon juice over fruit in large bowl.
2. Combine sugar, cinnamon, tapioca, and salt. Add to fruit, tossing lightly to combine. Let stand 15 minutes. Meanwhile, preheat oven to 425F.
3. Prepare Flaky Pastry; shape into ball.
4. On lightly floured surface, roll out half of pastry into 11-inch circle. Use to line 9-inch pie plate; trim.
5. Turn out fruit mixture into pastry-lined pie plate, mounding in center; dot with butter.
6. Roll out remaining pastry into 11-inch circle. Make several slits near center for steam vents. Adjust over filling; trim.
7. Fold edge of top crust under bottom crust; press together with fingertips. Crimp edge decoratively.
8. Bake 45 to 50 minutes, or until fruit is tender and crust is golden-brown.
9. Cool partially on wire rack; serve slightly warm.
Makes 6 to 8 servings.

# ❖ DEEP-DISH PEAR PIE

*2¼ to 2½ lb fresh pears*
*¾ cup light-brown sugar, packed*
*3 tablespoons all-purpose flour*
*⅛ teaspoon salt*
*Dash ground cloves*
*Dash ground nutmeg*
*⅓ cup heavy cream*
*2 tablespoons lemon juice*
*2 tablespoons butter or margarine*
*Flaky Pastry for 1-Crust Pie, page 354*
*1 egg yolk*
*1 tablespoon water*
*Heavy cream or vanilla ice cream*

1. Halve pears lengthwise; scoop out core. Cut V shape to remove stems. Pare and slice to make 6 cups.
2. In small bowl, combine brown sugar, flour, salt, cloves, and nutmeg. Stir in ⅓ cup cream.
3. Place sliced pears in shallow 8¼-inch round baking dish or 9-inch deep-dish-pie plate (about 1¾ inches deep). Sprinkle with lemon juice; add cream mixture. With wooden spoon, stir gently until well mixed. Dot with butter.
4. Preheat oven to 400F.
5. Prepare Flaky Pastry; shape into ball. On lightly floured surface, roll out pastry to 11-inch circle. Fold in half; make slits for steam vents.
6. Place over fruit in baking dish, and unfold. Press pastry to edge of dish. For decorative edge, press firmly all around with thumb.
7. Lightly beat egg yolk and water. Brush over pastry.
8. Place piece of foil, a little larger than baking dish, on oven rack below the one on which pie bakes, to catch any juices that may bubble over edge of dish. Bake pie 35 to 40 minutes, or until crust is golden and juice bubbles through steam vents.
9. Let pie cool on wire rack about 30 minutes. Serve warm with heavy cream or ice cream.
Makes 8 servings.
*Note:* To make pie with canned pears, use 2 cans (1-lb 13-oz size) sliced pears. Drain, reserving 2 tablespoons syrup. Make as above, reducing sugar to ½ cup and decreasing flour to 2 tablespoons. Add reserved syrup with the cream.

# ❖ SOUTHERN PECAN PIE

*9-inch Unbaked Pie Shell, page 355*

**FILLING:**

*4 eggs*
*1 cup sugar*
*1 cup light corn syrup*
*½ tablespoon all-purpose flour*
*¼ teaspoon salt*
*1 teaspoon vanilla extract*
*¼ cup butter or margarine, melted*
*2 cups pecan halves*

*Whipped cream*

1. Prepare pie shell, and refrigerate.
2. Preheat oven to 350F.
3. Make Filling: In medium bowl, with rotary beater or portable electric mixer, at low speed, beat eggs well.
4. Add sugar, corn syrup, flour, salt, and vanilla; beat until well combined.
5. Stir in butter and pecans, mixing well.
6. Turn out into unbaked pie shell. Bake 50 minutes, or until filling is set in the center when pie is shaken gently.
7. Cool pie completely on wire rack. Then chill slightly before serving.
8. Just before serving, decorate pie with whipped cream.
Makes 8 servings.

# ❖ OPEN-FACED PLUM PIE

*9-inch Kuchen Pie Shell, below*
*1½ lb Italian plums*
*2 tablespoons granulated sugar*
*1½ teaspoons grated orange peel*
*Confectioners' sugar*
*Light cream, vanilla ice cream, or*
*whipped cream (optional)*

1. Prepare pie shell; refrigerate until ready to fill.
2. Preheat oven to 400F.
3. Wash plums. Cut into quarters; remove pits. Arrange plums, in tight circular rows, in pie shell. Sprinkle with granulated sugar and orange peel.
4. Bake 15 minutes. Reduce oven temperature to 350F; bake 45 minutes longer.
5. Sprinkle with confectioners' sugar. Cool partially on wire rack; serve warm, with light cream, vanilla ice cream, or whipped cream, if desired.
Makes 8 servings.

## KUCHEN PIE SHELL:

*1½ cups all-purpose flour*
*¼ teaspoon baking powder*
*½ cup butter or margarine, softened*
*1 egg*
*⅓ cup sugar*
*Dash salt*

1. Sift flour and baking powder into medium bowl.
2. With portable electric mixer, or back of spoon, blend in butter until smooth.
3. In small bowl, beat egg until frothy. Gradually beat in sugar and salt, beating until mixture is thick and lemon-colored.
4. Add to flour mixture, mixing until smooth.
5. Turn out dough into center of greased 9-inch pie plate. Press dough evenly over bottom and side, not on rim, of pie plate.
6. Refrigerate until ready to fill.
Makes 9-inch shell.

# ❖ STRAWBERRY-RHUBARB LATTICE PIE

*1⅓ cups sugar*
*⅓ cup all-purpose flour*
*2 cups cut-up fresh rhubarb (about 1 lb), in 1-inch pieces*
*1 pint strawberries, washed, hulled, and cut in half*
*Flaky Pastry for 2-Crust Pie, page 354*
*1 tablespoon butter or margarine*
*Milk*
*Sugar*
*Ice cream (optional)*

1. In large bowl, combine 1⅓ cups sugar and the flour. Add rhubarb and strawberries, tossing lightly to combine; let stand 30 minutes.
2. Prepare Flaky Pastry. Shape into ball; divide in half.
3. On lightly floured surface, roll out half of pastry into 12-inch circle. Use to line 9-inch pie plate. Refrigerate until ready to use.
4. Preheat oven to 400F.
5. Roll out remaining half of pastry into 10-inch circle. With knife or pastry wheel, cut into 9 (1-inch-wide) strips.
6. Turn out rhubarb mixture into pastry-lined pie plate, mounding in center. Dot with butter.
7. Moisten rim of pastry slightly with cold water.

Arrange 5 pastry strips, ½ inch apart, over filling; press ends to pastry rim. Place remaining strips across first ones at right angles to make lattice, and press to rim. Fold overhang of bottom crust over ends of strips, and crimp decoratively. Brush lattice top, but not rim, lightly with milk, and sprinkle with sugar.

8. Bake 50 minutes, or until crust is golden and juice bubbles through lattice.

9. Cool on wire rack. Serve warm, with ice cream, if desired.

Makes 8 servings.

# ✖ CARAMEL CHIFFON PIE

9-inch Baked Pie Shell, page 355, or Baked Graham-Cracker Shell, page 356
1 cup granulated sugar
2 cups hot milk
4 eggs
1 env unflavored gelatine
¼ cup cold water
⅛ teaspoon salt
1 teaspoon vanilla extract
½ cup heavy cream, whipped
½ cup heavy cream
2 tablespoons confectioners' sugar

1. Prepare and bake pie shell; let cool completely.

2. Place ¼ cup granulated sugar in heavy 10-inch skillet. Stir over medium heat until sugar is completely melted and begins to boil. Syrup should be medium-brown color. Remove from heat. Slowly add hot milk, stirring constantly. Return to low heat; stir until all caramel is melted. Cool mixture to lukewarm.

3. Separate eggs, placing whites in large bowl of electric mixer and yolks in double-boiler top. Let whites warm to room temperature—about 1 hour.

4. Sprinkle gelatine over cold water to soften; set aside. With wooden spoon, beat egg yolks slightly. Stir in milk mixture and salt.

5. Cook, stirring, over hot, not boiling, water (water should not touch bottom of double-boiler top) until mixture thickens and forms coating on metal spoon —8 to 10 minutes. Add gelatine and vanilla; stir until gelatine is dissolved. Remove from water.

6. Turn out into medium bowl; set in larger bowl of ice cubes to chill, stirring occasionally, until as thick as unbeaten egg white—about 20 minutes. Meanwhile, at high speed, beat egg whites until soft peaks form when beater is slowly raised.

7. Beat in ¼ cup granulated sugar, 2 tablespoons at a time, beating after each addition. Beat until stiff peaks form when beater is raised. With wire whisk, gently fold gelatine mixture into whites just until combined. Fold in whipped cream; mound in pie shell. (See Note.)

8. Refrigerate until firm—3 hours. Beat ½ cup cream with confectioners' sugar. Transfer to pastry bag with medium star tip; make rosettes around edge, or use spoon to decorate edge with cream.

Makes 8 servings.

Note: If too soft, place bowl in ice cubes, stirring occasionally, until mixture mounds.

# ❖ FRESH STRAWBERRY GLACÉ PIE

*9-inch Baked Pie Shell, page 355*

## GLAZE:

*1 pint box fresh strawberries*
*1 cup granulated sugar*
*2½ tablespoons cornstarch*
*½ cup water*
*1 tablespoon butter or margarine*

## FILLING:

*1 pint boxes fresh strawberries*
*2 tablespoons Cointreau or orange juice*

*1 cup heavy cream, whipped*
*2 tablespoons sifted confectioners' sugar*

1. Prepare and bake pie shell; let cool.
2. Make Glaze: Wash strawberries gently in cold water. Drain; hull. In medium saucepan, crush strawberries with potato masher.
3. Combine sugar and cornstarch; stir into crushed strawberries. Add water.
4. Over low heat, stirring constantly, bring to boiling. Mixture will be thickened and translucent.
5. Strain; add butter. Cool.
6. Meanwhile, make Filling: Wash strawberries gently in cold water. Drain; hull. Measure 3 cups; reserve rest for garnish.
7. In medium bowl, gently toss strawberries with Cointreau; let stand about 30 minutes. Then arrange in baked pie shell.
8. Pour cooled glaze over strawberries. Refrigerate until well chilled—about 2 hours.
9. Just before serving, whip cream until stiff; fold in confectioners' sugar. To serve, garnish pie with reserved strawberries and whipped cream.
Makes 8 servings.

# ❖ FRESH COCONUT CREAM PIE

*9-inch Baked Pie Shell, page 355*
*1 cup sugar*
*½ cup cornstarch*
*¼ teaspoon salt*
*3 cups hot milk*
*3 egg yolks, beaten*
*1 teaspoon vanilla extract*
*½ teaspoon almond extract*
*2 cups grated fresh coconut (see Note)*
*1 cup heavy cream*

1. Prepare and bake pie shell; let cool completely before filling.
2. Combine sugar, cornstarch, and salt; gradually add to milk in medium saucepan, stirring until smooth. Bring to boiling, stirring, over medium heat; boil 2 minutes. Remove from heat.
3. Stir half of hot mixture into egg yolks; then combine with rest in saucepan.
4. Cook, stirring and over low heat, until it boils and is thick enough to mound from spoon—about 5 minutes.
5. Turn out into bowl; stir in extracts and half of coconut. Place waxed paper directly on filling; refrigerate 1 hour.
6. Turn out into pie shell; refrigerate 3 hours.
7. To serve: Whip cream, and spread over filling; top with remaining coconut.
Makes 8 servings.

*Note:* Or use 2 cans (3½-oz size) flaked coconut in place of grated fresh coconut.

## MOCHA CREAM PIE

*9-inch Baked Pie Shell, page 355*
*¾ cup sugar*
*⅓ cup cornstarch*
*1½ to 2 tablespoons instant coffee*
*2 squares unsweetened chocolate, cut up*
*½ teaspoon salt*
*2½ cups milk*
*3 egg yolks, slightly beaten*
*½ teaspoon vanilla extract*

**CREAM TOPPING:**

*1 cup heavy cream*
*2 tablespoons confectioners' sugar*
*½ teaspoon vanilla extract*

1. Prepare and bake pie shell; let cool completely before filling.
2. In top of double boiler, combine the sugar, cornstarch, instant coffee, chocolate, and salt; mix well. Then gradually stir in the milk.
3. Cook, over boiling water, stirring, until the mixture is thickened—about 10 minutes. Cook, covered, stirring occasionally, 10 minutes longer.
4. Gradually stir half of hot mixture into beaten egg yolks. Return to rest of mixture in double boiler; cook over boiling water, stirring occasionally, 5 minutes. Remove from heat; stir in vanilla. Pour chocolate filling into baked pie shell.
5. Refrigerate until well chilled—at least 3 hours.
6. Make Cream Topping: 1 hour before serving, with rotary beater, beat cream with confectioners' sugar and vanilla until stiff. Spread over pie. Refrigerate. Makes 8 servings.

## GRASSHOPPER PIE

*Chocolate-Cookie-Crumb Pie Shell, below*

**FILLING:**

*4 eggs, separated*
*2 env unflavored gelatine*
*¾ cup milk*
*¾ cup sugar*
*⅛ teaspoon salt*
*⅓ cup green crème de menthe*
*⅓ cup white crème de cacao*
*1½ cups heavy cream*

*Grated chocolate*

1. Make pie shell; refrigerate.
2. Make Filling: Let egg whites warm to room temperature in large bowl of electric mixer—about 1 hour.
3. Sprinkle gelatine over milk in top of double boiler; let soften 3 minutes.
4. Add egg yolks, ½ cup sugar, and the salt; beat with rotary beater or fork until well blended. Cook over boiling water, stirring constantly, about 5 minutes, or until gelatine dissolves and mixture thickens slightly and coats metal spoon.
5. Remove double-boiler top from bottom. Stir crème de menthe and crème de cacao into custard mixture.
6. Set double-boiler top in bowl of ice cubes and water. Cool, stirring occasionally, 10 to 15 minutes, or until custard mixture is consistency of unbeaten egg white.
7. Meanwhile, in medium bowl, whip cream; refrigerate. Also, beat egg whites until soft peaks form when beater is slowly raised. Gradually beat in remaining ¼ cup sugar. Continue beating until stiff peaks form.
8. With rubber spatula or wire whisk, fold custard mixture into egg whites. Then fold in whipped cream until mixture is just combined.
9. Mound high in prepared pie shell. Sprinkle grated chocolate around edge. Refrigerate 3 hours, or until filling is firm.
Makes 8 servings.

# ❖ CHOCOLATE-COOKIE-CRUMB PIE SHELL

25 crisp chocolate wafers (about 2 in-
    ches), broken
¼ cup butter or margarine, melted

1. In blender or food processor, place cookies and melted butter; blend just until cookies become crumbs.
2. Turn out into 9-inch pie plate. With back of spoon, press evenly into bottom and side.

# ❖ LEMON CHIFFON PIE

1 env unflavored gelatine
¼ cup cold water
4 eggs
½ cup lemon juice
1 cup sugar
¼ teaspoon salt
1 tablespoon grated lemon peel
Unbaked Graham-Cracker Pie Shell,
    page 356
1 cup heavy cream

1. Sprinkle gelatine over cold water in measuring cup; set aside to soften.
2. Separate eggs, placing whites in large bowl of electric mixer, yolks in double-boiler top. Set whites aside to warm to room temperature.
3. Beat yolks slightly with wooden spoon. Stir in lemon juice, ½ cup sugar, and salt.
4. Cook over hot, not boiling, water (water should not touch bottom of double-boiler top), stirring constantly, until mixture thickens and coats metal spoon—about 12 minutes.
5. Add gelatine mixture and lemon peel, stirring until gelatine is dissolved. Remove pan from hot water. Refrigerate, stirring occasionally, until cool and the consistency of unbeaten egg white—about 35 minutes.
6. Meanwhile, make Graham-Cracker Pie Shell.
7. At high speed, beat egg whites just until soft peaks form when beater is slowly raised—peaks bend slightly.
8. Gradually beat in remaining ½ cup sugar, 2 tablespoons at a time, beating well after each addition. Continue beating until stiff peaks form when beater is raised.
9. With rubber spatula or wire whisk, gently fold gelatine mixture into egg-white mixture just until combined.
10. Gently turn out into pie shell, mounding high. Refrigerate until firm—3 to 6 hours.
11. To serve: Whip cream until stiff. Spread about half over pie. Put remaining cream in pastry bag with medium star tip, and pipe rosettes around pie edge, or use spoon to decorate edge with cream.
Makes 8 servings.

# LEMON MERINGUE PIE

*9-inch Baked Pie Shell, page 355*

### LEMON FILLING:

*¼ cup cornstarch*
*3 tablespoons all-purpose flour*
*1¼ cups sugar*
*¼ teaspoon salt*
*2 cups water*
*4 egg yolks, slightly beaten*
*½ cup lemon juice*
*1 tablespoon grated lemon peel*
*1 tablespoon butter*

### MERINGUE:

*4 egg whites*
*¼ teaspoon cream of tartar*
*½ cup sugar*

1. Prepare and bake pie shell; cool completely before filling.
2. Make Lemon Filling: In medium saucepan, combine cornstarch, flour, sugar, and salt, mixing well. Gradually add 2 cups water, stirring until smooth.
3. Over medium heat, bring to boiling, stirring occasionally; boil 1 minute.
4. Remove from heat. Quickly stir some of hot mixture into egg yolks. Return to hot mixture; stir to blend.
5. Return to heat; cook over low heat 5 minutes, stirring occasionally.
6. Remove from heat. Stir in lemon juice, lemon peel, and butter. Pour into pie shell.
7. Preheat oven to 400F.
8. Make Meringue: In medium bowl of electric mixer, at medium speed, beat egg whites with cream of tartar until frothy.
9. Gradually beat in sugar, 2 tablespoons at a time, beating after each addition. Then beat at high speed until stiff peaks form when beater is slowly raised.
10. Spread over lemon filling, carefully sealing to edge of crust and swirling top decoratively.
11. Bake 7 to 9 minutes, or until meringue is golden-brown. Let pie cool completely on wire rack—2½ to 3 hours.

Makes 8 servings.

# NESSELRODE PIE

*9-inch Baked Pie Shell, page 355*
*2 eggs*
*1½ env unflavored gelatine*
*¼ cup cold water*
*2 cups light cream*
*⅔ cup sugar*
*Dash salt*
*3 tablespoons dark rum*
*¾ cup bottled Nesselrode sauce*
*1 cup heavy cream, whipped*
*1 square (1 oz) semisweet chocolate*

1. Make pie day before serving: Prepare and bake pie shell; cool completely before filling.
2. Separate eggs, placing yolks in medium bowl and whites in large bowl. Let whites warm to room temperature.
3. In small bowl, sprinkle gelatine over cold water to soften.
4. In top of double boiler, heat cream slightly (do not boil); add ⅓ cup sugar, the salt, and softened gelatine; heat, stirring to dissolve gelatine.
5. Beat egg yolks until thick; stir in some of cream mixture, mixing well. Return to rest of cream mixture in top of double boiler.
6. Place over boiling water; cook, stirring, until thickened—about 5 minutes. Set top of double boiler in bowl of ice, stirring occasionally, until gelatine mix-

ture just begins to set—20 to 25 minutes. Stir in rum and ½ cup Nesselrode. Remove from ice.

7. Meanwhile, beat egg whites just until soft peaks form. Gradually beat in remaining ⅓ cup sugar, 2 tablespoons at a time. Continue beating until stiff peaks form when beater is slowly raised.

8. With wire whisk or rubber spatula, gently fold thickened egg-yolk mixture into whites, to combine well. With rubber spatula, gently fold in half of whipped cream. Turn out into pie shell, mounding high and smoothing top with metal spatula. Refrigerate until well chilled and firm enough to cut—4 hours or overnight.

9. To serve, spread with rest of whipped cream. With vegetable peeler, shave chocolate over top. Decorate around edge with ¼ cup Nesselrode.

Makes 8 servings.

# ❖ McCALL'S BEST PUMPKIN CUSTARD PIE

9-inch Unbaked Pie Shell, page 355, with high fluted edge
3 eggs
¾ cup sugar
½ teaspoon salt
½ teaspoon ground cinnamon
½ teaspoon ground ginger
¼ teaspoon ground allspice
¼ teaspoon ground cloves
1 can (1 lb) pumpkin
2 cans (6-oz size) evaporated milk, undiluted
3 tablespoons light molasses
1 egg white, lightly beaten
½ cup heavy cream, whipped
Chopped walnuts

1. Prepare pie shell. Refrigerate until ready to fill.
2. Preheat oven to 400F.
3. In medium bowl, with rotary beater or portable electric mixer, beat eggs until frothy.
4. Combine sugar, salt, cinnamon, ginger, allspice, and cloves; mix well. Add to eggs with pumpkin, milk, and molasses; beat until smooth and well combined. Let stand ½ hour to dissolve sugar.
5. Brush pie shell with egg white. Stir filling to mix well; pour most of filling into pie shell. Place on lowest rack of oven. Pour in rest of filling; bake 30 minutes. Place foil collar lightly over edge of crust to prevent overbrowning. Bake 25 to 30 minutes longer, or until knife inserted in custard comes out clean and pie is set in center when gently shaken.
6. Cool on wire rack. To serve: Beat heavy cream until stiff. Transfer to pastry bag with medium star tip. Force cream through tip to form decorative edge, or use spoon to decorate edge with cream. Sprinkle with chopped nuts.

Makes 8 servings.

# ✦ FRUIT TARTS

## TART SHELL PASTRY:

½ cup butter or margarine, softened
¼ cup sugar
¼ teaspoon salt
1 egg white
1½ cups sifted all-purpose flour

Rum Cream, below

Fruits: Whole strawberries, blueberries, red raspberries, sliced bananas, seedless green grapes, apricot halves, black cherries (fresh, frozen, or canned), canned small pineapple rings or tidbits

Apricot Glaze or Currant-Jelly Glaze, below

1. Make Tart Shell Pastry: In medium bowl, with fork, blend butter, sugar, salt, and egg white until smooth and well combined.
2. Gradually stir in flour, mixing until smooth.
3. For each tart, use 2 teaspoons dough. Press evenly into 2½- to 3-inch tart pans of assorted shapes and sizes. Set pans on cookie sheet.
4. Refrigerate 30 minutes.
5. Preheat oven to 375F. Bake tart shells 12 to 15 minutes, or until light golden. Cool in pans on wire rack a few minutes; then carefully turn out, and cool completely before filling.
6. To fill tarts: Spoon several teaspoons of Rum Cream into each shell. Refrigerate.
7. Top with fruit. (Drain fruit very well before using.) Brush yellow or light fruit with warm Apricot Glaze and red or dark fruit with Currant-Jelly Glaze.
8. Refrigerate until ready to serve.
Makes 1½ dozen.

Note: If desired, make Tart Shells and Rum Cream day before. Then assemble tarts several hours before serving.

## RUM CREAM:

1 teaspoon unflavored gelatine
2 tablespoons granulated sugar
2 tablespoons all-purpose flour
Salt
1 egg yolk
½ cup milk
2 tablespoons rum
1 egg white, stiffly beaten
½ cup heavy cream
1 tablespoon confectioners' sugar
1 inch vanilla bean, scraped, or ½ teaspoon vanilla extract

1. In small saucepan, mix gelatine, granulated sugar, flour, and dash salt; mix well.
2. Beat egg yolk with milk and rum. Add to gelatine mixture; cook over medium heat, stirring constantly with wire whisk, until mixture is thickened and comes to boiling.
3. Pour into medium bowl; set bowl in pan of ice and water; let stand, stirring occasionally, until mixture begins to set—about 8 to 10 minutes. Fold in beaten egg white.
4. Beat cream with confectioners' sugar; fold into gelatine mixture. Stir in vanilla. Refrigerate until ready to use—at least 30 minutes.
Makes about 1½ cups.

## APRICOT GLAZE:

½ cup apricot preserves

1. In small saucepan, over medium heat, stir apricot preserves until melted. (If preserves seem too thick, thin with ½ to 1 tablespoon hot water.)
2. Strain. Use warm on tarts.
Makes about ½ cup.

## CURRANT-JELLY GLAZE:

½ cup red-currant jelly
1 tablespoon kirsch

1. In small saucepan, over moderate heat, stir currant jelly until melted. Remove from heat.
2. Stir in kirsch. Use warm on tarts. (If glaze becomes too thick, reheat gently, and add a little hot water.) Makes about ½ cup.

# ⬥ APPLE CUSTARD TARTS

Tart Shell Pastry (See Note)
4 (1½ lb) small tart apples (Granny Smith)
1¼ cups sugar
1 cup water
2 tablespoons lemon juice
¼ cup almond paste
2 eggs
¾ cup heavy cream
½ cup currant jelly
1 tablespoon light corn syrup
¼ cup chopped pistachio nuts or walnuts

1. On waxed paper, with palms of hand, roll tart pastry into roll 10 inches long; refrigerate 30 minutes. Divide into 10 (1-inch) pieces.
2. On lightly floured pastry cloth or surface, roll each part into 5-inch circle. Press pastry evenly into bottom and side of each tart pan (4 inches across and 1½ inches deep). Trim edges; use trimmings to fill spaces. Refrigerate until ready to fill.
3. Preheat oven to 375F.
4. Meanwhile, pare and core apples; cut each into 8 wedges. In large skillet, combine 1 cup sugar, the water, and lemon juice; bring to boiling. Add apple wedges, rounded side down, in single layer; simmer gently, covered, 5 minutes.
5. Turn apples; simmer 2 minutes, or just until tender but not mushy. With slotted utensil, remove apples. Drain on paper towels; cool.
6. Bake tart shells on large cookie sheet 10 to 12 minutes, or until golden-brown. Cool completely on wire rack.
7. Place 1 teaspoon almond paste in bottom of each baked tart shell. Top with 3 apple wedges.
8. In small bowl, beat together eggs, ¼ cup sugar, and heavy cream until combined. Pour 2½ tablespoons over each apple.
9. Bake on large cookie sheet 20 to 25 minutes, or just until custard is set. Cool on rack 15 minutes.
10. Remove tarts from pans. Combine jelly and corn syrup and brush over apples. Sprinkle edges with chopped nuts.
Makes 10.

Note: See recipe for Fruit Tarts (page 369). Make Tart Shell Pastry as directed in Steps 1 and 2.

# ❂ GLAZED-PEAR TARTS

1 pkg (10 or 11 oz) piecrust mix or
  Flaky Pastry for 2-Crust Pie, page
  354
8 Anjou pears (2½ lb)
¼ cup sugar
2 cups water
1 tablespoon lemon juice
1 jar (12 oz) apricot preserves
Whipped cream or vanilla ice cream
  (optional)

1. Prepare pastry; refrigerate. With vegetable peeler, pare pears, leaving them whole, with stems on. Carefully remove cores, working from bottom of pears.
2. In 3½-quart saucepan, combine sugar and water. Heat, stirring, until sugar is dissolved. Bring to boiling.
3. Add lemon juice and pears simmer, uncovered, over low heat 20 minutes, or just until pears are tender. Remove pears with slotted spoon; drain well.
4. Meanwhile, preheat oven to 425F. Divide pastry into 8 pieces. Roll each piece into 5-inch round. Fit into 2½- or 3-inch tart pans. Prick with fork, and bake 10 minutes, or until golden-brown.
5. Cool shells slightly; remove to serving platter or individual dessert plates. Carefully set 1 pear in each shell.
6. In small saucepan, heat preserves, stirring, until melted; boil 1 minute. Press through sieve. Brush over pears, coating well. Serve warm or chilled with whipped cream or vanilla ice cream, if desired. Makes 8 tarts.

# ❂ MINIATURE COCONUT TEA TARTS

## PASTRY:

1⅓ cups sifted all-purpose flour
⅓ cup sugar
¼ teaspoon salt
¾ cup butter or margarine
1 egg, slightly beaten

## FILLING:

1 egg
1 can (3½ oz) unsweetened flaked
  coconut
⅔ cup sugar

1. Make Pastry: Sift flour with sugar and salt into medium bowl. With pastry blender or 2 knives, cut in butter until mixture is like coarse cornmeal. With fork, stir in egg.
2. Knead slightly, with hands, until mixture holds together. Wrap in waxed paper; refrigerate several hours, or until firm.
3. Preheat oven to 375F.
4. Make Filling: With fork, beat egg in small bowl. Add coconut and sugar; mix well.
5. For each tart: Pinch off about 1 teaspoon chilled dough. Press into 2-by-½-inch tartlet pan, to make lining ⅛ inch thick.
6. Fill each tart with 1 teaspoon filling.
7. Bake tarts (about 24 at a time), set on cookie sheet, 12 minutes, or until coconut filling is golden-brown.
8. Place pans on wire rack; cool slightly. With small spatula, gently remove tarts. Makes about 47.

# ✜ TREACLE TART

Flaky Pastry for 1-Crust Pie, page 354
1 cup grated fresh bread crumbs
¼ teaspoon ginger
1 teaspoon grated lemon peel
½ cup currants
1 egg
1 cup dark corn syrup

1. Prepare pastry. Shape into ball; roll out to 10-inch round. Fit into 8-inch fluted tart pan with removable bottom or into 8-inch pie plate, with pastry extending ¾ inch up side.
2. Preheat oven to 350F. In medium bowl, toss together bread crumbs, ginger, lemon peel, and currants. Add egg and corn syrup. Stir with fork until well combined. Turn out into prepared pie shell. Bake 40 minutes, or until edge is golden and filling is set.
3. Remove to a wire rack; let cool completely.
Makes 6 servings.

# ✜ CRANBERRY-RAISIN TART

Flaky Pastry for 2-Crust Pie, page 354

## FILLING:

1 cup whole cranberries, chopped
1 cup chopped pared tart apples
1 cup raisins
½ cup chopped walnuts
⅓ cup butter or margarine
⅓ cup light-brown sugar, packed
⅓ cup granulated sugar
1 teaspoon ground cinnamon
¼ teaspoon ground nutmeg
¼ teaspoon salt
½ cup water
¼ cup light or dark rum
1 tablespoon cornstarch

1 egg yolk
2 teaspoons water
1 tablespoon granulated sugar

1. Prepare pastry. Shape into ball; divide in half.
2. Make Filling: In 3-quart saucepan, combine cranberries, apples, raisins, walnuts, butter, brown sugar, granulated sugar, cinnamon, nutmeg, salt, and water.
3. Bring to boiling; reduce heat, and cook, covered and stirring occasionally, 10 to 15 minutes.
4. Mix rum with cornstarch until smooth. Add to filling; bring to boiling, stirring constantly, about 2 minutes, or until thickened. Simmer 2 minutes. Remove from heat. Place saucepan in bowl of ice water to cool completely. Makes 3½ cups.
5. Preheat oven to 400F.
6. On lightly floured pastry cloth or board, roll half of pastry into 12-inch circle. Use to line fluted 9-inch pan with removable bottom; trim edge.
7. Roll out second half of pastry into rectangle 12 inches long and 6 inches wide.
8. With pastry wheel, cut 8 strips, each ½ inch wide and 10 inches long.
9. Turn out filling into pastry-lined pan. Place 2 strips, 1 inch apart, across each side of pie. Brush strips with egg yolk mixed with 2 teaspoons water. Sprinkle strips with sugar.
10. Bake 40 to 45 minutes, or until pastry is golden. (Cover with foil after 30 minutes to prevent overbrowning.) Remove to wire rack. Serve warm with vanilla ice cream.
Makes 8 servings.

# POULTRY

The proliferation of the forms in which poultry, especially chicken and turkey, are marketed is testimony to the popularity of poultry in our meals. There are small chickens, large chickens, chicken parts—legs, thighs, breasts for roasting, boneless breasts (cutlets), wings—even chicken livers, gizzards, and hearts sold separately to cater to every family preference. And in the freezer case there's a vast assortment of ready-to-heat chicken dishes, from parmigiana to fried parts. Turkeys are sold in parts—usually breasts or legs to suit taste preferences and as a convenience to smaller families who find a whole turkey too much to use.

Poultry is at once an economy and a festive dish. A whole chicken or turkey, roasted until it achieves a golden glaze, or a brace of Rock Cornish hens all say "Company Dinner" despite their reasonable price. The more expensive members of the poultry family, duck and goose, remain special treats for holiday occasions.

# CHICKEN

Ready-to-cook or oven-ready chicken is the only way whole chickens are sold in markets today. The birds are thoroughly cleaned, and the giblets are cleaned, wrapped, and placed in the cavity before the chickens are shipped to market in iced wooden crates in refrigerated trucks. At the market, chickens, whole or parts, are placed on trays and overwrapped with plastic and may be refrigerated in these wrappings 2 to 3 days. Chicken purchased in loose wrappings from a butcher shop should be rewrapped in fresh waxed paper or plastic wrap and refrigerated until used, within no more than 2 or 3 days.

Whole chickens are classified according to their age and size, and their names indicate their best uses.

*Broilers or broiler-fryers* are chickens about 9 weeks old weighing 1½ to 3½ lb. They are most suitable for broiling or frying but may be used for roasting or cooking in sauces.

*Roasters* are chickens about 12 weeks old weighing 2 to 5 lb. Newer versions of the roaster, bred to have a greater quantity of breast meat, weigh 5 to 7 lb at 12 to 14 weeks. These birds are intended to be roasted, stuffed or unstuffed, in dry heat.

*Stewing chickens* are less tender than roasters. They can be broiler chickens allowed to grow old or hens past egg-laying age. Full of flavor, they require long, moist cooking.

*Capons* are desexed (through surgery) male chickens weighing 4 to 8 lb. They are very tender, with a large amount of white meat.

*Rock Cornish game hens* are a particular breed of small chickens weighing 1 to 1½ lb. They are very tender and may be stuffed and roasted or roasted in parts with a basting sauce to prevent drying out.

## TIMETABLE FOR ROASTING STUFFED CHICKEN, AT 325F

| CHICKEN | READY-TO-COOK WEIGHT | APPROXIMATE ROASTING TIME |
|---|---|---|
| Broiler-fryer | 3 lb | 1½* hr |
| Roaster | 4 lb | 3½ hr |
| Large Roaster | 5–7 lb | 2–3† hr |
| Capon | 5 lb | 2½ hr |
| | 8 lb | 4½ hr |

Note: Chicken and dressing should be at room temperature.
*Broiler-fryers are roasted at 375F for 30 minutes per lb.
†Large roasters are roasted at 350F 25 to 30 minutes per lb.

# ❖ ROAST STUFFED CHICKEN

*4-lb roasting chicken*
*Bread Stuffing, below*
*2 tablespoons butter or margarine,*
  *melted*
*2 cups canned chicken broth*

1. Wash chicken well under cold running water; dry with paper towels. Remove excess fat.
2. Preheat oven to 350F.
3. Make Bread Stuffing.
4. Fill body cavity with stuffing. Close with poultry pins. Tie legs together with twine. Tuck wings under body.
5. Place chicken on rack in shallow roasting pan. Brush with melted butter. Roast, uncovered, 1¾ to 2 hours, or until leg joints move easily; baste occasionally with pan drippings.
6. Remove chicken to heated serving platter; remove poultry pins and twine. Let stand 15 minutes before carving.
7. Skim fat from drippings. Add chicken broth to pan. Cook over medium heat, stirring to dissolve browned bits; simmer until reduced to 1 cup. Strain into gravy boat.
Makes 4 servings.

## BREAD STUFFING:

*2 tablespoons butter or margarine*
*⅓ cup chopped onion*
*1 chicken liver, chopped*
*3 slices white bread, cubed*
*2 tablespoons chopped parsley*
*½ teaspoon dried thyme leaves*
*½ teaspoon salt*
*Dash pepper*
*¼ cup milk*

1. In hot butter in medium skillet, sauté onion until golden. Add liver, sauté 1 minute.
2. Remove from heat; stir in bread cubes, parsley, thyme, salt, and pepper. Add milk, tossing mixture with a fork.
3. Use to fill prepared chicken.
Makes enough to stuff 4-lb roasting chicken.

# ❖ ROAST CHICKEN WITH PECAN-RICE STUFFING

*6-lb roasting chicken*
*Salt*
*Pepper*
*1½ cups water*

1. Wash chicken, inside and out, and giblets under cold water; dry with paper towels. Remove excess fat. Sprinkle inside of cavity with salt and pepper. Chop liver. In medium saucepan, cook rest of giblets in 1½ cups water, covered, 2 hours, or until tender.
2. Make Pecan-Rice stuffing: In ¼ cup hot butter in 6-quart Dutch oven, sauté onion and chopped liver, stirring, until onion is golden—about 5 minutes.
3. Add wine and 1½ cups water; bring to boiling. Add rice, salt, pepper, nutmeg, and thyme. Return to boiling; reduce heat, and simmer, covered, 20 to 25 minutes, or until all liquid is absorbed. With fork, stir in raisins and pecans. Cool completely before stuffing bird.

## PECAN-RICE STUFFING:

¼ cup butter or margarine
¼ cup chopped onion
¾ cup dry white wine or condensed chicken broth, undiluted
1½ cups water
1 cup raw long-grain white rice
1 teaspoon salt
⅛ teaspoon pepper
⅛ teaspoon ground nutmeg
½ teaspoon dried thyme leaves
¼ cup raisins
1 cup coarsely chopped pecans

2 tablespoons butter or margarine, melted
1 can (10¾ oz) condensed chicken broth, undiluted

4. Preheat oven to 350F. Lightly fill body and neck with stuffing. Close body, and fasten neck with poultry pins. Lace body with twine, bootlace fashion; tie. Tie legs with twine; tuck wings under. Place on rack in roasting pan. Brush with melted butter. Roast, uncovered, 1¾ to 2 hours.
5. During roasting, baste chicken occasionally with pan drippings. Chicken is done when leg joint moves easily. Remove chicken to heated serving platter; remove poultry pins and twine. Let stand 15 minutes before carving. Meanwhile, skim fat from drippings.
6. Drain giblets, reserving broth. To ½ cup broth from giblets, add canned chicken broth; pour into roasting pan. Cook over medium heat, stirring to dissolve browned bits; simmer, uncovered, to reduce to 1 cup. Chop giblets; add to broth. Pour into gravy boat and pass with chicken.
Makes 8 servings.

# ✦ ROAST CAPON WITH HERBS

6-lb capon
Salt
Pepper
½ cup butter or margarine, softened
1 tablespoon lemon juice
1 tablespoon chopped chives
1 tablespoon chopped parsley
1 clove garlic, minced
1½ teaspoons chopped fresh tarragon or ½ teaspoon dried tarragon leaves
¾ teaspoon chopped fresh rosemary or ¼ teaspoon dried rosemary leaves
¾ teaspoon chopped fresh thyme or ¼ teaspoon dried thyme leaves
1 onion, sliced
2 carrots, pared and sliced
1 stalk celery, sliced
1 can (10¾ oz) condensed chicken broth, undiluted
½ cup dry white wine
3 tablespoons flour
Fresh tarragon sprigs (optional)

1. Preheat oven to 400F.
2. Wash capon well, inside and out, under cold water. Pat dry, inside and out, with paper towels. Sprinkle inside with 1 teaspoon salt and ¼ teaspoon pepper. Rinse giblets; set aside.
3. In small bowl, with electric mixer or wooden spoon, beat butter with lemon juice, chives, parsley, garlic, chopped tarragon, rosemary, thyme, ½ teaspoon salt, and ⅛ teaspoon pepper until well blended.
4. With fingers, carefully loosen skin from breast meat. Spread 2 tablespoons butter mixture over breast meat, under skin, on each side. Tie legs together; fold wing tips under back. Spread 1 tablespoon butter mixture over capon. Insert meat thermometer inside thigh at thickest part.
5. Place onion, carrot, celery, and giblets (except liver) in shallow roasting pan. Set capon on vegetables.
6. Roast, uncovered, 1 hour. Reduce oven temperature to 325F; roast 1¼ to 1½ hours, basting occasionally with remaining butter mixture, until meat thermometer registers 185F and leg moves easily at joint.

7. Remove capon to heated platter. Remove string. Let stand 20 minutes.

8. Meanwhile, make gravy: Pour undiluted chicken broth into roasting pan; bring to boiling, stirring to dissolve brown bits. Strain into 4-cup measure; skim off fat, and discard.

9. In small saucepan, stir wine into flour until flour is dissolved. Stir in chicken broth. Bring to boiling, stirring constantly, until mixture thickens; reduce heat, and simmer 5 minutes. Add salt and pepper, if necessary.

10. Garnish capon with tarragon sprigs, if desired. Pass gravy.

Makes 8 servings.

# ✺ BROILED CHICKEN WITH PARSLEY BUTTER

*3 (1½- to 2-lb size) broiler-fryers, split*
*3 teaspoons salt*
*1 teaspoon dried oregano leaves*
*1 teaspoon dried thyme leaves*
*3 tablespoons butter or margarine, melted*
*Parsley Butter, below*

1. Wash chicken; pat dry with paper towels.

2. Combine salt, oregano, thyme, and pepper.

3. Brush both sides of chicken halves with butter. Place, skin side down, in broiler pan without rack; sprinkle with salt mixture.

4. Broil, 8 inches from heat, 25 minutes; brush with pan drippings two or three times.

5. Turn halves skin side up; brush with pan drippings. Broil, brushing with pan drippings two or three times, 15 minutes, or until chicken is golden-brown and well done. (When done, drumstick will move easily at joint.)

6. Remove to heated platter. Top each chicken half with a piece of Parsley Butter.

Makes 6 servings.

**PARSLEY BUTTER:**

*¼ cup butter or margarine*
*2 tablespoons chopped parsley*
*1 tablespoon chopped chives*

1. In small bowl, let butter soften slightly. Beat until smooth.

2. Mix in parsley and chives until well blended.

3. Turn out onto waxed paper; shape into bar about 6 by ¾ by ¾ inches. Refrigerate or place in freezer 1 hour, or until hard.

4. Cut into 6 pieces. Serve on chicken, chops, or steaks, or hamburgers.

Makes 6 servings.

CHICKEN THIGHS PARMIGIANA (p. 390)

BEEF WELLINGTON (p. 277),
BEEF STROGANOFF (p. 285),
TOURNEDOS NIÇOISE (p. 282)

ROAST CAPON WITH HERBS
(p. 377), CROWN ROAST OF
PORK WITH FRUIT STUFFING
(p. 293), PARSLEY LEG OF
LAMB (p. 304)

CLOCKWISE FROM BOTTOM LEFT:
NESSELRODE (p. 367), McCALL'S BEST
PUMPKIN CUSTARD PIE (p. 368),
SCOTCH APPLE TART (p. 358), LEMON
MERINGUE PIE (p. 367), SOUR CREAM
APPLE PIE (p. 357)

**SPAGHETTI PRIMAVERA** (p. 339)

# ❖ BROILED CHICKEN OREGANO WITH GLAZED ONIONS

2 (2½-lb size) broiler-fryers, halved

**MARINADE:**

⅓ cup lemon juice
⅓ cup salad oil
1 clove garlic, crushed
⅛ teaspoon ground nutmeg
1½ teaspoons salt
⅛ teaspoon pepper
1½ teaspoons dried oregano leaves

**GLAZED ONIONS:**

8 medium onions
2 tablespoons butter or margarine
1 tablespoon sugar

Lemon quarters
Parsley

1. Wash chicken; pat dry with paper towels. Arrange in single layer in large shallow baking pan.
2. Make Marinade: Combine all marinade ingredients, and mix well. Pour over chicken. Refrigerate, covered, several hours or overnight, turning several times.
3. Pour off and reserve marinade. Broil chicken, skin side down, in same pan, about 8 inches from heat, 25 minutes, basting several times with reserved marinade. Turn chicken with tongs; broil 20 minutes longer.
4. Prepare Glazed Onions: Cook onions in 1 inch boiling salted water just until tender—20 to 25 minutes. Drain well.
5. In medium skillet, heat butter. Add onions; sprinkle with sugar. Cook over medium heat, shaking pan often, until onions are glazed—5 minutes.
6. Arrange chicken and onions on warm serving platter. Garnish with lemon and parsley.
Makes 8 servings.

# ❖ GOLDEN-FRIED CHICKEN

3- to 3½-lb broiler-fryer, cut up
⅓ cup all-purpose flour
1½ teaspoons salt
¼ teaspoon pepper
About 1¼ cups salad oil or shortening

1. Wash chicken pieces under cold running water. Thoroughly dry with paper towels. Fold under wing tips.
2. In clean bag, combine flour, salt, and pepper. Add chicken to bag, a few pieces at a time, and shake to coat evenly with flour mixture.
3. In electric skillet, pour in salad oil, or melt shortening, to measure one-fourth inch; heat at 375F. (Or slowly heat oil or shortening in large skillet with tight-fitting cover.)
4. Add chicken, a few pieces at a time, starting with meatiest pieces; brown on all sides, turning with tongs. Remove pieces as they are browned. It takes about 20 minutes to brown all the chicken.
5. Carefully pour off all but 2 tablespoons fat from skillet.
6. Using tongs, return chicken to skillet, placing pieces skin side down. Reduce temperature to 300F, or turn heat low. Cook, covered, 30 minutes. (If using electric skillet, leave steam vent open.) Then turn chicken skin side up, and cook, uncovered, 10 minutes, or until meat is fork-tender and skin is crisp.
7. Remove chicken to heated platter, or place in napkin-lined basket. Serve at once.
Makes 4 servings.

# ❖ POACHED CHICKEN WITH VEGETABLES

4- to 5-lb roasting chicken, with gib-
    lets
Salt
⅛ teaspoon pepper
¼ cup butter or margarine
8 leeks
1½ to 2 lb small carrots, pared
1½ small new potatoes, peeled
¼ cup butter or margarine, melted
4 teaspoons flour
½ cup dry white wine
½ cup canned chicken broth
Chopped parsley

1. Remove giblets from chicken; rinse giblets, and set aside on paper towels. Rinse chicken well; dry with paper towels. Sprinkle inside with 1½ teaspoons salt and the pepper. Tuck wings under body; tie legs together. If necessary, fasten skin at neck with skewer.

2. In ¼ cup hot butter in Dutch oven, brown chicken well all over—takes about 30 minutes. Turn chicken carefully with two wooden spoons; do not break skin.

3. Meanwhile, coarsely chop giblets. Wash leeks well; cut off roots, and discard. Remove some of top leaves, and add to giblets. Then halve leeks crosswise, and set aside.

4. Place giblet-leek mixture under browned chicken. Cover tightly, and simmer over low heat 30 minutes.

5. Arrange carrots (halved, if necessary) around chicken; simmer, covered, 40 minutes longer, or until chicken and carrots are tender. Remove from heat.

6. Meanwhile, cook potatoes in 1 inch boiling salted water in medium saucepan, covered, 20 to 25 minutes, or until tender. Drain; then drizzle with 2 tablespoons melted butter.

7. Also, cook halved leeks in 1 inch boiling water in medium saucepan, covered, 10 minutes, or until tender. Drain, and drizzle with 2 tablespoons melted butter.

8. Carefully remove chicken and carrots to heated platter; keep warm.

9. Strain drippings; return to Dutch oven. Stir in flour until smooth. Gradually stir in wine and chicken broth; bring to boiling. Reduce heat, and simmer 3 minutes. Taste, and add salt, if needed.

10. To serve: Arrange potatoes and leeks around chicken and carrots. Sprinkle potatoes with parsley. Pass gravy.

Makes 4 to 6 servings.

# ❖ CHICKEN PAPRIKASH WITH GALUSKA

*4-lb roasting chicken*
*1½ teaspoons salt*
*¼ teaspoon pepper*
*¼ cup butter or margarine*
*1 can (10¾ oz) condensed chicken*
  *broth, undiluted*
*2 tablespoons paprika*
*Giblets (gizzard, heart) and neck*
*3 medium onions, peeled and halved*
*8 small carrots, pared*
*Galuska, below*
*¼ cup all-purpose flour*
*¼ cup water*
*1 cup sour cream*
*1 tablespoon chopped parsley*

1. Remove giblets from chicken; rinse giblets, and set aside on paper towels. Rinse chicken well; dry with paper towels. Sprinkle, inside and out, with ¾ teaspoon salt and the pepper. Tuck chicken wings under body; then tie legs together at ends with twine. If necessary, fasten skin at neck with skewer.
2. In hot butter in Dutch oven, brown chicken well on all sides—about 30 minutes. Turn chicken carefully with tongs or wooden spoons—do not break skin.
3. When bird is browned, slip small rack under it. In small saucepan, combine ¼ cup chicken broth and 1 tablespoon paprika; heat, stirring until dissolved. Use to brush surface of chicken.
4. Heat remaining chicken broth with 1 tablespoon paprika, stirring until dissolved. Add to Dutch oven, along with giblets and neck (reserve chicken liver for another use).
5. Arrange onions and carrots around chicken in Dutch oven.
6. Simmer gently, covered, about 1 hour, or until chicken and vegetables are tender; baste with liquid frequently.
7. Meanwhile, make Galuska.
8. Remove chicken to heated serving platter. Cover loosely with foil; keep warm. Cut carrots into ¼-inch cubes; toss with galuska. Arrange around chicken.
9. Remove rack from Dutch oven. Remove giblets. Chop fine; set aside. Skim off any excess fat from surface of liquid in Dutch oven.
10. In small bowl, blend flour with water, to make smooth paste. Stir into hot liquid in Dutch oven until smooth. Add remaining ¾ teaspoon salt.
11. Bring to boiling, stirring; reduce heat, and simmer 2 minutes.
12. Remove from heat. Slowly stir in chopped giblets and sour cream; heat gently—do not boil.
13. Sprinkle galuska with parsley. Pass sauce.
Makes 8 servings.

## GALUSKA:

*3¼ cups sifted all-purpose flour*
*3 eggs*
*3 teaspoons salt*
*Water*
*2 tablespoons butter or margarine*

1. In large bowl, combine flour, eggs, 1 teaspoon salt, and 1 cup water. With portable electric mixer at low speed or with wooden spoon, beat until dough is smooth and bubbles appear on surface.
2. In 4-quart kettle, bring 2 quarts water and 2 teaspoons salt to boiling.
3. To shape galuska: Spread thin layer of dough (about 2 teaspoons ) on pancake turner. Then hold over kettle of boiling water, and with moistened spatula, cut off small pieces, letting them drop into

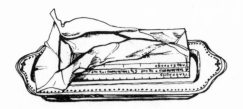

water. Continue until one quarter of dough is used.
4. Boil gently, uncovered, until galuska are firm and rise to top of water. Remove with slotted spoon, and place in colander or strainer. Quickly rinse with hot water; drain, and place in buttered casserole. Keep warm in 300F oven.
5. Repeat until all dough is used. When cooked, toss with butter.

# ❖ MOROCCAN CHICKEN AND CHICK-PEAS

2 cups (1 lb) dried chick-peas
Water
3½ teaspoons salt
4-lb roasting chicken
2 cloves garlic, crushed
½ teaspoon ground ginger
¼ teaspoon pepper
½ cup chopped onion
¾ teaspoon ground turmeric
2 tablespoons chopped parsley
1 (2-inch) cinnamon stick
2 tablespoons butter or margarine
1 cup condensed chicken broth, undiluted
1 cup sliced onion
¼ cup raisins

1. Pick over chick-peas. Cover with cold water; refrigerate, covered, overnight.
2. Next day, drain chick-peas. Place in large kettle; cover with 2 quarts water. Add 2 teaspoons salt. Bring to boiling. Reduce heat, and simmer, covered, 1½ to 2 hours, or until tender. Drain; set aside.
3. Meanwhile, rinse chicken well; dry with paper towels. Sprinkle inside with 1 teaspoon salt. Tuck wings under body; then tie legs together at ends with twine. If necessary, fasten skin at neck with skewer.
4. In large bowl, combine garlic, ginger, ½ teaspoon salt, the pepper, and 1 tablespoon water; mix well. Rub mixture over entire surface of chicken. Refrigerate chicken, covered, in large bowl 1 hour.
5. In 5-quart Dutch oven, combine chopped onion, turmeric, parsley, cinnamon stick, butter, and chicken broth; bring to boiling, stirring constantly. Add chicken, breast side down, and any juices left in bowl. Simmer, covered, turning chicken frequently in sauce, 1 hour, or until chicken is tender.
6. Remove cooked chicken. To liquid left in Dutch oven, add sliced onion, raisins, and drained chick-peas. Bring to boiling; cook, stirring frequently, until onion is soft and sauce has thickened—about 15 minutes.
7. Before serving, reheat chicken in sauce.
Makes 6 servings.

# ✦ COQ AU VIN

2 (2- to 2½-lb size) broiler-fryers, quartered
¼ lb bacon, cut into ½-inch pieces
15 small white onions (1¼ lb)
2 tablespoons butter or margarine
¼ cup cognac or brandy
4 shallots, coarsely chopped
½ lb small whole fresh mushrooms,
  washed and sliced ½ inch thick
1 clove garlic, crushed
Bouquet garni (see Note)
1½ teaspoons salt
½ teaspoon freshly ground pepper
1 teaspoon sugar
¼ teaspoon ground nutmeg
2 cups dry red wine
1 cup dry white wine

## CROÛTES:

4 slices white bread
¼ cup butter
2 tablespoons butter or margarine,
  softened

3 tablespoons all-purpose flour
2 tablespoons chopped parsley

1. Wash chicken under cold water; drain. Dry on paper towels. In 6-quart Dutch oven, over medium heat, sauté bacon until crisp; lift out with slotted spoon and drain.
2. In bacon fat, sauté onions over medium heat 5 minutes, stirring occasionally. Lift out, and set aside.
3. Add 2 tablespoons butter to drippings; heat. Add chicken, and brown over medium heat, one third at a time, turning with tongs until golden all over—about ½ hour in all; remove chicken as it browns.
4. Return chicken to Dutch oven. In small saucepan or ladle, heat cognac slightly. When vapor rises, ignite cognac and pour over chicken. Remove chicken.
5. To Dutch oven, add shallots, mushrooms, garlic, bouquet garni, salt, pepper, sugar, and nutmeg; mix well. Over low heat, simmer covered, 5 minutes.
6. Stir in the red and white wines. Return chicken to Dutch oven; bring to boiling. Reduce heat, and simmer, covered, ½ hour. Add onions; cook 25 minutes longer, until chicken and onions are tender. Remove bouquet garni.
7. Meanwhile, make Croûtes: With 3-inch round biscuit cutter, cut out centers from bread slices. Cut rounds in half. In ¼ cup hot butter in skillet, sauté until golden on both sides; place on paper towels.
8. In small bowl, mix softened butter with flour until smooth; stir into liquid in Dutch oven with chicken. Bring to boiling, stirring, until thickened.
9. Turn out into serving dish. Sprinkle with bacon and parsley. Garnish with croûtes.
Makes 8 servings.

*Note:* For bouquet garni, tie together large parsley sprig, 3 sprigs fresh or 1 teaspoon dried thyme, and bay leaf in small cheesecloth bag.

# ❖ CASSOULET

1½ lb dried white beans
4½ cups cold water
5 carrots
6 medium onions
4 whole cloves
2 cans (10¾-oz size) condensed chicken broth, undiluted
2 bay leaves, crumbled
½ cup coarsely chopped celery leaves
1 teaspoon salt
3 black peppercorns
3 cloves garlic, crushed
1½ teaspoons dried thyme leaves
1 teaspoon dried marjoram leaves
1 teaspoon dried sage leaves
¼ lb unsliced bacon
2 tablespoons butter or margarine
4-lb roasting chicken, cut into 8 pieces
⅛ teaspoon pepper
1 can (1 lb) peeled tomatoes, undrained
1 lb Polish sausage (whole)
2 tablespoons chopped parsley

1. In 8-quart kettle with cover, combine beans and cold water; let soak 2 hours, no longer. (They will burst easily in cooking.) Do not drain beans. Meanwhile, pare carrots; cut into quarters. Peel onions; stud one of onions with whole cloves.

2. To beans and soaking water, add chicken broth, bay leaves, one quarter of carrots, the onions (including onion studded with cloves), celery leaves, salt, peppercorns, garlic, thyme, marjoram, and sage. Bring just to boiling; reduce heat, and simmer, covered, 1 hour.

3. Add remaining carrots; cook, covered, 15 minutes longer. Meanwhile cut bacon into 2 pieces. In large skillet, sauté bacon until browned, turning on all sides. Drain off fat.

4. Preheat oven to 350F. Turn out bean mixture into 6-quart casserole. Add bacon. Bake, uncovered, 30 minutes.

5. Meanwhile, in hot butter in large skillet, brown chicken, half at a time, turning with tongs to brown well on all sides—this should take about 30 minutes in all. Sprinkle evenly with pepper.

6. Add browned chicken and undrained tomatoes to beans. With sharp knife, cut 9 diagonal slashes ⅛ inch deep in top of sausage. Place sausage on top of chicken and vegetables. Cover tightly (you may use aluminum foil); bake 45 minutes or until chicken is tender.

7. Bake, uncovered, 10 minutes longer. Sprinkle with parsley, and serve.

*Note*: Cassoulet is better made day before and refrigerated. To serve: Let warm to room temperature; reheat, covered, at 300F for 1 hour. If too dry, add 1 cup chicken broth.
Makes 8 servings.

# ❖ ARROZ CON POLLO

*3-lb broiler-fryer, cut into 8 pieces*
*½ cup olive oil*
*2 cups chopped onion*
*1 clove garlic, crushed*
*½ teaspoon crushed red pepper*
*2½ teaspoons salt*
*½ teaspoon pepper*
*2 cups raw converted white rice*
*¼ teaspoon saffron threads*
*1 can (1 lb 12 oz) tomatoes,*
  *undrained*
*1 canned green chile pepper, chopped*
*1 can (10¾ oz) condensed chicken*
  *broth, undiluted*
*½ cup water*
*½ pkg (10-oz size) frozen peas*
*½ cup pimiento-stuffed green olives,*
  *sliced*
*1 can (4 oz) pimientos, drained and*
  *sliced*

1. Wipe chicken pieces with damp paper towels.
2. In heavy 6-quart Dutch oven, heat olive oil. Brown chicken, a few pieces at a time, until golden-brown all over. Remove chicken as it browns.
3. Preheat oven to 325F.
4. Add chopped onion, garlic, and red pepper to Dutch oven; sauté, stirring, over medium heat until golden—about 3 minutes.
5. Add salt, pepper, rice, and saffron to Dutch oven; cook, stirring, until rice is lightly browned—10 minutes.
6. Add tomatoes, chile pepper, and chicken broth to rice mixture. Add chicken pieces. Bring just to boiling.
7. Bake, covered, 1 hour.
8. Add water. Sprinkle peas, olives, and pimiento strips over top; do not stir. Bake, covered, 20 minutes longer, or until chicken is tender and peas are cooked.
9. Serve hot right from Dutch oven.
Makes 6 servings.

# ❖ PÂTÉ-STUFFED CHICKEN BREASTS

*1 medium onion, sliced*
*1 celery stalk, sliced*
*1 carrot, sliced*
*1 parsley sprig*
*1 teaspoon salt*
*¼ teaspoon dried thyme leaves*
*1 small bay leaf*
*1 can (10¾ oz) condensed chicken*
  *broth, undiluted*
*1⅓ cups water*
*4 whole chicken breasts (4 lb), split*
*2 cans (4¾-oz size) liver pâté*

## GLAZE:

*¼ cup cold water*
*1 env unflavored gelatine*
*1 cup heavy cream*
*Pitted black olives, cut into diamond*
  *shapes*
*Pimiento-stuffed olives, sliced*

*Watercress sprigs*

1. In 6-quart kettle, combine onion, celery, carrot, parsley, salt, thyme, bay leaf, chicken broth, 1⅓ cups water, and split chicken breasts; bring mixture to boiling.
2. Reduce heat, and simmer, covered, 30 minutes, or just until chicken breasts are fork-tender.
3. Remove kettle from heat. Let chicken breasts cool in broth.
4. Remove chicken breasts from broth; reserve broth. Remove skin and bone from chicken breasts; trim edges evenly.
5. On underside of each chicken breast, spread about 1 tablespoon liver pâté, mounding it slightly. Refrigerate chicken breasts, covered, for 1 hour.
6. Meanwhile, strain broth; skim off fat. Reserve 2 cups of broth.
7. Make Glaze: In medium saucepan, bring reserved broth to boiling. Reduce heat; simmer broth, uncovered, 30 minutes, or until liquid is reduced to 1 cup.
8. In ¼ cup cold water in medium bowl, let gelatine stand 5 minutes to soften. Add hot broth, stirring to dissolve gelatine.
9. Add heavy cream, mixing until it is well combined with gelatine mixture.

10. Set bowl with gelatine mixture in ice water; let stand about 20 minutes, or until well chilled but not thickened. Stir occasionally. Remove from ice water.

11. Place chicken breasts, pâté side down, on wire rack; set rack on tray. Spoon glaze over chicken breasts.

12. Refrigerate, on tray, for 30 minutes, or until glaze is set.

13. Scrape glaze from tray; reheat it, and set in saucepan, in ice water again to chill. Spoon glaze over chicken breasts, coating them completely.

14. Press both kinds of olive into glaze, to decorate. Refrigerate until glaze is set—about 1 hour.

15. To serve: Arrange chicken breasts, in single layer, in large shallow serving dish. Garnish stuffed chicken breasts with sprigs of watercress before serving.

Makes 8 servings.

# ❖ BREAST OF CHICKEN IN MADEIRA SAUCE

*1½ cups raw long-grain white rice*
*4 whole chicken breasts (about 3 lb)*
*¼ cup butter or margarine*
*2 shallots, sliced*
*½ lb fresh mushrooms, washed and*
*    cut in half lengthwise*
*1 teaspoon dried thyme leaves*
*1½ teaspoons salt*
*Dash pepper*
*1½ cups dry Madeira wine*
*1 teaspoon cornstarch*
*1 cup light cream*
*½ cup heavy cream*
*1 cup grated natural Swiss cheese*
*2 tablespoons chopped parsley*

1. Cook rice as package label directs.

2. Wipe chicken breasts with damp paper towels. Cut breasts in half; with sharp knife, carefully remove skin and bone, keeping chicken breast intact.

3. In hot butter, in large skillet, cook shallots several minutes. Add chicken breasts; brown well over medium heat, about 10 minutes on each side.

4. Add mushrooms, thyme, salt, and pepper; cook about 3 minutes.

5. Preheat oven to 375F.

6. Turn out rice into lightly buttered 2-quart shallow casserole. Arrange chicken breasts, overlapping slightly, down center of casserole. Arrange mushrooms around chicken.

7. In same skillet, pour wine into drippings; stir to dissolve browned bits in pan.

8. Meanwhile, dissolve cornstarch in 2 tablespoons light cream.

9. Add heavy cream, rest of light cream, and the cornstarch to wine mixture; bring just to boiling, stirring. Remove from heat; add cheese.

10. Spoon half of sauce over chicken; bake in oven 10 to 12 minutes; then run under broiler several minutes to brown slightly. Sprinkle with parsley. Reheat rest of sauce; serve along with casserole.

Makes 8 servings.

# ❖ BREAST OF CHICKEN TARRAGON

3 whole chicken breasts (3 lb),
   skinned, boned, and cut in half
Flour
2 tablespoons salad oil
2 tablespoons butter or margarine
6 shallots, chopped
2 carrots, pared and cut into ⅛-inch
   rounds
¼ cup cognac or brandy
1 cup dry white wine
¼ cup water
¼ cup chopped fresh tarragon or 1 tablespoon dried tarragon leaves
1½ tablespoons chopped fresh chervil
   or 1 teaspoon dried chervil leaves
2 teaspoons salt
¼ teaspoon pepper
1 cup light cream
1 egg yolk
1 tablespoon flour
Chopped parsley

1. Wash chicken breasts; dry well on paper towels. Coat with flour.
2. In large skillet, heat oil and butter. Add chicken breasts; sauté on both sides until golden-brown, about 5 minutes on each side.
3. Remove browned chicken. To drippings, add shallots and carrots; sauté, stirring, 5 minutes. Return chicken to skillet; heat.
4. Reduce heat; sprinkle cognac over hot chicken, and ignite.
5. Add white wine, water, tarragon, chervil, salt, and pepper.
6. Bring to boiling; reduce heat, and simmer, covered, 30 minutes.
7. In small bowl, combine cream, egg yolk, and flour; mix well.
8. Remove chicken to heated serving platter. Keep warm.
9. Strain pan drippings, if desired. Return drippings to skillet.
10. Stir cream mixture into drippings in skillet. Bring just to boiling. Add a little white wine if sauce seems too thick. Strain over chicken. Sprinkle with parsley.
Makes 3 to 4 servings.

# ❖ BREAST OF CHICKEN LUAU

4 whole chicken breasts (4 lb), split
2 tablespoons butter or margarine
¼ cup chopped green onion
½ teaspoon salt
¼ teaspoon ground ginger
1 tablespoon brown sugar
1 can (8 oz) pineapple slices, packed
   in own juice
1 tablespoon soy sauce
1 tablespoon cornstarch

1. Wipe chicken breasts with damp paper towels.
2. Heat butter in large skillet. Add chicken, skin side down, three pieces at a time, and brown on all sides, about 5 minutes each side. Remove as browned.
3. In remaining fat in skillet, sauté green onion, stirring, about 2 minutes.
4. Return chicken breasts to skillet. Sprinkle with salt, ginger, and brown sugar.
5. Drain pineapple slices; reserve liquid. Cut slices in half. Add water to pineapple liquid to make 1 cup. Add soy sauce and cornstarch to liquid; stir until smooth. Pour over chicken breasts in skillet. Add pineapple.
6. Bring to boiling; simmer, covered, 20 to 30 minutes, or until chicken breasts are tender. Taste sauce, and add more salt, if desired.
7. Remove chicken breasts to heated platter. Spoon sauce remaining in skillet over chicken. Garnish with pineapple.
Makes 8 servings.

# ❖ STEAMED CHICKEN BREASTS AND VEGETABLES

3 whole chicken breasts (3 lb), split
  and boned, but not skinned
1 teaspoon salt
1 teaspoon dried tarragon leaves
1 cup cold water
2 large carrots, pared and sliced
  ⅛ inch thick on diagonal
6 new potatoes unpeeled, washed,
  and sliced ½ inch thick
3 zucchini, unpeeled and sliced
  ¼ inch thick on diagonal
1 bay leaf
2 tablespoons chopped parsley

1. Wipe chicken breasts with damp paper towels. On sheet of waxed paper, combine salt and tarragon. Use to coat chicken breasts on both sides. Reserve rest of tarragon mixture for later use.
2. Pour cold water in bottom of 12-inch skillet. Place 10-inch wire rack in bottom of skillet.
3. Layer chicken breasts, skin side up, on rack. Layer with carrot, potato, zucchini, and bay leaf in that order. Sprinkle with remaining tarragon mixture.
4. Over medium heat, bring to boiling; then lower heat, and steam, covered, 35 to 40 minutes, or until chicken and vegetables are tender. Remove from heat.
5. Arrange chicken breasts and vegetables on platter. Boil remaining liquid over medium heat until reduced to ½ cup. Pour over chicken breasts. Sprinkle with parsley.
Makes 6 servings.

# ❖ CHICKEN CURRY

4 whole chicken breasts (4 lb)
¼ cup butter or margarine
2 cans (10¾-oz size) condensed
  chicken broth, undiluted

## CURRY SAUCE:

¼ cup butter or margarine
1 clove garlic, crushed
1 cup chopped onion
2 to 3 teaspoons curry powder
1 cup chopped pared tart apple
¼ cup all-purpose flour
¼ teaspoon ground cardamom
1 teaspoon ground ginger
½ teaspoon salt
¼ teaspoon pepper
2 teaspoons grated lime peel
2 tablespoons lime juice
¼ cup chopped chutney

Saffron Rice, page 426
Lime slices

1. Wash chicken; dry well on paper towels. Using small sharp knife, carefully remove skin. Cut each breast in half, making 8 pieces.
2. In ¼ cup hot butter in large skillet, over medium heat, brown chicken, 4 pieces at a time, 5 minutes per side. Using tongs, remove chicken as it is browned.
3. Return chicken to skillet. Add 1 can chicken broth; bring to boiling. Reduce heat, and simmer, covered, 20 minutes, or just until tender. Remove chicken pieces; keep warm.
4. Measure liquid in skillet; add remaining can of chicken broth and enough water to make 3 cups; reserve.
5. Make Curry Sauce: In ¼ cup hot butter in same skillet, sauté garlic, onion, curry powder, and apple until onion is tender—5 minutes. Remove from heat. Stir in flour, cardamom, ginger, salt, and pepper; mix well.
6. Gradually stir in reserved 3 cups liquid and the lime peel and juice. Bring to boiling, stirring occasionally.
7. Stir in chutney; add chicken. Cover, and heat gently just to boiling, to reheat chicken—about 5 minutes.

8. Meanwhile, make Saffron Rice. Turn out rice into center of round platter. Arrange chicken breasts over rice; spoon sauce over chicken. Garnish with slices of lime. Serve with curry accompaniments (see Note).

Makes 8 servings.

*Note*: Chopped green pepper, chutney, salted peanuts, and flaked coconut are nice accompaniments for curry, as well as raisins, kumquats, sliced green onions, chopped unpared cucumbers, and pineapple chunks.

# ✠ CHICKEN-AND-HAM ROLLS À LA SUISSE

*3 whole chicken breasts (3 lb), boned, skinned, and halved*
*6 thin slices baked ham*
*1 egg*
*1 tablespoon prepared brown mustard*
*2 tablespoons water*
*¼ cup grated Parmesan cheese*
*½ teaspoon salt*
*¼ teaspoon white pepper*
*½ cup dry bread crumbs*
*6 tablespoons butter or margarine, melted*

## SAUCE:

*2 tablespoons butter or margarine*
*2 tablespoons all-purpose flour*
*½ teaspoon salt*
*¼ teaspoon white pepper*
*1 tablespoon prepared mustard*
*1½ cups milk*
*½ cup dry white wine*
*4 oz grated Swiss cheese*

1. Preheat oven to 425F. Line 12-by-8-by-2-inch baking dish with foil.
2. Wash chicken breasts; dry well on paper towels. To flatten chicken, place each half, smooth side down, on sheet of waxed paper; cover with second sheet. Using mallet, pound chicken to about ¼-inch thickness.
3. Place slice of ham on each piece of chicken. Roll up from short end; secure with wooden pick.
4. Combine egg, 1 tablespoon mustard, and 2 tablespoons water; mix well. Mix together Parmesan cheese, ½ teaspoon salt, ¼ teaspoon pepper, and the bread crumbs.
5. Dip chicken rolls in egg mixture, then in crumb mixture, coating evenly. Arrange in single layer in bottom of foil-lined pan; spoon 1 tablespoon melted butter over each roll.
6. Bake, uncovered, 45 minutes, or until richly browned and fork-tender.
7. Meanwhile, make Sauce: In small, heavy saucepan, melt butter. Remove from heat; stir in flour, salt, pepper, and mustard. Add milk gradually, stirring constantly. Return to heat. Bring to boiling, stirring. Add wine and cheese; simmer, stirring, 1 minute.
8. Pour three fourths of sauce into bottom of 12-by-8-by-2-inch baking dish. Place chicken rolls on top. Pour rest of sauce over chicken rolls. If desired, sprinkle with shredded Swiss cheese. Place under broiler 1 minute before serving.

Makes 6 servings.

# ❖ CRISPY CHICKEN DRUMSTICKS

12 broiler-fryer legs (3 lb)
¾ cup all-purpose flour
¾ cup crushed cornflake crumbs
2 teaspoons salt
½ teaspoon poultry seasoning
¼ teaspoon pepper
2 eggs, beaten
½ cup butter or margarine, melted

1. Preheat oven to 400F. Wipe chicken legs with damp paper towels.
2. In clean paper bag, combine flour, cornflake crumbs, salt, poultry seasoning, and pepper.
3. Dip chicken legs, a few at a time, into beaten egg; then shake in bag to coat with flour mixture.
4. Arrange in single layer in greased shallow baking pan. Brush chicken with melted butter. Cover pan with foil; bake 30 minutes.
5. Remove foil. Increase oven temperature to 450F, and bake 25 to 30 minutes, or until golden-brown. Makes 6 servings.

# ❖ CHICKEN THIGHS PARMIGIANA

8 chicken thighs (2 lb)
¼ cup butter or margarine
1 medium onion, sliced
2 cloves garlic, crushed
1 pkg (10 oz) frozen chopped spinach
½ teaspoon salt
1 teaspoon dried basil leaves
1 pkg (8 oz) spaghetti
¼ cup grated Parmesan cheese

1. Wash chicken thighs well; dry with paper towels.
2. In hot butter in large skillet, sauté chicken thighs, skin side down, 5 minutes, or until golden-brown.
3. Add onion and garlic; sauté, covered, 5 minutes.
4. Push chicken to one side. Add spinach. Sprinkle with salt and basil. Simmer, covered, 15 minutes.
5. Meanwhile, cook spaghetti as package label directs; drain.
6. Turn chicken right side up. Sprinkle with Parmesan cheese. Blend spinach with onion and butter. Simmer, covered, 10 minutes, or until chicken is tender. Serve on spaghetti.
Makes 4 to 6 servings.

# ❖ OVERNIGHT CHICKEN CASSEROLE

2 cups milk
2 cans (10¾-oz size) condensed cream
   of mushroom soup, undiluted
1 pkg (8 oz) elbow macaroni, uncooked
1 can (8 oz) water chestnuts, thinly
   sliced
2 cups diced cooked chicken
1 cup chopped onion
1½ cups grated Cheddar cheese (6 oz)
4 hard-cooked eggs, sliced
¼ teaspoon salt
⅓ cup chopped parsley
Canned pimiento strips (optional)

1. In large bowl, combine milk and soup; mix until smooth. Add macaroni, water chestnuts, chicken, onion, cheese, 3 hard-cooked eggs, and the salt. Mix well. Refrigerate overnight, tightly covered.
2. Next day, about 1½ hours before serving, preheat oven to 325F. Lightly grease 13-by-9-by-2-inch baking dish. Pour macaroni mixture into casserole. Bake 1 hour and 15 minutes, or until hot and bubbly. Garnish with chopped parsley, remaining hard-cooked egg, and pimiento strips.
Makes 8 servings.

# ❖ CHICKEN LIVERS WITH PASTA AND GREEN BEANS

2 tablespoons salad oil
1 lb chicken livers, washed, halved, and white part removed
1 clove garlic, crushed
1 teaspoon dried oregano leaves
½ teaspoon dried basil leaves
1 teaspoon salt
⅛ teaspoon pepper
1 can (14 oz) Italian tomatoes, undrained
½ pkg (16-oz size) tubular pasta (ziti)
½ pkg (12-oz size) frozen Italian green beans
2 tablespoons butter or margarine, melted
2 tablespoons grated Parmesan cheese

1. In hot oil in skillet, sauté chicken livers and garlic 6 to 8 minutes, or until brown; add oregano, basil, salt, and pepper; sauté, stirring, 1 minute. Remove livers.
2. Place tomatoes in skillet; mash with fork. Bring to boiling; simmer, uncovered, 5 minutes, or until thickened.
3. Return livers to skillet; simmer, covered, 5 minutes, or long enough to reheat.
4. Meanwhile, cook pasta and Italian green beans according to package directions; drain. In large bowl, toss pasta and beans with melted butter and Parmesan cheese.
5. Turn out into warm serving dish; spoon chicken livers into center.
Makes 6 servings.

# CORNISH HENS

## ❖ ROAST CORNISH HENS

6 (1¼-lb size) Cornish hens, with giblets

**BASTING SAUCE:**

¾ cup butter or margarine
¾ cup dry white wine
1 tablespoon dried tarragon leaves

Salt
Pepper
6 tablespoons dried tarragon leaves
6 cloves garlic
Garlic salt
1 can (13¾ oz) chicken broth
1 celery stalk, cut into large pieces
1 medium onion, quartered
1 medium carrot, pared and cut into large pieces
4 whole black peppercorns

1. If Cornish hens are frozen, let thaw overnight in refrigerator. Wash hens, inside and out, under cold water; drain. Dry well with paper towels. Wash giblets.
2. Make Basting Sauce: Melt ¾ cup butter in small saucepan; stir in wine and 1 tablespoon tarragon.
3. Preheat oven to 450F. Sprinkle inside of each hen with ¼ teaspoon salt, ⅛ teaspoon pepper, and 1 tablespoon dried tarragon leaves. Place one clove garlic, halved, inside each. Sprinkle outside of each hen liberally with garlic salt; tie legs together.
4. Place close together in shallow roasting pan without rack. Roast, basting often with sauce, 1 hour, or until browned and tender.
5. Meanwhile, place giblets (reserve livers) in large saucepan. Add chicken broth, celery, onion, carrot, 1 teaspoon salt, and the peppercorns. Bring to boiling; reduce heat, and simmer, covered, 45 minutes, or until tender. Add liver; simmer 10 minutes.
6. Make Pilaf: In medium saucepan, combine cracked wheat and chicken broth. Cover; bring to boiling. Reduce heat, and simmer 20 minutes.
7. Remove from heat. Let stand 10 minutes, or until

## PILAF:

*2 cups cracked wheat (bulgur)*
*2 cans (13¾-oz size) chicken broth*
*¼ cup butter or margarine*

*2 tablespoons all-purpose flour*
*¼ cup water*
*Watercress*

all liquid is absorbed. Add butter; toss gently to combine. Mound pilaf in center of heated platter; arrange hens around edge. Keep warm while making gravy.

8. Strain giblets and liver, reserving broth; chop. Combine flour and ¼ cup water; mix until smooth. Stir into drippings in roasting pan with 1 cup reserved broth and chopped giblets. Bring to boiling, stirring until thickened. Turn out into heated gravy boat. Garnish serving platter with watercress.
Makes 6 servings.

# ✠ ROAST CORNISH HENS WITH CARROT RICE

*4 (1¼-lb size) Cornish hens, with giblets*

## BASTING SAUCE:

*¼ cup butter or margarine*
*½ cup white wine*
*1 clove garlic, pressed*
*1 teaspoon dried tarragon leaves*

*½ teaspoon salt*
*¼ teaspoon pepper*
*2 teaspoons dried tarragon leaves*

## PILAF:

*¼ cup butter*
*¼ cup chopped onion*
*1 cup raw long-grain white rice*
*1 cup grated carrot*
*⅛ teaspoon pepper*
*¼ cup raisins*
*1 can (10¾ oz) condensed chicken broth, undiluted*

*½ cup hot water*
*Parsley (optional)*

1. If Cornish hens are frozen, let thaw overnight in refrigerator. Wash hens, inside and out, under cold water; drain. Dry with paper towels. Wash giblets. With kitchen shears, cut hens in half.
2. Make Basting Sauce: Melt ¼ cup butter in saucepan; stir in wine, garlic, and 1 teaspoon tarragon.
3. Preheat oven to 450F. Sprinkle cut sides of hens with ½ teaspoon salt, ¼ teaspoon pepper, and remaining 2 teaspoons tarragon.
4. Place hens, cut side down, close together in shallow roasting pan without rack. Roast, basting often with sauce, 1 hour, or until browned and tender.
5. Make Pilaf: Melt ¼ cup butter in medium skillet. Sauté onion and rice until golden. Stir in carrot, ⅛ teaspoon pepper, and the raisins. Add water to chicken broth to make 2 cups. Add to rice mixture, bring to boiling.
6. Turn out into 1½-quart casserole. Cover; bake 25 to 35 minutes, or until liquid is absorbed and rice is tender.
7. Spoon pilaf onto warm serving platter. Arrange hens on top. Pour any basting sauce remaining in pan over top. Add hot water to browned bits in pan. Bring to boiling, stirring. Pour over hens. Garnish with parsley, if desired.
Makes 8 servings

# TURKEY

Although a whole turkey, roasted until its crisp skin looks lacquered, served on a large platter with garnishes of cranberries, oranges, or grapes, is still the symbol of Thanksgiving time, it takes a large family to enjoy it. Today, with turkey parts available year-round, this low-fat meat is a good alternate main course for everyday or company dinners, not just on holidays. Think of turkey cutlets to fix Marsala-style for a company dinner. Think how well a cold whole turkey breast would go on a summer buffet table, with, perhaps, leftovers for sandwiches.

**TIMETABLE FOR ROASTING TURKEY, AT 325F**

| WEIGHT | COOKING TIME IN UNCOVERED PAN | INTERNAL TEMPERATURE (LEG JOINT MOVES FREELY) |
|---|---|---|
| Unstuffed ready-to-cook turkey | | |
| 6–8  lb | 3–3½ hours | |
| 8–12 lb | 3½–4½ hours | 180–185F |
| 12–16 lb | 4½–5½ hours | 180–185F |
| 16–20 lb | 5½–6½ hours | 180–185F |
| 20–24 lb | 6½–7 hours | 180–185F |
| | | 180–185F |
| Halves, quarters, and half breasts | | |
| 3–8  lb | 2–3 hours | |
| 8–12 lb | 3–4 hours | 180–185F |
| | | 180–185F |

# ◈ GOLDEN ROAST TURKEY

*14- to 16-lb turkey*
*Old-Fashioned Stuffing, below*
*1 cup butter or margarine, melted*
*Salt*
*Pepper*
*Giblet Gravy for Turkey, page 468*

1. Remove giblets and neck from turkey; wash, and set aside. Wash turkey thoroughly inside and out. Pat dry with paper towels. Remove and discard any excess fat.
2. Prepare Old-Fashioned Stuffing. Preheat oven to 325F.
3. Spoon some of stuffing into neck cavity of turkey. Bring skin of neck over back; fasten with poultry pin.
4. Spoon remaining stuffing into body cavity; do not pack. Insert 4 or 5 poultry pins at regular intervals. Lace cavity closed, with twine, bootlace fashion; tie.
5. Bend wing tips under body, or fasten to body with poultry pins. Tie ends of legs together. Insert meat thermometer in inside of thigh at thickest part.
6. Place turkey on rack in shallow roasting pan. Brush with some of butter; sprinkle with salt and pepper.
7. Roast, uncovered and brushing occasionally with remaining butter and pan drippings, about 4½ hours, or until meat thermometer registers 185F. Leg joint should move freely. When turkey begins to turn golden, cover with square of butter-soaked cheesecloth or loose tent of foil, to prevent too much browning.
8. While turkey roasts, cook giblets and neck as directed in Giblet Gravy for Turkey.
9. Place turkey on heated serving platter. Remove cheesecloth or foil, twine, and poultry pins. Let stand 20 to 30 minutes before carving. Meanwhile, make Giblet Gravy.
Makes 14 to 16 servings.

## OLD-FASHIONED STUFFING:

12 cups fresh white-bread cubes
½ cup chopped parsley
1 tablespoon poultry seasoning
2 teaspoons salt
½ teaspoon pepper
½ cup butter or margarine
3 cups chopped celery
1 cup chopped onion

1. In large bowl, combine bread cubes, parsley, poultry seasoning, salt, and pepper; toss to mix well.
2. In hot butter in medium skillet, sauté celery and onion until golden—7 to 10 minutes.
3. Add to bread mixture; toss lightly until well mixed.
4. Use to fill prepared turkey.
Makes 12 cups, enough to stuff 16-lb turkey.

# ✠ BREAST OF TURKEY WITH HAM STUFFING

## HAM STUFFING:

⅓ cup milk
2 eggs
1 tablespoon catsup
1 tablespoon prepared mustard
⅛ teaspoon pepper
⅔ cup fresh white-bread crumbs
1 lb ground smoked ham
2 tablespoons finely chopped onion
1 tablespoon chopped parsley

5- to 8-lb frozen turkey breast, thawed
2 teaspoons salt
½ teaspoon pepper
1 teaspoon dried thyme leaves
¼ cup butter or margarine, melted
2 cans (10¾-oz size) condensed chicken broth, undiluted
4 cups water
1 medium onion, quartered
3 stalks celery, cut up
1 medium carrot, cut up
1 bay leaf, crumbled
5 whole black peppercorns
2 parsley sprigs
2 tablespoons all-purpose flour

1. Make Ham Stuffing: In large bowl, combine milk, eggs, catsup, mustard, and ⅛ teaspoon pepper; beat until well blended. Stir in bread crumbs; let mixture stand several minutes. Add ham, chopped onion, and parsley; mix well.
2. Wash turkey breast inside and out under cold running water. Dry well with paper towels.
3. Preheat oven to 325F. With sharp knife, bone turkey, being careful not to cut skin of breast. Carefully cut around breastbone and remove; reserve bone. Lay breast flat, skin side down. Combine salt, pepper, and thyme leaves. Rub half of mixture into meat.
4. Spread ham stuffing evenly over inside surface of turkey. Close breast over stuffing and fasten with skewers; lace together with string. Place on rack, skewer side down, in shallow roasting pan. Rub rest of thyme mixture into skin of turkey. Brush top with melted butter. Roast, uncovered, 2 to 2½ hours, or until nicely browned. Baste with pan drippings every ½ hour or so.
5. Meanwhile, in large saucepan, cook turkey bones with chicken broth, 4 cups water, quartered onion, celery, carrot, bay leaf, peppercorns, and parsley. Simmer, uncovered, 2 hours, or until broth is reduced to about 2 cups.
6. When turkey is done, remove to heated platter. Make gravy: Into pan drippings, stir 2 tablespoons flour; cook, stirring, until slightly brown. Pour in 2 cups turkey broth, dissolving browned bits in pan. Bring to boiling; reduce heat, and simmer, stirring, until thickened—about 5 minutes. Strain.
7. Slice turkey breast thin. Serve with gravy.
Makes 12 servings.

*Note*: This is very nice served cold.

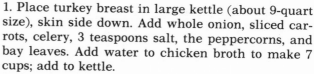

# ✦ DELUXE TURKEY PIE

4¾ lb frozen turkey breast
1 whole onion, studded with 4 whole
   cloves
3 carrots, pared and thickly sliced
3 stalks celery, thickly sliced
4 teaspoons salt
10 whole black peppercorns
2 bay leaves
2 cans (10¾-oz size) condensed
   chicken broth, undiluted
1 pkg (11 oz) piecrust mix
10 small white onions
4 medium carrots, pared and quartered
3 large potatoes (1¼ lb), peeled and
   cut into ½-inch cubes
6 slices bacon, quartered
½ lb pork sausage, formed into 12
   (1-inch) balls
Water
1 can (8 oz) sliced mushrooms
⅓ cup all-purpose flour
Dash pepper
2 tablespoons chopped parsley
1 egg, slightly beaten

1. Place turkey breast in large kettle (about 9-quart size), skin side down. Add whole onion, sliced carrots, celery, 3 teaspoons salt, the peppercorns, and bay leaves. Add water to chicken broth to make 7 cups; add to kettle.

2. Bring to boiling; reduce heat, and simmer, covered, 1 hour. Turn turkey; simmer ½ hour longer, or until turkey is tender.

3. Meanwhile, prepare piecrust mix as package label directs; refrigerate.

4. Remove turkey to large bowl. Strain broth, mashing vegetables, into medium saucepan. Add white onions, quartered carrots, and potatoes. Bring to boiling; reduce heat, and cook, covered, until carrot is tender—about 20 minutes.

5. At same time, in large skillet, cook bacon until crisp. Drain on paper towels; pour off fat. Crumble bacon.

6. In same skillet, cook sausage balls, turning until browned all over—about 15 minutes.

7. Cut turkey meat into 1-inch cubes; it should measure 6 cups.

8. Drain broth from vegetables into 1-quart measure. Add enough water to make 3½ cups liquid. Pour back into saucepan; bring to boiling.

9. Drain liquid from mushrooms into 1-cup measure; add water to make 1 cup. Combine with flour in small bowl, stirring until smooth. Add slowly to boiling liquid, stirring with wire whisk until smooth and thickened. Add remaining salt and the pepper.

10. Turn out vegetables into 3-quart oval casserole or Dutch oven. Add cut-up turkey, sausage balls, drained mushrooms, chopped parsley, and thickened sauce; stir just to combine. Top with bacon. Preheat oven to 400F.

11. On lightly floured surface or pastry cloth, roll out round of pastry ½ inch larger than top of casserole. Place on top of casserole, turning edge under; press to rim of casserole to seal all around. Cut several steam vents in top. Brush lightly with egg. Bake 30 to 35 minutes, or until crust is golden and mixture is bubbly.

Makes 12 servings.

# DUCK AND GOOSE

Duck and goose are the richer cousins of the poultry family. They must be cooked to release much of their fat but still keep the meat moist and full of flavor. Our directions tell you how to achieve that.

##  DUCKLING À L'ORANGE

5-lb duckling (if frozen, thaw completely)
1 teaspoon salt
1 large onion
1 clove garlic, chopped
3 whole black peppercorns
2 oranges, unpeeled and quartered
½ cup red Burgundy
2 cups water

### ORANGE SAUCE:

3 tablespoons butter or margarine
Liver from duckling
3 tablespoons brandy
2 tablespoons grated orange peel
¾ teaspoon chopped garlic
2 tablespoons all-purpose flour
2 teaspoons catsup
1 chicken-bouillon cube
Dash pepper
1¼ cups broth from giblets
⅓ cup Burgundy
¼ cup orange marmalade
¼ cup orange juice
1 cup orange sections

½ cup orange marmalade

1. Remove giblets and neck from duckling and reserve. Wash duckling under running water. Drain; dry with paper towels. Turn breast side down; using sharp scissors and knife, carefully cut out wishbone from breast for easier carving.
2. Preheat oven to 425F. Sprinkle inside of duckling with ½ teaspoon salt. Tuck onion inside neck; bring skin of neck over back. Fasten with poultry pins. Stuff body cavity with garlic, peppercorns, and oranges. Close cavity with poultry pins. Tie legs together; bend wing tips under body.
3. Place on rack in shallow roasting pan. Pour ½ cup Burgundy over duckling. Roast, uncovered, 30 minutes. Reduce oven to 375F; roast 1½ hours.
4. Bring giblets to boiling in 2 cups water and ½ teaspoon salt; reduce heat, and simmer, covered, 1 hour. Strain broth, and set aside.
5. Make Orange Sauce: In 2 tablespoons butter in skillet, brown liver. Remove from heat. Heat brandy slightly. Ignite and pour over liver. Remove liver; chop. In same skillet, in rest of butter, sauté orange peel and garlic 3 minutes. Stir in flour, catsup, bouillon cube, and pepper.
6. Gradually add giblet broth, the ⅓ cup Burgundy, ¼ cup marmalade, and the orange juice; mix well. Bring to boiling; reduce heat, and simmer, stirring, 15 minutes. Add liver and orange sections; heat.
7. Spread ½ cup marmalade over duckling. Roast 10 minutes longer.
8. Remove pins and twine. Place on heated platter. Using sharp knife, cut each side of breast into diagonal slices ½ inch wide, starting at leg. Then run knife down center of breast to separate two sides; run knife around outer edge to cut skin. Pass sauce with duckling.
Makes 4 servings.

Note: If desired, roast 2 ducklings at same time, leaving sauce recipe as is. Nice served with white rice combined with sautéed sliced mushrooms.

# ✜ ROSÉ DUCKLING

5-lb duckling, quartered
1 teaspoon salt
⅛ teaspoon black pepper
¼ teaspoon ground ginger
1 tablespoon grated onion
1 cup rosé wine
½ cup light-brown sugar
1 tablespoon cornstarch
1 teaspoon grated orange peel

1. Wipe duckling quarters with damp paper towels. Preheat oven to 400F.
2. Arrange duckling in roasting pan. Roast, uncovered, 30 minutes. Drain off excess fat.
3. Sprinkle duckling with salt, pepper, ginger, and grated onion. Pour ¼ cup wine into pan. Cover tightly with foil. Bake 45 minutes, or until tender.
4. In small saucepan, combine sugar, cornstarch, and orange peel; add remaining wine, and mix until well blended. Cook, stirring, until thickened.
5. Pour sauce over duckling; roast, uncovered, 10 minutes, basting frequently.
Makes 4 servings.

# ✜ ROAST GOOSE WITH CHESTNUT-SAUSAGE STUFFING

Chestnut-Sausage Stuffing, below
10- to 12-lb goose
2 tablespoons lemon juice
1 teaspoon salt
⅛ teaspoon pepper
Giblet Gravy for Goose, below
Parsley

1. Preheat oven to 400F. Make Chestnut-Sausage Stuffing.
2. Remove giblets and neck from goose, and set aside; discard liver. Wash goose, inside and out, under cold running water; dry well with paper towels. Remove and discard all fat from inside. Rub cavity with lemon juice, salt, and pepper.
3. Spoon stuffing into neck cavity; bring skin of neck over back, and fasten with poultry pins. Spoon stuffing lightly into body cavity; close with poultry pins, and lace with twine. Bend wing tips under body; tie ends of legs together. (Bake any leftover stuffing in 1-quart casserole during last 45 minutes of roasting.) Insert meat thermometer in inside of thigh at thickest part.
4. Prick skin only (not meat), with metal skewer or poultry pin, over thighs, back, and breast very well. Place, breast side up, on rack in large roasting pan.
5. Roast, uncovered, 1 hour. Remove goose from oven.
6. Pour off and discard fat from pan. Roast goose, uncovered, 2 hours longer. Pour off all fat. Roast ½ hour longer, or until skin is nicely browned and crisp. Meaty part of leg should feel soft and meat thermometer should register 185F.
7. While goose is roasting, make Giblet Gravy for Goose.
8. Place goose on heated platter. Garnish with parsley.
Makes 8 servings.

## CHESTNUT-SAUSAGE STUFFING:

*1 lb sausage meat*
*1 cup chopped onion*
*1 cup chopped celery*
*¼ cup chopped parsley*
*1 pkg (8 oz) herb-seasoned stuffing mix*
*2 cans (about 2-lb size) water-packed chestnuts (see Note), well drained and broken into pieces*
*½ teaspoon salt*
*¼ teaspoon pepper*
*1 cup chicken broth*

1. In large skillet, sauté sausage meat, stirring until lightly browned. Add onion, celery, and parsley; sauté 8 to 10 minutes.
2. In large kettle, combine stuffing mix, chestnuts, salt, and pepper; toss to mix well.
3. Add chicken broth, along with sausage mixture. Toss lightly, using 2 large forks.
Makes 8 cups.

*Note*: Or use 2 lb fresh chestnuts: To roast, make slit in each shell with sharp knife. Bake at 500F for 15 minutes. Remove shells and skins. Then chop coarsely.

## GIBLET GRAVY FOR GOOSE:

*Giblets and neck from goose*
*1½ cups water*
*2 celery stalks, cut up*
*2 carrots, pared and cut up*
*1 can (10¾ oz) chicken broth*
*Dash salt*
*Dash pepper*
*Goose drippings*
*¼ cup all-purpose flour*
*½ cup white wine*

1. While goose roasts, place giblets and neck in medium saucepan with water, celery, carrots, chicken broth, salt, and pepper.
2. Bring to boiling; reduce heat, and simmer, covered, 2 hours, or until giblets are tender.
3. Remove giblets; discard neck. Chop giblets finely; set aside. Strain broth, and reserve.
4. When goose is done, pour drippings into 1-cup measure; return ¼ cup of drippings to roasting pan. Stir in flour to make smooth mixture; gradually stir in 2 cups reserved broth and the white wine.
5. Bring to boiling, stirring. Reduce heat; simmer, stirring, 5 minutes, or until thickened and smooth. Add giblets and more salt and pepper, if needed. Serve with goose.
Makes 2½ cups.

# REDUCED-CALORIE COOKING

❖ **I**f Veal Stew Lafayette and Strawberries with Custard Sauce don't sound like reduced-calorie cooking to you, that's the intent. They are but two of our great-sounding and great-tasting recipes with pared-down calories.

Of course, you should use the recipes in this chapter when the scale begins to signal weight-gaining danger, but as you discover how good these dishes are, you will also learn how to slim down your own favorite recipes. Reducing the fat content, using skim milk instead of cream, cutting back on sugar, broiling rather than frying, are just a few of the secrets of the reduced-calorie cooking you'll find in this chapter.

# APPETIZERS

## ❖ CUCUMBER CANAPÉS

*2 medium cucumbers*
*1 jar (4 oz) red caviar*
*Parsley sprigs*

1. Wash cucumbers well. Slice crosswise into rounds ¼ inch thick, making about 50 rounds.
2. Arrange on tray; spoon ¼ teaspoon red caviar in center of each round; top each with parsley sprig. Makes 50; 15 calories each.

## ❖ HERB-MARINATED VEGETABLES

*Herb Marinade, below*
*Fresh green beans, ends trimmed*
*Green and red peppers, cut into strips ½ inch wide*
*Fresh cauliflower, separated into 1-inch flowerets*
*Fresh okra, ends trimmed*
*Eggplant, unpeeled and cut into 1-inch cubes*
*Fresh mushrooms, stems on, thickly sliced*
*Fresh broccoli, separated into 1-inch flowerets with stems*
*Frozen Brussels sprouts, thawed*
*Carrots, pared and cut into 5-inch sticks*
*Frozen artichoke hearts, thawed*
*Fresh zucchini, diagonally sliced ¼ inch thick*
*Radish roses, stems on*
*Fresh snow peas*
*Cherry tomatoes*

1. Make Herb Marinade.
2. Wash and prepare assortment of vegetables from list at left.
3. To blanch vegetables: Pour boiling water to cover green beans, red- and green-pepper strips, and cauliflowerets. Let stand 10 minutes; drain. Pour boiling water to cover okra. Let stand 3 minutes; drain. Pour boiling water to cover eggplant. Let stand 7 minutes; drain. The other vegetables need not be blanched.
4. Arrange vegetables in single layer in shallow baking dish or plastic container. Pour marinade over them, tossing gently to coat well. Refrigerate, covered, overnight, spooning marinade over vegetables 4 or 5 times.
5. To serve, drain vegetables; arrange on attractive platter.
About 3 calories each, depending on vegetable, with marinade: green beans, 3 calories each; peppers, 2 calories; cauliflowerets, 3 calories; okra, 3 calories; eggplant, 2 calories; mushroom slices, 1 calorie or less; broccoli, 3 calories; carrots, 3 calories; artichoke hearts, 2 calories; zucchini, 2 calories; radishes, 2 calories; snow peas, 2 calories; cherry tomatoes, 2 calories.

## HERB MARINADE:

1 bottle (8 oz) low-calorie Italian-style
    or herb-and-garlic salad dressing
2 teaspoons snipped fresh dill
¼ cup lemon juice
½ teaspoon salt

Combine all ingredients; mix well. Refrigerate.
Makes 1 cup, enough to marinate 2 lb assorted vegetables—about 16 calories per tablespoon of marinade.

# ✦ STUFFED MUSHROOMS

16 small mushrooms
1 tablespoon butter or margarine
3 tablespoons finely chopped green
    pepper
3 tablespoons finely chopped onion
1 teaspoon salt
⅛ teaspoon pepper

1. Preheat oven to 350F.
2. Wipe mushrooms with damp cloth. Remove stems, and chop stems finely; set aside.
3. Heat butter in large skillet. Sauté mushroom caps, on bottom side only, 2 to 3 minutes; remove. Arrange, rounded side down, in shallow baking pan.
4. In same skillet, sauté chopped stems, green pepper, and onion until tender—about 5 minutes.
5. Remove from heat. Stir in seasonings. Use to fill mushroom caps, mounding mixture high in center.
6. Bake 15 minutes. Serve warm from tray or chafing dish.
Makes 16 servings; about 3 calories each.

# ✦ MARINATED SCALLOPS AND SHRIMP

1 lb sea scallops, halved
1 lb fresh shrimp (about 22), shelled
    and deveined
¼ cup finely chopped onion
1 bay leaf
1 teaspoon salt
¼ teaspoon white pepper
1 lb small fresh mushrooms, thickly
    sliced right through stem

## LEMON DRESSING:

½ cup lemon juice
2 tablespoons olive or salad oil
2 teaspoons salt
½ teaspoon white pepper
½ to 1 teaspoon dried tarragon leaves

Chopped parsley

1. In medium saucepan, combine scallops, shrimp, onion, bay leaf, 1 teaspoon salt, and ¼ teaspoon pepper. Add water to cover.
2. Bring to boiling. Remove from heat, cover, and let stand 5 minutes.
3. With slotted spoon, remove scallops, shrimp, and onion to shallow baking dish. Add sliced mushrooms; toss with shellfish mixture.
4. Make Lemon Dressing: Combine well all dressing ingredients. Pour over shellfish; toss to mix well. Refrigerate, covered, overnight.
5. Just before serving, toss well. Turn out into serving dish; sprinkle with parsley. Serve with wooden picks.
Makes about 36 servings; 12 calories per shrimp, 15 calories per scallop half.

# ❖ SHRIMP-STUFFED TOMATOES

1 cup finely chopped deveined cooked
  shrimp
¼ cup finely chopped onion
½ teaspoon salt
¼ teaspoon pepper
2 tablespoons low-calorie mayonnaise
1 tablespoon lemon juice
1 lb cherry tomatoes
Parsley sprigs

1. In small bowl, combine shrimp, onion, salt, pepper, mayonnaise, and lemon juice; mix well. Refrigerate, covered, several hours to chill well.
2. Wash and dry tomatoes; refrigerate to chill well.
3. About 1 hour before serving, slice tomatoes across top to remove stem; scoop out some of seeds. Mound a little shrimp filling on top of each. Decorate each with parsley sprig. Arrange on tray. Refrigerate, covered, until serving time.
Makes 38; 17 calories each.

# ❖ SEVICHE

1 lb red snapper, halibut, or sole (see
  Note), boned and skinned
2 medium onions, thinly sliced
½ lb cherry tomatoes, halved
½ green pepper, cored, seeded, and
  thinly sliced
1½ teaspoons salt
¼ teaspoon black pepper
½ cup lime juice

1. Cut fish fillets crosswise into ½-inch strips. Turn out into large bowl. Add onions, tomatoes, green pepper, salt, and pepper; toss lightly to mix well.
2. Turn out into shallow baking dish. Sprinkle with lime juice. Refrigerate, tightly covered, overnight, tossing several times.
3. Drain; serve with wooden picks.
Makes 23 servings (2 pieces of fish); about 40 calories per serving.

*Note*: Number of calories depends on fish; halibut is higher in calories than sole or snapper.

# ❖ STEAK TARTARE TREATS

1 lb coarsely ground lean beef round
  or sirloin
½ cup finely chopped onion
½ clove garlic, crushed (optional)
1 teaspoon salt
1 teaspoon black pepper
½ cup finely chopped parsley

1. In medium bowl, lightly toss beef with onion, garlic, salt, and pepper just until combined.
2. Lightly form into 24 balls 1 inch in diameter. Do not handle any more than necessary.
3. Roll each ball in parsley, covering completely. Refrigerate.
Makes 24; 71 calories each.

# ⬖ YOGURT-DILL DIP

1 cup (8 oz) plain yogurt
½ cup low-calorie mayonnaise
2 tablespoons grated onion
2 tablespoons snipped fresh dill
¼ teaspoon salt

1. In small bowl, combine yogurt with rest of ingredients; mix well. Refrigerate, covered, several hours or overnight, or until thoroughly chilled.
2. Serve with assortment of raw vegetables for dipping.
Makes 1½ cups dip; 11 calories per teaspoon.

# SOUPS

# ⬖ VICHYSSOISE

1 lb leeks (see Note)
1 tablespoon salad oil
½ cup chopped onion
1 lb potatoes, peeled and cut into
    ½-inch cubes
½ teaspoon salt
Dash white pepper
Dash paprika
2 cans (13¾-oz size) clear chicken
    broth
2 cups skim milk
1 cup plain low-fat yogurt, chilled
2 tablespoons snipped chives

1. Trim leeks: Cut off roots and tips and most of dark green part, leaving some of light green. Wash leeks thoroughly, and drain. If leeks are very sandy, it may be necessary to remove outer leaves; wash and drain again.
2. Slice leeks crosswise ¼ inch thick. You should have 2 cups.
3. In hot oil in 5-quart Dutch oven or kettle, sauté leeks and onion over medium heat, stirring occasionally, until soft and golden—about 5 minutes. Do not brown.
4. Add potatoes, salt, pepper, paprika, and chicken broth to leek mixture. Bring to boiling; reduce heat, and simmer, covered, 45 minutes, or until potato is soft, almost mushy. Remove from heat.
5. Put potato-leek mixture into blender or food processor, 2 cups at a time, and blend until mixture is smooth; purée should measure 5 cups. Turn out into large bowl.
6. In small saucepan, heat milk until bubbles form around edge of pan. Remove from heat.
7. Add hot milk to potato-leek mixture; mix well with wire whisk. Refrigerate, covered, 6 hours or overnight.
8. Before serving, gradually add yogurt; mix well. Pour into 8 chilled soup cups; sprinkle with chives. Makes 8 servings; 129 calories per serving.

Note: If leeks are not available, substitute green onions.

# ❖ JULIENNE VEGETABLE SOUP WITH POACHED EGG

*1 small carrot*
*½ small zucchini*
*1 green onion*
*⅛ lb green beans*
*1 can (13¾ oz) chicken broth*
*½ cup water*
*Dash dried basil leaves*
*2 eggs*

1. Wash and pare carrot. Wash zucchini, green onion, and beans. Trim stem ends. Cut all into julienne strips.
2. Combine vegetables, chicken broth, water, and basil in medium saucepan. Bring to boiling; simmer 3 minutes.
3. Break one egg into saucer. With spoon, push vegetables to side of saucepan. Slip egg into broth. Repeat with second egg. Simmer, uncovered, 4 to 5 minutes, or until whites are firm but yolks are soft.
4. With slotted spoon, carefully lift eggs into center of 2 soup bowls. Divide broth between bowls.
Makes 2 servings; 132 calories per serving.

# ❖ TURKEY-VEGETABLE SOUP

**TURKEY BROTH:**

*2 frozen turkey legs (2½ lb), thawed*
*1 can (10¾ oz) condensed chicken*
  *broth, undiluted*
*2 medium carrots, pared and cut up*
*2 stalks celery with tops, cut up*
*1 large onion, quartered*
*2 teaspoons salt*
*1 teaspoon dried basil leaves*
*¼ teaspoon pepper*
*2 quarts cold water*

*2 large carrots, pared and thinly*
  *sliced*
*1 cup thinly sliced celery, on diagonal*
*½ cup chopped green onion*
*1 cup diced white turnip*
*2 small zucchini, sliced*
*2 tablespoons chopped parsley*

1. Make turkey broth: Rinse turkey legs, and place in 6-quart kettle. Add chicken broth, cut-up carrots and celery, onion quarters, salt, basil, pepper, and cold water.
2. Cover; bring to boiling. Reduce heat; simmer 1½ hours.
3. Remove turkey legs to platter. Strain broth; discard vegetables. Cool; refrigerate, covered, overnight.
4. Remove meat from turkey legs in large pieces; refrigerate (discard skin and bones).
5. Next day, remove and discard fat from broth.
6. Return broth to kettle; bring to boiling. Add sliced carrots and celery, green onion, and turnip; simmer, covered, 15 minutes. Add zucchini and turkey meat. Cook 5 minutes, or just until vegetables are tender.
7. Serve sprinkled with parsley.
Makes 6 servings; 248 calories per serving.

# SALADS

## ❖ FRESH-FRUIT AND SPROUT SALAD WITH FROZEN-YOGURT DRESSING

½ container (8-oz size) lemon yogurt
1 small ripe pineapple
8 strawberries
1 cup alfalfa sprouts

1. Spread yogurt in bottom of 8-inch baking pan. Place in freezer until just firm—20 to 30 minutes.
2. Wash pineapple; remove frond. Cut in half crosswise. Place halves, cut side up, on 2 salad plates. With grapefruit knife, remove pineapple to within ½ inch of shell on each half. Remove core, and cut pineapple into ¾-inch chunks.
3. Wash strawberries. Set aside 2 with stems. Remove stems from remaining strawberries. Cut in half.
4. In medium bowl, combine pineapple, strawberries, and alfalfa sprouts. Spoon into pineapple shells, dividing evenly. Refrigerate.
5. To serve: Stir frozen yogurt with fork. Swirl half on top of each salad. Top each with a strawberry.
Makes 2 servings: 126 calories per serving.

## ❖ COTTAGE CHEESE IN TOMATOES

3 medium tomatoes
1 container (1 lb) diet creamed cottage cheese
⅓ cup grated pared carrot
⅓ cup diced pared cucumber
⅓ cup finely chopped green onion
4 radishes, coarsely grated
¼ teaspoon salt
Crisp lettuce
Parsley or dill sprigs

1. Cut tomatoes in half crosswise. With spoon, scoop out pulp, and discard seeds. Drain; reserve pulp.
2. In medium bowl, combine cottage cheese, carrot, cucumber, onion, radishes, drained tomato pulp, and salt; mix lightly. Spoon cheese mixture into tomatoes.
3. Arrange on lettuce on salad plates. Garnish with fresh parsley or dill sprigs.
Makes 6 servings; 139 calories per serving.

# ❖ STEAMED VEGETABLES VINAIGRETTE

*3 zucchini (1½ lb)*
*1 lb carrots*
*½ lb snow peas*
*½ lb green beans*
*1 lb fresh asparagus*
*Water*
*1 teaspoon salt*
*1 cucumber, peeled and sliced*
*Cherry tomatoes*
*Watercress*
*Vinaigrette Dressing, below*

1. Prepare vegetables: Wash zucchini. Cut, unpeeled, into pieces 3½-inches long and ¼ inch wide. Using string, tie into 6 bundles.
2. Wash carrots. Pare, and cut into pieces 3½ inches long and ¼ inch wide. Using string, tie into 3 bundles.
3. Wash snow peas; remove stem ends.
4. Wash beans; cut off ends. Using string, tie into 3 bundles.
5. Break or cut off tough ends of asparagus. Wash under cold running water. With vegetable peeler, scrape skin and scales from stalks.
6. To steam vegetables: In 5-quart Dutch oven with 1 inch water and 1 teaspoon salt, place vegetable steamer tray or flexible steamer basket. Bring water to boil. Place each prepared vegetable on tray, and steam each separately. Steam zucchini, snow peas, and green beans 2 to 3 minutes, or just until tender but not soft. Steam carrots 3 to 4 minutes, and asparagus, 5 to 10 minutes, or until tender. Remove to bowl of ice water; drain. Refrigerate.
7. Remove from refrigerator about 30 minutes before assembling.
8. To serve: Remove strings. Arrange on large round platter, alternating vegetables around edge. In center, in ring, overlap cucumber slices; mound cherry tomatoes in center. Garnish edge with watercress. Pass Vinaigrette Dressing.
Makes 10 servings; 152 calories per serving.

## VINAIGRETTE DRESSING:

*½ cup lemon juice*
*½ cup water*
*⅓ cup salad oil*
*2 tablespoons grated onion*
*2 tablespoons chopped parsley*
*2 tablespoons chopped chives*
*½ teaspoon salt*
*½ teaspoon dried tarragon leaves*
*¼ teaspoon pepper*

1. Combine all ingredients in jar with tight-fitting lid. Shake vigorously.
2. Refrigerate dressing until ready to use. Shake again before using.
Makes 2 cups.

# ❖ CHICKEN-AND-ZUCCHINI SALAD

*1 cup cut-up cooked chicken breast*
*1 cup shredded zucchini (1 medium zucchini)*
*2 tablespoons low-calorie mayonnaise or salad dressing*
*Salt*
*Pepper*
*2 leaves Boston or iceberg lettuce*
*1 large tomato*

1. In medium bowl, combine chicken, zucchini, and mayonnaise. Add salt and pepper to taste.
2. Place 1 lettuce leaf on each plate. Arrange salad on lettuce, dividing evenly. Cut tomato into 6 wedges. Place 3 on each plate.
Makes 2 servings; 147 calories per serving.

# ❖ ROAST-BEEF SALAD WITH HORSERADISH DRESSING

¼ head green cabbage
¼ lb fresh spinach
2 medium carrots
¼ lb rare roast beef
½ cup plain low-fat yogurt
1 teaspoon grated fresh horseradish
½ teaspoon brown mustard

1. Wash and shred cabbage. Wash spinach, and drain well; cut into strips. Wash, pare, and coarsely shred carrots. Cut beef into julienne strips.
2. On 2 salad plates, arrange cabbage, spinach, and carrots around edge. Mound half the roast beef in center of each plate. Or toss vegetables together, and divide between 2 salad bowls. Top with roast beef.
3. In small bowl, stir together yogurt, horseradish, and mustard until well combined. Serve with salad.
Makes 2 servings; 220 calories per serving.

# ❖ CURRIED CHICKEN-AND-PINEAPPLE SALAD

3 whole chicken breasts, split (about 2½ lb)
2 carrots, pared and cut up
2 stalks celery, cut up
1 small onion, sliced
6 whole black peppercorns
2¼ teaspoons salt
1 bay leaf
3 cups boiling water
2 tablespoons lemon juice
½ cup thinly sliced celery, cut on diagonal
1½ cups diced unpared tart apple
½ cup coarsely chopped green pepper
2 teaspoons grated onion
¾ cup imitation mayonnaise
¼ cup unflavored low-fat yogurt
½ to 1 teaspoon curry powder
¼ teaspoon white pepper
1 medium-size fresh ripe pineapple (1½ lb)
Watercress sprigs

1. In 4-quart kettle, combine chicken breasts, carrots, cut-up celery, sliced onion, peppercorns, 1½ teaspoons salt, the bay leaf, and boiling water.
2. Bring to boiling; reduce heat, and simmer, covered, about 30 minutes, or until chicken is tender.
3. Remove chicken from broth. Cool; refrigerate until well chilled. (Refrigerate broth for use another time.)
4. Remove and discard skin from chicken; cut meat from bones in large pieces. Toss with lemon juice.
5. In large bowl, combine chicken, sliced celery, apple, green pepper, and grated onion.
6. In small bowl, combine mayonnaise, yogurt, curry powder, ¾ teaspoon salt, and the white pepper; mix well.
7. Add to chicken mixture; toss lightly to combine. Refrigerate until serving time—at least 1 hour.
8. Meanwhile, with sharp, long-bladed knife, cut pineapple in half, right through frond.
9. Remove pineapple, in one piece, from shells. Refrigerate shells. Cut and discard core from pineapple. Cut pineapple into chunks; refrigerate.
10. Before serving, add pineapple to chicken salad; toss lightly. Turn out into chilled pineapple shells. Garnish with watercress.
Makes 8 servings; 305 calories per serving.

# ❖ COTTAGE-CHEESE SALAD DRESSING

½ cup low-fat plain yogurt
½ cup low-fat cottage cheese
¼ cup chopped parsley
3 tablespoons vinegar
1 tablespoon prepared mustard
4 teaspoons sugar
2 cloves garlic, crushed
1½ teaspoons salt
Dash pepper

1. In small bowl, combine all ingredients, mixing well.
2. Refrigerate, covered, until ready to use. This is delicious on crisp salad greens.
Makes about 1 cup; 17 calories per tablespoon.

# PASTA

# ❖ PASTA AND BROCCOLI

1 bunch fresh broccoli (about 1½ lb)
½ cup boiling water
½ teaspoon salt
½ pkg (16 oz) spirelle or spaghetti twists
1 tablespoon salad oil
1 clove garlic, crushed
½ teaspoon dried basil leaves
½ cup canned condensed chicken broth, undiluted
¼ cup chopped parsley
2 tablespoons grated Parmesan cheese
Dash pepper
1 cup (8 oz) low-fat cottage cheese

1. Wash and trim leaves from broccoli. Remove flowerets. Split each stalk lengthwise into halves. Chop broccoli stalks. Arrange in single layer, along with flowerets, in bottom of large skillet.
2. Pour boiling water over broccoli; sprinkle with salt. Cook, covered, over medium heat 8 to 10 minutes, or until stalks are just tender and water is evaporated.
3. Meanwhile, cook pasta according to package directions; drain well.
4. In hot oil in medium skillet, sauté garlic and basil, stirring, about 1 minute.
5. Add chicken broth, parsley, Parmesan cheese, pepper, and broccoli. Stir over medium heat until blended—about 2 minutes. Remove from heat. Add cottage cheese.
6. Toss broccoli mixture with pasta. Turn out into heated serving dish.
Makes 8 servings; 168 calories per serving.

# ✦ ARTICHOKE STUFFED WITH PASTA SALAD

2 medium artichokes (1½ lb)
Boiling water
½ teaspoon salt
1 lemon
¼ cup small pasta shells
⅛ lb green beans
½ stalk celery
¼ red pepper
2 tablespoons low-calorie salad dressing

1. Wash artichokes. Trim off stems and 1-inch slice from tops. Remove discolored leaves; snip off spike ends.

2. Place artichokes in medium-size heavy saucepan. Pour in boiling water to measure 1 inch. Sprinkle with ¼ teaspoon salt. Slice ends from lemon; squeeze ends over artichokes, and add rinds to water. Wrap and refrigerate remaining lemon.

3. Cover saucepan, and cook artichokes gently 35 to 40 minutes, or until bases feel soft. Add more boiling water as necessary, to keep pan from boiling dry. Drain well. Cool to room temperature; then refrigerate until cold—several hours or overnight.

4. In small saucepan, combine 2 cups boiling water, ¼ teaspoon salt, and the shells. Bring to boiling; reduce heat, and cook 10 minutes.

5. Wash green beans; remove ends, and cut diagonally into ½-inch pieces. Add to simmering pasta, and cook until pasta is just tender—2 to 3 minutes longer.

6. Wash and thinly slice celery; wash and coarsely chop red pepper. Drain pasta and beans in colander. Set under cool running water until room temperature. Drain very well.

7. In small bowl, toss together pasta, beans, celery, red pepper, and salad dressing. Cover, and refrigerate several hours or overnight.

8. To serve: Spread open artichokes to reveal centers. Scoop out and discard prickly choke. Spoon salad into centers, dividing evenly. Place on salad plates. Slice reserved lemon; serve with artichokes.

Makes 2 servings; 115 calories per serving.

# ✺ LASAGNA FLORENTINE

1 pkg (10 oz) frozen chopped spinach,
    thawed, and well drained
1½ tablespoons salad oil
1 cup finely chopped onion
2 cloves garlic, crushed
¾ teaspoon dried basil leaves
½ teaspoon dried oregano leaves
½ bay leaf
1 can (2 lb 3 oz) Italian tomatoes
1 can (8 oz) tomato sauce
1½ teaspoons salt
⅛ teaspoon pepper
2 tablespoons chopped parsley
9 lasagna noodles (½ of 1-lb pkg)
2 cups (16 oz) low-fat cottage cheese
3 tablespoons grated Parmesan
    cheese

1. Drain spinach well on paper towels.
2. In oil in 5-quart Dutch oven or kettle, over medium heat, sauté onion, garlic, basil, oregano, and bay leaf, stirring, about 2 minutes.
3. Add tomatoes, tomato sauce, salt, pepper, and parsley; mix well, mashing tomatoes with fork.
4. Bring to boiling; reduce heat, and simmer, uncovered and stirring occasionally, 1 hour. Remove from heat. Makes 4 cups.
5. Preheat oven to 375F. Cook lasagna noodles according to package directions; drain very well.
6. Spoon 1 cup sauce into bottom of shallow 2-quart baking dish. Layer with 3 lasagna noodles, overlapping to cover, half of chopped spinach, 1 cup cottage cheese, and 1 cup tomato sauce.
7. Repeat layering. Top with remaining noodles; spread with remaining tomato sauce. Sprinkle with Parmesan. Cover with foil, tucking around edge.
8. Bake 25 minutes. Remove foil; bake, uncovered, 25 minutes, or until bubbly. Cool 10 minutes before serving.
Makes 8 servings; 206 calories per serving.

# MEATS

# ✺ VEAL STEW LAFAYETTE

1 tablespoon butter or margarine
2 lb boneless veal shoulder, cut into
    1-inch cubes
2 cups tomato juice
1 cup dry white wine
¾ teaspoon salt
½ teaspoon dried marjoram leaves
1½ cups pared carrot, cut into 1-inch
    pieces
1 cup thinly sliced celery
1 medium-size yellow summer
    squash, sliced ¼ inch thick (about
    2 cups)
2 medium zucchini, sliced ¼ inch
    thick (about 2 cups)
1 tablespoon flour
2 tablespoons water

1. In hot butter or margarine in 4-quart Dutch oven, brown veal well on all sides.
2. Gradually stir in tomato juice, wine, salt, and marjoram. Bring to boiling; reduce heat, and simmer, covered, ½ hour.
3. Add carrot and celery to meat mixture, and simmer, covered, ½ hour.
4. Add squash and zucchini, pressing them into liquid; cook 10 minutes, or until all vegetables are tender.
5. Remove meat and vegetables to heated serving dish; keep warm.
6. Mix flour with water until smooth. Stir into liquid in Dutch oven; bring to boiling, stirring, and boil 1 minute, or until slightly thickened. Spoon over meat and vegetables.
Makes 6 servings; 354 calories per serving.

# ✣ VEAL SCALLOPINI WITH PEPPERS

4 thin veal scallops (½ lb)
1 medium onion
1 small red pepper
1 small green pepper
½ teaspoon butter or salad oil
¼ teaspoon dried basil leaves
¼ teaspoon salt
Dash ground black pepper
1 tablespoon grated Parmesan cheese

1. Rinse veal; drain well. Peel and slice onion. Wash red and green peppers; remove seeds, and slice.
2. Heat butter in large skillet. Sauté veal until lightly browned on one side—about 3 minutes. Turn; add onion, red and green peppers, basil, salt, and black pepper. Sauté, stirring vegetables, until veal is browned on other side. Remove veal; keep warm.
3. Cover skillet; lower heat, and cook, stirring occasionally, until vegetables are just tender—about 3 minutes longer.
4. Fold veal into vegetables; turn out onto serving dish. Sprinkle with Parmesan.
Makes 2 servings; 214 calories per serving.

# ✣ LAMB-AND-VEGETABLE KEBABS WITH WHEAT PILAF

½ lb lean stewing lamb or leg-of-lamb cubes
1 large mushroom
¼ cup bottled low-calorie Italian-style salad dressing
½ small zucchini
1½ cups water
⅓ cup bulgur wheat
1 clove garlic, split
⅛ teaspoon salt
4 cherry tomatoes
Chopped parsley

1. Several hours or day before: Rinse lamb cubes; drain well. Trim off any visible fat. Wash mushroom. Cut into quarters. In small bowl, toss together lamb, mushroom, and dressing. Cover tightly, and refrigerate.
2. To prepare: Cut zucchini into 3 (1-inch) pieces. Cut each piece in half. Place in small saucepan; cover with water. Bring to boiling, and simmer 2 minutes. Drain well.
3. In medium saucepan, bring 1½ cups water to boiling. Stir in wheat. Add garlic and salt. Cook gently 15 minutes.
4. Preheat broiler. Arrange meat on 2 skewers, dividing equally. Arrange zucchini, mushroom, and cherry tomatoes on 2 skewers. Place skewers of lamb on broiling pan; brush with remaining dressing.
5. Broil, 3 to 4 inches from heat, 5 minutes. Turn lamb; place skewers of vegetables on broiling pan. Brush with more dressing, and broil 5 to 8 minutes longer, to desired doneness.
6. Drain wheat thoroughly. Remove and discard garlic. Spoon wheat onto small serving platter. Top with skewers; pour drippings from broiling pan over all, and sprinkle with parsley.
Makes 2 servings; 289 calories per serving.

# ✦ STIR-FRIED PORK AND PINEAPPLE

1 lb lean boneless pork
1 tablespoon salad oil
1 cup thinly sliced onion
2 medium zucchini, (1 lb), sliced ⅛ inch thick on diagonal
1 red pepper, washed, halved, ribs removed, and sliced ¼ inch thick
½ cup orange juice
3 tablespoons soy sauce
1 tablespoon sherry
½ teaspoon salt
⅛ teaspoon black pepper
1 tablespoon cornstarch
2 tablespoons water
2 cups fresh pineapple chunks (½ pineapple) or 2 cups pineapple chunks canned in its own juice, drained

1. Wipe pork with damp paper towels. Place in freezer 15 minutes for easier slicing. Trim off excess fat. Slice pork into ¼ inch thick and ½ inch wide strips.
2. In hot wok or heavy skillet, stir-fry pork until well browned—about 3 to 5 minutes. Remove pork from wok.
3. Add oil to wok, and stir-fry onion, zucchini, and red pepper about 2 minutes.
4. Return pork to wok. Add orange juice, soy sauce, sherry, salt, and black pepper. Reduce heat, and simmer, covered, 2 minutes.
5. Add cornstarch dissolved in 2 tablespoons water. Stir-fry until thickened and translucent.
6. Add pineapple.
Makes 6 servings; 299 calories per serving.

# ✦ BROILED CALF'S LIVER AND VEGETABLE PLATTER

1 large ripe tomato
Instant mashed potato for 2 servings
Skim milk
Dried chervil leaves
½ lb calf's liver (2 slices)
Salt
Dash ground black pepper
4 medium mushrooms
1 medium onion
Chopped parsley

1. Wash tomato; slice in half. Scoop out centers to make cups. Save centers.
2. Prepare instant mashed potato according to package directions, using skim milk and omitting butter. Stir in ¼ teaspoon chervil. Spoon into tomato cups. Place in baking pan.
3. Preheat broiler. Rinse and drain calf's liver. Place on rack of broiling pan. Set potato-filled tomatoes and liver under broiler 6 inches from heat. Broil 5 minutes. Turn liver. Sprinkle with dash salt and pepper. Broil 3 to 5 minutes longer, or until liver is of desired doneness and potato is browned.
4. Meanwhile, wash and slice mushrooms and onion. Combine with scooped-out tomato, dash salt, and dash chervil in small heavy skillet. Cover, and simmer until vegetables are just cooked.
5. Arrange tomato cups and liver on small platter. Spoon mushrooms, onion, and sauce over liver. Sprinkle with parsley.
Makes 2 servings; 305 calories per serving.

# POULTRY

## ✦ CHICKEN BREASTS NOUVELLE CUISINE

3 (12-oz size) whole chicken breasts,
    split
3 medium tomatoes (1½ lb)
Boiling water
2 medium carrots (½ lb), pared and
    thinly sliced
2 medium onions (½ lb), sliced
1 bay leaf
1 teaspoon salt
½ teaspoon dried rosemary leaves
⅛ teaspoon pepper
2 cans (10¾-oz size) condensed
    chicken broth, undiluted
2 medium cucumbers
Chopped parsley

1. Wash chicken breasts; dry with paper towels. Remove skin and excess fat.
2. Dip each tomato into boiling water for 1 minute. Lift out with slotted utensil; peel off skin. Cut 1 tomato in half; remove seeds, and chop pulp.
3. In heavy 6-quart Dutch oven, combine carrots, onions, bay leaf, and chopped tomato. Cook over medium heat, stirring occasionally, 5 minutes.
4. In small bowl, combine salt, rosemary, and pepper. Use this to sprinkle over chicken breasts. Place chicken breasts on top of sautéed vegetables. Pour 1 can chicken broth over vegetables. Bring to boiling; then cover tightly, and simmer over low heat 30 to 40 minutes, or until chicken breasts are tender.
5. Meanwhile, pare cucumbers. Halve lengthwise, and remove and discard seeds. Cut each cucumber half into 2 strips. In medium saucepan, bring to boiling remaining can of chicken broth. Add cucumber; simmer, uncovered, 10 to 15 minutes, or until tender.
6. Drain cucumber, reserving ½ cup broth. Remove chicken to warm serving platter. Discard bay leaf.
7. Make sauce: Place pan drippings, vegetables, and reserved chicken broth into blender or food processor; blend until smooth.
8. To serve: Cut remaining tomatoes into eighths. Cut cucumber strips in half crosswise. Arrange chicken breasts and cucumber on platter. Garnish edge of platter with tomato wedges. Pour 2 tablespoons sauce over each chicken breast. Sprinkle with chopped parsley. Pass remaining sauce.
Makes 6 servings; 275 calories per serving.

## ✦ CHICKEN BREASTS WITH JULIENNE VEGETABLES

1 medium carrot
½ medium zucchini
¼ lb green beans
¼ teaspoon butter
1 whole chicken breast (8 oz),
    skinned, boned, and split
⅛ teaspoon dried thyme leaves
1 cup water
Lemon slices

1. Wash and pare carrot. Wash zucchini and green beans. Cut each into long julienne strips. Keep separate.
2. Preheat oven to 300F. Melt butter in heavy skillet. Sauté chicken breast, uncovered, 5 minutes on one side. Turn; sprinkle with thyme, and sauté on other side until just done—5 to 7 minutes. Remove to serving platter, and set in oven.
3. Add vegetables to skillet (keep separate). Add 1 cup water. Bring to boiling; reduce heat, and sim-

mer, covered, until just tender—about 3 minutes. Remove with wide spatula to serving platter. Cook liquid in pan rapidly, to reduce to ¼ cup. Pour over chicken. Serve with lemon slices.

Makes 2 servings; 228 calories per serving.

# ⚜ LEMON CHICKEN WITH BROCCOLI

2½-lb broiler-fryer, quartered
1 tablespoon grated lemon peel
¼ cup lemon juice
2 cloves garlic, crushed
1 teaspoon dried thyme leaves
1 teaspoon salt
½ teaspoon pepper
1 pkg (10 oz) frozen broccoli spears
4 lemon wedges

1. Preheat oven to 350F. Wash chicken under cold water; dry well on paper towels.
2. Arrange chicken pieces, skin side up, in single layer in shallow roasting pan.
3. In small bowl, combine lemon peel, lemon juice, garlic, thyme, salt, and pepper.
4. Spoon over chicken. Bake, uncovered and basting every 20 minutes, 60 minutes, or just until chicken is brown and tender.
5. Meanwhile, cook broccoli as package directs; drain well.
6. Arrange chicken and broccoli on warm serving plate. Garnish with lemon wedges.

Makes 4 servings; 384 calories per serving.

# ⚜ LOW-CAL COQ AU VIN

2 (2- to 2½-lb size) broiler-fryers, cut into eighths
2 slices bacon, cut into ½-inch pieces
1 tablespoon diet margarine
12 small white onions
4 shallots, chopped
½ lb small whole fresh mushrooms
1 clove garlic, crushed
1 teaspoon dried thyme leaves
1 bay leaf
1 teaspoon salt
¼ teaspoon pepper
¼ teaspoon ground nutmeg
½ cup dry red wine
1½ cups dry white wine
2 tablespoons flour
¼ cup cold water
2 tablespoons chopped parsley

1. Wash chicken under cold running water; drain. Dry on paper towels. Remove all skin. In 6-quart Dutch oven, over medium heat, sauté bacon until crisp; lift out with slotted spoon, and drain on paper towels.
2. To bacon fat, add margarine; sauté onions over medium heat 5 minutes, stirring occasionally. Lift out.
3. Over medium heat, brown chicken, one third at a time, turning with tongs until golden all over—about ½ hour in all. Remove chicken as it browns. Drain fat.
4. Add shallots, mushrooms, garlic, thyme, bay leaf, salt, pepper, and nutmeg. Over low heat, simmer, covered, 5 minutes. Stir in red and white wines.
5. Return chicken to Dutch oven. Bring to boiling; reduce heat, and simmer, covered, ½ hour. Add onions; cook 25 minutes longer, or until chicken and onions are tender.
6. Mix flour and water until smooth; stir into liquid in Dutch oven. Bring to boiling, stirring, until thickened. Remove bay leaf.
7. Turn out into serving dish. Sprinkle with chopped parsley and reserved bacon.

Makes 8 servings; 320 calories per serving.

# ❖ TURKEY CUTLETS IN WHITE WINE

½ lb turkey cutlets (2 pieces)
½ teaspoon butter
4 medium mushrooms
1 large shallot
¼ teaspoon dried tarragon leaves
¼ teaspoon salt
¼ cup white wine
¼ cup water

1. Rinse turkey cutlets; drain well. Heat butter in medium skillet. Sauté cutlets over medium heat until golden on one side—5 minutes.
2. Wash and slice mushrooms. Peel and chop shallot. Turn cutlets; add mushrooms and shallot to pan. Sprinkle with tarragon and salt. Cook, stirring vegetables, until cutlets are just cooked through. Remove cutlets to platter. Keep warm.
3. Add wine and water to skillet. Simmer, stirring, 1 minute. Pour over cutlets.
Makes 2 servings; 216 calories per serving.

# SEAFOOD

# ❖ FILLETS OF SOLE DUGLÈRE

2 tablespoons diet margarine
2 shallots, chopped
1 medium onion, sliced
6 fillets of sole or flounder (about 2½ lb), see Note
2 tablespoons lemon juice
½ lb medium mushrooms, washed and sliced ¼ inch thick
1 teaspoon salt
⅛ teaspoon pepper
1 cup dry white wine
4 medium-size ripe tomatoes (1½ lb)
Dash ground red pepper
1 tablespoon flour
1 tablespoon chopped parsley

1. Melt 1 tablespoon margarine in large skillet. Add shallots and onion; sauté, stirring, 2 minutes.
2. Wash fillets; dry on paper towels. Brush with lemon juice. Fold crosswise. Arrange fish over shallot mixture, and top with mushrooms. Sprinkle with salt and pepper. Add wine.
3. Bring to boiling; reduce heat, and simmer, covered, 8 to 10 minutes, or just until fish flakes easily when tested with fork.
4. Meanwhile, dip each tomato into boiling water for 1 minute. Lift out and peel off skin. Cut into quarters; scrape out seeds and center pulp, and purée in food processor or blender. You should have ¾ cup purée. Set aside. Cut outer part of tomato into cubes.
5. With broad spatula, remove fish and mushrooms to warm serving dish. Keep warm.
6. Pour off liquid from fish and mushrooms into skillet. Bring to boiling; reduce liquid to 1 cup. Add tomato purée and red pepper. Cream together remaining 1 tablespoon margarine and the flour, and add to skillet. Cook over medium heat, stirring constantly, until mixture thickens and boils. Add cubed tomato.
7. Spoon sauce over fish. Sprinkle with chopped parsley.
Makes 6 servings; 228 calories per serving.

Note: If using frozen fish, let thaw completely; drain on paper towels.

# ✦ FLOUNDER EN PAPILLOTE

4 flounder fillets (1½ lb)
8 fresh shrimp
4 tomato slices, ¼ inch thick
Dried thyme leaves
1 clove garlic, slivered
Salt
Pepper
2 teaspoons salad or olive oil
2 tablespoons lemon juice
Lemon wedges

1. Preheat oven to 375F. Tear off four 12-inch squares of foil.
2. Wash flounder fillets in cold water; drain on paper towels.
3. Fold fillets in half. Place diagonally on half of each square of foil, 1½ inches from edges. Arrange 2 shrimp and 1 slice tomato on each fillet.
4. Sprinkle each with dash of thyme, sliver of garlic, dash salt, and pepper, ½ teaspoon salad oil, and 1½ teaspoons lemon juice.
5. Fold foil on diagonal; then fold edges over twice to seal securely.
6. Place foil packages on large cookie sheet or jelly-roll pan. Bake 25 to 30 minutes, or until fish is cooked through.
7. To serve: Slash cross in each package; fold back corners. Garnish with lemon wedges.
Makes 4 servings; 260 calories per serving.

# ✦ CHINESE-STYLE SCALLOPS WITH VEGETABLES

2 medium mushrooms
2 green onions
½ red pepper
2 leaves Chinese cabbage
¼ lb broccoli
½ cup fresh or canned bean sprouts
1 teaspoon salad oil
1 clove garlic, pressed
½ lb scallops
2 teaspoons soy sauce
1 teaspoon cornstarch
⅓ cup water

1. Wash and slice mushrooms, green onions, red pepper, and Chinese cabbage. Wash broccoli, and break top into flowerets. Pare and slice stems. Rinse and drain bean sprouts.
2. Heat oil in large skillet or wok. Add garlic, mushrooms, green onions, pepper, and broccoli. Stir-fry over medium heat 3 minutes.
3. Rinse and drain scallops. If using sea scallops, cut in half. Add scallops, Chinese cabbage, and bean sprouts. Stir-fry until scallops are cooked through—3 to 5 minutes.
4. In small cup, stir together soy sauce, cornstarch, and water. Add to vegetables and scallops. Cook, stirring, until thickened.
Makes 2 servings; 162 calories per serving.

# LIGHT CIOPPINO

1 can (10¼ oz) whole clams
2 cans (1-lb size) plum tomatoes, undrained
1 cup chopped onion
1 cup chopped green pepper
3 cloves garlic, crushed
1 can (8 oz) tomato sauce
¼ cup chopped parsley
2 teaspoons salt
½ teaspoon dried oregano leaves
¼ teaspoon dried basil leaves
¼ teaspoon black pepper
1 lb fresh cod fillets
1 lb fresh red snapper fillets

1. Drain clams, reserving liquid; set clams aside.
2. In 6-quart kettle or Dutch oven, combine tomatoes, onion, green pepper, garlic, tomato sauce, parsley, salt, oregano, basil, black pepper, and reserved clam liquid. Mix well.
3. Bring mixture to boiling; reduce heat, and simmer, covered, for 30 minutes.
4. Meanwhile, rinse cod and red snapper fillets quickly under cold water; pat dry with paper towels. Cut into large pieces.
5. Add fish and reserved clams to vegetable mixture. Return just to boiling; reduce heat, and simmer, covered, 30 minutes.
Makes 8 servings; 166 calories per serving.

# DESSERTS

## PEAR HALVES IN ROSÉ WINE

6 canned diet pear halves
1 teaspoon lemon juice
⅔ cup rosé wine or Chablis
2 sprigs mint (optional)

1. Several hours before serving, drain pears. Place in small bowl. Drizzle with lemon juice; pour wine over pears. Cover, and refrigerate.
2. Just before serving, place pear halves in 2 dessert dishes or wineglasses. Pour wine over pears, dividing evenly. Top each with mint sprig, if desired.
Makes 2 servings; 112 calories per serving.

## PEARS POACHED IN APPLE JUICE

2 tablespoons lemon juice
½ cup cold water
6 ripe pears (about 3 lb)
4 lemon twists (1½ inches long)
4 whole cloves
2 cups apple juice

1. In 4-quart Dutch oven or kettle, combine lemon juice and cold water.
2. Wash and peel pears; leave stems on. Add to lemon juice and water, and stir to coat well. Set upright in Dutch oven.
3. Add lemon twists, cloves, and apple juice.
4. Bring to boiling, uncovered; reduce heat, and simmer, covered, just until pears are tender—25 to 30 minutes, turning pears occasionally. Remove from heat.
5. With slotted utensil, carefully transfer pears to serving bowl. Discard cloves. Pour juice mixture over pears.
6. Refrigerate until well chilled—several hours, turning pears occasionally.
7. Serve pears with apple-juice mixture poured over top.
Makes 6 servings; 160 calories per serving.

# ❖ PEACHES WITH YOGURT

1 can (1 lb) diet peaches, drained
½ container (8-oz size) plain low-fat
  yogurt
Dash almond extract

1. Arrange peaches in small glass serving bowl.
2. Combine yogurt and almond extract; blend well with rubber spatula. Pour over peaches.
3. Refrigerate at least 2 hours, or until well chilled. Makes 4 servings; 50 calories per serving.

# ❖ STRAWBERRIES WITH CUSTARD SAUCE

1 pint strawberries

**CUSTARD SAUCE:**

2 egg yolks
2 cups skim milk
½ teaspoon vanilla extract
1 egg white
2 tablespoons sugar

5 chocolate curls

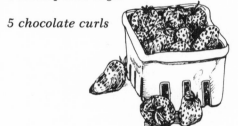

1. Wash strawberries under cold running water. Then hull them, and refrigerate.
2. Make Custard Sauce: In small saucepan, combine egg yolks and milk; mix with wire whisk or wooden spoon until well blended.
3. Cook over low heat, stirring, until thickened—about 10 minutes. Remove from heat. Add vanilla extract. Cool 10 minutes.
4. In small bowl of electric mixer, beat, at medium speed, egg white until foamy. Gradually add sugar, beating until moist stiff peaks form when beater is slowly raised.
5. With wire whisk or rubber spatula, fold beaten egg white into custard sauce, mixing until well blended. Turn out into bowl; refrigerate 2 hours, or until well chilled.
6. To serve: Spoon strawberries into 5 dessert glasses. Top each with ⅓ cup sauce and 1 chocolate curl. Makes 5 servings; 134 calories per serving.

# ❖ LOW-CALORIE COTTAGE-CHEESE CAKE

2 env unflavored gelatine
⅓ cup sugar
Dash salt
2 eggs, separated
2 cups skim milk
1 container (16 oz) low-fat cottage
  cheese
¼ cup lemon juice
¼ cup orange juice
2 teaspoons grated lemon peel
1 tablespoon grated orange peel
1 teaspoon vanilla extract
2 kiwis, peeled and thinly sliced
4 strawberries, washed

1. In small heavy saucepan, combine gelatine, sugar, and salt. In small bowl, with wire whisk, beat egg yolks with milk until light and frothy. Gradually stir into gelatine mixture; mix well.
2. Cook over medium heat, stirring, until gelatine is dissolved and custard is thickened slightly (should form coating on metal spoon).
3. Remove from heat. Let cool 30 minutes.
4. In large bowl, with electric mixer at medium speed, beat cottage cheese, lemon juice, orange juice, lemon and orange peels, and vanilla until well blended—3 minutes.
5. Slowly add cooled custard, beating at low speed just to blend. Place bowl in another bowl of ice water to chill, stirring occasionally, until mixture mounds when lifted with spoon—about 15 minutes.
6. In small bowl of electric mixer, beat egg whites

until foamy; continue beating until stiff peaks form when beater is slowly raised.

7. Add beaten egg whites to cheese mixture. With wire whisk or rubber spatula, gently fold in whites just until combined.

8. Pour into 8-inch springform pan. Refrigerate until firm—3 hours.

9. Before serving, gently remove side of springform pan. Decorate edge of cake with overlapping slices of kiwi. Arrange 1 whole strawberry and 6 halves in center.

Makes 12 servings; 82 calories per serving.

# ❖ LOW-CALORIE SPONGE CAKE

1 cup reconstituted nonfat dry milk
2 cups sifted all-purpose flour
3 teaspoons baking powder
Dash salt
6 eggs
1½ cups sugar
4 teaspoons grated lemon peel

1. In small saucepan, heat milk until bubbles form around edge of pan. Remove from heat; set aside.

2. Preheat oven to 350F. Sift flour with baking powder and salt, and set aside.

3. In large bowl of electric mixer, at high speed, beat eggs until thick and lemon-colored. Gradually add sugar, beating until mixture is smooth and well blended—about 10 minutes.

4. At low speed, blend in flour mixture just until smooth. Add warm milk and lemon peel, beating just until combined.

5. Immediately pour batter into ungreased 10-inch angel-food-cake pan. Bake 35 to 40 minutes, or until cake tester inserted in center comes out clean. Invert pan, placing center opening over neck of bottle; let cool completely. Serve plain.

Makes 20 servings; 107 calories per serving.

*Note*: If desired, make half the recipe. Turn out batter into ungreased 9-inch angel-food pan. Bake 30 minutes, or until cake tester inserted in center comes out clean. Invert pan over neck of bottle; let cool completely. Serve plain.

Makes 10 servings.

# ❖ COFFEE GRANITE

1½ tablespoons instant coffee
½ cup boiling water
2 tablespoons granulated sugar
1 cup cold water
Lemon peel, cut into julienne strips

1. Combine instant coffee and boiling water in measuring cup. Stir in sugar until completely dissolved. Stir in cold water.

2. Turn out mixture into 9-by-9-by-2-inch pan. Freeze until edges are firm and center is still a little soft—about 3 hours.

3. Spoon granite into chilled bowl. Beat quickly with electric beater until fluffy and separated into crystals. Turn out into plastic freezer container with tight-fitting lid, and freeze several hours.

4. To serve: Run fork through granite to loosen crystals, and spoon into serving dishes. Top with lemon peel.

Makes 4 servings; 27 calories per serving.

# RICE, GRAINS, DRIED BEANS, and PEAS

✦ Rice, dried peas, beans, lentils, and grain foods, such as cornmeal, farina, barley, and bulgur, have served mankind as staples since prehistoric times. Today, as we've learned more about the dietary benefits of whole grains and the desirability of "complex carbohydrates" in our diets, there has been a rush to find new ways of using these good foods—as extenders for meat, vegetables, cheese, or fish, main dishes, soups, and salads.

All grains and seeds are a nutritional bargain—low in cholesterol, high in fiber content, good providers of the B vitamins, iron, and phosphorus, and, at roughly 200 calories a cup, a nutrient-dense food. You'll find delicious ways to prepare and serve them in this chapter.

Rice is available in white or brown form and in long-, medium-, or short-grain form, polished or unpolished. White is most often sold in enriched form, with the vitamins and minerals lost in the processing replaced.

Long-grain white rice is most commonly used as a separate course because it is fluffier, drier, and holds its shape better. Short-grain white rice is more glutinous and is best suited for puddings, rice rings, and croquettes. Regular milled white rice will swell to three times its original size in cooking, and parboiled (converted) white rice, to four times its original size. Packaged, precooked white rice can also be purchased. It is processed to cook quickly, and it doubles in size.

Brown rice is highest in natural vitamins and minerals. It has a nutty flavor; only the hull and some of the bran have been removed from the natural rice. It requires more liquid and longer cooking than white rice. Substitute it for white rice by cooked measure only.

Wild rice is not actually rice at all but the seed of a wild grass that grows in the Great Lakes region. It is very expensive but has an unusually good flavor and a chewy texture. Reserve it for special occasions.

Dry beans and their close cousins, peas and lentils, are such nutritional nuggets that they were once considered worth their weight in gold. The jewelers' carat owes its origin to a pealike bean on the east coast of Africa. A serving of beans combined with a serving of rice may be used as a main dish; served together, they provide a complete protein. Overnight soaking of beans and peas rehydrates them close to their fresh state; it may be replaced by the short-soak method of boiling the dried peas or beans in water for 2 minutes than allowing them to soak for 1 hour (½ hour for split peas) before cooking. Lentils need no presoaking before cooking.

Many of the beans, for example, red and white kidney beans and chick-peas, come in cans. Rinsed and drained, they may be used like cooked beans in recipes.

Grain products, such as cornmeal, farina, grits, barley, cracked wheat (bulgur), and couscous, all provide the nutritional contribution of cereals. They are excellent quick-cooking budget foods, and a great way to add starch-food variety to menus.

# GRAINS AND RICE

## ✦ FLUFFY WHITE RICE

1½ cups raw long-grain white rice
1½ teaspoons salt
1½ tablespoons butter or margarine
3 cups cold water

1. In medium-size heavy saucepan with tight-fitting cover, combine rice, salt, butter, and cold water.
2. Bring to boiling, uncovered.
3. Reduce heat; simmer, covered, 15 to 20 minutes, or until rice is tender and water is absorbed.
4. Fluff up with fork.
Makes 4½ cups.

# ✦ BOILED RICE, ORIENTAL-STYLE

2 quarts cold water
1 tablespoon salt
1 cup raw long-grain white rice
2 tablespoons butter or margarine

1. In large saucepan over high heat, bring to boiling water and salt.
2. Slowly add rice; boil, uncovered, about 20 minutes, or until rice is tender.
3. Drain well. Fluff up with fork; add butter.
Makes 4 cups.

# ✦ WILD RICE

¾ cup wild rice
3 cups cold water
¾ teaspoon salt
1 tablespoon butter or margarine

1. Wash rice several times; drain.
2. In medium-size heavy saucepan with tight-fitting cover, bring water and salt to boiling.
3. Add rice very slowly. Boil, covered, stirring occasionally, 45 minutes, until rice is tender and water is absorbed. Add butter.
Makes about 2 cups.

*Wild and White Rice*: Combine 2 cups cooked wild rice and 4 cups cooked white rice; toss lightly with fork.

# ✦ RISOTTO WITH ARTICHOKE HEARTS AND TOMATOES

7 tablespoons butter or margarine
1 medium onion, chopped
2 cups raw long-grain white rice
3 cans (10½-oz size) condensed beef broth, undiluted
Water
1 teaspoon salt
¼ teaspoon pepper
1 pkg (9 oz) frozen artichoke hearts
3 medium tomatoes
½ cup grated Parmesan cheese
½ cup sliced pimiento-stuffed olives

1. Preheat oven to 350F. In 3 tablespoons hot butter in 4½-quart Dutch oven, sauté onion, stirring, about 5 minutes, or until golden and tender. Stir in rice; cook, stirring, several minutes, or until rice is golden.
2. Pour broth into 1-quart measure; add water to make 4 cups. Stir broth into rice mixture; bring to boiling. Cover Dutch oven; bake rice 20 minutes, or until tender and liquid is absorbed. Add salt and pepper.
3. Meanwhile, prepare vegetables: In medium skillet, cook artichokes as package label directs; drain. In same skillet, sauté artichokes in 2 tablespoons hot butter until golden. Meanwhile, peel tomatoes. Remove seeds; chop pulp fine. In 2 tablespoons butter in medium skillet, cook tomatoes 5 minutes.
4. With fork, fluff up rice and gently stir in tomatoes, artichokes, and half of grated cheese. Pile into warm serving dish. Sprinkle with remaining cheese and the olives.
Makes 8 servings.

# ✦ OVEN-STEAMED RICE

1½ cups raw converted white rice
1½ teaspoons salt
Dash pepper
2 tablespoons butter or margarine
3½ cups boiling water

1. Preheat oven to 350F.
2. In ungreased 2-quart casserole with tight-fitting lid, mix rice, salt, and pepper. Dot with butter.
3. Pour boiling water over rice; stir, with fork, to melt butter.
4. Bake, covered, 45 minutes (do not lift lid). To serve, fluff up rice lightly, with a fork, to mix well. Makes 6 servings.

*White Rice with Onions*: Add ¼ cup sliced green onions to cooked rice just before serving.

# ✦ CALIFORNIA CHEESE-AND-RICE CASSEROLE

¼ cup butter or margarine
1 cup chopped onion
4 cups freshly cooked white rice
2 cups sour cream
1 cup cream-style cottage cheese
1 large bay leaf, crumbled
½ teaspoon salt
⅛ teaspoon pepper
3 cans (4-oz size) green chilies, drained and halved lengthwise, leaving seeds
2 cups grated sharp natural Cheddar cheese
Chopped parsley

1. Preheat oven to 375F. Lightly grease 12-by-8-by-2-inch baking dish.
2. In hot butter in large skillet, sauté onion until golden—about 5 minutes.
3. Remove from heat; stir in hot rice, sour cream, cottage cheese, bay leaf, salt, and pepper; toss lightly to mix well.
4. Layer half of rice mixture in bottom of baking dish, then half of chiles; sprinkle with half of cheese. Repeat.
5. Bake, uncovered, 25 minutes, or until bubbly and hot. Sprinkle with chopped parsley. Makes 8 servings.

# ✦ OKRA RICE PILAU

2 cups raw converted long-grain white rice
6 slices bacon, chopped
2 medium onions, chopped
2 cans (1-lb size) stewed tomatoes
2 cups thinly sliced okra or 2 pkg (10-oz size) frozen okra
2 teaspoons salt
¼ teaspoon pepper

1. Cook rice as package label directs, or use double the recipe for Boiled Rice, Oriental-Style, page 424.
2. Meanwhile, in large skillet, cook chopped bacon; lift out with slotted spoon, and set aside. In hot bacon fat, sauté onion, stirring until tender—about 5 minutes.
3. Add stewed tomatoes and okra; cook, stirring, until most of the liquid is evaporated. Add salt and pepper.
4. Drain rice, if necessary, and combine with tomato mixture in top of double boiler. Cook, covered, over boiling water about 20 minutes. Add bacon just before serving. Makes 10 servings.

## SAFFRON RICE

*⅛ teaspoon saffron, crumbled*
*2 tablespoons olive or salad oil*
*2 tablespoons butter or margarine*
*1½ cups raw long-grain white rice*
*1½ teaspoons salt*
*3 cups water*

1. Mix saffron with 1 tablespoon hot water; set aside.
2. In medium saucepan, heat oil and butter. Add rice and salt; cook, stirring occasionally, 5 minutes.
3. Add saffron mixture and remaining water; bring to boiling. Reduce heat; simmer, covered, 15 to 20 minutes, or until liquid is absorbed.

Makes 8 servings.

## MEXICAN RICE

*2 tablespoons salad oil*
*1 cup chopped onion*
*½ cup cubed green pepper*
*½ lb ground beef*
*1 tablespoon paprika*
*1 teaspoon salt*
*1 teaspoon dried basil leaves*
*⅛ teaspoon pepper*
*1 can (1 lb. 14 oz) tomatoes, undrained*
*3 cups fluffy cooked rice*
*1 can (1 lb) red kidney beans, drained*
*¼ lb Cheddar cheese, cut lengthwise into 4 strips*

1. In hot oil in medium skillet, sauté onion, green pepper, and ground beef (break up meat with fork into small pieces) until meat is no longer red—about 10 minutes.
2. Stir in paprika, salt, basil, and pepper; mix well.
3. Add tomatoes; bring to boiling. Simmer, uncovered and stirring occasionally, 30 minutes.
4. Preheat oven to 375F.
5. Add rice and kidney beans to skillet mixture; mix well. Turn out into 2-quart casserole or baking dish. Arrange cheese strips over top.
6. Bake, covered with foil, 20 minutes. Remove foil; bake until cheese is melted.

Makes 8 servings.

## POLENTA

*4 cups water*
*1 tablespoon salt*
*2 cups yellow cornmeal*

1. In 9-or 10-inch skillet, bring water and salt to full, rolling boil.
2. Slowly add cornmeal, stirring constantly with wire whisk—mixture will get very thick. With spatula, smooth top.
3. Turn heat very low, and cook, uncovered and without stirring, until thick crust forms around edge and mixture is firm—about 20 minutes.
4. To serve: With spatula, loosen around edge and underneath. Invert onto large round platter. Serve with hearty Italian veal and chicken dishes with sauces.

Makes 6 to 8 servings.

# ✠ TAMALE PIE

4 cups water
1 teaspoon salt
1 cup yellow cornmeal
½ cup grated Cheddar cheese

## CHILI CON CARNE:

1 lb ground beef chuck (in chunks)
1½ cups sliced onion
1½ to 2 tablespoons chili powder
2 cans (1-lb size) dark-red kidney beans
1 can (1 lb 12 oz) whole tomatoes, un-drained
1 teaspoon salt
⅛ teaspoon pepper
¼ teaspoon garlic powder
½ teaspoon sugar
¼ cup catsup

1. Day before, cook cornmeal: In heavy 4-quart saucepan, bring water and 1 teaspoon salt to full, rolling boil. Slowly add cornmeal, stirring constantly with wire whisk—mixture will get very thick.
2. Turn heat low; cook, uncovered and stirring frequently, 20 minutes. Add ¼ cup cheese. Turn out into buttered 13-by-9-by-2-inch baking dish; let stand 20 minutes. Refrigerate, covered, overnight.
3. Next day, make Chili con Carne: In large heavy skillet, over medium heat, sauté ground chuck, stirring, until red color disappears.
4. Add onion and chili powder; cook, stirring, about 5 minutes, or until onion is tender.
5. Drain 1 can beans; use 1 can undrained. Add with rest of ingredients to meat, breaking up tomatoes with fork; stir to mix well. Simmer slowly, covered and stirring occasionally, until thickened and flavors are blended—30 minutes.
6. Preheat oven to 375F.
7. Cut cornmeal mixture into 24 squares. Pour meat mixture into shallow 3-quart casserole. Arrange 12 cornmeal squares, overlapping, around edge; top with second layer. Sprinkle with remaining cheese. Bake, uncovered, 25 to 30 minutes, or until cheese is melted.
Makes 8 servings.

# ✠ GNOCCHI

3 cups milk
1 cup farina
4 tablespoons butter or margarine
2 eggs, beaten
½ cup grated Parmesan cheese
½ teaspoon salt
Dash nutmeg

1. Lightly butter 13-by-9-by-2-inch baking pan. Heat milk slightly in heavy 3½-quart saucepan; do not boil.
2. Sprinkle in farina. Cook, over medium heat and stirring, until mixture is thick—about 5 minutes. Remove from heat.
3. Stir in half of butter, the eggs, ¼ cup Parmesan, the salt, and nutmeg; beat until smooth. Spread evenly in prepared baking pan. Refrigerate until firm—about 3 hours.
4. To serve: Cut the chilled mixture into 24 pieces. Arrange pieces, overlapping, in shallow baking pan. Melt remaining butter, and sprinkle over top with remaining Parmesan.
5. Broil, 4 inches from heat, until hot and golden—about 5 minutes.
Makes 8 servings.

# ❖ GRITS AND GRILLADES

## GRILLADES:

1 lb round steak, cut ½ inch thick
¼ cup all-purpose flour
1½ teaspoons salt
¼ teaspoon pepper
Salad oil
1 large onion, finely chopped
1 small green pepper, finely chopped
3 or 4 cloves garlic, crushed
1 can (16 oz) whole tomatoes or 2 cups
   chopped fresh tomatoes
¾ cup water
Dash Tabasco

## GRITS:

1 cup white hominy quick grits
1 teaspoon salt
4 cups boiling water
Butter or margarine

1. Make Grillades: Wipe steak with damp paper towels. Cut into strips about 3 inches long and ¼ inch thick.
2. On sheet of waxed paper, combine flour, 1½ teaspoons salt, and the pepper; mix well. Dredge meat in flour mixture; reserve remaining flour mixture.
3. In ¼ cup hot oil in large skillet over medium heat, brown beef strips, about one third at a time. Lift out as they brown; continue browning rest.
4. Remove skillet from heat; add flour mixture. Cook over low heat, stirring, to brown slightly. (Be careful not to burn.)
5. Add 2 tablespoons oil to browned mixture. Add onion, green pepper, and garlic; cook, stirring, 5 minutes, or until vegetables are tender-crisp.
6. Add beef, tomatoes, water, and Tabasco. Bring to boiling; reduce heat, and simmer, covered, about 1 hour, or until beef is tender.
7. Meanwhile, prepare Grits: Stir grits slowly into boiling salted water in heavy saucepan. Cook over low heat about 5 minutes, stirring occasionally.
8. Serve grillades over hot buttered grits.
Makes 6 servings.

# ❖ BEEF AND CRACKED WHEAT (Bulgur)

4 cups water
2 cups cracked wheat
1½ teaspoons salt
1½ teaspoons dried basil leaves
¼ teaspoon ground black pepper
1 clove garlic, pressed
½ lb beef chuck
1 large onion
2 firm tomatoes, at room temperature
2 tablespoons butter or margarine
Chopped parsley

1. In medium saucepan, bring water to boiling. Stir in wheat, 1 teaspoon salt, 1 teaspoon basil, the pepper, and garlic. Return to boiling; cover tightly, and cook over low heat until all water is absorbed—15 to 20 minutes.
2. Meanwhile, slice beef ⅛ inch thick. Cut into 1-by-½-inch cubes. Thinly slice onion.
3. Coarsely chop tomatoes. In small bowl, toss with ¼ teaspoon salt and ¼ teaspoon basil. Set in warm place but not on direct heat.
4. Just before wheat is ready, melt 1 tablespoon butter in large skillet. Sauté meat, a third at a time, over very high heat just until browned on each side and still rare inside. Remove to bowl. Add onion, and sauté, stirring, just until golden. Remove to bowl with meat. Toss with ¼ teaspoon salt and ¼ teaspoon basil. Keep warm.
5. Turn out wheat into same skillet. Add 1 tablespoon butter. Cook, stirring, until brown drippings from pan are well mixed with wheat.
6. To serve: Turn out onto serving platter. Spoon meat and onion in center. Surround with tomatoes. Sprinkle with parsley.
Makes 6 servings.

# ❖ BARLEY PILAF

½ cup butter or margarine
½ lb mushrooms, thinly sliced
½ cup coarsely chopped onion
1⅓ cups pearl barley
5 cups canned chicken broth

1. Preheat oven to 350F.
2. In 2 tablespoons hot butter in medium skillet, sauté mushrooms until tender—4 to 5 minutes. Lift out mushrooms with slotted spoon, and set aside.
3. Heat remaining butter in same skillet. Add onion; sauté until golden—about 5 minutes.
4. Add barley; cook over low heat, stirring frequently, until barley is golden-brown—about 5 minutes.
5. Remove from heat. Stir in mushrooms and 2 cups broth.
6. Turn out into 2-quart casserole; bake, covered, 30 minutes.
7. Stir in 2 more cups broth; bake, covered, 30 minutes, or until barley is tender.
8. Finally, stir in remaining cup broth; bake 20 minutes. Serve with veal or chicken.
Makes 8 servings.

# ❖ WEST AFRICAN COUSCOUS

4- to 5-lb roasting chicken, cut into 8
   pieces
½ cup peanut or salad oil
2 medium onions, sliced
2 teaspoons turmeric
1 teaspoon ground cumin
1 teaspoon ground allspice
1½ teaspoons salt
1 to 2 teaspoons ground red pepper
2 cloves garlic, crushed
3 bay leaves
2 cans (10½-oz size) condensed
   chicken broth, undiluted
3 carrots, pared and halved crosswise
3 white turnips, pared and cut into
   quarters
1 small head cabbage, cut into wedges
1 small eggplant, sliced crosswise,
   ¼ inch thick
3 zucchini, sliced
1 cup dark raisins
1 pkg (1 lb) couscous or semolina
½ cup butter or margarine, melted
1 can (1 lb) chick-peas, drained

1. Wash chicken pieces in cold water; drain on paper towels. In hot oil in 6-quart Dutch oven, brown chicken and onions, turning chicken on all sides, 15 to 20 minutes, or until nicely browned.
2. Add 1½ teaspoons tumeric, the cumin, allspice, salt, red pepper, garlic, bay leaves, and chicken broth; stir to mix well. Add carrots, turnips, and cabbage. Cook, covered, 20 minutes. Add eggplant and zucchini; cook 20 minutes longer.
3. Meanwhile, in small bowl, pour hot water over raisins to cover; let stand until needed. Prepare couscous as package label directs. Toss with butter, drained raisins, and ½ teaspoon turmeric. (Keep couscous hot in colander, lined with 2 towels and placed over hot water.)
4. Add chick-peas to chicken mixture; cook 5 minutes longer, or until heated through.
5. To serve: Mound couscous in center of large platter. Arrange chicken and vegetables around it. Serve with sauce.
Makes 6 to 8 servings.

# DRIED BEANS AND PEAS

## ❖ AMERICAN BAKED BEANS

3 cups (1½ lb) dried white navy beans
2 quarts cold water
¾-lb salt pork
1 large onion
4 whole cloves
¼ cup light-brown sugar, packed
2 teaspoons salt
2 teaspoons dry mustard
1 cup light molasses
1 cup tomato catsup
8 slices bacon

1. Wash beans, discarding imperfect ones. Cover beans with 2 quarts cold water, and refrigerate, covered, overnight.
2. Next day, turn out beans and water into 6-quart kettle.
3. Bring to boiling; reduce heat, and simmer, covered, 30 minutes. Drain, reserving liquid.
4. Preheat oven to 300F.
5. Trim rind from salt pork. Cut pork almost through, at half-inch intervals.
6. Place onion, studded with cloves, in bottom of 4-quart bean pot or casserole. Add beans; bury pork, cut side down, in center of beans.
7. Heat reserved bean liquid to boiling.
8. Combine sugar, salt, mustard, and molasses; mix well. Stir in 1 cup boiling bean liquid. Pour over beans. Add boiling liquid just to cover beans—about 1½ cups.
9. Bake, covered 4 hours. (Stir once every hour, so beans cook evenly, adding more water, if necessary.)
10. Remove from oven; add catsup. If beans seem dry after stirring, add a little boiling water. Arrange bacon strips over the top.
11. Bake, uncovered, 1 hour, or until tender.
Makes 8 servings.

## ❖ WHITE BEANS, COUNTRY-STYLE

2 cups (1 lb) dried white navy beans
   or baby lima beans
5 cups cold water
4 teaspoons salt
¼ teaspoon pepper
2 cloves garlic, pressed
2 bay leaves
6 tablespoons butter or margarine
2 onions, finely chopped
1 green pepper, finely chopped
1 can (1 lb) tomatoes, undrained
1 teaspoon dried oregano leaves
¼ cup finely chopped parsley
Tomato wedges (optional)

1. Wash beans, discarding imperfect ones. Cover with 2 quarts cold water; refrigerate, covered, overnight.
2. Next day, drain beans. Turn out into 4- or 5-quart Dutch oven; cover with 5 cups cold water. Add salt, pepper, garlic, and bay leaves. Bring to boiling; reduce heat, and simmer, covered, 1 hour, or until beans are tender. Stir several times during cooking. Drain; remove bay leaves and discard. Return beans to Dutch oven. Preheat oven to 350F.
3. Meanwhile, in medium skillet, in 4 tablespoons hot butter, sauté chopped onion until golden—about 5 minutes. Add green pepper, tomatoes, oregano, and parsley; cook 5 more minutes.

4. Stir vegetable mixture and remaining 2 tablespoons butter into drained beans. Bake, covered, 1 hour and 15 minutes; bake, uncovered, 15 minutes longer, or until tender. If desired, garnish top with tomato wedges.

Makes 6 servings.

# ✜ BEANS WITH TUNA SAUCE

2 cups (1 lb) dried white navy beans
  or dried pink beans
1 can (10½ oz) condensed beef broth,
  undiluted
3 cups water
½ cup salad or olive oil

## SAUCE:

1 can (7 oz) tuna, undrained
¼ cup lemon juice
½ cup salad or olive oil
½ teaspoon salt
Dash pepper
2 drops Tabasco
3 tablespoons grated Parmesan
  cheese
2 hard-cooked egg yolks
1 clove garlic, minced

Crisp romaine lettuce leaves
1 roasted red pepper, sliced
6 black olives
1 red onion, sliced

1. Wash beans, discarding imperfect ones. Cover beans with 2 quarts cold water; refrigerate, covered, overnight.

2. Next day, drain, then turn out beans, beef broth, and 3 cups water into 6-quart kettle.

3. Bring to boiling; simmer, covered, 2 hours, or until tender. If necessary, add 1 cup water during cooking. Drain. Turn out into large bowl; toss with ½ cup salad oil.

4. Make Sauce: In medium bowl, with fork, break up tuna. Stir in lemon juice, salad oil, salt, pepper, Tabasco, Parmesan cheese, hard-cooked egg yolks, and garlic; beat with wooden spoon until smooth and well blended. Refrigerate, covered, 1 hour.

5. Add sauce to beans; toss until well blended.

6. To serve: Line dish with romaine; mound beans in center. Garnish with red-pepper slices, olives, and onion slices.

Makes 8 servings.

# ❖ BAKED BEANS AU GRATIN

Boiling water
2 cups (1 lb) dried white navy beans
1 onion studded with 3 whole cloves
Bouquet garni (see Note)
5 teaspoons salt
2 tablespoons butter or margarine
1 onion, finely chopped
1 can (16 oz) tomatoes, undrained
1 clove garlic, crushed
1 can (10¾ oz) condensed chicken
  broth, undiluted
½ cup heavy cream
¼ teaspoon pepper
1 cup fresh white-bread crumbs
2 tablespoons butter or margarine,
  melted

1. Wash beans, discarding imperfect ones. In large saucepan, pour enough boiling water over beans just to cover. Bring to boiling; boil 2 minutes. Set aside, covered, 2 hours.

2. Drain beans; turn out into heavy 5-quart Dutch oven, along with onion studded with cloves, bouquet garni, and 3 teaspoons salt. Add enough water just to cover beans (about 1 quart). Bring to boiling; reduce heat, and simmer, covered, until tender—1½ to 2 hours. Drain, discarding onion and bouquet garni.

3. Meanwhile, in a large skillet, in 2 tablespoons hot butter, sauté chopped onion until golden—several minutes. Add tomatoes and garlic; cook, stirring, several minutes more. Stir in chicken broth and cream, blending well; simmer a few minutes. Meanwhile, preheat oven to 375F.

4. Stir in drained beans, 2 teaspoons salt, and the pepper, mixing just until combined. Turn out into 12-by-8-by-2-inch baking dish or 3-quart au-gratin dish.

5. Toss bread crumbs, with melted butter; sprinkle over top of beans. Bake, uncovered, 30 minutes, or until hot and crumbs are browned.
Makes 8 to 10 servings.

Note: Tie together 1 sprig parsley, 1 bay leaf, and ½ teaspoon dried thyme leaves in cheesecloth bag.

# ❖ BLACK BEANS AND RICE

2 cups (1 lb) dried black beans,
  washed
6 cups water
¼ lb bacon
1 cup chopped onion
1 large green pepper, chopped
2 cloves garlic, minced
2 bay leaves
1 teaspoon salt
¼ teaspoon pepper
½ cup red-wine vinegar
4 cups cooked rice
1 hard-cooked egg, sliced
Onion rings, raw

1. Wash beans discarding imperfect ones. Cover with 6 cups water, and bring to boiling. Boil 2 minutes; cover pan, and let stand 1 hour.

2. In medium skillet, sauté bacon until crisp. Remove from skillet and drain on paper towels. Crumble bacon into small pieces.

3. Add onion, green pepper, and garlic to bacon fat in skillet; sauté for 5 minutes, or until tender.

4. Add bacon, onion mixture, bay leaves, salt, and pepper to beans. Bring to boiling; reduce heat, and simmer, covered, 2 hours, or until beans are tender, adding more water if necessary.

5. Stir in red-wine vinegear. Serve with rice. Garnish with egg and onion slices.
Makes 8 servings.

# ❖ BAKED CREOLE LIMA BEANS

2 cups (1 lb) dried large lima beans
5 cups cold water
1 teaspoon salt

## SAUCE:

3 tablespoons salad oil
1 cup chopped onion
½ cup chopped celery
½ cup chopped green pepper
1 cup tomato catsup
½ cup light-brown sugar, packed
1 teaspoon Worcestershire sauce
1 teaspoon salt
½ teaspoon dry mustard
1 cup water

3 green-pepper rings

1. Wash beans, discarding imperfect ones. Cover beans with 5 cups cold water. Refrigerate, covered, overnight.
2. Next day, turn out beans and liquid (do not drain; there should be 4 cups) into 5-quart kettle or Dutch oven; add 1 teaspoon salt. Bring to boiling; reduce heat, and simmer gently, covered and stirring occasionally, 1 hour, or until beans are tender and liquid is almost absorbed.
3. Meanwhile, make Sauce: In large saucepan, heat oil, and sauté onion, celery, and green pepper until tender—about 5 minutes. Add catsup, brown sugar, Worcestershire, salt, mustard, and 1 cup water.
4. Bring to boiling, stirring; simmer, uncovered, 5 minutes.
5. Preheat oven to 350F.
6. Drain beans, reserving ¼ cup liquid.
7. In kettle, combine beans, ¼ cup liquid, and the sauce; mix well.
8. Turn out bean mixture into 2-quart casserole or baking dish. Bake, covered, 1 hour.
9. Remove cover from lima beans. Bake, uncovered, 10 minutes. To serve: Garnish with green-pepper rings.
Makes 6 servings.

# ❖ LIMA BEAN CHILI

1 pkg (1-lb size) dried baby lima beans
5 cups cold water
2 teaspoons salt
½ lb ground beef chuck
2 medium onions, sliced
1 to 1½ tablespoons chili powder
1 can (16 oz) stewed tomatoes
1 can (8 oz) tomato sauce
⅛ teaspoon pepper
½ teaspoon sugar
¼ cup catsup
½ cup grated Cheddar cheese
2 tablespoons chopped green pepper

1. Rinse beans thoroughly; drain. Cover with 5 cups cold water. Refrigerate, covered, overnight.
2. Next day, turn out beans and liquid (do not drain) into 4-quart kettle or Dutch oven; add 1 teaspoon salt. Bring to boiling; reduce heat, and simmer gently, covered and stirring occasionally, 45 minutes, or until tender, not mushy.
3. In large heavy skillet, over medium heat, sauté ground chuck, stirring until browned.
4. Add onions and chili powder; cook, stirring, about 5 minutes, or until onions are tender.
5. Add to beans, along with stewed tomatoes, tomato sauce, pepper, sugar, catsup, and 1 teaspoon salt.
6. Simmer slowly, covered and stirring occasionally, about 20 minutes.
7. Turn out into a 2-quart casserole. Garnish with grated cheese and green pepper.
Makes 8 servings.
*Note:* Pinto or kidney beans may be substituted for baby lima beans.

## ❖ BLACK-EYED PEAS WITH HAM

2 cups (1 lb) black-eyed peas
1- to 1½-lb smoked pork butt
5 cups cold water
Salt
2 bay leaves
1 medium onion studded with 4
  whole cloves
2 tablespoons butter or margarine
2 tablespoons salad oil
1 cup chopped onion
½ cup chopped celery
1 teaspoon dried thyme leaves
⅛ teaspoon pepper
¼ cup plus 2 tablespoons light-brown
  sugar
1 can (1 lb) whole tomatoes, undrained
½ cup dry red wine
Chopped parsley

1. Cover beans with cold water; refrigerate, covered, overnight.
2. Next day, place pork butt in 8-quart kettle; cover with 5 cups water, 3 teaspoons salt, bay leaves, and onion studded with cloves. Bring to boiling; reduce heat, and simmer, covered, 1 hour.
3. Drain beans; add to kettle with pork. Bring to boiling; reduce heat and simmer, covered, 1 hour, or until beans are tender.
4. Meanwhile, in medium saucepan, in hot butter and oil, sauté onion, celery, and thyme, stirring, 5 minutes. Add 1 teaspoon salt, the pepper, and ¼ cup brown sugar. Set aside.
5. Preheat oven to 350F. Drain beans, reserving liquid. Slice pork butt.
6. In 3-quart casserole, combine beans and tomatoes. Stir in onion-celery mixture and red wine; mix well. Arrange pork slices across top. Bake, covered, ½ hour, adding a little bean liquid if necessary. Sprinkle top with 2 tablespoons sugar; bake, uncovered, 30 minutes longer. Sprinkle with parsley.
Makes 8 servings.

## ❖ HONEY-BAKED BEANS

2 cups (1 lb) dried lima beans
2 quarts cold water
2 teaspoons salt
¼ lb sliced bacon, diced
1½ teaspoons dry mustard
1 teaspoon ground ginger
¾ cup honey
1 medium onion studded with 3
  whole cloves
1 cup sliced onion

1. Cover beans with 2 quarts cold water; refrigerate, covered, overnight.
2. Next day, over medium heat, cook beans, with 1 teaspoon salt, in same water, uncovered, until tender and skins burst. Drain, reserving liquid.
3. In 2½-quart casserole, place half of bacon, the beans, and remaining ingredients, combined with ½ cup bean liquid. Cover with rest of bacon.
4. Bake, covered, 1½ hours, or until tender. During last ½ hour, remove cover to brown. (Add more bean liquid during cooking if necessary.)
Makes 8 servings.

# SALADS and SALAD DRESSINGS

⬥ Salads, whether they are main courses for a summer luncheon or supper or mixed greens to serve as an appetizer course or an after-entrée refresher, deserve to be as carefully made as any other part of the meal. Today it is easy to find a variety of salad greens with different textures and colors and fresh herbs to spike them with interest. Learning to make a great salad is an achievement to make you proud and please your family and guests.

Also in this chapter you'll find main-dish salads and vegetable, pasta, fruit, and gelatine salads, as well as an assortment of dressings. When a recipe calls for mayonnaise or a cooked salad dressing, you may use a commercial dressing or our good, and easy, homemade dressings, beginning on page 452.

# GREEN SALADS

## KNOW YOUR SALAD GREENS

*Arugula,* also known as rugula, rochetta, or rocket, has a slightly bitter and peppery flavor. Its dark-green oak-shaped leaves add color and zest to any salad.

*Belgian endive* can be sliced lengthwise or crosswise into a salad. Although it is a member of the chicory and escarole family, it is a straight, pale, slender leaf, 6 inches or more in length. Endive can be eaten alone or served with greens. Some people enjoy eating it as they do celery.

*Bibb lettuce, or limestone lettuce,* is smaller and more delicate than Boston lettuce, but has something of the same shape and delicious flavor. Use the whole leaf in a salad. This lettuce gets its name from Jack Bibb, of Frankfort, Kentucky, who introduced it to his friends shortly after the Civil War. Still fairly expensive, it is growing less so, now that it has begun to reach the markets in greater quantity.

*Boston lettuce,* also known as "butterhead" and "big Boston," has velvety, spreading leaves, which can be easily separated. This tender lettuce will do much for a salad. It is available throughout most of the year. However, its distribution is rather limited.

*Curly endive, or chicory,* has a maze of narrow, thin, twisted leaves, shading from dark green at the edges to a pale-yellow heart. It is often used with grapefruit and orange sections or tomatoes. It has an almost bitter tang.

*Escarole* tastes a little like Belgian endive, though not as bitter. It is often called the broad-leaf endive. It resembles chicory, but its leaves are broader and not as curly. They are dark green, edging into yellow.

*Head lettuce, or iceberg lettuce, or Simpson lettuce,* is the most familiar of lettuces. It is the firm, tight, compact head of light-green leaves. Separated, the leaves make a lettuce cup as a container for potato salad, fruit salad, and so on. Cut in wedges, it is a favorite, particularly of those who like to pour blue-cheese dressing over it.

*Leaf lettuce* is a favorite with the home gardener. It is crisp and has a curly edge. It is a lovely green and has a good flavor, and it grows in large leafy bunches.

*Oak-leaf lettuce,* called thus because of the deeply notched leaves, which look so much like true oak leaves, has a delicate flavor. Bronze Beauty is another variety of this plant, with reddish-tinted leaves instead of green.

*Radicchio,* a red lettucelike plant from Italy, is a type of chicory. Its rose-colored leaves with distinctive white veins and its cabbagelike flavor add color and texture to your salad.

*Romaine lettuce* is more strongly flavored than several other varieties of lettuce. It can be recognized by its long head and spoon-shaped leaves, coarser and crisper than head lettuce. It is especially good served with tomatoes and avocados.

*Sorrel,* with its lemony flavor, is available in markets in the late spring and early summer and is easily cultivated in the home garden. French sorrel has a milder flavor than the more acidic wood and mountain sorrel. Use the tender young leaves in salads.

*Spinach* is not a lettuce; but the tender young leaves of spinach give an interesting taste and color to a tossed green salad.

*Watercress,* a dark-green leafy plant, with the unexpected bite in its taste, grows along the edges of brooks and springs. It gives an interesting color and taste contrast to a tossed green salad, adds a bright-green note as a garnish, and looks particularly attractive with the contrast of red tomatoes sliced over it.

# THE CARE OF SALAD GREENS AND FRESH HERBS

Once home from the market, where salad greens and fresh herbs should have been stored in refrigerated cases, plunge the greens and herbs briefly in a basin of tepid (not hot, not cold) water; tepid water removes any sand from vegetables more easily. (If head lettuces are not to be used the same day, don't break them apart.)

Remove the greens and herbs from the water and shake to release excess moisture. Let head lettuces dry, stem end up, in a paper-towel-lined colander, or spin them briefly in a salad dryer; wrap in a towel or plastic wrap, and store in the coldest part of the refrigerator. Let herbs dry on paper towels, store in covered jars, stems ends down, in the refrigerator. (You may cut down some of the stems for more compact storage.)

# MIXING SALAD GREENS

Tear dry, crisp, cold greens into bite-size pieces. Put the greens in a bowl large enough for tossing, and refrigerate until ready to serve. Don't add juice-bearing tomatoes or cucumbers until serving time.

Just before serving, add dressing, and toss gently. Add more dressing if necessary. Less is better; too much dressing wilts greens. Serve on chilled plates.

# ✤ CAESAR SALAD

*1 large head romaine*
*1 clove garlic*
*½ cup salad oil*
*1 cup French-bread cubes (½-inch),*
  *crusts removed*
*¾ teaspoon salt*
*¼ teaspoon dry mustard*
*¼ teaspoon freshly ground pepper*
*1½ teaspoons Worcestershire sauce*
*6 anchovy fillets, drained and*
  *chopped*
*¼ cup crumbled blue cheese*
*2 tablespoons grated Parmesan*
  *cheese*
*1 egg*
*Juice of ½ lemon (2 tablespoons)*

1. Trim core from romaine. Separate head into leaves, discarding any that are wilted or discolored. Place in wire salad basket; rinse under cold running water; then shake well to remove excess moisture. Or wash greens under running water; drain, and dry on paper towels or in salad dryer.

2. Now wrap in plastic wrap, and store in vegetable crisper in refrigerator until crisp and cold—several hours or overnight. Or put cleaned, drained greens in a plastic bag, and store on bottom shelf of refrigerator.

3. Several hours before serving, halve garlic. Set one half aside. Crush remaining half, and combine with salad oil in jar with tight-fitting lid. Refrigerate oil mixture at least 1 hour.

4. Heat 2 tablespoons oil-garlic mixture in medium

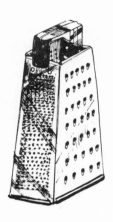

skillet. Add bread cubes; sauté until brown all over. Set aside.

5. To remaining oil-garlic mixture in jar, add salt, mustard, pepper, Worcestershire, and anchovies. Shake vigorously. Refrigerate until needed.

6. Bring 2-inch depth of water to boiling in small saucepan. Turn off heat. Carefully lower egg into water. Let stand 1 minute; then lift out. Drain, and set aside to cool.

7. Just before serving, rub inside of large wooden salad bowl with reserved ½ clove garlic; discard garlic.

8. Cut out coarse ribs from large leaves of romaine. Tear into bite-size pieces into salad bowl.

9. Shake dressing well, and pour over romaine. Sprinkle with cheeses. Toss until all romaine is coated with dressing.

10. Break egg over center of salad. Pour lemon juice directly over egg; toss well.

11. Sprinkle bread cubes over salad, and quickly toss it again. Serve salad at once.

Makes 4 to 6 servings.

## ❖ FRESH SPINACH SALAD

### WHITE-WINE FRENCH DRESSING:

*2 tablespoons white-wine vinegar*
*2 tablespoons lemon juice*
*½ cup salad oil*
*1 teaspoon salt*
*¼ teaspoon pepper*
*1 teaspoon sugar*
*½ teaspoon dry mustard*
*1 clove garlic (optional)*

### SALAD:

*¾ lb tender young spinach*
*6 green onions, thinly sliced (¼ cup)*
*½ cup sliced radishes*
*1 small cucumber, pared and thinly sliced*

1. Make White-Wine French Dressing: Combine all dressing ingredients in jar with tight-fitting lid; shake vigorously. Refrigerate until ready to use.

2. Make Salad: Wash spinach; dry leaves, and remove stems. Tear leaves into bite-size pieces into salad bowl.

3. Arrange other vegetables in groups on spinach. Refrigerate, covered, about 2 hours.

4. To serve: Remove garlic from dressing, and shake vigorously. Pour dressing over salad; toss until spinach is well coated. Serve at once.

Makes 4 to 6 servings.

# ❖ ENDIVE-AND-WATERCRESS SALAD WITH WALNUTS

## VINAIGRETTE DRESSING:

*⅓ cup olive or salad oil*
*¼ cup red-wine vinegar*
*1 teaspoon salt*
*1 teaspoon Dijon mustard*
*½ teaspoon freshly ground pepper*

*4 Belgian endives*
*2 bunches watercress*
*½ cup walnuts, halved*

1. Make Vinaigrette Dressing: Combine all ingredients in jar with tight-fitting lid. Shake vigorously.
2. Refrigerate dressing until ready to use. Shake again just before using.
3. Wash endive under cold running water. Drain on paper towels; separate and dry leaves. Store in plastic bag in crisper in refrigerator.
4. Remove stem ends from watercress. Wash; drain well. Store in plastic bag in crisper in refrigerator.
5. To serve: Arrange endive, spoke fashion, around edge of chilled serving dish.
6. Shake dressing well; pour half over watercress sprigs in large bowl. Toss until watercress is well coated with dressing. Turn out into center of dish. Sprinkle with walnuts. Pass remaining dressing.
Makes 12 servings.

# ❖ FRENCH GREEN SALAD

*1 small head Boston lettuce*
*1 small head Bibb lettuce*
*½ small head romaine lettuce*
*1 Belgian endive*
*½ clove garlic*
*6 tablespoons olive oil*
*3 tablespoons tarragon vinegar*
*1 teaspoon salt*
*Freshly ground black pepper*

1. Prepare salad greens: Wash lettuces and endive, and separate into leaves, discarding discolored or bruised leaves. Drain well, shaking in salad basket, placing on paper towels, or spinning in salad dryer, to remove excess moisture.
2. Place cleaned greens in plastic bag, or wrap in plastic wrap. Refrigerate until crisp and cold—several hours. Also refrigerate salad bowl.
3. At serving time, rub inside of salad bowl with garlic; discard garlic. Tear greens into bite-size pieces into bowl; leave small leaves whole.
4. In jar with tight-fitting lid, combine oil, vinegar, salt, and dash pepper; shake until well combined.
5. Pour half of dressing over greens. With salad spoon and fork, toss greens until they are well coated and no dressing remains in bottom of bowl. Add more dressing, if desired.
Makes 6 to 8 servings.

# ❖ CREAMED LETTUCE SALAD

2 quarts Boston or leaf lettuce, in bite-
  size pieces
½ cup sliced green onion
½ cup light cream
¼ cup lemon juice
4 teaspoons sugar
½ teaspoon salt
Dash white pepper

1. Place lettuce and green onion in salad bowl.
2. In small bowl, combine cream, lemon juice, sugar, salt, and pepper; mix well. Pour over lettuce, and toss well. Serve immediately.
Makes 6 to 8 servings.

# MAIN-DISH SALADS

# ❖ ANTIPASTO SALAD PLATTER

**DRESSING:**

½ cup olive or salad oil
¼ cup lemon juice
1 teaspoon salt
¼ teaspoon black pepper
⅛ teaspoon crushed red pepper
1 clove garlic, crushed
1 tablespoon chopped fresh basil or 1
  teaspoon dried basil leaves

1 tablespoon salt
1 tablespoon salad oil
8 oz radiatori or other pasta
½ cup cubed green pepper
½ cup cubed red pepper
4 medium mushrooms, washed and
  sliced
¼ lb provolone, cubed
1 can (1 lb 4 oz) garbanzos, drained
¼ lb sliced salami (slices cut into
  quarters)
¼ cup small black pitted olives
2 tablespoons chopped parsley

1. Make Dressing: In jar with tight-fitting lid, combine oil, lemon juice, 1 teaspoon salt, the black pepper, red pepper, garlic, and basil; shake until well combined.
2. Cook radiatori: In large kettle, bring 3 quarts water, the salt, and salad oil to rapid boil. Add pasta; bring back to boiling. Cook, uncovered and stirring occasionally with long fork to prevent sticking, just until tender—about 7 to 8 minutes. Do not overcook. Drain well; do not rinse.
3. Turn out into large bowl; add dressing, and toss to combine. Cool completely.
4. To radiatori mixture, add green and red peppers, mushrooms, provolone, garbanzos, salami, olives, and parsley; toss lightly to combine. Turn out into serving bowl; refrigerate, covered, 1 hour. Toss well before serving.
Makes 8 servings.

# ✦ CHEF'S SALAD

## CREAMY DRESSING:

*1 bottle (8 oz) herb-garlic salad dressing*
*¼ cup mayonnaise or cooked salad dressing*
*¼ teaspoon sugar*

## SALAD:

*1½ quarts bite-size pieces crisp salad greens*
*2 tablespoons snipped chives*
*2 cups slivered cooked ham (½ lb)*
*1½ cups slivered cooked chicken (½ lb)*
*½ lb natural Swiss cheese, slivered*
*2 medium tomatoes, cut into wedges*

1. Make Creamy Dressing: In small bowl, combine all dressing ingredients; with wire whisk or rotary beater, beat well. Refrigerate, covered, until ready to use.
2. Just before serving, make Salad: Place greens and chives in salad bowl. Add ham, chicken, and cheese.
3. Stir dressing well; pour over salad. Toss to coat meat and greens.
4. Garnish with tomato wedges.
Makes 6 servings.

# ✦ COBB SALAD WITH RUSSIAN DRESSING

*2 cups crisp iceberg lettuce, in bite-size pieces*
*2 cups crisp romaine lettuce in bite-size pieces*
*2 cups crisp chicory, in bite-size pieces*
*2 medium tomatoes, cut into eighths*
*2 medium avocados, peeled and sliced*
*3 cups slivered cooked chicken, chilled*
*6 crisp-cooked slices bacon, cut into ½-inch pieces*
*1 hard-cooked egg*
*2 tablespoons chopped chives*
*Watercress*
*Russian Dressing, page 453*

1. Just before serving, assemble salad: Place lettuces and chicory in salad bowl. Arrange tomato and avocado around edge of bowl. Mound chicken in center, and sprinkle with bacon. Chop egg white and egg yolk separately; sprinkle decoratively, along with chives, over top of salad. Garnish with watercress.
2. To serve: At the table, pour half of dressing over salad; toss well. Pass rest of dressing.
Makes 8 to 10 servings.

# ✛ CHICKEN SALAD

5- to 5½-lb ready-to-cook roasting
chicken
2 large carrots, pared and cut into 1-
inch pieces
2 stalks celery, cut into 1-inch pieces
1 large onion, sliced
6 whole black peppercorns
3½ teaspoons salt
1 bay leaf
1 quart water
1 cup mayonnaise or cooked salad
dressing
2 tablespoons lemon juice
2 tablespoons milk or light cream
Dash pepper
3 or 4 crisp large celery stalks
Crisp lettuce
Watercress
Tomato wedges

1. Remove giblets and neck from chicken. Then
rinse chicken well under cold water. Place, breast
side down, in 8-quart kettle.
2. Add carrots, cut-up celery, onion, whole peppercorns, 2 teaspoons salt, the bay leaf, and water.
3. Bring to boiling over high heat. Reduce heat, and
simmer, covered, about 2 hours, or until chicken is
tender. (After 1 hour, carefully turn chicken with
wooden spoons.) Remove kettle from heat.
4. Let stand, uncovered, and frequently spoon broth
in kettle over chicken, 1 hour, or until cool enough to
handle. Lift out chicken. Strain broth, and refrigerate, covered, to use as desired.
5. Cut legs, thighs, and wings from chicken. Remove
skin. Then remove meat from bones in as large
pieces as possible. Set aside.
6. Pull skin from remaining chicken. With sharp
knife, cut between the breastbone and meat, removing breast meat in large piece. Then check carefully,
and remove any additional meat. Refrigerate, covered, to chill—about 1½ hours.
7. Make salad: In large bowl, combine mayonnaise,
lemon juice, milk, 1½ teaspoons salt, and the pepper;
stir until blended.
8. Cut celery, on diagonal, into thin slices, to measure
2 cups. Add to dressing in bowl.
9. Cut large pieces of chicken meat into 1-inch
pieces; there should be almost 5 cups. Add all meat
to dressing. Toss lightly to coat well.
10. Refrigerate, covered, until serving time—at least
1 hour.
11. To serve: Spoon salad into attractive bowl; garnish with lettuce, watercress, and tomato wedges.
Makes 6 to 8 servings.

## CHICKEN WALDORF SALAD:

Chicken Salad, above
2 cups coarsely diced red apple
¾ cup broken walnut meats
Lettuce leaves
Watercress

1. Prepare Chicken Salad, reducing sliced celery to 1
cup.
2. Add apple to dressing as soon as it is cut, to prevent
darkening. Add walnuts and celery; toss lightly.
3. Garnish with lettuce leaves and watercress.
Makes 8 servings.

# ✠ SALADE NIÇOISE

## DRESSING:

*½ cup olive oil*
*¼ cup salad oil*
*¼ cup red-wine vinegar*
*1 teaspoon sugar*
*¾ teaspoon salt*
*¼ teaspoon cracked peppercorns*

## SALAD:

*1 lb fresh green beans, trimmed and washed, or 2 pkg (9-oz size) frozen whole green beans*
*1 medium red onion, thinly sliced*
*2 medium tomatoes, cut into wedges*
*½ cup pitted ripe olives*
*1 can (2 oz) anchovy fillets*
*2 cans (7-oz size) solid-pack tuna, drained and broken into chunks*
*2 hard-cooked eggs, sliced*

1. Make Dressing: In jar with tight-fitting lid, combine oil, vinegar, sugar, salt, and pepper; shake vigorously until well combined.
2. Cook whole fresh beans in small amount of boiling salted water, covered, 17 to 20 minutes, or until tender. Cook frozen beans, as package label directs, 5 minutes, or just until tender. Drain, then plunge beans into cold water to prevent further cooking. Drain well; turn out into shallow dish. Add ½ cup dressing; toss until beans are well coated.
3. Refrigerate beans, covered. Also refrigerate remaining dressing and the salad ingredients until well chilled—at least 2 hours.
4. To serve: Turn out green beans into salad bowl. Add all but a few onion slices, tomato wedges, olives, and anchovy fillets; toss gently. Then add tuna chunks and egg slices; toss again.
5. Garnish with reserved onion, tomato, olives, and anchovy. Drizzle remaining dressing over all.
Makes 6 servings.

# ✠ TABBOULEH

*1 cup bulgur (cracked wheat)*
*Boiling water*

## DRESSING:

*¾ cup olive or salad oil*
*3 tablespoons lemon juice*
*1 clove garlic, crushed*
*1½ teaspoons salt*
*¼ teaspoon black pepper*
*Dash ground red pepper*

*¾ cup finely chopped scallion*
*1 cup cucumber, pared and cut into ¼-inch cubes*
*1½ cups finely chopped parsley*
*¾ cup finely chopped fresh mint*
*4 medium tomatoes (1½ lb), peeled and cut into ½-inch cubes (see page 493)*
*Fresh mint sprigs*
*Romaine lettuce leaves (optional)*

1. Rinse bulgur under cold water; drain well. Place in large bowl; cover with boiling water. Let bulgur soak 1 to 2 hours. Drain; squeeze out excess moisture with your hands.
2. Make Dressing: In medium bowl, combine oil, lemon juice, garlic, salt, black pepper, and red pepper; mix well.
3. Add bulgur to dressing; toss lightly to mix well. Turn out into large glass bowl.
4. Layer scallion, cucumber, parsley, chopped mint, and tomato on top of bulgur. Garnish with mint sprigs.
5. Refrigerate, tightly covered, several hours or overnight.
6. Before serving, toss salad to combine. Nice served on romaine leaves.
Makes 10 to 12 servings.

# VEGETABLE SALADS

## ✥ LAYERED VEGETABLE SALAD

1 pkg (10 oz) frozen small peas
1 large head iceberg lettuce, washed and crisped
1 green pepper, chopped
1 cup finely chopped onion
3 celery stalks, washed and thinly sliced
2¼ cups mayonnaise
½ cup grated sharp Cheddar cheese
3 large tomatoes (1½ lb), peeled (see page 493)
½ cup bottled oil-and-vinegar dressing
¼ lb sliced bacon
Pitted black olives, drained and halved
6 hard-cooked eggs, peeled and sliced

1. Prepare salad day before serving: Cook peas as package label directs, omitting butter; drain. Shred lettuce.
2. In large shallow glass bowl, make a bottom layer of lettuce. Then layer green pepper, onion, celery, and peas. Spread with mayonnaise; sprinkle with cheese. Refrigerate, covered, until serving time.
3. Cut tomatoes into cubes. Arrange in single layer in large pie plate; sprinkle with some oil-and-vinegar dressing. Refrigerate, covered.
4. Next day, cook bacon until crisp; drain on paper towels, and crumble. Drain tomatoes.
5. Arrange tomato cubes on top of salad. Pour on rest of oil-and-vinegar dressing. Garnish with olives, eggs, and bacon.
6. To serve: Spoon down through layers so each serving has some of each layer; do not toss.
Makes 10 servings.

## ✥ FRESH ASPARAGUS VINAIGRETTE

2 to 2½ lb fresh asparagus
Boiling water
3½ teaspoons salt
3 tablespoons cider vinegar
¼ cup salad oil
2 tablespoons olive oil
½ teaspoon sugar
Dash pepper
1 hard-cooked egg, chopped
2 sweet gherkins, chopped

1. Break or cut off tough ends of asparagus stalks. Wash asparagus well with cold water; if necessary, use soft brush to remove grit. With vegetable peeler or paring knife, remove scales and skin from lower part of stalks.
2. Tie stalks into bunch with string. Stand up-right in deep saucepan. Add boiling water, to depth of 2 inches, and 1½ teaspoons salt.
3. Bring to boiling; cook, covered, 15 to 20 minutes, or just until tender. Drain well. Lay stalks in shallow baking dish.
4. In jar with tight-fitting lid, combine vinegar, oils, 2 teaspoons salt, the sugar, and pepper; shake well.
5. Pour dressing over asparagus. Refrigerate 1 hour, turning stalks several times.
6. Arrange asparagus on platter. Sprinkle with egg and pickle.
Makes 6 servings.

# ✠ MARINATED BEAN SALAD

## DRESSING:

½ cup salad or olive oil
¼ cup vinegar
1 teaspoon dried tarragon leaves
1 teaspoon sugar
½ teaspoon dry mustard
½ teaspoon salt
¼ teaspoon pepper

1 lb fresh green beans
1 teaspoon salt
Boiling water
1 pkg (10 oz) frozen Fordhook or large
    lima beans
1 can (1 lb) red kidney beans, drained

1. Make Dressing: In jar with tight-fitting lid, combine oil, vinegar, tarragon, sugar, mustard, ½ teaspoon salt, and the pepper; shake well.
2. Refrigerate until well chilled—about 2 hours.
3. Wash green beans; cut off ends. Place in large skillet. Add salt and boiling water to measure 1 inch.
4. Boil green beans gently, covered, 12 to 15 minutes, or just until tender-crisp. Run under cold water to set color. Drain well. Cool.
5. Cook lima beans according to package directions. Drain well. Cool.
6. Arrange green beans, lima beans, and kidney beans in single layer in shallow baking dish or plastic container.
7. Pour dressing over beans. Refrigerate, covered, several hours or overnight.
8. To serve: Drain vegetables, reserving dressing; arrange on chilled platter. Drizzle some dressing over beans.
Makes 10 to 12 servings.

# ✠ GARBANZO-BEAN SALAD

2 cups diced potato
1 cup thinly sliced carrot
1 large red onion, thinly sliced
¼ cup salad or olive oil
2 cans (1-lb size) garbanzo beans
½ cup bottled Italian-style dressing
1 or 2 cloves garlic, crushed
2 teaspoons salt
1½ teaspoons sugar
Chopped parsley

1. In large saucepan, in 1 inch boiling salted water, cook potato and carrot until tender—about 10 minutes. Drain; turn out into large bowl.
2. In medium-size heavy skillet, sauté onion in oil until soft but not brown. Add to potato and carrot.
3. Drain garbanzos. Add to potato mixture.
4. In small bowl, combine dressing, garlic, salt, and sugar; mix well. Pour over vegetable mixture.
5. Toss gently until well mixed. Serve warm. Or refrigerate 2 hours, or until well chilled. Sprinkle with chopped parsley.
Makes 8 servings.

# ❖ HARVEY HOUSE SLAW

*1 head green cabbage, slivered (10 cups)*
*1 large green pepper, cut into rings*
*2 medium Spanish onions, cut into rings*
*1 cup plus 2 teaspoons sugar*
*1 teaspoon dry mustard*
*1 teaspoon celery seed*
*1 tablespoon salt*
*1 cup white vinegar*
*¾ cup salad oil*

1. In large bowl, make layers of cabbage, green pepper, and onion; sprinkle 1 cup sugar over top.
2. In saucepan, combine mustard, 2 teaspoons sugar, the celery seed, salt, vinegar, and oil; mix well. Bring to a full boil, stirring; pour over slaw. Refrigerate, covered, at least 4 hours.
3. Before serving, toss salad to mix well.
Makes 8 servings.

# ❖ SOUR-CREAM COLESLAW

*1½ cups sour cream*
*2 egg yolks*
*2 tablespoons lemon juice*
*3 tablespoons prepared horseradish, drained*
*¼ teaspoon paprika*
*1 teaspoon sugar*
*1 teaspoon salt*
*2 quarts finely shredded green cabbage*

1. Combine sour cream and egg yolks in medium bowl; mix well. Blend in remaining ingredients, except cabbage.
2. Pour dressing over cabbage in large bowl; toss until well coated.
3. Refrigerate at least 30 minutes.
Makes 6 to 8 servings.

# ❖ SLICED CUCUMBERS IN SOUR CREAM

*2 large cucumbers, pared and very thinly sliced*
*1½ teaspoons salt*
*1 cup sour cream*
*2 tablespoons lemon juice*
*1 tablespoon finely chopped onion*
*¼ teaspoon sugar*
*Dash pepper*
*1½ teaspoons finely chopped parsley*

1. Lightly toss cucumbers with 1 teaspoon salt. Chill well.
2. Meanwhile, combine sour cream, lemon juice, remaining salt, the onion, sugar, and pepper.
3. Drain cucumbers. Toss with sour-cream mixture; refrigerate until well chilled—about 2 hours.
4. To serve: Turn out cucumber mixture into shallow serving bowl; sprinkle with chopped parsley.
Makes 4 to 6 servings.

# ⊡ PICKLED CUCUMBERS

*4 large cucumbers*
*2 tablespoons salt*
*1 cup white vinegar*
*¼ cup sugar*
*½ teaspoon white pepper*
*2 tablespoons snipped fresh dill or*
  *parsley*

1. Scrub cucumbers with vegetable brush; wipe dry with paper towels. Do not peel. Cut cucumbers into very thin slices.
2. In medium bowl, lightly toss cucumbers with salt. Cover with plate, and weight down with heavy can. Let stand at room temperature 2 hours.
3. Drain cucumbers well; pat dry with paper towels. Place in medium bowl.
4. In small bowl, combine vinegar, sugar, and pepper; mix well. Pour over cucumber slices. Refrigerate, covered, until well chilled—overnight.
5. To serve: Drain cucumber slices well. Turn out into serving dish. Sprinkle with dill.
Makes 8 to 10 servings.

# ⊡ DELICATESSEN DELUXE POTATO SALAD

*6 lb medium potatoes*

**DRESSING:**

*3 cups mayonnaise or cooked salad*
  *dressing*
*1½ cups finely chopped onion*
*1½ cups cubed pared cucumber*
*1 cup coarsely chopped green pepper*
*1 can (4 oz) pimientos, drained and*
  *diced*
*⅔ cup sliced sweet gherkins*
*⅓ cup pickle juice*
*3 tablespoons cider vinegar*
*2 tablespoons salt*

*Celery leaves*
*Cherry tomatoes*
*Ripe olives*

1. In boiling salted water to cover, cook unpeeled potatoes, covered, just until tender—about 35 to 40 minutes. Drain; refrigerate until cold.
2. Make Dressing: In large bowl, combine mayonnaise, onion, cucumber, green pepper, pimientos, gherkins, pickle juice, vinegar, and salt; mix well.
3. Peel potatoes; cut into 1-inch cubes. Add to dressing; toss until potatoes are well coated. Refrigerate, covered, until well chilled—several hours or overnight.
4. To serve: Garnish with celery leaves, cherry tomatoes, and ripe olives.
Makes 12 servings.

*Note*: For 6 servings, cut recipe in half; follow directions above.

# ✠ GERMAN POTATO SALAD

*3½ lb medium potatoes*
*1 cup chopped onion*
*½ lb bacon, diced*
*2 tablespoons flour*
*¼ cup sugar*
*2 tablespoons butter or margarine*
*1½ teaspoons salt*
*¼ teaspoon pepper*
*½ cup cider vinegar*
*1 cup water*
*1 cup sour cream*
*Chopped parsley*

1. Cook potatoes, covered in boiling salted water to cover, 35 to 40 minutes, until fork-tender. Peel warm potatoes, and slice; add onion.
2. In large skillet, cook bacon; remove from heat. Lift out with slotted spoon, and set aside. Pour off fat; return ¼ cup to skillet.
3. Stir flour into fat in skillet. Add sugar, butter, salt, pepper, vinegar, and water. Bring to boiling, stirring. Remove from heat; add sour cream.
4. Add potatoes, onion, and half of bacon; toss gently. Transfer to serving bowl; sprinkle with rest of bacon and parsley. Serve warm.
Makes 10 servings.

# ✠ FRENCH POTATO SALAD

*3 lb waxy or new potatoes*
*¼ cup wine vinegar*
*1½ teaspoons salt*
*1 teaspoon freshly ground pepper*
*3 tablespoons canned condensed con-*
  *sommé, undiluted (see Note)*
*⅓ cup dry white wine*
*1 tablespoon chopped fresh tarragon*
  *or 1 teaspoon dried tarragon leaves*
*2 teaspoons chopped fresh chervil or*
  *½ teaspoon dried chervil leaves*
*1½ tablespoons chopped parsley*
*1 tablespoon chopped chives*
*¾ cup salad or olive oil*

1. Cook potatoes, covered, in enough boiling salted water to cover, 30 minutes, or just until fork-tender.
2. Drain; peel, and slice while still warm into ¼-inch-thick slices into salad bowl.
3. In jar with tight-fitting lid, combine vinegar and rest of ingredients; shake to mix well.
4. Pour over warm potatoes; toss gently to coat with liquid. Serve warm, or let cool and refrigerate. Before serving, toss gently again.
Makes 8 servings.

*Note*: Remaining consommé may be reserved for use in soup or gravy.

# ✠ SPRING SALAD

*2 cups creamy cottage cheese*
*½ cup coarsely grated carrot*
*¼ cup thinly sliced green onion*
*½ cup coarsely chopped green pepper*
*6 radishes, sliced very thin*
*Dash ground pepper*
*Dash fresh or dried dill*
*1 tablespoon prepared oil-and-vine-*
  *gar dressing*

Combine all ingredients; toss lightly to mix well. Refrigerate until serving.
Makes about 3 cups.

# ✣ NEW-POTATO-AND-ZUCCHINI SALAD

**DRESSING:**

¼ cup tarragon vinegar
1½ teaspoons salt
1 teaspoon pepper
¼ cup canned condensed consommé,
    undiluted
⅓ cup dry white wine
1½ tablespoons chopped fresh tarra-
    gon or 1½ teaspoons dried tarragon
    leaves
2 tablespoons chopped fresh chives or
    dill
¾ cup salad or olive oil

2 lb very small new potatoes
Boiling water
1 teaspoon salt
1 lb zucchini (3 medium)
2 tablespoons salad or olive oil

1. Make Dressing: In jar with tight-fitting lid, combine vinegar and rest of dressing ingredients; shake
to mix well.
2. Scrub potatoes. Place in medium saucepan; add
boiling water to cover, along with salt. Bring to boiling; boil gently, covered, 30 minutes, or just until
fork-tender.
3. Drain, then peel potatoes; while still warm, toss
with dressing in large bowl until well coated.
4. Wash zucchini; cut into ⅓-inch-thick slices.
5. In oil in medium skillet, sauté zucchini, turning
occasionally, until just tender—about 3 minutes; cool
slightly. Add to potato mixture; toss gently.
6. Serve salad warm, or let cool and refrigerate, tossing several times in marinade. Before serving, toss
gently again.
Makes 8 servings.

*Note*: Remaining consommé may be reserved for use
in soup or gravy.

# ✣ MARINATED SLICED TOMATOES

4 large tomatoes (1½ to 2 lb)
¼ cup salad oil
1 tablespoon lemon juice
½ teaspoon minced garlic
½ teaspoon salt
1½ teaspoons dried basil leaves or
    1½ tablespoons chopped fresh basil
Chopped parsley

1. Peel and slice tomatoes. Arrange in shallow dish.
2. Combine oil, lemon juice, garlic, salt, and basil;
mix well.
3. Pour over tomatoes. Refrigerate, covered, several
hours, until well chilled. Serve sprinkled with
chopped parsley.
Makes 6 servings.

# ❖ ROSEDALE PASTA SALAD BOWL

## DRESSING:

½ cup olive or salad oil
¼ cup lemon juice
1 teaspoon salt
¼ teaspoon black pepper
⅛ teaspoon crushed red pepper flakes
2 cloves garlic, crushed
2 tablespoons chopped fresh chives
1 tablespoon chopped fresh basil or 1 teaspoon dried basil leaves
2 teaspoons snipped fresh dill or ½ teaspoon dried dill

1 pkg (8 oz) spirelle pasta or other similar pasta

## VEGETABLES:

2 tablespoons olive or salad oil
½ lb broccoli, cut into 1½-inch flowerets
½ red pepper, cut into ¼-inch-wide strips
¼ lb whole fresh snow-pea pods, ends trimmed

½ pint cherry tomatoes, washed, and stems removed
¼ cup chopped parsley

1. Make Dressing: In jar with tight-fitting lid, combine oil, lemon juice, salt, black pepper, red pepper, garlic, chives, basil, and dill; shake until well combined.
2. Cook spirelle as package label directs; drain. Turn out into large salad bowl. Add dressing; toss to combine.
3. Prepare vegetables: in oil in a large skillet, toss broccoli flowerets and red-pepper strips; stir-fry 5 minutes, or until vegetables are just crisp. Add pea pods; cook 1 minute. Cook vegetables, covered, 1 to 2 minutes. Do not overcook. Cool completely.
4. In salad bowl, lightly toss spirelle, vegetables, cherry tomatoes, and parsley until well coated with dressing. Refrigerate several hours, or until well chilled. Toss well before serving.
Makes 6 servings.

# ❖ TUNA-AND-MACARONI SALAD

1 pkg (8 oz) elbow macaroni
1 cup Italian-style dressing
1 tablespoon prepared mustard
1 small zucchini, sliced into thin rounds
1 cup cherry tomatoes, halved
½ cup diced green pepper
¼ cup coarsely chopped green onion
1 teaspoon salt
⅛ teaspoon pepper
2 cans (7-oz size) solid-pack tuna, drained
Chicory
Chopped parsley

1. Cook macaroni as package label directs. Drain; rinse with cold water.
2. In large bowl, combine Italian-style dressing and mustard. Add zucchini, tomatoes, green pepper, green onion, salt, pepper, tuna in large pieces, and macaroni; toss to mix well. Turn out into salad bowl.
3. Refrigerate, covered, until well chilled—about 4 hours.
4. Just before serving, garnish with chicory and parsley.
Makes 8 servings.

## ❖ FRESH ASPARAGUS IN ASPIC

### FRESH ASPARAGUS:

2½ lb asparagus
Boiling water
1½ teaspoons salt

### TARRAGON ASPIC:

1½ env unflavored gelatine
½ cup water
1½ cups chicken broth
½ cup dry white wine
2 tablespoons tarragon vinegar
1 teaspoon dried tarragon leaves
½ teaspoon salt

2 hard-cooked eggs
Lemon Mayonnaise, page 453

1. Break or cut off tough ends of asparagus, leaving asparagus as long as possible. Wash well under cold running water. If asparagus is sandy, scrub with brush. With vegetable peeler, scrape skin and scales from lower portion of stalks.
2. Bunch stalks together; tie with string. Place upright in deep saucepan. Add boiling water (about 1 inch deep) and 1½ teaspoons salt.
3. Return to boiling; cook, covered, 12 to 15 minutes. Pierce lower part of stalks with fork to see if tender. Be sure not to overcook.
4. Drain asparagus. Chill in ice water 30 minutes. Drain well.
5. Make Tarragon Aspic: Sprinkle gelatine over water to soften. In medium saucepan, combine chicken broth, wine, vinegar, tarragon, salt, and softened gelatine.
6. Over medium heat, stir constantly until mixture starts to boil. Remove from heat.
7. Strain gelatine mixture into medium bowl; discard tarragon.
8. Place bowl with gelatine mixture in large bowl filled with ice water. Chill, stirring occasionally, until consistency of unbeaten egg white—about 20 minutes.
9. To assemble: Remove string from asparagus. Divide asparagus into three even parts. Arrange one layer on chilled plate; spoon ½ cup aspic over top. Repeat twice; spoon any remaining aspic around edge. Refrigerate at least 1 hour, or until firm.
10. Chop whites, and put yolks through sieve. Sprinkle egg yolk and chopped white around edge. Serve with Lemon Mayonnaise.
Makes 6 servings.

# CREAMY DRESSINGS

Add a personal touch to your salad—make your own mayonnaise. It's not tricky to make if you follow our directions. The oil is beaten into the vinegar *drop by drop* to form a permanent emulsion. A boiled or cooked salad dressing is similar to mayonnaise but is easier and less expensive to make. A white sauce forms the base rather than the high proportion of oil as in mayonnaise.

# ✥ MAYONNAISE

2 egg yolks or 1 whole egg
1 teaspoon salt
Dash ground red pepper
1 cup salad or olive oil
2 tablespoons lemon juice or vinegar

1. Have all ingredients at room temperature. In small bowl, with wire whisk, with portable electric mixer at medium speed, or in blender, beat or blend egg yolks, salt, and red pepper until thick and lemon-colored.
2. Add ¼ cup oil, one drop at a time, beating or blending until thick.
3. Gradually add 1 tablespoon lemon juice, beating or blending after each addition. Then add ½ cup oil, in steady stream, beating or blending constantly.
4. Slowly add remaining lemon juice and then remaining oil, beating or blending constantly.
5. Refrigerate, covered, until ready to use. Makes 1¼ cups.
Note: Mayonnaise can be made easily and quickly in food processor; see our recipe for Processor Mayonnaise (page 208).
Lemon Mayonnaise: In small bowl, combine ⅓ cup mayonnaise, 1 tablespoon cream, and 1 teaspoon lemon juice. Stir until well blended. Refrigerate. Makes ⅓ cup.

# ✥ COOKED SALAD DRESSING

1 tablespoon flour
2 tablespoons sugar
1 teaspoon salt
1¼ cups milk
3 egg yolks, slightly beaten
¼ cup cider vinegar
1 tablespoon prepared mustard
2 tablespoons butter or margarine

1. In small heavy saucepan, stir flour with sugar and salt. With wire whisk, gradually stir in milk.
2. Cook, stirring, over medium heat until mixture starts to boil. Boil 1 minute; remove from heat.
3. Gradually stir hot flour-milk mixture, a little at a time, into beaten egg yolks in small bowl. Pour back into saucepan.
4. Add vinegar and prepared mustard. Cook, stirring constantly, until mixture starts to boil. Remove from heat. Stir in butter. Cool; then refrigerate, covered. Makes 1½ cups.

# ✥ RUSSIAN DRESSING

½ cup mayonnaise or cooked salad dressing
1 tablespoon chili sauce
2 tablespoons milk
2 tablespoons finely chopped stuffed olives
1 tablespoon finely chopped onion
1 tablespoon finely chopped green pepper
2 tablespoons lemon juice
¼ teaspoon salt
1 tablespoon prepared horseradish

1. In small bowl, combine mayonnaise with rest of ingredients; mix well.
2. Refrigerate, covered, until ready to use. Nice to use on chef's salads.
Makes ¾ cup.

# ⚙ CREAMY BLUE CHEESE OR ROQUEFORT SALAD DRESSING

¼ lb Roquefort cheese
1 cup sour cream
¼ cup mayonnaise or cooked salad
  dressing
¼ cup sherry
¼ cup wine vinegar
1 tablespoon grated onion
½ teaspoon salt
½ teaspoon garlic salt
¼ teaspoon paprika
Generous sprinkling pepper

1. Coarsely crumble cheese into medium bowl. Add remaining ingredients, stirring until well blended.
2. Refrigerate, covered, until well chilled—at least 1 hour. Serve on favorite combination of crisp greens, garnished with tomato and avocado slices if desired. Makes about 2 cups.

# ⚙ SOUR-CREAM DRESSING FOR VEGETABLES AND SALAD GREENS

1 tablespoon flour
1 tablespoon sugar
1½ teaspoons salt
½ teaspoon dry mustard
2 tablespoons salad oil
½ cup water
3 tablespoons cider vinegar
1 egg, slightly beaten
½ teaspoon celery seed
¼ cup sour cream

1. In top of double boiler, combine flour, sugar, salt, mustard, oil, and water. Bring to boiling, stirring, over medium heat. Mixture will be smooth and thickened.
2. In small bowl, gradually stir vinegar into egg; then stir in hot mixture, a little at a time.
3. Pour back into double-boiler top; cook, stirring, over hot, not boiling, water (water should not touch bottom of top part) until thickened—about 5 minutes. Remove from heat.
4. Stir in celery seed and sour cream. Refrigerate, covered, until ready to use.
Makes 1 cup.

# ⚙ SOUR-CREAM DRESSING FOR FRUIT

½ cup mayonnaise or cooked salad
  dressing
½ cup sour cream
2 tablespoons lemon juice
⅓ cup apricot preserves
Dash salt

1. In small bowl, combine all ingredients.
2. Refrigerate until well chilled.
Makes about 1 cup.

# ❖ THOUSAND ISLAND DRESSING

2 tablespoons chopped pickle
2 tablespoons finely chopped green pepper
2 tablespoons chopped red pepper or pimiento
2 tablespoons finely chopped onion
1 cup mayonnaise or cooked salad dressing
2 tablespoons chili sauce
2 tablespoons milk

1. Combine all ingredients in small bowl; stir until well blended.
2. Refrigerate, covered, at least 2 hours before serving. Good on lettuce wedges.
Makes 1¾ cups.

# ❖ HONEY-LIME DRESSING

1 cup mayonnaise or cooked salad dressing
½ cup honey
1 cup heavy cream, whipped
¼ cup lime juice

1. In small bowl, combine all ingredients well.
2. Refrigerate, covered, until ready to use. Delicious on fruit salad.
Makes 2½ cups.

# ❖ GREEN MAYONNAISE

1 cup mayonnaise or cooked salad dressing
2 tablespoons lemon juice
2 tablespoons chopped parsley
1 tablespoon chopped chives
1 tablespoon chopped watercress

1. In small bowl, combine mayonnaise, lemon juice, parsley, chives, and watercress; mix well.
2. Refrigerate, covered, overnight. Good on cold poached fish.
Makes 1¼ cups.

# ❖ AVOCADO DRESSING

1 medium-size ripe avocado (¾ lb)
1 cup mayonnaise
¼ cup coarsely chopped green onion
¼ cup coarsely chopped green pepper
2 tablespoons lemon juice
½ teaspoon salt
Few drops Tabasco
Dash pepper

1. Peel avocado, and cut into chunks. Blend in blender with rest of ingredients.
2. Refrigerate several hours to chill well. Good with fruit or vegetable salads.
Makes 2¼ cups.

# ❖ YOGURT-AND-BLUE-CHEESE DRESSING

*1 container (8 oz) yogurt*
*¼ cup crumbled blue cheese*

1. In small bowl, combine yogurt and blue cheese; mix well.
2. Refrigerate, covered, until serving. Use on salad greens.
Makes 1 cup.

# ❖ BASIC FRENCH OR OIL AND VINEGAR DRESSING

*⅓ cup vinegar (see Note) or lemon*
  *juice*
*⅔ cup salad or olive oil*
*1½ teaspoons salt*
*¼ teaspoon pepper*
*1 teaspoon sugar (optional)*
*1 clove garlic (optional)*

1. Combine all ingredients in jar with tight-fitting lid; shake vigorously to blend.
2. Refrigerate, covered, at least 2 hours before using.
3. Remove garlic; shake just before using.
Makes 1 cup.

*Note*: You may use white, cider, wine, or herb-flavored vinegar.

# ❖ SPECIAL FRENCH DRESSING

*⅔ cup salad or olive oil*
*⅓ cup cider vinegar*
*2 teaspoons salt*
*⅛ teaspoon pepper*
*¼ teaspoon paprika*
*Dash celery salt*
*1 teaspoon sugar*
*1½ teaspoons chili sauce*
*1½ teaspoons catsup*
*½ teaspoon prepared mustard*
*1 tablespoon lemon juice*
*1¼ teaspoons Worcestershire sauce*
*½ teaspoon prepared horseradish*
*Dash Tabasco*
*1 clove garlic*

1. Combine all ingredients, except garlic, in medium bowl. With wire whisk, beat until smooth and well blended.
2. Turn out into jar with tight-fitting lid. Add garlic. Refrigerate several hours. Before serving, shake well; remove garlic. Refrigerate leftover dressing for later use.
Makes 1⅓ cups.

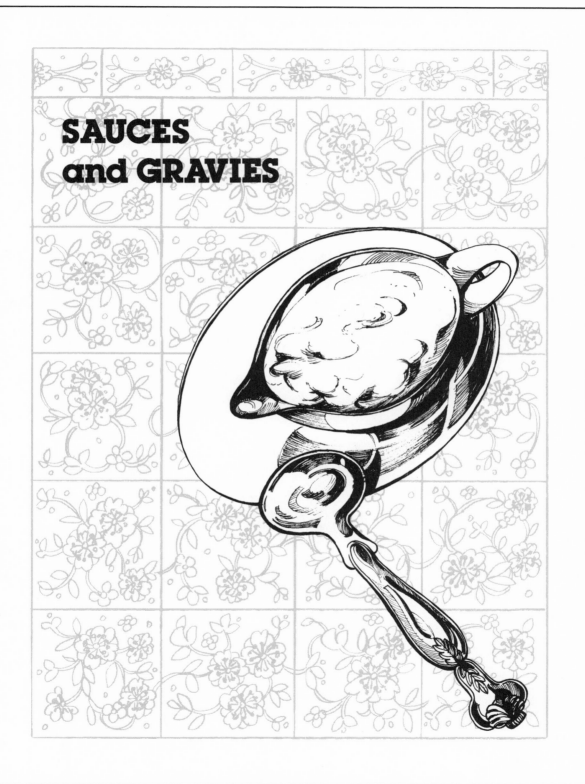

# SAUCES
# and GRAVIES

✦ **S**auces and gravies are frequently shunned by the weight-conscious and by many of us whose appetites have adjusted to lighter eating. But sauces too have changed their styles. Many use unusual ingredients, like yogurt; many are not thickened with starch or flour; and many are seasoned with vegetables puréed in a blender or food proces- sor. Though we may not use sauces as fre- quently, knowing how to make them satiny- smooth and perfectly seasoned is a worthwhile indulgence. And for the times we splurge on a roast, a really good gravy is thoroughly justified. In this chapter we give you a collection of our favorites and step-by- step directions for perfect gravy.

# SAUCES

## ✦ BASIC WHITE SAUCE

¼ cup butter or margarine
¼ cup all-purpose flour
½ teaspoon salt
⅛ teaspoon pepper
2 cups milk or light cream

1. In medium saucepan, slowly heat butter just until melted and golden, not browned, stirring all the while. Remove from heat.
2. Add flour, salt, and pepper; stir until smooth. Add milk, a small amount at a time, stirring after each addition. Return to heat.
3. Over medium heat, bring to boiling, stirring con- stantly. Reduce heat; simmer 3 minutes.
Makes 2 cups.

*Thin White Sauce*: Reduce butter and flour to 2 ta- blespoons each. Proceed as in Basic White Sauce. Use for soups.

*Mornay Sauce*: Add ½ cup grated natural Swiss cheese to Basic White Sauce. Stir, over low heat, just until cheese is melted.

### ONION SAUCE

*Basic White Sauce*
*1½ cups finely chopped onion*
*2 tablespoons butter*
*¼ cup grated Parmesan cheese*
*Dash ground red pepper*

1. Make Basic White Sauce.
2. In medium skillet, sauté onion in butter until ten- der but not brown—about 5 minutes. Add to Basic White Sauce, along with Parmesan cheese and ground red pepper. Cook over low heat, stirring, until cheese is melted. Serve with hamburgers or on green vegetables.
Makes 2½ cups.

# ❖ BASIC BROWN SAUCE

2 tablespoons butter
¼ cup chopped carrot
¼ cup chopped onion
2 mushrooms, washed and chopped
½ clove garlic, crushed
2 tablespoons flour
1 can (10½ oz) beef broth, plus water
    to make 2 cups
2 tablespoons tomato sauce
⅛ teaspoon salt
¼ teaspoon pepper
1 stalk celery, quartered
½ bay leaf

1. In hot butter in medium saucepan, sauté carrot, onion, mushrooms, and garlic, stirring, until onion is golden—about 5 minutes.
2. Remove from heat; add flour, stirring until smooth. Add beef broth, tomato sauce, salt, pepper, celery, and bay leaf.
3. Bring to boiling, stirring occasionally; reduce heat, and simmer until sauce is reduced by half. Remove and discard celery and bay leaf. Serve, warm, over meat.
Makes about 1 cup.

# ❖ BÉARNAISE SAUCE

¼ cup tarragon vinegar
¼ cup dry white wine
2 tablespoons finely chopped fresh
    tarragon or 2 teaspoons dried tarra-
    gon leaves
1 tablespoon chopped shallot or
    onion
⅛ teaspoon pepper
1 tablespoon chopped parsley
3 egg yolks
½ cup butter or margarine
1 tablespoon chopped fresh tarragon
    or parsley

1. In small saucepan, combine vinegar, wine, tarragon, shallot, pepper, and parsley; bring to boiling, stirring. Reduce heat, and simmer, uncovered, to reduce to ¼ cup—about 8 minutes. Strain into measuring cup, pressing herbs to extract juice.
2. In top of double boiler, with wire whisk, beat egg yolks with 2 tablespoons tarragon liquid just until blended. Cook over hot, not boiling, water, stirring constantly with whisk until mixture begins to thicken—about 1 minute.
3. Add butter, 1 tablespoon at a time, beating continuously after each addition until butter is melted, before adding next piece of butter (takes about 5 minutes). Hot water in base should not touch bottom of pan above; water should not be allowed to boil. If it should start to bubble, add a little cool water at once. Sauce curdles easily over high heat.
4. Remove double-boiler top from hot water. Using wire whisk, slowly beat in 2 more tablespoons tarragon liquid. Add chopped tarragon. Serve warm with beef.
Makes 1 cup.

# ❖ BORDELAISE SAUCE

¼ cup butter or margarine
2 shallots, finely chopped
2 cloves garlic, finely chopped
2 slices onion
2 slices carrot
2 sprigs parsley
10 whole black peppercorns
2 whole cloves
2 bay leaves
3 tablespoons flour
1 can (10½ oz) condensed beef broth,
    undiluted
1 cup red Burgundy
¼ teaspoon salt
⅛ teaspoon pepper
2 tablespoons finely chopped parsley

1. In hot butter in medium skillet, sauté shallots, garlic, onion, carrot, parsley, peppercorns, cloves, and bay leaves until onion is golden—about 3 minutes.
2. Remove from heat; stir in flour smoothly. Cook, stirring, over very low heat, until flour is lightly browned—about 5 minutes. Remove from heat.
3. Stir beef broth and ¾ cup Bugundy into flour mixture.
4. Over medium heat, bring just to boiling, stirring constantly. Reduce heat; simmer, uncovered, 10 minutes, stirring occasionally.
5. Strain sauce, discarding vegetables and spices. Return sauce to skillet. Add salt, pepper, parsley, and remaining ¼ cup Burgundy; reheat gently—do not boil.
6. Serve with fillet of beef, steak, or hamburger.
Makes about 2 cups.

# ❖ HOLLANDAISE SAUCE

3 egg yolks
2 tablespoons cold water
½ cup butter, cut into 8 pieces
2 tablespoons lemon juice
⅛ teaspoon salt
Dash ground red pepper

1. In top of double boiler, with wire whisk, beat egg yolks with water just until blended. Cook over hot, not boiling, water, stirring constantly with whisk, until mixture begins to thicken—about 1 minute.
2. Add butter, 1 piece at a time, beating continuously after each addition until butter is melted, before adding next piece of butter (takes about 5 minutes in all). Hot water in double-boiler base should not touch bottom of pan above; water should not be allowed to boil. (If it should start to bubble, add a little cold water at once to cool it.) Sauce curdles easily over high heat.
3. Remove double-boiler top from hot water. Using wire whisk, slowly beat in lemon juice, then salt and red pepper, beating just until sauce becomes as thick as mayonnaise. To keep warm, add cold water to hot water in bottom of double boiler, to make lukewarm; replace sauce, covered, over water, not heat. Hollandaise is the classic sauce to serve over asparagus or broccoli.
Makes 1 cup.

*Note*: See page 208 for making this sauce in food processor.

# ❖ BARBECUE SAUCE, CALIFORNIA-STYLE

⅓ cup cider vinegar
¼ cup chili sauce
1 can (8 oz) tomato sauce
¼ cup chopped onion
2 tablespoons brown sugar
1 tablespoon Worcestershire sauce
1 teaspoon dry mustard

In medium saucepan, combine all of sauce ingredients. Bring to boiling; reduce heat, and simmer, uncovered and stirring occasionally, 30 minutes. Serve with chicken, spareribs, hamburgers, or steak. Makes 1⅓ cups.

# ❖ BROWNED BUTTER SAUCE

½ cup butter
¼ cup beef broth
¼ cup lemon juice
Dash salt

1. In small saucepan, over low heat, brown butter; cool to room temperature.
2. Stir in beef broth, lemon juice, and salt. Cook, over low heat just until warmed. Serve with shrimp or lobster, or pour over cauliflower. Makes 1 cup.

# ❖ CHUTNEY SAUCE

½ cup light raisins
⅓ cup currant jelly
1 tablespoon coarsely grated orange
  peel
½ cup water
1 cup orange juice
1 cup chutney, undrained
¼ cup light-brown sugar, packed
1 tablespoon cornstarch
Dash salt
Dash ground cinnamon
4 thin slices orange, unpeeled

1. In medium saucepan, combine raisins, currant jelly, orange peel, water, orange juice, and chutney; bring to boiling.
2. Combine brown sugar, cornstarch, salt, and cinnamon; mix well. Stir into chutney mixture, along with orange slices.
3. Cook, stirring, until mixture is thickened and clear —5 to 10 minutes. Delicious with chicken, lamb, or beef. Makes 3 cups.

# ❖ CURRY SAUCE

½ cup onion, finely chopped
1 clove garlic, minced
2 tablespoons butter or margarine
1½ teaspoons curry powder
½ teaspoon ground ginger
2 teaspoons all-purpose flour
¼ teaspoon salt
Dash pepper
1 cup chicken broth
1 cup plain yogurt

1. In medium saucepan, sauté onion and garlic in butter until soft but not brown.
2. Stir in curry powder, ginger, flour, salt, and pepper. Cook, stirring, for 1 minute.
3. Add chicken broth, and bring to boiling, stirring constantly. Reduce heat, and simmer, covered, for 10 minutes.
4. Stir in yogurt and continue cooking just until heated through. Serve with chicken or vegetables, like cauliflower and broccoli. Makes 4 cups.

# ✦ EGG SAUCE

3 tablespoons butter or margarine
1 tablespoons chopped green or yellow onion
3 tablespoons flour
1¼ teaspoons salt
2½ cups milk
4 chopped hard-cooked eggs
4 teaspoons snipped fresh dill or 2 tablespoons chopped parsley
⅛ teaspoon Tabasco

1. In hot butter in medium saucepan, sauté onion until tender but not brown—about 5 minutes. Remove from heat.
2. Stir in flour and salt until well blended. Gradually stir in milk. Bring to boiling, stirring constantly; reduce heat, and simmer 1 minute.
3. Stir in eggs, dill, and Tabasco. Keep warm. Serve with salmon or tuna, or on toast.
Makes 3 cups.

# ✦ GARLIC SAUCE

¼ cup pine nuts
2 cloves garlic, crushed
2 teaspoons butter or margarine
1 cup plain yogurt

1. In small saucepan, sauté pine nuts and garlic in butter until golden.
2. Stir in yogurt and pour immediately into small serving bowl. Serve with lamb.
Makes 1 cup.

# ✦ MAÎTRE D'HÔTEL BUTTER SAUCE

¼ cup butter or margarine, melted
1 tablespoon lemon juice
½ teaspoon salt
1 tablespoon finely chopped parsley

1. Melt butter, stirring, in small skillet over low heat.
2. Remove from heat. Then stir in remaining ingredients. Serve hot or cold with London broil, lamb chops, or steaks.
Makes ⅓ cup.

# ✦ MUSTARD SAUCE

2 tablespoons butter or margarine
1½ tablespoons flour
½ teaspoon salt
⅛ teaspoon pepper
1 cup milk
¼ cup prepared mustard
1 tablespoon sugar
1 tablespoon cider vinegar
1 teaspoon Worcestershire sauce

1. Melt butter in small saucepan; remove from heat. Stir in flour, salt, and pepper until smooth. Stir in milk. Bring to boiling over medium heat, stirring, until thick.
2. Gradually stir in mustard, sugar, vinegar, and Worcestershire. Reduce heat, and simmer mixture, stirring, 2 minutes. Serve warm with pork, ham, or beef.
Makes about 1¼ cups.

# ❖ NEWBURG SAUCE

3 tablespoons butter or margarine
2 tablespoons flour
¼ teaspoon salt
⅛ teaspoon paprika
¾ cup light cream
½ cup fish stock (see Note)
2 egg yolks
2 tablespoons dry sherry

1. Melt butter in medium saucepan. Remove from heat; stir in flour, salt, and paprika until blended. Gradually stir in cream and fish stock.
2. Cook, over medium heat and stirring constantly, until mixture thickens and comes to boiling; boil 1 minute. Remove from heat.
3. In medium bowl, beat egg yolks well. Stir in about ½ cup hot sauce; then stir egg-yolk mixture into sauce in saucepan. Add sherry.
4. Cook over low heat, stirring, until heated through. Do not boil.
Makes 1½ cups.

*Note*: Use liquid from cooking fish or bottled clam broth.

# ❖ PIQUANT DILL SAUCE

1½ tablespoons butter or margarine
1½ teaspoons cornstarch
½ cup cold water
⅓ cup lemon juice
1 tablespoon snipped fresh dill or 1
    teaspoon dried dill
¼ teaspoon salt
⅛ teaspoon dried chervil leaves
Dash ground red pepper
3 thin slices lemon, unpeeled and cut
    into quarters

1. Melt butter in small saucepan; remove from heat. Combine cornstarch and cold water. Stir into butter.
2. Add lemon juice, dill, salt, chervil, and red pepper. Bring just to boiling, stirring. Remove from heat. Add lemon slices. Delicious with fish, lamb, chicken, or beef.
Makes ⅔ cup.

# ❖ RÉMOULADE SAUCE

1 cup mayonnaise
1 tablespoon chopped onion
1 tablespoon chopped parsley
1 tablespoon chopped celery
2 tablespoons Dijon mustard
1 tablespoon prepared horseradish
1 teaspoon paprika
½ teaspoon salt
Dash Tabasco
¼ cup salad oil
1 tablespoon vinegar
½ teaspoon Worcestershire sauce

1. Combine all ingredients in small bowl; mix until well blended.
2. Refrigerate several hours or overnight.
3. Serve with cold boiled shrimp, crabmeat, lobster, or tomatoes.
Makes 1½ cups.

# ✤ SAUCE VERTE

2 cups mayonnaise
⅔ cup chopped parsley sprigs (no stems)
⅔ cup chopped watercress (no stems)
¼ cup capers, drained
¼ cup tarragon vinegar
2 tablespoons chopped chives

1. Combine all ingredients in medium bowl, blender, or food processor. At high speed, beat with portable electric beater or blend until smooth.
2. Turn out into serving bowl. Refrigerate, covered, at least 2 hours. Serve with fish.
Makes about 2½ cups.

# ✤ SEAFOOD-COCKTAIL SAUCE

½ cup chili sauce
1 tablespoon prepared horseradish
1 tablespoon lemon juice
2 teaspoons Worcestershire sauce
¼ teaspoon salt
Dash ground red pepper

1. In small bowl, combine all ingredients; mix well. Refrigerate, covered, at least 3 hours.
2. Serve with cold boiled shrimp, crabmeat, or lobster.
Makes ⅔ cup.

# ✤ SOUR-CREAM SAUCE

½ cup mayonnaise
½ cup sour cream
2 tablespoons prepared horseradish
⅛ teaspoon salt

1. In small bowl, combine all ingredients; mix well.
2. Refrigerate, covered, until serving. Serve with cold seafood or beef.
Makes 1 cup.

# ✤ SWISS YOGURT SAUCE

2 tablespoons butter
2 tablespoons all-purpose flour
¾ cup milk
1 cup plain yogurt
1 teaspoon prepared Dijon-style mustard
¼ teaspoon salt
Dash pepper
1 cup grated Swiss cheese

1. Melt butter in medium saucepan; remove from heat, and stir in flour until well combined.
2. Add milk, yogurt, mustard, salt, and pepper; cook, stirring, over low heat until thickened.
3. Add cheese and simmer, stirring, just until cheese is melted. Serve with chicken, vegetables, or pasta.
Makes 2 cups.

# ❖ TARTAR SAUCE

*1 cup mayonnaise or cooked salad
   dressing*
*⅓ cup drained sweet-pickle relish*
*1 tablespoon lemon juice*
*1 tablespoon drained capers*
*1 tablespoon chopped parsley*
*1 teaspoon grated onion*
*⅛ teaspoon salt*

1. Combine all ingredients; mix well.
2. Refrigerate, covered, until well chilled—at least 2 hours. The classic accompaniment for fish.
Makes 1⅓ cups.

# ❖ VELOUTÉ SAUCE

*2 tablespoons butter*
*3 tablespoons all-purpose flour*
*¼ teaspoon salt*
*Dash pepper*
*1 can (13¾ oz) chicken broth*

1. In small saucepan, slowly heat butter, stirring, just until melted and golden, not browned. Remove from heat.
2. Add flour, salt, and pepper; stir until smooth. Cook, stirring, until slightly browned. Add chicken broth, a small amount at a time, stirring after each addition.
3. Over medium heat, bring to boiling, stirring constantly. Reduce heat; simmer 3 minutes. A delicate sauce to serve with chicken and veal or to use in casseroles.
Makes 1⅓ cups.

# ❖ WHITE WINE SAUCE

*1 cup dry white wine*
*2 shallots, chopped*
*1 tablespoon chopped fresh tarragon
   or ½ teaspoon dried tarragon leaves*
*½ cup heavy cream*
*¾ lb sweet butter*
*Juice of ½ lemon (1 tablespoon)*
*½ teaspoon salt*
*¼ teaspoon white pepper*

1. In medium saucepan, combine wine, shallots, and tarragon. Boil over moderately high heat to reduce to approximately ⅓ cup.
2. Add cream, and continue to reduce to ½ cup.
3. Lower heat, and whisk butter into mixture, 2 tablespoons at a time, being careful that mixture doesn't boil and doesn't get too cold (temperature must not change).
4. Add remaining ingredients. Taste, and adjust seasonings.
5. Strain; serve with fish.
Makes 1½ cups.

# GRAVIES

## ❖ BROWN GRAVY FOR ROAST BEEF

¼ cup meat drippings
3 tablespoons flour
1 can (10½ oz) condensed beef broth
½ teaspoon salt
Dash pepper

1. Lift roast from pan, and place on heated platter. Left stand 20 minutes.
2. Pour off drippings in roasting pan. Skim fat from surface and discard. Return ¼ cup drippings to pan.
3. Stir in flour to make smooth mixture; brown it slightly over low heat, stirring to loosen any brown bits in pan.
4. Add water to beef broth to measure 2 cups; gradually stir into flour mixture; add salt and pepper.
5. Bring to boiling, stirring gravy until smooth, and bubbly.
Makes 2 cups.

## ❖ BURGUNDY GRAVY FOR ROAST BEEF

6 tablespoons roast-beef drippings
¼ cup all-purpose flour
½ teaspoon salt
Dash pepper
2 cans (10½-oz size) condensed beef broth, undiluted
½ cup red Burgundy

1. Return the 6 tablespoons reserved drippings to roasting pan. Stir in flour, salt, and pepper to make a smooth mixture.
2. Gradually add beef broth and Burgundy to flour mixture, stirring until it is smooth and browned bits in pan are dissolved.
3. Bring to boiling, stirring. Reduce heat, and simmer, stirring, 5 minutes longer. Taste, and add more salt and pepper if necessary.
Makes 3 cups.

## ❖ CHICKEN GRAVY

3 tablespoons roast-chicken drippings
3 tablespoons flour
1½ cups condensed chicken broth, undiluted
½ teaspoon salt
⅛ teaspoon pepper
1 teaspoon coarsely chopped fresh marjoram leaves or ½ teaspoon dried marjoram leaves (optional)

1. Pour off drippings from roasting pan. Return 3 tablespoons drippings to pan.
2. Add flour; stir to make smooth paste. Gradually stir in broth; add rest of ingredients.
3. Bring to boiling, stirring. Mixture will be thickened and smooth. Simmer, stirring, 1 minute longer. Serve hot with roast chicken.
Makes 1½ cups.

# ❖ GIBLET GRAVY FOR ROAST TURKEY

*Turkey giblets and neck, washed*
*3 cups water*
*1 celery stalk, cup up*
*1 medium onion, peeled and quar-*
  *tered*
*1 medium carrot, pared and cut up*
*1 teaspoon salt*
*4 whole black peppercorns*
*1 bay leaf*
*1 can (10¾ oz) condensed chicken*
  *broth, undiluted*
*⅓ cup flour*

1. Refrigerate liver until ready to use.
2. Place rest of giblets and neck in 2-quart saucepan. Add water, celery, onion, carrot, salt, peppercorns, and bay leaf.
3. Bring to boiling; reduce heat, and simmer, covered, 2½ hours, or until giblets are tender. Add liver; simmer 15 minutes longer. Discard neck. Remove giblets from broth, and chop coarsely. Set aside.
4. Strain cooking broth, pressing vegetables through sieve with broth. Measure broth; add enough undiluted canned broth to make 2½ cups. Set aside.
5. When turkey has been removed from roasting pan, pour drippings into 1-cup measure. Skim fat from surface, and discard. Return ⅓ cup drippings to roasting pan.
6. Stir in flour until smooth. Stir, over very low heat, to brown flour slightly. Remove from heat. Gradually stir in broth.
7. Bring to boiling, stirring; reduce heat, and simmer, stirring, 5 minutes, or until gravy is thickened and smooth. Add giblets; simmer 5 minutes.
Makes about 3 cups.

# SOUPS

Soups served as a separate course before dinner are, in our lives today, reserved for formal occasions. But soups of the hearty variety can be a quick lunch or supper meal.

We suggest making up a batch of Hearty Beef and Vegetable Soup or Minestrone with Italian Sausage, or any other soup of your choice, to store in covered jars in the refrigerator, ready to heat and eat at the end of a busy day.

Most soups, like stews, improve in flavor the second day. Our Kapusta (Hot Cabbage Soup), for example, requires overnight refrigeration to "marry" the flavors.

In the summer, a well-chilled Senegalese Soup or Easy Raspberry Yogurt Soup will be a welcome refreshing lunch.

Most soups also freeze well, so they can be made ahead to use as needed.

# CURRIED AVOCADO SOUP

¼ cup butter or margarine
½ cup finely chopped onion
1¼ teaspoons curry powder
2 cans (13¾-oz size) clear chicken broth
1 cup heavy cream
2 ripe avocados (1½ lb)
1 tablespoon lemon juice
1½ teaspoons salt
Dash ground red pepper
½ cup sour cream

1. In hot butter in medium saucepan, sauté onion and curry powder, stirring occasionally, 5 minutes.
2. Add chicken broth; bring to boiling. Simmer, uncovered, 5 minutes. Slowly add heavy cream, stirring constantly; simmer, uncovered, 5 minutes more.
3. Peel avocados; remove pits. Cut flesh into chunks. Place half of avocado chunks and ½ cup hot chicken-broth mixture in blender. Blend, at high speed, 30 seconds, or until mixture is smooth. Turn out into small bowl. Repeat with remaining avocado and ½ cup broth.
4. Stir avocado mixture, lemon juice, salt, and red pepper into remaining broth mixture in saucepan; mix well.
5. Reheat gently—do not boil.
Serve in hot soup bowls. Garnish each serving with generous spoonful of sour cream.
Makes 8 to 10 servings.

# CHEDDAR-CHEESE SOUP

4 tablespoons butter or margarine
¼ cup finely chopped onion
½ cup finely chopped green pepper
½ cup finely chopped carrot
5 tablespoons flour
3 cans (10¾-oz size) condensed chicken broth, undiluted
3 cups grated sharp natural Cheddar cheese
2 cups milk
¼ teaspoon salt
Dash pepper
½ cup croutons (optional)
Chopped parsley

1. In hot butter in 3-quart saucepan, cook onion, green pepper, and carrot 10 minutes, stirring occasionally.
2. Remove from heat; stir in flour, and mix well. Cook 1 minute, stirring constantly.
3. Add broth to vegetable mixture. Bring to boiling, stirring constantly.
4. Gradually stir in cheese; cook over medium heat, stirring, until cheese has melted. Gradually add milk. Season with salt and pepper. Bring just to boiling, but do not boil.
5. Serve with croutons, and sprinkle with the parsley.
Makes 8 servings.

## ❖ LETTUCE-AND-GREEN-PEA SOUP

1 large head iceberg, romaine, or leaf
  lettuce, shredded (about 8 cups)
1 pkg (10 oz) frozen green peas
½ cup sliced green onion
1 can (13¾ oz) chicken broth
1½ cups light cream
1 teaspoon sugar
1 teaspoon salt
⅛ teaspoon ground nutmeg
Dash pepper
Thin lemon slices

1. In 4-quart kettle, combine shredded lettuce, peas, green onion, and chicken broth; bring to boiling over medium heat. Reduce heat, and simmer, covered, 10 minutes, or just until lettuce is soft.
2. In blender or food processor, place half of lettuce mixture and liquid; cover and blend at high speed 1 minute. Pour into bowl. Repeat with remaining lettuce mixture and liquid. Pour all lettuce mixture back into kettle.
3. Add cream, sugar, salt, nutmeg, and pepper to mixture in kettle. Cook over medium heat, stirring, until well blended.
4. Serve soup hot, or refrigerate until well chilled—several hours. Serve garnished with lemon slices.
Makes 8 servings.

## ❖ HOT CLAM BISQUE

¼ cup butter or margarine
3 slices onion
¼ cup flour
½ teaspoon salt
Dash pepper
1 cup milk
3 cups half-and-half or light cream
3 cans (6½-oz size) minced clams
⅓ cup dry sherry
Chopped parsley

1. In hot butter in large saucepan, sauté onion until golden—about 5 minutes. Remove from heat. Remove and discard onion.
2. Stir in flour until smooth. Add salt and pepper. Gradually stir in milk and half-and-half. Bring to boiling. Reduce heat, and simmer, stirring, until thickened—about 5 minutes.
3. Stir in clams and their liquid, and the sherry. Simmer gently, uncovered, until heated through—about 10 minutes. Serve hot with sprinkling of parsley over each serving.
Makes 8 servings.

## ❖ CREAM-OF-PUMPKIN SOUP

2 tablespoons butter or margarine
½ lb yellow onions, thinly sliced
½ tablespoon flour
1 can (10¾ oz) condensed chicken
  broth, undiluted
1 can (1 lb) pumpkin
2 cups milk
2 cups water
1 cup light cream
1 teaspoon salt
⅛ teaspoon pepper
¼ teaspoon ground ginger
⅛ teaspoon ground cinnamon

1. In hot butter in 6-quart Dutch oven, sauté onion, stirring occasionally, 10 minutes, or until tender. Remove from heat.
2. Stir flour into onion; gradually stir in chicken broth. Bring to boiling; reduce heat, and simmer, covered, 10 minutes.
3. Ladle mixture into blender. Blend, covered, at high speed 1 minute, or until completely smooth.
4. Return to Dutch oven; blend in pumpkin smoothly with wire whisk. Add milk, cream, water, and seasonings; beat with wire whisk to blend.
5. Heat soup slowly over medium heat just to boiling; reduce heat, and simmer, covered, 15 minutes, stirring occasionally. Serve hot.
Makes 6 to 8 servings.

# ✸ LOBSTER BISQUE

*1 small carrot, sliced*
*1 medium onion, quartered*
*1 teaspoon salt*
*2 whole black peppercorns*
*1 bay leaf*
*Pinch dried thyme leaves*
*1 sprig parsley*
*6 cups water*
*¾ cup dry white wine*
*3 (5-oz size) frozen rock-lobster tails*
  *(not thawed)*
*½ cup butter or margarine*
*3 tablespoons flour*
*2 cups heavy cream*
*1 to 2 tablespoons dry sherry (op-*
  *tional)*
*Paprika*

1. In 4-quart saucepan, combine carrot, onion, salt, peppercorns, bay leaf, thyme, parsley, and water.
2. Add wine and lobster tails; bring just to boiling. Reduce heat; simmer, covered, 5 minutes.
3. Remove lobster tails from cooking liquid; cool. Continue to cook liquid, uncovered, about 45 minutes, to reduce to about half of original volume. Strain; liquid should measure 2 cups.
4. Melt butter in same saucepan. Remove from heat; stir in flour to make smooth mixture.
5. Gradually add reserved cooking liquid, stirring until smooth. Bring to boiling, stirring; reduce heat; simmer 10 minutes, stirring occasionally.
6. Meanwhile, remove meat from shells; cut into very small pieces.
7. Gradually add cream, then lobster and sherry. Reheat gently—do not boil. Sprinkle with paprika before serving.
Makes 6 servings.

# HEARTY SOUPS

# ✸ FRENCH ONION SOUP

*⅓ cup bacon drippings or butter*
*5 medium-size yellow onions, thinly*
  *sliced*
*2 tablespoons flour*
*7 cups beef stock, or 3 cans (10½-oz*
  *size) condensed beef broth, diluted*
  *with 1 can water*
*¼ teaspoon pepper*
*⅓ cup dry sherry*
*6 slices Italian bread, 1 inch thick,*
  *toasted*
*6 slices Gruyère or Swiss cheese*
*¼ cup grated Parmesan cheese*

1. In heavy 5-quart saucepan or Dutch oven, heat bacon drippings. Add onion; sauté, stirring frequently, over low heat until golden-brown—about 20 minutes.
2. Stir in flour; cook, stirring, to brown flour slightly. Gradually add stock, stirring. Add pepper. Cook over low heat, covered, 30 minutes. Add sherry; taste for seasoning.
3. In each of 6 heat-proof bowls, place slice of toast. Cover each with slice of cheese; pour soup over top. Sprinkle each with Parmesan cheese. Broil, 6 inches from heat, just to melt cheese—about 10 minutes.
Makes 6 servings.

# ✦ BORSCHT

*3-lb fresh beef brisket*
*1 large marrowbone (3 lb), with marrow*
*4 teaspoons salt*
*2 quarts cold water*
*1 can (1 lb) tomatoes, undrained*
*1 medium onion, quartered*
*1 stalk celery, cut up*
*3 parsley sprigs*
*10 whole black peppercorns*
*2 bay leaves*
*¼ cup tomato purée*
*3 cups coarsely shredded cabbage*
*1½ cups thickly sliced pared carrot*
*1 cup chopped onion*
*2 potatoes, peeled and cubed*
*2 tablespoons snipped fresh dill or 3 teaspoons dried dillweed*
*¼ cup cider vinegar*
*2 tablespoons sugar*
*1 can (1 lb) julienne beets, undrained, or 1½ cups cooked fresh julienne beets*
*Sour cream*
*Snipped fresh dill or dillweed*

1. Day before: In 8-quart kettle, place beef, marrowbone, 3 teaspoons salt, and water. Bring to boiling; reduce heat, and simmer, covered, 1 hour. Add tomatoes, quartered onion, celery, parsley, peppercorns, bay leaves, and tomato purée; simmer, covered, 2 hours.
2. Remove from heat. Lift out beef. Discard marrowbone. Strain soup in colander. (There should be about 10 cups.) Return soup and beef to kettle. Add cabbage, carrot, chopped onion, potatoes, 2 tablespoons dill, the vinegar, sugar, and 1 teaspoon salt; bring to boiling.
3. Reduce heat; simmer, covered, 30 minutes, or until beef and vegetables are tender. Refrigerate overnight.
4. Next day, skim off fat. Remove beef. Cut into 1-inch cubes or slices; return to soup, along with beets.
5. Heat soup gently to boiling. Simmer, uncovered, 30 minutes. Serve with sour cream and dill.
Makes 8 servings.

# ✦ MINESTRONE WITH ITALIAN SAUSAGE

*1 cup dried white navy beans*
*2 cans (10¾-oz size) condensed chicken broth, undiluted*
*Water*
*Salt*
*1 lb sweet Italian sausage*
*1 small head cabbage (1½ lb)*
*4 carrots (½ lb)*
*2 medium potatoes (¾ lb)*
*1 can (1 lb) Italian-style tomatoes*
*2 medium onions (½ lb)*
*¼ cup olive or salad oil*
*1 stalk celery*
*2 zucchini (½ lb)*
*1 clove garlic*
*¼ teaspoon pepper*
*¼ cup chopped parsley*
*1 cup broken-up thin spaghetti*
*Grated Parmesan cheese*

1. Day before: In bowl, cover beans with cold water. Refrigerate, covered, overnight. Next day, drain. Turn out chicken broth into 1-quart measure; add water to make 1 quart. Pour into 8-quart kettle with 2 more quarts water, 2 teaspoons salt, and the beans. Bring to boiling; reduce heat, and simmer, covered, 1 hour.
2. Meanwhile, in medium skillet, simmer sausage gently in water to cover ½ hour. Drain well. Sauté over medium heat until browned all over. Slice sausage ¼ inch thick on diagonal; set aside.
3. Wash cabbage, and quarter. Remove core with sharp knife. Slice cabbage on diagonal ¼ inch thick. Pare carrots; slice on diagonal ¼ inch thick. Peel potatoes; slice ½ inch thick, and cut into ½-inch cubes. Add to beans with tomatoes. Cover; cook ½ hour longer.
4. Meanwhile, peel onions; cut in half, and slice thin. In hot oil in medium skillet, sauté onion, stirring,

PEPPERS AND BROCCOLI WITH WHOLE WHEAT FETTUCCINE (p. 346)

CLOCKWISE FROM TOP LEFT: COFFEE GRANITE (p. 420), EASY GAZPACHO (p. 206), PEARS POACHED IN APPLE JUICE (p. 418), SPINACH PASTA (p. 345) WITH RICOTTA CHEESE AND FRESH TOMATO SAUCE (p. 209), FRESH FRUIT AND SPROUT SALAD WITH FROZEN YOGURT DRESSING (p. 406), BROILED CALVES LIVER (p. 314) AND VEGETABLE PLATTER, PINEAPPLE SORBET (p. 218), ARTICHOKE STUFFED WITH PASTA SALAD (p. 410), CHICKEN BREASTS NOUVELLE CUISINE (p. 414)

TABBOULEH (p. 444), NEW POTATO AND ZUCCHINI SALAD (p. 450), ENDIVE AND WATERCRESS SALAD WITH WALNUT DRESSING (p. 440)

*OPPOSITE:* ARTICHOKE (p. 489) WITH HOLLANDAISE SAUCE (p. 461)

ZUPPA DI PESCE (p. 479), RASPBERRY YOGURT SOUP (p. 486)

*OPPOSITE:* OYSTER STEW (p. 478)

**STUFFED YELLOW SQUASH WITH PARMESAN SAUCE** (p. 515)

about 5 minutes. Remove from heat. Slice celery on diagonal ⅛ inch thick. Wash zucchini; slice into rounds ¼ inch thick. Press 1 clove garlic. Add vegetables to onion with ½ teaspoon salt and the pepper.

5. Cook slowly, uncovered and stirring occasionally, 20 minutes. Add to bean mixture with parsley and spaghetti. Cook slowly, covered and stirring occasionally, 30 minutes. Add sausage; heat through. Serve hot with Parmesan cheese.

Makes 10 servings.

# ❖ CALCUTTA MULLIGATAWNY SOUP

*4- to 5-lb roasting chicken, cut up*
*⅓ cup all-purpose flour*
*⅓ cup butter or margarine*
*1½ cups chopped onion*
*2 cups chopped carrot*
*2 cups chopped celery*
*1½ cups chopped pared tart apple*
*1½ tablespoons curry powder*
*4 teaspoons salt*
*¾ teaspoon mace*
*½ teaspoon pepper*
*¼ teaspoon chili powder*
*¾ cup canned flaked coconut*
*6 cups cold water*
*1 cup apple juice*
*1 cup light cream*
*1½ cups hot cooked white rice*
*½ cup chopped parsley*

1. Wash chicken; pat dry with paper towels. Roll chicken in flour, coating completely. Reserve any remaining flour.

2. In hot butter in large kettle or Dutch oven, sauté chicken until well browned on all sides. Remove chicken from kettle, and set aside.

3. Add to kettle onion, carrot, celery, apple, and any remaining flour; cook, stirring, 5 minutes.

4. Add curry powder, salt, mace, pepper, chili powder, coconut, chicken, and cold water; mix well. Bring to boiling; reduce heat, and simmer, covered, 2 hours. Stir occasionally. Remove from heat.

5. Skim fat from soup. Remove skin and bone from chicken. Cut chicken meat into large pieces; set aside.

6. Put soup through blender or food processor. Return to kettle, with chicken. Stir in apple juice and light cream; reheat.

7. To serve: Place 1 heaping tablespoon rice in each of 8 to 10 bowls. Add soup. Sprinkle each serving with parsley.

Makes 8 to 10 servings.

## TURKEY-AND-VEGETABLE CHOWDER
**(FROM TURKEY LEFTOVERS)**

*4 slices bacon, cut up*
*1 cup chopped onion*
*4 cups (1¾ lb) cubed peeled potato*
*2½ cups Turkey Broth, below*
*2 pkg (10-oz size) frozen whole-kernel corn, thawed*
*¼ cup butter or margarine*
*2½ teaspoons salt*
*¼ teaspoon pepper*
*2 cups cooked turkey, cut into large chunks*
*2 cups milk*
*1 cup half-and-half*
*2 tablespoons chopped parsley*
*Chowder crackers*

1. In 5-quart Dutch oven or heavy kettle, sauté bacon until crisp; remove and reserve. Make Turkey Broth.
2. In bacon fat, sauté onion, stirring, until golden—about 5 minutes. Add potato and Turkey Broth. Bring to boiling; simmer, covered, about 30 minutes, or just until potato is tender but not mushy.
3. Meanwhile, in medium saucepan, combine corn, butter, salt, pepper, turkey, and milk. Simmer, covered and stirring occasionally, 5 minutes.
4. Add to potato mixture, along with half-and-half. Cook, stirring occasionally, until hot—do not boil.
5. Turn out into warm soup tureen; sprinkle with reserved crisp bacon and the chopped parsley. Serve with chowder crackers.

Makes 10 servings.

### TURKEY BROTH:

*Carcass from turkey*
*6 cups water*
*2 carrots, pared and halved*
*3 parsley sprigs*
*3 celery tops*
*2 onions, halved*
*3 teaspoons salt*
*10 whole black peppercorns*
*1 bay leaf*

1. Break up carcass. Place in 6-quart kettle with water, carrots, parsley, celery tops, onions, salt, peppercorns, and bay leaf.
2. Bring to boiling; reduce heat, and simmer, covered, 2 hours. Strain.
3. Return to kettle; bring back to boiling, and boil gently, uncovered, to reduce to 2½ cups. Refrigerate.

Makes 2½ cups.

## KAPUSTA
**(HOT CABBAGE SOUP)**

*10 cups (2 lb) shredded cabbage*
*2 tablespoons salt*
*½ teaspoon white pepper*
*1 cup chopped onion*
*1½ quarts water*
*1½ lb beef chuck (flank-style ribs)*
*1 large soupbone*
*2 cans (1-lb size) tomato purée*
*8 peeled small whole potatoes (2 lb)*
*1 teaspoon sour salt (optional)*
*2 tablespoons sugar*
*2 cloves garlic, crushed*

1. In 6-quart kettle, combine cabbage, salt, pepper, onion, and water. Bring to boiling, covered. Add beef, soupbone and tomato purée. Bring to boiling; reduce heat, and simmer, covered, 1 hour.
2. Add potatoes; simmer, covered, 1 hour.
3. Twenty minutes before end of cooking time, add sour salt and sugar. Refrigerate overnight. Skim off fat.
4. Next day, reheat gently. Five minutes before serving, add garlic.
5. To serve: Pour into tureen or individual bowls. Beef can be served separately or cut up and added to soup.

Makes 8 servings.

## CORN CHOWDER

*4 slices bacon, finely chopped*
*1 medium onion, thinly sliced*
*4 cups cubed peeled potatoes*
*1 cup water*
*4 cups fresh corn kernels, cut from cob (see Note)*
*1 cup heavy cream*
*1 teaspoon sugar*
*¼ cup butter or margarine*
*2½ teaspoons salt*
*¼ teaspoon white pepper*
*2 cups milk*

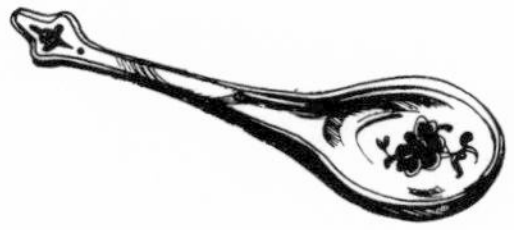

1. In large saucepan with cover, sauté bacon, over moderate heat, until golden.
2. Add onion, potatoes, and water. Cover; bring to boiling, and simmer about 10 minutes, or until potatoes are tender but not mushy.
3. Remove cover, and set saucepan aside.
4. In medium saucepan with cover, combine corn, cream, sugar, and butter. Simmer, covered and over low heat, 10 minutes.
5. Add to potato mixture with remaining ingredients. Cook, stirring occasionally and over low heat, until heated through—do not boil.
Makes 8 to 10 servings.

*Note*: Or use 2 pkg (10-oz size) frozen whole-kernel corn, thawed.

# FISH SOUPS

## MANHATTAN CLAM CHOWDER

*4 bacon slices, diced*
*1 cup sliced onion*
*1 cup diced carrot*
*1 cup diced celery*
*1 tablespoon chopped parsley*
*1 can (1 lb, 12 oz) tomatoes*
*2 cans (10½-oz size) minced clams*
*Water*
*2 teaspoons salt*
*4 whole black peppercorns*
*1 bay leaf*
*1½ teaspoons dried thyme leaves*
*3 medium potatoes, peeled and diced (3½ cups)*

1. In large kettle, sauté bacon until almost crisp.
2. Add onion; cook until tender—about 5 minutes.
3. Add carrot, celery, and parsley; cook over low heat 5 minutes, stirring occasionally.
4. Drain tomatoes; reserve liquid in 1-quart measure. Add tomatoes to vegetables in kettle.
5. Drain clams; set clams aside. Add clam liquid to tomato liquid. Add water to make 1½ quarts liquid. Pour into kettle. Add salt, peppercorns, bay leaf, and thyme.
6. Bring to boiling. Reduce heat; cover, and simmer 45 minutes.
7. Add potatoes; cover, and cook 20 minutes.
8. Add clams to chowder. Simmer, uncovered, 15 minutes. Serve hot.
Makes 8 large servings.

# ❖ NEW ENGLAND CLAM CHOWDER

2 slices bacon
1 cup finely chopped onion
2 cups cubed peeled potatoes
1 teaspoon salt
Dash pepper
1 cup water
1 pint shucked fresh clams or 2 cans
    (10½-oz size) minced clams
2 cups half-and-half
2 tablespoons butter or margarine

1. Chop bacon coarsely. Sauté in large kettle until almost crisp. Add onions; cook about 5 minutes.
2. Add potatoes, salt, pepper, and water. Cook, uncovered, 15 minutes, or until potato is fork-tender.
3. Meanwhile, drain clams, reserving clam liquid. Chop fresh clams coarse.
4. Add clams, ½ cup clam liquid, the half-and-half, and butter to kettle; mix well. Heat about 3 minutes; do not boil.
Makes 4 servings.

# ❖ OYSTER STEW

1 pint raw oysters with liquid
¼ cup butter
¾ teaspoon celery salt
¾ teaspoon salt
⅛ teaspoon white pepper
⅛ teaspoon paprika
1 quart half-and-half or light cream
Butter
Paprika
Oyster crackers

1. Pick over oysters to remove any bits of shell.
2. In large skillet, heat ¼ cup butter; stir in celery salt, salt, pepper, and ⅛ teaspoon paprika. Add oysters with liquid; heat just until edges of oysters curl slightly. Reduce heat to simmer.
3. Meanwhile, in top of double boiler, heat half-and-half. When hot, add oysters with liquid, and heat 15 minutes longer.
4. Serve in bowls or cups, each topped with pat of butter and dash of paprika. Serve along with oyster crackers.
Makes 6 servings.

# ❖ SHRIMP GUMBO

4 tablespoons butter or margarine
1 tablespoon flour
1 lb raw shrimp, shelled and deveined
2 cups water
2 teaspoons crab or shrimp boil (see
    Note), tied in cheesecloth bag
1 teaspoon salt
Dash pepper
1 pkg (10 oz) frozen whole okra,
    slightly thawed
½ cup chopped onion
2 tablespoons chopped green pepper
1 can (8 oz) tomato sauce
1 can (8 oz) stewed tomatoes
2 to 3 cups cooked white rice
Chopped parsley

1. In large saucepan or Dutch oven, melt 2 tablespoons butter. Remove from heat; blend in flour until smooth. Return to heat; add shrimp, and cook, stirring often, 3 to 4 minutes.
2. Add water, the crab or shrimp boil, salt, and pepper. Bring to boiling; reduce heat, and simmer, covered, 15 minutes.
3. Meanwhile, cut okra into 1-inch pieces. Heat remaining butter in medium saucepan. Sauté okra, onion, and green pepper until tender—about 10 minutes. Stir in tomato sauce and tomatoes.
4. Add tomato mixture to shrimp; simmer 30 minutes longer.
5. Mound ½ cup cooked rice in each large soup plate. Ladle gumbo over rice. Sprinkle with parsley.
Makes 4 to 6 servings.

Note: A special blend of spices and herbs for boiling crab and shrimp available in specialty food stores.

# ❖ ZUPPA DI PESCE

½ pkg (17¼-oz size) frozen puff pastry
1 egg yolk
3 slices bacon, diced
2 medium onions, coarsely chopped
3 cloves garlic, crushed
1 can (1 lb) stewed tomatoes
1 quart water
¼ teaspoon turmeric
¾ teaspoon ground cumin
½ teaspoon salt
Dash pepper
2 medium potatoes, diced
½ cup butter or margarine, softened
2 tablespoons lemon juice
Chopped parsley
1 pkg (16 oz) frozen cod or halibut
1 pkg (10 oz) frozen whole-kernel corn
1 tablespoon cider vinegar

1. Preheat oven to 350F. Line cookie sheet with brown paper. Using 2½-inch fish-shaped or other cookie cutter, cut as many pieces as you can from puff pastry. Arrange on cookie sheet.
2. Beat egg yolk. Brush tops of puff-pastry cutouts, being careful not to cover sides. Bake until puffed and golden—about 20 minutes.
3. In large saucepan, sauté bacon, onions, and 1 clove garlic until bacon is just crisp. Add tomatoes, water, turmeric, cumin, salt, and pepper. Bring to boiling. Add potatoes, and cook gently, uncovered, 15 minutes.
4. Make sauce: In small bowl, beat together butter, 2 cloves garlic, the lemon juice and 2 tablespoons chopped parsley. Transfer to serving bowl. Set aside at room temperature until serving.
5. Cut fish into ¾-inch chunks. Add to soup, along with corn and vinegar. Cook 5 minutes longer. Sprinkle with chopped parsley. Top with puff-pastry cutouts, and serve with garlic-butter sauce.
Makes 4 servings.

# ❖ FISH AND SHELLFISH STEW

⅓ cup olive or salad oil
1 cup chopped onion
1 cup chopped green onion
1 cup chopped green pepper
3 cloves garlic, crushed
1 dozen fresh littleneck clams or 1 can (10 oz) whole clams
1 can (1 lb 12 oz) tomatoes
1 can (8 oz) tomato sauce
1 cup dry red wine
¼ cup chopped parsley
2 teaspoons salt
½ teaspoon dried oregano leaves
¼ teaspoon dried basil leaves
¼ teaspoon pepper
1 cup water
1 lb fresh cod
¾ lb fresh red snapper or striped bass
½ lb small frozen rock-lobster tails

1. In hot oil in 6-quart kettle or Dutch oven, sauté onion, green onion, green pepper, and garlic, stirring occasionally, until onion is golden—about 10 minutes.
2. Open clams, reserving liquid; set clams aside. (If you are using canned clams, drain, reserving the liquid.)
3. Add clam liquid, tomatoes, tomato sauce, wine, parsley, salt, oregano, basil leaves, pepper, and water to sautéed vegetables; mix well.
4. Bring to boiling; reduce heat, and simmer, covered, 30 minutes.
5. Meanwhile, rinse cod, red snapper, and lobster tails under cold water; drain. Cut cod and snapper in large pieces.
6. Add fish and unthawed lobster tails in shell to vegetable mixture. Return just to boiling; reduce heat, and simmer, covered, 15 minutes. Add clams; simmer 15 minutes longer.
7. Serve with hot, crusty Italian bread.
Makes 8 servings.

# DRIED BEAN AND PEA SOUPS

## ✂ OLD-FASHIONED SPLIT-PEA SOUP

1½ cups quick-cooking split green peas
1 quart water
2½ lb fully cooked ham shank
⅔ cup coarsely chopped onion
¼ cup cut-up carrot
½ cup coarsely chopped celery
2 parsley sprigs
1 clove garlic, crushed
1 bay leaf, crumbled
½ teaspoon sugar
¼ teaspoon salt
⅛ teaspoon dried thyme leaves
⅛ teaspoon pepper
2 cans (13¾-oz size) clear chicken broth

1. In 3½-quart kettle, combine peas and water; bring to boiling. Reduce heat; simmer, covered, 45 minutes. Add more water if necessary.
2. Add ham shank and rest of ingredients; simmer, covered, 1½ hours.
3. Remove ham shank from soup; cool. Cut ham from bone; dice.
4. Press vegetables and liquid through coarse sieve.
5. Return to kettle. Add ham; reheat slowly, uncovered, until thoroughly hot, 15 minutes.
Makes 8 servings.

## ✂ THICK LENTIL SOUP

1 cup dried lentils
4 cups water
1 tablespoon salt
½ teaspoon dried thyme leaves
½ teaspoon dried marjoram leaves
4 large onions, finely chopped
4 carrots, pared and cubed
¼ cup salad or olive oil
¼ cup chopped parsley
1 can (1 lb) crushed tomatoes, undrained
2 tablespoons dry sherry
¼ cup grated Swiss or Gruyère cheese

1. Wash lentils. In 4-quart kettle, combine lentils and water; let stand 1 hour.
2. Add salt, thyme, and marjoram. Bring to boiling; reduce heat, and simmer, covered, 1 hour.
3. Meanwhile, slowly cook onions and carrots in hot oil until soft—10 to 15 minutes. Add to lentils, along with parsley, tomatoes, and sherry. Simmer, covered, about 1 hour, or until lentils are tender.
4. To serve: Sprinkle cheese over top of soup, or put 1 or 2 tablespoons grated cheese in each bowl, and then spoon lentil soup over cheese.
Makes 8 to 10 servings.

# ❖ OLD-FASHIONED BEAN SOUP

1 lb dried white navy beans
2½ quarts water
2 smoked ham hocks (2¼ lb)
1 cup finely chopped onion
2 cloves garlic, crushed
1 bay leaf
1 cup mashed potato (see Note)
1 cup sliced celery
1 cup thinly sliced carrot
1 teaspoon salt
⅛ teaspoon pepper
2 tablespoons chopped parsley

1. Wash beans, discarding imperfect ones. Combine beans and water; refrigerate, covered, overnight.
2. Next day, turn out beans and water (there should be 6 cups) into 6-quart kettle.
3. Add ham hocks, onion, garlic, and bay leaf. Bring to boiling; reduce heat, and simmer, covered tightly, about 2 hours, or until beans are almost tender.
4. Add mashed potato, celery, carrot, salt, and pepper. Return to boiling; simmer, covered, about 1 hour longer, or just until beans are tender.
5. Remove ham hocks; cut off meat. Dice meat, and return to kettle. Just before serving, sprinkle with chopped parsley.
Makes 8 servings.

*Note*: Use leftover mashed potato, or make instant mashed potato.

# ❖ TUSCANY BEAN SOUP

1 lb dried white navy beans or pink beans
3 teaspoons salt
3 quarts water
1 can (10¾ oz) condensed chicken broth, undiluted
½ teaspoon dried marjoram leaves
1 bay leaf
⅛ teaspoon pepper
2 tablespoons salad oil
1½ cups chopped onion
1 clove garlic, crushed
1 cup sliced carrot
2 large potatoes (¾ lb), peeled and cut into julienne strips
1 pkg (10 oz) frozen chopped spinach, thawed
Grated Parmesan cheese

1. Wash beans; drain. In 8-quart kettle, combine beans, 2 teaspoons salt, and the water. Bring to boiling; boil 2 minutes. Remove from heat; cover, and let stand 1 hour.
2. Add chicken broth, 1 teaspoon salt, the marjoram, bay leaf, and pepper. Bring to boiling; reduce heat, and simmer, covered, about 1 hour.
3. Meanwhile, in hot oil in medium skillet, sauté onion, garlic, and carrot, stirring, until onion is golden—about 5 minutes.
4. After bean mixture has cooked 1 hour, add onion mixture, potatoes, and frozen spinach. Cook, covered, until beans and vegetables are tender. Serve sprinkled with Parmesan cheese.
Makes 12 servings.

# ❖ BASIL-AND-BEAN SOUP

½ lb dried white kidney beans
Water
1½ lb zucchini
3 medium-size white turnips (1 lb)
1 large potato
6 medium carrots (1 lb)
2 celery stalks with leaves
2 cups coarsely chopped onion
1 onion, studded with 4 cloves
1 whole bay leaf
1 can (1 lb 1 oz) whole tomatoes, undrained
1 tablespoon dried basil leaves
⅛ teaspoon dried hot red pepper
flakes
1½ tablespoons salt
1 loaf French bread
Butter or margarine
Grated Parmesan cheese
2 tablespoons olive or salad oil
2 tablespoons chopped parsley

1. Cover beans with cold water; refrigerate, covered, overnight.
2. Next day, drain beans in colander; rinse under cold water.
3. Prepare vegetables: Slice zucchini. Peel and dice turnips and potato. Pare carrots; slice thin. Slice celery.
4. Turn out beans into 6-quart Dutch oven with 6 cups water; bring to boiling over medium heat.
5. Add prepared vegetables, and chopped onion, whole onion, bay leaf, tomatoes, basil, red pepper flakes, and salt. Bring back to boiling; reduce heat, and simmer, covered, 2½ hours, or until beans are tender.
6. Meanwhile, slice bread ½ inch thick. Toast bread slices in broiler until lightly browned on both sides.
7. Spread one side with butter; sprinkle with grated Parmesan cheese. Broil about 1 minute, or until cheese is bubbly.
8. To serve: Remove and discard onion with cloves and the bay leaf. Stir in oil. Taste for seasoning. Sprinkle with parsley. Top with toasted French bread. (Flavor is even better the next day.)
Makes 14 to 16 servings.

# ❖ BLACK-BEAN SOUP

1 lb black beans
2 quarts water
¼ cup salad oil
1 cup chopped celery
1½ cups chopped onion
2 teaspoons salt
½ teaspoon pepper
1 bay leaf
2 smoked ham hocks (2 lb)
½ cup sherry
1 hard-cooked egg, peeled and
chopped
½ cup chopped green pepper
Sour cream
Lime wedges

1. Wash beans; drain. In 8-quart kettle, combine beans and water. Bring to boiling; boil 2 minutes. Remove from heat; let stand, covered, 1 hour.
2. Add oil, celery, onion, salt, pepper, bay leaf, and ham hocks. Bring to boiling; reduce heat, and simmer, covered, 2 hours. Remove ham hocks. Discard bay leaf.
3. In food processor or blender, purée beans; return to kettle.
4. Remove meat from cooked ham hocks; discard fat and bones. Add meat and sherry to kettle (and more water if necessary); simmer, stirring, until hot.
5. Ladle soup into warm serving dishes; top each with chopped egg, green pepper, and 1 tablespoon sour cream. Serve with lime wedges.
Makes 8 servings.

# ✠ CABBAGE-AND-BEAN SOUP

1 lb dried white navy beans or baby lima beans
1½-lb fully cooked smoked boneless pork shoulder butt
3 cloves garlic, pressed
2 sprigs parsley
½ teaspoon salt
1 teaspoon dried thyme leaves
1 bay leaf
4 whole black peppercorns
4 potatoes (1 lb), peeled and quartered
3 carrots, pared and sliced
1 head green cabbage (2 lb), coarsely chopped

1. Cover beans with cold water; refrigerate, covered, overnight.
2. Next day, drain. Turn out into 6-quart kettle; cover with 6 cups cold water. Add pork butt, garlic, parsley, salt, thyme, bay leaf, and peppercorns.
3. Bring to boiling point. Reduce heat; simmer, covered, 2 hours, or until beans are tender.
4. Add 3 cups water, the potatoes, carrots, and cabbage; cook, covered, 25 to 30 minutes, or until potatoes are tender.
5. Before serving, remove pork butt; slice and return to kettle. (Add more water, if necessary.)
Makes 10 servings.

# COLD SOUPS

## ✠ GAZPACHO

3 medium tomatoes (1¾ lb)
1 large cucumber, peeled
1 large onion
1 green pepper (8 oz)
1 canned pimiento, drained
2 cans (12-oz size) tomato juice
⅓ cup olive oil
⅓ cup red-wine vinegar
¼ teaspoon Tabasco
1½ teaspoons salt
⅛ teaspoon pepper
2 slices white bread or ½ cup packaged croutons
2 cloves garlic, split
2 tablespoons olive oil
½ cup chopped chives

1. Prepare vegetables: To peel tomatoes, dip each tomato into boiling water for 1 minute; lift out with slotted utensil. Cut out stem end; peel off skin with paring knife. Or hold tomato on fork over heat just until skin splits, and carefully peel off skin with knife.
2. Cut cucumber into cubes. Cut onion in half. Wash green pepper; cut into quarters, and remove seeds. In large bowl, combine 2 tomatoes, sliced, and half of the cucumber, onion, and green pepper. Add pimiento and ½ cup tomato juice; stir to combine.
3. Put half of mixture at a time in blender. Blend, covered, at high speed 1 minute, to purée vegetables. Repeat with other half. Chop, separately, remaining tomato, cucumber, onion, and green pepper. Refrigerate, covered, each in a small dish.
4. In large bowl, with wire whisk, mix puréed vegetables, remaining tomato juice, ⅓ cup olive oil, the vinegar, Tabasco, salt, and pepper. Refrigerate, covered, until well chilled—3 hours or longer. Refrigerate 6 serving bowls and a tureen.
5. Cut bread into ¼-inch cubes. Rub inside of small skillet with garlic; reserve garlic. Add 2 tablespoons olive oil; heat over medium heat. Sauté bread cubes in hot oil until crisp and golden. Drain well on paper towels and turn out into small dish.

6. To serve, crush reserved garlic into chilled soup, mixing well with wire whisk. Ladle into chilled soup tureen. Sprinkle with chives. On tray, arrange reserved chopped vegetables and croutons to sprinkle over the top of each serving.
Makes 6 servings.

## ❖ SENEGALESE SOUP

*1 medium onion, chopped*
*1 medium carrot, pared and diced*
*1 stalk celery, sliced*
*3 tablespoons butter or margarine*
*2 tablespoons curry powder*
*1½ tablespoons flour*
*1 tablespoon tomato paste*
*2 cans (10¾-oz size) condensed*
  *chicken broth, undiluted*
*2 cups water*
*1 tablespoon almond paste*
*1 tablespoon red-currant jelly*
*10 whole cloves*
*1 cinnamon stick*
*1½ cups heavy cream*
*2 tablespoons shredded coconut*

1. In large saucepan, sauté onion, carrot, and celery in hot butter until golden—about 5 minutes. Remove from heat.
2. Stir in curry powder and flour until well blended. Add tomato paste; cook, stirring, 1 minute.
3. Gradually stir in undiluted chicken broth and water; bring to boiling, stirring constantly. Stir in almond paste and jelly; add cloves and cinnamon stick. Simmer, uncovered and stirring occasionally, ½ hour.
4. Strain; cool. Then refrigerate until very well chilled—several hours or overnight.
5. When ready to serve, skim off any fat from surface. Blend in cream. Serve in bouillon cups. Top each serving with coconut.
Makes 8 to 10 servings.

## ❖ COLD CUCUMBER SOUP

*1½ cucumbers (about 1 lb)*
*1½ tablespoons butter or margarine*
*1 tablespoon flour*
*¼ teaspoon salt*
*¾ cup chicken broth*
*½ cup milk*
*½ cup light cream*

1. Pare cucumbers; cut in half lengthwise. With teaspoon, scoop out and discard seeds. Cut cucumbers into ¼-inch pieces.
2. In large saucepan, sauté cucumbers in hot butter 5 minutes, or until transparent. Remove from heat. Stir in flour and salt until blended. Gradually add chicken broth and milk.
3. Cook over medium heat, stirring constantly, until mixture boils. Reduce heat; simmer, covered, 15 minutes.
4. Turn out into blender or food processor. Purée; turn out mixture into bowl.
5. Stir in cream. Refrigerate, covered, until very well chilled—at least 4 hours.
6. Serve in bouillon cups. Garnish with slice of cucumber, if you wish.
Makes 4 or 5 servings.

# ❖ COLD CURRY-CARROT SOUP

*1 lb carrots, pared*
*2½ cans (13¾-oz size) chicken broth*
*¼ teaspoon salt*
*Dash pepper*
*1 medium onion, halved*
*2 tablespoons butter or margarine*
*1½ teaspoons curry powder*
*1½ cups yogurt*
*3 thin unpared cucumber slices*
*Coarsely grated pared carrot*

1. In food processor, using slicing disc, slice carrots (or slice by hand).
2. In large saucepan, combine carrots, chicken broth, salt, and pepper. Bring to boiling; reduce heat, and simmer 10 minutes, or until carrots are fork-tender.
3. Slice onion in processor (or by hand). In hot butter in skillet, sauté onion and curry powder, stirring occasionally, until onion is tender—5 minutes.
4. In processor, or blender, purée half of carrot mixture at a time until smooth. Add onion mixture and yogurt; mix until smooth. Turn out into serving bowl; refrigerate until well chilled.
5. To serve, mix well; top with sliced cucumber and grated carrot.
Makes 8 servings.

# ❖ CHILLED CANTALOUPE SOUP

*1 (3-lb) ripe cantaloupe*
*½ cup dry sherry*
*¼ cup sugar*
*¼ cup orange juice*

1. Cut melon in half; scoop out and discard seeds. Scoop out cantaloupe meat.
2. In blender or food processor, combine cantaloupe and rest of ingredients. Blend until smooth—several times, if necessary. Turn out into bowl; chill over ice cubes, or refrigerate, covered, until very cold. Serve in chilled serving bowls.
Makes 4 servings.

# ❖ COLD PLUM SOUP

*2 cans (17-oz size) purple plums*
*⅛ teaspoon ground cinnamon*
*Dash ground cloves*
*⅓ cup lime juice*
*⅔ cup light rum*
*Whipped cream (optional)*
*Cinnamon (optional)*

1. Drain plums, reserving syrup. Remove pits from plums.
2. Combine plums, reserved syrup, and remaining ingredients. Blend in blender or food processor, about one third at a time.
3. Refrigerate, covered, until chilled (see Note)—4 hours or overnight.
4. Serve in chilled glasses or individual dishes set in ice. Garnish with dab of whipped cream, sprinkled with cinnamon, if desired.
Makes 6 servings.

*Note*: Place in freezer 1 or 2 hours to chill more quickly.

## ✠ RASPBERRY-YOGURT SOUP

2 pkg (10-oz size) frozen red raspberries
2 containers (8-oz size) red-raspberry yogurt
Fresh mint

In blender or food processor, combine raspberries and yogurt. Blend until smooth. Chill well. Garnish with mint.
Makes about 8 servings.

## ✠ STRAWBERRY SOUP

1 quart fresh strawberries
2 containers (8-oz size) strawberry yogurt
2 tablespoons lemon juice

1. Gently wash and hull berries. Set aside a few large berries for garnish.
2. In blender or food processor, combine rest of strawberries, the yogurt, and lemon juice. Blend to make purée.
3. Refrigerate until very well chilled. Serve in chilled serving bowl. Slice reserved berries; float several slices on top of each serving.
Makes 8 servings.

# VEGETABLES

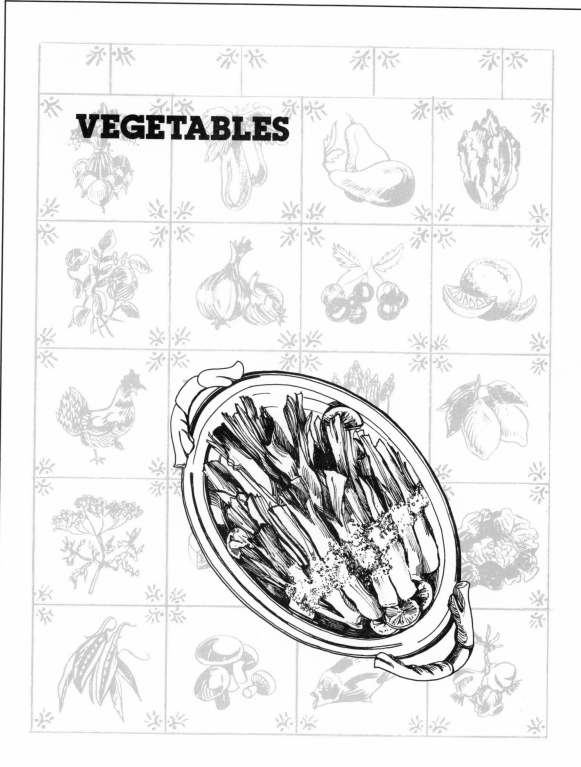

◆ **V**egetables, once treated as something that went along with a meat, poultry, or fish dish, have emerged as the bright flavorful meal accompaniment they should always have been. All-vegetable platters make beautiful and delicious main dishes and are being offered today on the menus of many prestigious restaurants.

Steaming, stir-frying, and simmering in a tightly covered pan with a small amount of water to retain the bright color and natural flavor are the proper methods for cooking vegetables on top of the range. Because of the increasing popularity of vegetarian diets, a lot more attention has been paid to interesting vegetable preparation, and those of us who are not vegetarians can share in the harvest of good new techniques and recipes.

## VEGETABLE BUYING GUIDE AND PREPARATION GUIDE

| VEGETABLE | BUYING GUIDE | PREPARATION | BASIC COOKERY |
|---|---|---|---|
| All vegetables | Best buys are in season. | Wash all vegetables before cooking. | Simmer, tightly covered, in 1 inch boiling water with ½ to 1 teaspoon salt per pound. |
| Artichokes, French or Italian | Compact, firm, heavy globes; free from brown blemishes. Good green color. Fleshy, tightly closed leaf scales. | Cut 1 inch from top. Cut stem close to base. Remove lower tough outer leaves. With scissors, cut thorny tip off each leaf. | 1 per serving. 20 to 45 minutes, standing upright in saucepan. |
| Artichokes, Jerusalem | Should be free from blemishes. | Pare thinly. Leave whole, dice or slice. | 3 or 4 servings. 15 to 35 minutes. |
| Asparagus | Green, firm stalk with close, compact tips; tender stalk is brittle and easily punctured. Should not be woody. Should be free from blemishes. | Break off woody end of stalk. Pare and remove scales. Leave stalk whole, or cut into 1-inch lengths. | 3 or 4 servings. 10 to 20 minutes. |
| Beans, green or wax | Clean, firm, crisp, tender pods. Should snap when broken. Free from blemishes | Remove ends. Cut into lengthwise strips for French-style. Cut on diagonal into 1-inch pieces; or serve whole. | 4 to 6 servings. French-style: 10 to 20 minutes. Cut or whole: 15 to 30 minutes. |

| VEGETABLE | BUYING GUIDE | PREPARATION | BASIC COOKERY |
|---|---|---|---|
| Beans, lima | Unshelled limas should be well filled, clean, free from blemishes; firm dark green pods. Shelled limas are highly perishable; should be light green or green-white; plump, with tender skins. | Shell just before cooking. | 2 servings. 20–25 minutes. |
| Beets | Sold in bunches. Smooth, free from blemishes or cracks; fairly clean, firm roots with green tops. Small to medium in size. | Remove tops (use as green vegetable); leave 1-inch stems. Scrub well. Peel and slice after cooking. | 3 servings. Cover with cold water. Cook, covered, 30–45 minutes (cook greens just with water that clings to leaves, 5–15 minutes). |
| Broccoli | Firm, tender stems with compact cluster of flower buds. Dark green or purple-green (depending on variety), free from bruises, or yellow. | Trim stem end; split heavy stalks. (Entire stalk is edible.) | 3 servings. 10–15 minutes. |
| Brussels sprouts | Firm, compact, bright green. Avoid yellow or worm-eaten leaves. | Cut off stem end. Soak in cold water 15 minutes. | 4 servings. 10–20 minutes. |
| Cabbage | Firm, heavy heads; crisp, tender leaves. Avoid yellowing or worm-eaten leaves. | Remove outer leaves; wash. Cut into wedges and remove most of core; or shred. | 3 or 4 servings. Green, in wedges: 10–15 minutes. Shredded: 3–10 minutes. Red, shredded: 8–12 minutes. |
| Carrots | Firm, clean, smooth, well-shaped, with good color. Free from bruises and cracks. | Remove tops. Scrape or pare thinly, or scrub well with brush. Cook whole or cut. | 4 servings. Whole: 15–25 minutes. Cut: 10–20 minutes. |

| VEGETABLE | BUYING GUIDE | PREPARATION | BASIC COOKERY |
|---|---|---|---|
| Cauliflower | Clean, heavy, compact head. White flowerets with crisp, green leaves. Avoid bruises or brown spots. | Remove outer leaves. Leave whole, removing stem, or cut into flowerets. | 3 or 4 servings. Whole: 15–20 minutes. Flowerets: 8–15 minutes. |
| Corn on cob | Plump, firm, milky kernels with bright color. Husks should be green; dried-out, yellow discolorations indicate stale corn. Immature corn lacks flavor. | Just before cooking, remove husks and silk. | 1 or 2 ears per serving. 5 to 10 minutes. |
| Eggplant | Heavy, firm, free from blemishes; shiny, smooth purple skin. | Peel if necessary. Do not soak in salted water. Cut as desired. | 4 or 5 servings. Cook as directed in recipes. |
| Endive, Belgian or French | Pale-white to slightly yellow heads; firm and fresh-looking. | Cut a small slice off base. Cut stalks in half lengthwise or separate whole leaves for salad. | 1 per serving. 5 minutes. |
| Greens (collards, dandelions, kale, spinach, Swiss chard) | Crisp, tender young leaves, free from bruises, excess dirt, and coarse stems. | Cut off root ends. Wash several times, lifting out of water, letting sand sink to bottom of vessel. | 3 or 4 servings. Thin leaf greens cooked just with water that clings to leaves. Thick leaf greens need only ½ inch water. |
| Leeks | Clean white bulbs with fresh crisp green tops. | Cut slice off root end, peel off tough outer layer from bulb. Take care to wash out all sand. | 3–4 servings. 15 minutes. |
| Mushrooms | Plump, unblemished, cream-colored or white, with short stems. | Wash briefly and dry with paper towels. Cut a thin slice off stem end. | 4–6 servings, depending upon use. Raw in salads. Sautéed or broiled, 5 minutes. |

| VEGETABLE | BUYING GUIDE | PREPARATION | BASIC COOKERY |
|---|---|---|---|
| Okra | Crisp bright-green pods, free from blemishes. | Trim off stem ends if woody. Cook whole or cut into ½-inch rounds. | 4–6 servings. 10 minutes. |
| Onions, small, white | Firm, clean, dry white skins, free from sprouts. | Remove outer skins under cold, running water. | 4 servings. 15 to 25 minutes. |
| Parsnips | Smooth, firm, clean, well-shaped, free from rot. Small to medium in size. | Scrape or peel. Cut as desired, or leave whole. | 3 or 4 servings. Cut: 10–20 minutes. Whole: 20–40 minutes. |
| Peas | Bright-green filled pods, free from yellow color or mildew, moisture, or bruises. | Shell just before cooking. | 2 servings. 8–20 minutes. |
| Peppers, sweet red or green | Firm, thick, shiny bright-green flesh. Bright red when mature. Avoid blemished or bruised peppers. | Remove stems and seeds. | 1 per serving. Raw in salads; cooked, 5–8 minutes. |
| Snow peas and snap peas | Fresh-looking bright-green pods. | Remove strings, if necessary, from sides of pods. | 4 or 5 servings. 4–6 minutes. |
| Spaghetti squash | Firm yellow skin, free from cuts and blemishes. Hard rind. | Cut in half, crosswise, remove seeds. Do not peel. | 3 or 4 servings. (2½ to 3-lb size). 30–35 minutes. |
| Potatoes, sweet (or yams) | Firm, plump, free from soft spots. Purchase small quantities; perishable. Sweet potatoes: Skins are pale to deep yellow; flesh is light orange. Yams: Skins are white to reddish; flesh is deep orange. | Remove bruised spots and root ends. Do not peel. | 2 or 3 servings. Cover with boiling water; cook, covered, 25–35 minutes, or until tender. |

| VEGETABLE | BUYING GUIDE | PREPARATION | BASIC COOKERY |
|---|---|---|---|
| Potatoes, white (mature or new) | Firm, uniform in shape (medium-size). Free from cuts and blemishes. Color varies with variety. Eyes should be shallow. | Peel; remove eyes; leave whole. Peel; cut into quarters. Peel; cut into 1-inch cubes, or slice ⅛ inch thick. Whole small new potatoes: Peel or scrape. Unpeeled, whole potatoes (medium-size). | 2 or 3 servings. 35–40 minutes. 20–25 minutes. 20 to 25 minutes. Cover with boiling water. Cook, covered, 35–40 minutes |
| Squash, Acorn | Dark green, ribbed. Hard rind. | Cut in half, lengthwise. Remove seeds. Do not peel. | 2 servings (1 large). 20–30 minutes (cook cut side down). |
| Squash, summer (zucchini included) | Heavy for size, free from blemishes. Thin, tender skin. | Remove stem and blossom ends. Paring not necessary. Cut as desired. | 2 or 3 servings. 10–20 minutes. |
| Squash, winter | Heavy for size, free from blemishes and bruises. Hard rind. | Cut as desired. Remove seeds. Remove rind, if desired. | 2 servings. 25–30 minutes. |
| Tomatoes | Bright red (or yellow); firm, heavy, not over-ripe. Green clear-skinned, for frying. | Remove skin if desired. Dip in boiling water 1-minute, skin will slip off easily. | 4 servings. 8–10 minutes. |
| Turnips (rutabagas) | Firm, smooth, clean, free from bruises, with few fibrous roots. Heavy for size. | Peel thinly just before cooking. Cut as desired. | 3 or 4 servings. 20–30 minutes. |
| Turnips, white | Firm, smooth, clean, free from bruises, with few fibrous roots. Small to medium in size. | Peel thinly just before cooking. Leave whole, or cut. | 3 or 4 servings. Whole: 20 to 30 minutes. Cut: 10 to 20 minutes. |

# ❖ ARTICHOKES WITH TARRAGON BUTTER

*3 cups water*
*¼ cup olive or salad oil*
*6 lemon slices*
*2 bay leaves*
*1 clove garlic, split*
*1 teaspoon salt*
*⅛ teaspoon pepper*
*4 large artichokes (about 3 lb)*

**TARRAGON BUTTER:**

*½ cup melted butter*
*2 tablespoons olive oil*
*2 tablespoons lemon juice*
*1 tablespoon dried tarragon leaves*

1. In large kettle, combine 3 cups water, ¼ cup olive oil, lemon slices, bay leaves, garlic, salt, and pepper; bring to boiling.
2. Meanwhile, trim stalk from base of artichokes; cut 1-inch slice from tops. Remove discolored leaves; snip off spike ends.
3. Wash artichokes in cold water; drain.
4. Add to boiling mixture. Reduce heat; simmer, covered, 40 to 45 minutes, or until artichoke bases feel soft. Drain artichokes well.
5. Meanwhile, make Tarragon Butter: In small bowl, mix butter, olive oil, lemon juice, and tarragon until well combined.
6. To serve: Place artichoke and small cup of sauce on individual plates. To eat, pull off leaves, one at a time, dip base in sauce, and nibble off only the fleshy parts. Discard prickly choke.
Makes 4 servings.

# ❖ FRESH ASPARAGUS MIMOSA

*2½ to 3 lb asparagus*
*½ teaspoon salt*
*Water*
*1 hard-cooked egg, peeled*
*¼ cup butter or margarine, melted*
*2 tablespoons lemon juice*

1. Cut off tough ends of asparagus. Wash stalks well. With vegetable peeler, scrape skin and scales from stalks.
2. In large skillet, add salt to 1½ inches water; bring to boiling. Add asparagus spears; boil vigorously, covered, 8 to 10 minutes.
3. Meanwhile, separate white and yolk of hard-cooked egg. Chop white and yolk separately.
4. Drain asparagus well. Arrange on platter. Drizzle with butter. Sprinkle egg white over asparagus, then egg yolk. Just before serving, sprinkle with lemon juice.
Makes 6 servings.

# ❖ FRESH ASPARAGUS WITH LEMON AND BUTTER OR HOLLANDAISE

*2 to 2½ lb asparagus*
*Boiling water*
*1½ teaspoons salt*
*¼ cup butter or margarine, melted*
*Lemon wedges*
*Hollandaise Sauce, page 461 (optional)*

1. Break or cut off tough ends of asparagus. Wash asparagus well under cold running water; if asparagus is sandy, scrub with brush. With vegetable peeler, scrape skin and scales from stalks.
2. Bunch stalks together; tie with string. Place upright in deep saucepan (see Note). Add boiling water (about 2 inches deep) and salt.

3. Return to boiling; cook, covered, 15 to 20 minutes. Pierce lower part of stalks with fork to see if they are tender. Be sure not to overcook.

4. Drain asparagus well, being careful not to break stalks. Arrange in heated vegetable dish; pour butter over all and serve with lemon wedges. Or, if preferred, omit butter and lemon wedges and serve with Hollandaise Sauce.

Makes 4 to 6 servings.

*Note:* You may use bottom of double boiler, with top inverted over asparagus as cover.

# ❖ FESTIVAL BEETS

*1½ lb beets*
*Water*
*½ cup sugar*
*1 tablespoon cornstarch*
*¼ teaspoon salt*
*½ cup cider vinegar*
*2 tablespoons orange or ginger marmalade*
*2 tablespoons butter or margarine*

1. Gently wash beets, leaving skins intact. Remove leaves, leaving 2 inches of stalk at top of beets.

2. Place beets in large saucepan. Cover with cold water; bring to boiling. Reduce heat; simmer, covered, 45 minutes, or until beets are tender.

3. Drain beets. Cover with cold water; cut off stalks, and slip off skins. Cut beets into ½-inch cubes; set aside.

4. In medium saucepan, combine sugar, cornstarch, and salt; mix well. Stir in vinegar.

5. Over medium heat, bring to boiling, stirring constantly. Mixture will be thickened and translucent.

6. Add marmalade and butter; heat, stirring, until butter melts.

7. Add beets; cook, over low heat, stirring occasionally, until beets are heated through—about 10 minutes.

Makes 6 servings.

# ❖ BROCCOLI AMANDINE

*1 bunch fresh broccoli (about 1½ lb)*
*½ cup boiling water*
*½ teaspoon salt*
*½ cup slivered almonds*
*¼ cup butter or margarine*
*2 tablespoons lemon juice*

1. Wash and trim leaves from broccoli. If stalks are very large, split lengthwise through flower and all. Arrange in single layer in bottom of large skillet.

2. Pour boiling water over broccoli; sprinkle with salt. Cook, covered, over medium heat 8 to 10 minutes, or until stalks are just tender and water is evaporated.

3. Meanwhile, sauté almonds in 1 tablespoon butter until golden. Add remaining butter and lemon juice. Heat until butter melts. Pour over broccoli.

Makes 4 to 6 servings.

## ❖ BROCCOLI AU GRATIN

2 pkg (10-oz size) frozen broccoli
    spears or 2 lb fresh broccoli
4 tablespoons butter or margarine
⅓ cup soft white-bread crumbs
4 teaspoons lemon juice

1. Cook broccoli as package label directs (cook fresh broccoli as directed on page 490).
2. Meanwhile, slowly heat 1 tablespoon butter in small skillet. Add bread crumbs, and sauté until golden-brown. Remove crumbs, and set aside.
3. In same skillet, melt remaining butter with lemon juice.
4. Drain broccoli. Add lemon butter; toss gently until evenly coated. Turn out into serving dish; sprinkle with browned crumbs.
Makes 6 servings.

## ❖ BRUSSELS SPROUTS IN CHEESE SAUCE

2 pkg (10-oz size) frozen Brussels
    sprouts or 2 lb fresh Brussels
    sprouts

**CHEESE SAUCE:**

2 tablespoons butter or margarine
2 tablespoons all-purpose flour
½ teaspoon dry mustard
¾ teaspoon salt
Dash black pepper
Dash ground red pepper
1 cup milk or light cream
1 cup grated natural sharp Cheddar
    cheese

1. Using large saucepan, cook Brussels sprouts as package label directs (cook fresh Brussels sprouts as directed on page 490).
2. Make Cheese Sauce: In small saucepan, slowly melt butter (do not brown). Remove from heat; stir in flour, mustard, salt, black pepper, red pepper, and milk until smooth.
3. Bring to boiling, stirring until thickened. Reduce heat; add cheese, and cook, stirring, until cheese is melted and mixture is smooth.
4. Drain Brussels sprouts; return to saucepan. Heat slightly to dry out. Pour cheese sauce over top.
Makes 6 servings.

## ❖ BUTTERED CABBAGE WEDGES

1 head cabbage (about 2½ lb)
½ cup water
1 teaspoon salt
½ cup butter or margarine
Freshly ground pepper

1. Discard outer leaves from cabbage. Wash head; cut into 8 wedges.
2. Pour water into large skillet; bring to boiling. Add salt, then cabbage. Cook, covered, over medium heat 8 minutes.
3. Add butter; stir until melted and cabbage is coated. Sprinkle with pepper before serving.
Makes 8 servings.

# ❖ BRAISED CARROTS

1 tablespoon butter or margarine
1 tablespoon salad oil
2 cups thinly sliced (on diagonal) pared carrots (about 9)
2 tablespoons water
½ teaspoon salt

1. In hot butter and oil in medium skillet, cook carrots, stirring, 1 minute.
2. Add water and salt; cook, tightly covered, over low heat until carrots are fork-tender—7 to 8 minutes. Stir once to prevent sticking.
Makes 4 to 6 servings.

# ❖ LEMON-GLAZED CARROTS

1 lb carrots
Salt
Boiling water
3 tablespoons butter or margarine
2 tablespoons sugar
4 thin slices lemon

1. Wash carrots; pare, and cut on diagonal into 1-inch pieces.
2. Place in medium saucepan with enough boiling salted water to cover; simmer, covered, 15 minutes, or until tender. Drain.
3. Melt butter in heavy medium skillet. Stir in sugar; add lemon slices and carrots. Cook over medium heat, stirring occasionally, until carrots are glazed.
Makes 4 servings.

# ❖ CAULIFLOWER POLONAISE

1 large cauliflower (about 2½ lb)
Boiling water
1½ teaspoons salt
3 slices lemon
1 hard-cooked egg, coarsely chopped
1 tablespoon chopped parsley
½ cup butter or margarine, melted
3 tablespoons lemon juice
½ cup prepared croutons

1. Trim leaves and stem from cauliflower. Place, stem side down, in large kettle. Cover with boiling water. Add salt and lemon slices. Bring to boiling; reduce heat, and simmer, covered, 20 to 25 minutes, or until tender. Drain.
2. To serve: Place whole cauliflower in warm serving dish. Sprinkle with hard-cooked egg and parsley. Combine butter with lemon juice and croutons. Pour over cauliflower.
Makes 6 to 8 servings.

# ❖ CORN ON THE COB

8 ears of corn
Water
Butter or margarine, melted
Salt
Pepper

1. Cook corn as soon as possible after purchasing. (Keep refrigerated until ready to cook.)
2. Remove husks and silk from corn, and break off stem ends.
3. In 6-quart kettle, cover ears with cold water. Cook, covered, just until water boils.
4. With tongs, remove cooked corn from water to heated serving platter. Serve at once, with melted butter, salt, and pepper.
Makes 4 servings.

# ❖ PERFECT FRIED EGGPLANT

2 eggs, beaten
1 teaspoon salt
Dash pepper
1 cup dry bread crumbs
2 tablespoons grated Parmesan
  cheese
1 medium eggplant (about 1 lb)
Salad oil or shortening for frying
Salt

1. In shallow dish, mix eggs, salt, and pepper.
2. Combine crumbs and cheese on waxed paper.
3. Cut unpeeled eggplant crosswise into ⅛-inch-thick slices. Dip in egg, then in crumb mixture, coating completely.
4. Meanwhile, in large heavy skillet, slowly heat salad oil (at least ¼ inch).
5. Sauté eggplant until golden-brown—about 3 minutes on each side. Drain on paper towels. Sprinkle lightly with salt.
Makes 4 servings.

# ❖ EGGPLANT-AND-TOMATO CASSEROLE

2 medium eggplants (about 2½ lb)
Boiling water
Salt
¼ cup salad oil
2 cloves garlic, finely chopped
2 tablespoons flour
2 cans (1-lb size) stewed tomatoes, undrained
2 teaspoons sugar
1 teaspoon paprika
⅛ teaspoon pepper
⅛ teaspoon dried basil leaves
½ cup grated Parmesan cheese

1. Preheat oven to 375F. Lightly grease 2-quart casserole.
2. Wash and peel eggplants; cut into 2-inch cubes. In 6-quart saucepan, in small amount of boiling salted water, simmer eggplant 10 minutes. Drain.
3. Meanwhile, in hot oil in large skillet, sauté garlic until golden—about 3 minutes. Remove from heat.
4. Stir in flour, tomatoes, sugar, paprika, pepper, and basil. Cook, stirring, over medium heat, until mixture boils and is thickened.
5. In prepared casserole, layer eggplant cubes, alternately with tomato mixture, to fill casserole. Top with grated cheese.
6. Bake 30 minutes, or until lightly browned.
Makes 6 to 8 servings.

# ❖ ENDIVES BRAISÉES

8 Belgian endives
½ cup water
Dash salt
¼ cup butter or margarine
2 to 3 tablespoons lemon juice
More butter (2 to 3 tablespoons)
Chopped parsley

1. Wash endives. Place in single layer in large saucepan or skillet. Add salt, water, ¼ cup butter, and lemon juice to barely cover endives.
2. Cut piece of aluminum foil to fit pan. Butter well; place on top of endives. Simmer over low heat until tender—30 to 40 minutes. Drain. Return endives to pan.
3. Add a little more butter; heat several minutes. Turn out into serving dish with butter from pan. Sprinkle with parsley.
Makes 4 servings.

# ❖ GREEN BEANS HOLLANDAISE

2 lb fresh green beans
2 cups boiling water
2 teaspoons salt
Hollandaise Sauce, page 461

1. Wash beans; cut off ends. Cut diagonally into 2-inch pieces.
2. Place in large skillet with boiling water and salt. Boil gently, covered, 12 to 15 minutes, or until tender.
3. Meanwhile, make Hollandaise Sauce.
4. Drain beans well; turn out into serving dish. Toss with Hollandaise Sauce, and serve immediately.
Makes 8 servings.

# ❖ FRENCH-STYLE GREEN BEANS

1 lb fresh green beans
1 teaspoon salt
Boiling water
3 tablespoons butter or margarine

1. Wash beans under cold running water; drain.
2. With tip of paring knife, trim ends of beans. Then cut each in half lengthwise. If beans are large and wide, cut in thirds (see Note).
3. Place beans in 2½-quart saucepan. Add salt and boiling water to measure 1 inch.
4. Boil beans gently, covered, 12 to 15 minutes, or just until tender-crisp.
5. Drain beans, and toss with butter.
Makes 4 servings.

Note: Some floating-blade vegetable peelers have device on one end for Frenching green beans.

# ❖ LEEKS MIMOSA

2 bunches leeks (about 8)
2 quarts water
1 teaspoon salt
1 hard-cooked egg
⅓ cup butter or margarine
3 tablespoons lemon juice

1. Trim leeks: Cut off root ends and green stems—leeks should be about 7 inches long after trimming. Cut each in half lengthwise, being careful not to cut through root end. Wash thoroughly.
2. In 4-quart kettle, bring water to boiling. Add leeks and salt; simmer, covered, 15 minutes, or just until tender. Drain leeks well.
3. Meanwhile, separate white and yolk of hard-cooked egg. Chop white; sieve yolk.
4. Arrange leeks in warm serving dish. Melt butter. Stir in lemon juice. Pour over leeks.
5. Sprinkle egg white and sieved egg yolk over leeks.
Makes 8 servings.

## ❖ SAUTÉED MUSHROOMS

18 large mushrooms (1¼ lb)
¼ cup butter or margarine
1 teaspoon dried marjoram leaves
½ teaspoon salt

1. Wash mushrooms, and pat dry; trim ends of stems.
2. Melt butter in large skillet. Add mushrooms; sprinkle with marjoram and salt.
3. Sauté mushrooms, turning frequently, 15 minutes, or until golden and tender.
Makes 6 servings.

## ❖ SAVORY STUFFED MUSHROOMS

12 to 16 fresh medium mushrooms
½ cup butter or margarine
3 tablespoons finely chopped green pepper
3 tablespoons finely chopped onion
1½ cups fresh-bread cubes (¼ inch)
½ teaspoon salt
⅛ teaspoon pepper
Dash ground red pepper

1. Preheat oven to 350F.
2. Wipe mushrooms with damp cloth. Remove stems, and chop stems fine; set aside.
3. Heat 3 tablespoons butter in large skillet. Sauté mushroom caps only on bottom side 2 to 3 minutes; remove. Arrange, rounded side down, in shallow baking pan.
4. Heat rest of butter in same skillet. Sauté chopped stems, green pepper, and onion until tender—about 5 minutes.
5. Remove from heat. Stir in bread cubes and seasoning. Use to fill mushroom caps, mounding mixture high in center.
6. Bake 15 minutes.
Makes 6 to 8 servings.

## ❖ FRIED ONION RINGS

1 large sweet onion (¾ lb)

**BATTER:**

1 cup all-purpose flour
1 teaspoon salt
1½ teaspoons baking powder
1 egg yolk
¾ cup milk
1 tablespoon salad oil
1 egg white

Shortening or oil for deep-fat frying

1. Peel onion. Slice about ¼ inch thick; separate into rings. Cover with cold water, and let stand 30 minutes. Drain, and spread out on paper towels.
2. Meanwhile, make Batter: Sift flour, salt, and baking powder into medium bowl; set aside.
3. Beat egg yolk slightly in bowl; then stir in milk and salad oil. Add to flour mixture, stirring until smooth.
4. Beat egg white until soft peaks form. Fold into batter.
5. Heat 1 inch of melted shortening in saucepan or skillet to 375F on deep-frying thermometer.
6. Dip onion rings in batter (let excess batter drip into bowl); drop several rings at a time into hot fat, and fry until golden. Remove with tongs. Drain on paper towels. Keep warm while frying rest.
Makes 4 to 6 servings.

## ❖ CREAMED ONIONS

2 lb small white onions
1½ teaspoons salt
Water
3 tablespoons butter or margarine
2 tablespoons flour
Dash pepper
Dash ground nutmeg
1¼ cups milk
2 tablespoons dry bread crumbs

1. In medium saucepan, place onions, 1 teaspoon salt, and enough cold water to cover.
2. Bring to boiling. Reduce heat, and simmer, covered, 20 to 25 minutes, or until tender. Drain onions, reserving ½ cup liquid.
3. Melt 2 tablespoons butter in medium saucepan; remove from heat. Stir in flour, ½ teaspoon salt, the pepper, and nutmeg until smooth. Gradually stir in milk and reserved onion liquid.
4. Bring to boiling, stirring constantly; boil gently 1 minute. Add onions, and simmer 2 minutes.
5. Melt remaining butter; mix with bread crumbs.
6. Turn out onions into serving dish; sprinkle buttered bread crumbs over top.
Makes 6 to 8 servings.

## ❖ ORANGE-GLAZED PARSNIPS

3 lb parsnips
1 large navel orange
Boiling water
½ teaspoon salt
¼ cup butter or margarine
½ cup orange marmalade
¼ teaspoon ground ginger
¼ cup water

1. Wash parsnips; peel. Cut thin end of each into 3-inch pieces. Cut rest of parsnip lengthwise into quarters; cut quarters into 3-inch pieces. Cut orange into ¼-inch-thick slices; cut slices in half.
2. Place parsnips in large skillet with tight-fitting cover. Add boiling water to measure 1 inch. Add salt. Simmer, covered, 15 minutes, or just until tender. Drain well.
3. Melt butter in same skillet; stir in orange marmalade, ginger, and ¼ cup water. Bring to boiling, stirring constantly. Add parsnips, and cook over medium heat, turning gently, until glazed on all sides.
4. Using slotted utensil, transfer parsnips to serving dish.
5. Over medium heat in skillet, heat orange, turning once. Garnish platter with glazed slices. Spoon remaining syrup over parsnips.
Makes 8 servings.

## ❖ CHINESE-STYLE SNOW PEAS

1 lb fresh snow-pea pods
¼ cup butter or margarine
⅓ cup water
½ cup chopped green onion (white part only)
½ teaspoon salt
Dash pepper

1. Cut off stems and pull off string of pods. Cover with cold water; drain well.
2. In medium skillet with tight-fitting cover, melt butter with ⅓ cup water. Add peas, green onion, salt, and pepper; cook, covered, a few minutes (adding a little more water if needed; pods should be tender-crisp when done, and water should have evaporated).
Makes 6 servings.

# ❖ FRENCH-STYLE BUTTERED PEAS

4 large lettuce leaves
3 lb fresh young peas, shelled (see Note)
1 teaspoon sugar
½ teaspoon salt
Dash pepper
2 tablespoons butter or margarine

1. Line medium-size heavy skillet with tight-fitting cover with 3 large lettuce leaves.
2. Add peas; sprinkle with sugar, salt, and pepper.
3. Dot with butter; top with another lettuce leaf. Cook, tightly covered, over medium heat 10 to 15 minutes, or until tender.
4. To serve, remove lettuce.
Makes 4 servings.

*Note*: Or use 1 pkg (10 oz) frozen tiny peas. Cook as directed in Steps 1 to 3, 8 minutes. Spread peas with fork; cook 8 minutes longer, or just until are tender. Makes 3 servings.

# ❖ PERFECT BAKED POTATOES

4 medium to large baking potatoes (about 2½ lb)
Salad oil (optional)
Butter or margarine
Salt
Pepper
Paprika
Sour cream (optional)
Crumbled crisp bacon (optional)
Finely chopped green onion (optional)

1. Preheat oven to 425F.
2. Scrub potatoes well under cold running water. Dry thoroughly with paper towels. With fork, prick skins over entire surface. (Brush potatoes with salad oil if you like skins soft after baking.)
3. Place potatoes right on oven rack, and bake 50 to 60 minutes, or until they are easily pierced with fork or feel soft when squeezed.
4. Slash X in top of each potato. Then, holding potato with potholders, squeeze ends so steam can escape and potato fluffs up.
5. Add pat of butter to each; sprinkle with salt, pepper, and paprika. Or top with sour cream and bacon or with green onion.
Makes 4 servings.

# COLCANNON

...oes
...ater
...s salt
...rsely shredded green cab-

...ed green onion

... or margarine
...epper

1. Peel potatoes. Cut each into quarters.
2. In medium saucepan, in ½ inch boiling water with 1 teaspoon salt, cook potatoes, covered, 15 to 20 minutes, or until fork-tender and completely cooked. Drain. Return pan to low heat, shaking to dry potatoes.
3. Meanwhile, in medium saucepan, in ½ inch boiling water with ½ teaspoon salt, cook cabbage, covered, 8 to 10 minutes, or just until tender. Drain well.
4. Also, heat green onion with milk and ½ teaspoon

salt. Bring to boiling; reduce heat, and simmer, un-covered, 10 minutes.

5. In saucepan, with electric mixer at medium speed, beat potato with 4 tablespoons butter, 1 teaspoon salt, and the pepper. Beat in green onion and hot milk, beating until potatoes are very light and fluffy.

6. Stir in cabbage, combining well. Heat over low heat 5 minutes.

7. Turn out colcannon into heated serving dish. Make depression in center; fill with remaining butter.

Makes 8 servings.

## ❖ POTATOES ANNA

½ cup soft butter or margarine
2 lb Idaho potatoes, peeled and thinly sliced
1 teaspoon salt
⅛ teaspoon pepper

1. Preheat oven to 425F. With 3 tablespoons butter, grease 8-inch skillet that has an oven-safe handle and tight-fitting cover.

2. Gently toss potatoes with salt and pepper. Layer one third of potato slices, circular fashion, around bottom and side of skillet. Dot with butter. Repeat twice.

3. Over high heat, cook potatoes 3 minutes. Then bake, covered, 30 minutes. (Place sheet of foil under skillet to catch any runover.) Remove cover; bake 5 minutes longer. Let stand 5 minutes; invert onto platter.

Makes 6 servings.

## ❖ LYONNAISE POTATOES

⅓ cup butter or margarine
6 medium potatoes (about 2 lb), peeled and thinly sliced
1½ cups sliced onion
½ teaspoon salt
Dash pepper
2 tablespoons chopped parsley

1. In hot butter in large heavy skillet, sauté potato and onion slices, turning frequently, until golden-brown and tender—15 to 20 minutes.

2. Sprinkle with salt, pepper, and parsley.

Makes 6 servings.

# ❖ FRENCH-FRIED POTATOES

**SINGLE-FRYING METHOD:**

1. Peel as many Idaho potatoes as desired. Cut lengthwise into ⅜-inch-thick slices. Then cut slices lengthwise into ⅜-inch-wide strips. Rinse in cold water; drain well on paper towels.
2. Meanwhile, heat salad oil or shortening in deep-fat fryer (filling at least one-third full) to 385F on deep-frying thermometer.
3. Cover bottom of fryer basket with single layer of potatoes; lower basket slowly into fat. Fry 5 or 6 minutes, or until potatoes are golden-brown and tender.
4. Remove potatoes; drain well on paper towels. Sprinkle with salt. Keep warm while frying rest of potatoes.

**DOUBLE-FRYING METHOD:**

1. Peel as many Idaho potatoes as desired. Cut lengthwise into ⅜-inch-thick slices. Then cut slices into ⅜-inch-wide strips. Rinse in cold water; drain thoroughly on paper towels.
2. Meanwhile, heat salad oil or shortening in deep-fat fryer (filling at least one-third full) to 360F on deep-frying thermometer.
3. Cover bottom of fryer basket with single layer of potatoes; lower basket slowly into fat. Fry 4 minutes, or until potatoes are tender but not browned.
4. Remove potatoes; drain well on paper towels. Keep at room temperature until ready to complete cooking. Reserve oil.
5. Before serving, reheat oil to 375F on deep-frying thermometer.
6. Cover bottom of fryer basket with 2 layers of potatoes; fry 1 minute, or until potatoes are golden.
7. Remove potatoes; drain well on paper towels. Sprinkle with salt. Keep warm while frying rest of potatoes.

# ❖ SCALLOPED POTATOES

*3 lb potatoes*
*4 medium onions, thinly sliced*
*Boiling water*
*3 teaspoons salt*
*3 tablespoons butter or margarine*
*2 tablespoons flour*
*¼ teaspoon pepper*
*⅛ teaspoon paprika*
*2¼ cups milk*
*2 tablespoons chopped parsley*

1. Preheat oven to 400F. Lightly grease 2-quart casserole.
2. Wash, peel, and thinly slice potatoes; measure 8 cups.
3. Cook potatoes and onions, covered, in small amount of boiling water, with 2 teaspoons salt, about 5 minutes, or until slightly tender. Drain.
4. Melt butter in saucepan. Remove from heat. Stir in flour, pepper, paprika, and remaining salt until smooth. Blend in milk.

5. Cook, stirring, over medium heat, to boiling point, or until thickened and smooth.

6. In prepared casserole, layer one third of potatoes and onions. Sprinkle with 1 tablespoon parsley; top with one third of sauce. Repeat. Then add remaining potatoes and onions, and top with remaining sauce.

7. Bake, uncovered, 35 minutes, or until top is browned and potatoes are tender when pierced with fork.

Makes 6 to 8 servings.

## ✣ FLUFFY MASHED POTATOES

8 medium potatoes (about 2½ lb)
Boiling water
1 tablespoon salt
1 cup milk
¼ cup butter or margarine

1. Peel potatoes; cut in quarters. Cook in 1 inch boiling water with salt, covered, until tender—20 minutes. Drain well; return to saucepan.

2. Beat with portable electric mixer (or mash with potato masher) until smooth. Heat, slowly, stirring, over low heat, to dry out—about 5 minutes.

3. In saucepan, heat milk and butter until butter melts—don't let milk boil.

4. Gradually beat in hot milk mixture until potatoes are smooth, light, and fluffy.

Makes 6 to 8 servings.

## ✣ SAVORY ROAST POTATOES

½ cup butter or margarine
8 large baking potatoes (about 4 lb)
1 tablespoon seasoned salt
½ cup chicken broth

1. Preheat oven to 350F. Melt butter in 13-by-9-by-1¾-inch baking pan.

2. Peel potatoes; roll in melted butter, to coat well. Sprinkle with seasoned salt.

3. Bake, uncovered, 1 hour. Remove pan from oven; turn potatoes. Add chicken broth.

4. Bake 1 hour longer, turning several times.

Makes 8 servings.

## ✣ NEW POTATOES WITH LEMON BUTTER

3 lb small new potatoes
Boiling water
1 teaspoon salt
½ cup butter or margarine
3 tablespoons lemon juice
2 tablespoons finely chopped chives,
   parsley, or mint

1. Scrub potatoes. Peel strip of skin about ½ inch wide around center of each potato. Place potatoes in medium saucepan; add boiling water to measure 2 inches and ½ teaspoon salt.

2. Bring to boiling; boil gently, covered, 20 minutes, or until potatoes are tender. Drain. Return to heat several minutes to dry out.

3. Melt butter in small saucepan. Stir in lemon juice, chives, and ½ teaspoon salt. Pour over potatoes, turning to coat well.

4. Turn out into serving dish.

Makes 8 servings.

# ❖ RUTABAGA IN CREAM

1 rutabaga (about 3 lb)
2 teaspoons salt
Boiling water
1 cup heavy cream
1 tablespoon flour
1 teaspoon sugar
Dash pepper
1 tablespoon chopped parsley

1. Cut rutabaga into quarters; peel. Cut into 1-inch cubes.
2. In 3-quart saucepan, add rutabaga and 1 teaspoon salt to 1 inch boiling water; bring back to boiling. Reduce heat; simmer, covered, 25 minutes, or just until rutabaga is tender.
3. Drain rutabaga well. Return to saucepan.
4. Combine cream, flour, sugar, pepper, and rest of salt. Pour over rutabaga; mix gently to combine.
5. Cook, uncovered, over low heat, about 15 minutes, or until rutabaga mixture is heated through; stir occasionally.
6. Turn out mixture into shallow heat-proof serving dish. Run under broiler, 6 inches from heat, until cream becomes golden and puffs up slightly. Sprinkle chopped parsley over top of rutabaga.
Makes 4 to 6 servings.

# ❖ ORANGE-GLAZED SWEET POTATOES

4 large sweet potatoes or yams (about 3 lb)
Boiling water
2 teaspoons salt
⅛ teaspoon pepper
4 tablespoons light-brown sugar
2 teaspoons grated orange peel
1 cup orange juice
¼ cup butter or margarine

1. Wash sweet potatoes. Place in large saucepan. Cover with boiling water; add 1 teaspoon salt.
2. Bring to boiling; reduce heat, and simmer, covered, 35 to 40 minutes, or until tender.
3. Drain potatoes; let cool. Peel; slice crosswise into ¼-inch-thick slices.
4. Meanwhile, preheat oven to 350F. Grease 12-by-8-by-2-inch baking dish.
5. Arrange half of potatoes in single layer, overlapping slightly, in prepared dish. Sprinkle with ½ teaspoon salt, dash pepper, 2 tablespoons brown sugar, and 1 teaspoon orange peel.
6. Repeat layering with rest of potatoes, salt, pepper, brown sugar, and orange peel. Pour over orange juice.
7. Cover dish with foil; bake, basting occasionally, 30 minutes, or until potatoes are bubbly.
8. Remove cover. Dot potatoes with butter; bake, uncovered and basting occasionally, 30 minutes longer.
Makes 4 to 6 servings.

# ❖ CANDIED SWEET POTATOES

¾ cup light-brown sugar, firmly
   packed
½ cup light corn syrup
¼ cup butter or margarine
¼ teaspoon salt
6 peeled cooked large sweet potatoes,
   halved lengthwise or 1 can (1 lb 1
   oz) vacuum-packed sweet potatoes

1. In large, heavy saucepan or Dutch oven, combine sugar, corn syrup, butter, and salt.
2. Bring to boiling over low heat, stirring until butter is melted and sugar is dissolved.
3. Reduce heat; add sweet potatoes, arranging in single layer. Baste well with syrup; cook, covered, over very low heat, turning once, 15 minutes.
4. Remove cover; cook, basting occasionally, 15 minutes longer, or until potatoes are well glazed.
Makes 6 servings.

# ❖ FRESH SPINACH MIMOSA

4 lb fresh spinach (see Note)
1½ teaspoons salt
1 clove garlic, split
3 tablespoons butter or margarine,
   melted
2 tablespoons lemon juice
1 hard-cooked egg yolk, sieved

1. Wash spinach thoroughly, and remove stems. Place in Dutch oven with only the water clinging to the leaves. Add salt and garlic.
2. Cook over medium heat, covered and stirring occasionally, 4 to 6 minutes, or just until leaves are wilted.
3. Drain spinach well; remove and discard garlic. Return spinach to Dutch oven. Add butter and lemon juice; toss until well blended. Turn out into serving dish; sprinkle with egg yolk.
Makes 8 servings.

Note: Or use 3 packages (10-oz size) frozen leaf spinach. Cook as package label directs, adding garlic to salted water. Drain; continue as above.

# ❖ CREAMED-SPINACH RING

2 lb fresh spinach or 2 pkg (10-oz size)
   frozen chopped spinach
Grated Parmesan cheese
4 tablespoons butter or margarine
½ cup chopped onion
1 cup light cream
1 teaspoon salt
½ teaspoon sugar
Dash pepper
Dash ground nutmeg
4 eggs
½ cup fresh bread crumbs (2 slices
   bread)
⅓ cup grated Swiss or Gruyère cheese

1. Wash spinach; remove and discard large stems. Place in large kettle with just the water clinging to the leaves. Cook, covered, tossing with fork once or twice, 5 minutes, or until spinach is just tender. Drain very well. Chop coarsely. If using frozen spinach, cook as package label directs; drain very well.
2. Preheat oven to 350F. Grease 4½-cup ring mold well, and dust with grated Parmesan cheese.
3. In hot butter in large saucepan, sauté onion until tender—about 5 minutes. Add spinach, cream, salt, sugar, pepper, and nutmeg; heat just to boiling. Remove from heat.
4. In large bowl, beat eggs slightly. Add bread crumbs and Swiss cheese; gradually stir in spinach mixture.

5. Turn out into prepared mold. Set mold in baking pan on oven rack; pour boiling water into pan to depth of 1½ inches. Place piece of waxed paper over top of mold.

6. Bake 30 to 35 minutes, or until knife inserted in center of spinach mixture comes out clean.

7. Loosen mold around edge with small spatula. Invert onto heated serving plate. Fill center of ring with Lemon-Glazed Carrots, page 497, if desired. Makes 6 to 8 servings.

# ❖ SUMMER SQUASH CREOLE

*2 lb small summer squash*
*4 bacon slices, diced*
*½ cup chopped green onion*
*1 teaspoon salt*
*Dash pepper*
*2 medium tomatoes, peeled and*
  *cubed*

1. Wash squash. Cut on diagonal into slices ½ inch thick.

2. In large skillet, sauté bacon until crisp; remove bacon, and reserve.

3. In bacon drippings, sauté green onion until tender —about 3 minutes.

4. Add squash, salt, and pepper; toss lightly. Cook, covered, over low heat, about 15 minutes, or just until squash is tender.

5. Add tomatoes; toss to combine. Cook, covered, 1 minute longer.

6. Turn out into serving dish; sprinkle with bacon. Makes 6 servings.

# ❖ SUMMER SQUASH WITH DILLED SOUR CREAM

*2½ lb small summer squash*
*¼ cup butter or margarine*
*½ cup sliced onion*
*1¼ teaspoons salt*
*⅛ teaspoon pepper*
*1 tablespoon snipped fresh dill*
*1 cup sour cream, at room temperature*
*Sprigs of fresh dill*
*Paprika*

1. Wash squash. Cut squash on diagonal into slices ½ inch thick.

2. In hot butter in large skillet, sauté onion until tender—about 5 minutes.

3. Add squash, salt, pepper, and snipped dill to skillet; toss lightly to combine.

4. Cook, covered, over low heat, 12 to 15 minutes, or just until squash is tender. Stir occasionally.

5. Drain squash if necessary. Turn out into serving dish. Spoon sour cream over squash. Top with dill sprigs; sprinkle with paprika.

Makes 6 servings.

# ❖ HONEY-SPICE ACORN SQUASH

3 medium acorn squash
¼ cup butter or margarine, melted
¼ teaspoon ground cinnamon
½ teaspoon salt
¼ teaspoon ground ginger
⅓ cup honey

1. Preheat oven to 375F.
2. Scrub squash. Cut in half lengthwise; remove seeds and stringy fibers.
3. Arrange, cut side down, in shallow baking pan. Surround with ½ inch hot water.
4. Bake 30 minutes.
5. Make sauce by combining remaining ingredients. Pour off excess liquid from baking pan; turn squash cut side up.
6. Pour sauce into cavities; bake 15 minutes, basting now and then with sauce.
Makes 6 servings.

# ❖ BAKED TOMATO HALVES

2 large tomatoes (about 1 lb)
4 tablespoons butter or margarine
¼ cup finely chopped onion
1 teaspoon prepared mustard
½ teaspoon Worcestershire sauce
2 slices white bread, torn into coarse crumbs
2 teaspoons chopped parsley

1. Preheat oven to 350F. Wash tomatoes and remove stems. Cut in half crosswise. Place, cut side up, in small shallow baking pan.
2. In 2 tablespoons hot butter in small skillet, sauté onion until tender. Stir in mustard and Worcestershire. Spread on tomato halves.
3. Melt remaining butter in same skillet. Stir in bread crumbs and parsley. Sprinkle over tomatoes.
4. Bake, uncovered, 20 minutes, or until tomatoes are heated through and crumbs are golden-brown.
Makes 4 servings.

# ❖ SQUASH AND TOMATOES

1 lb yellow summer squash or zucchini
¼ cup butter or margarine
1 cup thinly sliced onion
1 teaspoon salt
⅛ teaspoon pepper
¾ teaspoon dried basil leaves
1 can (8 oz) stewed tomatoes

1. Wash squash well, scrubbing with brush. Slice into ½-inch-thick diagonal slices.
2. In butter in medium skillet with tight-fitting cover, sauté onion, stirring, until golden—about 3 minutes.
3. Add squash and remaining ingredients; toss lightly to combine.
4. Cook, covered, over medium heat 10 to 15 minutes, or until squash is tender.
Makes 6 servings.

# ❖ TURNIPS FLORENTINE

1 lb white turnips (about 4 medium)
Boiling water
½ teaspoon salt
1 teaspoon instant minced onion
1 tablespoon lemon juice
2 tablespoons butter or margarine
½ cup finely chopped raw spinach

1. Wash turnips; peel. Cut each into quarters.
2. In 1 inch boiling water, in small saucepan, combine turnips with salt and onion.
3. Cook, covered, 25 to 30 minutes, or until turnips are tender.
4. Drain turnips well. Mash till smooth.
5. Return mashed turnips to heat. Cook over low heat 1 to 2 minutes to dry out.
6. Add lemon juice, butter, and spinach, mixing well. Serve at once.
Makes 4 servings.

# ❖ ZUCCHINI WITH FRESH HERBS

8 small zucchini (2 lb)
⅓ cup water
1 teaspoon salt
Dash pepper
¼ cup butter or margarine, melted
2 tablespoons chopped parsley
1 tablespoon snipped chives or dill
1 tablespoon lemon juice

1. Wash zucchini; cut on diagonal into ¼-inch-thick slices.
2. In medium skillet with tight-fitting cover, bring ⅓ cup water with the salt and pepper to boiling.
3. Add zucchini; cook, covered, over medium heat 10 minutes, or until just tender, not mushy; water should be evaporated.
4. Add butter, parsley, chives, and lemon juice; toss gently to combine. Turn out into heated serving dish.
Makes 6 servings.

# ❖ SAUTÉED ZUCCHINI AND GREEN PEPPERS

3 slices bacon, cut into 1-inch pieces
½ cup sliced onion
2 red peppers, cut into strips
1 green pepper, cut into strips
1 medium zucchini (½ lb), cut into
  ½-inch-thick slices
½ teaspoon salt
¼ teaspoon dried thyme leaves
Dash pepper

1. In large skillet, sauté bacon until crisp. Remove bacon bits, and set aside. In hot drippings, sauté onion until tender—about 5 minutes.
2. Add pepper strips and zucchini; sprinkle with salt, thyme, and pepper. Cook, covered, over medium heat 15 minutes, or just until vegetables are tender.
3. Turn out into serving dish. Sprinkle with bacon.
Makes 4 to 6 servings.

# ❖ STIR-FRIED MIXED VEGETABLES

1 tablespoon butter or margarine
1 tablespoon salad oil
2 cups thinly sliced carrot (sliced on
   diagonal)
1 cup (¼ lb) thinly sliced celery
   (sliced on diagonal)
½ lb fresh snow peas, ends trimmed
   and strings removed
¼ lb fresh mushrooms, washed and
   sliced lengthwise through stems
2 tablespoons lemon juice
½ teaspoon salt
Dash pepper
2 tablespoons chopped parsley

1. In wok or large heavy skillet, heat butter and oil. Add carrot and celery; stir to coat well. Stir-fry 3 to 4 minutes.
2. Stir in snow peas and mushrooms; stir-fry 2 minutes. Cover and cook 2 minutes longer, or until vegetables are cooked as you like them.
3. Add lemon juice, salt, and pepper; stir to mix well. Serve sprinkled with chopped parsley.
Makes 8 servings.

# ❖ RATATOUILLE

2 medium-size green peppers
2 medium zucchini
1 medium eggplant (about 1 lb)
½ cup salad or olive oil
1 cup thinly sliced onion
2 cloves garlic, crushed
1½ teaspoons salt
¼ teaspoon pepper
4 medium tomatoes, peeled and cut
   into wedges
2 tablespoons chopped parsley

1. Wash peppers; halve. Remove ribs and seeds. Cut lengthwise into ¼-inch-thick slices.
2. Scrub zucchini; cut crosswise into ½-inch-thick slices.
3. Wash eggplant. Cut lengthwise into quarters, then into ¼-inch slices.
4. In ¼ cup hot oil in large skillet, sauté green-pepper slices, onion, and garlic about 5 minutes. With slotted spoon, remove to medium bowl.
5. Add 2 tablespoons oil to skillet. Sauté zucchini, turning frequently, until tender—about 10 minutes. With slotted utensil, remove to large bowl.
6. Add remaining oil to skillet. In hot oil, sauté eggplant, turning occasionally, until tender—about 5 minutes.
7. Remove eggplant from skillet. Add to zucchini; toss lightly.
8. Spoon half of pepper mixture into skillet. Sprinkle with ¼ teaspoon salt and dash pepper. Top with half of zucchini-eggplant mixture; sprinkle with ¼ teaspoon salt and dash pepper.
9. Layer half of tomato wedges on top. Sprinkle with ¼ teaspoon salt, dash pepper, and 1 tablespoon parsley.
10. Repeat with remaining pepper mixture, zucchini-eggplant mixture, tomatoes, salt, pepper, and parsley.
11. Simmer mixture, covered and over low heat, 2 minutes, basting occasionally with pan juices. Remove cover; cook 5 minutes, basting occasionally, until liquid is evaporated.
12. Serve hot or very well chilled.
Makes 8 to 10 servings.

# MOSTLY-VEGETABLE MAIN DISHES

## ⊞ QUICK VEGETABLE PAELLA

⅓ cup salad oil
2 cups sliced onion
1 clove garlic, crushed
1 cup raw long-grain white rice
1½ teaspoons salt
½ teaspoon turmeric
⅛ teaspoon pepper
1½ cups cold water
1 can (10¾ oz) undiluted chicken
    broth
4 medium carrots
1 large red pepper
1½ cups boiling water
1 pkg (10 oz) frozen green peas,
    thawed
2 tomatoes, cut into eighths
2 tablespoons butter or margarine
½ cup blanched whole almonds

1. In hot oil in 6-quart Dutch oven, sauté onion and garlic, stirring, until golden—about 5 minutes. Stir in rice, 1 teaspoon salt, the turmeric, and pepper; mix well. Add cold water and chicken broth; bring to boiling, and simmer, covered, 20 minutes.
2. Meanwhile, pare carrots; cut in half lengthwise, then crosswise. Wash red pepper. Cut off end; remove seeds and ribs. Slice into ¼-inch-thick rings. Turn out carrots into 10-inch skillet. Add ½ teaspoon salt and the boiling water; simmer, covered, 15 minutes. Stir in red pepper and green peas; simmer, covered, just until carrots are tender—about 5 minutes.
3. Add cooked rice mixture to vegetable mixture; mix well. Top with tomatoes. Simmer, covered, 5 minutes. Turn out into serving dish.
4. Over medium heat, in hot butter, sauté almonds until golden—1 minute. Sprinkle over paella.
Makes 8 servings.

## ⊞ STUFFED CABBAGE ROLLS

Water
1 large head green cabbage (about
    3½ lb)
1 lb ground beef chuck
½ cup raw regular white rice
1 small onion, grated
2 eggs, beaten
1 teaspoon salt
¼ teaspoon pepper
⅛ teaspoon allspice
¼ cup water
1 large onion, sliced

### SAUCE:

2 cans (8-oz size) tomato sauce
1 can (1 lb 12 oz) tomatoes,
    undrained
⅓ cup lemon juice
¼ cup water
1 teaspoon salt
⅛ teaspoon pepper

¼ cup light-brown sugar, packed

1. In large kettle, bring 3 quarts water to boiling. Add cabbage; simmer 2 to 3 minutes, or until leaves are pliable. Remove cabbage; drain.
2. Carefully remove 12 large leaves from cabbage; trim thick rib. If leaves are not soft enough to roll, return to boiling water for 1 minute.
3. Preheat oven to 375F.
4. In large bowl, combine beef chuck, rice, grated onion, eggs, 1 teaspoon salt, ¼ teaspoon pepper, the allspice, and ¼ cup water. Mix with fork until well blended.
5. Place about ¼ cup meat mixture in hollow of each of 12 cabbage leaves. Fold sides of leaf over stuffing; roll up from thick end of leaf.
6. In Dutch oven, place a few of the remaining cabbage leaves. Arrange rolls, steam side down, on leaves. Top with onion slices.
7. Make Sauce: In large bowl, combine tomato sauce, tomatoes, lemon juice, ¼ cup water, the salt, and pepper. Pour over cabbage rolls.
8. Over medium heat, bring to boiling. Sprinkle with sugar; cover, and place in oven.
9. Bake 1½ hours. Uncover; bake 1½ hours longer.
Makes 6 to 8 servings.

# ❖ FRESH CORN CUSTARD

1 tablespoon butter or margarine
2 tablespoons chopped green pepper
2 cups fresh corn, cut from cob, or 2
  cups frozen corn, thawed
3 eggs
½ lb natural Cheddar cheese, grated
¼ cup all-purpose flour
½ teaspoon salt
⅛ teaspoon white pepper
1 tablespoon sugar
Dash ground nutmeg
2 tablespoons butter or margarine,
  melted
2 cups half-and-half
6 plum tomatoes, halved
6 strips green pepper, 2 inches long

1. In 1 tablespoon hot butter in small skillet, sauté chopped green pepper just until tender—about 2 minutes.
2. Preheat oven to 325F. Lightly grease shallow 1½-quart baking dish.
3. In large bowl, combine corn, eggs, cheese, and green pepper; mix well.
4. Combine flour, salt, pepper, sugar, and nutmeg. Stir into corn mixture.
5. Add butter and half-and-half; mix well. Pour into prepared baking dish. Arrange tomatoes and green-pepper strips around edge. Set baking dish in pan; pour hot water to 1-inch depth around baking dish.
6. Bake, uncovered, 1 hour and 10 minutes, or until custard is firm and knife inserted in center comes out clean. Serve hot.
Makes 8 servings.

# ❖ EGGPLANT PARMIGIANA

2 tablespoons butter or margarine
½ cup chopped onion
1 clove garlic, crushed
1 lb ground beef chuck
1 can (1 lb 1 oz) Italian-style
  tomatoes, undrained
1 can (6 oz) tomato paste
2 teaspoons dried oregano leaves
1 teaspoon dried basil leaves
1½ teaspoons salt
¼ teaspoon pepper
1 tablespoon brown sugar
1 cup plus 1 tablespoon water
1 large eggplant (1½ lb)
2 eggs, slightly beaten
½ cup dry bread crumbs
1¼ cups grated Parmesan cheese
¼ cup salad oil
1 pkg (8 oz) mozzarella cheese,
  sliced

1. In hot butter in large skillet, sauté onion, garlic, and beef chuck until meat is no longer red—about 5 minutes.
2. Add tomatoes, tomato paste, oregano, basil, salt, pepper, sugar, and 1 cup water; bring to boiling.
3. Reduce heat; simmer, uncovered, 20 minutes.
4. Preheat oven to 350F. Lightly grease 13-by-9-by-2-inch baking dish.
5. Wash eggplant; do not peel. Cut crosswise into slices ½ inch thick.
6. In pie plate, combine eggs and 1 tablespoon water; mix well.
7. On sheet of waxed paper, combine bread crumbs with ½ cup Parmesan cheese; mix well.
8. Dip eggplant slices into egg mixture, coating well. Then dip into bread-crumb mixture, coating evenly.
9. Sauté eggplant slices, a few at a time, in 1 tablespoon hot oil until golden-brown and crisp on both sides. Add more oil as needed.
10. Arrange half of eggplant slices in bottom of prepared dish. Sprinkle with half of remaining Parmesan cheese. Top with half of mozzarella; cover with half of tomato sauce.
11. Arrange remaining eggplant slices over tomato sauce. Cover with rest of Parmesan and tomato sauce.
12. Bake, uncovered, 20 minutes. Arrange remaining mozzarella over top; bake 20 minutes, or until mozzarella is melted and slightly browned.
Makes 6 servings.

# ❖ SPINACH-PASTA-AND-CHEESE LOAF

2 lb fresh spinach or 2 pkg (10-oz size)
   frozen chopped spinach
2 tablespoons grated Parmesan
   cheese
4 tablespoons butter or margarine
½ cup chopped onion
1 cup half-and-half
1 teaspoon salt
½ teaspoon sugar
Dash pepper
Dash ground nutmeg
4 eggs
½ cup fresh bread crumbs (2 slices
   bread)
½ cup grated Swiss or Gruyère cheese
1½ cups cooked elbow macaroni
1½ cups cooked carrot, in ½-inch
   pieces
1 cup coarsely chopped red pepper
Cheese Sauce, below

1. Wash spinach; remove and discard large stems. Place in large kettle with just the water clinging to leaves. Cook, covered, tossing with fork once or twice, 5 minutes, or until spinach is just tender. Drain very well. Chop coarsely. (If using frozen spinach, cook as package label directs; drain very well.)
2. Preheat oven to 350F. Grease well 9-by-5-by-2¾-inch loaf pan. Line bottom with aluminum foil; dust with Parmesan cheese.
3. In hot butter in large saucepan, sauté onion until tender—about 5 minutes. Add spinach, half-and-half, salt, sugar, pepper, and nutmeg; heat just to boiling. Remove from heat.
4. In large bowl, beat eggs slightly. Add bread crumbs and Swiss cheese; gradually stir in spinach mixture, macaroni, carrot, and red pepper.
5. Turn out into prepared pan. Set pan in larger baking pan on oven rack; pour water into pan to depth of 1½ inches. Place piece of waxed paper over top of pan.
6. Bake 35 to 40 minutes, or until knife inserted in center of spinach mixture comes out clean.
7. Loosen mold around edge with small spatula. Invert onto heated serving platter. Serve with Cheese Sauce.
Makes 8 servings.

## CHEESE SAUCE:

2 tablespoons butter or margarine
2 tablespoons all-purpose flour
½ teaspoon dry mustard
¾ teaspoon salt
Dash black pepper
Dash ground red pepper
1 cup half-and-half
1 cup grated sharp Cheddar cheese
   (¼ lb)

1. In small saucepan, slowly melt butter (do not brown); remove from heat. Stir in flour, mustard, salt, black pepper, red pepper, and half-and-half until smooth.
2. Bring to boiling, stirring until thickened. Reduce heat; add cheese. Cook, stirring, until cheese is melted and mixture is smooth.
Makes 1½ cups.

# ❖ SPAGHETTI SQUASH WITH FRESH SPINACH

1 spaghetti squash (2¾ to 3 lb)
Boiling water
1 lb fresh spinach
¼ cup salad oil
2 tablespoons butter or margarine
1 large onion, sliced
2 cloves garlic, crushed
½ teaspoon dried basil leaves
¼ teaspoon salt
Grated Parmesan cheese
2 tablespoons coarsely chopped walnuts

1. Wash spaghetti squash; cut in half lengthwise, and remove seeds. Pierce skin with fork. Set halves, skin side down, in large pot with cover. Add boiling water to measure 2 inches. Cover; return to boiling. Reduce heat, and simmer, 30 minutes, or until tender.
2. Meanwhile, make sauce: Remove stems from spinach, and wash leaves thoroughly; drain, and chop coarsely.
3. Heat oil and butter in medium skillet. Add onion and garlic. Sauté until golden—3 minutes. Add spinach, basil, and salt. Cover; reduce heat, and simmer until spinach has just wilted—5 minutes.

4. Drain squash. Run fork over inside of cooked squash to release strands. Place on warm platter. Stir ¼ cup Parmesan cheese into spinach mixture. Spoon over spaghetti squash. Top with nuts. Serve with more Parmesan cheese.

Makes 4 servings.

# ❖ STUFFED YELLOW SQUASH

*3 yellow squash (2 lb)*
*2½ cups water*
*2 teaspoons salt*
*1 tablespoon salad oil*
*1 clove garlic, crushed*
*½ lb ground beef*
*½ cup raw long-grain white rice*
*⅛ teaspoon pepper*
*1 can (16 oz) stewed tomatoes*
*Parmesan Sauce, below*

1. Wash squash; cut off and discard stem. Cut squash in half lengthwise. Scoop out and discard seeds.
2. In medium skillet with tight-fitting cover, bring 2 cups water and 1 teaspoon salt to boiling.
3. Add squash, cut side down; cook, covered, over medium heat 5 minutes, or until tender, not mushy. Drain well.
4. In hot oil in medium skillet, over medium heat, sauté garlic and beef, stirring until beef is no longer pink—about 10 minutes.
5. Add rice, 1 teaspoon salt, and the pepper; mix well. Cook stirring, 2 minutes. Preheat oven to 375F.
6. Stir in stewed tomatoes and ½ cup water; cook, tightly covered and over low heat, 20 minutes, or until rice is cooked and liquid absorbed. Meanwhile, make Parmesan Sauce.
7. Fill squash halves with rice mixture, dividing evenly.
8. Arrange in bottom of 13-by-9-by-2-inch baking pan. Pour a little cheese sauce over each. Cover tightly with foil. Bake 15 minutes, or until heated through.
9. Serve with remaining sauce.

Makes 6 servings.

## PARMESAN SAUCE:

*2 tablespoons butter or margarine*
*2 tablespoons all-purpose flour*
*½ teaspoon dry mustard*
*¼ teaspoon salt*
*Dash black pepper*
*Dash ground red pepper*
*1 cup milk*
*¼ cup grated Parmesan cheese*

1. In small saucepan, slowly melt butter (do not brown); remove from heat; stir in flour, mustard, salt, black pepper, red pepper, and milk until smooth.
2. Bring to boiling, stirring until thickened. Reduce heat; add cheese, and cook, stirring, until cheese is melted and mixture is smooth.

Makes 1¼ cups.

# ❖ STUFFED EGGPLANT CREOLE

2 small eggplants (about 2 lb)
2 teaspoons salt
Boiling water
2 tablespoons bacon fat or salad oil
½ lb ground beef
1 clove garlic, crushed
¼ cup finely chopped onion
¼ cup finely chopped green pepper
¼ cup finely chopped celery
1 can (1 lb) tomatoes, undrained
¼ teaspoon dried thyme leaves
½ teaspoon Tabasco
½ cup grapenuts
½ cup dry bread crumbs
¼ cup butter or margarine, melted

1. Wash eggplants; cut in half lengthwise. Add with ½ teaspoon salt to 1 inch boiling water in kettle; simmer, covered, 15 minutes. Drain; cool.
2. Preheat oven to 375F. Carefully scoop out pulp from eggplant halves, leaving ¼-inch-thick shell. Dice pulp.
3. In bacon fat in large skillet, sauté beef with garlic until brown. Add onion, green pepper, and celery; cook over low heat about 5 minutes.
4. Stir in tomatoes, 1½ teaspoons salt, the thyme, and Tabasco; remove from heat. Add eggplant and grapenuts.
5. Spoon meat mixture into eggplant shells. Place in shallow baking pan. Combine bread crumbs and butter; sprinkle over stuffed eggplants.
6. Bake, uncovered, about 45 to 50 minutes, or until hot and bubbly.
Makes 4 servings.

# ❖ FETTUCCINE AND SPINACH

½ pkg (1-lb size) fettuccine noodles
¼ cup salad oil
1 clove garlic, crushed
1 pkg (10 oz) frozen chopped spinach,
    thawed and drained
½ teaspoon dried basil leaves
¼ cup chopped parsley
1 cup (8 oz) cottage cheese
1 teaspoon salt
Dash pepper
2 tablespoons grated Parmesan
    cheese
Pimiento strips (optional)

1. Cook noodles according to package directions; drain.
2. Meanwhile, in hot oil in medium skillet, sauté garlic and spinach, stirring, 5 minutes. Remove garlic.
3. Add basil, parsley, cottage cheese, salt, and pepper. Stir over low heat until blended—about 2 minutes.
4. Toss cheese-spinach mixture with noodles. Turn out into heated serving dish. Sprinkle with Parmesan cheese. If desired, garnish with pimiento strips.
Makes 4 to 6 servings.

# ❖ ZUCCHINI AND TOMATO PARMIGIANA

2 tablespoons butter or margarine
2 tablespoons salad or olive oil
1 cup chopped onion
1 clove garlic, crushed
½ teaspoon salt
½ teaspoon dried basil leaves
Dash pepper
1 can (8 oz) tomato sauce
1 large zucchini (1½ lb)
½ cup water
2 large tomatoes (1 lb), sliced ⅓ inch
  thick
1 lb mozzarella cheese, sliced ¼ inch
  thick
2 tablespoons grated Parmesan
  cheese

1. Make sauce: In hot butter and oil in medium skillet, sauté onion and garlic, stirring, until golden—about 5 minutes.
2. Add salt, basil, pepper, and tomato sauce. Bring to boiling, stirring; simmer, uncovered, 10 minutes.
3. Preheat oven to 400F. Lightly grease 1½-quart casserole (10 inches in diameter).
4. Wash zucchini; cut into slices ½ inch thick. In large skillet, layer zucchini; add water. Bring to boiling; simmer, covered, 10 minutes, or until tender but not mushy. Drain well.
5. Spoon half of tomato sauce into bottom of prepared casserole.
6. Arrange zucchini, tomato slices, and mozzarella around inside edge of dish, overlapping.
7. Spoon remaining sauce on top. Sprinkle with Parmesan. Bake 15 minutes, or until cheese melts. If desired, place under broiler, 4 inches from heat, to brown.
Makes 8 servings.

# ❖ ZUCCHINI QUICHE

1½ lb zucchini
1 cup water
1⅛ teaspoons salt
1 pkg (10 or 11 oz) piecrust mix
8 slices bacon, quartered
½ lb natural Swiss cheese, grated
4 eggs
1½ cups light cream
⅛ teaspoon ground nutmeg
Dash pepper

1. Wash zucchini; trim ends. Slice into rounds ¼ inch thick.
2. In large skillet, bring water to boiling; add 1 teaspoon salt and the zucchini. Bring back to boiling; cook, covered, 3 minutes. Drain well.
3. Prepare piecrust as package label directs. On lightly floured pastry cloth, with a stockinette-covered rolling pin, roll pastry to form 14-inch circle. Use to line 11-inch pie plate. Flute edge. Refrigerate.
4. Preheat oven to 375F. Sauté bacon until crisp. Drain on paper towels.
5. Sprinkle bottom of pie shell with bacon, then cheese.
6. Arrange half of zucchini slices over cheese.
7. In medium bowl, with rotary beater, beat eggs with cream, nutmeg, ⅛ teaspoon salt, salt, and pepper just until combined.
8. Pour cream mixture into pie shell. Arrange remaining zucchini on pie.
9. Bake 40 minutes, or just until puffy and golden. Serve warm.
Makes 12 servings.

# ❖ ZUCCHINI MOUSSAKA

## MEAT SAUCE:

2 tablespoons butter or margarine
1 cup finely chopped onion
¾ lb ground beef chuck or lamb
1 clove garlic, crushed
½ teaspoon dried oregano leaves
1 teaspoon dried basil leaves
½ teaspoon ground cinnamon
1 teaspoon salt
Dash pepper
2 cans (8-oz size) tomato sauce

8 medium zucchini (2½ to 3 lb)
1 teaspoon salt
Boiling water

## CREAM SAUCE:

2 tablespoons butter or margarine
2 tablespoons all-purpose flour
½ teaspoon salt
Dash pepper
2 cups milk
2 eggs

3 tablespoons grated Parmesan
   cheese
3 tablespoons grated Cheddar cheese
2 tablespoons dry bread crumbs

1. Make Meat Sauce: In 2 tablespoons hot butter in 3½-quart Dutch oven, sauté onion, ground meat, and garlic, stirring, until brown—10 minutes. Add oregano, basil, cinnamon, 1 teaspoon salt, dash pepper, and the tomato sauce; bring to boiling, stirring. Reduce heat; simmer, uncovered, ½ hour.
2. Wash zucchini; cut off ends, then cut in half lengthwise. Add, with 1 teaspoon salt, to 1 inch boiling water; cook, covered, over medium heat just until tender, not mushy—8 to 10 minutes. Drain well.
3. Make Cream Sauce: In medium saucepan, melt butter. Remove from heat; stir in flour, salt, and pepper. Add milk gradually. Bring to boiling, stirring until mixture is thickened. Remove from heat. In small bowl, beat eggs with wire whisk. Beat in some hot cream-sauce mixture. Return mixture to saucepan; mix well. Set aside.
4. Preheat oven to 350F. To assemble casserole: In bottom of 12-by-7½-by-2-inch baking dish, layer half of zucchini, overlapping slightly; then sprinkle with 2 tablespoons each grated Parmesan and Cheddar cheeses.
5. Stir bread crumbs into meat sauce. Spoon evenly over zucchini in casserole. Layer rest of zucchini slices, overlapping, as before.
6. Pour cream sauce over all. Sprinkle top with remaining cheese. Bake 35 to 40 minutes, or until golden-brown and top is set. If desired, brown top a little more under broiler—1 minute. Cool slightly before serving. Cut into squares.
Makes 12 servings.

# ❖ BAGWELL'S VEGETABLE TERRINE HYATT
## (REGENCY WAIKIKI, HONOLULU)

Salt
Water
7 small carrots, pared
7 thin stalks asparagus, washed
¼ lb green beans, washed
1 large red pepper, washed
1 thin daikon (Japanese white radish) or 2 white turnips
½ lb fresh spinach
¾ cup broccoli flowerets
1 tablespoon chopped parsley
¾ lb boneless, skinless chicken breasts, cut into chunks
2 egg whites
1 teaspoon dried tarragon leaves
¼ teaspoon nutmeg
1¼ teaspoons salt
⅛ teaspoon pepper
2¼ cups heavy cream
Tomato Sauce, below
Assorted raw vegetables (optional)

1. Bring 1½ inches salted water to boiling in large skillet. Simmer carrots, covered, 5 minutes. Trim asparagus and green beans. Add to skillet; cover, and set aside 5 minutes.
2. Discard seeds from red pepper, and slice into ½-inch strips. Peel daikon, and cut into julienne slices. Add to skillet; cover, and set aside no more than 5 minutes.
3. Remove and discard stems from spinach. Wash leaves carefully, and blanch in boiling hot water until leaves are just flexible but haven't lost their color. Drain well.
4. Generously coat 9-by-5-by-2¾-inch loaf pan with olive oil; line with spinach leaves, leaving some of leaves hanging over edge. Preheat oven to 300F.
5. Combine broccoli, parsley, chicken, and egg whites in food processor with chopping blade. Process until smooth. Add tarragon, nutmeg, salt, pepper, and half of cream. Process until well combined. Gradually add remaining cream.
6. Drain vegetables well. Spread a little chicken mixture in bottom of prepared pan. Make layer of red pepper. Continue layering vegetables, alternating with chicken mixture, using asparagus, daikon, green beans, and carrots in that order.
7. Fold spinach leaves over mixture, adding more, if necessary, to cover. Brush with oil; cover with foil. Set pan in shallow baking dish. Pour boiling water around pan to measure 1 inch. Bake 1 hour and 15 minutes.
8. Cool completely. To serve: Pour off liquid; unmold and serve in slices surrounded by Tomato Sauce. Makes 12 servings.

## TOMATO SAUCE

1 lb ripe Italian plum or regular tomatoes
3 tablespoons red-wine vinegar
½ cup olive oil
1 drop Tabasco
¼ teaspoon Worcestershire sauce
Dash pepper
½ teaspoon salt
½ teaspoon chopped fresh tarragon leaves or ¼ teaspoon dried tarragon leaves

1. Blanch tomatoes in boiling water; remove skins. Cut in quarters.
2. In blender or food processor, combine vinegar, oil, Tabasco, Worcestershire, pepper, salt, and tarragon. Blend until smooth.
3. Add tomatoes, and blend just until tomatoes are chopped. Refrigerate.

# ❖ SAVORY STUFFED ZUCCHINI

6 small zucchini (1½ lb)
Boiling water
Salt
¼ cup butter or margarine
1 clove garlic, split
1 medium onion, chopped
1 cup chopped peeled fresh tomato
1 cup cooked white rice
½ teaspoon dried oregano leaves
⅛ teaspoon ground red pepper
½ cup grated Parmesan cheese

1. Wash zucchini; cut off stems. Cut zucchini in half lengthwise.
2. In large saucepan, in small amount of boiling water with ½ teaspoon salt, cook zucchini, covered, 5 minutes, or until just tender. Drain well; cool. Scoop out seeds.
3. In hot butter in skillet, sauté garlic until golden. Lift out and discard. Add onion; sauté, stirring, until golden. Add tomato, rice, oregano, 1 teaspoon salt, and the red pepper. Toss with fork to mix well.
4. Preheat oven to 450F. Sprinkle inside of each zucchini lightly with salt. Fill each zucchini half with some of rice mixture. Sprinkle each with Parmesan cheese.
5. Arrange in single layer in buttered baking dish. Bake, uncovered, 15 minutes. Run under broiler several minutes to brown tops.
Makes 10 to 12 servings.

# ❖ STIR-FRIED TOFU AND VEGETABLES

4 medium carrots (¾ lb)
2 large zucchini (1 lb)
4 green onions
1 tablespoon oil
½ teaspoon ground ginger
1 large clove garlic, crushed
1 lb fresh bean sprouts
2 blocks firm tofu
1 tablespoon cornstarch
¼ cup soy sauce
¼ cup water
Fluffy cooked rice

1. Pare carrots; cut into thin julienne strips. Scrub zucchini; slice thinly on diagonal. Wash and chop green onions.
2. In wok or large heavy skillet, heat oil. Add carrots; stir to coat well. Stir-fry 3 to 4 minutes.
3. Stir in zucchini, ginger, garlic, and all but 1 tablespoon green onions. Cover, and cook 2 minutes.
4. Rinse and drain bean sprouts. Slice tofu. Add to vegetables. Cover, and cook 2 minutes.
5. Stir cornstarch into soy sauce. Pour over tofu and vegetables, along with water. Stir-fry until sauce has thickened and vegetables are just tender. Sprinkle with reserved green onions, and serve with hot rice.
Makes 6 servings.

Note: Tofu, pressed bean curd, is available in oriental food stores.

# INDEX